ALL THE INGREDIENTS OF CULINARY SU...

"Just about every exotic, unusual, an... dishes in all corners of the world is ... to *zatar*, it's all here, explained in a very concise ...
—*Bon Appétit*

*

"Useful and imaginative."
—*Philadelphia Inquirer*

*

"An incredible wealth of information...a fascinating book for anyone who truly enjoys cooking or reading about food."
—Gannett News Service

*

"A valuable source."
—*Newsday*

*

"Chock-full of lore and irresistible for browsing."
—*Kirkus Reviews*

*

"The von Welanetz book has taken a solid place as a basic culinary reference book of international ingredients."
—*San Diego Tribune*

* * *

About the authors

Authors of *With Love from Your Kitchen, The Art of Buffet Entertaining,* and *The Pleasure of Your Company,* which won the French Tastemaker Award, Diana and Paul von Welanetz have studied cooking internationally and hosted a daily cooking show, *The New Way Gourmet.* To ensure the accuracy and completeness of the information in their *Guide to Ethnic Ingredients,* they assembled a special board of consultants from among the leading chefs, gourmets, and cookbook authors in the United States.

Also by Diana and Paul von Welanetz

The Pleasure of Your Company
With Love from Your Kitchen
The Art of Buffet Entertaining
Entertain with Style, the von Welanetz Hospitality Handbook

THE VON WELANETZ GUIDE TO ETHNIC
INGREDIENTS

DIANA & PAUL VON WELANETZ

WARNER BOOKS

A Warner Communications Company

Warner Books Edition
Copyright © 1982 by Diana and Paul von Welanetz
All rights reserved.

This Warner Books edition is published by arrangement with
J.P. Tarcher, Inc., 9110 Sunset Boulevard, Los Angeles, CA 90069

Warner Books, Inc., 666 Fifth Avenue, New York, NY 10103
W A Warner Communications Company

Printed in the United States of America
First Warner Books Trade Paperback Printing: September 1987
10 9 8 7 6 5 4 3 2 1

Library of Congress Cataloging-in-Publication Data

Von Welanetz, Diana.
  The von Welanetz guide to ethnic ingredients.

  Includes index.
  1. Cookery, International.   2. Food.
I. von Welanetz, Paul.   II. Title.   III. Title:
Ethnic ingredients.
TX725.A1V664 1987   641.59   87-10552
ISBN 0-446-38420-8 (pbk.) (U.S.A.)
      0-446-38421-6 (pbk.) (Canada)

FOR MIMI, JACK, MARGE, AND LEXI

BOARD OF CONSULTANTS

The authors wish to thank the following for sharing their knowledge and expertise.

GIULIANO BUGIALLI, the foods of Italy
HUGH CARPENTER, the foods of Asia
MARION CUNNINGHAM, the foods of Regional America
BARBARA HANSEN, the foods of Latin America
FAYE LEVY, the foods of Europe
JIM AND JULIE NASSRAWAY, the foods of the Middle East
RUE PINE, the foods of Mexico
NORISHIGE AND MELINDA TAKEUCHI, the foods
  of Japan
PAULA WOLFERT, the foods of the Middle East
JEAN YUEH, the foods of China

CONTENTS

ACKNOWLEDGEMENTS 10

HOW TO USE THIS BOOK 10

INTRODUCTION 11

HERBS, SPICES, AND
    SEASONING BLENDS 13

THE FOODS OF AFRICA 91

THE FOODS OF ASIA 121

THE FOODS OF EUROPE 309

THE FOODS OF LATIN AMERICA 473

THE FOODS OF THE MIDDLE EAST 563

THE FOODS OF REGIONAL
    AMERICA 625

RECOMMENDED
    ETHNIC COOKBOOKS 691

SHOPPING SOURCES 700

RECIPE INDEX 707

GENERAL INDEX 710

ACKNOWLEDGMENTS

Our most joyous appreciation is for our editor, Janice Gallagher, whose passion for this project was at least equal to ours. Thanks, as well, to all of those at J. P. Tarcher who have worked so hard to bring this book into being.

The following people have been helpful in many ways, some with recipes, others with words of encouragement: James Beard, Andrea Bell, Penny Birnbaum, Julie and Frank Boone, Genevieve Davis, Patrick Dunavan, Jennifer Edwards, Julienne Edwards, Mary and John Erpelding, Andrea Fenster, Evangeline Garcia, Lloyd Gaynes, Annette and Steve Grob, Neil Grosman, Susie Gross, Lenore and Tony Hatch, Phyllis Hoffman, Cyndi James-Reese, Nancy Kehoe, Pauline Kelbly, Candace Kommers, Dr. Ron Krolik, Dolly and Dick Martin, Richard Milton, Dr. Ernie Nagamatsu, Ty Nutt, Ann Pappas, Frances Pelham, Stu Rosen, Karen Rubin, Mimi and Jack Schneider, Judi Skalsky, Harold Solursh, Bill Stetz, Michel Stroot, Barbara Swain, Gretchen and Bob Vernon, Marilyn Domoto Webb, Marge Welanetz, Mary Poulos Wilde, and Chef Richard Wing.

HOW TO USE THIS BOOK

We have divided the culinary world into six sections: Asia, Africa, Europe, Latin America, the Middle East, and Regional America. Ingredients are listed alphabetically within each section. In cases where ingredients are used in the cuisines of two or more of those sections, cross-referencing indicates where the main entry is located. Further cross-referencing is indicated by the use of SMALL CAPS within an entry, followed by the name of the section where the listing can be found if not within the same section. There is a separate section on Herbs, Spices, and Seasoning Blends, because they are used extensively in most of the world's cuisines.

With most entries you will find the proper pronunciation and various foreign-language names for the entry item. The introductory portion of an entry deals with background information, the forms in which the item is available, and general suggestions on where to seek it out. Brand names and other shopping tips are given where appropriate. STORAGE describes the ways in which the item can or should be stored. PREPARATION AND USE tells quantities to buy and basic preparation (i.e., how to clean, peel, etc.) This is followed by suggestions for use and classic affinities. Often a very basic recipe appears here. Specific dishes that are examples of how and in which countries the item is used are often followed by one of our own recipes using the items as an ingredient.

Recipes that appear in the book are capitalized and can be found in the RECIPE INDEX.

Following the main body of the work there are two other sections. SHOPPING SOURCES lists many mail-order sources for bringing hard-to-find ingredients to your doorstep. RECOMMENDED ETHNIC COOKBOOKS is a listing of those we most enthusiastically recommend.

INTRODUCTION

Culinarily speaking, America is coming of age. The telltale signs are everywhere: the proliferation of cooking schools and ethnic restaurants, extraordinarily good food magazines, and the creation of the International Cooking School Association, which has yearly conventions and is setting high standards in the field. We seem to be on a nationwide tasting spree, and delighting in the sheer sensuality and fun of it all.

Springing up everywhere are food societies that hold seminars and symposiums. It was at one of these, in San Francisco in the spring of 1981, that the idea for this book was born.

We were invited to hear James Beard and Julia Child, along with Barbara Kafka and Giuliano Bugialli, at an evening symposium on the "Future of Cooking in America." It was a lively discussion, during which each panelist, without exception, commented on the surprisingly rapid expansion of interest in ethnic cuisines here in America, the startling rate at which we absorb new information, and how the cooking sophisticate is digging deeper and deeper into more ethnicity, and into broader tastes.

It was as if a flashbulb had gone off in both our heads at the same time. We asked ourselves, "If that many Americans are taking such an interest in ethnic cooking, are they having the same problems shopping for ingredients that we are?" We have studied cooking internationally, have written three books on food, and have taught cooking for years yet, as sophisticated as we feel ourselves to be, we have often felt confused, if not awkward, in some ethnic markets.

Just after that meeting in San Francisco, we were having dinner with friends, and our host, a dedicated cook and tenacious shopper, commented, "If only I knew how to buy all those exotic foods I see in a Chinese or other ethnic market, and, once I bought something, how to store and use it." That idle comment focused our resolve and was the springboard that launched us into this new endeavor.

During our many months of research, we had some exciting times searching out ethnic markets. We traveled about with pocket tape recorders, notebooks, and cameras, asking questions of shopkeepers like big-time spenders. For the most part, we were tolerated but, more than once, we were scowled at and accused of price-shopping for the market's competition. You can imagine how difficult it was trying to explain our innocent project to someone who didn't speak or understand English very well, and our nerves were shot after writing the Asian chapter alone. Although we did feel at this point that there wasn't much we hadn't learned about Asian ingredients, we decided to establish a board of consultants and asked some of the world's foremost experts in ethnic cooking to review our chapters in order to double-check our information for accuracy.

Our main purpose in writing this book is to provide as much assistance as possible to the shopper in ethnic markets. Language and pronunciation always seem to be a difficulty when shopping for foreign foods, so we have tried to be as accurate as possible with both (considering that everyone pronounces everything differently anyway). We see this guide as a companion volume to your favorite ethnic cookbooks, and we hope that it will inspire greater interest in the exciting foods of the world. We have included our own list of favorite ethnic cookbooks, as well as over 150 of our own favorite ethnic recipes using the ingredients in this book. In choosing those to be included, our goal has been authenticity of use, except in a few innovative instances that foreshadow America's trend toward a new "melting pot" kind of cookery.

We have not included obscure and elite products flown in by exotic restaurants because they are never available to the consumer. Nor have we described such items as fried caterpillars and chocolate-covered baby bees, novelty items no one takes seriously, but that are included in some fancy food catalogues. In short, if it is beyond the reach or use of even the most devoted shopper, we have excluded it. We have also shunned such items as "crêpe mix," Swiss Birchermuesli cereal, and the like, because they are self-explanatory and complete unto themselves. Missing also are most liqueurs. They are already widely known and generally available in most liquor stores. A few, such as South African Van der Hum, are mentioned because they are often homemade, and then are used in recipes. And, in choosing ethnic ingredients of Regional America, we made a decision to describe only the generally unfamiliar. Though apples, melons, and the like may indeed qualify as ethnic, we don't believe our readers will expect to find those items here. All the listed items are ingredients, so prepared foods are not listed unless they, themselves, become an ingredient in another dish.

We have, during the writing of this book, often felt as though we were at an international food fair. The things we found for sale were often so aromatic, so enticing, that we actually felt deprived for never having tasted them. We were continually amazed at how busy these little markets were, and how willing the American cook is to try something new, to take a traditional ethnic ingredient and inventively substitute it for an ingredient in a classic dish. America's kitchens have been exposed to an enormous amount of ethnic influence. In fact, there is practically nothing to which they have not been exposed, and this tends to bring about confidence, innovation, improvisation—the daring to try something new.

We hope this volume inspires you to do just that, that it will provide an open sesame for you. We offer it as a friendly and helpful companion for your marketing explorations.

Diana and Paul von Welanetz
Pacific Palisades, California
April, 1982

Herbs, Spices, and Seasoning Blends

Much of the history of the world is the story of humankind's search for spices and how the trade routes for obtaining these spices crisscrossed the known world and were established and fought over. Spices, the pungent roots, seeds, dried berries, and bark of tropical and subtropical plants, were valued as flavorings and food preservatives and were as much a symbol of wealth as money is today. Herbs, the fragrant leaves of plants grown in temperate zones, have a long history both as seasonings and as medicines.

Since almost all of the major cuisines of the world have, in some way or other, made use of the more common herbs and spices, it will be easier for the reader to find them collectively here rather than in specific sections. Supermarket and ethnic market spice shelves carry an array of herbs and spices. Some may have to be sought out or ordered by mail, but the effort is repaid a hundredfold by the adventure of new tastes. Large metropolitan areas have all kinds of ethnic markets to explore. Those who must order by mail should not be dismayed— just consult our extensive listing of SHOPPING SOURCES in the back of this book. In the following listings, we have attempted, as best we could, to give tips for buying and storage, and guidelines for use.

HERBS

Fresh herbs are available more and more in supermarkets and specialty produce markets. Look for crisp leaves and a strong aroma.

Dried herbs are sold everywhere, and the secret is to shop for them where there is a rapid turnover, so they won't already be old and faded when you buy them. Quite often, excellent herbs can be purchased inexpensively in ethnic markets, dried on branches or in small cellophane bags and, if they are bright and fresh looking when you buy them, you can store them at home after transferring them to airtight containers.

STORAGE: Fresh, tender varieties of fresh herbs, such as chives, can be wrapped in damp paper towels and stored in a plastic bag in the refrigerator for use within a few days. Hardier types, such as rosemary, will keep a week or more. For longer storage, we prefer to freeze herbs rather than dry them. We remove the leaves from the stalks and wrap them tightly in plastic wrap or pack them tightly into a small jar. They will keep, frozen, for up to a year. In the following listings, we give specific directions for those that need special treatment for storing and freezing.

Freshly harvested herbs can also be dried by hanging them in bunches in a warm, dry room. They should be covered loosely with paper to prevent dust from landing on them, with an opening left at the bottom to allow air to circulate. Another good drying method is to place what is to be dried on racks or trays in your oven. The heat from the pilot alone in many gas ovens is sufficient for this drying. However, if your stove is electric, the oven should be turned on to a very low temperature (150°) and then turned off, and this process repeated until the drying is complete. It is better to over-dry than to encourage the possibility of mildew or rot. Alternatively, if you have a microwave oven, herbs can be quick-dried, 3 or 4 large sprigs at a time, by placing them between paper towels, and heating on "high" for 2 to 3 minutes until the leaves are brittle. Finish drying on a rack, and then remove leaves from stalks and store as dried herbs.

Dried herbs lose their flavor quickly, and some delicate herbs, like chervil, don't have all that much to begin with. All should be stored in a cool, dark place, *not* next to the stove! Heat and light are the enemies of the essential oils in dried herbs, and the ultraviolet rays of sunshine and some lightbulbs have a tendency to affect these delicate oils. And so, as a matter of course, we prefer to place ours in a cool, dark place, lined up alphabetically. We use a marking pen to write the names of the herbs on the caps of the bottles so we can spot them quickly. (Dried herbs would last even longer if placed in the refrigerator, but we don't enjoy that luxury of space.)

Dried herb leaves keep in this way for up to a year; ground herbs only six months. As you can see, it is really best to buy no more than you think you will be able to use up quickly. Older herbs and spices cannot hurt you, but they have lost much of their original flavor, and eventually will have no more taste than hay.

PREPARATION AND USE: Always crumble dried herbs between your fingers, or rub them between your palms before adding them to recipes. Your body heat will release their fragrance and oils. A good rule of thumb for substituting dried for fresh is to use one-third to one-fourth the amount of dried as you would fresh.

As a general rule, 1 teaspoon of chopped fresh herbs will be enough for 4 servings. At least it is a starting point, and it is easy to add more after tasting, but difficult to remedy a concoction that is too "herby." If substituting fresh herbs for dried in a recipe, a good rule of thumb is to use 3 to 4 times the amount of fresh as dried.

SPICES

Whole spices are your best buy. They keep their flavors much longer than ground spices, and are most flavorful when freshly ground for each recipe.

STORAGE: Spices should be stored in the same manner as dried herbs. A general rule for storing spices is:
Whole peppercorns: 5 years or longer.
Whole spices: 2 years.
Ground spices and blends: 6 months to 1 year.

PREPARATION AND USE: Whole spices are often used in broths or marinades, and are easily strained out. A recipe may specify that spices be tied in a cheesecloth bag (a BOUQUET GARNI, see SEASONING BLENDS), in which case cut a small square of several layers of cheesecloth and rinse well to remove any sizing or stiffening. Place spices in center of cheesecloth, bring corners together, and tie securely with string. The bag is easily removed at a specific point in the recipe.

Whole spices can be pulverized with a mortar and pestle, or powdered in a blender if you have more than just a few small berries to crush. The best tool of all is an electric coffee mill. We have two; one for coffee and one for spices. Often the spices are lightly toasted in a dry skillet just before grinding to bring out their flavors. Freshly ground spices must be packed tightly into a measuring spoon to be equivalent to the same measure of pre-ground spices because they become highly aerated during the grinding.

SEASONING BLENDS

The blending of spices and herbs has acquired national characteristics: Mexican Chile Powder, Chinese Five Spice Powder, Madras-Style Curry Powder, France's Fines Herbes, Italian Herb Seasoning, and Pickling Spice, an international blend used not only to pickle meats, but to season vegetables, relishes, and sauces. Our listings include the familiar and some lesser known that may be specified in ethnic cookbooks. We have tried to be as helpful as possible in guiding you to create your own and in finding substitutes.

STORAGE: Store as herbs and spices.

USE: Blends have a place in ethnic cooking, but cooks have a tendency to rely on them, which we think is a mistake. No Indian we know would use ready-made curry powder, but would always roast and grind the spices needed to curry a dish. He or she would, however, reach for a homemade blend of Garam Masala. And no Mexican we know would use blended chile powder, unless it were the type concocted of only dried chiles, without the addition of herbs. A French cook would readily reach for Quatres Épices, and a Moroccan cook for Ras El Hanout, but would not hesitate to improvise with a pinch of this and a sprinkling of that if the blends were not available.

HERBS AND SPICES

AJWAIN

See FOODS OF ASIA section

ALLSPICE

OTHER: Jamaica pepper

ARABIC: *bahar* FRENCH: *poivre de la Jamaïque* or *toute-épice* GERMAN: *Allgewürz, Jamaikapfeffer* ITALIAN: *pimiento* LATIN: *Pimienta dioica* IN MOROCCO: *noioura* SPANISH: *pimiento de Jamaica* IN THE SPANISH CARIBBEAN: *pimienta de Jamaica* or *pimienta gorda* SWEDISH: *kryddpeppar*

A dried, reddish-brown berry, allspice is so named because it has a flavor and aroma that resemble several spices: cinnamon, clove, and nutmeg. It is of the myrtle family and native to tropical America and is exclusive to the Western Hemisphere, with most being produced in Jamaica. It is sold whole or ground on the spice shelves of most supermarkets and, like all whole spices, produces the most flavor if you grind it yourself just before use.

STORAGE: Whole berries keep well in a dark, cool place for up to 2 years without much loss of flavor. Ground allspice should be used within 6 months.

USE: Whole berries flavor pickling liquids and spiced syrups for fruit, and are used in spiced wines or punches. Two to three whole berries per pound of meat are used in broth for cooking fish and pot roasts, such as Sauerbraten, and in marinades and sauces for game and smoked meats.

Ground allspice is often used in fruitcakes and in German honey cakes, spice cookies, and other desserts. The English use it in plum puddings and mincemeat. It is a favorite in the Middle East where it is used in pilafs, such as the Turkish Pilaf Ali Pasha (rice with currants and nuts), and vegetarian dishes as well as in sweets. A Greek dish, Midea Yemisya, consists of cooked mussels in their shells topped with a rice and currant stuffing that is flavored with allspice. In Italy, rice-meatballs, called Arangini, are popular. In Morocco it is part of the spice blend, RAS EL HANOUT, and it is used in some Cous Cous and chicken dishes, and some varieties of Kefta (meatballs). In South Africa, it flavors Denningvleis (spiced lamb fricassee), and Boerewors (home-made sausage). It is sometimes substituted for the blend known as ÉPICE FINE or SPICE PARISIENNE in the making of French pâtés.

ANISE

OTHER: aniseed

ARABIC: *yanisun* DUTCH: *anijs* FRENCH: *anis* GERMAN: *Anis*
GREEK: *anise* INDIAN: *sonf* ITALIAN: *anice* LATIN: *Pimpinella anisum* IN MOROCCO: *nafaa* or *habbt hlewa* PORTUGUESE: *eruadoce* RUSSIAN: *anis* SPANISH: *anís* IN THE SPANISH CARIBBEAN: *semilla de anís*

This licorice-tasting seed is native to the Middle East and widely cultivated throughout the world. It is slightly stronger in flavor and less sweet than FENNEL, and is available on the spice shelf of any supermarket. The size and shape of the seeds vary from country to country, and the best are said to be the green ones from Spain, but most in the United States are imported from Mexico. Anise oil, pressed from the seeds, is the distinctive flavoring of liqueurs such as the French anisette, Turkish *raki*, and Latin American *aguardiente*.

STORAGE: As any whole spice.

USE: Anise has a special affinity for garlic and is used in all sorts of Mediterranean fish stews, sausages, and marinades. It is used extensively in India, usually lightly toasted, in all kinds of curried dishes, and is also chewed after meals to aid the digestion and sweeten the breath. It is used in Springerle-type German cookies and in Italian anise cookies (1½ to 2 teaspoons in recipes yielding 5 dozen cookies). An anise-flavored Greek Easter bread, Tsoueki, is wreath-shaped and studded with colored eggs. It is an important flavor in the highly spiced Mexican national dish, Mole Poblano de Guajolote.

BASIL

OTHER: sweet basil, holy basil (in India)

FRENCH: *basilic* GERMAN: *Basilienkraut* HINDI: *babuitulsi*
INDIAN: *tulsi* INDONESIAN: *kemangi* ITALIAN: *basilico* LAOTIAN: *phak itu lao* LATIN: *Ocimum basilicum* MALAYSIAN: *kemangi selaseh*
IN THE MIDDLE EAST: *habekh* IN MOROCCO: *hboq*
PORTUGUESE: *manjericão* RUSSIAN: *bazilik* SINHALESE (Sri Lanka): *kus kus* SPANISH: *albahaca* THAI: *horapa, bai ka-prow* (seeds)

Basil is a bright green, leafy, aromatic herb native to Asia and Africa. It is often sold fresh, in bunches, and is available dried in all supermarkets though the flavor does not really compare favorably with aromatic fresh basil, one of the easiest herbs to grow in a summer garden. Its season is from midsummer until the first frost, and we have even had it continue growing into February in our Southern California herb garden. One variety with huge leaves is called "lettuce leaf" basil. Tiny black seeds known as "holy basil" are sold only in Indian markets.

STORAGE: Dried basil can be stored indefinitely in a cool, dark place. Fresh basil, washed, dried, and stems removed, can be preserved in several ways. It can be layered between coarse salt in tightly sealed jars, in which case it loses a bit of its bright color but retains much of its flavor. Alternatively, the whole leaves can be wrapped in plastic wrap and frozen for up to 6 months. Our favorite method is to chop it, mix with olive oil, coating it generously, and then freeze it in teaspoon-sized mounds, which are easily added, usually without thawing, to many recipes.

USE: Basil is used, fresh or dried, in a wide range of cuisines, but is indispensable to Mediterranean cooking. It has a special affinity for tomatoes, zucchini, and other summer vegetables. In Italy, it is the base for PESTO (see THE FOODS OF EUROPE section) in which it is combined with olive oil, garlic, grated Romano or Parmigiano cheese, and pine nuts, to be used as a pungent sauce for pasta or as an ingredient in many other dishes. It is essential to minestrone. Basil blends beautifully with vinegar and olive oil to spoon over sliced tomatoes and mozzarella cheese.

In the south of France it flavors the Provençal soup, Pistou. Portuguese Fish Soup contains basil and ground almonds. Hindus plant it around their homes and temples as a symbol of happiness, and float the tiny, black, flavorless seeds atop sweet drinks in tropical areas because they are thought to be cooling to the body. It is a versatile herb that can be used in fresh salads, garlic-scented soups, stews, and pasta sauces, cooked or uncooked.

The following is one of our favorite uncooked pasta sauces.

PASTA TRICOLORE

For 8 servings

We named this dish after the Italian flag because of its distinct white, green, and red colors.

FOR THE SAUCE:
⅔ cup "extra-virgin" olive oil
2 medium cloves garlic, minced
2 large bunches fresh basil

½ bunch parsley, leaves only, minced
½ a medium size red (Bermuda) onion, minced
5 large, ripe tomatoes, seeded and diced
2 teaspoons coarse salt
¾ teaspoon freshly ground black pepper
1½ pounds dried pasta of your choice, or 3 (12-ounce)
    packages frozen TORTELLINI, cooked according to
    package directions

Variation: Substitute 8 ounces of frozen PESTO for both the olive oil and basil called for in the recipe.

Combine the sauce ingredients in a serving bowl, cover, and leave at room temperature for at least an hour to blend the flavors.

Just before serving, cook the pasta according to package directions until barely tender and still chewy (*al dente*). Drain well and toss immediately with the sauce.

TO PREPARE IN ADVANCE: The sauce will only improve if allowed to marinate for several hours at room temperature. If necessary, the sauce ingredients, except for tomatoes, can be assembled a day or two ahead of time and stored in the refrigerator. Several hours before serving, bring to room temperature and add tomatoes. Any leftovers can be refrigerated to serve as a pasta salad the next day.

BAY LEAF

OTHER: bay laurel

ARABIC: *ghar* DUTCH and FRENCH: *laurier* GERMAN: *Lorbeer*
ITALIAN: *lauro* LATIN: *Lauris nobilis* PORTUGUESE: *loureiro*
RUSSIAN: *lavr* SPANISH: *laurel* SWEDISH: *lagr*

Bay leaf is native to the Mediterranean. Dried leaves can be purchased in all supermarkets and in Mediterranean markets. Fresh are only available through people who happen to own a tree. Those labeled "imported" are most likely from Turkey and are more squat-shaped and only half as pungent in flavor as the longer, tapered California bay laurel. It can be used as a substitute for the Southeast Asian DAUN SALAAM (see THE FOODS OF ASIA section).

STORAGE: If fresh, bay leaves should dry thoroughly before being stored in covered jars in a cool, dark place or they will mildew. Dried leaves should be used within a year.

USE: Use half as much fresh bay as you would dried, and only half as much again of the California type as you would imported. A general rule is to use 1 leaf to 2 quarts of liquid, but a single leaf should be ample for any recipe, even if you are doubling or tripling the amounts called for. Bay leaves are used in almost every known cuisine to flavor stews, beans, marinades, and stocks.

They are one of the basics of a BOUQUET GARNI (see SEASONING BLENDS) in French cooking. They add dimension to all kinds of sauces, soups, and braised dishes, especially those containing beef, and are almost always used in *court-bouillon* for poaching fish, and add an important flavor to fish soups, such as the Spanish Zarzuela de Mariscos (seafood soup).

BAY RUM BERRIES

IN THE FRENCH CARIBBEAN: *bois d'Inde* LATIN: *Pimienta acris*

These dried berries are from the bay rum tree in the Caribbean, which produces berries almost identical to MALAGUETA peppercorns (see under PEPPERCORNS), that come from a West African tree. They are interchangeable. The berries can be found in some Caribbean markets, but are not widely available. Substitute black peppercorns.

STORAGE: As any whole spice.

USE: In the Caribbean they are used in Blaff, fresh-caught fish plunged into broth.

BORAGE

LATIN: *Borago officinalis* ITALIAN: *boraggine*

Borage has rather hairy, cucumber-tasting leaves and tiny bright blue flowers. It has a long history as a medicinal herb, and is native to southern Europe. It is seldom called for in recipes, probably because it is not widely available. It is often grown in herb gardens, and plants or seeds can be ordered by mail.

STORAGE: As any fresh herb.

USE: The leaves are usually chopped to add to salads, or steeped to make a medicinal tea. In Italy, the leaves are used in a stuffing for ravioli, or are batter-dipped and fried to make Frittelle (fritters). They can be cooked like spinach and flavored with butter. The brilliant flowers are ideal for garnishing salads (as are other herb flowers, because one needn't be concerned about toxicity as with flowers from non-edible plants). The flowers are often crystallized, like violets in Europe, but this is done in the home and they are not available commercially.

CAPERS

FRENCH: *câpres* GERMAN: *Kaper* ITALIAN: *cappero* SPANISH: *alcaparra*

Capers are small, unopened flower buds from a Mediterranean bush that are pickled in vinegar. They are available in many supermarkets and gourmet specialty shops, as well as in all European markets, and tend to be expensive. Usually they are sold in jars packed in vinegar, but some Italian markets will have salted capers loose for sale in bulk. The tiny *nonpareille* variety from the South of France are considered the finest, though we often prefer the larger, brined type sold in Italian markets.

STORAGE: Those in vinegar will keep for months in the refrigerator in a nonmetal container in their original liquid though they tend to get softer and mushier on standing. Loose ones can be stored in a nonmetal, airtight container at room temperature for 3 months or longer.

PREPARATION AND USE: Salted capers should be rinsed well and dried before use. Bottled ones are usually drained, but their vinegar brine is sometimes used in dishes such as Eggplant Caponata.

Most Americans are familiar with the flavor of capers because they are almost always an ingredient in the ubiquitous "tartar" sauce, but French sauces such as Rémoulade, Gribiche, and Ravigote contain them as well. The French variety almost always accompanies thinly sliced smoked salmon. They combine very well with lemon and with anchovies, and complement most fish and veal dishes, such as Austria's Wiener Fischfilets (fish in sour cream with bacon and mustard), and Sweden's Biff à la Lindström. They are an important garnish for eggs or calves brains cooked in "black butter" and in many cold dishes and salads. Capers are at their finest when they are served as a pungent garnish and flavor contrast with very rich dishes, such as Vitello Tonnato (veal with tuna, anchovy, and cream sauce). In Italy, Caponata, a delicious Sicilian antipasto dish of eggplant, tomatoes, olives, and capers is also very popular, and can be found in Italian delis, freshly made, and imported in jars or cans.

Capers lend a pungent flavor to the uncooked sauce of olive oil and diced tomato for the dish called Pasta alla Puttanesca, which was reputedly created by "ladies of the evening" for a quick meal between appointments. No matter its origin, it makes a tasty lunch or supper dish and is suitable for buffet serving. Here is our recipe.

PASTA ALLA PUTTANESCA

1 pound dried pasta, cooked   For 6 servings
   according to package directions

SAUCE:
  6 very ripe tomatoes, peeled, seeded, and diced
  ½ cup "extra-virgin" olive oil
  ¾ cup pitted black olives (Italian or Greek), sliced or
     chopped
  2 tablespoons salted capers, rinsed and drained
  ¼ cup chopped fresh basil
  2 tablespoons chopped fresh parsley (Italian flat-leaf
     preferred)
  2 cloves garlic, minced
  ½ cup freshly grated Parmesan
     Optional: 1 (2-ounce) can flat anchovy fillets, drained,
        rinsed, and blotted dry, then minced
     Freshly ground black pepper, to taste

Combine the sauce ingredients in a large serving bowl and keep at room temperature. Cook pasta according to package directions, drain, and place directly in the bowl of sauce. Toss and serve immediately.

TO PREPARE IN ADVANCE: The sauce can be prepared in the morning and left, covered, at room temperature. Cook and add pasta just before serving.

CARAWAY SEED

ARABIC: *hub-et il barary* (a black variety) FRENCH: *carvi* or *cumin de près* GERMAN: *Kümmel* ITALIAN: *carvi* or *comino dei prati* LATIN:

Carum carvi IN MOROCCO: *karwiya* PORTUGUESE: *alchravia*
RUSSIAN: *tmin* SPANISH: *alcaravea* SWEDISH: *kummin*

Caraway seed is native to Europe and the Middle East and is very popular in the cooking of Germany, Austria, Hungary, and the Scandinavian countries. It is slightly sweet and has a faintly acrid, anise undertone. It is often mistranslated as CUMIN, a similar looking seed, which has an entirely different taste. (A glance at the Swedish name will tell you why this happens.) An oil pressed from the seed is the base for the liqueur, kümmel.

STORAGE: Store as any spice in a cool, dark place for up to a year, though these seeds harden on standing and may require longer cooking if they are old.

USE: The seeds commonly flavor rye bread. In Europe, they are widely used in the cooking of stews, such as Hungarian Székely Gulyás, which teams them with pork, paprika, sauerkraut, and sour cream, and in a Viennese version of goulash that contains sweet green peppers. In Latvia, the seeds are steeped in boiling water to make an extract to flavor a salad made of beets.

In Bavaria, they season pork dishes, sausages, noodles, cabbage, and sauerkraut. One German dish that uses them is Fische Mit Kümmelkraut (fish with caraway seed cabbage). The Alsatian meat-and-sausage-garnished sauerkraut, Choucroute Garni, is properly flavored with the tiny seeds, as is the German Gefülte Gans (goose stuffed with prunes and apples). A Polish dish, Sztufada, consists of short ribs cooked with bacon, vinegar, caraway, and cauliflower, and is usually served with noodles. Caraway seeds have a special affinity for cheese, and the Norwegian cheese, Kuminost, is studded with them. They are usually added to the seasonings for Hungarian LIPTAUER cheese (see THE FOODS OF EUROPE section). In the Middle East they are used in sweet cookies.

CARDAMOM

SOMETIMES SPELLED: cardamon

ARABIC: *hal* or *hab-hal* BURMESE: *phalazee* FRENCH: *cardamome*
GERMAN: *Kardamome* GREEK: *kardamomon* INDIAN: *illaichi* or
elaichi INDONESIAN: *kapulaga* ITALIAN: *cardamomo* LATIN:
Elletaria cardamomum MALAYSIAN: *buah pelaga* IN MOROCCO:
qaqula RUSSIAN: *kardamon* SINHALESE (Sri Lanka): *enasal*
SPANISH: *cardamomo* THAI: *kravan*

Cardamom is an aromatic spice native to the tropical jungles of southern India and of Ceylon. It belongs to the ginger family and is one of the world's most expensive spices—the most expensive, in fact, next to saffron. Dried cardamom seedpods are either white, pale green, or brown, depending upon whether they were bleached (white), dried in the oven (green), or dried in the sun (brown). Each pod contains two clusters of approximately six seeds each. Most cardamom pods found in the United States are imported from Sri Lanka or Guatemala and are of the bleached variety. They can be found in the spice sections of most supermarkets. But the green pods found in Indian markets are more aromatic. The outer pod is not usually used in cooking, but is broken away from the small dark seeds inside and discarded. The seeds have a lemon-eucalyptus flavor which, in the East, is believed to have a cooling effect on the body. There is a black variety, found in Indian stores, called *bara elaichi,* which is cheaper and much more earthy tasting. Ground cardamom is widely available in spice bottles, but should be used only if pods are not available because it loses its aromatic qualities quickly.

STORAGE: Store cardamom pods in a cool, dry place to prevent the aromatic oils of the seed from evaporating. The pods have a shelf life of about 1 year, the powder only a few months.

PREPARATION AND USE: Crush the pods between your fingers to reveal the small dark seeds. When ground to a powder, its use is very popular in Indian and Indonesian curried dishes and pastries, and in ground spice combinations such as GARAM MASALA. Cardamom is very popular in Scandinavia and Germany for its sweet pungency, and is added to meat dishes, such as sauerbraten and Swedish Meatballs, and to cakes and desserts, and is more widely used in those countries than cinnamon. It is a popular flavoring for mulled wine and Danish pastries and, in Norway, it is added to ground-meat dishes. A Finnish bread, Paasiaisleipa, flavored with cardamom and lemon is baked in shiny buckets to celebrate the arrival of spring calves. Some devoted coffee drinkers claim that a whole pod added to a cup of coffee mellows the coffee without changing the flavor.

In the Middle East, cardamom coffee, called Gahwa, is given to visitors as a symbol of Arab hospitality. It is a tradition that the ritual of coffee drinking not be interrupted by any discussion of business. To make it, roasted coffee beans are crushed with cardamom seeds, sugar, and a pinch of cloves, and then simmered for 2 to 3 minutes. It is served black, in small cups, with sweet pastries.

In Saudi Arabia, it is one of the most highly favored spices, not only for its purported cooling effect, but because it is thought to have aphrodisiac qualities. Iranian Shir Berent (rice pudding with fruit) often teams this flavor with pistachios. In Ethiopia, it flavors Kitfo (raw chopped beef with spices) and Yegoman Kifto (chopped collards with buttermilk). In Asia, the green cardamom pods are used as breath fresheners as well as in teas. In India, the bruised pods flavor Parsi Pilau (spiced rice with saffron, raisins, and nuts), and the whole pods are simmered in Thai Muslim Curry with chicken, TAMA-

RIND, and coconut milk. In Indonesia, cardamom pods are an important ingredient of Pacari (pineapple coconut curry). We crush them to add to homemade applesauce instead of cinnamon.

CASSIA
See CINNAMON

CAYENNE
OTHER: ground red pepper, Guinea pepper, Spanish pepper

LATIN: *Capiscum frutescens* IN MOROCCO: *felfla soudaniya*

Cayenne is a pure, orange-red, ground chili powder made from the dried pods of ripe, pungent chiles. Its color varies from orange to dark red, and it varies in hotness as well. Waverly Root, noted food historian, writes that it is not named for the Cayenne district of French Guiana in South America but derives its name from a modification of the Brazilian Tupi Indian word for it, *kyinha* or *quiynha*. For the most part it is now sold as "ground red chile," because it may be made with any of a variety of tiny, dried red chiles. It is produced in various countries—India, China, Japan, Africa—and even our own state of Louisiana. That which is purchased in Korean and Indian markets is usually brighter in color and of finer quality than that found on supermarket spice shelves.

STORAGE: Store all red spices (paprika, chili powder, etc.) tightly sealed in the refrigerator to prevent infestation of bugs.

USE: Because it can vary so much in pungency, it is really not possible to give measurements for crushed or dried red chiles. Use it with caution, and let your tongue tell you when you've added enough. We suggest you start out with ⅛ teaspoon, which should be ample to flavor any dish of 4 servings to a reasonable pungency. Asians, who eat lots of fiery dishes, would find that amount ludicrously lacking. It is used in some of the seasoning blends found in this book. A few grains of cayenne are often added to French sauces during the final seasoning: Béarnaise, hollandaise, mayonnaise and stews such as bouillabaisse. It adds piquancy and accentuates the flavors of soups, spreads—in fact, most savory dishes.

CELERY SEED
ARABIC: *karafs* DUTCH: *selderij* FRENCH: *céleri* GERMAN: *Sellerie*
INDONESIAN: *seldri* ITALIAN: *sedano* LATIN: *Apium graveolens*

MALAYSIAN: *daun seladri* RUSSIAN: *syel'derey* SPANISH: *apio*
SWEDISH: *selleri* THAI: *pak chi farang*

This very tiny seed is not from cultivated celery but from a wild celery known as "smallage," native to Southern Europe. It is available on the spice shelf of any supermarket as a whole seed and, when ground and mixed with salt, as "celery salt."

STORAGE: As any whole spice.

USE: Use a light hand with this because it tends to be bitter. It does not actually substitute for fresh celery in a dish, but is widely used in pickling and in dressings for potato salad, coleslaw, and for fruit salad. It is added to melted butter to brush over breads and rolls before baking, and is used in meat loaves, sauerkraut, and stuffings. A few seeds in oyster stew and other chowders give a slight celery flavor without the addition of chopped fresh.

CHERVIL

ARABIC: *maqdunis afranji* FRENCH: *cerfeuil* GERMAN: *Kerbel*
ITALIAN: *cerfoglio* LATIN: *Anthriscus cerefolium* RUSSIAN: *kervel'*
SPANISH: *perifollo* SWEDISH: *körvel*

Chervil is an aromatic herb with feathery leaves and a delicate anise flavor which is used almost as commonly in France as parsley is used in the United States. Though native to southwest Russia, it is one of the classic FINES HERBES called for in French recipes. It is seldom sold commercially either fresh or dried, because there is not much demand for it, though Spice Islands does package dried chervil in jars. It is such a delicate herb that it loses most of its flavor in the drying process. Chervil is an annual that is easily grown in a pot in a shady spot. Plants and seeds are available in nurseries.

STORAGE: Wrap fresh chervil in damp paper towels and store in a plastic bag in the refrigerator for up to 3 days. It does not freeze well because it is delicate.

PREPARATION AND USE: Chervil is believed to bring out the flavor of other herbs with which it is used. Some experts claim chervil should never be cooked, but added only at the last moment to soups, stews, and braised dishes, sprinkling it as one would minced parsely over the top. It is especially good with chicken, veal, lamb, and rabbit. It is used extensively in French and Belgian cooking. We have always used it, along with tarragon, in making Béarnaise sauce. It has a special affinity for fish and for eggs.

CHIVES

ARABIC: *basal* DUTCH: *bieslook* FRENCH: *ciboulette* GERMAN: *Schnittlauch* ITALIAN: *erba cipollina* LATIN: *Allium schoenoprasum* PORTUGUESE: *cebolinha* RUSSIAN: *luk-resanyets* SPANISH: *cebolleta* SWEDISH: *gräslök*

Chives are a subtle member of the onion family, growing in delicate, long, green shoots, which are snipped off with scissors. They are sold in many supermarkets, fresh, freeze-dried, or frozen. Fresh plants, which are always best, are usually available at nurseries and are easy to grow in a pot on a sunny windowsill, where they can be snipped as needed, and thrive by regular trimming. Frozen chives are next best in flavor, followed by the freeze-dried type, which are not at all bad if they are not old. Chinese chives (See CHIVES, CHINESE, in THE FOODS OF ASIA section), found in Asian markets, are considerably heartier and stronger flavored.

STORAGE: Fresh chives, wrapped in damp paper towels and placed in a plastic bag, can be stored in the crisper of the refrigerator for up to 5 days. Or freeze them after rinsing, drying, and cutting. Freeze-dried chives are stored as any dried herb to be used within 3 months. Frozen chives should be used within a few months.

PREPARATION AND USE: Fresh chives shoots are used to decorate aspics and other elegant food preparations, but are usually snipped with scissors to sprinkle over prepared dishes. If they are to be cooked, add them only at the last minute to preserve their flavor and fresh color. Freeze-dried and frozen chives are already snipped, but are treated in the same manner as fresh, and the frozen-type needn't be thawed before use. They are delicious with vegetables, in omelettes, and in Sauce Verte (herbed mayonnaise). They are classically used in Vichyssoise (potato and leek soup, served cold).

CILANTRO
See CORIANDER

CINNAMON (and CASSIA)

ARABIC: *qurfa* (cassia is *darasini*) BURMESE: *thit-ja-bob-gauk* CHINESE: *jou-kuei* (cassia is *kuei*) FRENCH: *cannelle* (cassia is *casse*) GERMAN: *Zimt* (cassia is *Kassie*) INDIAN: *dalchini* or *darchini* INDONESIAN and MALAYSIAN: *kayu manis* ITALIAN: *cannella* (cassia is *cassia*) JAPANESE: *seiron-nikkei* (cassia is *kashia keihi*) LATIN: *Cinnamomum zylanicum* (cassia is *Cinnamomum lauri*) MOROCCAN: *dar el cini* (cassia is *karfa*) RUSSIAN: *koritsa* SINHALESE (Sri Lanka): *kurundu* SPANISH: *canela* (cassia is *casia*) SWEDISH: *kanel* (cassia is *kassia*) THAI: *op chery*

Because cinnamon and cassia are so often sold as the same thing, we are pairing them here for comparison. Cinnamon is the sweetly pungent, reddish-brown spice that is the dried bark peeled from the evergreen cinnamon tree. It is native to Sri Lanka. In the United States, we rarely see true cinnamon, or Ceylon cinnamon but, instead, find cassia, which usually comes from Saigon and is much stronger in flavor and less expensive. Buy either cinnamon or cassia bark in its natural quill-shaped, sun-dried form, which has curled to form sticks. True cinnamon is tan-colored and much more slender than cassia, which is reddish-brown. Both are less expensive in ethnic markets than in supermarket spice sections.

STORAGE: Tightly wrapped and stored in a cool, dry, dark place, it will keep indefinitely.

USE: Many Asian cooks prefer using this spice in sticks rather than in its ground form because it does not darken the color of the finished dish as much. The stick form is used to flavor Malaysian rice dishes, and is simmered in sauce for Thai Muslim Curry and the Vietnamese national dish, Pho, a soup with beef and rice noodles, garnished with bean sprouts and other salad ingredients. In the Middle East, whole sticks of cassia are preferred because they have less tendency to break up in the cooking of rice pilaf.

Ground cinnamon, in India, is used primarily as a garnish for desserts. In Morocco, it flavors Bastilla (the succulent chicken-filled pastry) and Cous Cous, and is sprinkled over Harira soup and desserts. In South Africa, it flavors Kaltschale (cold buttermilk soup with lemon, raisins, and nutmeg). In Lebanese cooking it is used with all fowl and meat, and is widely used in Greece in meat dishes, such as Pastitsio (marcaroni and beef with a custard topping). It is used in the Israeli almond dessert, Halvah. In Europe, it is used in Irish Chocolate Potato Cake, Danish rice fritters with raisins and nuts, and the Portuguese fried bread dessert, Rabanadas.

In most cuisines, ground cinnamon is one of the most important spices in baking. If you grind your cinnamon from sticks as needed, it will not be much more aromatic than the spice purchased already ground, so it is not worth the effort. Use whole or powdered to flavor foods and beverages. A cinnamon stick makes a wonderful utensil to stir coffee, tea, or mulled cider, lending its special spiciness to those drinks. We love its flavor in a rich, meaty Greek stew with tomatoes, called Papou's Greek Stew (see OLIVES, KALA-MANTA in the FOODS OF THE MIDDLE EAST section).

CLOVES

ARABIC: *qaranful* BURMESE: *ley-nyim-bwint* CHINESE: *ting hsiang*
FRENCH: *clou de girofle* GERMAN: *Nelke* INDIAN: *laung* or
lavungam INDONESIAN: *tjengkeh* ITALIAN: *chiodo di garofano*
JAPANESE: *choji* LATIN: *Syzygium aromaticum* MALAYSIAN: *bunga
cingkeh* IN MOROCCO: *oud el nouar* PORTUGUESE: *cravo*
RUSSIAN: *gvozdika* SINHALESE (Sri Lanka): *karabu* SPANISH: *clavo*
SWEDISH: *kryddnejlika* THAI: *gahn plu*

Cloves are the dried, nail-shaped flowerbuds of the tall evergreen clove trees that are native to southern Asia and the West Indies. They are the most aromatic spice and contain an oil that is not only antiseptic, but also has powerful preserving action. They are expensive because they must be hand-picked at just the proper time and sun-dried. Ground cloves consist of only the pulverized heads.

STORAGE: Whole cloves will keep indefinitely in an airtight container in a cool, dark place.

USE: Always use cloves sparingly. In Europe, a whole clove is often stuck into an onion to season soups and stews, and one is plenty in most cases. In marinades, 4 or 5 cloves are usually used for 2 pounds of meat because their flavor is not released by heat. Whole cloves are an important seasoning for Glögg, the traditional hot wine and brandy served in Sweden at Christmas, which is also flavored with cardamom and cinnamon sticks. They are essential to the German dishes Schweinebraten (fresh ham served with sauerkraut, dumplings, and sour cream sauce), and to sauerbraten. Whole cloves are pushed into oranges and other citrus fruits to make pomander balls. This practice results in what James Beard refers to as "a domestic ailment known as clove pusher's thumb." And Americans use them often in pickling and preserving and in the decoration and flavoring of baked ham.

Powdered cloves are used as a seasoning throughout India in various mixed spices such as GARAM MASALA, and are used to flavor betel nuts, which are chewed as a stimulant. In South Africa, they are used in Tomato Bredie (lamb and tomato stew), Swartzuuer (lamb stew with tamarind and dumplings) and, in East Africa, in Zanzibar Duck. In Europe and many other parts of the world they are an important ingredient in cookies, spice cakes, and all sorts of baked goods. In the United States, the powdered form is popularly used to season desserts such as gingerbread and apple pie.

CORIANDER

(Often referred to in this book as CILANTRO).
OTHER: Chinese or Japanese parsley

ARABIC: *kuzbara* BURMESE: *nannimbin* CHINESE: *yuen sai*
DUTCH: *koriander* FRENCH: *coriandre* GERMAN: *Koriander*
INDIAN: *dhania sabz* ITALIAN: *coriandolo* JAPANESE: *koyendoro*
LAOTIAN: *phak hom pon* LATIN: *Coriandrum sativum* IN LATIN
AMERICA: *cilantro, culantro* MALAYSIAN: *daun ketumbar* IN
MOROCCO: *kosbour* PORTUGUESE: *coentro* RUSSIAN: *koriandr*
SPANISH: *coriandro* SWEDISH: *koriander* THAI: *pak chee*

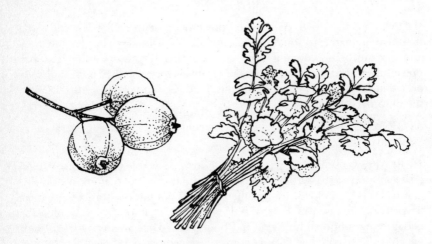

Fresh coriander is an herb and coriander seeds are a spice. They differ greatly in flavor and in use. For clarity, let us separate them.

FRESH CORIANDER

A very pungent and aromatic herb with a taste very unlike the flat-leaf Italian parsley it closely resembles. In Asian cooking, all parts of this plant are used: the seeds, as an essential ingredient in curries; the fresh green leaves, indispensable as an herb; and the roots, the secret ingredient of some Thai dishes. It is available all year by the bunch in oriental markets and in many supermarkets in the southern and western parts of the United States, where there are large Asian or Latin American populations. Buy it with its roots attached. We are among its legion of fans, though we admit it was an acquired taste. The uninitiated often remark that it tastes like hand soap.

Coriander seeds, available in all supermarket spice sections, can, if fresh, be planted to grow this aromatic herb.

STORAGE: Place the roots and stems in a tall jar of water. Cover the leaves with a plastic bag. Store in the refrigerator for up to a week. It doesn't freeze very well, as it is a very tender herb. Paula Wolfert, cookbook author, prefers making "coriander water" to freezing whole leaves, and her method works for all recipes except salads, which require fresh leaves. To make "coriander water," cut off and discard half the stalks from a bunch of fresh coriander. Wash well and chop to puree in a blender, using half the amount of water as you have of packed leaves. Freeze in ice-cube trays and, when solid, transfer to a plastic bag for freezer storage. Each cube is equivalent to 2 tablespoons of chopped fresh coriander.

USE: Use leaves to add a robust flavor and aroma to soups, stews, sauces, chutneys, and DAL (see THE FOODS OF ASIA section). It is widely used in the cooking of Asia, where it is used in Indian, Sinhalese, and Laotian curries and in Indian chutneys. It is mixed with chopped onion and lemon juice to make a raw salad in Thailand, where it is used in great quantities, especially in their Chile Fried Rice. The roots are often called for in Thai and Burmese recipes. A Chinese dish from Szechuan province calls for a whole plant to be used in the making of roast duck, the roots being placed inside the cavity.

Fresh coriander is also widely used in the Middle East, especially in Morocco, where it seasons many spicy dishes, and is used in many dishes in Mozambique. In Mexico it is often teamed with tomatoes or tomatillos, or both, and is essential to many types of fresh table sauces and some recipes for guacamole (avocado dip). The leaves make a fragrant garnish for dishes containing fish or poultry.

CORIANDER SEEDS

Ethnic names are listed only if they differ from those used for the fresh herb.

INDIAN: *dhania* BURMESE: *nannamzee* MALAYSIAN: *ketumbar* IN MOROCCO: *kosbour* THAI: *mellet pak chee*

Coriander seeds (actually a misnomer, as they are the fruit of the plant) taste nothing at all like fresh coriander but have a delightful aroma, reminiscent of lemon and caraway. The flavor is sweeter than that of fresh coriander. They are yellow-orange, almost round, and are available in all supermarkets either whole or ground. If the seeds are fresh, they can be planted, watered daily, and will soon sprout fresh coriander.

STORAGE: As any spice. The seeds keep their flavor much better than the ground spice, and can be stored on the pantry shelf for up to 2 years. Use up ground spice within a few months.

PREPARATION AND USE: Toast coriander seeds lightly before using to bring out their full flavor and make them easier to grind.

Whole seeds are used in India in curried dishes and pastries, and to decorate desserts and sweetmeats covered with VARK (silver foil—see THE FOODS OF ASIA section). The ground seeds are an indispensable ingredient in many Asian curried dishes and for GARAM MASALA (see SEASONING BLENDS). They are widely used, often along with the fresh herb, in Indonesian, Burmese, Malaysian, and Thai dishes.

In the Middle East, they are teamed with garlic and salt to make a mixture called taklia, used as an Arab condiment-seasoning for MULOUKIA (see THE FOODS OF THE MIDDLE EAST section), meatballs, and many other dishes, and added just at the last minute of cooking. In Morocco, they are rubbed into lamb with other seasonings before roasting. In Europe, they season roast meats, sausages such as frankfurters, and anything prepared *à la Grecque* (marinated in a dressing of olive oil, lemon or vinegar, and herbs).

CUMIN

OTHER SPELLING: cummin

ARABIC: *kammun* CHINESE: *ma ch'in* DUTCH: *komijn* FRENCH: *cumin* GERMAN: *Kreuzkümmel* GREEK: *kimino* INDIAN: *zeera* or *jeera* INDONESIAN: *jinten* ITALIAN: *cumino* JAPANESE: *kumin* LATIN: *Cuminum cyminum* MALAYSIAN: *jintan puteh* IN MOROCCO: *habet el soudane* PORTUGUESE: *cominho* SINHALESE (Sri Lanka): *suduru* SPANISH: *comino* THAI: *yira*

This amber-colored, strongly aromatic, kernel-shaped dried fruit of a plant of the parsley family is available either whole or ground. The whole seeds are often mistaken for CARAWAY and often mistranslated in Asian recipes. Cumin seeds, whole or ground, are available on all supermarket spice shelves. White cumin (*safed zeera*), found in Asian markets, can be used interchangeably with the amber-colored. Black cumin seeds are called *kala zeera*. They are not the same spice as white cumin. Though aromatic and peppery, the taste of black cumin is more complex and the seeds are darker.

STORAGE: As any whole or ground spice.

PREPARATION AND USE: This spice is always best freshly ground. For a mellow flavor, it is recommended to roast cumin seeds lightly before grinding. To roast, place about ¼ cup of cumin seeds in a heavy skillet. Stir constantly with a wooden spoon over medium heat until they have turned a light chocolate color. Reduce to a powder in either a coffee mill or mortar to use in curried dishes, chili power, pickles, or to sprinkle over DAL (see THE FOODS OF ASIA section), and yogurt dishes, salads, and soups.

Cumin is one of the most important ingredients in Madras-Style CURRY POWDER (see SEASONING BLENDS). It is considered a digestive and is made into a refreshing drink with tamarind water in India. It is used in Mozambique in Shrimp in Coconut Milk. Any cumin called for in European cooking, except in Spain and Portugal, is probably CARAWAY. In the Middle East, it is widely used as a seasoning for hard-cooked eggs sold as a street snack, and in Greece as a seasoning for a sausage called Soutzoukakia. In Morocco, it is considered an indispensable spice for all kinds of chicken, meat, and fish dishes. It is one of the most important culinary herbs in Mexico, adding a distinctive flavor to many dishes, and is purported to be a stimulant for the appetite. In Peru, it flavors a popular dish called Antichuchos (skewered, marinated beef heart, which is charcoal-grilled).

DILL

ARABIC: *shibith* FRENCH: *aneth* GERMAN: *Dill* INDIAN: *sui bhati*
ITALIAN: *aneto* LAOTIAN: *phak si* LATIN: *Antheus graveolens*
POLISH: *koper* PORTUGUESE: *endro* RUSSIAN: *ukrop* SINHALESE
(Sri Lanka): *enduru* SPANISH: *eneldo*

Dill is native to Asia Minor. Like coriander, fresh dill is an herb and dill seeds are a spice. For clarity, let us separate them.

FRESH DILL

A feathery green herb that is popular in Russia, Scandinavia, and southern Asia. Fresh dill is available in most supermarkets during most of the year, and dried dill weed is sold in the spice section of every supermarket, but should be used only when the fresh is unavailable. You will often find bright yellow flowers on fresh dill, which can be used as an attractive garnish for salads and vegetable platters.

STORAGE: The weed loses its flavor and aroma rapidly. Fresh dill should be rinsed well and wrapped in a moist paper towel and stored in a plastic bag in the crisper of the refrigerator. The feathery leaves can be wrapped tightly in plastic or packed into a small jar and stored in the freezer for up to 6 months. Dried dill loses flavor rapidly and should be used within a few months.

PREPARATION AND USE: Dill weed must be rinsed and dried carefully before use. It is very popular in Scandinavian cooking—in their GRAVLAX (cured salmon) (see RECIPE INDEX) and in their open-faced sandwiches, where tiny sprigs are a traditional garnish. It is a common ingredient in Piroshki (Russian meat turnovers) and flavors Tshakhohbili (Russian chicken stew, made with tomato and vinegar). In Poland, it flavors Zupa Koprowa (dill soup), Barszczyk (beet soup), and a warm, creamy sauce served with fish, beef, or chicken. A German potato and cheese soup is flavored with it. It is used hardly at all in France, Italy, or Spain.

In the Middle East, especially in Iran and Turkey, it is used in pastries called Börek, and in Balik Corbasi (fish chowder with garlic and coconut). It flavors Iranian salads and is often paired with fresh mint. It is a very popular flavoring in Sri Lanka, where it is used in Frikkadels (deep-fried meatballs) and in fish curries. Dill combines well with creamy foods, such as sour cream and yogurt, and is classically used with fish and vegetables, particularly cucumber. Combined with sour cream, a dill sauce complements any cooked fish. Dill vinegar is good on salads and is easily made by steeping sprigs of fresh dill in white or red vinegar.

DILL SEED

Dill seed is the form of dill used primarily in Asian cooking. It can be found in the spice sections of supermarkets. Its flavor is more pungent than fresh dill, and is slightly camphorous. Most is imported from India.

STORAGE: Dill seeds should be stored as a spice.

PREPARATION AND USE: Dill seeds can be used directly in a dish, but will benefit from steeping or a brief dry-roasting in a skillet to bring out their full flavor. They are usually used whole, but can be ground after roasting for some curry recipes.

They have a pungent flavor and should be used with discretion. They are a substitute for fresh dill and are used in very small amounts to flavor the same dishes. In India, they are an essential ingredient in some fish curries. In Scandinavia, the seed is used in breads and potato dishes. In the United States, the seeds are fundamental to cucumber pickles and are often used in cole slaw and potato salad.

EPAZOTE

See FOODS OF LATIN AMERICA section

FENNEL

OTHER: "sweet" cumin

ARABIC: *shamar* BURMESE: *samouk-saba* DUTCH: *venkel* FRENCH: *fenouil* GERMAN: *Fenchel* INDIAN: *sonf* or *vendhyam* INDONESIAN: *adas* ITALIAN: *finocchio* LATIN: *Foeniculum vulgare* MALAYSIAN: *jintan manis* NORWEGIAN: *fennikel* PORTUGUESE: *funcho* RUSSIAN: *fyenkhel'* SINHALESE (Sri Lanka): *maduru* SPANISH: *hinojo* SWEDISH: *fänkål* THAI: *yira*

Fennel is native to southern Europe and the Mediterranean. Like coriander and dill, fennel is both an herb (the feathery leaves are used) and a spice, but it is the licorice-flavored seed that is used primarily in cooking. One variety is also a vegetable—see FENNEL, FLORENTINE in THE FOODS OF EUROPE section. Fennel seeds are available on every supermarket spice shelf, and are milder, sweeter-flavored, and plumper than anise seeds. They are the same shape as cumin seeds but are larger and lighter in color. The dried woody stalks of fennel, available through mail order, are also used as fuel for grilling meats and fish in French Provençal cooking, to give them a special fragrance.

STORAGE: Store the feathery fronds as a short-lived fresh herb, and the dried seeds as a spice.

USE: Chopped fennel leaves can be used as a dill-like garnish or sprinkled in salads or vegetable dishes. Fennel seeds are used throughout the Mediterranean in soups, sauces, and stews. It is sometimes referred to as the "fish herb" and is used especially for seafood dishes. The seeds are widely used in Italian cooking and are the distinctive flavor in Italian "hot" and "sweet" link sausages and in lasagna.

In Norway, fennel is popular in pickling. The French use it in Bouillabaisse de Chapon (capon in spicy tomato sauce). In Asia, fennel seeds are toasted until dark brown, and then ground, to become the distinctive flavor in Sinhalese curries, and as a flavoring for liqueurs. They appear in Malaysian curries as well, but not in Indian ones. In India they are lightly roasted to serve as a mouth freshener after dinner. A few lightly crushed seeds lend a delicious flavor to the water in which fish, artichokes, beans, or lentils are cooked.

FENUGREEK

(FEN-yoo-greek)

ARABIC: *helba* DUTCH: *fenegriek* FRENCH: *fenugrec* GERMAN: *Bockshornklee* INDIAN: *methi* ITALIAN: *fieno greco* LATIN: *Trigonella foenumgraecum* MALAYSIAN: *alba* IN MOROCCO: *helbah* PORTUGUESE: *alforva* RUSSIAN: *pazhitnik* SINHALESE (Sri Lanka): *uluhaal* SPANISH: *fenogreco*

The fresh leaves of this plant are used as a vegetable in India, but it is very unlikely that you will find them here, as they are used in this country primarily as animal fodder. The very small, square, red-brown seeds, available in Indian markets and in health food stores, are used either whole or ground as a spice. It is almost always part of any blend labeled "curry powder."

STORAGE: The seeds should be stored as a spice.

PREPARATION AND USE: The small, square seeds are best freshly ground, and should be carefully roasted to develop their full aromatic flavor. If overheated in roasting, however, they turn red and become intolerably bitter and no longer useful. After roasting, soak them to soften, and then pulverize with a mortar and pestle or grind to a powder.

Fenugreek is a very important spice in India, and considered essential to curried dishes (especially those containing fish), and chutneys. They flavor Indian Patrani Machchi (fish steamed in banana leaves with fresh coriander, coconut, garlic and chiles), a Malaysian dish, Gulai Ayam (curried whole chicken), and are often used in making mango pickles. In Ethiopia, it is used in most recipes for Wat, the national stew, and in South Africa it is used in Lemon Atjar, spiced lemon pickles. In Morocco it is used to flavor a flat bread called Therfist, which is called Hulba by the Arabs in Egypt and Abish in Ethiopia. In Greece, the seeds, toasted or not, are mixed with honey for a light snack. Steeped to make tea, they are used medicinally to clear the mucous membranes.

In the United States, fenugreek is used primarily as a source for an extract used in flavoring imitation maple syrup. When the plant can be found, the leaves make a tangy, astringent addition to salads.

FILÉ

See THE FOODS OF REGIONAL AMERICA section

GALANGA ROOT

There are two types of this root used in Asian cooking. They are quite different, one from the other, and are used in various ways in different areas. Powdered and dried forms of both may sometimes be found in Asian markets, but they are never available fresh. Dutch markets are an excellent source for such Indonesian and Malaysian ingredients, especially spices. Ginger is not used as a substitute even though the two plants have certain similarities. For clarity of terminology, we will separate them.

STORAGE: As any spice.

PREPARATION AND USE: In Asia, where these are widely available in fresh form, they are sliced or pulverized. Dried slices, available in some Asian markets, should be ground in a coffee/spice mill or blender. The powdered form may be called for. A ⅛″ slice equals approximately ½ teaspoon of the powdered, and this is the usual amount specified for a dish of 4 to 6 servings.

GREATER GALANGAL

OTHER: Java root, galingale

FRENCH: *souchet long* GERMAN: *Galangawurzel* INDONESIAN: *laos*
LAOTIAN: *kha* MALAYSIAN: *lengkuas* IN MOROCCO: *kedilsham*
SPANISH: *galanga* THAI: *kha*

A rhizome, like ginger, greater galangal has white flesh and a mild flavor, and is used more widely in Southeast Asian cooking than the lesser galangal. It is native to Indonesia. If it is not available, substitute a combination of 4 parts powdered ginger to 1 part powdered cinnamon or cardamom.

USE: See main entry for equivalents. In Morocco, it appears often as part of the spice mixture, RAS EL HANOUT. This is widely used throughout Southeast Asia. It flavors the Indonesian SAMBAL, Bajak, a fiery condiment (see THE FOODS OF ASIA section), as well as corn fritters, fish curries, and peanut wafers made with rice flour. It is used, as well, in the Balinese dish of fish steaks, Ikan Bali, and in Thai Chicken in Coconut Milk, Tom Kha Kai.

LESSER GALANGAL

OTHER: aromatic ginger

CHINESE: *wong geung fun* FRENCH: *souchet odorant* GERMAN: *Galantwurzel* INDONESIAN and MALAYSIAN: *kentjur* or *kachai* SINHALESE (Sri Lanka): *ingurupiyali* THAI: *krachai*

Native to southern China, this peppery-flavored rhizome with orange-red flesh can be found in jars, sliced or chopped.

USE: Lesser galangal is seldom used in Chinese cooking, but is used in Southeast Asia for its aromatic qualities in some dishes, such as the Indonesian dish, Rendang, a "dry" meat curry with tamarind, spices, and coconut milk, and in Malaysian Spiced Coconut Fish. In China, it is used primarily for medicinal teas.

GARLIC

ARAB: *tum* BURMESE: *chyet-thon-phew* CHINESE: *suen tau*
FRENCH: *ail* GERMAN: *Knoblauch* INDIAN: *lasan* or *vellay poondoo*
INDONESIAN and MALAYSIAN: *bawang puteh* ITALIAN: *aglio*
LATIN: *Allium sativum* IN MOROCCO: *tourma* RUMANIAN: *usteroi*
RUSSIAN: *chesnok* SINHALESE (Sri Lanka): *sudulunu* SPANISH: *ajo*
THAI: *krathiem*

Garlic is a member of the lily family, the same family as onions, shallots and leeks, and used, though in moderation, in similar ways. The entire garlic bulb is called a "head" and each finger-section of the bulb is a "clove." The size of these cloves can vary enormously and, generally, the largest cloves are the sweetest. There are three types of garlic available in the United States. The most common is the white-skinned American or Creole. The pink- or purple-skinned variety is Mexican or Italian garlic, and the relatively rare huge one is Tahitian. Garlic is in season all year, with its peak during the summer. When purchasing it, press the cloves—they should feel firm.

We have been told that there is a new Japanese variety specially cultivated to leave no odor on the breath. It is not yet being marketed, but if its flavor is comparable to the garlic we are used to, we predict enormous success for it.

Various kinds of dehydrated garlic are sold in the spice sections of supermarkets: garlic powder, chips, and salt. The flavor of these cannot be compared to the real thing, and should be used only if absolutely necessary.

STORAGE: Individual cloves of garlic will lose their moisture fairly quickly so, if possible, keep the head together and store in a topless glass jar in a cool, dry, dark place. Garlic heads tend to sprout if placed in the refrigerator.

We find it handy to keep minced garlic on hand. To make it, we peel a whole head of garlic, and then chop it in the food processor by dropping one clove after another into a dry processing bowl using the steel blade while the machine is running. (It can, of course, be chopped by hand, or even pressed in a garlic press.) When it is finely minced, we transfer it to a small jar and stir 2 tablespoons of vegetable oil into it to keep it moist. This will keep for months in the refrigerator. When minced garlic is called for in a recipe, simply spoon out ¼ to ½ teaspoon of this per clove of garlic required.

Dried garlic, in all its forms, becomes stronger-flavored as it ages on the pantry shelf.

PREPARATION AND USE: To peel garlic, cut off a small slice from the stem end and discard. Lay the clove on its side on a chopping board and smack it smartly with the side of a chef's knife or cleaver—the papery skin will pop right off. Mince or press, according to preference. Minced garlic is only half as strong-flavored as that which is put through a garlic press.

Garlic is used extensively in most of the world's cuisines, with the exception of England and Scandinavia, where chives are the preferred members of the onion family. It is practically never used in Japan, where its flavor is considered gross. (Adding garlic to Teriyaki Sauce is an American idea.)

It is especially popular in Mediterranean cooking where it flavors seafood stews, pastas, and summer vegetables. An Italian dip, Bagna Cauda, is a warm, creamy, garlicky coating for raw vegetables. Italians use it a great deal in such dishes as Spezzatino di Pollo (garlic-fried chicken). The French use if for Aïoli, garlic mayonnaise, as well as for Rouille, the mayonnaise-type of sauce traditionally served with bouillabaisse. The French also make use of it in the aromatic sauce traditionally served with escargots (snails), and the popular "Chicken with Forty Cloves of Garlic." In Spain, it is important in the flavoring of the national stew, Olla Podrida (literally, "forgotten pot").

In the Middle East, it is teamed with yogurt and eggplant and often used to flavor pilaf. In Morocco, garlic is used in meat stews to which honey has been added. It is used in South Africa in such dishes as Gesmoorde Vis (salt cod and potatoes) and in Sosaties (skewered, curried lamb). In Ethiopia, it is essential to Wat, the spicy national stew.

Ginger is the usual companion to garlic in Chinese cooking, and both are very widely used, especially in Szechuan and Hunan cooking. Garlic is used in many dishes and always with fermented black beans (see BEANS, BLACK, SALTED, AND FERMENTED, in THE FOODS OF ASIA section). It is used in many Thai dishes with ginger, such as Kai Kang (garlic chicken) and Phat Wun Sen (a combination of rice noodles with garlic, pork, prawns, mushrooms, and fresh coriander). It is used in Philippine Pork or Chicken Adobo, Malaysian curried dishes, and in Singapore to flavor spareribs and barbecue-style pork. It is consumed in Burma in great quantities in dishes such as Mon Hin Gha (fish with coconut milk, chiles, and noodles) and Tha Hnat (cucumber pickles served as an accompaniment to rice). In Laos, one dish named Sousi Pa (fish with coconut cream) calls for 15 cloves of garlic for 4 servings, and in the Philippines, 10 cloves are used in Arroz Caldo (rice with chicken) for 6 servings. Indians often swallow a whole clove of garlic following a meal in the belief that it eliminates a gaseous feeling.

Whole garlic cloves that have been baked in a slow oven in their skins until very soft are surprisingly mild in flavor, and can even be spread on toast as an appetizer.

One of our favorite uses of garlic is in the fresh tasting Gremolata, which is used as a garnish for Osso Bucco (veal shanks cooked in wine), and also with a simpler version of this dish, which we call simply Veal Stew alla Milanese.

VEAL STEW ALLA MILANESE

For 8 servings

This easy-to-make stew is based on a traditional recipe for Osso Bucco alla Milanese, veal shanks braised in wine. We use cubes of veal stew meat here to make the dish more manageable as a buffet dish. Gremolata, the tasty topping of minced garlic, citrus rind, and parsley, highlights not only the flavor but makes for a very colorful presentation. Serve with Risotto alla Milanese (see RICE, ITALIAN), or ORZO (see PASTA).

STEW:
    3 cloves garlic, peeled
    2 stalks celery
    1 large carrot, scraped
    1 large leek, halved and cleaned

1 large onion
4 tablespoons (½ stick) butter
1 (28-ounce) can Italian-style pear shaped tomatoes,
    drained, seeded, and chopped (reserve juice)
1 tablespoon fresh basil, chopped, *or* 1 teaspoon dried,
    crumbled
¾ teaspoon fresh thyme, *or* ¼ teaspoon dried, crumbled
3–3½ pounds boneless veal, cut into 1″ cubes*
1½ teaspoons coarse salt
    Freshly ground black pepper
    Flour for coating the veal
½ cup olive oil
1 cup dry white wine
1¼ cups strong beef stock
1 Bouquet Garni containing 2 (1″) strips of lemon zest,
    the stems of 1 bunch parsley, and 1 bay leaf

GREMOLATA:
2–3 large cloves garlic, minced
¼ cup minced parsley (Italian flat-leaf parsley preferred)
1 tablespoon minced lemon zest
1 tablespoon minced orange zest

*Note: Use leg, shoulder, or stew meat cut from the rib area. Do not buy white, milk-fed veal for this purpose. Pink veal will be just as good here, and much more economical.

To prepare the vegetables for the stew, use a very sharp knife to mince the garlic, celery, carrot, leek, and onion very, very fine. This mixture is called the *soffrito*. (Alternatively, if you have a food processor, use it to chop the vegetables. Start with the garlic and chop 6 cloves, so you will have the garlic needed for the Gremolata later. Make sure the processor bowl is bone dry and insert the steel blade. With the motor running, drop the garlic, a clove at a time, through the feed tube. As it is chopped, it will spray up on the sides of the bowl. Remove the garlic with a rubber spatula and set half of it aside for the Gremolata and half for the *soffrito*. Cut the celery, carrot, and leek, into 1″ lengths and process until minced. Cut the onion into eighths and process in on-and-off bursts with the other vegetables until minced. When combined with the garlic, this is the *soffrito*.)

In a large, heavy sauté pan, melt the butter and sauté the *soffrito* for 7 to 8 minutes until the vegetables are wilted. Add the chopped tomatoes and about half of their reserved juice along with the basil and thyme. Cook briskly, uncovered, until most of the liquid has evaporated. (If desired, transfer the mixture at this point to an earthenware casserole in which the stew can be cooked and served.)

Sprinkle the veal with 1½ teaspoons salt and ground black pepper to taste. Shake the cubes in a bag containing some flour to coat them. Heat about ¼ cup of the olive oil in the sauté pan. Shake off the excess flour and brown the veal, 10 or so cubes at a time, without crowding. Remove each piece when browned and continue in this manner until all the veal is browned, adding more oil to the pan if necessary. Place the browned veal on top of the *soffrito* in the casserole.

Add the wine to the drippings in the sauté pan. Boil hard over high heat while scraping any browned bits from the bottom. When most of the wine has cooked away, stir in the broth and bring to a simmer. Pour over the veal. Place the Bouquet Garni in the liquid and cover the pan. Cook the stew slowly, either on top of the stove or in a 375° oven for an hour, until the veal is tender when pierced with a fork.

While the stew is cooking, combine the ingredients for the Gremolata. When ready to serve, either sprinkle the Gremolata over the surface of the stew, or serve separately to be added to each diner's individual taste.

TO PREPARE IN ADVANCE: This tastes best if made a day ahead and reheated to serve. Reheat at 350° for 30 minutes or until piping hot. It can be frozen successfully for up to 2 months; thaw before warming.

GINGER

See also GINGER, PICKLED and RED CANDIED, in THE FOODS OF ASIA section

BURMESE: *gin* CHINESE: *jeung* or *sang keong* DUTCH: *gember* FRENCH: *gingembre* GERMAN: *Ingwer* INDIAN: *adrak* or *ingee* INDONESIAN: *jahe* or *aliah* ITALIAN: *zenzero* JAPANESE: *shoga* LATIN: *Zingiber officinale* MALAYSIAN: *halia* IN MOROCCO: *skinjbir* PORTUGUESE: *gengibre* RUSSIAN: *imbir'* SINHALESE (Sri Lanka): *inguru* SPANISH: *jengibre* SWEDISH: *ingefära* THAI: *khing*

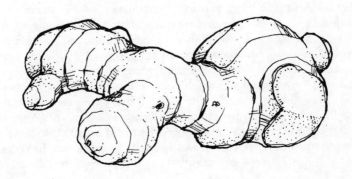

A gnarled and knobby fibrous root with light brown skin and an ivory interior, ginger has a crunchy texture and very pungent taste. Fresh gingerroot is available all year, but the youngest and most tender can be found in the springtime in China, and in early fall in markets in the United States. The "spring" type is milder in flavor and has no tough outer skin to peel away. Most of the fresh ginger sold in the United States is imported from Jamaica and is more pungent than Asian ginger. When buying mature roots, make sure they have a firm skin; if wrinkled they are too old. The flesh that lies right underneath the skin is the youngest and most delicate, so peel the root carefully to preserve that highly valued portion.

Powdered ginger is *not* a substitute—it has an entirely different flavor. Dried ginger is sometimes available, but it has a flavor similar to the powdered. Candied, preserved ginger, available in most supermarkets, can be washed of its sugar crystals to use as a substitute only if fresh ginger is not available, but there will be a substantial flavor difference.

STORAGE: Wrap the root in plastic and store in the refrigerator for up to a week or in the freezer for up to 3 months. Or peel by scraping, and store in the refrigerator in a jar of dry sherry, which will have some effect on the flavor in long-term storage. A mixture of lemon juice and salt can be substituted for the sherry if you prefer. It is even possible to keep the root alive in a pot of damp, sandy soil. Dig it up, cut off what you need, and return to the pot and, if you are very lucky, it will even sprout new shoots. Richard Wing, the award-winning California chef, always keeps a supply of peanut oil in which chopped ginger and garlic are steeping in the refrigerator to use as an all-purpose cooking oil. We are told that old ginger, which has dried and shriveled, can be reconstituted by soaking it in water, but we are certain it would never regain its full flavor. Dried ginger should be stored as any ground spice.

PREPARATION AND USE: Peel sparingly with a vegetable scraper (except for "spring" ginger, which needn't be peeled at all). Slice, mince, or grate to use in cooking many dishes. A fresh ginger paste can be made in the food processor, but it is really best to use one of the inexpensive Japanese ginger graters with fine teeth, available in Japanese hardware stores.

Fresh ginger is one of the most important of all Asian ingredients and is used as a flavor-booster in most dishes. Chinese cooks almost always use it in meat dishes, usually in combination with garlic. (A recipe for Lemon Chicken is unusual because ginger is not teamed with the garlic.) It is considered a must in the cooking of fish because it neutralizes fishy odors. In stir-frying, it is added to the oil (with garlic, if desired) in the wok and stir-fried briefly before adding the other ingredients. In Japan, it is commonly used in Sunomono (vinegared cucumber salad), and is pickled to serve as a garnish with many dishes. Ginger is widely used in Asian curries. In Malaysia, it flavors Semur Ati (spiced, braised liver) and lamb curry. One Laotian dish,

Pa Khing (steamed fish with young ginger), uses 4 ounces of it for 4 servings. It is widely used in Thailand, fresh in spicy dishes with coriander and garlic, and candied (see GINGER, RED CANDIED in THE FOODS OF ASIA section) in a ginger sauce for whole fried fish. It heightens the flavors of vegetables, so we almost always add some to the cooking water, or grate fresh ginger over cooked vegetables just before serving.

In Morocco it is usually teamed with ground black pepper in flavoring Tagines (meat stews). In West Africa, it is essential to Groundnut Stew. Dried ginger is used primarily in canned fruits and preserves and in making CRAB BOIL (see SEASONING BLENDS). The ground dried spice is used a great deal in baking, especially in Europe. It is essential to German gingerbread and to all kinds of spice cookies.

HARISSA

See THE FOODS OF THE MIDDLE EAST section

HORSERADISH

ARABIC: *fujl har* DANISH: *peberrod* DUTCH: *mierikwortel*
FINNISH: *piparjuuri* FRENCH: *raifort* GERMAN: *Meerretich, Kren*
ITALIAN: *rafano* LATIN: *cochlearia amoracia* RUSSIAN: *khren*
SPANISH: *rábano picante* SWEDISH: *pepparrot*

Horseradish is the cylindrical root of a plant of the mustard family, native to eastern Europe. Bottled horseradish is available in 4- to 6-ounce jars in the refrigerator deli sections of most supermarkets, and is labeled with the degree of hotness. It is grated and packed in vinegar with spices and is usually white, but a red type, which is colored with beet juice, is almost as commonly found. There is little difference in taste, so the choice is primarily a matter of aesthetics. Fresh horseradish is easiest to find at the time of the Jewish Passover holidays because it represents the "bitter herb" in the traditional Seder observance. A dried type can also be found in some European markets, and can be an excellent substitute for fresh.

STORAGE: Once opened, bottled horseradish quickly loses its pungency. Store in a nonmetal container in the refrigerator for up to a month. Fresh horseradish can be stored in a paper bag inside a plastic bag in the crisper of the refrigerator for up to a week, but it is best to clean (as described below), wrap tightly, and store in the freezer. It can be grated without thawing. After grating, it quickly loses pungency, and should be treated like commercially bottled horseradish. Dried horseradish can be stored indefinitely in an airtight container, though it does lose flavor gradually.

PREPARATION AND USE: To grate fresh horseradish root, scrub and scrape away only the very outside portion of the root. Cut in half lengthwise and cut out most of the tough center core; then cut in 1″ lengths. It can be grated on a hand-grater or put through a meat grinder, but it is easier to place in an electric blender or food processor and process until finely chopped. (Its fumes are more powerful than an onion's, and your tears will flow copiously unless the process of grating is enclosed.) Add ½ cup of white vinegar and 2 teaspoons salt. Store in a glass jar in the refrigerator for at least 3 days before using to allow the flavor to develop fully. Frozen whole horseradish should be grated without thawing and the unused root returned to the freezer immediately. Dried horseradish can be made by slicing the root in thin crosswise slices and drying them in a 200° oven for several hours; then pulverizing to a powder. Add water to rehydrate before use.

Horseradish, in any of its forms, is rarely cooked, because it loses its pungency. It is primarily a condiment. As an ingredient, it most often finds its way into sauces, and the one with which most Americans are familiar is the ubiquitous red "cocktail" sauce, called the "red menace" by James Beard, which is served with shrimp or crab cocktails. Plain, or folded into whipped cream, it is a traditional accompaniment to English Roast Beef, but also complements smoked fish and tongue. In France, it is often combined with lemon juice. It is an excellent ingredient to spice up a drab mustard. In Russia and in the Scandinavian countries, it is often mixed with sour cream to serve as an accompaniment to boiled meats. In East European Jewish cooking it is served with gefilte fish.

JUNIPER BERRIES

DUTCH: *jenever* FRENCH: *genièvre* GERMAN: *Wacholder* ITALIAN: *ginepro* SPANISH: *enebro*

These are the dried, blue berries of a small evergreen shrub native to Europe, but now widely grown throughout Asia and North Africa. Most of what is found on supermarket spice shelves is from Hungary or Italy. Juniper gives gin its distinctive flavor, and some chefs flame a dish with gin to give it a juniper flavor.

STORAGE: As any spice for up to 2 years.

PREPARATION AND USE: Use juniper berries sparingly, no more than 1 per serving. Toast them lightly in a dry skillet, just for a minute or so to bring out their full flavor, before adding to recipes. If they are to be used in sauces or stuffings, they should be finely crushed, but can be left almost whole for use in marinades.

Their bittersweet flavor is excellent in marinades and sauces for game, such as venison. They are often used with lamb, with reindeer in Scandinavia, and with wild duck in Ireland. They are classically used in the pork-and-sausage-garnished sauerkraut of Alsace called Choucroute Garnie. They are used in France in the famous Beurre de Genièvre, served with some classic French game dishes, by crushing and mixing with butter. Dried juniper stalks are often used as fuel in the smoking of sausages such as CHORIZO (see SAUSAGE, FRESH in THE FOOD OF EUROPE section).

KALONGI

OTHER: *nigella*

FRENCH: *Quatre Épices* or *nigelle* GERMAN: *Schwarzkümmel*
MIDDLE EASTERN: *siyah-daneh* SPANISH: *neguilla, pasionara*

This is a tiny, spicy, black seed used in Indian and Iranian cooking that is often confused with onion seeds or black cumin seeds. It can be found in Indian and some Middle Eastern markets. The Middle Eastern name means "black seeds." It tastes a bit like onion.

STORAGE: As any spice.

USE: In Indian cooking, the seeds are added to hot oil along with any other whole spices and cooked until sizzling before other ingredients are added. Kalongi adds an intriguing flavor when used with vegetables or in breads. Occasionally it is mixed with an equal amount of sesame seeds to sprinkle on bread before baking.

KENTJUR

See GALANGAL, LESSER

LAOS

See GALANGAL, GREATER

LAVENDER

LATIN: *Lavandula spica* IN MOROCCO: *khzama*

The flowers of this English herb are used in Middle Eastern cooking as part of spice mixtures, such as the Moroccan RAS EL HANOUT (see FOODS OF THE MIDDLE EAST section). Dried flowers, which may be white or purple, are available in Middle Eastern markets, and in stores that sell dried flowers for potpourri.

STORAGE: Stored as a spice in a cool, dry, dark place, it will keep indefinitely.

PREPARATION AND USE: The flowers have a rather strong, sweet, lemony flavor, and should always be used sparingly. They can be crushed using a mortar and pestle, or ground to be used in marinades for venison or lamb, and in some English jellies. A few flowers are sometimes added to tea as it steeps to add a floral flavor.

MACE

FRENCH: *macis* or *fleur de moscade* GERMAN: *Muskatblute* INDIAN: *javatri* LATIN: *Myristica fragrans* IN MOROCCO: *bsibsa* SINHALESE (Sri Lanka): *wasa-vasi* SPANISH: *macia* or *macis*

Mace is the highly flavorful, web-like filament cage surrounding the seed of the nutmeg native to the Moluccas, the "Spice Islands." East Indian mace has a bright scarlet color; West Indian is more golden. Both have a more delicate flavor than nutmeg. It is difficult to grind because it is oily, so you will find it ground only on supermarket spice shelves, where it is usually higher priced than nutmeg. Dried blades of mace can be found in Asian and Caribbean markets. It has been cured, so it has a golden appearance rather than the original red color. The island of Granada now produces 40% of the world supply.

STORAGE: Mace, which is one of the "red" spices, is more highly perishable than other spices (and attracts bugs), so store it in the refrigerator.

USE: In Indian cooking, this is one of the ingredients of GARAM MASALA (see SEASONING BLENDS) and is often added to curries in southern Asia, particularly in the cooking of Sri Lanka, Sumatra, and Java. In South Africa, it flavors Cape Malay Bean Soup. It is an indispensable ingredient in Moroccan RAS EL HANOUT (see SEASONING BLENDS). In Mexico, it is used in some recipes for Huachinango Relleno (stuffed fish fillets).

It adds a very special quality to pastries and combines particularly well with chocolate. It is very often used in Europe and America in chowders, cakes, cookies, and puddings, and is the distinctive flavoring in doughnuts and pound cake. Blades of mace are often used in pickling and in clear soups and, like stick cinnamon, they give off less color when used in this way.

MAHLEB

See FOODS OF THE MIDDLE EAST section

MARJORAM

OTHER: sweet marjoram, knotted marjoram

ARABIC: *marzanjush* DUTCH: *marjolein* FRENCH: *marjolaine*
GERMAN: *Marienkraut* ITALIAN: *maggiorana* LATIN: *Origanum
majorana* IN MOROCCO: *mrdeddouch* PORTUGUESE: *manjerona*
RUSSIAN: *mayoran* SPANISH: *majorana*

A perennial herb of the mint family native to the Mediterranean, marjoram
is frequently confused with OREGANO (wild marjoram). It is slightly sweeter
and more delicate than its cousin. It is rarely available fresh, but is always
available in its dried form on supermarket spice shelves.

STORAGE: Fresh marjoram, wrapped in damp paper towels and stored in
a plastic bag in the refrigerator will keep for up to 4 days. It loses much of
its delicate flavor if frozen. Store dried as any herb.

PREPARATION AND USE: This is a delicate herb that is best added to
cooked dishes shortly before serving, or added fresh to salads. Marjoram has
a special affinity for dishes containing tomatoes, and is delicious rubbed into
lamb before roasting or used in stuffing for boned leg of lamb. It also flavors
cooked beans, poultry, liver, and veal. Northern Italian cooks favor marjoram,
whereas those in the south prefer the more assertive oregano. It is often
added to sausages: in Poland, Kielbasa, in Germany, Liverwurst, in Italy,
Bologna. In Morocco, it flavors meatballs, called Kefta, and is brewed in
sweetened hot milk as a cold remedy. In Chile, it flavors a fish soup, Caldillo
de Pescado.

MINT

ARABIC: *na nal* FRENCH: *menthe* GERMAN: *Minze* GREEK:
diosmo INDIAN: *podina* ITALIAN: *menta* LAOTIAN: *pak hom ho*
LATIN: *Mentha viridis* IN MEXICO: *yerba buena* IN MOROCCO:
nana MALAYSIAN: *daun pudina* SINHALESE (Sri Lanka): *meenchi*
SPANISH: *yerbabuena* or *menta* THAI: *by kaprow* VIETNAMESE: *que,
rauthom, tia to, hung* (different varieties)

This culinary herb grown throughout the world is much used both as a
flavoring and as a garnish. Fresh mint can be found in many supermarkets,
and is very easy to grow in an herb garden. Dried mint, which is surprisingly
good, can be found on supermarket spice shelves and in many Asian and
Middle Eastern markets. Spearmint is the type most often used in cooking,
but other varieties are often substituted. Those with purple stalks are considered the most flavorful. Peppermint has more of a menthol taste and is

47

not much used in recipes, though it is the basis for crème de menthe liqueur. There are many varieties of mint including pineapple mint, apple mint, and orange bergamont mint. Plants and seeds can be ordered through plant catalogues, or obtained at nurseries.

STORAGE: Wrapped in a moist paper towel in a plastic bag, fresh mint should stay usable for a week in the crisper of the refrigerator. Store dried as any herb.

PREPARATION AND USE: Rinse and dry fresh mint well and remove the leaves from the stalks. Then chop or use whole as directed in the recipe.

Mint is widely used in Asian cooking as a flavoring in curries, mint SAMBALS (see THE FOODS OF ASIA section), raw chutney, dipping sauces, for jellies, and as a garnish for many spicy dishes . In Vietnamese cooking, mint garnishes vegetable platters served with every meal and is part of the filling of Vietnamese Spring Rolls made with rice-flour skins. It is widely used in Thai cooking in such dishes as Yam Nang Mu (pork skin salad) and in Malaysian and Indian curries. In Morocco, it is the basis of the sweet mint tea traditionally served after meals, and in South Africa it flavors a popular Green Pea Soup. In the Middle East, it is often added to yogurt, to soaked BULGHUR WHEAT to make the popular salad, Tabooli, and flavors a popular cheese, HALOUMI (see THE FOODS OF THE MIDDLE EAST section). Greeks use it in salads, stews, and sauces. In Mexico, it is used sparingly in Albondigas (meatballs for soup) and occasionally in the cooking of beans and, as in Morocco, it makes a soothing tea to serve after a meal. The English make mint sauce with vinegar and sugar to serve with lamb. In our own South, it characterizes the famous mint julep of Kentucky. We like to add a few chopped mint leaves to peas before cooking. One of the tastiest of all Indian chutneys is this simple uncooked one.

MINT CHUTNEY

For approximately 1½ cups

2 large bunches fresh mint, leaves only
½ cup fresh coriander leaves
1 medium white onion
1 tablespoon ANARDANA (dried pomegranate seeds)
2 fresh green CHILES SERANOS or JALAPEÑOS
1 teaspoon salt
½ cup yogurt

Combine all ingredients, except yogurt, in the container of an electric blender. Process until pureed and transfer to a serving bowl. Stir in the yogurt.

Served chilled or at room temperature.

TO PREPARE IN ADVANCE: This will keep, covered, in a nonmetal container in the refrigerator for up to 3 days.

MUSTARD

WHOLE YELLOW OR BROWN SEEDS

ARABIC: *khardal* CHINESE: *chieh* DUTCH: *mosterd* FRENCH: *moutarde* GERMAN: *Senfsaat* ITALIAN: *senape* JAPANESE: *karashi* LATIN: *Sinapis alba* (white or yellow), *Brassica juncea* (brown) PORTUGUESE: *mostarda* RUSSIAN: *gorchitsa* SPANISH: *mostaza* SWEDISH: *senap*

BLACK MUSTARD SEED

INDIAN: *rai* or *kudoo* LATIN: *Brassica nigra* MALAYSIAN: *biji sawi* SINHALESE (Sri Lanka): *abba*

There are two primary types of mustard seed, white (or yellow), and brown, both native to southern Europe, that you will find on the spice shelves of supermarkets and gourmet specialty shops, and they differ slightly in flavor and pungency. The white (or yellow) is the flavor most of us associate with American-style yellow mustard (which gets its bright color from TURMERIC). The brown is stronger in flavor, and is the only seed used in the making of French Dijon-style mustards. Powdered mustard, such as the English Colman's Mustard, which is the best known brand, as well as that sold in Chinese markets *(gai lat)*, is made from a combination of the two. The seeds in themselves are not "hot" until liquid (usually water) is added, and enzymes are activated that produce the pungency. The black variety, found only in Asian markets, is slightly milder in flavor.

STORAGE: Store the European types as you would any whole or ground spice. You can store black mustard seeds in an airtight container in a cool spot for up to 3 months, or in the refrigerator indefinitely. Mustard powder should be stored as any ground spice. Dry mustard mixed to a paste with water loses flavor quickly and will not keep. If stored, it should be mixed with an acid liquid such as vinegar, beer, or wine, which will stop the enzyme activity so it retains its "hot" quality. It does, however, develop a brown skin, and loses pungency on standing.

USE: The whole seeds are often used in pickling and in the cooking of cabbage and sauerkraut. Two teaspoons, for instance, will flavor the brine for 8 pints of Bread and Butter Pickles.

The black ones are invariably added to hot oil in the first stage of making curries. As they hit the oil they make a popping sound, exploding their pungent flavor into the oil. Our recipe for Alu Gobi (see under ASAFETIDA in THE FOODS OF ASIA section) features them, as do many Indian potato dishes. They are sometimes ground to use as one would other spices and seeds, and are used in Sri Lanka to make a mustard not unlike European coarse ground mustard, called Abba.

Dry mustard is considered a preservative because it retards, to some extent, the growth of bacteria in mayonnaise, curries, etc. It has an emulsifying effect on mayonnaise and salad dressings, and is a very common ingredient in both, as well as in the cheese sauce for Welsh Rarebit. As children, we remember dry mustard mixed to a paste and served as a strong, pungent dip along with catsup for the proverbial fried shrimp always served as an appetizer in Chinese restaurants. To use it in that manner it must be mixed to a paste with water or other liquid 30 minutes before using so it will lose its raw taste and develop its "hot" quality.

NUTMEG

ARABIC: *basbasa* or *jos-teeb* CHINESE: *tau kau* DUTCH: *notemoskaat* FRENCH: *muscade* GERMAN: *Muskat* INDIAN: *jaiphal* or *jathikka* INDONESIAN: *pala* ITALIAN: *noce moscato* or *moscata* JAPANESE: *nikuzuku* LATIN: *Myristica fragrans* MALAYSIAN: *buah pala* IN MOROCCO: *gouza* RUSSIAN: *oryekh muskatny* SINHALESE (Sri Lanka): *sadikka* SPANISH: *moscada* SWEDISH: *muskot* THAI: *look jun*

Nutmeg is the aromatic seed of a tree native to the Moluccas. Ground nutmeg is sold on the spice shelf of every supermarket, and whole nutmegs can be found in fine grocery stores everywhere. East Indian nutmegs are stronger in flavor than those from the West Indies. Freshly grated nutmeg has a fragrance beyond compare. Nutmeg graters are available at cookware shops.

STORAGE: The grated spice should be stored in the refrigerator to keep its aroma fresh as long as possible. Whole spices can be stored on the pantry shelf, or right in a handy nutmeg grater near the stove.

USE: Nutmeg is an essential spice in Italian cooking, especially in Tuscany, and flavors the traditional Salsa Balsamella (in France it's Bechamel), the white sauce so important to many Italian dishes, and the equally famous Salsa Bolognese, the sauce flavored with ham, tomatoes, and cream. It is an important flavor in Filosoof (Dutch meat and potato pie) and Lofschotel (baked Belgian endive). The Germans always put some in Kartoffelklösse (potato dumplings).

In France, nutmeg flavors the famous Quenelles de Brochet (fish dumplings) and Blanquette de Veau (our recipe appears under SEASONING BLENDS,

BOUQUET GARNI). The British use it in Bubble and Squeek, a dish of leftover meat or chicken served with cabbage that sizzles noisily when sprinkled with vinegar after it is sautéed, and in Marlborough Pudding. Russians enjoy Cotletki Pojarski (chicken cutlets flavored with nutmeg and served with hollandaise sauce). It is widely used in Scandinavian cooking, especially in baked goods and spice cakes. In Greece, it is added to Kotopita (chicken pie baked in pastry with garlic and onions).

Nutmeg is used primarily in Asia in curries and as a flavoring for pastries. In Thailand, it is often used in fried meatballs. In Africa, it flavors many dishes, both sweet and savory, particularly the Wat (stew) of Ethiopia. And in England and the United States, nutmeg is a popular condiment to sprinkle over eggnogs and puddings. Nutmeg has a special affinity for spinach. Grate it fresh over fruits and desserts as a garnish. We like it especially in Sauce Sancerre, a recipe given to us by Penny Birnbaum, the best amateur cook we know. She developed it from a Belgian recipe and serves it over rolls of thinly sliced ham.

SANCERRE SAUCE

For about 1½ cups, or 4 to 6 servings

    1 tablespoon butter
  2–3 shallots
    1 cup Sancerre wine (white wine from the Loire Valley)
    1 tablespoon wine vinegar
    1 cup (½ pint) CRÈME FRAÎCHE
    2 tablespoons tomato puree
    2 egg yolks
       Freshly grated nutmeg, to taste
       Salt and cayenne, to taste

Melt the butter in a heavy skillet. Sauté the shallots briefly; then add the wine and vinegar. Simmer, uncovered, until almost all liquid has evaporated, about 10 minutes. Add the crème fraîche, tomato puree, and simmer briefly. Whisk some of the hot sauce into the egg yolks and then add the mixture to the skillet, whisking briefly over medium heat, just until thickened. Take care not to boil the sauce or the yolks will curdle. Season with freshly grated nutmeg, and salt and cayenne, to taste.

Serve with any type of plain cooked ham.

OREGANO

OTHER: wild marjoram

ARABIC: *anrar* DUTCH: *wilde marjolein* FRENCH: *origan*
GERMAN: *Oregano* GREEK: *rigani* ITALIAN: *origano* LATIN:
Marjoram vulgaris RUSSIAN: *dushitsa* SPANISH: *oregano* SWEDISH:
vild mejram

Oregano is a fragrant and strong-flavored Mediterranean herb of the mint family, spicier and more assertive than its cousin, MARJORAM. Its name comes from two Greek words: *oros* (mountain) and *ganos* (joy), which refer to its jolly appearance growing on mountainsides. It is seldom found fresh in markets, but will be found dried on the spice shelves of all supermarkets, and in dried bunches in Mediterranean or Latin American markets. There are over 30 varieties, but generally only two types are offered for sale by nurseries or through seed catalogues. The European variety is milder than the Mexican, which is more aromatic and pungent. Bottles of dried oregano are usually labeled with their country of origin. Americans are familiar with the robust flavor in the traditional thick tomato sauce that is spread over pizza.

STORAGE: As any fresh or dried herb.

USE: Use this herb sparingly as its flavor can be overwhelming. It combines very well with sweet basil and with tomatoes, zucchini, and eggplant. It is extensively used in Greek cooking and in salads, and those dishes that contain it often have the word "riganato" following their names to indicate its presence. It is popular in all Middle Eastern cooking, as well as in the cooking of southern Italy (northern Italians prefer marjoram). Italians use it in pasta sauces, Zuppa di Vongole (clam soup), and Spaghettini Zingarella (with white clam sauce). It is used a great deal in Spain and Latin America. Mexicans use it in many dishes including Ceviche (seafood marinated in lime juice), and in Sopa Seca ("dry" vermicelli soup). In Puerto Rico, it flavors Cerdo Asado (roast pork).

PAPRIKA

LATIN: *Capsicum annum* IN MOROCCO: *felfla hlouwa*

Paprika is a red powder made from grinding chiles, and is "sweet" or "hot" depending on which chiles are used. The finest is Hungarian paprika, which comes in three varieties. That found on supermarket shelves is usually labeled "sweet" and is very mild in flavor. The finest "noble sweet rose" type is sold in large, colorful cans, and has the words "Hungarian" and "sweet" on the label. The other two varieties, "half sweet" and "hot" paprika, can be found in European markets. A concentrated paprika paste is sold in 3-ounce tubes in gourmet specialty shops. Fine imported Hungarian paprika can be ordered from Paprikás Weiss. Spanish paprika (called *pimentón*) is coarser in texture and a bit stronger flavored, and can be found in European and Latin American markets. Look for bright red color, as brown is an indication of age.

STORAGE: Paprika loses its pungency very rapidly and, like all other red spices, should be stored in the refrigerator to prevent infestation of bugs.

USE: Too many Americans consider paprika a mere decoration for casseroles and baked dishes. Paprika is used extensively in Hungarian cooking, where it is considered the national spice, and flavors such dishes as Gulyás (or goulash, as it is called in this country) and Chicken Paprikás, as well as most Hungarian soups. The very hot paprika is used in hearty soups and stews. Spanish paprika flavors many Andalusian dishes such as fish soup and Cocido, a meat stew, Pato y Arroz (duck and rice) and Pollo Valenciano (chicken and duck, Valencian style). In Austria, paprika flavors Hühnerlebarragout (chicken liver ragout with mushrooms and noodles) and, in Germany, Käsepudding (cheese pudding soufflé). It is popular in Yugoslavia on skewered meats, and in a bean soup called Popina Janja Yante (literally "priests lunch"), which is brisket of beef cooked with garlic, vegetables, and a generous amount of paprika.

The favored type in the Middle East is the Spanish *pimentón*, which is a bit stronger in flavor than the Hungarian. It is used extensively there, especially in cold dishes, such as the delicious walnut-sauced Cerkes Tavugu (Circassian chicken), and in marinades for fish. In North Africa, it is often used in marinades with cumin, coriander, garlic, and lemon juice. It is the primary spice in Ethiopian BERBERÉ (see THE FOODS OF AFRICA section), used to season the national stew called Wat, which may be made with meat, chicken, or just vegetables.

In Asian cooking, paprika is used to give a red color to curries when diners have a low chili tolerance. We enjoy it in a simple sauce of seasoned cream, as in the following, somewhat innovative, recipe, which is best served with tiny, shaped pasta.

Chicken Suprêmes in Paprika-Champagne Sauce

For 8 servings

The sauce for this quick entrée was inspired by one we tasted at the Four Seasons restaurant in New York. We've taken an idea from the Chinese for tenderizing chicken and making it especially succulent.

- 4 whole chicken breasts, skinned and boned
- 2 tablespoons cornstarch
- 2 egg whites

  2 teaspoons sherry or white wine
1½ teaspoons salt
  3 tablespoons sweet Hungarian paprika
  ½ stick (4 tablespoons) butter
  4 large shallots, minced
  2 cups champagne (fresh or flat)
  2 cups heavy (whipping) cream
     Optional: 1 cup sorrel leaves, cut in thin shreds

TO GARNISH AND SERVE:
 12 ounces small pasta*, cooked
     Minced parsley or chives (if sorrel is not used)

*Note: Hungarian style *Valodi Tojasos Teszta*, which is a tiny bow tie-shaped pasta available at German and Hungarian delicatessens, is especially appropriate for this recipe. Any small, shaped pasta will do.

Remove the tendons and trim the chicken breasts neatly. In a glass pie plate or other shallow dish, combine the cornstarch, egg whites, sherry (or wine), and salt, beating with a fork until frothy. Marinate the chicken in this mixture for 20 minutes (or up to 2 hours), turning them over from time to time.

Within 20 minutes of serving, remove the breasts from the marinade and sprinkle them on both sides with a heavy dusting of paprika to coat them evenly. Melt the butter in a large, heavy skillet and sauté the breasts briefly on each side. Add the shallots and cook for a few seconds; then pour in the champagne. Cover the skillet, lower the heat, and allow the chicken to simmer very slowly for 10 minutes. Remove the chicken with tongs and keep warm. Turn the heat to high and boil the liquid in the pan until it has reduced to about ⅓ its original volume. Stir in the cream (and optional sorrel) and simmer, uncovered, until the sauce has thickened to the desired consistency. This will take only a minute or two, depending on the size of your skillet.

Place a portion of cooked pasta in the center of each warmed serving plate. Top with one piece of chicken and cover with sauce. Garnish with a sprinkling of parsley or chives if you haven't added sorrel to the sauce. Serve immediately. Chilled champagne is an appropriate accompaniment.

TO PREPARE IN ADVANCE: Bone and prepare the chicken for cooking the day before and wrap tightly for refrigerator storage. Marinate no longer than 2 hours and cook just before serving.

PARSLEY

ARABIC: *baqdunis* FRENCH: *persil* GERMAN: *Petersilie* GREEK: *maítano* ITALIAN: *prezzemolo* LATIN: *Petroselinum crispum* (curly), *Petroselinum sativum* (flat-leaf) IN MOROCCO: *madnouss*

NORWEGIAN: *persille* PORTUGUESE: *salsa* RUSSIAN: *pyetrushka*
SPANISH: *perejil* SWEDISH: *persilja*

Parsley is the most used of all culinary herbs. Curly parsley is a bit more delicate in flavor than the Italian flat-leaf variety specified in Mediterranean recipes. Curly is, however, more widely available in supermarkets. The Italian type is very easy to grow, year 'round, in a small, hydroponic herb garden. Dried parsley is so tasteless and faded looking that we refuse to discuss it here. Why anyone would waste money on it with the fresh so widely available we cannot imagine.

STORAGE: When you bring home fresh parsley, rinse it well, shake off excess moisture, and wrap it in paper towels to store inside a plastic bag in the refrigerator for up to a week. (If it is not wrapped in paper towels, it will begin to mildew immediately.) Chopped fresh parsley can be stored in a covered jar if a damp paper towel is placed in the jar with it. It can also be chopped and frozen with some success.

USE: Parsley is one of the FINES HERBES (see SEASONING BLENDS) so often mentioned in French cookery, and is used in France to flavor mayonnaise, Jambon Persillé de Bourgogne (cubed ham and minced parsley in wine aspic), and herb butters. It is combined with fresh breadcrumbs and shallots to make a mixture called *persillade,* which is used to top rack or shoulder of lamb. Parsley is a very common ingredient in the cuisines of all Mediterranean countries. On its own it makes a delicious Middle Eastern salad, Tabooli, combined with BULGHUR WHEAT (see FOODS OF THE MIDDLE EAST section), mint, tomatoes, and lemon juice. It is delicious when deep-fried (it should be very carefully dried before deep-frying) and served as an accompaniment to grilled meats. One of our favorite salads is based on it. We call it:

PARSLEY SALAD

For 5 or 6 servings

This recipe doesn't sound special but it is—very! It is our interpretation of a recipe that came to us through James Beard and Marion Cunningham. We serve it in very small portions on overlapping thin slices of ripe tomatoes as a first course.

    4   cups parsley, leaves only, washed and dried (depending on
            size, 1 to 2 bunches)
    1   clove garlic, peeled
    ½   cup "extra-virgin" olive oil
    3   tablespoons finest quality red wine vinegar
    ¾   cup finely grated imported Parmesan (Parmigiano) cheese
        Course salt and freshly ground pepper, to taste

Place the parsley flowers in a bowl. Combine garlic, olive oil, and vinegar in blender container, and process until garlic is pureed. Pour the dressing over the parsley and toss lightly until evenly coated. Sprinkle the Parmesan cheese over and toss well. Season to taste with salt and pepper.

Serve in small portions, on top of thin slices of tomato overlapping on a salad plate as a first course.

TO PREPARE IN ADVANCE: This is best freshly made at room temperature, but keeps quite well in the refrigerator for up to 2 days.

PEPPERCORNS

ARABIC: *filfil aswad* BURMESE: *nga-youk-kaun* CHINESE: *hu-chiao* DUTCH: *peper* FRENCH: *poivre* GERMAN: *Pfeffer* INDIAN: *kali mirich* INDONESIAN: *merica hitam* ITALIAN: *pepe* JAPANESE: *kosho* LAOTIAN: *phik noi* LATIN: *Piper nigrum* MALAYSIAN: *lada hitam* IN MOROCCO: *elbezar* RUSSIAN: *pyerets* SINHALESE (Sri Lanka): *gammiris* SPANISH: *pimienta* SWEDISH: *peppar*

BLACK AND WHITE PEPPERCORNS

We refer here to the small berries of the plant *Piper nigrum,* native to Asia, and the world's most commonly used spice. There are other spices referred to as peppercorns, which are listed under the heading OTHER PEPPERCORNS.

Black peppercorns and white peppercorns are the same basic berry, most of which are grown in the far East. The black one is picked when it is red and underripe, and is then allowed to dry and shrivel and turn black. It has more bite than the white peppercorn, which is simply the mature berry from which the outer coating has been removed. Fine types of black peppercorns are Allepeppy, Lampong, and Tellicherry. The best white ones are Muntok (from near Sumatra), Brazilian, and Sarawak. Both white and black are sold on supermarket spice shelves, whole or ground, and the more exotic varieties are sold in gourmet specialty shops. White is generally more expensive, and the whole berries are harder to find. We would always prefer using whole berries and grinding them ourselves, but there are times when the pre-ground is a great convenience.

STORAGE: Unlike other whole spices, these may be stored in a cool, dark place for many years without loss of quality.

PREPARATION AND USE: We cannot give equivalents for whole berries as compared to ground because the berries vary so much in size. If you use a pepper grinder to grind whole berries it is virtually impossible to measure the amount, so it is best to use it to your own taste, unless a recipe specifies a certain number of berries, or a teaspoon measure of ground.

As you may have noticed in the extensive listing of foreign names, this spice is used in almost every cuisine on earth. Whole berries are used in stocks and pickling brines. Some recipes, such as Thai Garlic Chicken, use them slightly crushed, in which case the flavor is milder than if it were ground. Ground black pepper adds a sharp tang to so many spicy dishes that we cannot begin to list them. White pepper, which is milder in flavor, is preferred in pale sauces, fish mousses, and the like because it is less visible. For the finest flavor from ground pepper, have two good pepper grinders, such as those manufactured by Peugeot, to grind both kinds of berries fresh as you need them. Take care never to burn pepper because it takes on an unpleasant bitterness. A recipe that gives the cook a chance to taste and compare peppercorns is the following:

STEAK WITH FOUR PEPPERCORNS

For 4 servings

If the controversy over pink peppercorns is settled and they are proclaimed safe, feel free to add 1 teaspoon of these as a final garnish (they don't require cooking) and make this into "Steak with Five Peppercorns."

- 2 sirloin or New York steaks, 1½" thick, or 4 thick filet mignon steaks
- 1 teaspoon whole black peppercorns
- 1 teaspoon whole white peppercorns
- 1 teaspoon SZECHUAN PEPPERCORNS
- ½ cup vegetable oil
- 1 tablespoon butter
- 3 tablespoons minced shallots
- ⅓ cup cognac or brandy
- ½ teaspoon beef extract
- 2 cups heavy (whipping) cream
- 1 teaspoon GREEN PEPPERCORNS (freeze-dried preferred)
- 1 tablespoon Dijon mustard

Trim the steaks of all fat. Wrap the black, white, and Szechuan peppercorns in an old kitchen towel, place on a chopping board, and pound with the bottom of a heavy skillet until crushed. Press the crushed pepper into both sides of the steaks.

Place a heavy skillet (an iron one is a good choice) over medium-high heat. Pour in the vegetable oil and, when it just begins to smoke, add the steaks and cook 3 to 4 minutes on one side. Turn and brown the other side. When well browned, check for doneness. If necessary, lower the heat and continue cooking.

When done to your liking, remove the steaks to a warm platter and cover with foil to keep them hot while you make the sauce. Wipe out the skillet with a paper towel and let it cool slightly. Add the butter and minced shallots, and cook over medium heat for a few seconds. Add the cognac or brandy and beef extract. Simmer until the liquid has nearly evaporated. Stir in the cream and green peppercorns (drained if canned), and simmer for about 5 minutes, until the cream has thickened to a sauce consistency. Whisk in the mustard and remove from the heat. Taste, and add salt if needed.

Large steaks should be sliced diagonally to serve. Pour some of the hot sauce over the steak slices, spooning any loose peppercorns with it. Extra sauce can be served separately at the table.

GREEN PEPPERCORNS

FRENCH: *poivre vert*

Fresh green peppercorns are simply that—undried peppercorns. They have become very popular in French cooking in recent years, and are available in this country in cans or jars, packed in water or vinegar, or freeze-dried. They have an intriguing, fresh and rather pungent flavor. We especially like the freeze-dried ones, sold by the ounce in specialty shops.

STORAGE: Green peppercorns packed in water won't last long after opening. Store them in the refrigerator for up to a week, or freeze them for longer storage. Those preserved in vinegar will keep for a month in the refrigerator after opening, but need to be rinsed well before using. If they turn dark, they have oxidized and should be tossed out. Freeze-dried peppercorns, if stored airtight in a cool place, will keep their full flavor for 6 months.

PREPARATION AND USE: Rinse canned or bottled peppercorns and drain. They can be mashed or left whole, as you prefer. Freeze-dried ones can be added directly to sauces and need not be reconstituted. Green peppercorns are popping up all over in pâtés, sauces, and mayonnaise, with Steak au Poivre, and as a garnish for many dishes. The French enjoy them especially in sauces for duckling and for duck liver. Stirred or mashed into soft butter to spread over grilled fish, lamb, or vegetables, they add flair to simple dishes. Green peppercorn mustard is easily made by mixing a few into a good Dijon mustard, which makes an excellent accompaniment to sausages and cold cuts. We like them in the following recipe.

CRISP DUCKLING WITH GREEN PEPPERCORNS AND KUMQUATS

For 4 to 6 servings

Fournou's Ovens in the Stanford Court Hotel in San Francisco rates high on our list of preferred restaurants. This is our adaptation of their crisp roast ducklings, which are served partially boned for easy eating. A simple Celery Root or Turnip Purée, and a fine Burgundy make the best accompaniments.

    2   ducklings, each weighing 4 to 5 pounds
    2   small onions, cut in half
    2   stalks celery
        Salt

THE SAUCE:
    4   preserved KUMQUATS in syrup
    2   tablespoons red wine vinegar
    ⅓   cup sugar
    ¾   cup fresh orange juice
    ¼   cup fresh lemon juice
    2   cups Sauce Espagnole (see SAUCES, FRENCH)
    ⅓   cup Grand Marnier *or* Cointreau
   ½–1 teaspoon green peppercorns*

*Note: Green peppercorns vary in color, taste, and texture. Sample the brand you buy to test the pungency. If the flavor is very strong, use the smaller amount. If the flavor is subtle, use more.

Rinse the ducks and dry well, reserving the necks and giblets for another purpose. Place two onion halves and stalk of celery inside of each and place on a rack over a large roasting pan. Salt the ducks lightly and use a fork to prick the skin all over. (This will allow the excess fat to run out from underneath the skin during the roasting and produce a very crispy skin.) Roast at 325° for 1½ hours; then increase the temperature to 450° and roast 30 minutes longer. (The ducklings can be roasted ahead of time—simply set them aside at room temperature, covered loosely with a towel, for up to 4 hours. When ready to serve, reheat at 300° for 30 minutes.)

To make the sauce, cut the kumquats in half lengthwise. Using the tip of a spoon, scrape out and discard the inner white pith; then slice the kumquat skins into thin, lengthwise slivers. Combine the vinegar and sugar in a heavy skillet. Set out the orange and lemon juices next to your work space along with the remaining ingredients. Stir the vinegar and sugar over medium-high heat until the syrup turns translucent and begins to darken (caramelize). Stir in the two juices and simmer for 3 or 4 minutes. Add the Sauce Espagnole and half the sliced kumquats. Simmer, uncovered, 5 minutes longer until a sauce consistency is obtained. (Sauce can be prepared ahead up to this point—cover and set aside.)

Just before serving, stir the Grand Marnier or Cointreau and green peppercorns into the hot sauce and simmer for 2 to 3 minutes. To serve the ducks, cut in half along both sides of the backbone with poultry shears—discard the backbones or reserve for stock. Using your fingers, lift away as many of the breast bones as possible to make the ducks easier to eat. If serving the ducks quartered, cut each half crosswise. Top each serving with the warm sauce and sprinkle with the remaining kumquat slices.

TO PREPARE IN ADVANCE: The ducks and the sauce can be prepared in the morning. Reheat, and finish the sauce as described in the recipe.

OTHER PEPPERCORNS

The following are unusual pepper-type berries that may be specified in ethnic recipes.

CUBEBE PEPPER

LATIN: *Piper cubeb* IN MOROCCO: *kabbaba*

Sometimes called "tailed" pepper, this is a sharp-flavored, rather bitter, gray, oval berry from Ceylon and Java. It is available only at stores that specialize in importing exotic spices.

STORAGE: As any whole spice.

USE: This is used in Morocco in RAS EL HANOUT (see SEASONING BLENDS), the aromatic spice blend used to flavor Tajines.

MALAGUETA PEPPER

OTHER: grains of paradise, Guinea pepper

LATIN: *Amonum melegueta* IN MOROCCO: *gooza sahraweea*

These small brown berries that are about half the size of peppercorns are grown only in West Africa. They are a relative of cardamom, and are considered to be both a stimulant and aphrodisiac. They were once used in Europe as an inexpensive pepper substitute, but are available now only through specialty spice shops such as Aphrodisia in New York City.

STORAGE: As any dried spice.

USE: The seeds are still widely used in West Africa, but are not often exported because there is not a great demand. They are used as a flavorful pepper substitute by some restaurants, such as the Four Seasons in New York.

PINK PEPPERCORNS

FRENCH: *poivre rose*

There is a good deal of controversy raging over these pungent pink berries, which are not related to pepper (*Piper nigrum*) at all. A recent article by Daniel P. Puzo in the food section of the *Los Angeles Times* tells us that the U.S. Food and Drug Administration is investigating this French import because several university botanists claim that they are "blatantly mislabeled and a potentially toxic substance." The article states that "Furthermore, there is a strong resemblance between the pink berries being marketed as peppercorns and the fruit of an ornamental tree found in Florida and California . . . which belongs to the poison ivy family of plants and can cause toxic reactions in both animals and humans." The fate of these pungent little berries will soon be determined by the FDA.

At the time of this writing, the freeze-dried berries are sold in gourmet specialty shops by the ounce or in jars of brine. They are very expensive. The freeze-dried type have the best flavor.

STORAGE: Store both dried and those packed in brine as you would green peppercorns.

USE: Pink peppercorns make a colorful and flavorful garnish for cooked dishes, especially Nouvelle Cuisine restaurant creations, which feature seafood with Beurre Blanc Sauce.

SZECHUAN PEPPERCORNS

OTHER: wild pepper, fagara, anise pepper, flower pepper, Chinese or Japanese peppercorns

CHINESE: *faah jiu, hua chaoi* JAPANESE: *sansho, kona sansho* LATIN: *Zanthoxylum piperitum*

These mildly peppery berries are speckled brown and come from the prickly ash tree, which is not a member of the pepper family. The kernels have seeds in the center. They are often heated to bring out their full aroma, and then combined with salt to make a table seasoning. They lend a distinctive fragrance and tongue-tingling spiciness to many foods. They can be purchased in oriental markets, and a fine, flaky, powdered type is sold in Japanese markets in small tin boxes.

STORAGE: They will keep for up to 6 months in a cool, dark place, though they lose flavor on standing. When stale, they develop an unpleasant odor, and should be tossed out.

PREPARATION AND USE: Roast the kernels lightly in a dry skillet, stirring until you smell their fragrance. Transfer to the container of a blender, food processor, or spice mill. Process until finely ground. If desired, strain to remove the husks of the peppercorns. These ground berries are used as

61

a fragrant seasoning for many Chinese and Japanese dishes and, in particular, by the Japanese as a seasoning for grilled eel, Unagi. To make a popular table seasoning, combine the ground berries with salt and place in a container with a shaker top. We like it in this Szechuan dish:

FANCY TASTE CHICKEN

For 8 servings

Serve this cold as an appetizer, or as one of several dishes at a Chinese meal.

4   whole chicken breasts, split and boned, but with skin
      attached
½   cup chicken broth
2   tablespoons Szechuan peppercorns
⅓   cup light soy or mushroom soy sauce
2   tablespoons finely sliced scallions
2   tablespoons CHILI OIL, or more to taste
2   tablespoons rice wine or other wine vinegar
1   tablespoon sesame oil
2   teaspoons grated or minced ginger
2   cloves garlic, minced
½   teaspoon sugar
1   long English cucumber (this need not be peeled or
      seeded)
      Optional: a few sprigs of fresh coriander (cilantro or
      Chinese parsley)

Place the chicken breasts in a shallow baking dish large enough to hold them without crowding. Pour the chicken broth over them, cover the pan with foil, and bake at 350° for 25 to 30 minutes, until they are tender when pierced with a fork. Cool slightly; then remove the skin from the breasts, and trim any ragged ends so they look very neat.

Meanwhile, toast the peppercorns as described above, grind, and sieve to remove the husks. Place in a small bowl with the remaining ingredients, except cucumber, to make the dressing.

To serve, cut the chicken breasts lengthwise and crosswise into ½" cubes, and then press back together into original shape. Slice the cucumber as thinly as possible and spread on a round or oval serving dish. Arrange the still oval-shaped breasts, petal-fashion, on top of the sliced cucumbers. Stir the dressing and pour over the breasts. Garnish the platter with fresh coriander (cilantro or Chinese parsley).

TO PREPARE IN ADVANCE: The chicken can be cooked, cooled, and wrapped in plastic wrap, a day ahead. The dressing can be prepared a day ahead as well. Bring both to room temperature and assemble just before serving.

POPPY SEEDS

ARABIC: *khashkhash* CHINESE: *ying-shu* DUTCH: *slaapbol* FRENCH: *pavot* GERMAN: *Mohn* HUNGARIAN: *mákos* INDIAN: *khas khas* (white variety) ITALIAN: *papavero* LATIN: *Papaver somniferum* POLISH: *makom* PORTUGUESE: *dormidiera* RUSSIAN: *mak* SPANISH: *adormidera* SWEDISH: *vallmo*

These are tiny seeds that range in color from dark blue-gray to white and are native to the Eastern Mediterranean and Asia. The dark-colored ones can be found on the spice shelf of any supermarket. White poppy seeds, which have a nutlike taste very much like the more familiar black ones, are preferred in India, and are available in Asian markets. Poppy-seed oil, pressed from the seeds, is used like olive oil in French cookery and is known as *olivette*.

STORAGE: Black poppy seeds should be stored as any spice. White poppy seeds get rancid quickly, so store in the refrigerator.

PREPARATION AND USE: Toast poppy seeds in a dry skillet, stirring continuously, to crisp them slightly and bring out their full nutty flavor. They are usually used whole, but can be ground if they are soaked overnight, drained, and then processed in a blender or crushed with a rolling pin.

Dark poppy seeds are very popular in the cooking of eastern Europe, where they are used as a filling for baked strudel, and tossed with noodles to accompany stews. They are often sprinkled as a topping over rolls, breads, or cakes. The Lithuanian national dish, Loksinu su Aguonais, combines them with almonds and noodles in a creamy sauce. Makovy Dort, a Czech poppy-seed cake with raisins and lemon rind, and Lomanci Z Makom, Polish poppy-seed pastries, are examples of their use in sweet dishes.

White poppy seeds are often toasted lightly and then ground and used in Eastern curries and masalas for their thickening effect.

ROSEMARY

ARABIC: *iklil aljabil* DUTCH: *rosmarijn* FRENCH: *romarin* GERMAN: *Rosmarin* ITALIAN: *rosmarino* LATIN: *Rosmarinus officinalus* PORTUGUESE: *alecrim* RUSSIAN: *rozmarin* SPAIN: *romero* SWEDISH: *rosmarin*

Rosemary is a strong-flavored, spiky, perennial herb, native to the Mediterranean. It is a member of the mint family and has a slight camphor taste that is very pleasant if not used in excess. It is an extremely hardy, ornamental evergreen shrub with leaves like pine needles. It is easy to grow in mild climates and, unlike most herbs, grows best during the winter months. Dried rosemary is available in the spice section of any supermarket. Avoid any that is powdered.

STORAGE: Fresh rosemary can be dried and kept in a cool, dry place or frozen in small packages. Use dried rosemary within a year because it loses flavor on standing.

PREPARATION AND USE: This is a pungent herb, so use with discretion. Use only twice as much of the fresh as you would the dried, rather than following the usual 3 parts to 1 part rule. Chop fresh or dried rosemary or pulverize with a mortar and pestle to release the flavorful oils from inside the needles. A sprig of rosemary, or ½ teaspoon dried, placed in the cavity of a chicken before roasting does wonders. It has a special affinity for roast lamb, grilled fish, and new potatoes. It combines well with thyme to flavor stuffings, etc. It is one of the most popular herbs in Italian cooking, particularly in Pasta e Fagioli (macaroni and bean soup), Anitra Farcita e Arrostita (roast stuffed duck), and is always used in Roast Suckling Pig. In Austria and Hungary, it flavors Ungarishes Bohengulyas (dried bean goulash with ham and potatoes). The English traditionally put some in Steak and Kidney Pie.

SAFFRON

ARABIC: *za'faran* DUTCH: *saffraan* FRENCH: *safran* GERMAN: *Safrangewurz* GREEK: *krokus* INDIAN: *kesar* ITALIAN: *zafferano* JAPANESE: *safuran* LATIN: *Crocus satvius* IN MOROCCO: *zafrane* PORTUGUESE: *açafrão* RUSSIAN: *shafran* SPANISH: *azafran*

The world's most expensive spice is not only golden, but worth its weight in gold. It is made by drying crocus stamens and it takes more than 80,000 blossoms to yield a mere pound. Fortunately, it is used very sparingly. Fine quality saffron comes from Spain, Turkey, and from India, near Kashmir. It adds delicate, bittersweet flavor and vivid color to the dishes in which it is used. Whole thread-like strands keep their flavor longer than powdered saffron, and are safer to buy because they cannot be adulterated with turmeric or other less expensive powders. You will find it in gourmet specialty shops, fish markets, and in many ethnic markets. If you don't see it, be sure to ask for it, because it is usually kept in a dark place (and sometimes under lock and key)! Beware of some that is sold in Latin American markets under the name Mexican saffron, or the Spanish name AZAFRÁN (see THE FOODS OF LATIN AMERICA section), which is not saffron, but safflower.

STORAGE: Saffron must be kept in the dark because it loses flavor when exposed to light. Store in a cool, dark place and use as soon as possible.

PREPARATION AND USE: The usual amount for 4 servings is ½ teaspoon of crumbled saffron threads or ⅛ teaspoon powdered saffron. Take care not to use too much, or you will have a medicinal-tasting dish. For finest flavor, gently roast the saffron threads in a hot skillet until they turn dark red. Saffron should be soaked in hot water or other liquid to make a tea and the threads can then be strained out if desired, but it is not usually necessary.

This saffron tea is usually added to dishes that are almost finished cooking, such as curries, rice, bouillabaisse (the famous Mediterranean fish stew), Paëlla (the classic rice dish of Spain), Bacalao à la Vizcaina (salt cod, Spanish style) and many of the world's finest dishes. In Italy, it flavors and colors the famous Risotto alla Milanaise and, in Morocco, it is often added to Cous Cous (see THE FOODS OF THE MIDDLE EAST section). It flavors Shirini Polo (an Iranian orange-flavored chicken pilaf), Pescado Guisado (a Puerto Rican fish stew), and Ajiaco (a Columbian potato, corn, and avocado soup). Saffron is often used to flavor European breads and cakes, such as Swedish Saffransbröd, which are traditionally served at Easter. In Pennsylvania Dutch cooking, it is almost always used in the preparation of chicken dishes, such as Chicken Stoltzfus. Indian curries are often flavored with saffron, and one of our favorite dishes to serve to guests is:

CHICKEN MOGLI

For 6 to 8 servings

Loving to prepare party food ahead, as we do, we have substituted heavy cream for the sour cream specified in the original recipe so we won't have to worry about the sauce separating on reheating. It can be made with sour cream, or even yogurt, if care is taken not to overheat them.

    4   chicken breasts, split and boned
        Flour, salt, and pepper
    4   ounces GHEE or ¼ pound (1 stick) butter
    3   large onions, minced
    5   large cloves garlic, minced
  ½″   cube fresh ginger root, finely minced
    2   cups water
    2   large tomatoes, peeled and chopped
    1   cup heavy cream, sour cream, or yogurt*

SPICE MIXTURE 1:
    2   teaspoons caraway seed
    2   teaspoons whole cumin seed
    2   teaspoons ground cumin
    2   teaspoons ground turmeric
  ¾   teaspoon ground red pepper (cayenne)

SPICE MIXTURE 2:
    3   tablespoons JAGGERY (or substitute ¼ cup dark brown
            sugar)
    2   teaspoons ground cloves
    2   teaspoons ground cardamom seeds
    1   teaspoon saffron threads, soaked in 2 tablespoons warm
            water, or ¼ teaspoon of saffron powder

*Note: Yogurt curdles if allowed to boil. To prevent this, whisk 2 teaspoons cornstarch into the yogurt before adding it to the hot sauce.

Rinse the chicken breasts and dry them well with paper towels. Combine flour, salt, and pepper in a paper bag. Melt the ghee or butter over medium heat in a 12″ to 14″ sauté pan or skillet. Shake the breasts in the bag of flour to coat them evenly, and place them in the sizzling butter, skin side down. When lightly browned, use tongs to turn them over to brown briefly on the second side. Remove the chicken from the pan. In the pan drippings, sauté the onion, garlic, and ginger, stirring until the onion is transparent. Stir in SPICE MIXTURE 1, and cook for 2 to 3 minutes to toast it lightly. Return the chicken to the pan, add 2 cups of water and the diced tomatoes. Simmer for 5 minutes or so until chicken is tender when pierced with a knife. Add SPICE MIXTURE 2 and the cream, sour cream, or yogurt. Heat 2 to 3 minutes, without boiling, to warm through. Serve with Rice Pilaf, RAITA, and curry condiments.

TO PREPARE IN ADVANCE: This has a mellower flavor if it is reheated to serve the second day. Refrigerate it in a shallow baking dish. Reheat in a 350° oven for 15 to 20 minutes, only until warmed through.

SAGE

ARABIC: *mariyamiya* DUTCH: *salie* FRENCH: *sauge* GERMAN: *Salbei* ITALIAN: *salvia* LATIN: *Salvia officinalis* RUSSIAN: *shalfey* SPANISH: *salvia*

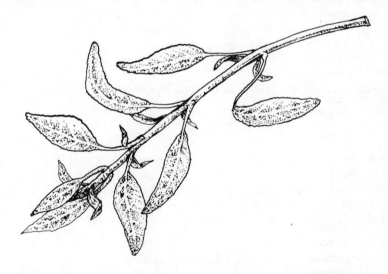

Garden sage with its grayish, furry-looking leaves is native to southern Europe and is one of the most important herbs in Italian cooking. Fresh sage is seldom sold in supermarkets, so it is best to grow your own and preserve it as described below, or seek it out in an Italian or Middle Eastern market where it can be purchased dried on small branches. There are several varieties of sage plants available in nurseries, including "pineapple" sage, "golden" sage and "dwarf" sage, but "garden" sage is your best bet for cooking. All varieties are quite hardy and require full sun. Bottled dried sage, available in the spice sections of all markets, should be used only if no other is available, and dried leaf sage is far superior to ground sage.

STORAGE: To preserve fresh sage, alternate layers of washed fresh sage leaves with layers of salt in a jar or other container and store in the refrigerator or freezer. Remove leaves as needed and brush off salt to use as you would fresh sage.

USE: "Parsley, sage, rosemary, and thyme," as they were once put together in the old folksong, are still a good combination. Sage has a rather pungent flavor, which can become camphorlike if it is exposed to high heat. Add it with discretion near the end of the cooking time. It is especially good with fatty meats or poultry, and is the flavor most of us associate with our domestic breakfast sausage and turkey stuffings. It has a special affinity for pork. In Italy, it is often added to the rice dish, Risotto, and the traditional Tuscan-style cannellini beans. Other well-known Italian dishes that are characterized by it are Saltimbocca Romana (Roman-style veal and prosciutto medallions), and Involti di Vitello (veal birds). It is popular in Yugoslavia, as well, where it is added to fish and pasta dishes, and even to pastries.

SALT

Several types of salt are sold in supermarkets and ethnic markets:

KOSHER SALT

May also be called "dairy" salt or "flake" salt. This is sold in almost all supermarkets these days. It is a coarse salt without additives, and we like it because it is less salty than an equal measure of table salt, and because it has a nice crunch to it in salads. Julia Child says she likes it because it is easy to pick up in the fingers for salting water for vegetables, pasta, etc.

PICKLING SALT

Fine ground, pure salt, used to make pickles, sauerkraut, etc.

ROCK SALT

Sometimes called "ice cream" salt because it is used in some ice cream freezers. This is a crude salt used as a bed for cooking Oysters Rockefeller, and is also handy to pick up and use for salting pots of boiling water for vegetables. The French name is *sel gris,* literally "gray salt," because it is not as refined as white salt. It contains valuable minerals, and cannot harm you.

SEA SALT

Salt processed from sea water. May be large crystals or fine grains. The world's finest is said to be Malden salt from England. Large crystals (the French name is *gros sel*) must be crushed in a salt mill.

TABLE SALT

Fine-grained salt that often contains additives to make it free-flowing. These additives will cloud a brine for pickles.

STORAGE: Stored airtight, it will last indefinitely. Salt is a natural preservative and cannot lose freshness.

USE: Salt is essential to human existence, and heightens the flavors of foods, but the tastebuds so quickly adapt to a taste for it that cooks have a tendency to overuse it. Since many fresh foods naturally contain salt, it is not really necessary to add but a minimum amount for flavor. Through history, it has been used in the preserving of meats, and in making brine to preserve many foods. Gastronomes claim to be able to tell a vast difference between sea salt, evaporated from sea water, and rock salt, mined from salt flats in land areas.

SAVORY

ARABIC: *nadgh* DUTCH: *bonenkruid* FRENCH: *sarriette* GERMAN: *Bohnenkraut* ITALIAN: *santoreggia* LATIN: *Satureja hortensis* (summer), *Santureja montana* (winter) PORTUGUESE: *segurelha* RUSSIAN: *chabyok* SPANISH: *sabroso* SWEDISH: *kyndel*

There are two types of savory. "Summer" savory is a bushy annual and is slightly milder than the sharper, more resinous "winter" variety. Their names have no relation to the time of year they are produced. Both are sold dried on supermarket spice shelves. Fresh savory must usually be grown in the home herb garden.

STORAGE: As any fresh or dried herb.

USE: Both types of savory are very strong and should be used with great discretion. Use approximately ¼ teaspoon for 4 servings. Neither appears often in recipes, perhaps because neither is a commonly available herb. Summer savory, which has a flavor slightly like thyme, complements summer vegetables and creamy chowders. Throughout Europe, it is used in sausages and stuffings for veal. Winter savory is even more pungent, and complements cooked beans, especially lentils, rich stews, and roast meats. Savory is often used in the classic French fish stew, bouillabaisse, in the summertime. We enjoy it in a simple lamb stew.

CREAMY LAMB STEW WITH HERBS

For 6 servings

2 large onions, thinly sliced
4 tablespoons butter
2 cloves garlic, minced
3 pounds lean lamb stew meat, cut in bite-sized pieces
¼ cup flour
2 cups fresh, peeled tomatoes, or canned tomatoes with their liquid
1 cup dry white wine
¾ teaspoon fresh summer savory, chopped, or ¼ teaspoon dried, crumbled
¾ teaspoon fresh basil, chopped, or ¼ teaspoon dried, crumbled
¾ teaspoon fresh marjoram, chopped, or ¼ teaspoon dried, crumbled
½ teaspoon fresh thyme, chopped, or a pinch of dried, crumbled
¼ teaspoon fresh rosemary, crushed, or a small pinch of dried, crumbled
2 tablespoons chopped parsley
1 cup whipping cream or sour cream

Sauté the onions and garlic in the butter in a skillet until lightly browned. Add the lamb, and brown lightly for a few minutes. Sprinkle with the flour; then add the tomatoes and wine. Bring to a simmer, cover the pot, and cook slowly for 1 hour. Or use a Dutch oven and cook in a 325° oven, covered, for the same amount of time. Add the herbs and simmer 30 minutes longer, until the lamb is tender.

Add the parsley and cream. If using sour cream, use very low heat under the pan, and take care not to let the mixture boil or it will separate. Serve with hot, buttered noodles and simply cooked vegetables, such as peas or green beans.

TO PREPARE IN ADVANCE: Refrigerate overnight. Reheat very gently, especially if sour cream is an ingredient.

SESAME SEEDS

ARABIC: *simsim* IN THE CARIBBEAN: *ajonjolí* CHINESE: *jee mah*
DUTCH: *sesam* FRENCH: *sésame* GERMAN: *Sesam* INDIAN: *til*
ITALIAN: *sesamo* JAPANESE: *goma shiro goma* (white, unhulled) *muki goma* (tan, hulled) *kuro goma* (black seeds) LATIN: *Sesamum indicum* IN THE MIDDLE EAST: *benne* IN NEW ORLEANS: *benne* RUSSIAN: *kunzhut* SPANISH: *ajonjolí* SWEDISH: *sesam*

Sesame seeds, white (hulled), tan (unhulled), or black oval, are available by the ounce in health food stores and in Middle Eastern and Asian markets, where they cost only a fraction of what they do in the spice section of the average supermarket. Use the pale-colored ones, hulled or unhulled, unless otherwise specified in recipes. Sesame seeds (or *benne*, as they are called in the Middle East) are a very rich source of calcium and protein. The black ones have a more pungent and slightly bitter flavor. (In China, the black ones are said to promote hair growth.)

STORAGE: Sesame seeds will keep indefinitely in the refrigerator or freezer, but their natural oils will turn rancid if stored long at room temperature. After roasting, they lose flavor very rapidly, so seeds should be toasted as close to serving time as convenient.

PREPARATION AND USE: For most purposes, toasted sesame seeds, widely used in Asian cooking, have a much finer nutty flavor than the plain seeds. Just before using, toast them in a dry skillet, stirring to prevent burning, until they are golden and fragrant. They have a tendency to fly out of the pan, so you may wish to cover it with a metal mesh cover. (There is a special sesame seed toaster sold in Japanese markets especially for this purpose.) Turn the seeds out of the pan to cool, lest they continue to cook. They are used whole or ground.

The toasted seeds can be used to season and garnish many dishes, and are a staple in the cooking of China, Japan and Korea. The Korean dishes, Bulgogi (brazier-cooked beef), and Gun Sae Sun (grilled fish) are characterized by their use. A sesame seed sauce is used for dipping cooked foods from the Korean dish, Steamboat, and the Japanese dish, Shabu-Shabu, which diners cook for themselves at the table. To make a sesame-salt to use as a table seasoning, grind the toasted seeds in a blender or spice mill with an equal amount of salt, and transfer to a shaker bottle. The Japanese product, *goma shio*, is the same sesame-salt, except it is made with black sesame seeds. The black seeds are used in China in a batter for deep-fried apple slices called Chinese Toffee Apples.

The pale seeds are very widely used in the Middle East to make sesame-seed paste, TAHINI (see THE FOODS OF THE MIDDLE EAST section), which is used in cooking and as a dip for bread. Unlike the Chinese sesame-seed paste, the seeds are not roasted before being ground, so it has a much more delicate flavor. The sauce for the Mexican national dish, Mole Poblano, has a very spicy sauce thickened with various seeds, including sesame, and they are often used to garnish the finished product. They are often sprinkled as a topping over bread to be baked. Sesame seeds are used in the Jewish candy, Halvah, and are widely used in confections and pastries. We enjoy them in our very easy recipe for:

SESAME SEED BRITTLE

For 1¼ pounds

Why the soda? It makes the mixture just slightly foamy, lending an airy texture to the finished candy.

- 1 teaspoon vanilla extract
- ½ teaspoon baking soda
- 2 tablespoons (¼ stick) butter
- 2 cups granulated sugar
- 1 cup sesame seeds, lightly toasted in a skillet until golden, and cooled

Set out on your work surface two pieces of heavy aluminum foil measuring about 20″ x 20″, and a rolling pin.

Combine the vanilla and soda in a small cup and set aside. Melt the butter or margarine in a *heavy* 3- or 4-quart saucepan. (Don't make the mistake of using a flimsy pan or the sugar will burn.) Add the sugar and stir constantly with a wooden spoon over medium heat until the sugar dissolves and becomes a smooth, golden brown liquid. The sugar will turn into lumps before dissolving. Just at the moment when all lumps are dissolved, immediately remove from the heat and stir in the sesame seeds and vanilla-soda mixture, mixing well. Quickly pour the contents of the pan onto the center of one sheet of foil. Cover with the second sheet of foil and roll the covered brittle with a rolling pin to spread it out to an even thickness of approximately ¼″, taking care not to burn your fingers, as the mixture is very hot.

Cool at room temperature. Peel off the top piece of foil and break into serving pieces.

TO PREPARE IN ADVANCE: This will keep, stored in airtight containers, for up to 3 weeks.

STAR ANISE

OTHER: anise

CHINESE: *bot gok* or *peh kah* INDONESIAN AND MALAYSIAN: *bunga lawang* THAI: *poy kak bua*

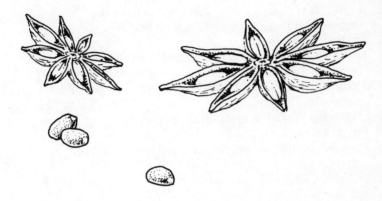

Star anise is so named because it comes from brown pods in an eight-pointed star-shaped cluster. It is native to China, and can be found in Chinese markets or spice shops. This "anise" is not actually related to the anise family, but to the magnolia family. ANISE seeds can be substituted in a pinch, but differ in flavor. Substituting FIVE SPICE POWDER (see SEASONING BLENDS), which usually has this spice as an ingredient, will give a better result.

STORAGE: As any whole spice.

PREPARATION AND USE: A "point" or "clove" refers to both the seed and its barklike covering. Break off the number of points specified in the recipe. This is a strong-flavored, aromatic spice, so 1 or 2 points are usually ample for most recipes. If substituting Five Spice Powder, use ⅛ teaspoon per point. Use crushed, broken, or whole, tying them in cheesecloth for easy removal from a finished dish. Star anise is a common flavoring in Chinese "red" sauces for poultry and meat with soy sauce, ginger, and garlic. They add fragrance and a subtle spiciness to many Chinese dishes and marinades. They are used as an ingredient in Malaysian curries. We like the flavor in the following recipe for oxtails.

OXTAILS CHINOISES

For 4 servings

Chef Richard Wing of the award-winning Imperial Dynasty restaurant in Hanford, California, gave us a taste of this unusual dish prepared for the kitchen help. It may be doubled or tripled, in which case you will end up with a good deal of sauce, which can be condensed over high heat at the end of the cooking time.

THE SAUCE:
- 2 pounds fresh tomatoes *or* 1 (28-ounce) can crushed tomatoes in tomato puree (Progresso brand)
- 1 cup dry white wine
- 1 BOUQUET GARNI consisting of: 2 medium cloves garlic, peeled and cut in half; a strip of orange or tangerine peel, 2 whole cloves, 2 points (seed pods) from a whole star anise
- 1 tablespoon minced or grated fresh ginger
  Worcestershire sauce
  Cayenne (ground red pepper) or a pinch of red pepper flakes
- 2½ pounds oxtails, cut in 1½" to 2" sections
- ¼ cup peanut oil, for browning

Combine the sauce ingredients, except for the Worcestershire and cayenne, in a heavy stew pot. Simmer over low heat. Meanwhile, rinse and dry the oxtails. Heat the oil in a wok (or sauté pan) until it is almost smoking. Brown the oxtails, three pieces at a time, turning often to color evenly on all sides. When browned, lift them out with tongs and place them in the pot with the sauce. When all have been browned and are in the sauce, cover and simmer very slowly for 3½ hours, until the meat is very tender and nearly falls from the bones. Remove and discard the bouquet garni.

Lift the oxtails with a slotted spoon to a warm bowl or platter. Cook the sauce over high heat to thicken it slightly while you season it to taste with Worcestershire and cayenne. (The oxtails will have given off very little fat, so you will probably not find it necessary to skim the sauce at the end of the cooking time.)

Serve in wide soup bowls, with French bread for mopping up the delectable sauce, and plenty of napkins.

TO PREPARE IN ADVANCE: This is even tastier reheated the next day.

SUMAC
See THE FOODS OF THE MIDDLE EAST section

TARRAGON
OTHER: French tarragon

ARABIC: *tarkūhn* FRENCH: *estragon* GERMAN: *Estragon* ITALIAN: *targone* or *dragoncelle* LATIN: *Artemesia dracunculus* PORTUGUESE: *estragão* RUSSIAN: *estragon* SPANISH: *estragón*

There are two types, French and Russian, but the only one with culinary value is French tarragon. It is a perennial herb, one of the FINES HERBES (see SEASONING BLENDS) of French cooking. You will find it sold in bunches during the summer and early fall in fine produce markets. If buying plants at a nursery, make sure they are labeled French tarragon. Dried tarragon is always available in the spice sections of supermarkets. Tarragon leaves packed in vinegar are sold in gourmet specialty shops.

STORAGE: Fresh tarragon, wrapped in damp paper towels and stored in a plastic bag in the refrigerator will keep up to a week, or it can be preserved in vinegar for indefinite storage. Strip the leaves from the stems and pack them into a small jar, crowding them; then cover with vinegar. Store in the refrigerator for up to a year. Dried tarragon should be stored as any dried herb.

PREPARATION AND USE: As a general rule, use one-third the amount of dried herb as you would fresh. To use tarragon preserved in vinegar, squeeze out as much of the vinegar as possible, and then use as you would the fresh herb leaves. Tarragon can be overpowering, so use with discretion.

It is one of the most important herbs used in French cooking, and is an essential ingredient in the herb-flavored, hollandaise-type sauce known as Béarnaise, which is superb with grilled beef and lamb. It is not used much in Italy except for a bread stuffing for artichokes that is a specialty of Siena, and occasionally in recipes for Pollo alla Cacciatoria (hunter's style chicken). It is the perfect herb to place inside a chicken to be roasted; the pan juices, when mixed off the heat with sour cream, are sublime. Steep a sprig of tarragon in the vinegar you use for salads and mayonnaise. Mix chopped fresh leaves with softened butter to make Beurre à L'Estragon to melt over grilled fish, chicken, or meats.

THYME

ARABIC: *sa'tar* (See ZA'ATAR for hybrid) DUTCH: *tijm* FRENCH: *thym* GERMAN: *Thymian* ITALIAN: *timo* LATIN: *Thymus vulgaris* PORTUGUESE: *tomilho* RUSSIAN: *tim'yan* SPANISH: *tomillo*

There are several varieties of this perennial herb of the mint family that are native to southern Europe. Garden thyme is most often used in cooking, but lemon thyme (*Thymus citriodorus*) is also widely used and preferred by some for its delicate lemony flavor. Fresh thyme is seldom available in produce markets, but can usually be found in nurseries. Garden thyme is available dried on the spice shelf of every supermarket.

STORAGE: Fresh thyme sprigs, wrapped in paper towels and stored in a plastic bag in the refrigerator will keep for up to a week. The leaves, removed from the stems and frozen, and tightly sealed in plastic or foil will keep for up to a year. Dried thyme should be stored in a cool, dark place, as any herb.

USE: Thyme is seldom the predominant herb used in a dish. It is, however, an essential ingredient of a BOUQUET GARNI (see SEASONING BLENDS) used in the cooking of most French stews and braised dishes. Thyme is widely used in the cooking of France where it often flavors dishes containing beef, chicken, game, and eggs. It is used in boulliabaisse (fish stew), onion soup, and Bisque de Homard (lobster bisque), to name a few. Lemon thyme complements fish, chicken, and veal. Hymettus honey, one of the finest in the world, is made by bees who feed on the thyme flowers growing wild on Mount Hymettus in Greece. It characterizes Fassoul Yahnia (a Bulgarian bean stew), and Apfel Mit Leberfülle (a German dish of baked apples stuffed with liver). In Norway, it is added to potato dumplings and, in Belgium, to Boeuf à la Flamande (beef, Flemish style). The Irish add it to potato soup.

Thyme is used in some African recipes (the Gallic influence) and is a predominant herb in American Creole cooking, as a major seasoning for gumbo. On the island of Aruba, it seasons Acra L'en Mori (fish fritters). It has a special affinity for tomato and corn dishes, and also for beans.

TURMERIC

ARABIC: *kurkum* BURMESE: *fa nwin* CHINESE: *wong gueng fun* or *yu-chin* DUTCH: *geelwortel* FRENCH: *circuma* or *safran d'Indie* GERMAN: *gelbwurz turmer* INDIAN: *haldi* or *munjal* INDONESIAN and MALAYSIAN: *kunyit* ITALIAN: *circuma* JAPANESE: *ukon* LATIN: *Curcuma longa* IN MOROCCO: *quekoum* PORTUGUESE: *acafrão-da-India* RUSSIAN: *zholty imbir'* SPANISH: *curcuma* THAI: *kamin*

This is a rhizome of the ginger family and is native to southern Asia. It lacks the spicy flavor of ginger, but has the bright orange-yellow color of saffron and lends its color and slightly musty flavor to commercial curry powders, American-style mustard, and mustard pickles. Its flavor is nothing at all like saffron and it is never used as a substitute for that spice except for its color. It is often used as a dye. It is available on the spice shelves of all supermarkets, usually imported from India. It is never purchased in its whole form because it is almost impossible to grind.

STORAGE: As any ground spice.

USE: Turmeric has a slight thickening effect upon liquids. The flavor of turmeric can be bitter if too much is used in a dish. A good rule of thumb is to use ⅛ to ¼ teaspoon per cup of cooked food, be it rice or sauce. Add it to rice dishes and curried dishes where a yellow color is desirable. Women in India use it on their cheeks to give a golden glow, which is preferred over the rosy blush affected in the West.

It is often a part of Asian spice mixtures and MASALAS (see THE FOODS OF ASIA section), and commercial curry powders and pastes derive their bright color from turmeric. In Indonesia, rice dyed with turmeric is an important part of the wedding ritual and, in Bali, the whole root is rubbed into the skin of a pig before roasting. It is a common ingredient in Molee (coconut milk curry). In Indonesia, it lends its bright color to Nasi Kuning Lengkap (festive yellow rice, served in a cone shape with a large assortment of condiments). In Malaysia, it colors glutinous rice cooked in coconut milk, and Satay (skewered grilled beef). In Burma, it is used specifically in Pazoon Kyau (skewered fried prawns), and in Beef and Pumpkin Curry.

Turmeric is used in the soup, Harira, traditionally served to break the fast at Ramadan in the Middle East. And in Morocco, it almost always appears in recipes for Cous Cous. In East Africa, it flavors Muhogo, a beef and cassava stew. In England, it is used in Piccalilli (pickle relish) and Mulliga-tawny Soup.

VANILLA BEAN

OTHER: vanilla stick, crystallized vanilla

ARABIC: *wanila* FRENCH: *vanille* ITALIAN: *vaniglia* LATIN: *Vanilla plantifolia* IN MEXICO: *vainilla de papantla* RUSSIAN: *vanil* SPANISH: *vainilla* SWEDISH: *vanile*

Vanilla, native to Mexico, the West Indies, and Central America, derives its name from the Spanish word for "small sword." The pods of an orchid plant are yellow and tasteless when picked, but develop their strong, sweet flavor and darken as they are aged. There are several varieties, all expensive, which can be purchased in gourmet specialty markets or baker's supply houses in glass tubes. Look for pliable beans labeled "fine vanilla" with white surface crystals (technically called *givre*). Today, 90 percent of the world's production is from Madagascar.

Beware of artificial, chemically produced flavor when buying extracts—the words "pure vanilla extract," which indicate that it was made with vanilla beans, should appear on the label. "Mexican vanilla" sold in Latin American markets has a very different flavor from the vanilla extract found in the spice sections of supermarkets. It is stronger and smoother in flavor, and much less expensive. We strongly recommend that you seek some out to experiment with.

STORAGE: Vanilla beans dry and harden on standing. Store them tightly wrapped or in a jar in the freezer or refrigerator if you won't be using them within a week or so. Extracts will keep indefinitely in a cool place.

PREPARATION AND USE: Many French pastry chefs prefer using the podlike bean to the use of vanilla extract, but Julia Child says she doesn't have much luck with them and we agree. The bean can be used two or three times in the making of custards if it is thoroughly dried and stored, tightly wrapped as above, between uses. Vanilla sugar is often sprinkled over fruit and desserts. It is made by burying a split vanilla bean in granulated sugar and storing for several days in a tightly covered jar to let the aroma permeate the sugar.

Many of the world's cuisines make use of vanilla. In Europe, it flavors desserts from French pastries to Yugoslavian Hazelnut Cookies to Swedish Äpplekaka med Vaniljsas (applecake with vanilla sauce). We wouldn't dream of making Flan, the creamy, molded custard dessert of Latin America without Mexican vanilla. It gives an authentic Mexican flavor and aroma to all Mexican *postres* (sweets) that call for vanilla. Mexican vanilla is stronger in flavor than American extract, so use about one-third less. Vanilla is not widely used in Asia except where there has been a strong European influence. In Sri Lanka it is used in cakes and fried pastries and, in the Philippines, it is used in rice fritters.

FIESTA FLAN

For 16 to 20 servings

This is a festive dessert to serve at large parties. To make it, you will need an 11″ ring mold of 12-cup capacity, and a larger pan containing an inch or more of hot water (water bath or "*bain marie*") in which to place the ring mold when you bake it in the oven. The finished dessert requires a serving plate with a rim that will catch the overflow of caramel when the custard is turned out of the mold. For a garnish, set a shallow container of flowers in the center of the flan.

3   cups granulated sugar
8   whole eggs
8   egg yolks
4   (13-ounce) cans evaporated milk
1   tablespoon Mexican vanilla (Vainilla de Papantla) *or* 4
     teaspoons pure vanilla extract
     Grated peel (zest) of 1 orange
     Grated peel (zest) of 1 lemon

First, caramelize 1½ cups of the sugar to line the mold. Use a *heavy* saucepan over medium-high heat for this process, stirring constantly with a wooden spoon just until the sugar melts and turns golden brown. Take care not to touch the liquid—caramel can give a bad burn. Quickly pour into ring mold and rotate the mold to coat its sides with the caramelized sugar; set aside to cool. The caramel will harden as it cools, but will become liquid again during the baking.

To make the custard, beat the whole eggs and yolks together in a large mixing bowl. Add the milk, the remaining 1½ cups sugar, vanilla, and grated peels and stir for at least a minute to dissolve the sugar. Pour the mixture into the caramel-coated mold, cover and set it in a larger pan containing 1″ or more of hot water. Bake the custard in its water bath at 350° for 1 hour and 15 minutes, or until a knife inserted into the center of the custard comes out clean. Let cool for 10 to 15 minutes before inverting it carefully onto a serving plate with a rim. Serve warm or chilled.

TO PREPARE IN ADVANCE: The flan can be prepared up to 2 days in advance and refrigerated, loosely covered with plastic wrap. Do not freeze.

YERBA BUENA

See MINT

ZA'ATAR

See FOODS OF THE MIDDLE EAST section

SEASONING BLENDS

The following are blends that you will find specified in recipes from ethnic cookbooks. We have tried to be as helpful as possible in guiding you to create your own and in finding substitutes.

BERBERÉ

See FOODS OF AFRICA section

BHARAT

See FOODS OF THE MIDDLE EAST section

BOUQUET GARNI

(boo-KAY gahr-NEE)

Bouquet garni is a French term that has now come to refer to the small muslin bags of dried herbs that are commercially available in gourmet specialty shops, and that have supposedly magical flavors for soups and other specified uses. Far preferable is the classic meaning of a bundle of herbs tied together with string or tied inside cheesecloth, easily removable from soups, stews, and braised dishes at the end of the cooking time. We suggest using only freshly assembled bouquets garnis.

STORAGE: Keep in mind that dried herbs lose flavor on standing and should be stored airtight, in a cool, dark, dry place where they will keep for up to a year.

PREPARATION AND USE: A true bouquet garni can be assembled very quickly from what is at hand, the traditional combination being 1 bay leaf, 1 or 2 sprigs of fresh thyme, parsley stems, and celery leaves tied together with string. If dried herbs are used rather than sprigs of herbs, use ¼ to ½ teaspoon dried thyme, the same of celery seeds and the bay leaf, but skip the parsley unless you have fresh. The combination should be placed inside well-rinsed cheesecloth and tied with string to keep it contained.

Do not simmer more than 30 to 40 minutes, which will give maximum flavor without the risk of any bitterness that might result from overlong exposure to heat.

This is used in most French stews and braised dishes, such as Boeuf Bourguignonne and Coq au Vin, and has become international in use.

CHILI POWDER

This is a confusing term. Any red spice labeled chili powder in an Asian market is made from pure, ground, dried red Asian chiles. It is, as a general rule, much hotter than Latin American chili powder, which is made from any of various dried chiles, or the blend of chili powder found in every supermarket, which has various herbs, such as cumin and oregano added to it. For the Asian type, you can substitute CAYENNE, or grind your own from dried Bird's Eye Peppers, available in Thai markets.

STORAGE: All red spices should be stored in the refrigerator to prevent infestation by bugs.

USE: It is very important when cooking from ethnic cookbooks to be aware that chili powder may refer to any of a number of products. American recipes, for the most part, specify Mexican-style chili powder.

Following is a recipe for the type of chili powder found in supermarkets. It is not intended for purists seeking Mexican flavors. It is more of a Tex-Mex product, used to flavor everything from Chile con Carne to Tamale Pie.

CHILI POWDER

For ¼ cup

Most blends of this type contain a large amount of garlic powder, which we consider a disadvantage because we prefer fresh garlic. You can add 2 teaspoons of granulated dried garlic to this recipe if you wish. It is necessary to toast the spices lightly to bring out their flavors.

2   large, dried CHILES PASILLA or negro
1   large, dried CHILE ANCHO
1   tablespoon cumin seeds
¼   teaspoon whole cloves
4   allspice berries
2   tablespoons dried oregano leaves
1   tablespoon paprika

81

Remove the stems and seeds from the chiles and tear the skins into small pieces. Place in a heavy, dry skillet with the remaining ingredients except the oregano and paprika, and toast over medium-low heat, stirring constantly until the chile skins have toasted and browned lightly, but take care not to scorch them. Pour the mixture into the container of an electric blender or electric coffee grinder/spice mill, add the oregano and paprika, and process until pulverized. Transfer to an airtight container.

VIVI'S TAMALE PIE

For 12 servings

This is a recipe from Genevieve Davis, renowned fiction author, and one of the most creative cooks we know. Serve Vivi's Tamale Pie as a main course, or as an accompaniment to barbecued ribs or steaks.

    8 tamales*
    1 tablespoon butter
    1 tablespoon vegetable oil
    2 large onions, finely diced
    1 bunch scallions, thinly sliced
    ½ pound fresh mushrooms, chopped
    4 cloves garlic, crushed
    1 tablespoon chili powder
    2 pounds ground sirloin, or lean ground beef
    8 ounces sharp Cheddar cheese, grated
    2 cups tomato sauce
    1 (16-ounce) can creamed corn
    1 (7-ounce) can diced mild green chiles (Ortega brand)
    1 (4-ounce) can chopped black olives
       Butter to grease a 3-quart (or larger) baking dish

TO GARNISH AND SERVE:
    6 ounces Monterey Jack cheese, grated, *or* QUESO BLANCO,
          crumbled
       Sliced scallions

*Note: Vivi uses the large XLNT brand tamales, sold in most supermarkets in the West. If not available, substitute an equivalent amount of canned tamales.

Remove paper wrappers from the Tamales and mash them with a fork. Place in a very large mixing bowl.

Heat butter and oil in a large skillet, and sauté the onion, scallions, and mushrooms until the onion is transparent and the liquid resulting from cooking the mushrooms has evaporated. Add the garlic and chili powder and cook, stirring, for a minute or so longer; then transfer the contents of the pan to the bowl with the Tamales.

In the same skillet, cook the ground beef, breaking it up with the back of a spoon, until crumbly but still pink. Add it to the mixing bowl followed by the remaining ingredients. Mix well and pour into a buttered baking dish.

Bake at 350° for one hour. Top with Monterey Jack cheese or queso blanco, and continue baking 10 minutes longer until melted. Sprinkle the top with sliced scallions.

TO PREPARE IN ADVANCE: This can be baked several days in advance; cool and refrigerate. Reheat in a 350° oven for about 30 minutes, or until hot.

CRAB BOIL

OTHER: shrimp boil, New Orleans seafood boil

This mixture is often specified in American seafood recipes. It is sold in supermarkets and gourmet specialty shops, especially in the southern states. We are including a recipe for a homemade version.

STORAGE: As any spice mixture.

PREPARATION AND USE: The mixture is added to the water in which shellfish, such as shrimp, crab, and lobster are cooked, to give them extra flavor. The water in which they are cooked cannot be reused because it is too salty. If you remove a good deal of the salt from the homemade blend, the cooking liquid could function as the base for a spicy soup, after the seasonings are strained out.

SHELLFISH BOIL

Up to 4 tablespoons salt   For 5 pounds of shellfish
2 teaspoons yellow mustard seeds
1 teaspoon dill seeds
12 allspice berries
2 blades mace
4 cloves
2 bay leaves
2 small, dried, red chiles, crumbled

Combine and mix well. Store in an airtight jar until used. Add directly to boiling water and simmer 5 minutes before adding the shellfish to be cooked.

CURRY POWDER/PASTE

OTHER: *kari*

FRENCH: *poudre de cari* GERMAN: *Indisches Currypulver* ITALIAN: *curry* SPANISH: *polvo de curry*

Curry powder is not a natural spice, but a combination of anywhere from 7 to 20 separate ingredients. An Indian cook will generally grind the spices daily in combinations that depend upon the curry to be served that day. In India, a hundred curry stews will be made with a hundred different combinations.

The bottled curry powders and pastes found on grocer's shelves are merely convenience items. For this convenience, we must accept one of only a few formulas for all of our various uses. It is best either to make the blend called for in a particular recipe, or make your own for an all-purpose curry powder/paste. As a general rule, the brands of curry powder from India are the best. One favorite, widely available brand that you will probably find in specialty food shops is Sun Brand Madras Curry powder. Ceylon curry powder is especially flavorful with well-roasted spices. It is sold in some Asian markets, and a recipe for it appears in *The Complete Asian Cookbook* by Charmaine Solomon. (McGraw-Hill)

STORAGE: The aromatic powdered spices and herbs of curry powder will deteriorate quickly if not packaged in an airtight container and stored in a cool, dark spot. Curry paste will keep several months in the refrigerator.

PREPARATION AND USE: Commercial curry powder should be cooked briefly in a little fat (oil, butter, etc.) to bring out its full flavor and remove the floury taste before it is added to foods. Chinese and Japanese cooks usually dry-roast it in a skillet to a color the Japanese call "fox-colored," and this may be done as an alternative to cooking in oil. This step is unnecessary with the paste product, or a homemade powder in which the spices were roasted. Add paste or powder to your own taste when curry is called for in a recipe.

Asian curries seldom call for these blends, but for individual spices or a blend such as GARAM MASALA. These blends are often called for in American and British recipes, for such things as Kedgeree (a garnished rice, served as a main course), or curried rice, used as a starch substitute for potatoes. The Netherlands use such blends a great deal, in such dishes as Kerry Kool Sla (hot curried slaw). Curried dishes are an important part of the cooking of Mozambique. In Africa, curry sauces often contain tomato sauce, a European influence. A South African curry will contain pieces of dried fruit, such as peaches, apples, or prunes, a Middle Eastern influence. Madras-style curry powder is often used in that port city, especially on the very popular grilled lamb and apricot dish called Sosate, and in lamb meat loaf.

Following is a recipe for an Indian curry powder given to us by our editor, Janice Gallagher.

HOT CURRY POWDER

For 1½ cups

½ cup ground turmeric
½ cup coriander seeds
5 tablespoons black peppercorns
1 tablespoon whole cloves
2 tablespoons cumin seeds
2 tablespoons shelled cardamom seeds
1 tablespoon ground mace
1 tablespoon ground cinnamon
1 tablespoon fenugreek seeds
1½ teaspoons ground ginger
½ teaspoon cayenne

Grind the whole seeds coarsely. Place all ingredients in a large, heavy skillet or baking pan. Roast, either on top of the stove or in a 375° oven, stirring often, until they have darkened in color slightly and the aroma permeates the kitchen. This will take only 5 minutes or so on top of the stove; about 20 minutes in the oven. Turn out of the pan and let cool; then transfer to a container for storage.

Use in place of commercial curry powder. It is not necessary to cook it before use.

And, here is a Madras-style curry paste, which we developed.

MADRAS CURRY PASTE

For 1 cup

The advantage of a curry paste is that the spices have been cooked in oil so they have no raw, powdery taste as they do in commercial curry powders, which must be cooked in fat before use. As a general rule, use 1 tablespoon of curry paste per pound of meat, or simply substitute this paste for powder or for the paste called for in recipes. (If cooking from authentic Indian recipes, substitute it for the spices, ginger, and garlic in the recipe—then precooking of spices won't be necessary. For depth of flavor, be sure to add GARAM MASALA, as well.)

½ cup ground coriander
¼ cup ground cumin
1½ teaspoons cayenne (ground red pepper)
1½ teaspoons ground turmeric
1½ teaspoons ground black pepper
1½ teaspoons salt
6 large cloves garlic, pressed
1 tablespoon pureed ginger
¼ cup cider vinegar
3 ounces MUSTARD OIL

Combine spices and salt in the container of an electric blender. Add garlic, ginger, and vinegar. Blend until puréed.

Heat the oil in a heavy skillet. Pour in the spices and stir constantly over medium heat for about 10 minutes until the mixture has darkened. (The strong aroma of the mustard oil disappears as the spices are cooked.)

Stir in 3 ounces of water to make the mixture into a paste. Let cool and transfer to a jar for storage.

Use in place of the curry powder or paste called for in a recipe (using 3 parts of this paste to 1 part GARAM MASALA). You can omit any directions that call for cooking the curry powder or spice blends in oil at the beginning of the recipe because the spices, in this case, have already been cooked. The aroma and flavor of the vinegar disappears when the paste has simmered for a few minutes in the sauce.

TO PREPARE IN ADVANCE: Stored in a cool place or in the refrigerator, it will keep indefinitely.

ÉPICES FINES

OTHER: Spice Parisienne

Épices Fines is a more complex herb and spice combination than QUATRE ÉPICES both of which are used in French cooking. Chefs usually create their own blends, though such mixtures are packaged commercially in France, and can be found in some American specialty shops under the name Spice Parisienne.

STORAGE: Stored in an airtight container in a cool, dark place, it will keep for up to a year.

PREPARATION AND USE: To make this all-purpose blend, which is adapted from a recipe of Julia Child's, grind together in a blender or spice mill 3 parts white peppercorns, 2 parts *each* crumbled bay leaves, whole cloves, crumbled dried thyme, ground mace, nutmeg, and sweet paprika, and

1 part *each* ground cinnamon, crumbled dried basil, and winter savory. This is sprinkled as a seasoning over pork roasts and into pâté mixtures.

FINES HERBES

This is a delicately flavored, classic French blend of sweet herbs, which traditionally consists of finely chopped parsley, chervil, tarragon, and chives, with the occasional addition of basil, marjoram, fennel, or sage. A bottled dried version is sold in the spice section of most markets. Look for uniform blending and size of particles. It is easy enough to create your own.

STORAGE: As any dried herb for use within a year.

PREPARATION AND USE: A typical blend contains 1 tablespoon *each* of minced parsley, snipped chives, fresh tarragon, and chervil. (If using dried tarragon and chervil, use only 1 teaspoon of each.) A sprinkling of this herb mixture can do wonders for dishes containing eggs, cheese, fish, or poultry. It is also widely used to flavor simple soups and stews. The mixture, blended into ½ pound of soft butter becomes Beurre aux Fines Herbes, which is handy to keep in the freezer in a foil-wrapped roll. A small slice of it can be spread over grilled liver, steaks, or chops. It is said that one of the favorite dishes of the Duke and Duchess of Windsor was the classic Omelette aux Fines Herbes, a dish in which these fresh herbs are lightly sautéed in butter with a bit of minced fresh leek before the addition of beaten eggs. It is a dish we enjoy often, especially when we have a bit of Gruyère cheese to tuck inside when the omelette is folded.

GARAM MASALA

Garam masala is a mixture of ground aromatic spices used as a seasoning in Indian foods. There are hundreds of variations, but the basic ingredients will be black pepper, coriander, cumin seeds, cloves, and cinnamon. It is not a curry powder, and blends may vary, but they are never "hot." Many cooks choose to add some of this, homemade or purchased, to curried dishes, even those containing curry powder or paste, because the more highly aromatic spices contained in a garam masala are generally not present in packaged curry blends.

STORAGE: Once prepared, garam masala loses its aromatic essence quickly. If more is made than is required, pack tightly into a jar and store in a cool, dry, dark place for use as soon as possible, or up to 6 months in the refrigerator.

USE: The spices are, as a rule, roasted before grinding to bring out their flavors. This mixture is used along with other spices to flavor many Asian curries, added either toward the end of cooking or sprinkled over the finished dish.

GARAM MASALA

For about 1¼ cups

This is easy to make, especially if you have an electric coffee grinder, but a blender works well, too. The following is our preferred combination. You may wish to consult Indian cookbooks for other ideas, or simply add more or less of some of our chosen spices. All of the following spices, except perhaps black cumin seeds, are available in supermarkets.

6″ piece of stick cinnamon
⅓ cup cardamom pods
3 tablespoons black peppercorns
2 tablespoons coriander seeds
2 tablespoons cumin seeds, either "black" or regular
1 teaspoon whole cloves
½ a whole nutmeg

Crush the cardamom pods between your thumb and forefinger to break open the husks and reveal the brown seeds inside. Discard the husks.

Place all the spices on a baking sheet and toast them in a 200° oven for 30 to 45 minutes. (Your kitchen will be fragrant beyond words.) Remove from the oven. Grind the spices together in the container of an electric coffee grinder or blender in several batches until pulverized and powdered.

RAITA

For 6 cups

A traditional yogurt-and-chopped-vegetable side dish served with many Indian meals. It also makes a fine topping for baked potatoes, and a dip for cooked artichokes or raw vegetables.

1 cucumber, peeled and seeded (preferably the long English
    type which need not be seeded)
2 teaspoons salt
1 quart plain yogurt
1 green bell pepper, seeded and diced
2 firm but ripe tomatoes, diced

1 tablespoon minced fresh coriander (cilantro or Chinese
    parsley)
2 teaspoons garam masala
2 teaspoons sugar
1 teaspoon ground cumin
    Additional salt, to taste

Chop or grate the cucumber. Toss with 2 teaspoons salt and let it rest at room temperature for 10 to 15 minutes to draw out excess moisture. Rinse with cold water and place in rinsed cheesecloth or a clean kitchen towel and squeeze out as much of its liquid as possible. Stir it gently into the yogurt along with the other ingredients. Refrigerate for an hour or more for the flavors to develop.

TO PREPARE IN ADVANCE: This will keep in the refrigerator for up to 4 days.

HERBES DE PROVENCE
See FOODS OF EUROPE section

PICKLING SPICES

This mixture of whole spices can be found on the spice shelf of every supermarket. Some of the traditional ingredients, such as mace and dried ginger, are difficult if not impossible to obtain in their whole form, so it is easiest to buy this mixture, which is readily available.

STORAGE: As any whole spice.

USE: These are usually tied in cheesecloth so they can be fished out of a kettle of pickles easily. They are used because powdered spices darken pickles (and these will, too, if left too long). In the southern United States, such spices are used in making pickled shrimp. In the Middle East, they are used in Tourlu Guvech (pickled vegetable salad with turnips and cabbage), and in Czechoslovakia they are essential to Ryba Na Cerno (fish in a "black sauce" of prunes, vinegar, beer, rye bread, and gingersnaps).

QUATRE ÉPICES

Quatre Épices, literally "four spices," is usually a mixture of white pepper, cloves, nutmeg, and ground ginger. It is sold commercially in France but is easily made at home. Some cooks substitute ground ALLSPICE, in equal measure. Some recipes contain more than the usual 4 spices. A typical blend is 4 tablespoons ground white pepper, 1 tablespoon ground nutmeg, 2 teaspoons ground ginger, and ¾ teaspoon ground cloves.

STORAGE: Such blends lose flavor on standing. Keep in a cool, dark place for up to a year.

USE: This is a seasoning for pâtés, stews, soups, and meats to be grilled.

RAS EL HANOUT

See FOODS OF THE MIDDLE EAST section

SPICE PARISIENNE

See ÉPICES FINES

THE FOODS
OF
AFRICA

EAST AFRICA
NORTH AFRICA
 (see THE FOODS
 OF THE MIDDLE
 EAST section)
SOUTH AFRICA
WEST AFRICA

THE TAMING OF THE STEW

Culinarily, as well as geographically, Africa can be divided into distinctive areas.

North Africa, by its very location, is a "Mediterranean" area, enjoying almost the same climate and air as Spain and southern Italy. This part of Africa, being entirely Muslim and attached physically by land to the Middle East is, regardless of its French "connections," gastronomically Middle Eastern. And that is where we have placed it in this book.

From just below the tip of North Africa, stretching 1,400 miles down a full one-third of this continent, will be found the forbidding wasteland of the Sahara Desert. Africa, then, as we think of it and personally know it, is the Africa below the Sahara.

It can logically be assumed that out of the 50 or so nations that Africa comprises there will be among them some that have, for a variety of reasons, developed their cooking more quickly than the others—nations where the indigenous cuisine has advanced beyond the basic techniques of spitted and boiled foods. To us, the three most obvious front-runners in this race are Nigeria, in West Africa; Ethiopia, in East Africa; and, in the south, the Republic of South Africa. But, before we highlight the differences among these remarkable cuisines, it would be interesting to look at the general similarity of all African foods.

The most characteristic native African meal consists of a starch as a major ingredient, accompanied by a stew, either thick or thin, containing vegetables or meat, or both. This fairly standard native diet is similar in many ways to the rice cuisine of Asia, both being basically subsistence diets that supply the necessary nutritional needs of a high-density population with a minimum of agricultural technology. These starchy filler foods, though they are the main ingredient of the meal, are never eaten by themselves. They are always enlivened with a spicy stew or soup. This starch and stew cuisine is wonderfully well reflected by Nigeria, in West Africa.

West Africa contains over 30 percent of the population of the entire African continent. In Nigeria alone, there are over 33,000,000 people, and over 300 different languages. These are huge numbers, and they take on greater meaning when we realize that almost one-third of Africa's population is existing on a subsistence agriculture. Each family must have its own garden from which to gather cooking ingredients, and the yam or the cassava is the popular crop.

Nigeria has evolved an inventive cuisine based upon a filler-food with the delightful name of Fufu, a boiled and pounded yam mush, served with imaginative stews that have been highly seasoned with native spices. Fufu is the general name given to this rather stiff mush throughout West Africa, whether it is made from flour derived from corn (*mealie*), or cassava, or whether it is made from yams. Nigerian African slaves brought their Fufu to the kitchens of the American south, and influenced our cuisine forever with Cornmeal Mush and spoon bread. In Nigeria, Fufu is generally rolled between the palms of the hands and served molded into neatly shaped balls.

A second popular Fufu in West Africa is made with cassava, which has been grated, dried, and then roasted before mixing with water, to produce Gari Fufu. In one or two areas farther down the coast from Nigeria, cassava flour is mixed with water to make a paste, which is placed into greased molds and steamed. This is known as Miondo.

In the parts of North Africa that come under Mediterranean influence, the kitchens have over 200 herbs and spices to choose from; Nigeria, on the other hand, accustomed to using what can be locally grown, generally embraces the fiery pepper, known there as *piripiri*. Not only Nigeria, but the dozen or so other countries hugging the shoreline beneath the bulge of Africa, are extremely fond of chiles in their dishes. In neighboring Ghana, there is a delicious fried rockfish or mullet that is marinated in a mixture of ginger, onion, tomato, and cayenne, cooked in groundnut (peanut) oil, and traditionally served with sliced tomatoes and boiled yams. And then there is the French touch in neighboring Senegal, farther west. They, too, use cayenne pepper as a fish marinade, but more subtly, in a blend of lime juice, chopped parsley, peppers, scallions, and garlic. The fish is simmered in this marinade for half an hour with cauliflower, cabbage, turnips, and eggplant and then served on fluffy rice. This composition is musically called Thiebou Diene. Pepper Chicken is a favorite Nigerian dish that can be prepared in many ways, but is most often cooked as a stew. The chicken is first browned, and then added, with an equal volume of peeled tomatoes, to sautéed onions in a heavy stewing pan with groundnut oil, cayenne, and thyme. No liquid is added—the chicken cooks in its own juice and that from the tomatoes, with the oil. This is traditionally served with balls of yam Fufu.

One of the tastier stews of Nigeria is a Chicken Groundnut Stew with balls of corn Fufu. "Groundnut" is the African name for a peanut. In its role as an ingredient, it is not only a nutritious thickener, but imbues the chicken with a rich, peanut butter flavor.

As modern and metropolitan as the principal cities of West Africa are, very few restaurants, if any, are recommended by travel agents to visitors to sample this culinary fare. In fact, visitors are earnestly advised to eat in their hotels where the water is filtered and the food preparation is "certified, sanitary." If one follows these "for safety's sake" recommendations, one is bound to be disappointed, as there is then no chance to try the ethnic foods or experience the ethnic table. The hotel restaurants, though employing native cooks in their kitchens, offer menus right out of Paris, if you are in a previously French territory, such as Senegal; or foods right from a London menu, if you are in Nigeria, which at one time was an English possession. The only variation in Nigeria is the "curry lunch," served regularly every Saturday. Rarely, if ever, is a native stew or Fufu served. However, in many of the major cities of the world, there has been a blossoming of West African and Ethiopian restaurants, encouraged perhaps by the success of Moroccan restaurants but proving, certainly, the growing popularity of these unusual ethnic cuisines.

As the major East African nation, Ethiopia has a classic and distinctive cuisine, and as in West Africa, a spicy stew is most popular—in Ethiopia, called Wat. Its national dish is Doro Wat, composed of chicken, onions, tomato puree, chicken stock, and hard-cooked eggs, seasoned with a fiery spice paste. It has earned its place of honor because it's just too good to be in second place. And, if you can believe it, East Africans surpass West Africans in their penchant for hot chiles, here incorporated in the spice paste called Berberé (a paste of paprika, chiles, and spices), a formidable ingredient met in Chicken Wat, Meat Wat, Fish Wat, Vegetable Wat, or as an essential dip for raw meat. There is an alternate, of course, for those among the 25,000,000 Ethiopians who don't like their stew quite that "hot"—they have a version called Alechas, which is made in the same manner, but without the cayenne.

The staff of life in this country is bread—wheat, barley, or millet—which is generally shaped into a rough loaf. There is also an unusual bread, called Injera, a thin, round, spongy bread made of very finely ground millet, called Teff. Teff flour is mixed with water and left for three or four days to ferment in a cool place. It's then poured onto a hot, flat griddle, covered with a lid and, in about five minutes, you have something that looks like a flat, round piece of moist sponge rubber, pockmarked with tiny air holes, that has a sourdough flavor. This tangy, thin, yellow, pancake-like bread serves as the plate, tray, or tablecloth for your food combinations. No forks or spoons are required; you just tear off a three- to four-inch square of bread, and dip, wrap, fold, or roll your selection in it, and eat.

Since Ethiopia is not Muslim, alcohol is a welcome social drink. Aside from good native beers, the national drink of this dignified country is Tej, a type of heady, fermented honey mead that reminds one of an apricot liqueur mixed with plain raw alcohol. Dinner is usually concluded with a super-rich, spiced Ethiopian coffee that is twice boiled into a concentrate and served unsweetened.

In Africa, there are over 800 languages and, as a consequence, there is little communication between cuisines, little recipe exchanging or sharing of techniques. The Republic of South Africa, with its universality of language, is the exception. South Africa is the most progressive, the richest, and the most advanced country in Africa. The steel and glass high-rise office buildings, museums, manicured parks, sidewalk cafés and thousands of tempting restaurants give the cities of Johannesburg, Durban, and Cape Town an air of familiarity, as if you were really in Amsterdam or San Francisco, but have found yourself on an unknown street. Europeans have been encouraged to emigrate to South Africa, and World War II convinced hundreds of thousands to take up permanent residency. Consequently, a variety of international foods are offered by restaurants, including Portuguese, Dutch, English, Malaysian, West African, Ethiopian, Old Cape, or exclusively South African seafood. The breadth of their seafood is extensive, and they are justly famous for their lobster tails, Cape Salmon, and oysters. It is also possible to order springbok or impala, eland, kudu, buffalo, or other wild game native to South Africa, and certainly the stews made by the native Bantus, with their accompanying cornmeal (mealie meal) mush called Putu.

Three hundred years ago, the Bantu country of South Africa was settled by the Dutch so that food and water could be supplied to their ships traveling to and from plantations and spice holdings in East India. As the settlement grew and moved northward, the Dutch imported Malaysian slaves into Cape Town to supply the necessary muscle for their farms. The Cape Malay adapted well to this new country and added a welcome Asian influence to a fairly dull, Middle European diet. The resulting cuisine is what is known as "Old Cape cookery." Another interesting factor in this development of South Africa's table was the early immigration of French Huguenots, who carried among their trappings grape vine cuttings that flourished on the Cape of Good Hope, below the Tropic of Capricorn.

So, here is a curious ethnic mixture—the Dutch, who were to model the agriculture, the English, who were the townspeople and traders, the French, who developed the vineyards, the imported Asians, who brought their curries, and the local Bantu natives, with their preferred starch-and-stew diet. Some foods resulting from this cultural blend that are well worth our attention are Frikkadels (highly spiced hamburger patties made from pork, beef, or lamb, and served either by themselves or wrapped in cabbage leaves and simmered in seasoned stock), Gesmoorde Hoender (braised chicken with chiles), and Denningvleis (spiced lamb stew). The Dutch, the English, and the Malayans are all old curry hands, and they have combined their talents expertly in a dried fruit and meat curry served with fluffy rice, and again in Bobotie (lamb meat loaf).

Good, hearty meals are served in South Africa and meat, generally, is the major ingredient. The English still serve breakfast on the sideboard and take great pride in their "mixed grills." The Dutch are equally proud of their barbecues, which they call Braaivleis. However, South Africa's most unusual meat is a wind-dried beef called Biltong, similar to our jerky, but spicier, moister, and more elegant. It finds its way naturally to the sports arena, racetrack, into lunch bags and back packs. It is a typically African food and can be found country-wide below the Sahara wherever meat is available.

South African brandies and sherries are distinguished and their wines are very good, but the South Africans tend to fancy beer. With most family meals, they prefer a glass of Castle or Lion, both good lagers, or an imported Hansa Beer from southwest Africa. A real treat, though, which must be tried, is a brandy-based, tangerine-flavored liqueur called Van Der Hum.

This world of Africa, below the Sahara, was hidden from outsiders for over 50 centuries. Since its discovery by Western man, this awakening continent has been greatly influenced by half a dozen European powers. These influences are visible in all of Africa's cuisines, not only in the imposed cooking style of a country's occupying population, but in the African cook's preference for non-native ingredients, such as tomatoes, cassavas, chiles, and corn. To the casual eye, African cooks may all seem to use these ingredients in somewhat the same manner. But, a closer look will disclose a definite individual style specific to each area and culture, as you will see when browsing through the following pages.

BAOBAB

OTHER: "cream of tartar" tree

No part of this large African tree is wasted in African cooking. Its large oval fruit, which can weigh several pounds and is eaten raw, has a slightly sweet, yet acid, dry pulp, somewhat like a grapefruit. The juice of the fruit is used as a drink or as a seasoning in cooking. The leaves, which can be cooked like spinach or used in soups, are usually blanched, dried, and powdered to make KUKA powder. The seeds, called "monkey bread," are steeped in water to make a naturally sweet drink, roasted and eaten, or made into LALU powder. Explorers in the bush often place the seeds under their tongues to keep away thirst. The ashes from its wood are used as a salt-like seasoning. Even the trunk is a source of water for jungle explorers who become dehydrated. Baobab trees also grow in Florida, but their products are not sold commercially in this country. We mention them here for their intrinsic interest.

95

BERBERÉ

OTHER: *ber-beri*

In Amharic, the official language of Ethiopia, the word "berberé" means pure red chili powder, but most often refers to a fiery red pepper-spice paste that is the essential ingredient of Ethiopian cuisine. The paste is not a commercial ingredient, but one that is made in the home and used to season Wat (stew), the national dish of Ethiopia, which can be made from meat, chicken, fish, or simply vegetables on one of the many fast days, and as a dip for raw meat and bread. To make it, very "hot" red chiles are sun-dried, and then ground with aromatic seasonings including garlic and ginger. (See the recipe following this entry.) A passable substitute can be made by combining 1 part CHILE PASTE WITH GARLIC (see THE FOODS OF ASIA section) with 3 parts paprika, though it will lack the depth resulting from the variety of spices used in the real thing. Most African cookbooks containing Ethiopian recipes recommend that paprika and ground red pepper (cayenne) be used for seasoning a dish to taste, and ignore this paste altogether.

STORAGE: If a ¼" covering of oil is replaced over the paste after each use, this spice-paste will keep in the refrigerator indefinitely. All red spices, such as paprika and cayenne, should be stored in the refrigerator to prevent infestation of tiny bugs.

PREPARATION AND USE: In the making of various Ethiopian Wats (stews), 1 to 4 tablespoons of the paste will flavor 4 servings, 1½ pounds of meat, or 1 to 2 chickens. The paste is often cooked with other spices in a spiced butter called NITER KIBBEH before meat and liquids are added. In Ethiopia, this paste is also rubbed into meat along with salt and pepper. The meat is then hung in a cool place for two weeks to make BILTONG (dried beef), used as a snack ration.

BERBERÉ

For about ⅔ cup

This is most easily made in an electric blender. Our version is medium "hot"—adjust the amount of cayenne to your own taste.

- 1   clove garlic, peeled
- 1   scallion, white part only *or* ½-inch cube of onion
- 1   tablespoon red wine vinegar
- ½   cup water
- ½   cup paprika
- 2   tablespoons ground red pepper (cayenne)

2   teaspoons salt
½   teaspoon ground black pepper
¼   teaspoon ground ginger
¼   teaspoon ground cardamom
¼   teaspoon ground coriander
⅛   teaspoon ground fenugreek seeds
⅛   teaspoon ground nutmeg
    Pinch ground cloves
    Pinch ground cinnamon
    Pinch ground allspice
1   tablespoon palm, peanut, or vegetable oil

Combine the garlic, onion, vinegar, and water in the container of an electric blender and process to a smooth puree. Set aside.

In a small, heavy skillet, combine all remaining ingredients *except* oil. Place these ground spices over medium heat, stirring constantly until the mixture is hot to the touch, taking care not to scorch it. Remove from the heat and let cool for 2 to 3 minutes; then stir in the blended mixture, mixing until smooth. Return the pan to the heat and cook over very low heat, stirring often, for 10 minutes. If the paste seems too dry, stir in more water, a little at a time, to keep it at a paste consistency.

Transfer the berberé to an 8-ounce jar or other nonmetal container for refrigerator storage. Pour the oil over the surface of the paste to cover it completely.

To use, sauté the desired amount of the spice mixture in oil or butter at the beginning of sauce preparation, as in the following recipe for Ethiopia's national stew.

DORO WAT

For 4 servings

This is the national dish of Ethiopia, chicken stewed in a bright red sauce of fragrant African spices. It is traditionally garnished with hard-cooked eggs and served with Injera (see TEFF), a pancake which is torn into pieces and used as an edible utensil to lift the stew to the mouth.

2   tablespoons NITER KIBBEH
3   pound chicken, cut in serving pieces
2   large onions
2   medium cloves garlic
½   inch piece fresh peeled ginger, chopped
¼   cup BERBERÉ
¼   teaspoon ground fenugreek

¼ teaspoon ground cardamom
¼ teaspoon ground nutmeg
1 cup chicken broth or water
2 tablespoons lime juice (or lemon juice)

TO GARNISH AND SERVE:
4 hard-cooked eggs, sliced
   Chopped parsley

Rinse the chicken pieces well and dry with paper towels. Heat the NITER KIBBEH in a heavy deep skillet. Brown the chicken, a few pieces at a time, in the hot oil, and remove from the pan. When all pieces are browned, add the onion to the drippings in the skillet. Stir often over medium heat until they start to brown, then add the garlic, ginger, spices and berberé. Cook, stirring, for 2 to 3 minutes. Add the broth and lime juice and simmer for 3 to 4 minutes until the sauce has thickened slightly. Return the chicken to the pan, cover the pot and simmer slowly for 30 minutes. Lift the lid from time to time to stir the contents of the pot and turn the chicken over in the sauce.

To serve, transfer the stew to a platter. Garnish decoratively with hard-cooked eggs and a sprinkling of parsley.

TO PREPARE IN ADVANCE: The stew tastes even better the second day. Reheat in a saucepan or in the oven until the chicken is warm.

BILTONG

OTHER: dried meat, "jerky"

The South African word for air-dried, seasoned meat is *"biltong,"* which is a staple food in Ethiopia and other African countries. Pioneers in South Africa traditionally prepared it from the finest pieces of meat from game animals. Beef replaced game when beef cattle became popular as farm animals. The meat is cured by rubbing salt, brown sugar, and spices mixed with a bit of SALTPETER (see THE FOODS OF EUROPE section) into fresh pieces of lean meat that have been cut or pulled into pieces along the grain. It is then hung to dry in a cool, clean spot for two weeks or longer. At its finest, it can be compared to the PROSCIUTTO of Italy, which is served thinly sliced as an appetizer (see under HAM in THE FOODS OF EUROPE section). Our domestic equivalent, called JERKY (see THE FOODS OF REGIONAL AMERICA section), which is not truly comparable, can be found in most supermarkets, but African biltong is not available.

STORAGE: If thoroughly dried, this will keep indefinitely in an airtight container at room temperature.

USE: In central Africa, biltong is used as a snack ration by both hunters and villagers. It is sometimes skewered to roast over open fires, or finely grated to sprinkle as a seasoning on buttered toast. In South Africa, it has reached restaurant status to be served as an appetizer.

BLACK-EYED PEA

OTHER: cowpea

Beans rather than peas, these are a staple food of West Africa, though they are widely grown in India, China, and in the southern United States. They are available both dried and canned in many supermarkets. Fresh ones can be found occasionally in produce markets, especially in the South, during the fall.

STORAGE: Store fresh beans in the refrigerator for use as soon as possible. Dried beans will keep indefinitely in an airtight container on the pantry shelf. Canned beans, after opening, can be stored in a nonmetal container in the refrigerator for up to a week.

PREPARATION AND USE: Buy 3 pounds of fresh peas in their pods for 4 servings. One pound of shelled ones, fresh or dried, will serve 4 to 6. Fresh peas should be removed from their pods, and this job is made easier if a vegetable peeler is used to peel a strip from the outer curve of the pod. Fresh peas take 1 to 1½ hours to cook, as do the dried. Most American recipes recommend that these be cooked with salt pork or ham.

In West Africa, they are cooked and then mashed with minced onion and cayenne and formed into Akara (bean cakes), which are fried in PALM OIL or vegetable oil to be served as an appetizer or main dish. In East Africa, they are cooked with onion, ground peanuts, and tomato to make a sauce; cooked with coconut milk and a bit of curry powder to make a soup; or cooked with onion and ground peanuts to make a mush-like porridge called Ugali. In Nigeria, they are cooked with corn, bell peppers, and tomatoes to flavor a fish stew called Adalu, and in Ghana in a soup called Nkakra. In Central Africa, they are made into a Burundi sauce called Ibiharage in which they are flavored generously with onions, garlic, cayenne, and salt. In South Africa, they are curried with lamb to make Kerrieboonjjies Bredie.

CASSAVA

One of the most important foods in Africa, the cassava, is native to South America and was brought to Africa by the Portuguese in the 17th century. (General information on CASSAVA, cassava flour [TAPIOCA], and CASSAVA

MEAL will be found in THE FOODS OF LATIN AMERICA section.) Over half the world's supply of cassava is now produced in Africa. Cassava flour is called GARI in Africa, where it is an extremely important African staple. It is also the source of true tapioca, which can substitute for it in areas where it is not available, because the taste and consistency are similar, and both are nearly flavorless when cooked. An alternative substitute, and one that we prefer, is adding 1 tablespoon of instant tapioca to 1 mashed potato. Cassava can be purchased in Latin American markets, fresh or frozen, as can cassava flour and meal.

STORAGE: The whole root or pieces of it can be wrapped in plastic wrap to store in the refrigerator for up to 4 days, though the flesh discolors on standing. Frozen cassava can be stored for up to 4 months.

PREPARATION AND USE: (See THE FOODS OF LATIN AMERICA section for basic cooking directions.) In West Africa, cassava is preferred over other starches such as yam or plantain to make Fufu, the unseasoned glutinous starch eaten with most meals. To make it, raw cassava is usually soaked in water for several days to soften it. It is then grated or pounded into a pulp, which is placed in a sack, and weighted to press out the liquid, for two more days. It is then pounded into flour, which is dampened and formed into balls. It can be purchased in markets in Africa in this form. These balls are mixed with water to make a paste. The mixture is cooked very slowly for 30 minutes or so, stirring almost constantly, until it is translucent and forms a cohesive mass. This thick, smooth paste, Fufu, is then formed into either a loaf or a mound. Diners pull some off, form it into a rough ball, and dip it into the stew before eating. There are several variations—it is sometimes steamed instead of boiled; and it can also be sliced or diced to place in soups or stews.

Americans may be best off starting with frozen cassava, which is partially cooked before it is frozen. Frozen cassava needn't be thawed before cooking. One-inch chunks of cassava are boiled in water to cover, to which salt and lemon juice are added, for about 45 minutes until tender and thoroughly soft; then pounded and made into a sticky substance, which is called Dumboy and is the national dish of Liberia, and very much like the Fufu made by the previously described method. All of these types of mixtures should be served very quickly after they are prepared, because they harden quickly on standing.

Cassava Fufu or Dumboy is served as an accompaniment to soups and stews and, in some areas, is steamed inside greased plantain leaves and is called Miondo. In Sierra Leone, the Fufu is sometimes mixed with egg, onion, and garlic, and formed into balls that are fried until brown. In Liberia, it is made into "cassava pone" flavored with coconut, and almond and vanilla extracts. Raw cassavas are thinly sliced to fry like potato chips, which can be kept for several days in an airtight container and reheated in a low oven. The following recipe for EBA is a typical African cassava recipe.

EBA
(Cassava Porridge)

For 4 servings

This is often served as a very bland breakfast porridge or as a starchy accompaniment to African soups and stews.

⅔ cup GARI (about 4 ounces)
1⅔ cups water

Sift the gari to remove any large lumps. Bring the water to a boil in a small heavy saucepan. Remove from the heat and lightly sprinkle the gari into the hot water, stirring rapidly as you add it. It will thicken very rapidly into a glutinous mass and requires vigorous beating. Rinse a 2- to 3-cup bowl with cold water and turn the mixture into it. Press it down firmly, smoothing the top. Turn out onto a serving plate.
Serve immediately.

TO PREPARE IN ADVANCE: Not advisable. Serve as soon as possible because it hardens rapidly on standing.

COCONUT

See THE FOODS OF ASIA section

COCOYAM

See TARO ROOT in THE FOODS OF ASIA section

COLA NUT

OTHER: kola nut, ombene, temperance nut, guru nut, bissybissy

Many popular carbonated drinks, such as Coca Cola, are flavored by the kola nut. This reddish-brown, rather flat seed from a tree native to West Africa contains a large amount of caffeine and other stimulants. It is very important in African ceremonial life. It is also purported to have aphrodisiac properties. Like BAOBAB, it is also believed to lessen thirst. We have not located a source for the seeds, but surely it must be available somewhere because the nut is widely grown in most tropical areas, and it is used as an ingredient in cola drinks.

STORAGE: Cola nuts will keep indefinitely in a cool dry place.

USE: Africans chew the cola nut as a stimulant. The ground seeds are often made into a simple drink.

EFO

This term applies to any of a multitude of tender greens used in African cooking. Many of them are dried and stored to be added to stews and rice dishes. Among the hundreds of African greens are cassava, SORREL (see THE FOODS OF EUROPE section), *craincrain* (which has a thickening effect upon liquids, and is similar to MULOUKIA (see THE FOODS OF THE MIDDLE EAST section), and carrot tops. Spinach is an easy substitute in African recipes, but other greens such as beet tops, MUSTARD GREENS, COLLARDS (see THE FOODS OF REGIONAL AMERICA section), chard, and turnip greens provide more interest. Adjust the cooking time accordingly, depending on how tough the greens are. Some, such as spinach, cook in less than 5 minutes; others, such as collards, may require up to 20 minutes to become tender. As a general rule, 2 ounces of dried greens are equal to a pound of fresh. We mention this even though you are not likely to find, or use, dried greens.

EGUSI
OTHER: *epusi*

Egusi are the seeds of an African "watermelon," a small, round fruit with pink or white flesh, cultivated in West and central Africa. It is a cross between a gourd and a pumpkin. The seeds are a popular food item in West Africa. They are imported in bulk and in cans and can be found only in West African markets.

STORAGE: After opening, egusi can be stored in the refrigerator for up to a month.

PREPARATION AND USE: The seeds are eaten whole as snacks, but are more commonly dried, ground, and mixed to a paste to use as a thickener for stews and soups. Recommended substitutes for ½ cup ground egusi seeds used in thickening 4 cups of liquid are: 1 beaten egg, 2 finely chopped hard-cooked eggs, 1 cup mashed kidney, navy, or pinto beans, or ½ cup dried, peeled eggplant. In Africa, egusi seeds are often roasted and pounded into cakes with black pepper to use as a seasoning of the same name, which must be pulverized before use.

ELUBO

(Yam flour)
See YAM

FISH, DRIED

Salted, preserved fish are used in South Africa for seasoning soups and stews, and are the basis for one of the national dishes, Smoor-vis, in which the salted fish (*snoek* is the favored variety) is soaked for at least 8 hours in several changes of water to rid it of excess salt, and then flaked and braised in a sauce with onions, chiles, and tomatoes. The resulting dish is not unlike the Bacalao of the Mediterranean. In Central Africa, a dried perch called *kapenta* is used in the same manner. A wide variety of dried fish can be found in Asian markets. See THE FOODS OF ASIA section for general information.

GARDEN EGGS

Garden eggs are a variety of small, green-skinned African eggplant. Substitute Japanese eggplant, or ordinary eggplant if the small ones are not available.

GARI

(GAH-ree)
OTHER: cassava meal, manioc meal, *gari, gali, garri*

IN LATIN AMERICA: *farinha de mandioca*

Gari is a starch made from the CASSAVA, which has been peeled, sliced, and sun-dried, and then ground into a coarse flour. It is available in Latin American markets. (See CASSAVA MEAL, in THE FOODS OF LATIN AMERICA section, for general information.) Gari is a specialty of Ghana and other parts of West Africa.

STORAGE: Gari can be stored indefinitely in an airtight container in a cool, dry place.

PREPARATION AND USE: As in Brazil, this starch is often toasted to bring out its flavor. The toasting is done by heating the flour, or meal, with PALM OIL, stirring it constantly until it is golden brown. It is often mixed with just enough water to make it swell to serve without cooking as a porridge for breakfast and, if this porridge is then cooked, it is served in a ball or loaf and is called Eba (see recipe under CASSAVA). Once prepared, either mixture must be served immediately, because it quickly hardens. In West Africa, gari is often made into Gari Foto, a dish in which the gari is seasoned with onion, garlic, and tomato, and then combined with scrambled eggs. This is served for breakfast or lunch and is usually accompanied by red beans.

In most parts of Africa, cassava flour and other starches, such as plantain, yam, and cornmeal, are made into a type of mush, called Fufu (or Foofoo), described in this section under CASSAVA, which is steamed or boiled, and then molded or made into balls to serve as a starchy accompaniment to many dishes, particularly soups and stews. (Some African cookbooks mention that it is supposed to be eaten without chewing, lest one's jaws stick together, but it doesn't really happen that way.)

The gari can be used toasted or untoasted, and is sometimes fermented in the same way as TEFF, to give it a sourdough flavor. In Nigeria, the untoasted flour is mixed with coconut, sugar, and water to make a paste, and baked into cookies called Gurudi.

GROUNDNUT

OTHER: peanut, monkeynut, goober

IN AFRICA: *nguba* CHINESE: *fah sang* FRENCH: *cacouette* or *arachide* GERMAN: *Erdnuss* INDONESIAN: *katjang tanah* ITALIAN: *arachide* MALAYSIAN: *kachang tanah* SPANISH: *cacahuete* THAI: *thua lisong*

The peanut was introduced to Africa from its native Brazil by the Portuguese and quickly became one of the most commonly used ingredients in African cooking. It is actually a legume that grows underground, not a nut. Peanut oil is the second most commonly used cooking oil in Africa, after PALM OIL.

STORAGE: Raw peanuts do not keep well. Store them in the refrigerator or freezer for use as soon as possible. Roasted peanuts can be stored on the pantry shelf for a month or longer, but are also best kept in the refrigerator or freezer to prevent rancidity.

PREPARATION AND USE: Peanuts are widely used in African cooking and are generally used roasted, but unsalted. They are occasionally eaten raw or boiled, in which case they taste a good deal like green peas. Roasting or frying develops their flavor. The use of commercial, supermarket-variety peanut butter can save a good deal of time in preparing African recipes that specify that peanuts be roasted, skinned, and ground, but the taste is not exactly the same.

THE FOODS OF AFRICA

The most famous African peanut dish is Groundnut Stew. It usually con-tains a combination of chicken and beef with ground, roasted peanuts, to-matoes, onions, ground chiles, and hard-cooked eggs. Groundnut Sauce is similar except that the meats are ground, and dried shrimp are added. Both are served with some sort of smooth starch dish. A Senegalese variation called Mafé uses a number of vegetables, including green peppers, in the preparation of the stew, and also thyme, showing a Gallic influence. The Senegalese make a peanut ice cream as well.

In Nigeria, peanuts are ground into flour and made into a dough, which is formed into balls and fried to become a snack called Kulikuli. Other parts of Western Africa make a peanut brittle-like confection called Groundnut Cakes. In East Africa, peanuts are cooked with greens, with beans, and are made into sauces; in Kenya, they are cooked with spinach and coconut milk in a chile-spiced Spinach and Groundut Stew. In Tanzania, they are mashed with yams and pumpkin and seasoned with a bit of curry to make a starchy mush called Mchanyanto. In Central Africa, peanuts are cooked with to-matoes, onions, and a soup bone to make Groundnut Soup. Another soup, Shorba, made with lamb (the Middle Eastern influence), bones, garlic, rice, and peanut butter, is popular in the Sudan.

On the island of Mozambique, they are not only added to curries and desserts, but combined with clams and tender greens, such as spinach, to make a stew called Matata. The following recipe is for a West African spicy stew.

CHICKEN GROUNDNUT STEW

For 4 to 6 servings

This is a very popular West African dish, with as many ways of preparing it as there are cooks. Freshly ground roast peanuts have a finer flavor than commercial peanut butter.

4–6 chicken legs and thighs, attached or separated
    Salt and pepper
2 tablespoons peanut or palm oil
1 large onion, minced
2 teaspoons grated or chopped fresh ginger
2 pounds ripe tomatoes, peeled and chopped, or a 28-ounce can crushed tomatoes in tomato puree
1½ teaspoons chopped fresh thyme or ½ teaspoon dried thyme, crumbled
1 teaspoon crushed red chiles*
6 ounces roast peanuts, ground to a paste or ⅔ cup cream-style peanut butter

TO SERVE:

> 1   green bell pepper (seeds and membranes removed), cut
>   in very fine slivers
>   Steamed rice or Eba (see RECIPE INDEX)

*Note: In South Africa, this type of stew would very likely contain curry powder in place of the chiles. Our favorite, hot curry powder, needs no precooking (see RECIPE INDEX).

Rinse the chicken and dry it with paper towels. Sprinkle lightly with salt and pepper. In a large, deep pan, brown the chicken lightly in the oil. Add the onion to the pan and cook until transparent; then add the ginger and cook briefly, followed by the tomatoes, thyme, and chiles. Cover and simmer slowly for 20 minutes. Stir in the peanut paste or peanut butter until well blended and the sauce has thickened. Heat, uncovered, over very low heat for just a minute or two. Taste, and correct the seasoning. Do not heat long after adding the peanuts or the sauce may separate.

Arrange in a serving dish, sprinkling very thin slivers of green bell pepper over the chicken as a garnish and flavor accent. Serve with steamed rice.

TO PREPARE IN ADVANCE: Cook up to 2 days before serving; cool, and refrigerate. If overheated, the sauce can separate, so reheat gently over very low heat, or in a baking dish in the oven, just until hot.

KUKA

Kuka is a powder made from the leaves of the BAOBAB tree, which have been blanched, dried, and powdered. It is used as a slippery thickening for stews, to which it also adds a slightly tart flavor. It is a similar product to FILÉ (see THE FOODS OF REGIONAL AMERICA section) and, because kuka is not exported, you would be wise to substitute filé in equal measure.

LALU

Lalu is a powder made from the dried, crushed seeds of the BAOBAB tree. It functions as a crude baking powder and as a flavoring for stews. It is not exported, nor will you miss it in recipes. If it is indicated in an African recipe as a baking powder, substitute ½ the given amount with our domestic baking powder.

MALAGUETA PEPPER

See PEPPERCORNS, OTHER, in the HERBS, SPICES, AND
SEASONING BLENDS section

MEALIE AND
MEALIE MEAL

Maize or American Indian corn, introduced to Africa from America, is
mealie in South Africa. It is not the sweet corn we are familiar with, but a
drier type of "field" corn. Ground into a white meal, it is *mealie meal*, a staple
food of the Bantu tribe. (The term "Bantu corn" refers to MILLET.) When
this fine cornmeal is roasted it is called *ablemanu*. The best substitute for
mealie is canned whole hominy. The best substitute for mealie meal is stone-
ground white cornmeal, available in natural-food stores.

PREPARATION AND USE: Mealie is the staple starch of South Africa.
It is made into a stiff mush, like the West African Fufu, called Pap by the
Dutch, Putu by the Bantus, and Nshima by the Sambians, seasoned only
with salt. This mush is served with stews or soups, which tend to be a great
deal less spicy than those of West Africa and Ethiopia. Fritters, cakes
(muffins), and puddings are also made with mealie. Mealie meal is most
commonly made into porridge, which is a major part of the African diet. In
West Africa, mealie meal is made into cornmeal cakes to serve with their
more robust stews. *Ablemanu* is used in making Tsitsinga, barbecued skewered meat, which is coated with the toasted flour halfway through the grilling.
A basic mush to serve with stew is made as in the following recipe.

MEALIE MEAL PORRIDGE

For 6 to 8 servings

Serve this as a breakfast porridge with maple syrup or honey, or as a starchy
accompaniment to African stews such as the following South African Fruit
Curry.

1   cup white stone-ground cornmeal
1   cup cold water
1   teaspoon salt
4   cups boiling water

In the top of a double boiler stir together the cornmeal, cold water, and
salt. Slowly pour in the boiling water (a teapot is handy here), stirring
constantly. Place over boiling water and cook, covered, for 20 minutes or

so, until it is thickened. (Alternatively, it can be cooked in a heavy saucepan over low heat, but requires almost constant stirring.) Serve immediately.

TO PREPARE IN ADVANCE: Pour leftover porridge into a loaf pan lined with plastic wrap and chill. To reheat, slice in ½" slices and heat in butter or bacon drippings to serve as a starchy accompaniment to South African meals, or as Fried Mush, a breakfast treat in America's Deep South.

SOUTH AFRICAN FRUIT CURRY

1   5-pound leg of lamb
1   pound firm dried peaches (can be found in
        health food stores)
    Salt and pepper
½   cup oil or GHEE (NITER KIBBEH can be used)
1   large onion, chopped
2   cloves garlic, minced
1   large, tart apple, chopped
1   green bell pepper (seeds and membranes removed), finely
        diced
2   fresh mild green chiles, peeled and seeded, *or* 2 canned
        chiles, rinsed and seeded
2   tablespoons Madras curry powder *or,* better yet,
        homemade HOT CURRY POWDER (see RECIPE INDEX)
1½ teaspoons chopped fresh thyme, *or* ½ teaspoon dried
        thyme, crumbled
2   tablespoons Major Grey's mango chutney
1   tablespoon cider vinegar or lemon juice

For 6 to 8 servings

TO SERVE: MEALIE MEAL PORRIDGE (see the preceding recipe) or steamed rice and condiments such as roasted peanuts, chopped hard-cooked egg, raisins, crumbled bacon

Cut the meat from the leg of lamb into 1" cubes. Place the bone in a pot with water to cover and bring to a boil, skimming any foam that rises to the surface during the first 10 minutes. Add the peaches to the pot and simmer about 20 minutes, until they are soft. Remove pot from heat.

Dry the meat well and sprinkle with salt and pepper. In a large stew pot or Dutch oven, brown the meat in the oil or ghee, a few cubes at a time, until all are browned. After all the meat has been browned, remove meat and add the onion, garlic, apple, pepper, chiles, curry powder, and thyme to the drippings in the pot. Cook slowly, stirring for 10 minutes or so, until the onions are transparent. Return the meat to the pot along with 3 cups of the lamb broth from cooking the lamb bone and peaches. Simmer, covered, for

1½ to 2 hours until the lamb is tender. Add the peaches, chutney, vinegar or lemon juice to the pot, and simmer 10 minutes longer to blend flavors. Thin the curry with lamb broth or water if it is too thick. Taste, and add salt and pepper and more vinegar or lemon juice as needed.

TO PREPARE IN ADVANCE: Cooled and then refrigerated, this will keep for up to 4 days; frozen, for up to 4 months. Thaw before reheating.

MILLET

There are many varieties of this cereal from grain-bearing grass, and most are native to Africa. In the United States, we seldom see millet except in birdseed, but it is a delicious and highly digestible grain with a nutty flavor. Millet and millet flour can be found in health food stores and Korean markets. *Bajra,* or bullrush millet, is ground into flour to make unleavened bread in India and Africa. (Millet flour lacks gluten, so it should not be substituted for other flours when a high-rising bread is desired.) TEFF is a particularly fine grade of millet that is usually ground into flour. *Raji,* or finger millet, is coarse and is served like rice, made into breads, and even fermented into beer. "Kaffir corn" and *milo,* other seedlike grains, are sometimes referred to as millet, but are actually SORGHUM. Buy plain millet without additives. Puffed millet, which is eaten as a breakfast cereal, is sold in health food stores as well, but should not be substituted for the grain.

STORAGE: Millet does not keep as well as other grains. Store it in an airtight container in a cool place for up to 3 months, or store in the refrigerator or freezer indefinitely.

PREPARATION AND USE: In Africa, millet is cooked whole, or ground to be cooked into a basic porridge. The tiny hulled grains, which triple in bulk during cooking, can be cooked with rice or in place of rice to accompany many meals and provide an intriguingly firm, yet fluffy, texture. Or it can be pureed after cooking to make a sort of mush which is, as we have seen, a very popular texture in African cooking, and may even be formed into balls to serve with soups and stews.

Millet can be cooked until tender in a large amount of boiling water and then drained and tossed with butter, or it can be steamed like rice. To steam 4 servings, place 1 cup millet (¼ cup raw millet per person is a good general rule) in a heavy saucepan and stir constantly over medium heat until it is lighty toasted. (This step adds flavor and speeds cooking.) Add 1½ cups water (1½ parts to each part millet) and ½ teaspoon salt, cover the pan, and cook over lowest possible heat for 30 minutes. Add 3 tablespoons boiling water to moisten the grains, stir, cover, and let stand 15 minutes before serving. Butter can be added just before serving, or add chopped cooked vegetables or raisins to make a pilaf-type dish. Millet adapts well to Western treatment—try seasoning it with sautéed mushrooms and a sprinkling of sage to accompany roast chicken or turkey.

NIGER OIL

This is an oil from the African niger seed, which is yellow and very flavorful. It can be found only in African and some East Indian markets and has usually been blended with other oils for cooking. GHEE (see THE FOODS OF ASIA section) can be substituted.

STORAGE: The oil will keep indefinitely in the refrigerator. Bring to room temperature for an hour or two before pouring.

USE: Use as a cooking oil for Ethiopian dishes in place of NITER KIBBEH, and in Indian vegetarian dishes, to which it adds a nutty flavor.

NITER KIBBEH

To make this Ethiopian spiced butter oil, butter is clarified in the same manner as for GHEE (see THE FOODS OF ASIA section) except that garlic, ginger, and aromatic spices, such as nutmeg, cinnamon, and cardamom seeds are added along with a generous amount of turmeric to give the resulting oil a bright yellow color. After boiling slowly for 45 minutes, the milk solids have browned and the clear, flavorful oil is strained through several layers of damp cheesecloth. GHEE can be substituted, but it won't add the spicy flavor.

STORAGE: Stored in a nonmetal, airtight container, it will keep for up to 2 months on the pantry shelf, or indefinitely in the refrigerator.

USE: This is a basic cooking oil in Ethiopia, where it is used in most dishes, including Mokoto (tripe), Teré Sega (raw beef), and Wat (stew). It, along with the spicy seasoning BERBERÉ, plus generous use of other spices, makes Ethiopian cooking one of the most interesting and complex of all African cooking. We make it as in the following recipe.

NITER KIBBEH

		For ½ cup
4	ounces (1 stick) sweet (unsalted) butter	
1	quarter-sized slice fresh ginger	
1	clove garlic, peeled and crushed but left whole	
¼	teaspoon turmeric	

1   whole clove
½" piece stick cinnamon
1   small piece whole nutmeg
    The seeds from 1 pod cardamom

In a small saucepan, combine all ingredients. Cook slowly for 20 minutes, and then strain through several layers of damp (rinsed and wrung out) cheesecloth. If any milk solids manage to sneak through, strain again through fresh cheesecloth.

OKRA

OTHER: *ochro*, ladyfingers

IN AFRICA: *gumbo* ARABIC: *bamiya* IN THE FRENCH
CARIBBEAN: *gombo* IN THE SPANISH CARIBBEAN: *quimbombó*
IN THE DOMINICAN REPUBLIC: *molondron*

Okra are the pale to dark green hairy pods of a tropical plant native to Africa. When cooked, they give off a mucilaginous substance that thickens soups and stews. Fresh cooked okra have a slippery texture that may take some getting used to. Some countries in the Middle East go to great lengths to rid the okra of their slimy texture by soaking them in lemon juice or sprinkling them with salt for an hour before cooking, and then frying them whole. Okra are available fresh in many supermarkets, especially in the southern United States, all year, with their peak season in late summer and early fall. Look for small, firm, blemish-free pods, less than 4 inches long. Avoid stiff pods. Frozen okra are available almost everywhere and make an excellent substitute for fresh. Canned okra are a third choice. Dried okra (see OKRA, DRIED in THE FOODS OF THE MIDDLE EAST section for general information), are not a desirable substitute for fresh because they lack the mucilaginous quality for which okra are prized in Africa. For those who absolutely detest okra (there are many), green beans can be substituted in equal quantity, but there will be a considerable difference in consistency.

STORAGE: Store in a paper bag, not sealed in plastic, in the refrigerator for up to 4 days.

PREPARATION AND USE: Do not cook okra in iron cookware or they will discolor, and be aware that the water or other liquid in which okra cook will have a tendency to boil over very easily. Buy 1 pound to serve 3 as a vegetable. Leave pods whole if they are small; cut in 1-inch lengths if they are large. Okra can be boiled or steamed (about 4 minutes for sliced, 8 minutes for whole), or can be coated with egg, seasonings, and cornmeal and fried until golden. They lose their crisp quality and their color if over-cooked.

Throughout Africa, chopped okra are added to soups and stews to thicken them. In East Africa, okra are cooked with shrimp and chiles to make a stew called Pombo, or are slit lengthwise to be stuffed with a curried garlic paste and then deep-fried. In the United States, they are often sliced to be cooked as a vegetable, along with other vegetables such as corn and tomatoes, or pickled. Whole ones, with stems still attached, can be breaded and fried, or boiled to serve cold in a vinaigrette dressing. Okra are also fried in India in a dish called Behendi Bhasi and are used in several classic Indian curries. But most famous of all is the African-inspired dish of Creole Gumbo, a rich stew with many variations, which is thickened either with okra or with FILÉ (powdered sassafras leaves—see THE FOODS OF REGIONAL AMERICA section), but *never* with both.

PALM BUTTER

OTHER: cream of palm fruits

This liquid, obtained from pounding and boiling palm nuts, is exported from Ghana in cans but is almost impossible to find in the United States. It is creamy, pale yellow, and highly saturated. Palm nuts are not exported, so you can't even make it yourself. Creamy peanut butter can be substituted but will have an entirely different flavor.

STORAGE: After opening, transfer to a nonmetal container for refrigerator storage of up to 6 months.

USE: Palm butter flavors African soups and sauces. Dishes using it always combine meat or chicken with seafood.

PALM OIL

OTHER: palm nut oil, palm kernel oil, dende oil

IN LATIN AMERICA: *aciete de dende*

Palm oil varies in color and strength of flavor depending on whether it comes from the whole fruit or just the palm kernels. The former is orange-red in color and quite strong in flavor. Palm kernel oil is clear and mild in flavor, and is used primarily in cosmetics. Both are available in African and some Latin American markets. The orange type is the oil most used in African cooking, but that which is exported is generally inferior. A substitute is 1 cup COCONUT OIL (see THE FOODS OF ASIA section) in which 1 tablespoon paprika has been steeped for 30 minutes and then strained out.

STORAGE: Store indefinitely in a cool place. Because it is a highly saturated oil, it solidifies in the bottle. Place the bottle in a pan of warm water for a few minutes to reliquefy it to a pourable consistency.

USE: Bright orange palm oil is commonly used in West Africa to fry eggs, and in vegetable or rice dishes. It adds both color and flavor to stews. In the Congo, it is used in the national dish, Chicken Moambe, chicken cooked in palm oil and served on rice with steamed EFO (greens).

PEANUT

See GROUNDNUT

PIGEON PEA

OTHER: red gram, Congo pea, yellow dahl (when split)

IN THE CARIBBEAN: *gunga peas, goongoo* INDIAN: *arhar, tur, turvaram* SPANISH: *gandul*

The pigeon pea, a type of field pea, is native to Africa, but it has become a very important food in India and the Caribbean. When fresh from their rather hairy, twisted, tightly packed pods, they are small and round like garden peas and can be eaten raw, but are more commonly allowed to mature and dry, after which they are usually yellow or grayish in color, and have developed a strong flavor and a rather mealy texture. Fresh ones are available in some Latin American and Indian markets and dried ones are often available where dried beans are sold. Split dried pigeon peas are available as *arhar dahl* in Indian markets. Latin American markets often have canned pigeon peas, and occasionally have frozen green ones, which are best avoided because they don't freeze well.

STORAGE: Fresh pigeon peas should be stored in their pods in a paper bag inside a plastic bag in the refrigerator for use as soon as possible. Dried ones, whole or split as DAL (see THE FOODS OF ASIA section), can be stored as any bean, in an airtight container on the pantry shelf indefinitely, though they harden on standing and require longer cooking.

PREPARATION AND USE: Cook fresh peas as you would green peas, or English peas as they are sometimes called. Dried pigeon peas are cooked in the same way as dried beans, either soaked or not, as you prefer. They are then simmered in approximately 3 parts water to 1 part peas for 1½ to 2 hours until tender, salting only during the last 30 minutes of cooking.

Pigeon peas are widely used in Africa in a sort of succotash, combined with corn, chiles, and a bit of curry powder, and served with meat dishes. When cooked, they can be used interchangeably in recipes that call for cooked black-eyed peas. In Nigeria, they are puréed with coconut milk, making a dish called Frejon, or Mbaazi in Kenya. In India, where these are called *arhar dal* or red gram, they are made into porridge or DAL (see THE FOODS OF ASIA section) and are almost as important as the chick-pea to that country's diet. In Western Africa, these or other beans are ground and seasoned with onion and cayenne pepper to be fried into the very popular fritters called Akara.

PIRIPIRI
OTHER: *peri-peri, pili-pili, peli-peli*

This African term refers to both the long, fiery, red chiles and the national dish of Mozambique, which contains seafood, fowl, or meat that has been marinated in a mixture of lemon juice, garlic, and chiles, and then grilled and served with rice. A seasoned oil and a ground spice of the same name may sometimes be found in well-stocked African markets, but are not used in the authentic dish. Your best bet is to use dried red chiles, available in Asian and Latin American markets, when following African recipes for this dish. The name has come to apply to any chile-based sauce served as a condiment, and may very well not even be made with red peppers. If piripiri "sauce" is desired for use as a condiment, SHATTA is probably what you are looking for.

STORAGE: Dried chiles should be kept in a cool place or in the refrigerator to prevent infestation of bugs.

PREPARATION AND USE: In making Piripiri, use 2 tablespoons of crumbled, dried red chiles, 1 tablespoon chopped garlic, and ½ cup lemon or lime juice to marinate 1 to 1½ pounds shrimp, chicken, or meat for 4 servings. The meat is then charcoal-grilled, and the marinade is sometimes strained and simmered to make a fiery sauce to serve as a table condiment.

PLANTAIN
See THE FOODS OF LATIN AMERICA section

PLAYER'S #3 CIGARETTE TIN

This is not an ingredient, but a measuring device so often mentioned in African recipes that we felt it should be included. Lacking a measuring cup, an African cook uses this empty tin. It equals approximately 1 cup.

114

RICE FLOUR

(See THE FOODS OF ASIA section for general information.) Rice flour is often used in Africa to make Fufu, the smooth starch that accompanies most meals. Blend 1 cup rice flour with 2 cups water and 1 teaspoon salt, simmer until thickened, and serve with stews or soups.

SAMBAL

See THE FOODS OF ASIA section

SHATTA

OTHER: *ata*

This spicy condiment is popular in the Sudan. It is another item you are unlikely to find commercially available, though it can be sought out. It is easily made by combining 1 cup lemon or lime juice, 3 cloves mashed garlic, 3 tablespoons crumbled, dried red chiles, 1 teaspoon salt, and ½ teaspoon ground black pepper.

STORAGE: Store in the refrigerator for use within a week.

USE: In the Sudan, this is served in small ramekins to accompany an assortment of soups, stews, and starches. It is a spicy seasoning that we enjoy as an accompaniment to most African meals.

SORGHUM

OTHER: guinea corn, dura

Sorghum is a tropical, cane-like grass that yields a seed-like cereal grain that looks like bird seed. It is often confused with MILLET. The "Kaffir corn" variety is small and pink; "milo" is larger. You can find sorghum grain in well-stocked natural-food stores, but the best and least expensive source is a feed and grain store, where it is sold at a ridiculously low price. **Take care it has not been sprayed with pesticides.** (Any specified as chicken feed is usually purest.) MILLET can be substituted.

STORAGE: It will keep for up to two months in an airtight container in a cool place.

PREPARATION AND USE: Prepare as you would millet, using 4 times as much water as sorghum. Cooking time will vary depending on the variety and age of the grain, and the result will be chewy when cooked. In Africa, this is one of the major foods used to make porridge or mush. It can be cooked, like millet, to serve as a starch in place of rice. The Bantus of South Africa grow "Kaffir corn" as an important crop, and continue to use it for porridge and to brew beer. It can be popped like popcorn or millet, but the popped corn is very tiny, and it has a tendency to burn.

STAR BEER

This is not much used as an ingredient in African cooking but, like the previously mentioned Player's cigarette tin, an empty Star Beer bottle is often used for measuring in West African recipes. It equals approximately 2¾ cups.

TEFF

OTHER: *tef*

Teff is flour made from the finest quality MILLET, which is widely grown in Ethiopia. Only very well-stocked African markets carry it. Substitute finely ground millet flour, grinding your own from millet grain, if necessary, or use buckwheat flour, which somewhat resembles millet in flavor. Millet flour lacks gluten, so it should not be substituted for other flours when a high-rising bread is desired.

STORAGE: It can be stored like any flour, in an airtight container in a cool place indefinitely.

PREPARATION AND USE: In West Africa, millet flour is made into small pellets in the same manner as COUS COUS (see THE FOODS OF THE MIDDLE EAST section), which are cooked as a breakfast cereal, sweetened with brown sugar and vanilla, and served with a type of cottage cheese. In Ethiopia, teff is mixed with water to make a thin dough, which is then allowed to ferment at room temperature for three days to develop a sourdough flavor. The fermenting also produces holes in the dough which, when cooked, create a sponge-rubber appearance. The dough is used for Chechebsa (pancakes), and for Injera, the "bread of Ethiopia," a lacy griddle-cooked bread that is served with most meals. Injera is used as an edible "plate" or "tablecloth," often covering the table. Various stews are placed upon it and one tears it into small squares and uses it to wrap the cooked food into mouthful-sized pieces that are eaten with the fingers rather than with fork or spoon. Following is our version.

INJERA

2½	cups water	For 6 to 8 (10″) pancakes
1½	teaspoons (½ packet) active dry yeast	
½	teaspoon honey *or* ¼ teaspoon sugar	
1½	cups teff or finely ground millet flour*	
¼	teaspoon baking powder	

*Note: If the millet flour you purchase is not very finely ground, grind it again in a blender or an electric coffee/spice mill until it is as finely ground as teff.

Heat the water until lukewarm—no hotter than 115°. Place ¼ cup of it in a measuring cup and stir in the yeast and honey or sugar. Set aside for 5 minutes to "proof" the yeast; it will begin to bubble and foam. Place the remaining water in a large mixing bowl, add the yeast mixture and the millet flour, and mix. When well blended, cover with plastic wrap and set aside to ferment at room temperature for 24 to 48 hours. It should have a fermented, sourdough odor.

Mix baking powder with a teaspoon of water and stir it into the batter. Heat a 10- to 12-inch, heavy nonstick skillet that has a lid (or a very well-seasoned cast iron skillet) over medium heat. If desired, wipe the pan with a very small amount of oil, GHEE, or NITER KIBBEH on a paper towel. To test the heat, place a small spoonful of batter in the center—it should solidify rather quickly without browning. Pour ⅓ to ½ cup of batter, spiral-fashion, into the pan, starting at the outside of the pan and working toward the center. As soon as the batter is poured, cover the pan and cook approximately 1 minute. Lift the lid to check doneness—the top of the injera should be cooked and dimpled with many holes, and the bottom should be firm but not at all browned. Slide out onto a tray to cool and continue making injera until all the batter is used.

Serve warm or at room temperature, topped with various spicy stews and relishes.

TO PREPARE IN ADVANCE: Injera can be made several hours before serving and stacked on a serving platter. Leftover batter can be used as a starter for making the next batch of injera.

VAN DER HUM LIQUEUR

This tangerine-flavored, brandy-based liqueur is very popular in South Africa. It also contains various spices such as cardamom seeds, cloves, cinnamon, and nutmeg. It is very often made from family recipes in the homes of South Africa, but you may find a commercially made version in well-stocked liquor stores. Grand Marnier makes an excellent substitute, as it also has a brandy base, if a sprinkling of a mixture of the previously mentioned aromatic spices is added to any dessert recipe calling for it.

STORAGE: It will keep indefinitely at room temperature.

USE: This liqueur is served as an after-dinner drink, and is also used as a flavoring for Bavarian Cream (called Chippolata in South Africa), dessert sauces, and soufflés.

YAM, GIANT OR WHITE

OTHER: *tria* yam, *yautia, tannia,* or new *cocoyam*

The name "yam" comes from the African word *ñame,* and is properly applied to the several varieties of "true" yam. The African variety of this starchy tuber, which is not the variety of orange-fleshed sweet potato called yam or Louisiana yam that we are all familiar with, has white flesh, bark-like skin, and can weigh up to 100 pounds! It is native to West Africa where it is highly revered, not only as a staple food but as an important symbol of survival in that area. Yam feast days are common, and the yam is cooked into many dishes, which are served at every holiday and at other celebrations.

Fresh white yams can be found year 'round in some Latin American and Caribbean markets. Look for firm, unblemished ones that show no signs of wrinkling and, for finest flavor, stick to those that weigh a pound or less. Canned white yams are imported from West Africa, but will only be found in some African and Latin American markets. Boiling potatoes can be substituted with not a great deal of difference in flavor or texture.

STORAGE: Fresh whole yams can be stored in a cool place or in the refrigerator for up to a week.

PREPARATION AND USE: Peel the yams and slice in ½" pieces. They can be cooked in stews, boiled in water, or deep-fried after partial cooking, like French-fried potatoes. To boil, cook in salted water to cover until soft, about 45 minutes.

In West Africa, the most common way of preparing yams is to pound the cooked yams into a paste called Fufu, which is often formed into balls to serve as a starchy accompaniment to many stews. The same paste is also used as a thickener for soups and stews. In Ghana, they are boiled, and then sliced or diced, and sometimes deep-fried to make Ampesi, which is served with any meat or fish dish. Thinly sliced raw yams are also deep-fried, like potato chips, and are then salted and eaten as snacks. In West Africa, croquettes of yam and flaked fish are fried in palm or peanut oil and are served with a spicy chile-based sauce such as SHATTA. When sliced, sun-dried, and ground into flour (called *elubo*), this tuber can be made into a pudding called Amala, which is served with bean soup, or into a thick, creamy porridge called Ugali. In East Africa, yams are cooked with pumpkin, groundnuts, and a bit of curry to make a stew called Mchanyanto.

The Foods
of
Asia

Australia
Burma
Mon Khmer
  (Cambodia)
  and Laos
China
India and
  Pakistan
Indonesia
Japan
Korea
Malaysia and
  Singapore
New Zealand
Philippines
Polynesian
  Islands
Sri Lanka
  (Ceylon)
Thailand
Vietnam

The Rice Cuisine

For thousands of years, while Europe still slept, highly developed civilizations flourished in Asia. China was the cultural center of this world and the motherland to the majority of islands in Polynesia, the South China Sea, as well as to a good number of those in the Indian Ocean. Consequently, a basic similarity in cooking techniques, ingredients, presentation, and dishes shows through the veneer of local ritual and language differences throughout Asia and the South Pacific. A brief tour of several Asian countries will show why they are grouped together culinarily.

Rice is the unifying Asian ingredient. Asians depend upon this grain for 80 to 90 percent of their dietary intake. Here, rice is the main dish, and the rest of the meal is considered an accompaniment, or a condiment. However, at the latitude north of Peking called the "rice line," wheat replaces rice as the staple food, and we find such dishes as *chapatis* (Indian flatbreads), noodles, steamed cakes, rolls, and Dim Sum (Chinese snack foods).

Steamed rice is the basis of a Chinese meal, and the Chinese prefer a small- or medium-grain rice, not cooked dry, but left fluffy and clinging, so it can be picked up easily with chopsticks. Small amounts of fish, shellfish, or pork in sauces such as sweet-and-sour, curried, or spicy, round out the meal.

Indonesians, like the Chinese, prefer small-grained rice; however, they like the grains to be separated, extremely firm, and not clinging. The national dish of Indonesia is Rijsttafel, which literally means "rice table" in Dutch (most of these islands were formerly part of the Dutch East India Company). This national dish (or perhaps we should say institution) is made up of a series of many different foods, which the diner places in small amounts upon his or her own plate of boiled rice. The many peppery dishes of spiced meats, such as Gulai Ikan (spicy fish in coconut milk), Gulai-Cumi-Cumi (curried squid), and Ayam Panggang Pedis (spicy hot chicken), can be cooled down with an additional selection of different palate refreshers such as cucumbers, chopped peanuts, or grated coconut. Indonesian cooking never seems to get very far away from their beloved chiles. Malaysian rice cuisine, with its traditionally Indonesian-style foods, is in so many ways similar to Indonesian family and ceremonial cooking that the minor differences that may exist are not worth mentioning here.

The rice of Japan is preferably small- or medium-grained and cooked fluffy, not dry, and slightly clinging, to be manageable with chopsticks, in a similar manner to that of China and their culinary foster-child, Korea. In Japan, where eating is an aesthetic pursuit, rice is the basis for the most elegantly simple of all the world's great cuisines. The Japanese cuisine is unique because it emphasizes basic ingredients used in their most natural state—the raw fish in Sushi presentation, for example, and the beautiful raw vegetables that garnish so many dishes. Unlike China, where foods are traditionally stored between harvests by fermenting, pickling, or salting, the Japanese, with so little tillable soil and so huge a population, are continually eating "land to mouth." Japanese farmers are pressed to produce multiple crops, and over 700,000 Japanese make their livings from fishing. In Japan, the farthest point from the sea is only 80 miles. With this continuously fresh protein supply there has been little need to preserve food, as their land-bound Chinese neighbor does. Curiously enough, the two Japanese dishes with the greatest appeal to Western palates are their newest creations. Sukiyaki was created less than 100 years ago, when the Buddhists relaxed their prohibition against meat. And Tempura, that delicate, deep-fried vegetable- and shrimp-in-batter treat, was improvised by the Japanese for the Portuguese traders in the 16th century to comply with their meatless days of Lent.

Korea, a peninsula finger of eastern China, points directly at Japan across the East China Sea. Hugged as it is between these two distinctively great cuisines, it is not surprising that Korean food should in many ways resemble both, and it does. The first similarity is in their national staple, rice. And, because the Koreans prefer the use of chopsticks, they have borrowed from China their method of preparing food in bite-sized pieces. From Japan, they have borrowed the individual charcoal grill that produces such savories as Bulgogi (marinated beef, charcoal-grilled at the table), and have adopted into their cuisine the seaweed that the Japanese call *nori*. The Koreans call it *kim*, and use it as a wrapper for steamed rice, turning out a dish similar to the Japanese rolled Sushi. Koreans are fond of chicken and pork, but their most popular meat is beef, which they are expert at slicing very thin. This sliced beef is then marinated for two to four hours to tenderize it. A representative example of this traditional technique is found in Gogi Bokum, deep-fried beef slices, accompanied by a tangy Bulgogi dipping sauce, and white rice. If there were only one item that Korea should be considered famous for, it would be their unique pickled dish, Kimchi, prepared in the tradition of an age-old system of preserving vegetables by natural fermentation through long, bitter winters. This far from subtle, garlicky Korean passion finds its way into every meal of the day, including breakfast, right along with the rice.

"Come and eat rice," literally translated, is the invitation to a meal in Thailand. Here the words for food and rice are the same, and everything else is referred to as "with the rice." The Thais prefer their rice to be long-grained, cooked firmly, and yet to have each grain remain separate, because in Thailand they don't use chopsticks. They prefer to eat with the fingertips of the right hand, or with spoons and forks. Thailand, along with her Southeast Asian neighbors of Burma, Cambodia, Laos, and Vietnam, harvests almost 10 percent of the world's rice, and their meals are naturally built around it. In Thailand, the standard family meal consists of heaping individual servings of rice and five to seven various Kaengs, colorfully sauced dishes placed in the center of the table. There might be a red beef curry (Kaeng Phed Nuer), the bright color coming from a Thai red curry paste made with red chiles and paprika. Another Kaeng might feature a green curry of duck, or a green curry of chicken (Kaeng Khieu Wan Kai), the color here imparted by a green curry paste composed of fresh herbs and finely chopped green chiles, and the sauce, of course, structured on Thai coconut milk. There would be at least one other Kaeng, perhaps either prawn or fish, with as many side dishes as seemed appropriate or were handy. Unlike the Koreans, Chinese, or Japanese, Thais have a bit of a sweet tooth and desserts are welcome indeed. They are usually made with a coconut milk or palm sugar base, and are followed by some of their beautifully carved fruits: melons shaped into huge blossoms, pineapple slices intricately fashioned into tiny fans, or the luscious sapodilla, shaped to look like a blooming rose.

Thailand and India are separated by the Bay of Bengal, but the similarities between these two countries, as indeed the similarities of India's cuisine to all of Asia's cuisines, is remarkable. India shares common culinary aspects with each, from foods like curries and rice, to cooking utensils like the round-bottomed Chinese wok-like pan, which they depend on absolutely and which is found in all of their kitchens. In Malaysia, this pan is called a kuali; in Indonesia, a wajan; in Burma, dare-oh; in Vietnam, chao; in the Philippines, carajay; and in India, karahi.

India is too large and complex to be neatly categorized, but it does tend to divide into two food groups: wheat and meat in the north, rice and vegetables in the tropical south. Indians prefer eating with their fingers so, in the north, they have invented many forms of flat, unleavened breads that they use as edible scoops and wrappers. Wheat, the grain of the north, also thickens their curries, which is one of the reasons that the curries of northern India are considered drier than those in the south. The more liquid curries of the south are served with long-grained, nonsticky, fluffy rice as the absorbent base.

The lavish use of spices is the very heart and soul of Indian cooking, and the curry (masala) stone upon which individual spices are ground fresh daily is found in every home. The aromatic freshness of these spices is undoubtedly responsible for the high quality of India's curries, whether meat, chicken, fish, vegetable, coconut, or peas and *panir,* the Indian version of cheese— the variety is endless and their goodness unforgettable.

The curries, spices, cuisines and customs of Sri Lanka (Ceylon) are remarkably similar to those of southern India. In fact, the island-nation of Sri Lanka seems as though it could be the broken off tip of India. Like southern India, the Sinhalese diet is primarily vegetarian, with thin curry sauces of incredible delicacy. However, there are times when they can be positively volcanic with chili. Typical of their tropical food is Lamprai (rice boiled in stock with dry curries, and then baked in a banana leaf). Because it is a tropical island only five or so degrees off the equator, its naturally heavy rainfall produces an abundance of tropical vegetables and exotic fruits, such as pineapples, pawpaw, avocados, mangoes, rambutans, oranges, grapefruit, guava, jackfruit, cherimoya, pears, watermelon, passion fruit, sapodilla, pomegranates, custard apples, mangosteens, and durians. The natural abundance, as well, of fish, long-grained rice, and coconut makes an exciting and varied cuisine.

Another tropical area that produces an abundance of fruit and produce is the 7,000-some islands of the Philippines. Fewer than one-third of these islands are inhabited today, but visible on the sides of whole mountain ranges are gigantic steppes carved by ancient farmers for the terracing of rice crops, thousands of years ago. Unquestionably the favored meat of the Philippines is pork, whether it is served whole, as a barbecued suckling pig (Lechón), or as one of the ingredients in an infinite variety of spicy casseroles, known as Adobos. With every dish served, rice will have an important part, as in any Asian cuisine.

In the 1600s, these islands were conquered by the Spanish, and the Catholic Church has exerted a powerful influence for over 400 years. Consequently, passed down as part of Filipino-Spanish heritage are a great many zesty, meatless Lenten dishes, such as Sinigang, a stewed fish with vegetables, or Lumpia, a very popular vegetable roll whose wrapper is made of rice flour, a departure from the traditional Chinese egg roll.

Looking at the huge panorama of Asian food from a great distance, the major characteristics are apparent. Rice is unquestionably the major staple food, and everything else is an addition to it. There are differences, to be sure, in ingredient uses and cooking techniques among Asia's people, but the similarities are striking, as you will discover when you browse through the exciting grouping of Asian ingredients that follows.

ABALONE

IN AUSTRALIA: mutton fish CHINESE: *bow yew* JAPANESE: *awabi* or *turbo*

This shellfish has silky textured meat that is often used as an ingredient for holiday dinners by the Chinese and Japanese. Fresh abalone, which must be vigorously pounded to make it tender, is available to Westerners only in California and coastal Mexico, and has become very scarce even in those places. Canned abalone, especially that imported from Japan, is excellent—delicate and very tender. It is very expensive. Asian markets also carry a similar mollusk labeled "abalone-type" shellfish in cans. Dried abalone, also expensive, is available in oriental markets. It has a much stronger flavor than fresh or canned.

STORAGE: Fresh or frozen—cook as soon as possible or store in the freezer for up to 3 months. Canned—once opened, it can be kept in a covered container of water in the refrigerator for up to a week if the water is changed every 2 days. Dried abalone can be stored, tightly wrapped, in a cool, dry spot indefinitely.

PREPARATION AND USE: One fresh abalone in the shell contains approximately ⅓ pound of meat, which is enough for 1 main-course serving. If whole, cut into thin steaks across the grain and pound each with a mallet until it is limp and velvety. Frozen abalone has usually been pounded. To cook steaks, sauté in butter, either lightly breaded with beaten egg and bread crumbs or PANKO, or plain, only 1 minute or so on each side. Cook all types of abalone only briefly to avoid toughness. Slice it thin for stir-fry dishes, in which it is commonly combined with asparagus or straw mushrooms in Cantonese cooking, or add with its liquid to soups or chowders. Canned abalone needn't be cooked, and is very convenient to use compared to the fresh or frozen product—we like to cut it into julienne strips to serve as a Japanese-style appetizer with a squeeze of lime juice or a sprinkling of rice vinegar and some toasted sesame seeds. Dried abalone must be soaked for several days in cold water before it is used.

ACCENT

See MONOSODIUM GLUTAMATE

ACHIOTE OR ACHUETE SEEDS

See ACHIOTE SEED in THE FOODS OF LATIN AMERICA section

ADUKI

See BEANS, AZUKI

ADZUKI

See BEANS, AZUKI

AGAR

(AY-gar)

OTHER: Chinese or Japanese gelatin, vegetable gelatin

BURMESE: *kyauk kyaw* CHINESE: *dai choy goh* JAPANESE: *kanten* or *tengusa* MALAYSIAN: *agar-agar* SINHALESE (Sri Lanka): *chun chow*

Agar is a vegetable gum made by freeze-drying *tengusa* seaweed to make a product used either in dried form as a crisp-textured ingredient for cold dishes or in powdered form as unflavored gelatin. The dried form comes in 4-ounce packages of either red or white translucent, brittle, crinkled sheets, which must be soaked before use. If soaked in cold water, it becomes a delightful, slightly crunchy ingredient that can be added to cold dishes in fine strips.

In powdered form, it is the gelatin preferred by vegetarians because it is a vegetable product. (Ordinary gelatin is derived from animal bones and is a protein; agar is a carbohydrate.) The powder is available in some Asian markets and health food stores, but always in pharmacies, where it is used in the mixing of medicines. If soaked in hot water, the powder dissolves and can be used as any unflavored gelatin. It jells at 110°, a much higher temperature than the American product, which makes it excellent for use in summer dishes to be served at room temperature on even the hottest days. You will find that molded, gelatin-type dishes are much easier to unmold when this product is used.

Kanten, the Japanese variety, is usually sold in rectangular cakes or in flake form. It is often used to make very stiff, colored gelatin that is cut into shapes for garnishing platters of various foods. *Ito-kanten* is kanten cut into thin strands that look like cellophane noodles.

STORAGE: Wrapped tightly, all types will keep indefinitely in a cool pantry.

PREPARATION AND USE: Soften the sticks in cold water, and then cut in fine strips for cold dishes and salads. It will have no real flavor of its own, but will pick up the flavor of any sauce used. Dissolve powder or flakes (breaking up sticks to make flakes if necessary) by sprinkling a small amount of cold water over them and setting aside for 5 minutes. Heat just until dissolved to use as a thickening agent, but do not boil it overly long in an acidic liquid such as vinegar or it will eventually lose its thickening power. As a general rule, 1 tablespoon powder will thicken 4 cups liquid, and ½ stick kanten equals approximately 1 tablespoon powdered agar (or 1 packet ordinary gelatin). As a jelling agent, it can even be used for mixtures containing pineapple, an ingredient that prevents ordinary gelatin from setting. In Malaysia, agar is used to thicken Coconut Milk Jelly and, in Burma, a similar jelly is flavored with ROSE WATER.

AJI-NO-MOTO

See MONOSODIUM GLUTAMATE

AJWAIN

OTHER: *ajowan,* carom seeds

This spice, available in Indian markets, looks a great deal like celery seed, but has a flavor that resembles thyme.

STORAGE: It will keep for up to 6 months in an airtight container in a cool, dark place.

PREPARATION AND USE: Crush the seeds lightly before adding them to recipes. In Indian cooking, this delicate seed is used primarily to flavor lentil dishes, batters for frying fish or Pakoras (fritters), and in the making of pickles. (It is often soaked in water to make a medicine to treat stomach disorders.)

We have found it to be a delicious flavoring for cookies.

ALIMENTARY PASTE

See KONNYAKU

ALMOND POWDER

This powder made of very finely ground almonds, is available either sweetened or unsweetened in Chinese grocery stores.

STORAGE: It will keep a few weeks on the pantry shelf; indefinitely in the freezer.

USE: The sweet type is used in making desserts. The unsweetened is used as an extra-crispy coating on foods for deep frying.

AMARANTH

OTHER: Chinese spinach, pigweed (one variety), tampala

IN THE CARIBBEAN: *callaloo* CHINESE: *hsien ts'ai* or *hin choy*
INDIAN: *bhaji* JAPANESE: *hiyu*

There are several varieties of this nutritious, dark green, small-leaved vegetable with red or green stems, which is sold by the bunch. The term Chinese spinach is a misnomer because there is a spinach in China just like the spinach in the United States. Waverly Root, the food historian, describes amaranth as an "edible symbol of immortality." Its flavor is slightly sweet. You will find it in some Asian or Caribbean produce markets and health food stores. (See also CALLALOO GREENS in THE FOODS OF LATIN AMERICA section.)

STORAGE: Place in paper bag inside a plastic bag. Store in the crisper section of the refrigerator for up to a week.

PREPARATION AND USE: To serve as a vegetable, buy 1 pound for 3 servings; to use as a soup or stir-fry ingredient, 1 pound will serve 6. Rinse and shake off excess water. Steam as you would spinach, or stir-fry with other ingredients, but only very briefly or it becomes mushy.

AMCHOOR

OTHER: *amchur*

This is dried, unripe mango, and is available in either powdered form or in slices in Indian markets. It is used as we would use lemon, to give an acidity to various dishes.

STORAGE: As any ground spice.

PREPARATION AND USE: One teaspoon amchoor equals 2 tablespoons lemon juice in acidity. The powder is added to various dishes such as Samosas (fried pastries) and cooked vegetables to add a tart flavor. Stir it with salt and other spices to make any lumps disappear. (See recipe for alu gobi under ASAFETIDA.)

ANARDANA

OTHER: *anardhana,* dried pomegranate seeds

These are seeds from sour pomegranates dried to use as a seasoning. They are available in Indian markets.

STORAGE: As any whole spice.

PREPARATION AND USE: This is a common seasoning in DAL and Samosas (fried pastries), and adds a delightful acid flavor to stuffings, chutneys, etc.

ANCIENT EGGS

See EGGS, 1000 YEAR OLD

ANISE PEPPER

See PEPPERCORNS, SZECHUAN in the HERBS, SPICES, AND SEASONING BLENDS section

ANNATO SEEDS

See ACHIOTE SEED in THE FOODS OF LATIN AMERICA section

AO NORI

See SEAWEED, DRIED

AO NORIKO

See AO NORI, under SEAWEED, DRIED

ARROWROOT

OTHER: arrowhead

CHINESE: *chok wo*

There are many varieties of this bland, slightly nut-flavored rhizome or tuber in various parts of the world. The type most often found in Asian markets is 5″ to 8″ long and about 1″ in diameter, and is usually imported from St. Vincent in the West Indies. Some sources say it derives its name from the *aru* root of the Arucu Indians, others say from its history of being used to treat poisoned-arrow wounds. Some types are poisonous in the raw state. When cooked, arrowroot has a mealy texture and a slightly sweet taste.

STORAGE: Wrapped in a paper bag inside a plastic bag, arrowroot will keep in the crisper of the refrigerator for up to 2 weeks.

PREPARATION AND USE: Boil until tender; then peel to serve like boiled potatoes. In Chinese cooking, it is often served with steamed chicken. A Cantonese dish, See Gu Lap Chang, is made by braising the cooked tubers with Chinese sausage, and then garnishing with fresh coriander. Its mealy texture makes it a good accompaniment to fatty dishes.

ARROWROOT POWDER

OTHER: arrowroot starch

FRENCH: *arrowroot* GERMAN: *Pfeiwurz* ITALIAN: *maranta tubero edule* SPANISH: *arrurruz*

Arrowroot powder, the easiest to digest of all the many starches used as thickeners, has a long history of use in cooking for infants and invalids. It is sold on the spice shelves of most markets and in Asian and Caribbean markets, and is more expensive than other starches. It is preferable to corn-starch because of its very neutral flavor and because it lends such a beautiful glaze to sauces.

STORAGE: It will keep indefinitely on the pantry shelf if tightly sealed.

PREPARATION AND USE: Arrowroot has more thickening power than cornstarch—use 1 teaspoon arrowroot powder for each 1½ teaspoons corn-starch or 1 tablespoon flour called for in a recipe. Make a paste by stirring 1 part arrowroot powder with 3 parts water. Stir gradually into boiling soups or sauces until they reach the consistency you desire. Once thickened, sauces containing arrowroot should not be boiled for any length of time, as any starch will break down and lose its thickening power if cooked too long.

ASAFETIDA

(ahs-ah-FEHT-eh-dah)
OTHER: *asafoetida*

BURMESE: *sheingho* FRENCH: *assafoetida* or *ferule perisque* GERMAN: *Teufelsdreck* INDIAN: *hing* or *heeng* SPANISH: *asafetida* TAMIL (Ceylon): *perunkaya*

A tan or reddish-brown dried gum resin with a very strong fetid odor and somewhat garlicky flavor, asafetida is used very sparingly in various Asian dishes to add flavor and as an aid to digestion. It is available in boxes in

Indian markets, either in powdered or lump form. The lump form is supposed to be the purest, but the powder is certainly easier to use. It can be omitted from recipes when not available.

STORAGE: It will keep in a cool, dark place indefinitely if tightly sealed.

PREPARATION AND USE: The lump form must be flaked before using. Place the flakes between two pieces of paper and press with a pestle or hammer to make a powder. Use only the tiniest bit, no more than $1/8$ to $1/4$ teaspoon. It is added along with other spices to curried fish or vegetarian dishes and other highly seasoned foods, and used in lentil soup.

ALU GOBI
(Curried Cauliflower and Potatoes)

For 8 to 10 servings

This is one of our very favorite vegetarian dishes. We were taught how to make it by the owner of the award-winning Los Angeles restaurant, Paul Bhalla's Cuisine of India. It hails from Punjab, India. The tiny amount of asafetida gives it an indescribably hearty flavor.

2	pounds potatoes, cut in $1/2''$ dice
4	ounces GHEE or $1/4$ pound (1 stick) butter or margarine
$1/2$	cup MUSTARD OIL
$1/2$	teaspoon black mustard seeds
1	medium onion, chopped
2	tablespoons finely slivered fresh ginger
2	teaspoons AMCHOOR
$1\frac{1}{2}$	teaspoons turmeric
$1\frac{1}{2}$	teaspoons ground coriander
$1\frac{1}{2}$	teaspoons ground cumin
1	teaspoon paprika
1	teaspoon cayenne (ground red pepper)
$1/4$	teaspoon asafetida
3	pounds cauliflower, cut into flowerets
2	fresh tomatoes, peeled and diced

In a large wok, melt butter and brown the potatoes lightly. Transfer to another container and set aside. Pour in the mustard oil and turn the heat to high. When the oil is hot (but not smoking) drop in the black mustard seeds. Almost immediately they will begin to pop. Stir in the onion, tossing until lightly browned. Lower the flame and add the rest of the ingredients *except* remaining butter, cauliflower, and tomatoes. Cook, stirring constantly, until lightly toasted. Add the cauliflower to the wok along with the browned potatoes. Toss to coat them with spices. Add the tomatoes, cover tightly and cook over low flame for 15 minutes until the vegetables are tender but still crisp.

Serve hot with almost any meal. It goes well with Rotis, and other Indian breads, and is usually accompanied by Raita (spiced yogurt). (See RECIPE INDEX for these recipes.)

TO PREPARE IN ADVANCE: This is at its best when freshly made, though it reheats beautifully and leftovers are to be treasured.

ATTA

OTHER: *ata,* chappati flour

Atta is a fine whole wheat flour made from hard, low-gluten wheat and is available in Indian markets. It is used for making Chappatis, Parathas, and other Indian breads. As a substitute, you can use finely ground whole wheat flour mixed with an equal amount of cake flour.

STORAGE: As any flour.

USE: Used in the making of many kinds of Indian breads.

AZUKI

See under BEANS, DRIED

BACON, CHINESE

CHINESE: *lop yuk* or *yin yoke*

This is a smoked, reddish-brown meat with layers of yellow fat, often seen hanging in Chinese kitchens. It is available by the pound in Chinese delicatessens and in supermarkets in areas with large Oriental populations. Chinese pork sausage can be substituted.

STORAGE: Wrapped tightly and stored in the refrigerator, it will keep indefinitely.

PREPARATION AND USE: Sliced or diced, a small amount of this lends a delicious smoky, salty flavor to steamed or simmered dishes. Like Chinese sausages, it is often steamed to serve on top of rice as a seasoning for a main course. (For this dish, allow approximately 2 ounces per person.)

BAGOONG
See SHRIMP PASTE, SOUTHEAST ASIAN

BAGOONGALAMANG
See SHRIMP PASTE, SOUTHEAST ASIAN

BALSAM PEAR
See MELON, BITTER

BAMBOO LEAVES
CHINESE: *jook yip*

These long, narrow leaves are used to wrap foods for steaming and to line steamer baskets. They are available in oriental markets. LOTUS LEAVES, which are used for the same purpose, can be substituted.

STORAGE: Wrapped loosely and stored in the refrigerator, they will keep for weeks.

PREPARATION AND USE: Soak overnight until soft. Bamboo leaves are never eaten, but are used as we would parchment or foil to enclose foods for steaming. They often enfold a filling of glutinous rice to make Dim Sum (Chinese snack foods).

BAMBOO SHOOTS
CHINESE: *jook sun* or *dung shung* FRENCH: *pousse de bamboo*
INDONESIAN: *rebung* ITALIAN: *germoglio di bamboo* JAPANESE:
takenoko MALAYSIAN: *rebong* SPANISH: *cana de bamboo*

The cream-colored young shoots of the bamboo plant are crisp and have a slightly sweet taste reminiscent of artichokes. They are one of the most commonly used Asian ingredients, adding texture and contrast to many dishes. The best canned ones are packed in water, not brine, and are available whole (preferred) or sliced, but canned ones always have a tinny flavor. Fresh bamboo shoots and their tips, which resemble asparagus and can be used interchangeably, are sometimes available during the winter and spring months, but only in oriental markets. The winter variety is smaller and more tender. Sun-dried bamboo shoots, which are really very good, are sometimes available and range in color from white to black, the black being the most flavorful. Pickled or "soured" bamboo shoots, *sun yee,* are also available, but are not often seen because they are not popular in America.

STORAGE: Fresh bamboo shoots should be refrigerated for use as soon as possible. After opening, store canned bamboo shoots in cold water in a covered jar in the refrigerator. If the water is changed every other day, they will keep for up to two weeks. For longer storage, freeze, covered with water; they will keep for several months, but will lose crispness.

PREPARATION AND USE: Fresh shoots must be blanched for 15 minutes after the hairy husk has been cut away; or they can be cooked for an hour or so in their husks and then peeled. Some Chinese cooks simmer the canned shoots in broth or water for a minute or two to help rid them of their canned taste. Rinse the shoots thoroughly to remove any white calcium residue (which is harmless to eat) from the ridges, and slice or cut into pieces of the desired size. They can be stir-fried or deep-fried or used in soups, though it is best to cook them no longer than 5 minutes so they will retain their crispness. Dried shoots must be soaked for 3 hours, and then simmered for approximately 2 hours until tender. Pickled bamboo shoots are often steamed with meat as a seasoning.

BANANA LEAVES
See THE FOODS OF LATIN AMERICA section

BARBECUE SAUCE, CHINESE

This name appears on jars and cans in Chinese markets. It is the same type of sauce as HOISIN and CHEE HOW.

BARBECUED ROAST DUCK
See DUCK, ROAST

BARLEY, PRESSED
JAPANESE: *oshi-mugi*

Pressed barley is a popular starch in Korea and Japan, where it is often cooked with rice. It cooks faster than regular barley.

STORAGE: In a covered jar, it will keep indefinitely on the pantry shelf.

PREPARATION AND USE: Soak 30 minutes; then drain and cook as you would rice.

BEANS

(General purchasing information, storage, and basic cooking of dried beans are described in THE FOODS OF LATIN AMERICA section.) Following are the beans, dried and fresh, most commonly called for in Asian recipes. Other bean products, such as BEAN CURD and BEAN SAUCE, follow this listing.

AZUKI

(AH-zoo-kee)
OTHER: "red beans," *aduki, adzuki, azuki-sarashian* (a powdered form), *feijao*

CHINESE: *saang see* or *wu dow*

These small, dark red or black beans, known in Japan as the "king of beans," become very tender when cooked and have an unusual, strong, sweet flavor. They are available in natural-food stores and in Asian markets, and are considered to have medicinal properties.

STORAGE: They will keep for up to a year in a cool, dry place.

PREPARATION AND USE: Cook as you would any legume.
The Japanese and the Chinese enjoy sweetened azuki as a filling for tea cakes (see BEAN PASTE, RED). In Japan, they are used to prepare the festival dish called Sekihan, and are often served in combination with cooked rice, either sweet (glutinous) or long-grained, in which case the dish is often sweetened with sake and toasted sesame seeds. Oshiruko is a sweet soup made from azuki. They are also often used in the confection called Yokan, and even appear in ice cream. In India, they are cooked as DAL and are seasoned with spices, garlic, and ginger, and then lightly mashed.

BEANS, BLACK, SALTED AND FERMENTED

CHINESE: *dow see* VIETNAMESE: *tuong*

Very strong-flavored, pungent and salty, fermented black soybeans are available in Chinese markets in bags or in jars or cans. They are more widely used in Cantonese cooking than that of other regions, and are almost always cooked with garlic. There is no American counterpart or substitute.

STORAGE: In a glass jar, these will keep on the pantry shelf indefinitely. On long standing, salt crystals may form on the surface but they can be rinsed away. Stir in a bit of peanut oil or sesame-flavored oil from time to time to prevent drying.

PREPARATION AND USE: Always rinse well before using. These beans are usually mashed as a seasoning for sauces, allowing 1 teaspoon per serving. Use with fresh garlic as a seasoning for sauces to accompany meats, fish, shellfish of all types, poultry, and vegetables. They are especially good with steamed clams.

BLACK BEAN SAUCE

For about 1½ cups or 6 servings

This is a Cantonese sauce for steamed clams, chicken, or fish.

2 tablespoons fermented black beans
1 tablespoon peanut oil
2 tablespoons sherry or *shao hsing* (Chinese rice wine)
4 large cloves garlic, minced
2 tablespoons minced fresh ginger
1 cup water or chicken broth
3 tablespoons OYSTER SAUCE
1 tablespoon mushroom soy sauce *or* light soy sauce
1 teaspoon sugar
1½ tablespoons cornstarch mixed with
3 tablespoons water

TO SERVE:
2 tablespoons peanut oil
2 scallions, cut in 2″ lengths, then slivered
 Fresh coriander (optional)

Rinse the beans very well in a strainer under cold water. Place them in a small skillet with the oil and mash them. Add the sherry, garlic, and ginger. Cook over low heat for 2 to 3 minutes, stirring constantly. Stir in the broth, oyster sauce, and soy sauce. Bring to a simmer; pour in the blended cornstarch and water, and cook and stir until thickened.

Spoon over steamed clams, fish, or chicken. As a final flavoring, heat the 2 tablespoons of peanut oil in a small skillet until it just begins to smoke. Meanwhile, garnish the top of the dish with scallions and coriander. Pour the hot oil over the sauce and garnishes.

TO PREPARE IN ADVANCE: The sauce can be refrigerated for up to a week, or frozen for up to 6 months. Reheat gently before serving, adding water to thin if necessary.

BEANS, LONG

OTHER: Chinese green beans, yard-long beans, ribbon beans, chopstick beans, asparagus beans

IN THE CARIBBEAN: *boonchi* CHINESE: *dow gok, p'ien tou*

These beans resemble American green beans in taste and in looks but are 12″ to 30″ long, and are a bit more chewy-textured. They are available fresh, by weight, in many supermarkets, as well as in Chinese and some Caribbean grocery stores. The height of their season is in the fall, but they are available year 'round in many places. When purchased, they should be velvety and pliable, not tough and shriveled.

STORAGE: If placed in a paper bag stored inside a plastic bag, these can be kept for up to a week in the refrigerator.

PREPARATION AND USE: Dice or cut into 2″ lengths to stir-fry. They are cooked in the same manner as string beans, but care should be taken not to overcook them—they get mushy. In the dish Doh Goh Ngau Yuk, the cooked beans are added to sautéed beef with oyster sauce. They are also combined in a Chinese stir-fry dish with thin-sliced beef and rice vermicelli. In Aruba, they are wrapped around skewered lamb and vegetables in the grilled dish called Lamchi and Boonchi.

STIR-FRIED LONG BEANS

2	tablespoons peanut oil	For 4 servings
2	cloves garlic, peeled and halved	
2	quarter-sized slices ginger root	
¾	pound long beans, cut in 2″ to 4″ lengths	
1	teaspoon salt	
¼	cup chicken stock	
2	teaspoons sesame oil	

Heat wok until hot. Pour in oil, swirl around, and add garlic and ginger. When nearly smoking, add beans and stir-fry for 1 minute. Sprinkle in salt and pour in chicken stock. Cover and cook 2 to 3 minutes. Remove lid and stir-fry until liquid has evaporated, about 5 minutes. Test for doneness. Remove from heat, drizzle sesame oil over the beans. Toss lightly, discard garlic and ginger, and turn out onto a warm serving platter.

MUNG BEANS

OTHER: green gram

CHINESE: *lok doe* INDIAN: *mung dal* INDONESIAN: *katjang hidjau*
MALAYSIAN: *kachang hijau* THAI: *thua khiaw*

Mung beans are actually dried peas with yellow flesh that have green, brown, or black outer skins. They are available in Asian markets. They have a rather soft texture when cooked, and a slightly sweet flavor. This is the bean usually used to grow BEAN SPROUTS. They are widely used in India and in China. MUNG BEAN FLOUR, made from ground mung beans, is used to make Chinese CELLOPHANE NOODLES (see under NOODLES) and various Indian and Malaysian sweet dishes.

STORAGE: Mung beans can be stored in an airtight jar in a cool spot for up to 6 months.

PREPARATION AND USE: One cup of soaked mung beans will serve 4 to 6, depending on the other ingredients. These are more often cooked whole than split as DAL. Like any bean, they should be soaked, but only up to 4 hours. They are then cooked with 3 parts water to 1 part beans, and will be tender in about 30 minutes. They can be combined with rice and spices in Indian dishes.

SOYBEANS, DRIED

OTHER: yellow bean, soya bean, great bean

CHINESE: *wang dow* JAPANESE: *daizu* and *edamame*

According to food historian Waverly Root, the world's most important bean is the small, oval soybean. They have been cultivated for over 4,000 years and are processed into all sorts of products, which supply nutrition to much of the world: bean curd, soy sauce, MISO, and others too numerous to list. There are yellow, green, red, and black varieties, all of which are high in protein, calcium, and lecithin. The United States is now the world's largest grower, supplying even China. They have a rather sweet flavor and a floury texture. A variety called "soy splits" is precooked. There is even such a thing as "soy grits," hulled and coarsely ground soybeans, sold in health food stores.

STORAGE: They can be stored indefinitely on the pantry shelf.

USE: Dried soybeans can be sprouted in the same manner as mung beans to develop large, crisp BEAN SPROUTS. If used whole, they require long cooking and are often simmered in seasoned stock to serve as a side dish. Soak overnight in cold water, or quick-soak for 1 hour in boiling water.

138

Place in a saucepan with 3 parts water to 1 part soaked beans and boil hard for 10 minutes, skimming away any scum; then simmer 1½ to 2 hours or until tender.

SOYBEANS, FRESH YOUNG

CHINESE: *mou tou* JAPANESE: *daizu* or *edamame* (EH-dah MAH-MEH)

These are the beans found in the fresh, dark green soybean pods that are available in Japanese markets throughout the summer and early fall. Each pod contains two to four beans. Our friends, Melinda and Nori Takeuchi, tell us these are the quintessential Japanese drinking accompaniment in the summer. They can be shucked and cooked like peas, or cooked in the pod to be shucked as they are eaten.

STORAGE: The fresher these are when eaten the better, so use them as soon as possible after they are picked. They will keep, stored in a paper bag inside a plastic bag in the refrigerator, for up to 3 days.

USE: The outer fuzz can be removed from the pods by rubbing them vigorously with salt, though this step is unnecessary. Drop into boiling, salted water and blanch them for 3 minutes. Drain and dry immediately on paper towels. Shuck, and sprinkle with more salt if you like them well salted. They are usually served with cocktails in Japan, and if they are to be shucked before cooking, this task will be made easier if they are blanched for 5 minutes and allowed to cool. One pound of pods will yield approximately 1½ cups of shucked beans. For use in stir-fried dishes, or to serve as a starch, place beans in salted water just to cover and simmer for 10 to 20 minutes or until they are tender. For a delicious snack, roast the cooked beans in butter and salt at 350° until they are lightly browned.

BEAN CURD

OTHER: soy bean cake, bean custard

CHINESE: *dou-fu, dow foo* JAPANESE: *tofu*

Fresh bean curd, white and custardlike, is formed into 1″ by 4″ square cakes, or 1-pound blocks packed in water, and sold in plastic containers in the refrigerator sections of many supermarkets and in health food stores. It may be labeled "soft," "medium," or "firm." As a general rule, the Chinese type is firmer and a bit sweeter than the Japanese. One type, *yakidoufu,* labeled "broiled" or "grilled," is quite firm, and excellent for those who dislike a very soft, custardy consistency.

Bean curd is quite inexpensive and is such a powerhouse of protein that it is often called "meat without bones" by the Chinese. Made from soybeans that have been soaked, pureed, cooked, and solidified into curds by the addition of epsom salts, vinegar, or a natural solidifier from distilled sea water, called *nigari,* bean curd is the richest natural source of lecithin and contains all the essential amino acids. Nutritionists claim it is the only vegetable that contains a complete protein. It is very low in calories and in cholesterol and is much more easily digested than plain soybeans.

STORAGE: Use as soon as possible. If the water is changed daily, it can be stored in the refrigerator for up to a week. It develops a sour taste when it is spoiled. Do not freeze.

PREPARATION AND USE: Fresh bean curd absorbs flavors from other ingredients so it is an easy way to extend and to add protein to many dishes. If it seems too soft for the use it is to be put, it can be placed on paper towels and topped with a plate on which a weight is placed for up to an hour to firm it. It may be cubed, cut in strips, or crumbled, depending on the recipe. Simmer it in soups, steam it, stir-fry, or deep-fry. There are hundreds of uses for it. In Japan in the summertime it is iced and garnished with grated ginger, shredded NORI (see SEAWEED, DRIED), sliced scallion, KATSUO-BUSHI flakes, and *shoyu* (Japanese soy sauce). In winter, it finds its way into soups, hot pots, is fried, etc. A spicy Szechuan dish, Ma Po Dofu, is made with ground pork, "hot" bean paste, and green onions. In Vietnam, it is served in chicken stock with fresh coriander. We have seen recipes for every type of dish from salad dressings to tacos!

BEAN CURD, DRIED STICKS

OTHER: bean curd sticks, bean curd skin, bean curd film, second bamboo

CHINESE: *tim jook* or *foo jook*   JAPANESE: *yuba*   THAI: *forng tawhu*

This is soybean milk residue, lifted from the top of boiling soybean "milk," dried, and then folded into thin, stiff sheets or long sticks. It can be found in Chinese markets in packages of various sizes. The Japanese type comes in thin rolls tied with strips of KOMBU. It is sometimes called "bamboo" because it resembles that plant in texture. It has a bland and creamy, nutlike flavor and lends a firm, chewy texture to stir-fried dishes. It must be soaked before use to become white and pliable enough to cook.

STORAGE: These dried bean curd sticks can be stored on the pantry shelf for 2 to 3 months. They contain oil, so they will eventually turn rancid.

PREPARATION AND USE: They are often used as a main ingredient, especially in vegetarian dishes and soups to which they lend a meaty texture. Allow approximately 2 ounces, before soaking, per serving. Soak for 10 to 60 minutes—the Japanese type will require only about 15 minutes, the Chinese, up to 1 hour—then cut or slice as desired. Add to soups or stir-fry dishes only near the end of cooking time or they will fall apart. They absorb a great deal of liquid, so you will want to compensate for this in the dish you are cooking. They can also be stuffed and then steamed to serve as Dim Sum (Chinese snack foods).

BEAN CURD, FERMENTED

OTHER: red bean curd, Chinese cheese, pickled bean curd, soybean cheese

CHINESE: *foo yoo* or *narm yoo*

Made from fermented soybeans and crushed rice or barley, fermented bean curd is available in its brining liquid in cans or jars. It is soft and creamy in consistency, and its color is either white or red. The white is commonly sold in jars. The red, which is fermented with wine and colored with red rice, usually comes in ½" squares in cans or jars that have a drawing of a square cake covered with a thick red sauce on the label. The flavor of the white is strong and salty, reminiscent of Camembert cheese. The red is somewhat milder and spiced. Some brands are very spicy from the addition of chiles.

STORAGE: After opening, transfer to a glass with a tight lid and store in the refrigerator for up to 3 months.

PREPARATION AND USE: Both types are used in small quantities as a seasoning or as a condiment. The white type is often eaten raw with a sprinkling of oil or sugar, on top of rice. Or it may be tossed with cooked vegetables, such as spinach or watercress, in which case it has a sour-cream flavor. The red is most commonly cut into small cubes to use as a seasoning in sauces and in braised dishes, especially with poultry and pork, to which it adds a nutlike flavor. In China, the winey-flavored red type is very popular as a flavoring for the hot breakfast porridge made from rice called Congee. A little bit goes a long way. Cubes of either may be mashed until smooth to use as a spread, and, if a milder taste is desired, it is often mixed with shredded romaine lettuce.

BEAN CURD, FRIED

JAPANESE: *age* or *aburage* (Ah-BOOR-Ah-GAY)

Japanese-style fried soybean curd in pouches, *aburage,* rectangular sheets, *age,* or strips is available in the refrigerator or freezer sections of oriental markets. It is sometimes available canned with seasoning added, though the spongy texture suffers in the canning process. It has a stronger bean flavor than fresh bean curd.

STORAGE: Store in refrigerator for up to three days. If it is purchased frozen and not allowed to thaw, it can be kept frozen for months.

PREPARATION AND USE: Each sheet of aburage makes two pouches, or pockets, to be stuffed. Pour boiling water over fried bean curd in a colander to remove excess oil. It is popularly used for a type of Sushi (vinegared rice dish) in which case it is stuffed with seasoned rice, toasted sesame seeds, and vegetables, and often tied with pieces of dehydrated gourd, KAMPYO. In China, diced bean curd is fried to serve as an appetizer or to add to vegetable dishes, and Yeung Dofou is made by stuffing fried bean curd with pork, shrimp, and seasonings to serve in a sauce of soy sauce, sherry, and fresh coriander. In Thailand, it is stuffed with pork, garlic, and fresh coriander.

BEAN CURD, PRESSED

CHINESE: *doufu-kan*

A weight is used to press out much of the water from fresh bean curd cakes. It is then simmered with soy sauce and seasonings to make a delicious, high protein meat replacement, which is available in the refrigerator sections of many supermarkets and in Chinese grocery stores.

STORAGE: Pressed bean curd, unopened, will keep for up to 1 week in the refrigerator, or for up to 3 months in the freezer. After opening, it will keep for up to a week in the refrigerator submerged in fresh water, which should be changed daily.

PREPARATION AND USE: Cut into thin strips or dice to add to soups; stir-fry with vegetables; or serve in thickened Chinese sauces.

BEAN PASTE, RED

CHINESE: *dow cha* JAPANESE: *an* (smooth: *koshi-an,* chunky: *tusbushi-an*)

This sweetened puree of red beans or AZUKI beans is available in cans in Chinese and Japanese markets.

STORAGE: It will keep indefinitely in a glass jar in the refrigerator.

USE: It is used in Chinese pastries, such as "moon cakes" and sweet steamed buns, and in many Japanese sweet dishes.

BEAN SAUCE

OTHER: brown bean sauce, brown bean paste
soybean condiment

CHINESE: *min sze jeung* or *mor sze jeung* MALAYSIAN: *tauceo* THAI: *dow jeeoh dam*

Bean sauce is a thick, aromatic paste made from fermented yellow soybeans, flour, water, and salt, and is available in 1-pound jars or cans. There are two kinds, regular and ground, which have the same flavor but different textures. Regular, *min sze jeung,* which contains some whole beans, is similar to the Malaysian product called *taucheo.* Ground bean sauce, *mor sze jeung,* is smooth and similar to Korean-style bean sauce. Chinese cooks prefer the regular because the appearance of the whole beans assures them that it is made with high-quality beans. When added to cooked foods, it colors, thickens, and seasons them. Bean sauce is salty and somewhat pungent. It must be cooked before it is eaten. Equal parts of pale and dark MISO make an adequate substitute.

STORAGE: Transfer to a tightly sealed jar and store in the refrigerator. It will keep indefinitely. If it becomes too thick and begins to dry out, stir in some peanut oil or sesame-flavored oil to moisten it.

PREPARATION AND USE: The flavor combines well with garlic. Stir, a teaspoon at a time, into cooked sauces to flavor, color, and thicken them, and allow the sauce to simmer a minute or so to cook it. Delicious with spareribs and with beef and bean curd. The ground sauce is a bit saltier than the regular, so add a bit of sugar to it for better flavor. It is often served as a relish with Korean foods, and is used in the sauce for Bulgogi (brazier-cooked meat). It is served as a dip for scallions in northern China. When cooking from most Chinese and Malaysian recipes, use the regular, *min sze jeung.* In Malaysia, it is combined with onion, garlic, chiles, and ginger to make a sauce for fried fish. A good example of the use of bean sauce is in the following recipe for beef noodles, from Jean Yueh's book, *Dim Sum and Chinese One-Dish Meals,* published by Irena Chalmers Cookbooks, Inc., New York. It appears here with permission of the publisher.

AROMATIC BEEF NOODLES

Serves 3 as a one-dish meal, 6 as a snack

The Chinese often serve noodles in a bowl of soup and top it with meat and vegetables. This is called soup noodles, and it can be served as a between-meal snack or a full meal. Aromatic Beef Noodles is modified from a well-known soup noodles recipe of the Szechuan region where the soup is cooked with hot bean sauce. The subtle and aromatic soup in this recipe is equally good without the hot flavor, with hot chili oil added instead at the table.

    2   tablespoons cooking oil
    4   slices fresh ginger
    5   cloves garlic, peeled
    1   pound boneless beef chuck, cut into 1" cubes
    5   cups water
    2   tablespoons sugar
    5   tablespoons brown bean sauce or to taste
    ¼   cup dry sherry
    2   whole star anise
    1   tablespoon Szechuan peppercorns
        Salt to taste
        Soy sauce to taste
  ¾–1   pound fresh egg noodles (or dry noodles or dry extra
            thin spaghetti)
    2   cloves garlic (optional), mashed into a paste or crushed
            through a garlic press
    2   tablespoons sesame oil or to taste (optional)
    1   large scallion, finely minced
        Hot CHILI OIL to taste (optional) (or use Tabasco
            sauce, or Chinese chili paste)

Heat oil in a 3-quart saucepan, fry ginger and garlic for 30 seconds, then add beef. Cook until beef loses its red color. Add water, sugar, brown bean sauce, and sherry. Place star anise and Szechuan peppercorns in a stainless steel tea strainer or tie them in a cheesecloth bag, then place them in the saucepan.

Cook for 1½ to 2 hours until beef is tender. Add salt or soy sauce to taste. There are about 4 cups of soup in the saucepan. Remove the spice bag. (The recipe may be made ahead of time to this point.)

In another pot, cook fresh egg noodles for about 2 minutes or until just cooked. Do not overcook. (Cook spaghetti according to the package directions.) Quickly drain noodles in a colander. They should be soft but resistant to the bite.

Add garlic paste to the simmering soup just before serving. Add sesame oil, and remove from the heat.

Place noodles and soup in a tureen, or dish into individual bowls. Garnish with minced scallions. Let each diner add hot chili oil to taste.

TO PREPARE IN ADVANCE: The beef and soup can be cooked several days ahead, then served with freshly cooked noodles.

BEAN SAUCE, HOT

OTHER: Szechuan bean paste, black bean sauce with chili, chili bean sauce

CHINESE: *yuan shai chi*

In Szechuan province, hot ground chiles are added to this bean sauce. You will find it under different labels in jars or cans in Asian markets. It has a delicious spiciness, and is especially good when combined with garlic. The Lan Chi brand, in 8-ounce jars, is widely distributed.

STORAGE: Transfer to a glass jar and store in the refrigerator. It will keep indefinitely.

USE: Thickens, colors, and adds a spicy flavor to foods. Delicious when combined with garlic. If not available, substitute bean sauce mixed with CHILI OIL or CHILI PASTE WITH GARLIC.

HOT AND SPICY SZECHUAN SHRIMP

MARINADE: For 6 to 8 servings
   1   egg white   when other dishes are served
   2   cloves garlic, minced
   2   quarter-sized slices fresh ginger, minced
   1   teaspoon cornstarch
   ½   teaspoon FIVE SPICE POWDER
   2   pounds raw shrimp, medium or large, shelled and
         deveined
  12   scallions
   3   tablespoons peanut or vegetable oil

SAUCE:
   1   cup chicken broth
   ⅓   cup sherry or *shao hsing* (Chinese rice wine)
   ⅓   cup tomato sauce
   3   tablespoons light soy or mushroom soy sauce
   2   tablespoons cornstarch

4 teaspoons sugar
1½ teaspoons hot bean sauce, or more to taste
1 teaspoon white wine vinegar
½ teaspoon salt

Combine the marinade ingredients in a small mixing bowl. Cut the shrimp into bite-sized pieces, and marinate them in the mixture for at least 15 minutes, or up to 2 hours, in the refrigerator.

Meanwhile, combine the sauce ingredients in another bowl. Clean the scallions and cut them crosswise where the green shoots separate from the white stalks. Cut the white portions into thin lengthwise strips. Cut the green shoots into 1" sections.

Just before serving, heat a wok or heavy skillet until very hot. Pour in the oil, and when just beginning to smoke add the shrimp mixture and stir-fry for several minutes until most of the shrimp have turned pink. Turn the shrimp out of the pan. Stir the sauce mixture well and pour it into the hot pan—it will thicken almost immediately. Return the shrimp to the pan along with the scallions, and toss together for 2 to 3 minutes until the shrimp is just cooked through. Serve immediately.

BEAN SPROUTS

CHINESE: *gna tsoi* or *lo do ya* INDONESIAN: *taoge* JAPANESE: *moyashi* MALAYSIAN: *taugeh* THAI:*thua ngork*

These crisp, bland sprouts of mung or soybeans have a light, nutlike flavor and are very low in calories while high in nutrients. Available fresh or canned in most supermarkets and in all Asian markets. The canned variety is of very poor quality and is really not worth using.

It is a very simple matter to sprout your own. Place 2 tablespoons mung beans in a glass jar with a screened lid (available in health food stores). Fill with water and soak overnight. Drain and put in a cool, dark place. Rinse and drain two times a day. Mung bean sprouts appear in 3 to 4 days; soybean sprouts take twice as long. Refrigerate them until ready to use. When buying fresh sprouts, make sure they are white and plump. The shorter they are, the younger.

STORAGE: Fresh sprouts should be used as soon as possible. They will stay fresh for more than a week if placed in water in a covered jar. Canned sprouts, once opened, should be rinsed very well and then crisped in ice water for at least 30 minutes before using, which will give them a somewhat fresher flavor. They can be stored as fresh once opened.

PREPARATION AND USE: Bean sprouts needn't be cooked before eating so they make a superb addition to salads and sandwiches. Stir-fry briefly, or add to soups just before serving. If unavailable, substitute thinly sliced celery—the texture will be similar but the flavor will be a bit different.

BEAN THREADS
See NOODLES, CELLOPHANE

BÊCHE-DE-MER
OTHER: sea cucumber, sea slug, trepang

CHINESE: *hoy sharm*

This dried, shiny black mollusk, measuring 4″ to 12″ in length, is considered a great delicacy in China, so it is frequently served at banquets. It is available in packages, either whole or in segments. It must be soaked and cleaned meticulously, which is a tedious chore. Once that is accomplished, however, it expands in size to become soft and gelatinous in texture and very delicate in flavor.

STORAGE: Tightly wrapped, this will keep on the pantry shelf indefinitely.

PREPARATION AND USE: Soak in cold water for several hours. Brush well. Soak 24 hours in warm water, changing the water 3 or 4 times. Cut open to remove the internal organs. Rinse. Simmer 4 hours until soft. Rinse thoroughly. Now it is ready to be cut into thin strips or in halves to be used as an ingredient for stir-fry dishes. In Cantonese cooking, it is classically served in Sea Cucumber and Abalone Soup. It is also served with chicken or meat flavored with various sauces, and is often "red-cooked" (with soy sauce and spices), to serve with sliced bamboo shoots.

BEEFSTEAK LEAVES
See SHISO

BENI SHOGA
See GINGER, PICKLED

BESAN

OTHER: chick-pea flour, channa flour

FRENCH: *farine de pois chiches*

Besan is a very nutritious, pale yellow, high-protein flour made by grinding small chick-peas, *channa,* and straining out the husks. It can be found in most Asian markets. This flour has a distinctive taste, and ordinary wheat flour cannot be substituted. Strained pea flour may be substituted. Besan can be made at home by gently roasting Channa Dal (see under DAL) or yellow split peas, cooling, and grinding to a powder in a blender. It must be sieved to remove the husks.

STORAGE: Besan is somewhat more perishable than wheat flour, so it should be refrigerated and used within a few months.

USE: Besan is used to make batters for all types of fried foods, and as an excellent stabilizer for Indian and Burmese yogurt-based sauces (curries) and souplike dishes, called Karhis, to prevent separation. It is very widely used as a thickener for sauces in India and Burma (it is mixed to a paste with water and used as any other thickener). It is also mixed with GARAM MASALA (see HERBS, SPICES, AND SEASONING BLENDS section) and turmeric to coat fish to be deep-fried. A popular Indian fudgelike dessert, Barfi, which contains almonds, sugar, syrup, and GHEE, is made with besan, as are Boondi (besan fritters soaked in syrup), and many other Indian sweets. In northern India, it is used as a basis for an onion and ginger tortilla-like bread and for various pancakes and dumplings. Chick-pea flour is also used as a thickener in African cooking.

BIRD PEPPERS

See DRIED CHILES under CHILES, ASIAN

BIRD'S EYE CHILES

See DRIED CHILES under CHILES, ASIAN

BIRDS' NESTS

OTHER: swallows' nests

CHINESE: *yeen waw*

The nests of Salangane swallows or swifts near the South China Sea are gathered by men who climb the sides of cliffs to seek them out. They are formed of a pre-digested seaweed. They are considered a great delicacy in China, a sign of gracious hospitality, so they are a must at formal dinners and banquets. They are sold in boxes with windows through which the contents can be viewed. The finest in quality, and the most expensive by far, are whole and almost white. Broken pieces, known as "Dragon's Teeth" (and sometimes referred to as "black"), are of medium quality and price. Both must be scrupulously cleaned. Ground birds' nest, which is formed into cakes, is the least expensive, and by far the easiest to use because no cleaning is necessary. It is the variety usually served in restaurants.

On their own, birds' nests have a very bland flavor, but in cooking they take on the flavors of the other ingredients. They are almost pure protein.

STORAGE: They can be stored in a cool place indefinitely.

PREPARATION AND USE: For 6 servings, buy ¼ pound dried birds' nests. To clean whole nests, soak in cold water overnight. Remove any feathers and impurities with tweezers. Rub in a few drops of peanut oil and soak again in cold water. More feathers will float to the surface. Repeat until very clean. Parboil for 10 minutes. To clean birds' nest chips, pour boiling water over them and let cool. Simmer in water to cover for 30 minutes; drain, and let cool. Squeeze out water. Remove any feathers or impurities with tweezers. Simmer in stock and serve as soup, or in sugar syrup to serve as a traditional Chinese dessert. A Chinese banquet soup, Chicken Velvet and Bird's Nest Soup, contains shredded chicken, ham, and snow peas.

BLACHAN
See SHRIMP PASTE, SOUTHEAST ASIAN

BLACK MUSHROOMS
See MUSHROOMS, DRIED

BITTER MELON
See MELON, BITTER

BOMBAY DUCK
OTHER: *bummalo*

149

Bombay duck is not a duck at all, but a variety of small, sun-dried, salted fish sold in small packets or flat tins in Indian markets. They have a strong fish taste.

STORAGE: They will keep indefinitely in a cool, dry place.

PREPARATION AND USE: These tiny fish are crisped in the oven or in a skillet with hot oil. When served as a condiment with curried dishes, they are crumbled; when eaten as a snack, they should be nibbled in small bits.

BOTTLE GOURD

See SQUASH, BOTTLE

BREADFRUIT

See THE FOODS OF LATIN AMERICA section

BRINJAL

Indian name for eggplant

BROCCOLI, CHINESE

CHINESE: *guy lan*

Chinese broccoli is longer, leafier, and more sharply flavored than our familiar domestic broccoli, and is sold only in oriental produce markets. It is extremely easy to grow from seed. Domestic broccoli can be substituted when necessary.

STORAGE: It will keep for up to one week in the refrigerator.

PREPARATION AND USE: One to 2 pounds will serve 4 as a vegetable dish. Scrape any tough stalks, as you would domestic broccoli, and cut in diagonal sections ½″ to 1″ thick, depending on the recipe. Cook the same length of time as domestic broccoli, just until crisp-tender. This is especially crunchy in texture and is excellent for stir-frying, especially with pork and beef. It is often added to slow-cooked dishes.

BROWN BEAN SAUCE OR PASTE

See BEAN SAUCE

BROWN GRAVY SAUCE

See MOLASSES, CHINESE BEAD

BURDOCK ROOT

See GOBO

CABBAGE, ORIENTAL

There are several types of oriental cabbage, all of which look very much alike. Following are brief descriptions and drawings to help you in your shopping. It doesn't help matters at all when markets mislabel them!

BOK CHOY (AND CHOY SUM)

OTHER: chard cabbage, Chinese chard, white mustard cabbage

CHINESE: *bok choy* or *baak choy*; (heart): *bok choy sum* or *choy sum*
JAPANESE: *shirona*

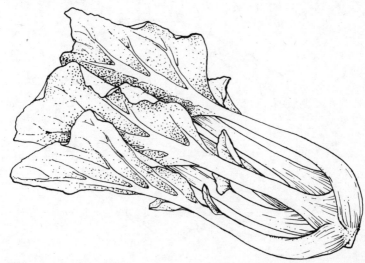

Bok choy is an extremely versatile oriental vegetable with limp, dark green leaves on smooth white stalks. It may have an especially delicate and tender center with yellow flowers called *sum* or "heart of cabbage," in which case it is called *bok choy sum* or *choy sum* . The tender center (choy sum) is sometimes sold separately, and is more delicate in flavor. Bok choy is best during its winter peak season but is available all year. The small ones are the choicest.

STORAGE: Place in a paper bag inside a plastic bag and store in the crisper of the refrigerator. Use as soon as possible, certainly within 4 days.

PREPARATION AND USE: For 4 servings as a vegetable, buy 2 heads of either type (plain dark green, or with yellow centers). This vegetable requires very little cooking. Cut in pieces to stir-fry with any meat, poultry, or seafood. Add the cut up stems sooner than the quick-cooking leaves. When using in soups, add 10 minutes before serving. The hearts can be served raw in salads or steamed or blanched briefly to serve as a vegetable. (Any yellow flowers which stem from the center are not usually used in cooking.) One Szechuan dish serves the deep-fried heart with a sauce containing cream, butter, and flour, a very unusual occurrence in China where those dairy products seldom appear in recipes. In Korea, choy sum is often used to make KIMCHI, the staple pickle served with almost every meal.

CELERY CABBAGE

OTHER: napa or nappa, Chinese lettuce

CHINESE: *petsai, tientsin* cabbage, *wong nga bok* or *sui choy* JAPANESE: *hakusai* (HAH-ku-sa-ee)

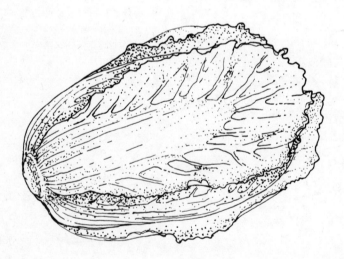

There are several varieties of this soft green and off-white leafy vegetable, which looks like a pale and compact head of romaine lettuce. We are grouping the varieties here to avoid confusion as they all taste the same. Do not become confused by the name as we were. Celery cabbage does not refer to the Chinese cabbage with long celerylike stalks. It is not related to celery, nor does it look like it, but is so named because it tastes like it—in a mild sort of way. The flavor is a happy combination of mild cabbage, iceberg lettuce, and celery. It can be served raw in salads or coleslaw, or cooked briefly in many dishes. The flavor is delicate and there is no strong cabbage odor in cooking. Small heads have the finest flavor.

STORAGE: Place unwashed in a paper bag inside a plastic bag and store in the crisper of the refrigerator for up to 2 weeks.

PREPARATION AND USE: Remove the tough outer leaves and wash well. Shred or dice to use in salads or in stir-fry dishes. Cook only briefly. In Japan, celery cabbage is served in soups and one-pot dishes and made into pickles. In China, it is briefly stir-fried, or added to a pale green soup of chicken broth, scallions, rice, and sesame oil. In Singapore, it is stir-fried with ginger, soy sauce, and oyster sauce, to accompany fried rice. It is an important ingredient in Vietnam's Shrimp Drop Soup.

CALPIS
(KAH-ru-PEES)

Calpis is an extremely sweet, white, soft-drink concentrate, made from nonfat dry milk and lactic acid, and is very popular with children. It is available in bottles in Japanese markets. Grape and orange flavors are also available, but are not quite so popular as the original.

STORAGE: Unopened this will keep indefinitely on the pantry shelf. After opening, it will keep for up to 3 months in the refrigerator.

PREPARATION AND USE: Dilute to taste with water (usually 1 part calpis to 4–6 parts water) and serve warm, or over ice, as a snack.

CALTROP
See WATER CHESTNUT

CANDIED RED GINGER
See GINGER, PRESERVED

CANDLENUT

DUTCH: *kemirie noten* INDONESIAN: *kemiri*-nut MALAYSIAN: *buah-keras*

The name of this hard, oily, tropical nut derives from the fact that it is used locally to make primitive candles. Candlenuts are available roasted in Dutch and Indian markets, usually in 3-ounce bags, either whole or in pieces. Blanched almonds make an excellent substitute— in fact, many Malaysians prefer using almonds. Brazil nuts or macadamia nuts, which they resemble in appearance, can be substituted, but both are sweeter and more expensive.

STORAGE: They will keep indefinitely in a cool, dry place.

PREPARATION AND USE: Candlenuts are highly toxic in their raw state so are always sold roasted. After roasting, they can be crushed into soups and ground into curry pastes for flavoring and thickening. In Malaysia, they flavor Soto Ayam (spicy chicken soup) and are used in various SAMBALS that accompany rice and curries. In Singapore, they are freshly grated to flavor spicy roast chicken.

CANTONESE SAUSAGE

See SAUSAGE, CHINESE PORK

CARAMBOLA

OTHER: star fruit

INDIAN: *kamrakh*

Carambola is a thin, waxy, yellow-green tropical fruit, native to India, about 4″ long which, when cut in cross-section, is star-shaped. It is popular in Chinese and in Indian cooking. Now cultivated in tropical areas of the United States, it can often be found in markets in Florida and Southern California. For eating raw, look for yellow fruit to indicate ripeness; green ones are best for cooking.

STORAGE: Refrigerate for use as soon as possible, within 3 or 4 days.

USE: In Indonesia, this is eaten raw or used in cold drinks. Depending upon the variety, the mild-tasting, watery pulp can be either sweet or sour. If sweet, it can be used in fruit salads or jellies. If sour, it can be used in place of TAMARIND.

CARDAMOM

See HERBS, SPICES, AND SEASONING BLENDS section

154

CASHEW NUT

FRENCH: *noix d'acajou* GERMAN: *Elephantlaus* HINDU: *kaju*
ITALIAN: *noce d'Anacardo* IN LATIN AMERICA: *nuez de anacardo*
MALAYSIAN: *gaju* SINHALESE (Sri Lanka): *cadju*

An evergreen shrub, native to the West Indies, Brazil, and India, produces a red- or yellow-skinned, pear-shaped apple, from the bottom of which grows a kidney-shaped nut. This is the cashew! The shell is highly toxic, so the nuts are always shelled and carefully cleaned. They are sweet in flavor and are considered a great delicacy in southern India. You will find them in supermarkets, usually roasted. Raw ones can be found in health food stores and Asian markets.

STORAGE: It is best to store cashews in the refrigerator or freezer as they become rancid even more rapidly than other nuts.

PREPARATION AND USE: Use whole as snacks or chopped in recipes when a sweet and crunchy texture is desired. It is usually best to add them at the end of the cooking time to preserve their texture. They are widely used in Chinese stir-fry dishes. In Vietnam, they are cooked with bananas and coconut in a cake. In the making of many Indian and Sinhalese curries, cashews are ground and added to the sauce as a thickening agent.

CASSAVA

See THE FOODS OF LATIN AMERICA section

CASSIA BLOSSOMS

CHINESE: *kwee hwa*

These tiny yellow flowers from the cassia tree are preserved in salt and sugar. They are an unusual ingredient that can be found only occasionally in Chinese specialty food shops.

STORAGE: Stored in a cool dry place or in the freezer, they will keep indefinitely.

USE: Their fragrance is a delightful addition to sweet dishes. Use to garnish foods as you would candied violets or rose petals.

CAUL FAT

See CAUL in THE FOODS OF EUROPE section

CELLOPHANE NOODLES

See under NOODLES

CENTURY EGGS

See EGGS, 1000 YEAR OLD

CHAPPATI FLOUR

See ATTA

CHARD, CHINESE

See CABBAGE, ORIENTAL

CHAROLI

OTHER: *chironji*

Charoli are small, round-shelled nuts found in Indian markets. They are mild in flavor, and MELON SEEDS, easily found in Chinese markets, can be substituted.

STORAGE: Store in a tightly sealed jar in a cool dry place.

USE: This lightly flavored nut is used in Indian stuffings and to garnish sweetmeats and noodle-based desserts.

CHASOBA

See under NOODLES

CHEE HOW SAUCE

This is a slightly spicier version of HOISIN, which is stored and used in exactly the same way. It is sold in Chinese grocery stores in jars or cans, but is not quite as readily available as hoisin. We use it in the following recipe.

HUGH'S FILLING FOR PEKING PANCAKES

Filling for 20 pancakes

Hugh Carpenter, Chinese cooking authority, invented this eclectic and perfectly delicious filling for Mandarin Pancakes (often called Doilies or Po Ping). His recipe for the pancakes can be found under SESAME OIL in this section. The filling can be used in LUMPIA WRAPPERS as well, and demonstrates wonderfully what can be improvised from available ingredients.

THE SAUCE:
- 2 tablespoons dry sherry
- 2 tablespoons OYSTER SAUCE
- 1 tablespoon mushroom soy *or* dark soy
- 1 teaspoon sugar
- 1 teaspoon Chinese sesame oil
- 1 teaspoon curry paste
- 1–2 teaspoons cornstarch mixed with water, to thicken if necessary

THE SEASONINGS:
- 3 cloves garlic, minced or pressed
- 3 thin slices ginger, minced

THE EGG MIXTURE:
- 2 tablespoons peanut oil
- 3 eggs, beaten with
- 1 teaspoon sesame oil and a
  Sprinkling of black pepper

THE MEAT MIXTURE:
- 1 pound ground pork or "meatloaf mix" (available in any supermarket)
- 1 tablespoon mushroom soy *or* dark soy
- 1 tablespoon sesame oil

THE VEGETABLES:
- 2 medium onions, halved, then slivered
- ½ large green cabbage, diced
- 4 mushrooms, sliced through the stems

GARNISH:
- HOISIN or chee how sauce, to brush over the pancakes with
  Scallion brushes

Combine the sauce ingredients in a small mixing bowl and set aside until needed. Combine seasonings in a separate bowl.

Heat a large, well-seasoned wok over highest heat until very hot. Add peanut oil, rolling oil around sides of wok. Pour in the beaten egg mixture and scramble lightly. Remove from pan and roll up. Cut in ½" sections to form noodle-like strips. Set aside.

Return the wok to the heat and cook the meat while tossing constantly until it is cooked and crumbly. Transfer to another container and drain off fat, reserving 3 tablespoons. Set aside.

Return the reserved drippings to the wok and place over high heat. Add seasonings. At once, stir-fry the onions, cabbage, and mushrooms just until they soften slightly. Pour in the sauce ingredients and stir-fry until well combined; then return the eggs and meat to the pan. Toss well; taste and correct the seasoning, adding more of anything you think it needs. If necessary, thicken slightly with a paste of cornstarch and water.

Make scallion brushes by shredding the ends of 3-inch scallion lengths with a sharp paring knife or razor blade and then soaking them in ice water until needed—the ends will open and curl. To serve, brush Hoisin or CHEE HOW sauce over a warm Po Ping pancake (or substitute LUMPIA WRAPPERS or even small, thin FLOUR TORTILLAS) with a scallion brush. Place some of the hot filling in the center. Fold up one portion of the pancake to form the bottom of the roll, then fold in both sides. Eat out of hand or with a fork, depending on the formality of the occasion.

TO PREPARE IN ADVANCE: The filling keeps beautifully for up to 4 days in the refrigerator. Bring to a simmer over medium heat, stirring until heated through.

CHEESE, CHINESE
See BEAN CURD, FERMENTED

CHESTNUTS, PRESERVED
See KURI NO KANRO NI

CHICK-PEA FLOUR
See BESAN

CHILES, ASIAN

Chiles are native to Latin America, and general information on types, storage, and use will be found in THE FOODS OF LATIN AMERICA section. They are widely used in Asian cooking, however, and are sold in Asian markets, so we are listing the types you are most likely to find in those markets. You will find the word "chiles" spelled "chillis" and "chillies" in Asian cookbooks.

DRIED CHILES

BURMESE: *nil thee* CHINESE: *la-jiao* HINDU: *lal mirich*
INDONESIAN: *lombok* JAPANESE: *togarashi* LAOTIAN: *mak phet kunsi* MALAYSIAN: *cabai* IN THE PHILIPPINES: *siling labuyo*
SINHALESE (Sri Lanka): *rathy miris* TAMIL (Ceylon): *kochikai* THAI: *prik chee pha*

Dried chiles are used extensively in Asian cooking, especially the small, fiery, red ones. Various kinds, 1″ to 2″ long, will be found in oriental, Latin American, and Italian markets. Bird's Eye chiles, or Bird Peppers, are an especially fiery, tiny Thai chile. Kashmiri chiles are fairly mild and are usually ground and sieved to make ground red pepper. In most cases, crushed red chiles, available in the spice sections of most markets, can be substituted —as a general rule, ¼ teaspoon equals 1 dried chili. Sambal Oelek (see SAMBAL) can be substituted as well: 1 teaspoon equals 2 dried chiles, but this product contains some salt, which you may care to compensate for in the recipe. CHILE PASTE WITH GARLIC can be substituted in equal measure for a combined amount of garlic and chiles.

Like all red spices, these should be stored in the refrigerator. There are usually tiny eggs present in these spices, which hatch on long standing at room temperature.

In Chinese stir-frying, especially in dishes of Hunan and Szechuan provinces, dried chiles are often fried whole in oil until the skins darken, and play a large part in such dishes as Kung Pao Chicken. Some Sinhalese dishes have as many as 30 dried chiles in them! These chiles are also used to make CHILI OIL, a popular seasoning in many Chinese and Japanese dishes. The Japanese don't go in much for "hot" foods, so dried chiles find their way only into Tsukemono (pickled salad), and are ground to make Shichimi Togarashi (see SEVEN SPICE SEASONING in the HERBS, SPICES, AND SEASONING BLENDS section, under SEASONING BLENDS).

KUNG PAO CHICKEN
(CHICKEN WITH CHARRED CHILES AND PEANUTS)

For 6 to 8 servings when other dishes are served

If the fiery flavor of this Szechuan dish is too hot for your tastes, use fewer dried chiles.

2 whole chicken breasts, or 1 pound boned chicken breasts
6 to 8 small dried red chiles
4 teaspoons minced fresh ginger root
4 scallions
2/3 cup roasted peanuts
1/3 cup peanut oil

MARINADE:
2 tablespoons dry sherry or shao hsing (Chinese rice wine)
1 egg white
4 teaspoons cornstarch
4 teaspoons light soy or mushroom soy sauce
1 teaspoon salt

SAUCE:
1 cup chicken broth
2 tablespoons cornstarch
2 tablespoons dry sherry or shao hsing (Chinese rice wine)
2 tablespoons light soy or mushroom soy sauce
4 teaspoons sugar
2 teaspoons white vinegar
1 teaspoon sesame oil

Remove bones and skin from chicken breasts, and cut the meat into 3/4-inch pieces. In a medium bowl, combine the marinade ingredients. Mix in the chicken and leave, covered, at room temperature for at least 15 minutes or in the refrigerator for up to 2 hours.

In a measuring cup or small bowl, combine the sauce ingredients.

Make a slit in the side of each chile to shake out and discard the seeds. Cut the scallions in 1½-inch lengths using part of the green shoots, then sliver each section by cutting it lengthwise into thin strips. Set out the ginger and peanuts next to your work surface.

Just before serving, heat a wok or heavy skillet over high heat. Add the oil and swirl until it is nearly smoking. Add the chiles and stir-fry until they turn dark brown, then add the chicken with its marinade. Stir-fry until the chicken is white, then add the ginger, shredded scallions, and peanuts. Stir the sauce ingredients until smooth, then pour into the pan. Toss the ingredients together just until the sauce has thickened. Remove from the heat and turn out onto a warm serving platter. Serve immediately.

TO PREPARE IN ADVANCE: The chicken pieces may marinate in the refrigerator for up to 24 hours.

FRESH CHILES

HINDU: *sabz mirch* INDONESIAN: *lombok hijau* MALAYSIAN: *cabai hijau* SINHALESE (Sri Lanka): *amu miris* THAI: *nil thee sein*

Fresh, hot green chiles are used to season many Asian dishes, especially in Indian and Southeast Asian cooking, where they are ground into SAMBALS or cooked in seafood dishes. The exact Asian varieties won't be found, even in Asian markets, but any small, hot green chili, such as JALAPEÑO or SERRANO can be substituted (see under CHILES, FRESH in THE FOODS OF LATIN AMERICA section). Asian recipes occasionally specify that they be ground, in which case the seeds and veins, which are the hottest parts, are removed before grinding. An easier substitute, which lacks the green color but is more than adequate in flavor, is Sambal Oelek (see SAMBAL): use 1 teaspoon for each 2 fresh, hot chiles called for in an Asian recipe. However, this product contains salt for which you may care to compensate in the dish you are making.

CHILI OIL

OTHER: hot chili oil, chili-flavored oil

CHINESE: *la yu* JAPANESE: *rayu*

This is a red oil in which chiles have released their flavor. It can be purchased in varying intensities of flavor in dispenser bottles or it can be easily made at home. To make it, heat 1 cup of peanut, vegetable, or corn oil (or sesame oil, if a sesame flavor is desirable) in a small saucepan until it is hot, but not smoking. Remove from the heat. Add any one of the following: 30 small, dry red chiles, broken; 3 tablespoons red pepper flakes; or 1 tablespoon ground red pepper (cayenne). Stir, and cover the pot. When cool, strain through a paper towel.

STORAGE: This oil loses more and more of its spicy flavor the longer it stands. Store in an 8-ounce dispenser bottle. It can be stored for up to 6 months on the pantry shelf. We prefer to store it in the refrigerator because it seems to keep its flavor longer.

USE: Adding chili oil is the easiest way to spice up a dish. Add gradually to stir-fry dishes or cooked foods when you wish a fiery flavor. It is used in the classic Chinese dish, Cold Shredded Chicken Salad. It can be used (with caution!) as a table condiment, too.

CHILI PASTE WITH GARLIC

This thin paste of hot red chiles, garlic, and salt is available in 6- to 8-ounce bottles in Asian markets. The Lan Chi brand, from Taiwan, is widely distributed.

STORAGE: It will keep indefinitely refrigerated in an airtight jar.

USE: Add a small amount to the oil when stir-frying to add a spicy tang.

CHILI SAUCE

CHINESE: *lar dew din* THAI: *prik dong*

Most of the countries of Southeast Asia have their own versions of this bottled spicy seasoning sauce—a mixture of hot, sweet, and salty flavors, made of chiles, onions, apricots, lemon, garlic, and vinegar. They vary widely, but most are very spicy, so they should be used sparingly. Lingham's Chilly Sauce from Malaysia, made of only sugar, chiles, vinegar and salt, is particularly fine.

STORAGE: Refrigerate after opening. It will keep indefinitely.

USE: Use chili sauce as a table condiment, a SAMBAL, or as a marinade or dipping sauce for skewered grilled meat. It is widely used in Singapore as a seasoning for rice, noodles, and prawn dishes.

CHIVES, CHINESE

OTHER: garlic chives

CHINESE: *gow choy* JAPANESE: *nira* or *asatuki*

Several types of Chinese chives are available—green-leaved, yellow-leaved, and chive flowers. All look like large, very flat chives, but the flavor is sharper and more pungent than the domestic variety. Sold fresh, by the bunch, in spring and summer months.

162

STORAGE: Wrapped in a paper towel and stored in a plastic bag in the crisper of the refrigerator, they will keep for up to a week. They become stronger in flavor the longer they are kept, which is not necessarily desirable. Chinese chives can also be frozen.

PREPARATION AND USE: Approximately ½ teaspoon of chopped chives per serving is the usual amount to use. If frozen, do not thaw before adding to cooked dishes. The leaves add robust flavor to noodle dishes, eggs, and stir-fry dishes. The flowers, which have a distinct garlic flavor, make an attractive garnish for many dishes.

CHRYSANTHEMUM GREENS

OTHER: *pyrethrum,* garland chrysanthemum, chop suey greens

CHINESE: *ting how chai* JAPANESE: *shungiku* or *kikuna*

Chrysanthemum greens are spicy flavored greens available fresh, by the bunch, in oriental produce markets in spring and summer. These are not the same as the American nursery variety. Try to buy them with the stems attached because these will last longer, and look for bright green, perky leaves with no flower buds. This green can be grown in containers—the seeds are available at nurseries that have oriental vegetables. Spinach and MITSUBA make good substitutes, though they lack the special fragrance.

STORAGE: Wrapped in damp paper towels inside a plastic bag and stored in the crisper of the refrigerator, they will keep for up to a week. The leaves will wilt on standing, but they will not lose flavor.

PREPARATION AND USE: Chrysanthemum greens develop a bitter flavor if overcooked so, if adding to stir-fry dishes (for spiciness), cook only a few minutes. For use as a vegetable, steam as you would spinach or other greens, just until tender; serve with a topping of ground toasted sesame seeds and soy sauce. These greens are a classic ingredient in the famous Japanese Sukiyaki (beef, vegetables, and yam noodles cooked in broth) and in MISO soup. Delicious in all kinds of soups.

CHUKA SOBA

See NOODLES, JAPANESE

CHUTNEY

OTHER: *chatni*

Chutneys are highly seasoned Indian relishes, either cooked or raw, usually made with fruits, vegetables, spices, sugar, and vinegar, or with any ingredient that is considered refreshing to the palate (mint, tamarind, etc.). They are most often freshly made in India to be served as a side dish with curried dishes. For the most part, those found in American markets are golden-colored mango chutneys often labeled "Major Grey's," which are more British than Indian, but which have become popular to serve with Indian food. Indian markets carry a well-rounded variety of bottled or canned chutneys, and occasionally carry their own fresh versions.

Indian cookbooks have recipes for chutneys of all descriptions: tomato, fresh mint, pineapple, coconut, onion, garlic. We urge you to experiment with them, using some of the more exotic ingredients described in this section of the book. Our recipe for MINT CHUTNEY appears under MINT in the HERBS, SPICES, AND SEASONING BLENDS section.

STORAGE: Bottled Major Grey-type chutneys can be stored indefinitely, like preserves, in the refrigerator. Storage of homemade chutneys will vary depending on the ingredients: the fresh will keep only a day or two; the cooked ones with sugar will keep a week or longer.

USE: Several different chutneys are taken in small amounts to add a palate-pleasing accent to a heavily spiced meal.

TOMATO CHUTNEY

For 2 cups

This recipe has been adapted from *The Cooking of India*, by Santha Rama Rau, one of the books in the Time-Life series on Foods of the World. The addition of currants or golden raisins was our idea.

1   pound fresh ripe tomatoes, chopped (do not peel)
1   cup malt or cider vinegar
1   cup JAGGERY (palm sugar)
1   medium onion, minced
⅓ cup currants or golden raisins
¼ cup chopped fresh coriander (cilantro or Chinese parsley)
2   teaspoons salt
¼ teaspoon ground cinnamon
3   cloves garlic, minced
1   small hot green chili, minced
½ cup MUSTARD OIL
2   tablespoons black mustard seeds

Combine all ingredients, except mustard oil and mustard seeds, in a 3-quart saucepan (not iron). Bring to a simmer and cook slowly for 5 minutes.
   Heat the mustard oil in a skillet just until it begins to smoke, and then add the mustard seeds—they will make a popping sound. Add the oil and seeds to the saucepan mixture and simmer, stirring often, for 10 minutes. Cool. Serve at room temperature.

TO PREPARE IN ADVANCE: This will keep, refrigerated, for up to 3 weeks. For best flavor, bring to room temperature before serving.

CILANTRO

See CORIANDER, in the HERBS, SPICES, AND SEASONING BLENDS section

CINNAMON

See HERBS, SPICES, AND SEASONING BLENDS section

CITRUS LEAVES

OTHER: dried keffir lime leaves

INDONESIAN: *djeroek poeroet* or *djeroek* MALAYSIAN: *limau purut*
THAI: *makrut* or *bai maikrut* (powdered)

Citrus leaves are the dried leaves of the wild keffir lime tree, and are sold in some Asian markets, either whole or powdered. Fresh lemon or lime leaves can be substituted.

STORAGE: As any dried herb.

PREPARATION AND USE: The leaves are used whole or ground to add a lemony flavor to many Southeast Asian curried dishes. One leaf is equal to ¼ teaspoon of the powder, and is the usual amount used for four servings.

CLAMS, DRIED

CHINESE: *gup guy* IN THE PHILIPPINES: *bagoon tahong*

These are dehydrated razor clams sold in packages by weight. They are not really a substitute for fresh clams as they have a strong distinctive flavor of their own.

STORAGE: They will keep indefinitely on the pantry shelf.

PREPARATION AND USE: Soak 1 hour in cold water. Wash to remove surface sand. Soak 8 hours in warm water, changing the water several times. Slit the hard portion, clean out the sand, and rinse. Use, whole or sliced, to flavor soups, noodles, and stir-fry vegetables. Because they have a strong flavor, they are best used with other ingredients, or in an aggressive sauce, such as Black Bean or Sweet and Sour. For most dishes, allow only 1 per serving.

CLOUD EARS

See MUSHROOMS, DRIED

COCONUT

OTHER: cocoanut

FRENCH: *noix de coco* INDIAN: *narial* ITALIAN: *noce di coco*
IN LATIN AMERICA: *nuez de coco*

Coconut comes from the hard-shelled seed of the coconut palm tree. This nut, unless cracked, will contain coconut water and coconut flesh. A good coconut should feel heavy and sound full of water when shaken. In unripe or green nuts, not generally available except in tropical areas where they grow, the flesh is gelatinous and can be scraped from the inside of the nut with a spoon. In a ripe nut, this gelatinous flesh has firmed into a fine-textured inside coating, ½" thick. When this flesh is removed and shredded it can be easily processed into coconut milk, coconut oil, coconut syrup, and various other familiar coconut products.

As a general rule, 1 coconut, weighing 1½ pounds, will usually yield up to 4 cups of flesh. To use fresh coconut, use an icepick to poke holes in 2 of the three "eyes," and then drain out the inside water (reserve for use as a storage liquid). To facilitate the removal of the thick, brown outer covering, place the whole coconut in a 400° oven for 20 minutes, let cool slightly and then, holding it over a large bowl, hit it all the way around with the back of a knife or cleaver until it splits open. At this point, taste the meat. It should have a fresh, sweet taste. If it tastes at all sour, it is rancid and should be discarded (and better to do it now than after you have gone to a lot more work). Use a screwdriver to chip away the heavy outer shell from the meat. The remaining thin brown skin can be scraped away with a vegetable peeler. The coconut pieces should then be washed and dried. To grate the coconut meat, use a food processor or blender. Process 1 cup of chunks at a time into fine pieces. It can also be grated by hand on a fine grater.

Frozen grated coconut, a convenience product that is excellent, can be purchased in some markets these days. Dried grated coconut, (or "dessicated," as it is referred to in many Asian cookbooks), the unsweetened type, found in supermarkets, is an adequate substitute for making coconut milk. Coconut jam is sold in some Asian markets, as well as various coconut SAMBALS, such as Serundeng, served as a condiment with Nasi Goring (an Indonesian rice dish) and with curries.

STORAGE: Store whole coconuts in the refrigerator until needed. The flesh, grated or in pieces, should be used as quickly as possible or frozen with the reserved water that was inside the coconut. Dried coconut can be stored indefinitely in an airtight container in a cool place.

PREPARATION AND USE: The coconut is one of the major food products of southern Asia, and is used as well in Latin America, Africa, and the Middle East. Its various products are used either by themselves, as flavoring ingredients, as aids to preparation, or as spoons and ladles (the shells). A Thai dessert, Songkaya, is a custard of coconut milk, PALM SUGAR, and eggs and is served in a coconut shell. In Bali, coconut is cooked with vegetables in a dish called Sayur Urap. In Ghana and Nigeria, it is added to rice. Grated coconut to be used as a chutney ingredient or curry condiment is especially delicious if it is toasted in a skillet or in the oven until golden, before it is used. We like it in the following Indonesian condiment.

SERUNDENG

For 3 cups

Coconut and spices are toasted together to use as a condiment or garnish for curries and rich dishes.

3 tablespoons peanut or vegetable oil
1½ cups dried, unsweetened coconut
1 medium onion, minced
1 clove garlic, minced
2 (½″) pieces fresh ginger, peeled and minced
1 tablespoon lemon juice *or* 1½ teaspoons TAMARIND
   soaking liquid
1½ teaspoons salt
1 teaspoon ground coriander
1 teaspoon ground cumin
1½ cups unsalted peanuts, roasted until golden

Heat the oil in a wok or large, heavy skillet. Add the coconut, onion, garlic, and ginger. Cook, stirring often, over medium heat until the coconut has turned golden. Add the remaining ingredients except peanuts and continue cooking over very low heat for 30 to 40 minutes, until the mixture is crisp. Cool. Add the peanuts.

TO PREPARE IN ADVANCE: This will keep in the refrigerator for up to 5 days. For best flavor, refresh by warming in a skillet or a low oven until crisp before serving.

COCONUT MILK/CREAM

INDIAN: *nariyal ka duhd* or *thengai pal* INDONESIAN: *santan* or *santan kental* (thick) MALAYSIAN: *santan* THAI: *kathi* (thin), *hua kathi* (thick)

Canned coconut milk and coconut cream are available in Asian markets and many supermarkets. They are excellent, and it is much easier to buy them than to make your own. They can be thinned with water to the desired consistency.

Do not confuse the water inside the coconut with coconut milk. Coconut milk or cream is an extraction made by steeping the freshly grated flesh of a ripe coconut in boiling water (or milk). The basic recipe is as follows:

Place 1 cup of shredded coconut in a blender or food processor fitted with the steel blade. Add 1 cup boiling water (or milk or cream if using dried coconut, which is not as rich) and blend for 5 minutes. Let steep for 30 minutes, then wring out in cheesecloth, squeezing out as much of the juice as possible. Repeat the process with the *same* coconut and *fresh* boiling water or milk to make a second pressing, which will be milder in flavor, but also useful. One coconut will yield 3 to 4 cups of coconut "milk." The coconut used to make the milk will have no flavor left at all, so it should be discarded. As the coconut milk cools, a coconut "cream" will rise to the top. This can be spooned off to use in recipes, or simply reblended into the milk.

STORAGE: Coconut milk spoils very quickly. It can be stored in the refrigerator for 2 to 4 hours; in the freezer, it will keep indefinitely. It is convenient to freeze in ice-cube trays and, when solid, transfer to a plastic bag for freezer storage.

USE: Both coconut milk and cream are used throughout southern Asia in the preparation of sauces, desserts, and beverages. It is commonly used as the liquid in Balinese and other curries, and is used in Rendang (beef in coconut milk), which is a popular dish in Sumatra. In most Southeast Asian countries it is used in the cooking of prawns or fish, which are often flavored with garlic and ginger. In Thailand, it is used to make a dessert custard steamed in a pumpkin shell, or cooked with glutinous rice and sugar to serve as a snack, and the thick type is used in Pork and Crab Sausage. It is the base for a Laotian soup with mushrooms and coriander, and for the Vietnamese Kilaw (marinated fish salad with sweet pepper).

In Latin America, coconut milk is used in many pastries and sweets and, in Puerto Rico, in the cooking of rice.

COCONUT OIL

This is a standard cooking oil in tropical Asia and elsewhere where coconuts are abundant. It is a highly saturated oil with a distinctive flavor and, for some people, difficult to digest. Any village in southern India, Ceylon, or Malaysia has its own *chekku* or oil press. Coconut oil is generally available throughout the United States in either liquid or solid form. If not available, substitute peanut oil.

STORAGE: Store in the refrigerator to prevent rancidity.

USE: It is generally used for frying, and particularly when the recipe calls for a coconut taste. It can withstand high heat very well (up to 480°). Use only the liquid oil in dishes that are to be served cool.

169

COCONUT SYRUP

This molasseslike, caramelized syrup of sugar and coconut juices is available in bottles in gourmet food stores. It is extremely sweet.

STORAGE: Refrigerate after opening.

USE: It is used to sweeten beverages and flavor desserts, and is poured as a condiment over a Thai appetizer salad that consists of seasoned meat or seafood wrapped in lettuce leaves.

COLTSFOOT
OTHER: butterbur

JAPANESE: *fuki*

This perennial plant has leaves that are flat and look like lily pads, and stems that resemble rhubarb stalks and, like rhubarb, only the stalks are edible. It can be found only occasionally in Japanese markets. It is similar to celery in flavor, and it is much easier to substitute celery than to seek out this rather rare item, which is always expensive. Look for only green in the stalks, no pink.

STORAGE: It will keep for up to a week in the refrigerator.

PREPARATION AND USE: Salt the stalks and let rest on paper towels for 10 minutes to draw out any bitter flavor. Then simmer in water to cover for 5 minutes, let cool, and strip away the fibrous strings. In Japan, this vegetable is sometimes wrapped up in very thin strips of raw beef to be charcoal grilled.

CORIANDER, FRESH
See HERBS, SPICES, AND SEASONING BLENDS section

CORN, BABY SWEET
OTHER: young corn, young sweet corn, miniature ears of baby corn

CHINESE: *yu mi sun*

These tiny whole ears of corn are available in jars or cans in Chinese markets or gourmet specialty shops. They are often used in stir-fry dishes to add color and texture. They look wonderful but, unfortunately, always seem to have a tinny taste.

STORAGE: After opening, store them in a jar in their own juice.

PREPARATION AND USE: Rinse well in cold water before using. The ears need only warming, so add them to stir-fry dishes shortly before serving. One or 2 per serving is usually adequate.

CORNSTARCH
OTHER: corn flour

This powdered corn product is sold by weight in boxes in every supermarket. Of all the starches (arrowroot, tapioca, lotus root) cornstarch has the most noticeable taste in bland foods.

STORAGE: It will keep indefinitely on a pantry shelf.

USE: Use as a thickener and glaze for sauces, as a coating for foods to be deep-fried, and as a binder with minced meat. To use as a thickener for soups and sauces, mix with cold water or chicken stock to a smooth paste. (Adding a drop or two of oil helps to prevent it from lumping.) Stir gradually into simmering liquid until liquid has thickened to desired consistency. Do not boil the sauce much after thickening because the cornstarch will "break" or lose its thickening power. To use as a coating for deep-frying, dredge fish or meat in cornstarch to coat. Juices will be sealed in and the coating will be light and crispy. Cornstarch produces a very light texture in cakes. To turn all-purpose flour into cake flour substitute 2 tablespoons cornstarch for 2 tablespoons flour in each 1 cup flour in the recipe.

CUCUMBER, SWEET
See MELON, TEA

CURRY LEAVES
OTHER: *kari* leaves

BURMESE: *pyi-naw-thein* INDIAN: *kitha neem* or *karipattar*
MALAYSIAN: *daun kari* or *karupillay* SINHALESE (Sri Lanka):
karapincha TAMIL (Ceylon): *karuvepila*

Kari is the Tamil word for "seasoned sauce" and the source word for the English "curry." Curry leaves are small, shiny, aromatic leaves that resemble bay leaves, but when bruised or crushed give off a strong curry fragrance. Outside of Asia, they are generally dried, and cannot be compared to the fresh ones so abundant in Asia. Do not buy them unless they have a strong aroma. Indonesian bay leaves, DAUN SALAAM, are a good substitute.

STORAGE: Store in an airtight container in a cool, dark place.

PREPARATION AND USE: In India, the leaves are usually heated in oil in the early stages of preparation of Sinhalese and Indonesian dishes, allowing 1 or 2 leaves per serving. When powdered in a grinder or blender they can be used in marinades or sprinkled on vegetables or yogurt.

CURRY POWDER/PASTE

See HERBS, SPICES, AND SEASONING BLENDS section

CUTTLEFISH, DRIED

CHINESE: *muck yee* JAPANESE: *ika*

This dehydrated, yellowish mollusk has 10 appendages and resembles a squid, but is thicker and larger. It is available in packages by weight. A seasoned and roasted variety is called *sarume*.

STORAGE: It will keep indefinitely on a pantry shelf.

PREPARATION AND USE: One of our sources tells us this can be eaten dried, like beef jerky, though we think for most people that would take some getting used to. Before cooking, soak overnight in cold water to cover. Rinse well and peel off any membranes. Cut away the cuttle bone. Cut into 1″ squares or into large strips. This is used primarily as a soup ingredient. *Sarume,* the roasted and seasoned type, is delicious as an accompaniment to cocktails.

DAIKON

OTHER: Japanese white radish, Japanese radish, giant white radish, icicle radish

CHINESE: *loh baak* JAPANESE: *daikon* VIETNAMESE: *cu cai*

One variety of this crisp white radish, a member of the turnip family, looks like a very large white icicle. Another variety is round, but both have green stems and leaves, and are available fresh in Japanese markets and many supermarkets nationwide. There are many varieties, all slightly different, but interchangeable in recipes. (The Chinese is slightly shorter and wider than the daikon of the Japanese, which is usually at least 12″ long.) This is one of the staple vegetables of the Japanese diet and is in season most of the year. It has a rather sharp, yet sweet, flavor. Look for firm white ones with healthy dark-green leaves. Smaller ones are usually moister and more delicate. A shredded and dried form, *kiri-boshi daikon,* is also available in plastic bags in Japanese markets. In many parts of Asia, this vegetable is considered to be an aid in the digestion of fats. In fact, its primary enzyme, *diatase,* is used commercially in digestion-aid tablets.

STORAGE: Fresh daikon, if tightly wrapped in plastic wrap, will stay fresh for up to 2 weeks in the refrigerator. It does not freeze well. Wilted ones can still be grated to use as a soup or salad ingredient or in the traditional dipping sauce for Tempura (deep fried shrimp, fish, and vegetables). Grated daikon can be stored in the refrigerator for up to 3 days, but cover it tightly, as it develops a stronger odor as it stands. Dried daikon can be stored for up to a month in a plastic bag in the refrigerator.

USE: The leaves, which taste a bit like cabbage, can be steamed to serve as a vegetable or added to salads, and are often pickled. The radish itself can be used raw, peeled and sliced to use in salads, or grated to use in soups and in slow-cooked dishes, and in dipping sauce for Tempura. Grated raw daikon should be wrung out in a towel or cheesecloth to prevent it from becoming soggy. We enjoy it prepared as we prepare celery root, with a *rémoulade* sauce. Dried daikon should be softened and cooked slowly in broth until it is tender. Serve it as a vegetable.

DAIZU

(DAH-ee-zoo)

"Daizu" is the Japanese name for dried soybeans (see SOYBEANS, DRIED, under BEANS).

DAL

OTHER: *dhal* or *dhall*

"Dal" is the Hindi name for grains, legumes, or pulses (seeds) that are split, like split peas, into two halves. The varieties, textures, tastes, and uses of dal seem to have no end, and it finds its way into almost every Indian meal as a recipe ingredient, a flavoring agent, or a thickener. It contains more protein than any other food available to India's lower classes, and dishes made of dal are especially popular in southern India, where the people are generally vegetarians. One variety should not be substituted for another in recipes because they differ enormously.

STORAGE: Store in airtight containers in a cool, dark, dry place. After cooking, let cool, and then store in an airtight container in the refrigerator for up to 3 days or in the freezer for up to 6 months.

PREPARATION AND USE: All dal should be picked over very carefully and rinsed well as they are usually adulterated with gravel. Unless dal is to be ground into paste, it can be cooked without presoaking. As with all beans, salt should be added only at the end of the cooking time. The different varieties of dal have as many flavors, and it is used for everything from pancakes to soups to desserts. As a basic accompaniment to an Indian meal, it is usually cooked with spices to a consistency of thin oatmeal and topped with some freshly fried spices to heighten the flavor. When served, it is either spooned over rice or placed next to the rice, or is placed in a small bowl to be served with Indian breads that are dipped into it. We repeat—do not substitute one variety for another in recipes. Cooking methods and times vary widely, so use each as the recipe specifies. The listings that follow are the most readily used dals:

ARHAR DAL

OTHER: pigeon pea, red gram, *toovar dal, tur dal*

The flesh of this rather large split pea, referred to sometimes as a pigeon pea, is a dull, pale yellow, and the pea itself has a slightly irregular shape. Arhar is the most commonly used dal of southern and western India. It has a fine earthy taste and is easily digested. Occasionally in western India, this dal is rubbed with oil to act as a preservative and to discourage the hatching of bugs. This oil will rinse away after several washings. Two cups of dried arhar dal make 6 servings. It should be covered and simmered slowly for 1½ hours, stirring often. Spices will depend upon the recipe used.

BLACK GRAM

OTHER: *mash dal*

This is a black-jacketed pulse (seed) about the size of a small pea which, when split to make dal, reveals a white flesh. It is a staple ingredient, grown and used throughout India and, though it is the most expensive pulse, it is considered essential to many northern Indian dishes. One variety of black gram, which sometimes has a green jacket, is often mistaken for its sister, the mung bean, or green gram which, when split, reveals a yellow flesh, but they are not interchangeable in recipes. Black gram does not require prior soaking but does take longer to soften in cooking than similar whole beans or dals.

Roasted, it is added as a flavoring to vegetarian curries. Soaked and ground to a fine paste, it is the usual basis for PAPPADUM (dal wafers) and Dosas (rice wafers). There is a totally white variety called *dhuli urd*.

CHANNA DAL

OTHER: Bengal gram

Channa dal, a type of small chick-pea, is the most common Indian pulse (seed). When split for use as dal, it is a bit more oval in shape than the common chick-pea of the Middle East, and has a nutty flavor. Some channa is sold roasted as a snack food. It can be ground into BESAN flour, used as a seasoning, or made into sweetmeats, but is most commonly used for Indian cooked and spiced dal. Canned CHICK-PEAS (see under BEANS in THE FOODS OF THE MIDDLE EAST section) can be substituted for cooked channa in most recipes.

LOMBIA

"Lombia" is the Indian word for BLACK-EYED PEA (see THE FOODS OF AFRICA for general information).

MASUR DAL

OTHER: *masoor dal,* red lentils

This type of lentil is one of the most easily recognized dals because it is bright orange, and is one of India's most common split legumes. As it cooks, the bright orange color turns slowly to a light yellow. Other lentils can be substituted, but keep in mind that, if not split, they will take longer to cook.

MUNG DAL

OTHER: green gram

When hulled and split this small yellow-fleshed bean with green, black, or brown jacket makes the most digestible of all dals. In Korea, it is made into Bindae Duk (bean pancakes).

RAJMA

OTHER: red-eye bean

These are split and hulled red kidney beans. They are sold in various sizes. Common kidney beans can be substituted.

URAD DAL

This dal, which is made from hulled and split, extremely fine-textured, small yellow urad kernels, is used for cakes, pancakes and is, sometimes, lightly roasted before using as a recipe ingredient.

DASHEEN

See TARO ROOT

DASHI

(DAH-SHEE)

OTHER: *dashi-no-moto* (brand name of an "instant" type of mix to make *dashi*), *hon-dashi* (*dashi* granules)

Dashi is a clear, fish-and-seaweed-flavored stock brewed from KOMBU (kelp) and KATSUOBUSHI (dried bonito shavings). It has a subtle flavor, and is the base of many Japanese dishes. *Dashi-no-moto* (literally "stock essence") is a combination of properly measured ingredients, packaged to use as an "instant" mix to make dashi. The time it saves is only in the measuring, not the brewing. Granules, called *hon-dashi,* are also widely available and have excellent flavor, though most of these "instant" products contain MONOSODIUM GLUTAMATE.

STORAGE: Store granules in the refrigerator after opening. It is best to brew dashi fresh just before use, though any that is left over can be stored for up to 3 days in the refrigerator. Do not freeze.

PREPARATION AND USE: Add 1 tablespoon of bonito shavings and a 2″ by 1″ sheet of KOMBU (or 1 tablespoon of dashi mix) to 1 cup boiling water. Let stand 5 minutes; then strain. To use the granules, add 1 teaspoon to 1 quart water. Any one of these methods makes a thin soup, which forms the base of Osuimono (clear soup) and Miso Shiro (miso soup), of dipping sauce for Tempura (deep-fried shrimp and vegetables), and of Oden (fish hot pot). If the dashi is to be used for dipping sauce, you may wish to make it double strength.

SHABU-SHABU

For 4 servings

Each diner cooks his own portion of thinly sliced meat and vegetables, stirring them about with chopsticks, and then dips them in sesame seed sauce.

176

A Mongolian hot pot is a good utensil to use, but any attractive pot with a flame under it can be used.

SESAME SEED SAUCE:
- ½ cup white sesame seeds
- ½ cup dashi
- ¼ cup Japanese soy sauce
- 2 tablespoons MIRIN
- 2 tablespoons SAKE
- 2 teaspoons sugar

- 2 pounds prime, well marbled, boneless beef or lamb
- 4 long onions, *or* 8 scallions, cut diagonally in 2″ lengths
- 1 pound Chinese cabbage (CELERY CABBAGE or *hakusai*—see CABBAGE, ORIENTAL), cut in 2″ slices crosswise
- 1 bunch CHRYSANTHEMUM GREENS, washed and trimmed of stalks
- 12 fresh, or dried and soaked, SHIITAKE mushrooms, stems removed, and cut in ½″ shreds
- 1 (2″) square of KOMBU, wiped clean and slashed
- 2 quarts dashi
  Optional: 4 small pieces wheat gluten (FU), soaked for 5 minutes in warm water, and squeezed of excess moisture

TO SERVE:
Cooked rice for 4 servings.

To make the sauce, toast the sesame seeds in a small skillet over medium heat, stirring constantly until golden. Place in an electric coffee grinder/spice mill or in an electric blender. Grind to a paste; then add the remaining ingredients. Place in 4 individual serving dishes, cover, and set aside.

Place meat in freezer for about 30 minutes until partially frozen to make it easier to slice in paper-thin slices using an electric slicer or serrated knife. The slices should measure approximately 6″ by 2″—if larger, cut into smaller pieces or they will be difficult to eat. Arrange on chilled serving plates with the prepared vegetables.

Wipe the kombu with a damp paper towel, slash it in a few places, and bring to a simmer in a casserole or Mongolian firepot with the 2 quarts dashi. Bring just to a simmer and remove the kombu. Bring pot to the table and light flame under it to keep broth hot. Each diner, provided with chopsticks or fondue forks, cooks his own meat and vegetables by dipping them into the pot, and then places them on rice in a small rice bowl. They are then dipped in sesame sauce before eating. We usually serve Miso Salad Dressing (see RECIPE INDEX) as a second dipping sauce. The broth should be skimmed of any surface foam from time to time and, garnished with sliced scallion, is served to sip from bowls at the end of the meal.

DATES, CHINESE

OTHER: jujubes, red dates

CHINESE: *hoong jo, tsa*

Chinese dates are small, dried, wrinkled red fruit, not actually of the date family, with an apple-prunelike taste. They are imported from northern China, and are available here in small packages by weight. They are also grown in the western United States and are occasionally available fresh in markets in the West. Fresh ones are brown when ripe. Other Chinese dates— black dates *(huk jo)* and white honey dates *(mut jo)*—are used in the same way, but are not nearly as common.

STORAGE: Fresh Chinese dates can be stored for 2 weeks in the refrigerator. The dried can be stored in the refrigerator or freezer indefinitely.

PREPARATION AND USE: Fresh Chinese dates should be dried on a rack in the oven at 120° to 150° for 3 to 4 days, turning them often. Use to add a subtle, sweet taste to braised or steamed dishes or soups. The usual amount specified is 3 dates per pound of meat, or 1 date per serving. They are often diced to cook with other ingredients. In some recipes cooked whole dates are split to scrape out the pulp, which is added to sauces. For sweet dishes, soak the dried dates for several hours in cold water before using. Candied dates are eaten as a confection.

DAUN PANDAN

OTHER: pandanus, screwpine

SINHALESE (Sri Lanka): *rampé* THAI: *bai toey*

"Daun Pandan" is the Malaysian and Indonesian name for a leaf with a floral flavor that is as popular in southeast Asia as vanilla is in America. It may occasionally be found in Asian markets, as may an essence made from a plant of the same family, called KEWRA. If not available, either omit, or add the tiniest amount of kewra.

STORAGE: Wrap airtight and store in a cool place for use within a few months.

USE: The leaves are used a great deal in the cooking of Sinhalese yellow rice and Indonesian Nasi Kunyit (glutinous yellow rice). They are added to the cooking oil with other spices before the rice and liquid are added to the pot.

DAUN SALAAM

OTHER: Indonesian bay leaves

Daun Salaam are aromatic Indonesian laurel leaves, larger than curry leaves, but almost identical in flavor. They are available only in dried form in Asian markets. Make sure they are fragrant when purchased. Two or 3 CURRY LEAVES can be substituted for each of these, depending on size, with little appreciable difference in flavor.

STORAGE: Use as soon as possible, as the flavor dissipates rapidly in storage.

PREPARATION AND USE: One or 2 whole leaves are the usual amount specified to add fragrance to Indonesian dishes of 4 servings. They can be ground to a powder to use in marinades or in the making of Indonesian cookies.

DRAGON EYES

See LONGAN

DRIED BLACK MUSHROOMS

See MUSHROOMS, DRIED CHINESE, BLACK OR "WINTER"

DUCK FEET

Dried, cured duck feet are considered a delicacy in China. You will find them in Chinese poultry shops. They are used most often for stock, but are also served stuffed or braised.

STORAGE: They will keep indefinitely on a pantry shelf.

PREPARATION AND USE: Wash; cover with boiling water and soak for 5 minutes; drain. Remove the skin, nails, and bones. For stock, split in two. They are usually cooked until tender to serve with OYSTER SAUCE or sweet-and-sour sauce as an appetizer, allowing 1 duck foot per serving.

DUCK LIVER, CURED

CHINESE: *opp geoke bow*

Dark-colored, hard duck liver wrapped in cured duck feet (which may be found in some Chinese poultry or meat markets) has a very strong meaty flavor. Smoked ham can be substituted.

STORAGE: Store up to 1 month in the refrigerator or indefinitely in the freezer.

PREPARATION AND USE: Soak 2 hours in cold water. Rinse and drain; then chop. It is most often steamed with minced pork.

DUCK, PRESERVED or SALTED

CHINESE: *lop opp*

Preserved salted duck has been pressed, partially cooked, and then immersed in peanut oil, or sun-dried. You will find them stacked, unrefrigerated, in Chinese markets.

STORAGE: They will keep indefinitely in a cool, dry place.

PREPARATION AND USE: Preserved duck is usually parboiled for 10 minutes, and then steamed with other ingredients until it is tender, about 30 minutes. Dice and use in small quantities to flavor soup, or serve atop rice.

DUCK, ROAST

OTHER: barbecued roast duck, plum duck (a variation with plum sauce marinade)

CHINESE: *shew opp*

Deliciously seasoned Cantonese-style roast duck is sold by weight, whole, or in pieces, at Chinese barbecued-meat markets or delis. They are an excellent buy because ducks raised for Chinese butchers are meatier than the Long Island variety sold frozen in supermarkets. A container of the cooking juices is usually given to the purchaser of this delicacy. You would be wise to take a large plastic bag with you when purchasing these, however, as the containers tend to leak. In our opinion, roast duck is one of the most versatile ingredients it is possible to have on hand for impromptu cooking.

STORAGE: Refrigerate for up to 3 days, or freeze right in its carton from the deli.

USE: Roast duck can be eaten cold, lukewarm, or hot. Cut in small pieces to use as a noodle or stir-fry ingredient. We like to serve it warm with PEKING PANCAKES (or with flour tortillas, in a pinch) in the style of Peking Duck with scallions and HOISIN, CHEE HOW, or other spicy Chinese barbecue-type sauce. It is very often diced to toss with green pepper, pickled scallions, and fresh pineapple to serve as a summer dish garnished with LITCHIS.

DUCK SAUCE

See PLUM SAUCE

DURIAN

Sometimes called the "king of fruit," these huge, spiky, and very heavy football-shaped fruit from Malaysia and Indonesia are often tied to the tree branches from which they hang to prevent them from falling and being bruised. The interior consists of soft, bananalike sections. It is not available fresh in the United States, but is sold canned in water, in sweetened syrup with AGAR, or as a preserve, in some Asian markets. It has a strong odor, which most people find offensive, but an excellent sweet taste and a creamy texture. Indonesians consider it to be an aphrodisiac.

STORAGE: After opening, store canned durian in a nonmetal container with a tight-fitting lid in the refrigerator for up to 5 days.

USE: In Southeast Asia, durian is cooked as a vegetable and used as a curry ingredient. Canned durian may be served as a fruit to accompany meals or as a simple dessert. It also makes an intriguing ice cream ingredient. The preserve is often served as a dessert.

EGGPLANT, JAPANESE

JAPANESE: *nasu*

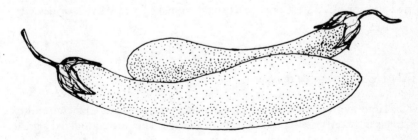

These small purple eggplants are smaller and sweeter than the American variety. They can be found in many fancy-produce shops, and in oriental and some Middle Eastern markets.

STORAGE: Store in a plastic bag in the refrigerator for up to 4 days.

USE: Sauté, deep-fry, or grill *robata*-style. These are superb for pickling.

EGG ROLL SKINS
See EGG ROLL WRAPPERS

EGG ROLL WRAPPERS
CANTONESE-TYPE: egg roll skins SHANGHAI-TYPE: spring roll wrappers or skins, Shanghai wrappers

These Cantonese-style wrappers, identical to the smaller WON TON WRAPPERS except in size, are pastry squares measuring 5″ to 8″, and there are approximately 24 wrappers in a pound. Shanghai-type wrappers come in 8″ rounds or squares, but are thinner, more delicate, and crisper after frying. Both are available in 2- to 5-pound packages in the refrigerator sections of Chinese markets and many of America's supermarkets. They are filled with a meat or vegetable mixture, and then deep-fried to serve as a snack with dipping sauces. A Vietnamese type, RICE PAPER wrappers, are sold in some Asian markets.

STORAGE: The wrappers will keep at least 5 days in the refrigerator. It is best to rewrap what you can't use in a short time and freeze for future use. Frozen wrappers eventually become brittle, so use them up within 3 months.

USE: Roll portions of your chosen filling in the wrappers, sealing with beaten egg yolk and fry in hot oil until crisp and golden brown. The detailed method is described in most Chinese cookbooks. This type of food is not served in China as part of a main meal, but as Dim Sum, or snack foods. The wrappers themselves, when cut into bite-size pieces, can also be deep-fried and sprinkled with powdered sugar to make an easy snack or dessert.

EGGS, QUAIL
JAPANESE: *uzura no tamago*

In large metropolitan areas, most Japanese markets and Chinese poultry markets now carry tiny speckled fresh quail eggs. They are considered a great delicacy, but their flavor is quite similar to chicken eggs. They are also available cooked, in cans or jars.

STORAGE: Store up to 2 weeks in the refrigerator.

USE: At sushi bars, fresh quail eggs are broken over sushi. Hardcooked and shelled they are served in soups or are breaded and deep-fried. They are sometimes served raw with DAIKON as a relish to accompany meals.

EGGS, SALTED OR PRESERVED

CHINESE: *harm don*

These duck eggs are cured in brine for 30 to 40 days, and sold individually. They must be cooked before eating (those purchased in Filipino markets are usually already cooked). The whites are very salty and the yolks are bright orange.

STORAGE: They will keep for up to 6 months in the refrigerator.

PREPARATION AND USE: One egg will serve 2 to 4, depending on how it is used. Unlike 1000 Year Old Eggs, these must be cooked. Remove the salt covering and wash. To hard-cook, simmer slowly for 60 minutes. (If you change the water several times during the cooking, the cooked egg will be less salty.) Cool until the egg can be handled; then shell and cut into quarters. These eggs can also be mixed raw with meats before cooking. In China, they are often hard-boiled to serve with rice and meat, which is called "poor man's dinner," or served as a garnish for Pork Patty (seasoned ground meat, which is steamed).

EGGS, SHRIMP

See SHRIMP EGGS

EGGS, THOUSAND YEAR OLD

OTHER: ancient eggs, century eggs, 100-year-old eggs, Ming Dynasty eggs

CHINESE: *pay don*

These are duck eggs that have been artificially aged with a black coating of lime, salt, ashes, and tea, and then cured for 100 days. The whites are firm and amber colored, the yolks are dark green. Used primarily by the Chinese as an appetizer or breakfast food but quite often served at banquets, they are favored for their very pungent, cheesy taste and smooth, creamy texture.

STORAGE: Wrap tightly in a plastic bag to store in the refrigerator for up to a month. They can be kept at room temperature for up to 10 days.

PREPARATION AND USE: These are very strongly flavored, so one egg will serve 2 to 4 as one of several appetizers. Soak in cold water for 1 hour until the black coating can be scraped away. Crack gently all over and remove the shell. Slice, or cut in quarters to serve as an appetizer. Often served with a dipping sauce of soy, vinegar, and minced fresh ginger root or with OYSTER SAUCE. Delicious accompanied by red (pickled) ginger (see GINGER, RED CANDIED) and pickled scallions (see SCALLIONS, PICKLED).

ELEPHANT EARS
See GOBO

FAGARA
See SZECHUAN PEPPERCORNS under PEPPERCORNS, OTHER in the HERBS, SPICES, AND SEASONING BLENDS section

FAVA BEANS
See under BEANS, in THE FOODS OF THE MIDDLE EAST section

FEIJAO
See BEANS, AZUKI

FISH, CHINESE DRIED OR SALTED

CHINESE: *hom yee*

This is a very common home-style ingredient sold by weight in oriental markets in many varieties. Domestic dried flounder has a much milder flavor than the imported varieties.

STORAGE: Tightly wrapped, this will keep indefinitely in a cool, dry place.

PREPARATION AND USE: This is strong-flavored, so it should be used very sparingly. Soak only the amount you will be using, in the same manner as for BACALAO (see THE FOODS OF LATIN AMERICA section). Drain well, and steam with ginger and minced pork or other meats until tender. In China, this is often served steamed as the main course for dinner, by itself or with available vegetables. Chinese dry salt cod *(tai tze)* is highly thought of in southern France to use as bacalao.

FISH, DRIED, SOUTHEAST ASIAN

OTHER: dried sprats, "silver fish"

INDIAN: *nethali* INDONESIAN and MALAYSIAN: *ikan bilis*
SINHALESE (Sri Lanka): *baal masso* THAI: *plasroi*

These tiny, sun-dried fish of the anchovy family are popularly used in Southeast Asian cooking. They are sold in small packets in Asian markets.

STORAGE: Wrap in dry paper towels in an airtight container and store in the refrigerator.

PREPARATION AND USE: This is not the moist salted anchovy popular in Europe. These tiny dried fish should be rinsed and have their intestines removed, then dried well on paper towels before frying to serve as a crisp accompaniment to rice and curried dishes, in the same manner as BOMBAY DUCK.

FISH MAW

See SWIM BLADDER, DRIED

FISH SAUCE

OTHER: fish's gravy

BURMESE: *ngan-pya-ye* or *ngapi* CAMBODIAN, LAOTIAN, AND VIETNAMESE: *nuoc nam* CHINESE: *yu lu* or *yu chiap* IN THE PHILIPPINES: *patis* THAI: *nam pla*

This thin, salty, brown or brownish-gray flavoring agent is as important an ingredient in Southeast Asia as soy sauce is in Japan and China. Many types are available in Asian markets and some are highly fermented, with a strong fish taste. Many cooks consider the Thai version to be the finest. Fish sauces from Vietnam and Burma are very strong in flavor, and not likely to appeal to Western tastes. When buying Vietnamese *nuoc nam,* such as Squid brand, look for the word *nhi* on the label, which indicates that it is of the highest quality. It is a good deal stronger in flavor than the Philippine *patis.*

STORAGE: This is best stored in the refrigerator though it will keep on the pantry shelf for up to 3 months.

PREPARATION AND USE: It is used sparingly to add a hint of seafood flavor to many Chinese dishes. The strong odor disappears when cooked. It is often preferred to soy sauce in Thailand and, in Vietnam, it is used as a table condiment and as a flavoring ingredient in almost every dish. It is used as is for a salad dressing. The Vietnamese add other seasonings, such as garlic, citrus juice, and chiles to it to make a SAMBAL-type dish called Nuoc Cham.

FIVE SPICE POWDER

OTHER: five heavenly spices, five fragrant spices, five fragrance powder, Chinese five spices

CHINESE: *heung new fun* or *hung liu* FRENCH: *cinq épices chinoises*

This fragrant and spicy flavoring is a combination of ground anise seed, star anise, clove, cinnamon or cassia, and Szechuan peppercorns, in approximately equal measure. Some blends contain cardamom or orange peel. It is available in plastic bags in Chinese markets and is becoming, these days, increasingly available in jars in supermarkets. Avoid any that smell only of anise.

STORAGE: As any ground spice.

USE: Use very sparingly when a fragrant anise flavor is desired. For most dishes, ¼ teaspoon is ample for 4 servings.

This spice is used a great deal in Chinese dishes, such as Fragrant Chicken, Five Flavor Pork, and in the cooking of duck. In Indonesia, it is used in cooking spareribs along with JAGGERY (palm sugar), and in Singapore it flavors Mah Mee (noodles with seafood and pork). It is the essential spice in Chinese "red-cooked" dishes, as demonstrated by the following recipe.

BARBECUED ROAST PORK

For 6 to 8 servings as a main
course or many servings as a flavoring

This is our method for making one of the most popular Chinese "red-cooked" dishes.

4   pounds pork shoulder
    Water
½   cup sherry or *shao hsing* (Chinese rice wine
6   quarter-sized slices fresh ginger
1   clove garlic, minced
1   cup light soy sauce
¼   cup rock sugar, light brown sugar, or honey
½   teaspoon five spice powder

Place the pork in a wok or Dutch oven. Add 3 cups water, sherry, ginger, and garlic. Bring to a boil and simmer 10 minutes, skimming any scum that rises to the surface. Add the remaining ingredients, cover, and simmer, turning the meat over from time to time, until it is very tender when pierced with a fork (about 2½ hours). Lift the meat to a warm serving platter, cover loosely with foil, and keep warm.

Skim fat from the top of the liquid in the pan. Lift out and discard the ginger. Simmer the sauce, uncovered, adding any accumulated juices from the platter, until it has reduced to about 1½ cups and is syrupy. Slice the meat as desired, and spoon sauce over it. Serve with rice and cooked mustard greens.

TO PREPARE IN ADVANCE: Wrapped tightly in plastic wrap and over-wrapped with foil, this will keep in the refrigerator for up to 4 days, or in the freezer for up to 4 months.

FU

(FOO)
OTHER: wheat gluten

CHINESE: *miiti* or *mien chen*

Fu is a spongelike substance made from gluten flour, which is high in protein and low in starch. In Japan, it comes in two varieties, *nama fu* (fresh fu) and *yaki fu* (literally "roasted" fu), which has been dried and puffs up when water is added. The latter, by far the most popular, is sold in cellophane packages in oriental grocery stores. It is one of the ingredients found in "instant noodle" packages. *Kohana fu* ("little flower" fu) is so named for its fanciful resemblance to a flower. Fresh or frozen fu is sometimes found in Asian markets. (See GLUTEN FLOUR for information on making fresh fu from gluten flour.)

STORAGE: Fresh *(nama fu)* is perishable and should be stored in the refrigerator for up to 3 days or frozen up to 6 months. Dry *(yaki fu* and *kohana fu)* will keep indefinitely in a tightly sealed container.

PREPARATION AND USE: In Japan, fresh fu is excellent for dishes cooked at the table, such as Sukiyaki. It is also occasionally served in MISO soup. Dried fu is used as a delicate, light garnish, like croutons, or is softened in warm water for 5 minutes, during which time it puffs up like spongy bread. The water is then pressed out and the fu is added to soups and noodle dishes. In China, balls of fresh or frozen fu are added to soups or stews, or are stuffed to make Dim Sum (snack foods).

FUKI
See COLTSFOOT

FUNGUS
See CLOUD EARS, under MUSHROOMS, DRIED

FUZZY MELON
See MELON, HAIRY

GADO GADO

This term is used for several things: a salad dressing, a prepared vegetable dish, and a condiment base, extremely popular in Indonesia, made from peanuts and hot ground chiles. Recipes for all may be found in Asian cookbooks. The paste may be found in Asian markets.

STORAGE: After opening, store in the refrigerator for use within a month or so.

PREPARATION AND USE: Mix to a paste with water. Serve as a condiment with rice and Indonesian vegetable dishes.

GALANGA ROOT

See HERBS, SPICES, AND SEASONING BLENDS section

GARAM MASALA

See HERBS, SPICES, AND SEASONING BLENDS section, under
SEASONING BLENDS

GARLIC

See HERBS, SPICES, AND SEASONING BLENDS section

GELATIN, CHINESE

See AGAR

GENMAI CHA

(GEHN-ma-ee CHA)

Though we have not listed all the world's teas in this volume because they are not truly "ingredients," we decided that Genmai Cha deserved a mention because of the rice kernels that are a part of it, and because it is so delicious with Japanese food. It is a combination of green tea and toasted rice kernels used to prepare a delicious, smoky flavored tea. It is sold in plastic bags in Japanese markets.

STORAGE: It will keep indefinitely in an airtight container at room temperature.

PREPARATION AND USE: For one cup, steep 1 tablespoon of Genmai Cha in water that is slightly below the boiling point for 30 seconds. Serve with Sushi (vinegared rice dishes) or other Japanese dishes.

GENUINE MALTOSE

See SUGAR, MALT

GHEE

Ghee is a rich, nutty tasting cooking medium, commonly used in India. The finest ghee, made with butter, is called *usli ghee*. It is prepared by slowly heating unsalted (sweet) butter over very low heat until all water is dissipated and milk solids have turned almond-brown and cling to the sides or have fallen to the bottom of the pan. The remaining clear liquid is then strained off and is sometimes combined with groundnut (peanut) oil. Because of the slow cooking and the resultant nutty flavor from browning the milk solids, this product is not exactly the same thing as clarified butter but both have the advantage over regular butter of taking high heat without burning. Ghee can be purchased in Asian or Indian markets in bottles or tubs.

Another type of ghee, which resembles solid shortening, is made from various oils. You can substitute your preferred cooking medium for ghee with the exception of olive oil, which is not used in Indian cooking.

STORAGE: Store in a cool place, preferably in the refrigerator, for up to 4 months.

USE: Ghee is the preferred cooking medium in Indian and Sinhalese and some Burmese dishes.

GINGER

See HERBS, SPICES, AND SEASONING BLENDS section

GINGER, PICKLED

Two types will be found in Japanese markets.

AMAZU SHOGA

(ah-MAH-zu SHO-gah)
OTHER: *hajikami su-zuke*

This is thinly sliced pink ginger pickled in sweet vinegar. It is available in small plastic tubs in the refrigerator sections of oriental markets and some supermarkets. *Hajikame* means "youthful blush" and describes the pale pink color of pickled young ginger. We have also seen it unrefrigerated in plastic bags and in jars. It has a wonderfully pungent spiciness.

STORAGE: After opening, it can be stored in its brine in the refrigerator for up to 6 months.

USE: This is popularly served with Sushi (vinegared rice) platters in Japanese restaurants to clear the palate between tastes of different types of raw fish. It can be used as a garnish for many Asian meals.

BENI SHOGA

This is vinegared ginger, similar to *amazu shoga,* but artifically colored bright red. Use and store in the same way.

190

GINGER, PRESERVED

CHINESE: *seen jeung*

Stems of young ginger preserved with sugar and salt are available in 20-ounce jars. *Mee Chun* is a widely available brand.

STORAGE: Unopened, it will keep up to 3 months on the pantry shelf; after opening, it will keep indefinitely in the refrigerator.

PREPARATION AND USE: Recipes for ginger ice cream, the perfect ending to a Chinese meal, abound in cookbooks. You can also dice preserved ginger to sprinkle over many desserts, or even use it to flavor a soufflé.

GINGER, RED CANDIED

OTHER: preserved red ginger

This is a sweet, pungent seasoning packed in jars with red syrup.

STORAGE: After opening, it will keep stored in the refrigerator indefinitely. It can also be frozen.

PREPARATION AND USE: Drain and dice to use very sparingly as a seasoning and garnish for chicken or fish dishes, fruit dishes, and salads. It colors a Chinese dish called Coral and Jade Prawns. In Thailand, it is the main ingredient of Ginger Sauce, which accompanies Whole Fried Fish. We always put some in Shredded Chinese Chicken Salad.

GINGER, SUBGUM

OTHER: mixed Chinese pickles, ginger pickles

CHINESE: *subgum jeung*

Subgum ginger is a sweet, tangy combination of preserved ginger, vegetables, fruits, and spices, and comes in jars and cans.

STORAGE: After opening, it can be stored in the refrigerator indefinitely.

USE: Serve as a relish just as it comes, or cook with spareribs and sweet-and-sour dishes.

GINKGO NUTS

(GING-ko or JING-ko)
OTHER: white fruit

CHINESE: *bok gwa, pai kuo* JAPANESE: *ginnan* (GEEN-nan)

A ginkgo nut is the buff-colored pit from the center of the inedible ginkgo fruit of the maidenhair tree, and is available dried, or packed in brine in cans. Occasionally, during the fall and winter months, ginkgo nuts are available fresh, in which case they must be shelled and blanched. They are used primarily as a garnish for soups and vegetable dishes and are highly prized for their meaty flavor and texture. They are a traditional food at Japanese weddings.

STORAGE: Opened canned gingko, drained of its brine, can be stored in a covered jar of water in the refrigerator for up to 2 weeks. Change the water every other day. Prepared fresh ginkgo can be stored in the same way.

PREPARATION AND USE: One to 3 gingko nuts per serving is the usual amount specified. If fresh or dried, they must be shelled with a nutcracker and then blanched. Pour boiling water over them and let soak for 5 to 10 minutes. Drain, let cool, and remove skins. Then stir-fry or deep-fry with batter, or skewer and roast to serve as a snack. They will turn bright green as they cook. Drain and rinse canned ones before using. They will add interest to soups, poultry stuffings, and vegetable stir-fry dishes. They are added to the fish baked in foil in the Japanese dish, Sakan No Gingami Yaki.

GLUTEN FLOUR

Gluten is a protein substance obtained from flour (usually wheat flour) from which all starch has been removed. It is made into gluten flour and, when formed into balls and precooked, is used as a chewy ingredient in Chinese and Japanese dishes. See FU.

STORAGE: Gluten flour, stored in an airtight container in a cool place, will keep for several months.

PREPARATION AND USE: Excellent instructions for making wheat gluten "from scratch" appear in Madhur Jaffrey's *World of the East Vegetarian Cooking* (Knopf, 1981). To make gluten balls, mix gluten flour with water in equal proportions and knead until smooth. Cover with a towel and let rest for 1 hour. Cut in pieces or form into balls and precook by boiling or steaming for about 30 minutes. The balls or pieces are then diced and added as a high-protein ingredient with a light, chewy texture to soups, stews, and many other dishes. Gluten balls are also stuffed and made into vegetarian Dim Sum (snack foods). If gluten is to be stir-fried, pieces should be simmered in water or stock for 15 minutes and then diced. Frozen gluten balls need not be thawed before use; just simmer in stock. Allow one ball per serving.

GOBO

(GOH-boh)
OTHER: burdock root, elephant ears

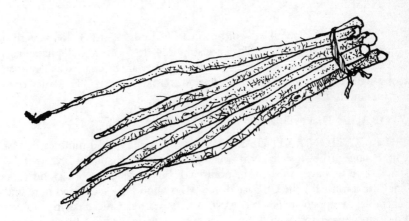

Gobo is a slender root vegetable with white flesh and an edible brown covering. It has a delightful, earthy flavor and crisp texture and is considered a delicacy. Buy young, tender ones only—those that are an inch or less in diameter. They will be about 18″ long. Canned gobo is not a good substitute because it loses much of its character in the canning process.

STORAGE: Do not wash away any of the attached soil until just before cooking. Store in paper wrapping, not plastic, in the crisper of the refrigerator for up to 2 weeks. It is best to use it as soon as possible after purchase because it loses much of its flavor on standing.

PREPARATION AND USE: One pound of gobo will serve 4 to 6, depending on its use. Scrub, and rinse it well, but do not peel. (Some people have sensitive skin and may wish to wear gloves to prevent an itching sensation.) It discolors quickly when exposed to air so drop it into water to which you have added some vinegar or lemon juice if it is not to be used immediately. It is most commonly cut into 2″ julienne strips and cooked briefly as a stir-fry ingredient, or it is used as a stuffing for meats to be grilled. Thin shavings cut from the tip (as if the cook were sharpening a pencil) are another way of cutting this root. The finest flavor lies closest to the skin. Drop the shavings into cold water as you work so they won't turn brown. Gobo is also good when diced, sautéed, and sprinkled with sesame seeds, sesame oil, and hot chili oil. (The same cooking technique used for strips of carrots in place of gobo is called *kimpira gobo*.)

GOLDEN LILIES

OTHER: lily buds, golden needles, tiger needles, tiger lily stems, lotus buds

CHINESE: *gum jum*

Golden lilies are wrinkled gold-brown lily buds, 2″ to 3″ long, with a delicate, slightly sweet taste. They are sold in 4- to 8-ounce cellophane bags and are quite nutritious and very inexpensive. They are often used as a garnish along with CLOUD EARS (see under MUSHROOMS, DRIED). The paler ones are the finest.

STORAGE: They will last on a pantry shelf indefinitely.

PREPARATION AND USE: Soak in cold water for 10 minutes or just a little longer (they lose flavor if oversoaked). Pinch off and discard any hard stems. Use to flavor meat, fish, poultry dishes, especially with cloud ears. They are a must for the Chinese dishes Moo Shoo Pork (seasoned pork and vegetables wrapped in PEKING PANCAKES), Braised Chicken with Golden Lilies, and Sweet and Sour Soup. They are popularly used in Korean cooking as well. In Vietnam, they are added to a stuffing used for squid made of cellophane noodles and pork. They are used also in sweet dishes. We like to knot each one in the middle to make it more decorative. Some Chinese cooks cut them in half crosswise for easier eating.

GOLDEN NEEDLES

See GOLDEN LILIES

GOOSEBERRY, CHINESE

See KIWI

GRAM

See DAL

GRASS JELLY

OTHER: Chinese-style gelatin

This is a black jelly made with seaweed and cornstarch, with a slight iodine flavor. It can be purchased in 19-ounce cans in Asian grocery stores.

STORAGE: Refrigerate after opening and use within a few days.

PREPARATION AND USE: It is cut in ½″ dice and served in sweet drinks and fruit salads throughout China, Burma, Cambodia, Singapore, and Malaysia. To make the sweet drink, put 1 tablespoon chopped grass jelly in a tall glass with 2 tablespoons GOLDEN SYRUP (see THE FOODS OF EUROPE section) and a few drops of ROSE WATER ESSENCE. Add crushed ice and fill with water or COCONUT MILK.

GRASS MUSHROOMS

See MUSHROOMS, STRAW

GREEN BEANS

See BEANS, LONG

GUAVA

See THE FOODS OF LATIN AMERICA section

HAAK

"Haak" is the Indian term for collard greens. They are usually seasoned with mustard oil and, like many vegetables, with just a bit of ASAFETIDA. For general information, see COLLARDS in THE FOODS OF REGIONAL AMERICA section.

HAIRY BRINJAL

See MELON, HAIRY

HAISEIN SAUCE

See HOISIN SAUCE

HAKUSAI

See CELERY CABBAGE, under CABBAGE, ORIENTAL

HAM, CHINESE

OTHER: gammon

CHINESE: *gum waw tuey*

This very salty red Chinese ham is seldom available in the United States. The best substitutes are Smithfield and Virginia hams, which are sold by the pound in Chinese markets and usually must be cooked (see HAMS in the FOODS OF REGIONAL AMERICA section), or Westphalian ham, which needn't be cooked. The redder the ham, the better.

STORAGE: Wrapped tightly, it will keep in the refrigerator for up to 6 months. It can also be frozen.

PREPARATION AND USE: Slice or cut into small pieces to use as a flavoring for soups, fried-rice, and many other dishes. In fine dice, it is used to garnish steamed dishes and is also scrambled with eggs. It is especially flavorsome in soup with mustard greens.

HASU

See LOTUS ROOT

HICHIMI TOGARASHI

See SEVEN SPICE SEASONING

HIJIKI

See under SEAWEEDS, DRIED

HIYAMUGI

See under NOODLES

HOISIN SAUCE

OTHER: haisein sauce, Peking sauce

CHINESE: *hoy sin jeung*

Hoisin is a thick, sweet, mahogany-colored sauce made from soybeans, flour, vegetables, chili, red beans, and red color, and is available in cans or jars. It has a sweet, pungent, and slightly garlicky taste, and is used as a seasoning or condiment. CHEE HOW is a slightly spicier variation of the same sauce and can be used interchangeably.

STORAGE: If canned, transfer to a glass jar with a lid. It will keep refrigerated indefinitely. If it thickens on standing, thin with sesame-flavored oil or peanut oil.

USE: Hoisin is used as is, or mixed with SESAME OIL or orange rind to spread on PEKING PANCAKES (or flour tortillas, in a pinch) to serve with Peking Duck, or Barbecued Duck or Pork. Used as a stir-fry ingredient, it adds an interesting flavor and depth to the other ingredients. Add to marinades for poultry. The Jade West restaurant in Los Angeles is known for its rather unusual hoisin-flavored version of Shredded Chinese Chicken Salad.

HOLY BASIL

See BASIL in the HERBS, SPICES, AND SEASONING BLENDS section

HOT CHILI OIL

See CHILI OIL

HUNDRED-YEAR-OLD EGGS

See EGGS, 1000 YEAR OLD

INDIAN MUSTARD

See MUSTARD GREENS, ORIENTAL

ITO-KEZURI-KATSUO

These shavings of dried bonito look like pink excelsior. You will find them in boxes in Japanese markets.

STORAGE: They will keep for several months in an airtight container at room temperature.

PREPARATION AND USE: These make a delightful garnish with a taste of the sea. They are sprinkled over soups or cooked dishes without presoaking.

JACKFRUIT

OTHER: *jak, jaca,* jakfruit

The fruit of the jack tree in southern Asia is one of the world's largest fruits, and is related to the breadfruit and fig. There are two types, one sweet and the other more acid. Its very size (up to 100 pounds per fruit) discourages importation, but it can be found packed in syrup in 20-ounce cans in those markets carrying Indian, Southeast Asian, or Latin American products.

STORAGE: After opening, transfer to a nonmetal container and store in the refrigerator.

USE: It is used in Asia when it's unripe as well as when it's ripe. When underripe, the pulp, seeds, and flower are used in curried dishes, or are baked and served as a vegetable. Ripe, it can be eaten raw, or sweetened and used in desserts. The large white seeds, when dried and roasted, taste a bit like chestnuts. Indonesian dishes in which it is used are Jackfruit With Coconut Milk, Jackfruit Salad, and Jackfruit With Beef.

JAGGERY

OTHER: *gur* or palm sugar

BALINESIAN: *gula bali* BURMESE: *tanyet* INDONESIAN: *gula Jowa*
MALAYSIAN: *gula Melanka* IN THE PHILIPPINES: *kaong*
SINHALESE (Sri Lanka): *hakuru*

Jaggery is an unrefined, very dark, strong-flavored sugar made from the juice of certain types of palm trees or from sugar cane. It has a delicious winey taste and aroma. When buying it in solid cake form, look for a piece that crumbles easily and is not rock hard. It also comes in a softer form, like a smooth nut butter, and can be found in jars in some Asian markets. To make an adequate substitute, combine 1 part molasses to 8 parts dark brown sugar.

STORAGE: It will keep indefinitely in a covered jar in a cool, dark place.

PREPARATION AND USE: The cakes must be grated before use. Jaggery is a major sweetener in India and throughout Southeast Asia. It is used especially in vegetarian curries, teas, milk, desserts, and gives KETJAP its specific sweet taste. In Sri Lanka, it is used for Jaggery Satay (skewered beef); in Indonesia, it is essential to the flavor of Peanut Sauce which is served with grilled meats or a topping for cooked vegetables.

INDONESIAN PEANUT SAUCE

For about 1½ cups

This is best made with freshly ground roast peanuts, but crunchy peanut butter makes a convenient and very acceptable substitute.

½   cup peanut oil
½   cup minced onion
2   cloves garlic
1   teaspoon dried SHRIMP PASTE *(trasi or blacan)*
4   teaspoons jaggery
1   tablespoon lemon juice
1   tablespoon dark soy sauce *or* 2 teaspoons KETJAP MANIS
12 ounces roasted peanuts (or crunchy peanut butter)
1   teaspoon SAMBAL *oelek (or* HARISSA)
½   teaspoon salt
    COCONUT MILK *or* water, to thin to the desired
      consistency

Heat the oil in a wok or skillet. Sauté the onions until transparent; add the garlic. Add and sauté the shrimp paste, breaking it up with the back of a spoon. Add the jaggery, lemon juice, and soy. Remove from heat and cool.

In a blender or food processor, grind the peanuts until nearly smooth, leaving a few larger chunks for texture. When the mixture in the skillet is cool, add the ground peanuts, sambal oelek, and salt. Taste, and add more salt or sambal oelek if needed.

This can be used as a spread for Satays, or as a relish just as it is. It can be thinned to the desired consistency with coconut milk or water to use as a sauce for dipping, and even as a salad dressing.

TO PREPARE IN ADVANCE: The paste can be stored in the refrigerator for up to a week.

JELLYFISH, DRIED

CHINESE: *hoy jit pay*

Jellyfish from which the tentacles have been removed are dried in opaque shriveled discs and sold in oriental markets by weight, in sheets approximately 24″ square and ⅛″ thick. They are also sold shredded and heavily salted in refrigerated packets. Dried jellyfish has a bland flavor and crisp texture and is not expensive.

STORAGE: The completely dried variety can be stored in the pantry indefinitely. The refrigerated form will keep for 2 to 3 weeks in the refrigerator.

PREPARATION AND USE: In China, this is usually soaked in cold water until soft, and then shredded to serve as part of an appetizer platter of cold seafood and vegetables. The refrigerated variety is heavily salted, so it must be soaked for 2 to 3 hours in several changes of cold water.

JUDA'S EAR

See CLOUD EARS, under MUSHROOMS, DRIED

JUJUBES

See DATES, CHINESE

JUNSAI

(JOON-sa-ee)
OTHER: water shield

This tiny water plant, related to the lotus, is sold in glass bottles in Japanese markets. It is considered a great delicacy in Japan.

STORAGE: It will keep in the refrigerator for up to 3 months.

PREPARATION AND USE: In Japan, it is often sliced thin and added to soups to give a delicious flavor and texture.

KALONGI

See HERBS, SPICES, AND SEASONING BLENDS section

KAMABOKO

(Kahm-Ah-BOH-Koh)
OTHER: fish cakes

Kamaboko is a loaf (sometimes referred to as a "sausage") of steamed, pureed fish often bound with potato starch. It usually has a white outer surface, less often pink-tinted, and is available in 6″ logs in the refrigerator section of Japanese markets. It is often packed on a cypress wood plank, in which case it is called *ita-kamaboko. Chikuwa* (CHEE-ku-wa) is a tube-shaped relative. Both varieties are also sold canned.

STORAGE: Store it in the refrigerator for up to a week, using it as soon as possible. It is sometimes sold frozen, but we do not recommend that kind, as the texture suffers dramatically.

PREPARATION AND USE: Slice and serve hot or cold with or without a dipping sauce. Kamaboko is served in Japan as a New Year's dish, as part of Oden (fish hot pot), in soups, and sometimes as an appetizer with WASABI. *Chikuwa* is delicious when stuffed with cucumber and then steamed and grilled. Both are sliced to serve as a garnish for UDON (noodles in broth—see NOODLES).

KAMPYO

(KAHM-pyoh)
OTHER: kanpyo

Kampyo are the long, beige, ribbon-like shavings of a gourd, dried to use as a garnish and to tie foods to be steamed. These strings are available in 1-ounce plastic bags in Japanese markets.

STORAGE: After opening, they will keep indefinitely stored in an airtight container on the pantry shelf.

PREPARATION AND USE: Wash and knead with salt; then soak for 20 minutes until softened or as long as overnight. It is used as a filling for seaweed wrapped Sushi, called Norimaki-zushi, and for garnishing. It is also used as an edible string to keep fragile food compositions from falling apart, such as the unusual mushroom-stuffed Chicken Kiev (see ENOKI-DAKE, under MUSHROOMS, FRESH).

KANTEN

See under AGAR

KARASHI

(kah-RAH-shee)
OTHER: Japanese mustard powder

Karashi is a powdered mustard similar to the English and Chinese varieties, sold in Japanese markets in cans or tubes. It is extremely strong-flavored. Substitute Chinese or English powdered mustard.

STORAGE: As any spice.

PREPARATION AND USE: Mix with water to a paste, cover, and let stand 10 minutes to develop flavor. Serve with Oden (fish hot pot), stuff into the holes in LOTUS ROOT before making Tempura, or serve with KAMABOKO (steamed fish cakes).

KATAKURIKO

(kah-tah-KOO-ree-koh)

This is a white, powdered potato starch. It is similar to arrowroot and cornstarch and is used in Japan as a binder for sauces or to give a very crisp coating to foods that are deep-fried. It is available in Japanese markets in plastic bags. It is moderately priced and tasteless.

STORAGE: It will keep indefinitely in an airtight container on the pantry shelf.

PREPARATION AND USE: Use in the same proportions as ARROWROOT POWDER (it is a more powerful thickener than cornstarch). Mix into a paste with water and stir gradually into simmering liquid to be thickened. Do not boil long after adding, or it will "break." To coat foods to be deep-fried, dredge them in the powder and let stand for 3 minutes before frying. They can be fried with that simple coating, or further coated by dipping into beaten egg and PANKO (bread crumbs).

KATSUO-BUSHI

(kah-tsu-OH-boo-shee)
OTHER: *hana-gatsuo* or *kezuri bushi*

These are dried pinkish flakes of bonito used in making DASHI (fish stock). They are available in boxes or plastic bags in Japanese markets. Be sure to buy these in a shop that has a large turnover, because the flakes lose flavor on standing.

STORAGE: They will keep up to 6 months in an airtight container in a cool place.

USE: The flakes are occasionally used as a garnish for vegetable dishes, but are primarily used along with dried kelp to make DASHI.

KEMIRI NUT

See CANDLENUT

KETJAP MANIS

OTHER: *ketjap benteng*

Ketjap Manis is a syrupy, sweet, Indonesian soy sauce, much thicker, darker, and sweeter than Chinese or Japanese soys. The Indonesian word "ketjap" means a sauce added to food for extra flavor, and is the root of our word "catsup" (sometimes spelled ketchup). This is sometimes available in Indonesian markets. A passable substitute can be made by combining 1 cup Chinese or Japanese soy sauce with ⅓ cup molasses, 3 tablespoons dark brown sugar or JAGGERY (palm sugar), and ¼ teaspoon each ground coriander and cayenne. Simmer until sugar is melted.

STORAGE: It will keep indefinitely in a cool, dry place.

USE: Use as a table condiment or an ingredient in Indonesian recipes, and especially as a marinade for grilled foods. Interestingly, our domestic catsup, which is not the same thing at all, is often used as an ingredient in Chinese dishes.

KEWRA

OTHER: screwpine

Kewra is an aromatic essence made from the flower of a tree in tropical Asia. This perfume is used as a flavoring throughout Asia, and it is possible to buy it infused in either water or syrup in Asian markets.

STORAGE: It will keep indefinitely in an airtight container on the pantry shelf.

USE: Kewra is very strong and only a few drops are needed for most recipes. On holidays and other special occasions, kewra and rose essences are combined in sweet dishes, and it is also used to flavor an Indian rice dish called Biriani. It is added as a special ingredient to Sinhalese curries.

KIKURAGE

See CLOUD EARS, under MUSHROOMS, DRIED

KIMCHI

Kimchi is Korean pickled cabbage, in all its countless variations. Before winter closes in on the country people of Korea, the families get together and jointly put up quantities of fermented vegetables—onions, radishes, garlic, chiles, and cabbages—and bury the results in the ground, retrieving them throughout the winter as needed. And they need some with every meal and generally in several varieties. A large selection of kimchi is generally available in oriental markets.

STORAGE: It will keep indefinitely in a closed container in the refrigerator.

USE: At least one is served as a relish with every Korean meal.

KINAKO
(KEE-nah-koh)
OTHER: soy flour

Kinako is flour made from soybeans and is high in protein. It is sold in natural-food stores.

STORAGE: We always store this in the freezer because it spoils so quickly (within a few weeks, if at room temperature).

USE: Kinako has a rather strong flavor. Add it sparingly to your favorite bread recipe to add more protein. In Japan, the most popular use of this product is in making confections. Kinako sweetened with sugar is loved by children, who sprinkle it over steamed white rice.

KINOME
(KEE-noh-meh)

These aromatic, new green leaves of the prickly ash, the same tree that gives us SANSHO (see PEPPERCORNS, SZECHUAN in the HERBS, SPICES, AND SEASONING BLENDS section) are only rarely available in Japanese produce markets in the spring. They have a very fresh, somewhat minty, flavor.

STORAGE: Store in damp paper towels in the crisper section of the refrigerator and use as soon as possible (within a week).

PREPARATION AND USE: This is used as a garnish for broiled fish, in soups or in salads. Elizabeth Andoh in her superb book *At Home With Japanese Cooking* (Knopf) says, "Just before eating rinse the leaves lightly, then gently pat them dry. Open your hand, lay several leaves in the center of your open palm, then slap down on them with your other hand. This will release the unique aroma of the leaf." This is a favorite garnish with Japanese chefs, who use it in just about any dish.

KISHIMEN

See under NOODLES

KIWI

OTHER: actinidia, Chinese gooseberry

This delicious fruit has a fuzzy brown skin and a bright green interior with tiny black seeds. It is widely available in American supermarkets today and, at this writing, is the darling of the Nouvelle Cuisine of France. A fruit native to China, it was introduced to New Zealand in 1906.

STORAGE: If ripe, store in the refrigerator and use as soon as possible. Unripe fruit can be ripened very quickly by placing it in a brown paper bag overnight with a ripe apple or banana.

PREPARATION AND USE: Kiwi makes a delicious dessert as is, and is also used as a garnish for tarts and ice creams. Take care not to touch the skin to your lips—it may cause blisters. The skin is sometimes used as a meat tenderizer.

KOBE BEEF

This is a superb grade of beef of unbelievable tenderness from cattle raised in Kobe. The cattle are fattened on beer and massaged daily with SAKE, resulting in highly marbled beef of excellent flavor. It is rarely available in this country because, at last report, it cost more than $50 a pound in Japan!

KOCHU CHANG

Kochu Chang is a very "hot" bean paste made with red pepper and fermented soybeans, with garlic added occasionally, available in Korean or Chinese markets.

STORAGE: Kept in an airtight container in the refrigerator, this should last indefinitely.

USE: Use moderately, as a flavoring addition to stews, soups, and sauces.

KOHLRABI

OTHER: turnip cabbage, knol-kohl

CHINESE: *dai toe choy* FRENCH: *chou-rave* GERMAN: *Kohlrabi*
ITALIAN: *cavolrapa*

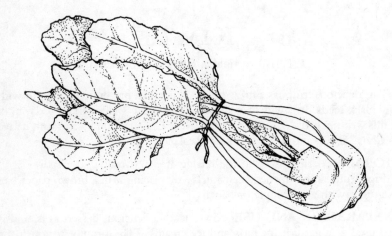

A light green or purplish, round root vegetable of the cabbage family that looks like a turnip that has grown above ground. It is available fresh, with stemmed leaves, or preserved, Szechuan-style with chiles, in cans or jars. The fresh variety has a crisp, mild, turnip-like taste. You will find them in markets year 'round, with the peak of their season from late April to early October. Look for small ones as they are especially choice.

STORAGE: Fresh kohlrabi can be stored in a brown paper bag inside a plastic bag in the crisper of the refrigerator for up to a week. The preserved variety, once opened, can be stored in a glass jar for several months in the refrigerator.

PREPARATION AND USE: The bulb, if young and tender, can be used as a salad vegetable with a vinaigrette dressing or mayonnaise, or eaten raw with salt and pepper. Or, it can be peeled, if the outer skin is tough, and then diced or sliced and steamed or boiled until tender, buttered, and seasoned with a bit of grated nutmeg. Allow 1 per person. The tender leaves are delicious, but are seldom used by American cooks. Try them steamed or in soups. Use the preserved kohlrabi as a spicy condiment, or as a seasoning in stir-fry dishes, steamed dishes, and soups.

KOMBU

See SEAWEED, DRIED

KONNYAKU

(KOHN-nee-yah-koo)
OTHER: yam cakes, alimentary paste (both misleading), shiru konnytaku
(white, refined), kuro konnyaku (dark, unrefined)

Konnyaku is a gelatinous cake made from a yam-like tuber known as
"Devil's Tongue," and is available canned or in tubs in the refrigerator sections
of Japanese markets. It is the solid form of SHIRATAKI noodles (see NOODLES),
and the thicker form of the shirataki noodles known as *ito-konnyaku*. You
will see this cake in white (refined) and black (unrefined) forms. It is purported to be an excellent digestive and is often prescribed for its cleansing,
soothing (and nonlaxative) effect on the stomach.

STORAGE: The canned form will keep indefinitely on the pantry shelf. The
refrigerated form will keep for several weeks if unopened. After opening,
cover either kind with cold water and store in the refrigerator for up to 5
days.

PREPARATION AND USE: Bring to a simmer in water to cover and
then drain and cool. Cut into cubes or strips to cook with meat or vegetables
in a seasoned broth. This is an essential ingredient in Oden (fish hot pot).
Slices are often served with dipping sauces as a vegetarian snack. In noodle
form, it is used in Sukiyaki.

KRUPEK

OTHER: shrimp slices

CHINESE: *har peen* INDONESIAN, MALAYSIAN, and THAI: *krupek*

These reddish-pink, orange, green, or yellow chips look like potato chips
but are made of dried shrimp, egg white, and tapioca powder and are sold
in cellophane bags, boxes, or tins in many Asian markets. They have a delicate,
sweet, seafood taste and must be deep-fried before serving. They are especially
popular in Thailand.

STORAGE: They will keep a month or longer on the pantry shelf if tightly
sealed. (Keep in an airtight container in the refrigerator for long storage.)
After deep-frying, they will keep well for 2 to 3 days in an airtight tin.

PREPARATION AND USE: If exposed to humidity, shrimp chips don't puff well when fried. Damp ones can be oven-dried at 200° for 10 to 15 minutes, and then stored or fried. Deep-fry 4 to 6 at a time. They will sink to the bottom of the oil, triple in size, and rise to the surface in a matter of seconds. These are served as an accompaniment to many dishes, such as Gado Gado, or as an appetizer, accompanied by a SAMBAL for dipping.

KUMQUAT

CHINESE: *gum quot, jin jin* JAPANESE: *kinkan*

Kumquats are the small (about an inch long), oval, shiny orange fruit of the Fortunella genus, closely related to citrus. They have a pungent, orange-ginger taste. The skin of fresh kumquats is sweet, but the center is tart. Fresh ones, available from November through February—should be plump and firm, not shriveled. Two other types are available—those preserved in syrup, and the preserved and sugared ones available for only a short time before and after Chinese New Year. They are used in Japan as a condiment and garnish.

STORAGE: Fresh ones will stay fresh for up to 2 weeks in the refrigerator. Those in syrup can be kept indefinitely on the pantry shelf (where they may darken on long standing), or in the refrigerator. The preserved and sugared ones can be stored for up to 6 months in a covered jar in a cool, dark place.

PREPARATION AND USE: Fresh kumquats make a delicious addition to fruit salads and can be used as a garnish for many dishes. When preserved kumquats are used as an ingredient, they are usually cut in half lengthwise, the seeds are scraped out, and the rind is slivered. When served as a sweetmeat after a meal, they are sometimes rolled in sugar.

KURI NO KANRO NI

(KOO-ree-noh KAN-roh-NEE)
OTHER: preserved chestnuts in syrup

These are very similar to the French preserved chestnuts, *marrons glacés,* (see under CHESTNUTS, CANNED, in THE FOODS OF EUROPE section), but are much less expensive, and are available in jars in oriental markets.

STORAGE: Unopened, they can be stored indefinitely on the pantry shelf, though they darken slightly on standing. After opening, they can be stored in the refrigerator indefinitely. We learned, to our dismay, that they begin to ferment very quickly at room temperature.

PREPARATION AND USE: A confection in themselves, they are often served with cha (green tea). Drained, they can be used to garnish desserts or served as *marrons glacés*.

KUZU
OTHER: *kudzu*

Kuzu is a powdered starch, high in minerals, made from the kuzu vine, and can be found in Japanese markets and health food stores, usually in 4-ounce boxes. It has a lumpy appearance when raw, but it makes beautiful translucent sauces. It is even more expensive than ARROWROOT POWDER .

STORAGE: It will keep indefinitely in an airtight container.

PREPARATION AND USE: Sift to remove the lumps. Use kuzu as you would arrowroot powder, but use only half as much. Mix to a paste with 3 parts water for thickening sauces, especially sweet ones. Use it also to coat foods for deep-frying when you wish an extra-crispy white crust.

LARD
OTHER: leaf fat, leaf lard

FRENCH: *graisse de porc* GERMAN: *Schweinefett* ITALIAN: *strutto*
SPANISH: *manteca de cerdo*

Pure leaf lard is the finest kind of this soft white pork fat. It is highly prized in China to lend a rich flavor to stir-fry dishes, particularly vegetables. Contrary to public opinion, it is highly digestible. As it increases in price throughout the world, its popularity is waning, and it is being replaced by vegetable oil. Because Americans have become suspicious of highly saturated fats, it is not used much in the United States.

STORAGE: Store fresh leaf lard for up to 1 week in the refrigerator, 2 to 3 months in the freezer. Rendered lard will keep in a covered container in the refrigerator for up to 3 months.

PREPARATION AND USE: To obtain about 1½ cups of rendered lard, cut 1 pound fresh leaf lard into 1″ pieces. Place in a saucepan with ¾ cup of water and bring to a boil. Boil it uncovered for about 20 minutes until the water has boiled away and all the fat has cooked out of the solids. Then strain, pressing all the fat from the crackling. Pour into a jar to store in the refrigerator. It is never used in cold dishes because it congeals at room temperature, and is seldom used for deep-frying because it makes the coating soft, not crisp. Foods cooked in lard do not reheat well.

LEAF FAT

See LARD

LEAF LARD

See LARD

LEAF MUSTARD

See MUSTARD GREENS, ORIENTAL

LEMON GRASS

OTHER: citronella root

BURMESE: *zabalin* INDIAN: *sera* INDONESIAN: *sereh* LAOTIAN: *Bai mak nao* MALAYSIAN: *serai* THAI: *takrai* or *da kri* VIETNAMESE: *xa*

This is a tall, gray-green grass with an aromatic, scallionlike base and is one of the most important Thai flavorings. It is available in the produce sections of most Asian markets. Also available is a dried variety, labeled *daun sereh,* which must be soaked, or ground to a powder. Powdered lemon grass can be found in natural-food stores and herb shops where it is used as an herb tea.

You can grow it in your garden from seed, or by planting purchased lemon grass that still has roots attached. To do the latter, place in a jar of water until roots develop further, and then transplant into a large pot where the plants will have room to spread sideways. Harvest by cutting into the soil and through the roots, taking only the number of stalks you need.

Lemon verbena, in equal quantity, or 2 strips of lemon peel (or 1 teaspoon finely grated lemon rind) per stalk, make acceptable substitutes.

STORAGE: Fresh lemon grass can be kept up to 2 months in the crisper of the refrigerator. Store the dried as you would any herb and use as soon as possible.

PREPARATION AND USE: Use the portion of the white base up to the place where the leaves begin to branch, discarding the gray-green leaves. Bruise the fresh stalks to release their flavor. Soak dried grass in warm water for 2 hours and then chop before adding to recipes. If you use the powdered type, add it directly to recipes, substituting 1 teaspoon for each stalk of fresh. Lemon grass is very widely used in Thai, Malaysian, and Vietnamese cooking.

It flavors Malaysian Chicken Curry with Coconut, Vietnamese Chicken with Lemon Grass, Chiles and Peanuts, and Burmese Dry Pork Curry with Tamarind.

LILY BUDS
See GOLDEN LILIES

LITCHEE
See LITCHI

LITCHI
OTHER: lychee, litchee

CHINESE: *lay jee*

Litchis are tropical fruit from the tree of the same name, and are grown in China and in the United States. They are available in three forms: Fresh (in markets only in July and very expensive), dried, and canned in syrup. The fresh fruit has a crimson skin or hull, which makes it look like a strawberry, but which is removed to expose a silky, white, jellylike flesh and a single seed. The taste is sweet and distinct. The dried fruit (known as litchi nuts or Chinese nuts) has a shriveled brown flesh similar to a sweet raisin. Canned litchis are excellent.

STORAGE: If you love fresh litchis, buy them in generous amounts when you see them. They do not need to ripen and will keep for up to 3 weeks under refrigeration or indefinitely in the freezer. Dried litchis will keep indefinitely in the refrigerator or freezer.

PREPARATION AND USE: Fresh and canned litchis are delicious served with poultry, shellfish, and pork, especially in sweet-and-sour sauce. Chilled litchis make a refreshing dessert when combined with other fruits in season. We use them to garnish our favorite curried turkey salad. Dried litchis are usually eaten as an out-of-hand snack, like raisins.

LONGAN
OTHER: lungan dragon eyes

CHINESE: *loan ngon*

This is a cherry-sized, round, yellowish fruit with a soft, smooth center and a pit. Fresh longans are very rare, but two other forms are widely available. Dried longans are sold in boxes by weight. Canned and pitted longans in syrup are the most commonly available. They have a delicate, refreshing taste. They are closely related to the litchi, but are smaller and considered inferior in taste and texture.

STORAGE: Dried longans will keep indefinitely in the refrigerator or freezer. After opening, canned longans will keep in a nonmetal container in the refrigerator for up to 4 days.

USE: In China, they are often used to flavor sweet soups. They can be used in sweet-and-sour dishes, as a garnish with many dishes, and as a dessert. They are interchangeable with litchis in recipes, though not as flavorful.

LOQUAT
OTHER: Japanese medlar

CHINESE: *pay pa gwor*

The loquat is a downy, yellow-orange, subtropical fruit similar in size and texture to the apricot. Its juicy yellow flesh has a delicate taste and crisp texture. Fresh loquats are very rare because they must be tree-ripened and do not travel well, but they are available either dried or preserved in syrup.

STORAGE: Dried loquats will keep indefinitely in the refrigerator or freezer. After opening, canned will keep in a nonmetal container in the refrigerator for up to 4 days.

USE: These are peeled to eat fresh. In Japan, they are commonly served with chicken dishes or as a dessert.

LOTUS LEAVES
CHINESE: *leen gnow yip*

These large leaves, measuring 11″ to 14″ in diameter, are available in Asian markets. They are used fresh to add both flavor and fragrance to food, and dried to wrap foods such as glutinous rice to create a Tamale-like dish to serve as Dim Sum (Chinese snack foods).

STORAGE: Tightly wrapped, these will keep indefinitely in a cool, dry place. They can also be frozen.

PREPARATION AND USE: Soak overnight or for at least 1 hour in warm water until soft. Use as a wrapping for Beggar's Chicken or various rice stuffings. They are often used to wrap fish or pork that is to be steamed.

LOTUS PASTE

OTHER: lotus jam

Lotus paste is made of sweetened cooked lotus seeds and is available in cans in oriental markets. It is stored and used in the same manner as sweetened BEAN PASTE, RED, and as a filling for tea cakes.

LOTUS ROOT

OTHER: water lily root

CHINESE: *leen ngow* JAPANESE: *renkon, hasu* INDIAN: *bhain*

Fresh lotus root is an ivory or brown-colored, smooth stalk vegetable that looks a great deal like sugar cane. It is available fresh from July to February. It grows in 6″ increments and is crisp in texture with a taste not unlike coconut. Hollow spaces, which run the length of each root, form a snowflake-like mandala pattern when the root is cut crosswise. These roots can grow up to four feet long and 30 inches in diameter. Look for firm, unblemished roots. If bruised on the outside, it is likely that they will be discolored inside. Besides fresh, three other forms are available (but are not interchangeable in cooking): Chinese dried slices, sugared slices, and canned slices. The canned variety is very much inferior to the fresh.

STORAGE: Fresh lotus root will keep 2 to 3 weeks in the crisper section of the refrigerator, but once the root is cut it should be used within a few days. Dried lotus root and sugared lotus root will keep indefinitely on the pantry shelf. Canned lotus root, after opening, will keep for 1 week in the refrigerator in water, if the water is changed every other day.

PREPARATION AND USE: Fresh lotus root must be peeled with a potato peeler. Cut it crosswise or diagonally into thin slices. If not cooking it immediately, place it in acidulated water until needed to prevent darkening. Dried lotus root should be soaked in acidulated water as well for an hour or until soft. Canned lotus root needs no cooking, merely warming.

Deep-fried slices, which have the mandala-like holes filled with hot mustard or *wasabi,* are delicious as a snack like potato chips, and are often part of a Tempura platter. Lotus root is a very popular ingredient to use in place of potatoes in soups, stews, and in vegetarian dishes, but is probably at its most exquisite when pickled. (To pickle, cook the slices just until tender, then marinate in 4 parts vinegar to 1 part sugar and season with salt to taste.)

It is a tradition in Japan to serve it as part of the New Year's feast. In India, fresh lotus root is used in chutneys, and is also boiled, mashed, and mixed into meatballs, or mixed with lentils and curry spices. In Vietnam, it is cooked with pork in a soup flavored with fish sauce. To retain the crisp texture of fresh or canned lotus root, stir-fry only briefly—if overcooked it becomes starchy in texture.

LOTUS ROOT FLOUR

CHINESE NAME: *ou fen*

This starch, available by the ounce, is used as a thickener in China (much like cornstarch) for soups and sauces, or to give a particularly crispy coating to foods to be deep-fried. It browns more quickly than other starches.

STORAGE: It will keep indefinitely on the pantry shelf.

PREPARATION AND USE: As a thickener for soups and sauces, mix with cold water to a smooth paste. (The starch turns purple when combined with liquid, but don't let that worry you.) Stir gradually into simmering liquid until thickened to the desired consistency. Do not boil the sauce much after thickening because it will "break" (lose its thickening power). Use it to dredge foods for deep-frying that you want to brown quickly to retain their crispness.

LOTUS SEEDS

CHINESE: *leen jee* VIETNAMESE: *hat sen*

Lotus seeds are traditionally served in tea at weddings in China because they are a symbol of fertility. They are expensive and are considered a great delicacy. When very young and fresh, they look like peanuts with green skins, and are eaten raw as a fruit or are cooked, pickled, or made into Lotus Jam (see LOTUS PASTE). Dried lotus seeds, which have dark brown skins like filberts, are found in Chinese markets, and must be blanched and peeled before eating. Canned seeds need no preparation.

STORAGE: Store fresh and dried lotus seeds in the refrigerator. Use them as soon as possible because they lose some of their delicate texture on long standing. Canned lotus seeds, once opened, can be stored in the refrigerator for up to 4 days.

PREPARATION AND USE: Blanch dried lotus seeds until tender; then use a toothpick or needle to push out the bitter green heart. Lotus seeds are traditionally used to flavor desserts or sweet soups, and are often made into lotus paste to use as a pastry filling for Moon Cakes. They can also add interest to poultry dishes. The dried seeds are used in Chinese slow-cooked dishes and desserts. In India, they are popped like popcorn.

LUMPIA WRAPPERS

OTHER: Shanghai-style egg roll wrappers

FILIPINO: *balat ng lumpia*

Lumpia is a Filipino version of egg roll. Thin pancakes or "skins" made of either flour and water, or cornstarch, eggs, and water, are sold frozen in many Asian markets. A 1-pound package contains approximately 32 wrappers.

STORAGE: They will keep frozen for up to 6 months.

PREPARATION AND USE: Lumpia wrappers can be filled in several ways and are eaten either without cooking, or deep-fried. If they are to be eaten without cooking, a lettuce leaf is placed over the wrapper and the desired filling is placed in the center of the leaf. The filling can be as simple as a salad, or a mixture of cooked meat (pork is preferred in the Philippines) and vegetables. Three sides of the wrappers are folded in around the filling and it is eaten in the hand. The most prized filling in the Philippines is HEARTS OF PALM *(ubod)*—see THE FOODS OF LATIN AMERICA section. Fried lumpia are similar to Chinese Spring Rolls, but more delicate. The lettuce leaf is omitted and the wrapper completely encloses the filling. They are fried in 375° oil for only 2 to 3 minutes until they are golden and crisp. Both types are served with a slightly sweet sauce.

LUNGAN

See LONGAN

LYCHEE

See LITCHI

MACADAMIA NUT

OTHER: Queensland nut

Although this sweet and creamy golden nut is native to the coastal tropical forests of northeastern Australia, it has, within the last 100 years, been successfully transplanted to Africa, South America, and to Hawaii, which is now the largest exporter. It is is named after its discoverer, a Dr. MacAdam. It can be found in most supermarkets and is very expensive.

STORAGE: We prefer to store nuts in the freezer to prevent rancidity.

PREPARATION AND USE: In Indonesia, the macadamia nut is used as a substitute for CANDLENUT in certain dishes. They are also a dessert nut and, when lightly salted, are a popular appetizer. We like to use macadamia nuts in Asian stir-fried dishes, and in place of almonds for sautéed fish "almandine."

MACE

See HERBS, SPICES, AND SEASONING BLENDS section

MAIN FUN

See under NOODLES

MALDIVE FISH

SINHALESE (Sri Lanka): *umbalakada*

Pulverized dried fish of several species peculiar to the Maldive Islands, southwest of Sri Lanka, are used in many Sinhalese dishes. You will find them in Indian markets. If not available, substitute KATSUO-BUSHI (bonito flakes) that have been finely ground.

STORAGE: As any other spice.

PREPARATION AND USE: Maldive fish needs to be ground fine, so use a mortar and pestle or a blender until you have achieved a fine powder. This fish powder is used in making various SAMBALS, and as a seasoning where fish flavor is desirable.

MALTOSE, GENUINE

See SUGAR, MALT

MANDARIN ORANGE

See MIKAN

MANGETOUT

See SNOW PEAS

MANGO

Mangoes are the magic ingredient in Major Grey's famous chutneys, and the unripened or green mangoes are the basis of many homemade Indian chutneys and pickles. For general information on fresh mangoes see THE FOODS OF LATIN AMERICA section. Dried mango strips are sold in Philippine markets. They are also ground into powder called AMCHOOR. As a mango ripens, its greenish skin will begin to turn yellow and develop red spots.

STORAGE: Since mangoes ripen rather quickly, store them in the crisper of your refrigerator if you don't want them to ripen. Use firm, green mangoes in recipes that call for them unripe. To ripen mangoes, store them in separate, small paper bags in the warmth of your kitchen until they turn yellow and develop red spots; then eat, or refrigerate for up to 3 days.

PREPARATION AND USE: Always use firm, unripe mangoes to make chutney (ripe ones are far too soft). Green ones are also used in curries and to make pickles.

Ripe mangoes make delicious desserts and snacks. See THE FOODS OF LATIN AMERICA section for directions.

MANGOSTEEN

Mangosteen is a large, tender, white-fleshed berry, widely cultivated in Southeast Asia. The berry is surrounded by a tough, reddish-brown rind and its orange-like segments are usually eaten with the fingers. It is seldom found in the United States.

217

MASALA

Masala is an aromatic seasoning for sauces made of spices ground together. Any number of spices may be combined. Masalas are made by cooks throughout India for their own use. If moistened with vinegar, coconut milk, or yogurt, they are called "wet." Various masalas will be found in Asian markets, especially GARAM MASALA (see HERBS, SPICES, AND SEASONING BLENDS section, under SEASONING BLENDS).

MELON, BITTER

OTHER: balsam pear, bitter gourd

CHINESE: *foo gwa, mo gwa*

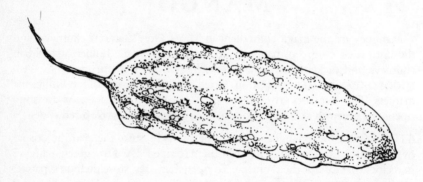

Bitter melon is a yellowish-green fruit that looks like a very wrinkled cucumber with bumpy skin. Fresh ones, which are available from April through September in most Asian markets, are picked while they are still green because it is then that they are most delicate in flavor. As they ripen, they turn yellow, and even orange, and become progressively stronger in flavor. The seeds are melonlike, and the firm flesh has a pungent aroma and a bitter, almost acrid, taste, which is due to the high quinine content (which takes some getting used to). Asians believe that bitter foods cleanse the blood and prevent all types of disease.

Bitter melon is also available dried and canned, but neither of these is anywhere near as good as the fresh.

STORAGE: Store fresh melons in the refrigerator for up to 1 week. Canned melon, once opened, can be stored in the refrigerator in a nonmetal container for up to 3 days.

PREPARATION AND USE: Do not be concerned if bitter melon turns a bit brown during cooking. Use sparingly, especially if you are trying it for the first time. One melon will be enough for 6 or 8 servings as part of another dish.

Trim off and discard the stem ends, cut in half lengthwise, and scoop out the spongy center along with the seeds. You may peel it or not as you wish. Slice or dice; then either sprinkle with salt and drain on paper towels for 20 minutes, or soak in salted water for up to 1 hour, in order to rid it of some of its bitterness.

Use as a stir-fry ingredient (especially tasty in a sauce of black beans with garlic) or add to dishes containing meat as the main ingredient. It can also be steamed or added to soups, or stuffed with pork or seafood and topped with OYSTER SAUCE. A Philippine dish, Ampalaya, pairs it with pork, prawns, and a substantial amount of garlic. In China, it is often stuffed with fresh prawns to be served with Black Bean Sauce.

MELON, HAIRY

OTHER: fuzzy melon, hairy brinjal

CHINESE: *jit gwa* or *mo gwa*

Hairy melon is a green or yellow, cylindrical, squash-shaped melon with a dull-colored, hairy skin, and is available during the summer months. It has a fleshy, soft interior and a delicate, bland taste that takes on the flavors of the foods it is cooked with.

STORAGE: Hairy melon can be kept for up to 2 weeks in the crisper section of the refrigerator.

PREPARATION AND USE: Peel, and then slice or dice to use in Cantonese-style soups, stir-fried, or braised dishes.

MELON SEEDS

CHINESE: *gwa tzee*

These dried watermelon seeds are available in red or black by the ounce in plastic bags. They have a rather sweet, nutlike taste and are very popular in China where they are expertly cracked with the teeth to reach the delicate inner kernel.

STORAGE: They will keep indefinitely on the pantry shelf.

USE: In China, these are served as a snack food or used as a dessert ingredient.

MELON, SILK

See OKRA, CHINESE

MELON, TEA

(When preserved: **Chinese pickle, pickled cucumber, preserved melon shreds**)
OTHER: sweet cucumber

CHINESE: *cha gwa*

Tea melon is a 2" long, cucumber-shaped fruit with a sweet, delicate taste and a very crisp texture. It is available only preserved in honey, with or without ginger flavoring, in jars or cans. Its name comes from the fact that it turns a dark tea color during the preserving process. It is also available pickled in soy sauce. It is not sold fresh in the United States.

STORAGE: Both preserved forms can be stored indefinitely in the refrigerator if transferred to a glass jar with a tight-fitting lid.

PREPARATION AND USE: Both of the preserved forms are most often served cold as condiments or pickles, but are also used as seasonings for steamed meat or fish, salads, and soups. Chop fine and sprinkle over ingredients to be steamed.

MELON, WINTER

CHINESE: *doan gwa*

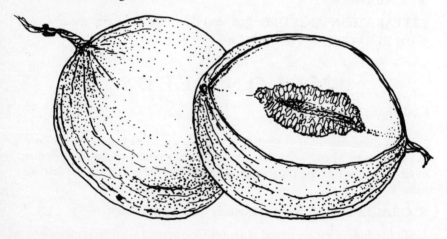

Winter melon is a large oval or round vegetable of the squash family with pale green skin covered with "bloom" (a frostinglike coating) and snowy white, porous flesh. It has a delicate, subtle, somewhat zucchini-like taste and is never eaten raw. In its most glorious form, a half melon with its pulp removed is ornately carved, then steamed, and used as a tureen or serving bowl for the well-known Winter Melon Cup served at banquets. In its fresh form, it is available whole (some weigh 20 pounds or more) or cut into pieces. Just before and after Chinese New Year it is available in cellophane bags as a sugared confection.

STORAGE: Whole melons can be stored, without any kind of wrapping, in a cool, dark place for up to 3 months. Once cut, it can be stored in the refrigerator for up to 6 days with the cut edges covered with plastic wrap.

PREPARATION AND USE: This is never eaten raw. Remove the rind and scrape out the seeds. Slice or dice the flesh to use as a soup or stir-fry ingredient, especially with chicken or shellfish. Most comprehensive Chinese cookbooks have detailed instructions for making Winter Melon Cup with its decorative container, and for a simpler soup in which the melon is combined with ham and snow peas. In Vietnam, it is cooked in chicken broth to make a soup flavored with fish sauce.

MIKAN

(MEE-kahn)
OTHER: Japanese orange, winter tangerine

Mikan is a citrus fruit of the same family as the tangerine and the mandarin orange but less "orangy" in flavor and firmer in texture than either. It is available fresh during the winter in Japan, but is rarely found fresh in the United States. Fresh ones should feel heavy for their size. Mikan is available in sections, canned in syrup, in many oriental grocery stores. Friends from Japan tell us that in Japan they are sold on the famous "bullet train" (Shinkansen), frozen, out of season, and that they are a wonderful treat.

STORAGE: Store fresh mikan in the refrigerator for up to 1 week. Canned mikan, once opened, can be stored in its syrup in the refrigerator for a week or longer.

USE: The traditional Japanese dessert is fruit, and so mikan is often served as is. In fancy Tokyo restaurants, the hollowed out rind is sometimes filled with dessert ice or cold seafood dishes, though California oranges are more often used because they are now more highly prized than mikan in Japan.

MING DYNASTY EGGS

See EGGS, 1000 YEAR OLD

MINT

See HERBS, SPICES, AND SEASONING BLENDS section

MIRIN

OTHER: "sweet rice wine for cooking"

Mirin, a sweet, syrupy rice wine, is an essential Japanese ingredient, and is used to flavor perhaps half of all Japanese dishes—as a seasoning, as a cooking ingredient, and as a glaze for cooked dishes. You can make an acceptable substitute by cooking together equal parts of sake (or even sherry or white wine) and sugar to make a syrup, though several Japanese cooks have advised us to simply substitute 1 teaspoon of sugar for each tablespoon of mirin called for.

STORAGE: It will keep stored on the pantry shelf for several months or, refrigerated, indefinitely. After using, be sure to wipe the neck of the bottle with a damp cloth before recapping or the cap will stick and be difficult to remove later.

USE: Delicious any time a sweet-wine taste is desired in cooking. To name but a few: a basic ingredient in Teriyaki sauce; also used in broth for SOBA and UDON noodles (see under NOODLES).

MISO

(MEE-soh)
OTHER: bean paste, soybean paste

Soy paste combined with yeast is allowed to ferment for several months to create this delicious seasoning and soup base. Several varieties of miso are available in tubs, jars, or plastic bags in the refrigerator sections of oriental markets and many metropolitan supermarkets. *Shiromiso,* or "white" miso, is made with rice. It is pale beige and slightly sweet. *Akamiso,* or "red" miso, is made with barley and can actually be quite brown in color and has a much stronger flavor.

STORAGE: This is very high in salt content so it can be stored for a short time on the pantry shelf. It is best to refrigerate it though, and use it up within 3 months because it loses flavor on standing.

PREPARATION AND USE: Miso should be softened by thinning it with warm DASHI and whisking until smooth, otherwise it may not dissolve smoothly. (A blend of the white and red misos will produce a pleasing combination.)

Miso soup is often served for breakfast in Japan, and is used as a first course in most Japanese restaurants, with a garnish of cubed bean curd and sliced scallions. It is popularly used in marinades and to season sauces. It is delicious mixed with MIRIN and used as a topping for Dengaku, foods that are skewered and charcoal-grilled.

It can be thinned to use as a salad dressing and is also used as a base for making pickles.

In Vietnam, red miso (called *misu*) is made into a sauce with tomatoes, onion, garlic, and vinegar to serve over fish, and it is also used in Korean dishes. We like the following salad dressing made from white miso.

MISO SALAD DRESSING

For ⅔ cup, or about 4 servings

Use this as a dressing over mixed green salads, cooked shellfish, or as a dip for raw vegetables. It makes an excellent sauce for steamed vegetables such as asparagus, broccoli, or cauliflower.

¼ cup light, mild miso *(shiromiso)*
2 teaspoons sugar
½ teaspoon dry mustard powder
2 tablespoons rice wine vinegar or white wine vinegar
¼ cup mayonnaise
2 teaspoons thinly sliced scallion greens

Combine miso, sugar, mustard, and vinegar in a small saucepan (or glass measuring cup if using microwave oven). Heat, stirring, until smooth. Remove from heat and cool. Mix in mayonnaise. Scallions can be mixed in or sprinkled on top, depending on use.

TO PREPARE IN ADVANCE: This will keep, covered, in the refrigerator, for up to a week; longer, if scallions are omitted.

MITSUBA

(MEE-tsoo-bah)
OTHER: trefoil, honewort

Mitsuba is a delicate and aromatic leafy green of the parsley family, and is sold in bunches in oriental produce markets most of the year. It looks a bit like fresh mint. Look for strong stems and fresh young leaves.

STORAGE: Rinse, and wrap in paper towels. Place inside a plastic bag and store in the crisper section of the refrigerator for up to a week.

PREPARATION AND USE: Mitsuba loses flavor if cooked too long. It is often served in Osuimono (clear soup) as well as in Miso soup, and in Chawanmushi (a custard-like soup with shrimp). It makes a delicious garnish for broiled fish, pork, etc., and is often served as a vegetable. It is often used in Shabu-Shabu, the traditional country dish (see our recipe under DASHI).

MOCHI

(MOH-chee)
OTHER: *omochi,* glutinous rice cakes

Chewy cakes made of cooked glutinous (sweet) rice that has been pounded or processed to a paste. Mochi can be made at home or purchased in Japanese markets, either freshly made by the store or packaged in squares or sheets. They should feel soft.

STORAGE: Freshly made mochi will keep in the refrigerator for a week. Tightly wrapped and frozen, they will keep for up to 4 months. Thaw completely before using.

PREPARATION AND USE: If hard, soften 6 to 8 hours in cold water. To serve, charcoal-grill them, basting them with MIRIN or SAKE, during which time they will double in size and develop a delicious crust. They are sometimes simmered in soups such as Ozoni, the traditional soup served for New Year. Leftover dried mochi can be flaked and deep-fried to serve as a snack.

MOCHIKO

See RICE FLOUR

MO-ER

See CLOUD EARS, under MUSHROOMS, DRIED

MOLASSES, CHINESE BEAD

OTHER: brown gravy sauce

CHINESE: *ju yow*

This thick black sauce, available in cans or bottles, is used primarily as a coloring agent. It has a pungent aroma and a bittersweet taste.

STORAGE: It will keep indefinitely on the pantry shelf.

USE: Small quantities are used to add color to such specialties as Peking Duck and Cantonese Fried Rice. This is an interesting ingredient for the American cook to use for darkening and flavoring sauces and to give an appetizing color to those pale foods cooked in microwave ovens.

MONOSODIUM GLUTAMATE

OTHER: M.S.G., Accent (brand name)

CHINESE: *wei ching* or *mei chen* JAPANESE: *Aji-no-Moto, Vetsin* (brand names)

These white crystals, which are an extract of various grains and vegetables and have no real flavor of their own, are used in Chinese and Japanese cooking to enhance flavors. The Chinese names mean "essence of taste." This product has come under fire lately because, when used in excessive quantities, it has unpleasant side effects for some people. We do not recommend its use at all. If ingredients are first-rate, there is no need to enhance flavors with chemicals. Most of the authors of our best known Chinese cookbooks claim that it should be used only sparingly, if at all, because overuse tends to make all the flavors in a dish taste the same. A Japanese salt *aji-shio* is coated with this product.

STORAGE: It will keep indefinitely on the pantry shelf.

USE: Not recommended. It is a sodium-related product, so it is not safe to serve to those on sodium-restricted diets.

M.S.G.

See MONOSODIUM GLUTAMATE

MUNG BEAN FLOUR

This very smooth flour is made from mung beans and is available in Asian markets in white, pale pink, or pale green.

STORAGE: It will keep indefinitely in an airtight container in a cool place.

USE: This pastel-colored flour is used primarily in the making of Asian confections and desserts. Like other starches, it clears and becomes translucent as it thickens. If not available, use ARROWROOT POWDER or cornstarch in equal amounts.

MUSHROOM SOY
See SOY SAUCE, CHINESE

MUSHROOMS, DRIED

There are a number of delicious dried mushrooms sold in Asian markets, and they are a very important part of many Asian recipes. They are packaged and sold by the ounce.

STORAGE: Dried mushrooms will keep indefinitely in an airtight container in a cool pantry. Once soaked, drain and wrap in plastic wrap for refrigerator storage of up to 5 days.

BLACK OR "WINTER" MUSHROOMS
OTHER: Northern mushrooms, fragrant mushrooms

CHINESE: *doong gwoo, leong goo* MALAYSIAN: *cindauwan* THAI: *hed hom*

Dried Chinese and Japanese mushrooms are probably the most versatile of all oriental ingredients because their distinctive, meaty flavor combines well with any other kind of ingredient. There are several varieties of Chinese dried mushrooms and it is not always easy to tell the difference between them. Winter (or black) mushrooms are large with rather flat caps; the Northern have rounder, speckled caps. As a general rule, the larger, light-colored ones are the most tender and flavorful. There is one expensive variety, somewhat flower-shaped, that is often used for banquets. All have a distinctive, meaty flavor and are available by weight in simple cellophane bags or beautifully arranged in gift boxes in Asian markets. All are expensive, and the finest quality ones are very expensive.

PREPARATION AND USE: All dried mushrooms require soaking to bring them back to their original shape. The first step is to rinse very well in cold water to remove any sand. They can be soaked in hot water or stock for 30 to 90 minutes, depending on their size. (Some cooks prefer to soak them 8 hours or longer in cold water, saying they retain more flavor with this method.) Squeeze out excess moisture from the soaked mushrooms and cut away the woody stems before using. Usually the soaking liquid, minus any grit, is used in the recipe for additional flavor. Save the stems and soaking liquid (if not otherwise used) to add flavor to stocks.

Small mushrooms are generally cooked whole; large ones are shredded. They can be braised or simmered, or added to stir-fry dishes or soups. In Vietnam, they are steamed with chicken to serve with CELLOPHANE NOODLES (see NOODLES).

CLOUD EARS

OTHER: tree ears (large and thick), wood ears, dried black fungus
THE ALBINO FORM: Juda's ears, fungus silver ears, white fungus,
snow mushrooms

CHINESE: *mo-er* or *wun yee, sewt yee* (the albino form) JAPANESE: *kikurage, shirokikurage* (the albino form) INDONESIAN: *kuping jamu* MALAYSIAN: *kuping tikus* THAI: *hed hunu*

These extraordinary fungi look like dried, black (or black and ivory) chips when they are purchased. When they are soaked in water, they expand to five or six times their original size, and look almost like double petunias. They are available in two sizes: large and thick, or small and thin. The small ones are best and are most expensive. Silver ears or white fungus (the albino form) are most expensive and are considered a health tonic.

PREPARATION AND USE: Pour boiling water over them and soak for 30 minutes. Rinse and cut away the woody stem. (Large ones, the tree ears, may have a tough "eye" in the center, which should also be cut away.) Rinse again. Cut into bite-size pieces. Cloud ears really have no flavor of their own, but take on the flavors of the other ingredients. Their resilient texture, crunchy and somewhat gelatinous, and their appearance add interest to many dishes.

They are most often combined with GOLDEN LILIES in Chinese dishes. They are also excellent in soups, and combine well with pork, noodles, chicken, eggs, and vegetables, and are an important ingredient in Vegetarian Fried Rice.

They can also be stir-fried, braised, or steamed, and are often aggressively seasoned, as in one Chinese dish that teams them with garlic and HOISIN. In Singapore, they are served in sweet soup with litchis or longans. White cloud ears are most often used in soup or vegetarian stir-fried dishes.

SHIITAKE

The Japanese shiitake is the most popular variety of dried mushroom used in oriental cooking. To cultivate them, the spawn is planted into holes in

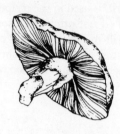

dead trees, where they grow quickly and may be harvested for years. They are then sun-dried, or dried artificially, and packaged in 1-ounce plastic bags containing 8 to 10 mushrooms, which are available in oriental grocery stores and many supermarkets.

STORAGE: Shiitake will keep indefinitely in an airtight container in a cool pantry. Once soaked, drain and wrap in plastic wrap for refrigerator storage of up to 5 days.

PREPARATION AND USE: Shiitake mushrooms are generally very clean, and need only a brief rinsing. They should be soaked in hot water or stock for 10 to 60 minutes, depending on their size. (Some cooks prefer to soak them 8 hours or longer in cold water, saying they retain more flavor with this method.) Squeeze out excess moisture from the soaked mushrooms and cut away the woody stem before using. Usually the soaking liquid, minus any grit, is used in the recipe for additional flavor. Save the stems and soaking liquid (if not otherwise used) to add flavor to stocks.

Small shiitake are generally cooked whole; large ones are shredded. They can be braised or simmered, or added to stir-fry dishes or soups. They are a delightful and flavorful ingredient to use in all kinds of experimental dishes. One of our favorite dishes resulted when we sliced them in thin strips, and then simmered their soaking liquid with heavy cream until it reduced to a sauce consistency. We stirred in the mushroom strips and tossed this delicious, creamy sauce with hot drained pasta.

FETTUCCINE WITH SHIITAKE CREAM SAUCE

1½	ounces dried shiitake mushrooms	For 4 servings
2	cups heavy (whipping) cream	
	Salt and ground red pepper (cayenne), to taste	
12	ounces dried fettuccine, or other pasta of your choice	
1	tablespoon butter	

Soak the mushrooms in boiling-hot water to cover for 10 minutes. Strain the soaking liquid through a clean kitchen towel or several layers of rinsed and wrung out cheesecloth into a large skillet and simmer over high heat until only ½ cup or so remains in the skillet. Meanwhile, cut away the tough stems from the mushroom caps. (Save the stems for soups or broths, as they are flavorful.) Slice the caps into thin strips. When the liquid has reduced, add the cream to the pan and simmer for 5 minutes or so until thickened to a sauce consistency. Add the sliced mushrooms to the skillet and simmer briefly to heat through. Season with salt and cayenne to taste.

Spoon the sauce over pasta that has been cooked until barely tender and then drained and tossed with butter. Serve immediately on warm plates.

TO PREPARE IN ADVANCE: The sauce can be made several hours ahead of time. Cover, to prevent a surface skin from forming. Reheat gently before serving.

MUSHROOMS, FRESH

Certain Asian mushrooms are available fresh in markets; others are available canned. We have taken the liberty of including both here rather than having a separate listing for canned mushrooms.

STORAGE: Store fresh mushrooms wrapped in paper towels in the refrigerator, and use as soon as possible. Never seal in a plastic bag, or they will deteriorate rapidly. After opening, transfer canned mushrooms to a nonmetal container to store in their original liquid for up to 4 days. They lose flavor on standing, so use them as soon as possible.

ENOKI-DAKE

(e-NOH-kee dah-KEH)
OTHER: *enokitake,* enok mushrooms

These tiny, slender-stalked, cream-colored mushrooms appear in produce markets everywhere from September to December. They are new to the Western marketplace where they have become an attention-getting garnish for many Nouvelle Cuisine dishes, but have been appreciated in northern Japan for centuries. We even enjoyed them recently in an Italian restaurant in Los Angeles, where they were served as an imaginative salad garnish. You will find them packaged in cardboard boxes or 3½-ounce plastic bags. Canned, they are called "golden mushrooms." They suffer greatly in the canning process so we recommend using only fresh ones.

PREPARATION AND USE: The bases of the stems are brownish in color; trim those away before use. Rinse with cold water. They need very little, if any cooking.

We like to sprinkle these little mushrooms over salads or cooked dishes as a garnish. Our good friend, Dr. Ernie Nagamatsu, makes an elegant Japanese version of Chicken Kiev by filling pounded chicken breasts with enoki mushrooms, chopped leeks, and herbs, and then tying each with KAMPYO, dipping in egg, flour, and the super-crispy Japanese breading called PANKO. We enjoy them, too, batter-coated to deep-fry for the Japanese dish, Tempura, or pickled in lemon juice or vinaigrette. Sauté briefly in butter to serve as a vegetable, but take care not to overheat them or they will develop a bitter flavor. In Japan, they are traditionally used in soups and often in Nimono (stewed and seasoned vegetables and/or fish).

MATSUTAKE

(Maht-soo-TAH-keh)
OTHER: pine mushroom

These large, dark brown Japanese mushrooms, which grow only in the wild on red pine trees, are sought out and gathered as eagerly in Japan as truffles are in France and Italy. They are delicate in flavor and valued primarily for their texture and their extraordinary, woodsy fragrance. Fresh ones are in season for only a short time in the fall, during which time you may be able to find them in Japanese or Korean specialty food stores where they may cost up to $70 apiece if in their prime. They are being successfuly cultivated now in the Pacific Northwest and in the Rocky Mountains, so we may soon find them more available. Canned matsutake, packed in water, are exported from Japan, but do not compare to the fresh. They are never dried.

PREPARATION AND USE: If you are fortunate enough to have fresh matsutake, do not wash them. Trim away only the tiniest tough part of the stems. Because they are so highly prized, you would be wise to simply broil them lightly and enjoy them with only a bit of Japanese soy sauce for dipping. Or make them the primary flavor of a dish such as Chawan Mushi (steamed custard, eaten as soup) or Tori Mushiyaki (steamed chicken garnished with mushrooms).

OYSTER MUSHROOMS

OTHER: summer oyster mushrooms, tree oyster mushrooms, tree mushrooms

CHINESE: *how-goo* JAPANESE: *shimeji, hiratake*

Known as the "shellfish of the forest," these grayish mushrooms grow in close clusters. They may be purchased fresh or canned in some Asian markets, and in fancy food shops. There are many strains, so there are slight variations in color and shape. The flavor is robust and rather like oysters, thus their name.

PREPARATION AND USE: Just before use, rinse fresh mushrooms quickly and dry. Rinse canned mushrooms. Slice if large.

Raw oyster mushrooms have a strong flavor and should be used only sparingly in salads. Cooked oyster mushrooms are milder and may be used in Chinese stir-fry dishes, or other Asian dishes, in place of shiitake or black mushrooms. They make excellent appetizers when breaded with flour, egg, and crumbs, then briefly deep-fried.

SHIITAKE

(shee-TAK-keh)
OTHER: black forest shiitake

Fresh shiitake have two seasons each year in Japan, spring and autumn. They are dark brown with velvety brown or striated caps and are available in specialty produce shops and Japanese markets. The best ones are thick with edges that curl under. Edges that curl upward indicate that the mushroom is getting old. We have seen advertisements in food magazines for logs and spores to grow your own shiitake at home.

PREPARATION AND USE: Trim away the stems because they are tough and take much longer to cook than the caps. Save them for stocks though, as they are flavorful. Fresh shiitake can be used interchangeably with dried shiitake that have been soaked, though the fresh, because of their especially fine aroma and flavor, are best used in dishes where they are the featured ingredient and are left whole. They are often placed atop UDON noodles (see NOODLES) in Osaka, cut in half or decoratively notched. They are especially good when lightly salted and grilled over charcoal or under the broiler.

In the making of the relish Shiitake Karani, 8 ounces of fresh mushrooms are thinly sliced and simmered slowly in a partially covered saucepan in ½ cup each of SAKE and soy sauce until the liquid has thickened and the mushrooms are cooked. This is served with rice and other dishes as a condiment.

They add delicious flavor to Chawan Mushi, the steamed egg custard eaten as a soup.

STRAW MUSHROOMS

OTHER: grass mushrooms, jelly mushrooms, paddy straw mushrooms

BURMESE: *hmo* CHINESE: *chao gwoo* JAPANESE: *nameko*

These canned mushrooms are yellowish in color and have pointed caps that look like half-open umbrellas. They are highly fragrant and very tasty, so they are considered a great delicacy in the Orient. Because they are extremely perishable, even the Japanese usually use them canned. Their texture is soft and silky. Canned straw mushrooms come both "unpeeled," in which case the cap completely surrounds the stem and "pecled," which have finer flavor and texture. They have a distinct rich flavor; don't be put off by their natural slippery coating. A dried form is only rarely available and not worth the cost because the delicate flavor and umbrella shape are lost in drying.

PREPARATION AND USE: A 15-ounce can will be enough for 4 servings when used as part of a stir-fry dish. (If dried, they must be soaked for 15 to 45 minutes in warm water until softened. Rinse and squeeze out excess liquid.) Drain canned mushrooms and rinse well before using. They can be used in place of button mushrooms in any recipe. Delicious with crab, abalone, and steamed chicken. In Szechuan province, they are often cooked with ground pork and hot chiles. Another Chinese dish uses them with walnuts and a bit of FIVE SPICE POWDER. In Japan, these are used primarily in MISO soup and on grated DAIKON as an accompaniment to cocktails.

MUSHROOMS, JELLY
See STRAW MUSHROOMS

MUSTARD GREENS, ORIENTAL
OTHER: leaf mustard, Indian mustard

CHINESE: *guy choy, kai choy* JAPANESE: *karashina*

Oriental mustard greens have textured, dark green leaves and stalks and are available fresh all year in Chinese markets and some supermarkets. They have a tangy, slightly bitter after-taste, but are much milder than the American type. Look for round leaves of good color, not spotted or wilted; the smaller leaves are the tenderest. Do not confuse with mustard cabbage. If you cannot find this vegetable where you live, seeds are readily available through seed catalogues. Like other leafy green vegetables, mustard greens are very high in vitamins A and C and in iron and folic acid. Other available forms are salted (*ham choy*), sold loose by the pound; and pickled, sold in jars.

STORAGE: Wash, wrap tightly in paper towels and store in a plastic bag in the crisper of the refrigerator for up to a week. The salted form can be stored in a jar in the refrigerator for up to a week. Pickled mustard greens can be stored indefinitely in the refrigerator.

PREPARATION AND USE: One pound of greens will serve 2 to 4 depending on how used. Remove stems, and chop leaves if they are large. (If using the salted form, rinse well and use as you would fresh.) Add to soups or stir-fry dishes, especially with pork and bamboo shoots, and in dishes containing rice flour noodles. Or cook as you would spinach in a heavy saucepan, covered, with salt and only the water that clings to the leaves after washing for about 15 minutes or until tender, which is quite a lot longer than it takes to cook spinach. Drain and chop. As a vegetable, it should be served with highly seasoned dishes, not delicate ones, and is often specified in Chow Mein recipes. These are especially delicious when accompanied with a shake of lemon juice or vinegar. The stems are often pickled.

MUSTARD OIL

INDIAN: *sarsou ka tel* or *kapwatel*

This pale yellow oil, flavored with black mustard seed, is available in Indian markets. It is a flavorful ingredient, often used in Indian cooking.

STORAGE: It can go rancid quickly, so store in a cool place or in the refrigerator.

USE: Delicious for stir-fry vegetables. (See our recipe for ALU GOBI, under ASAFETIDA.) It is often used for pickling but is seldom used raw.

NAM PRIK

"Nam Prik" is the generic term for Thai dipping sauces and condiments, in many varieties, which are sold in Asian markets. *Nam prik gapee* is FISH SAUCE to which chiles and shrimp paste are added. *Nam prik pow* is a paste of dried fish, shrimp, chiles, and oil.

STORAGE: After opening, store in the refrigerator for up to 3 months.

USE: These are used as dips for SHRIMP CHIPS, or as a table seasoning for soups and other Thai dishes, such as Yam Nang Mu (pork skin salad).

NATTO

(na-TOH)

These light brown fermented soybeans are used as a seasoning (primarily in Tokyo), and are available in refrigerated packages in Japanese grocery stores. More traditionally, they will be in a straw wrapping, to allow them to breathe. They have a strong, cheesy odor and a slippery, stringy texture that are offensive to nearly all Westerners and to many Japanese as well. They are, however, highly nutritious and easily digested.

STORAGE: If transferred to a plastic container, they will keep for up to 2 weeks in the refrigerator.

USE: In Japan, natto are used to make a pungent soup called *nattojiru*, which is a combination of MISO and NATTO, or are served as a nutritious topping for rice accompanied by raw egg and seasoned NORI (see under SEAWEED, DRIED). They can add a salty tang to dishes.

NET FAT

See CAUL, in THE FOODS OF EUROPE section

NIBOSHI

(nee-BOH-shee)

These sun-dried sardines are used for making a fish stock that is stronger in flavor than DASHI, which is made with bonito shavings. Niboshi are usually about 2″ long and are sold in small plastic bags in most oriental markets. Those of finest quality are whole and straight-bodied.

STORAGE: After opening, they can be stored indefinitely in an airtight container on the pantry shelf.

PREPARATION AND USE: These are often enjoyed as a snack, just as they are, with a soy dipping sauce. To make Dashi (stock), remove and discard the heads, put in pot of cold water (or cold stock made with kelp), bring to a boil, and simmer for 7 to 8 minutes. Use for UDON noodles (see NOODLES), or to make MISO soups.

NIGARI

(nee-GAHR-ee)
OTHER: magnesium chloride, calcium chloride, bittern

Nigari is a solidifier contained in distilled seawater used as a coagulant for making bean curd. A flake form is available in Japanese markets and in health food stores.

234

STORAGE: They will keep indefinitely in a cool, dry place.

USE: Making fresh bean curd is a complicated process, but excellent directions can be found in several of the books mentioned in the RECOMMENDED ETHNIC COOKBOOKS section.

NOODLES, BUCKWHEAT

See CHASOBA, JAPANESE NOODLES, AND SOBA under
NOODLES

NOODLES

Following is an alphabetical listing of Asian noodles found in ethnic markets.

STORAGE: Fresh noodles should be refrigerated and used as soon as possible—within a day or two. Most can be frozen for up to 2 weeks. Dried noodles keep indefinitely in a cool, dry place.

PREPARATION AND USE: There are many different ways of cooking Asian noodles. Some need only soaking, some should be cooked just until tender, others can be deep-fried to use as a textural ingredient in salads or as a base for cooked dishes. One Singapore specialty, Htamin Letholke, consists of three types mounded separately with many sauces and accompaniments.

CELLOPHANE NOODLES

OTHER: bean threads, shining noodles, soybean vermicelli, glass noodles

BURMESE: *kyazan* CHINESE: *fun see, sei fun, bi* or *ning fun*
INDONESIAN: *sotanghoon* or *laksa* JAPANESE: *harusame* (made from *satsumo-imo* starch) MALAYSIAN: *sohoon, tunghoon, laska, beehoon* IN THE PHILIPPINES: *sotanghon* THAI: *woon sen* VIETNAMESE: *bun*

These shiny, thin, translucent noodles made from ground mung beans are not really noodles in the traditional sense, but a vegetable product made from various bean starches. The Japanese name for these gossamer, hair-like noodles means "spring rain." Available in packages of various sizes, they need only soaking to make an inexpensive and easy extender for many dishes. When cooked, they become bouncy and slippery, and have a delicate blandness that takes on the flavors of other foods.

STORAGE: Uncooked, they will keep indefinitely on the pantry shelf. After soaking or cooking, they should be consumed as quickly as possible because they become mushy on standing.

PREPARATION AND USE: As a soup ingredient these needn't be soaked, but before stir-frying or adding to other dishes, soak 10 minutes in hot water or until softened. Drain, place in cold water, and drain again. They need only brief cooking.

They are very often stir-fried with meat and seafood in such dishes as Bean Thread and Beef, or Cellophane Noodles and Shrimp, or the Vietnamese dish, Mien Ga, with chicken, mushrooms, and scallions, to stretch those expensive items and to add an intriguing texture. A Szechuan dish combines them with pork, hot bean sauce, and fresh coriander. They are used interchangeably with RICE FLOUR NOODLES and are used in many Thai, Cambodian, Laotian, Burmese, and Filipino dishes. In Japan, they are often soaked, then cooked in broth with meat or fish and vegetables, as in the well-known dishes, Sukiyaki and Yosenabe. In Thailand, they are served with steamed fish with ginger, garlic, and fresh coriander and, in Vietnam, they are served in fish soup.

They can be deep-fried in the same manner as Rice Flour Noodles to use as an ingredient in Chinese chicken salad, or in the Thai fried-noodle dish, Mee Krob. A whimsical Japanese method of using these noodles is to break them up into small pieces and sprinkle them over foods that have been dipped in batter for deep-frying. They puff up and give the food a lacy, flower-like appearance.

CHASOBA

(cha-SOH-ba)

This soup noodle, available only occasionally fresh or dried in Japanese markets, is made from a rather unusual combination of buckwheat flour and green tea. Regular SOBA noodles can be substituted.

STORAGE: If fresh, use as soon as possible; or freeze for up to a month if they haven't been previously frozen. Dried noodles will keep indefinitely in a cool, dry place.

PREPARATION AND USE: Boil in unsalted water until barely tender. Drain, and rinse with cold water. They are usually served cold with a dipping sauce, but can be served warm in the same manner as SOBA noodles. They are served on special occasions, traditionally in conjunction with the tea ceremony but otherwise are not so commonly used.

CHINESE EGG NOODLES

CHINESE: *lo mein* INDONESIAN: *mie* JAPANESE: *ramen* MALAYSIAN: *mee* THAI: *bamee* VIETNAMESE: *mi*

These shoelace-like noodles made from wheat flour and eggs are available, dried, in cellophane bags, or fresh in the refrigerator sections of Chinese markets and many supermarkets. In large Chinese grocery stores, you can often just reach in and grab what you need from a large cardboard box, transfer to a plastic bag, and pay for them by the pound. They are used in much the same ways as other kinds of pasta. Fresh or dried SPAGHETTI or SPAGHETTINI (see under PASTA in THE FOODS OF EUROPE section) can be substituted.

Under the Japanese name, *ramen*, these very popular noodles are available in some form in almost every market in the United States. The "instant" soup-noodle version has become a new food fad—simply add boiling water and you have an instant meal complete with vegetables and, if you read the label, a huge list of chemical additives. The best *ramen* are available in oriental grocery stores either freshly made, or dried.

STORAGE: Dried egg noodles will keep indefinitely on the pantry shelf. The fresh noodles can be stored in the refrigerator for 3 to 4 days, or can be frozen for up to 3 months. Do not thaw before cooking.

PREPARATION AND USE: Cook according to package directions until nearly tender but still firm in the center, or *al dente*. A dish of "Chinese Noodles" is one of the most common of all meals on the menu in Chinese restaurants. Simply place the cooked noodles in a flavorful broth with any kind of sliced cooked meat, such as Red Roast Pork or Barbecued Duck, and add a few sliced scallion greens for flavoring. The cooked noodles can also be stir-fried, or used as you would any pasta, or even fried like a pancake to serve with meat dishes.

An Indonesian soup, Soto Ayam, combines them with chicken, garlic, chiles, and a long list of spices. In Singapore, they are fried with pork, prawns, and fermented black beans, to be garnished with fresh coriander. Vietnamese Pancit combines them with pork, chicken, prawns, ham, and lots of garlic.

HIYAMUGI

(HEE-yah-MOO-gee)

Hiyamugi are thin, white Japanese dried noodles.

STORAGE: As any dry noodle.

PREPARATION AND USE: These are cooked in the same manner as SOBA noodles and, like them, are usually eaten cold, with a dipping sauce. Very fine Italian VERMICELLI (see PASTA in THE FOODS OF EUROPE section) makes a good substitute.

JAPANESE NOODLES

There two main types of Japanese noodles, those made with wheat flour and those made with buckwheat flour. Chinese-style egg noodles, known as *ramen*, are also popular in Japan. All are available, dried, in Japanese markets but, like pasta, all are best when fresh. You will find fresh noodles in some Japanese markets but, if unavailable, they are easy to make at home, and directions appear in some of the Japanese cookbooks listed in our RECOMMENDED ETHNIC COOKBOOKS section. In Japan, it is considered *de rigueur* to eat hot noodles while very hot, making a delicate slurping sound as you cool them on their way into your mouth.

KISHIMEN

This flat, Nagoya-style Japanese wheat noodle is thicker than UDON, but prepared and served in the same way.

MAIN FUN

OTHER: Chinese water noodles

These fresh, shoelace-like noodles made with flour and water are much whiter in appearance than egg noodles. They are available packaged by weight in the refrigerator sections of Chinese markets and in many supermarkets.

STORAGE: Store up to 5 days in the refrigerator, or 3 months in the freezer. Do not thaw before cooking.

PREPARATION AND USE: Cook according to package directions until almost tender, but still firm in the center, or *al dente*. Use as you would egg noodles, or any pasta.

RICE FLOUR NOODLES

OTHER: rice sticks, long rice

CHINESE: *mai fun* MALAYSIAN: *beehoon, meehoon* THAI: *wun sen, mee* (extra thin) VIETNAMESE: *banh pho*

These very thin, white hair-like noodles made from rice that has been pounded into flour are starchier and have a more distinctive flavor than cellophane noodles. They are available in Asian markets, as well as in many supermarkets, in 8-ounce packages. Thicker ones are sometimes available as well.

STORAGE: Uncooked, they will keep indefinitely on the pantry shelf. Once simmered, they should be consumed as soon as possible. Deep-fried noodles can be kept fresh-tasting in a closed brown paper bag for up to 8 hours.

PREPARATION AND USE: Thin ones require only brief soaking before they are steamed or added to stir-fry dishes. Soak for 15 minutes in cold water, or for 5 minutes in warm water. Larger ones may need longer soaking and even a bit of simmering, or can be soaked in boiling-hot water for 3 minutes. Drain well and add to soups or stir-fry dishes. If preparing them ahead of time, rinse well and keep chilled until they are added to dishes. They combine especially well with oysters, mussels, scallions, pork, and cloud ears (dried mushrooms) in dishes that have a lot of sauce.

Unsoaked ones, which can be deep-fried in seconds, puff up dramatically and become crisp. To deep-fry the noodles, heat about 5 cups of oil in a skillet or wok. Pull off a tuft of the rice sticks from the wad and loosen it slightly. Drop it into the oil. It will puff and crisp on one side immediately. Use slotted spoons or large flat spatulas to turn, and cook on the other side for a few seconds. Drop into a brown paper bag, which will absorb the excess oil. When deep-fried, these (or cellophane noodles) become the essential ingredient of what has become popularly known as "Chinese Chicken Salad," and the Thai dish, Mee Krob. In Singapore, they are soaked, drained, and topped with chili sauce, soy sauce, HOISIN, and toasted sesame seeds, to serve as a snack. They are used also in Laksa, a very spicy soup of noodles in coconut milk with cucumber and mint.

SEAWEED NOODLES

CHINESE: *yang fun*

Available in boxes by weight, these are threadlike noodles made from seaweed. They are transparent and are thinner and more gelatinous than cellophane noodles.

STORAGE: They will keep indefinitely on the pantry shelf.

PREPARATION AND USE: Place in a small bowl. Pour boiling water over the noodles to cover them and let stand for 20 minutes. Rinse in cold water. Use as an extender and to add texture to cold dishes.

SEVIYAN

OTHER: *sev*

A very, very fine wheat or potato flour verimicelli type of noodle sold in Indian markets. Some are white, and some have been browned. They are sold in varying degrees of fineness, with the finest being marked "thinnest." "Elephant" brand is widely distributed.

STORAGE: As any dried noodle.

PREPARATION AND USE: This type of noodle is mostly used in India for making milk desserts such as Sheer Korma, with saffron and pistachio nuts. One ounce of dried noodles will be ample per serving. The unbrowned type is fried in GHEE until browned; then milk and spices are added and they are cooked together until the noodles are cooked. These desserts are usually served warm, and are often topped with VARAK (silver leaf).

SHIRATAKI

(sheer-ah-TAH-kee)

Gelatinous transparent noodles, the shredded form of KONNYAKU, made from a tuber known as "Devil's Tongue" are used in many Japanese dishes including Sukiyaki. They are available in cans or refrigerated plastic tubs in oriental markets and some supermarkets. They are thought to have a highly beneficial cleansing effect on the intestines and are often served to those suffering from stomach ailments and ulcers. The name means "white waterfall."

STORAGE: After opening, store packaged or canned shirataki up to 2 days in the refrigerator. Packaged shirataki can be stored unopened for up to a week. Do not freeze.

PREPARATION AND USE: Drain any liquid and drop the shirataki into simmering water for a few seconds to freshen it. They need very little cooking. Add to broths to create interesting soups, or to various dishes as an extender.

SOBA

Soba is a buckwheat flour noodle that is buff-colored and very thin. There is a variation, made with powdered green tea, which is pale green and called CHASOBA. A thin variety is called *ki-soba*. A very thin Korean type, for which *ki-soba* can be substituted, is called *naeng myon*.

STORAGE: Store as any dry noodle.

PREPARATION AND USE: Soba are cooked until barely tender in un-salted boiling water, and then cooled under cold running water. Often they are served cold with a dipping sauce. They can be reheated by placing in a sieve and dipping into boiling water to serve topped with Tempura (deep-fried shrimp and vegetables).

SOMEN

Somen is a fine white Japanese noodle, sometimes made with egg yolk.

STORAGE: Dried somen can be stored for years and many Japanese allow them to mellow on a cool shelf for a year before eating.

PREPARATION AND USE: Allow 1 ounce per serving. Somen are almost always served cold as a summer food, but occasionally a few are dropped into a clear, hot soup. A popular summer dish in Japan is Hiyashi Somen, in which the cold, rinsed noodles are served in bowls with ice cubes. They are topped with sliced scallions and served with a dipping sauce of DASHI, MIRIN, and SOY SAUCE mixed with WASABI. This dish is often topped with cooked shellfish.

UDON

(OO-Don)

These thick Japanese wheat noodles, which look very like square-edged spaghetti, are available in fresh or dried form in oriental groceries and in many supermarkets. You will find them in varying thicknesses. They are very similar to main fun and to spaghetti, both of which can be substituted.

STORAGE: Use up fresh noodles within a day or two. If you know they are freshly made, as in some family-run grocery stores, they can be frozen with great success. Commercial brands may have been already frozen once, so it is best not to freeze them again. Dried udon can be stored as you would any type of dried noodle, indefinitely on the pantry shelf.

PREPARATION AND USE: Follow package directions, which will vary according to the thickness of the udon. Bowls of noodles in broth with various flavorings are one of the most common (and delicious!) of oriental dishes. Cooked noodles are often added to meat and vegetable dishes as well, or are fried.

NUKA

(NOO-Kah)
OTHER: rice bran

Nuka is a rice bran sold in plastic bags that is used mostly for making very crisp, nutritious pickles. You will find it in Japanese markets located next to the rice and grains. Check the date on the package to make sure it is very fresh for best flavor. Several varieties are available: nuka is plain rice bran for pickling, *iri-nuka* is roasted and somewhat less perishable, *nuka-zuke no moto* is a pre-seasoned pickling mixture.

STORAGE: After opening, store in an airtight container in a cool place for up to 2 months. It loses flavor quickly on standing.

USE: Layer soft-skinned vegetables such as Chinese cabbage, cucumber, eggplant, with water, salt, and nuka and let stand until vegetables are pickled. The usual proportions are 4 pounds nuka to 4 pounds salt to 1 large cabbage. The length of time will depend on outside temperature, season, climate, etc. Consult a Japanese cookbook for detailed instructions.

In Japan, nuka is also used as a dishwashing agent when wrapped in a cotton bag, and as a polishing agent for woodwork and wooden floors.

OIL, SESAME

See SESAME OIL

OIL, TEMPURA

See TEMPURA OIL

OKRA, CHINESE

OTHER: pleated squash, silk squash, silk melon, ridged melon

CHINESE: *sing gwa*

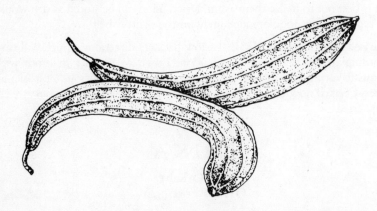

Chinese okra is a dark green, slightly sweet-tasting vegetable that looks like a large American okra or a tough-skinned cucumber and has a fibrous, spongy flesh. It is available during the summer months. There is no substitute.

STORAGE: If wrapped in a brown paper bag inside a plastic bag, it will keep for up to a week in the refrigerator.

PREPARATION AND USE: Peel away the tough skin and sharp edges before cooking. Slice thin for stir-frying, or dice to add to soups. In soups, it is usually combined with straw mushrooms and bean curd.

OKOME
See RICE, SHORT GRAIN

ONE HUNDRED UNITIES
CHINESE: *bok hop* or *bai ho*

"One Hundred Unities" is the name for the small, dried, irridescent white petals of a lily plant that are used as a condiment or spice. This is very rarely found in Chinese specialty shops and, when it is, it is very expensive.

STORAGE: It will keep indefinitely in a cool, dark place in a covered jar.

USE: Use sparingly as a condiment or spice to flavor soups and "red-cooked" dishes.

OLIVE, CHINESE-CURED
CHINESE: *larm gok*

Chinese-cured olives are salty, blackish-brown dried fruit with a pungent aroma and slightly sweet anise taste. They are sold in Chinese markets.

STORAGE: They will keep indefinitely in a covered jar in the pantry.

PREPARATION AND USE: Soak for 30 minutes in cold water. Drain and chop fine to use as a seasoning for steamed fish, meat, and vegetable dishes. It is used especially in banquet dishes. It can be steamed with oil, ginger, and sugar to serve as a snack.

ONION, LONG
OTHER: Japanese leek

JAPANESE: *negi* or *nagenegi*

A long onion looks a great deal like a giant-sized, slender scallion. They are very popular, especially in Tokyo, and we see them often in Japanese grocery stores in the United States. They are 14″ to 16″ long and have a flavor slightly more bitter than scallions and quite different from leeks. Scallions can be substituted.

STORAGE: They will keep for up to a week in the crisper of the refrigerator.

PREPARATION AND USE: Slice the white part thin and soak briefly in cold water to use as a garnish or as an ingredient in dipping sauces.

ORANGE, JAPANESE
See MIKAN

ORANGE PEEL, DRIED
See TANGERINE PEEL, DRIED

OSHIMUGI
See BARLEY, PRESSED

OSHINKO
"Fragrant things" (Japanese name for pickles)

OYSTER MUSHROOMS
See MUSHROOMS, OYSTER

OYSTER SAUCE

CHINESE: *ho yo jeung, how yow*

This popular Cantonese seasoning is a velvety brown, free-flowing oyster extract with a meaty aroma. It intensifies flavors and adds body to many dishes. Available in jars and cans of varying sizes, the best brands by far, such as Lee Kum Kee, are imported from China.

STORAGE: It will keep indefinitely in the refrigerator.

PREPARATION AND USE: The sauce contains cornstarch, so it has a thickening effect on sauces it is added to. Do not expose overly long to high heat or it will lose its thickening power. It is best used sparingly as a seasoning or table condiment, and the amount of salt in a recipe should be reduced when adding it. It can be used in meat, poultry, and seafood dishes, and it does something sublime to bean curd. We team it with broccoli in the following recipe.

BROCCOLI WITH OYSTER SAUCE

For 4 servings

This is a variation of the popular Chinese restaurant dish, "Beef and Broccoli with Oyster Sauce."

2½ pounds broccoli (1 large bunch)
2 teaspoons minced fresh ginger
2 cloves garlic, minced
2 tablespoons sherry or *shao hsing* (Chinese rice wine)
2 tablespoons light soy or mushroom soy sauce
2 tablespoons peanut oil
¼ teaspoon salt
½ teaspoon sugar
3 tablespoons oyster sauce

Rinse broccoli, peel and discard tough skin from the stalks. Cut off the flowers. Cut tender stems about 2″ long. Cut thick stems into quarters, and then into 2″ lengths. Mince ginger and garlic and place in a small bowl. Combine sherry and soy in a small bowl.

Heat a large wok over high heat. Pour in the oil and roll it around the sides of the wok to heat it. When just starting to smoke, add the ginger and garlic, stir; then add the broccoli and ¼ teaspoon salt. Stir-fry for 1 minute; add the sherry–soy mixture, and sugar. Stir-fry briefly, cover, and cook 30 seconds. Remove the lid, and stir-fry until most of the liquid has evaporated, glazing the broccoli. Test for doneness, and add a bit more liquid (either sherry or soy) if the broccoli must cook longer. Pour the oyster sauce over the broccoli, toss just until it begins to simmer; then transfer to a warm platter to serve immediately.

TO PREPARE IN ADVANCE: The vegetables and all ingredients can be set out several hours in advance, but the final cooking must be done just before serving.

OYSTERS, DRIED CHINESE

CHINESE: *ho she gawn* or *how see* FILIPINO *ba goon sisi* THAI *nahm man hoi*

These reddish-brown dried oysters are available in 8- or 16-ounce cellophane bags. They have a delicate fishy taste and are used as a seasoning.

STORAGE: They will keep indefinitely on the pantry shelf.

PREPARATION AND USE: One per serving is ample for most dishes. Rinse well with cold water to remove any sand. Soak in warm water for at least 8 hours. Rinse again to remove any remaining sand. Can be stir-fried, steamed, or added to soups or stews.

PALM SUGAR

See JAGGERY

PANCH PHORA

OTHER NAMES: *panchphoran,* 5-spice mixture

Panch means "five" in Hindi, and this is a combination of the raw seeds of five spices, in equal amounts, which is often used in Bengalese dishes. The spices are cumin, fennel, black mustard, fenugreek, and kalonji or black cumin. The mixture can be purchased in Indian markets, or mixed at home.

STORAGE: As any spice.

USE: The spices are cooked in oil at the beginning of preparation of certain Indian recipes, and are often used in vegetable and chutney dishes. It is added, along with GARAM MASALA and, on its own, to Alu Mattar Sukhe (potato and pea curry) and to Piaz Bahhi (spicy fried onions with turmeric and ginger).

PANIR

OTHER: *paneer*

Panir is a fresh, crumbly cheese made from coagulated milk solids that have been separated from the liquid whey of milk and curdled with lemon juice. It may be found in Indian markets, or made at home using recipes found in Indian cookbooks (see the RECOMMENDED ETHNIC COOKBOOKS section).

STORAGE: Store in the refrigerator as you would yogurt.

USE: Panir is very bland, so it is almost always cooked with other foods. It is usually cut in pieces and fried (use a nonstick pan) before being added to other dishes. When diced and fried, it is an important ingredient in Indian vegetable dishes, and is often combined with peas or with pureed spinach. It is often crumbled between layers of rice to be baked. It is occasionally eaten plain, garnished with chopped vegetables or fruit.

PANKO

(PAHN-Koh)

Panko is equivalent to our coarse, white bread crumbs, and is available is cellophane packages in Japanese markets.

STORAGE: Unopened, it will keep indefinitely, but, like any bread crumbs, once the package is opened, panko will turn stale quickly.

PREPARATION AND USE: Use as you would any coarse bread crumbs— to coat foods for deep-frying, to create a crispy Japanese-style breading. In Japan they are used for Tongatsu (deep-fried pork cutlet) and for shrimp. We use panko as a topping for all kinds of casseroles and *au gratin* dishes.

PAPPADUM

OTHER: *papar*

Pappadum are thin Indian breads, plain or seasoned, that resemble tortillas in appearance. They will be found in varying diameters in small packages in Indian markets. They are made of DAL flour and are often seasoned with garlic, red chiles, black pepper, or Madras seasonings. As a general rule, those in tins are not very good.

STORAGE: Transfer to an airtight container and use as quickly as possible.

PREPARATION AND USE: Grill over flame or fry quickly. They will puff and expand. Serve as an appetizer or as an accompaniment to Indian meals.

PAPAYA

See THE FOODS OF LATIN AMERICA section

PASSION FRUIT

See GRANADILLA in THE FOODS OF LATIN AMERICA section

PATIS

See FISH SAUCE

PAWPAW

See THE FOODS OF REGIONAL AMERICA

PEANUT OIL

CHINESE: *far sung yow* INDIAN: *moongphali ka tel*

The clear oil from peanuts is the most highly prized cooking oil to the Chinese for several reasons. It has a distinctive flavor that enhances the flavors of Chinese ingredients and it can be heated to higher temperatures than other oils without burning. It can be used over and over without losing its clarity because it absorbs practically nothing from the foods being cooked. Planters and Skippy brands are widely available in supermarkets in the United States, but it is much less expensive purchased in large cans in Chinatown. A cold-pressed (unprocessed) type can be found in health food stores.

STORAGE: At very low temperatures, peanut oil turns cloudy, but this does not affect the flavor. It will keep indefinitely in a cool, dark place. The cold-pressed type is more perishable and should be stored in a cool place and used within a few weeks.

PREPARATION AND USE: Use for deep-frying or stir-frying. Heat some in a wok with sliced ginger and garlic just until they start to brown. Strain, cool and store in the refrigerator to use as an all-purpose cooking oil for Chinese dishes. After deep-frying, strain the oil through a paper towel or coffee-filter to clarify it.

PEKING PANCAKES

OTHER: Mandarin pancakes, *moo shoo* pork skins

CHINESE: *po ping*

Moo Shoo Pork has become one of America's most popular restaurant dishes in recent years. It consists of a filling of stir-fried pork, GOLDEN LILIES, soy sauce, scallions, and CLOUD EARS (see under MUSHROOMS, DRIED) enfolded in a thin, crêpe-like pancake on which HOISIN has been spread. The pancakes, which are also traditional with Peking Duck, are now available in the freezer sections of oriental markets. They can be used for other fillings as well.

STORAGE: If tightly wrapped for freezer storage, these will keep frozen for 6 months or longer.

PREPARATION AND USE: Thaw if frozen. Wrap any fillings you like in these. Follow directions for steaming in the following recipe.

HUGH'S PEKING PANCAKES

For 20 pancakes

We had no great success at making the delicate wrappers until our friend, Hugh Carpenter, Chinese-cooking authority, taught us this method.

2   cups unbleached white flour
1   cup boiling water
    Chinese sesame oil

Combine flour and boiling water in mixing bowl and mix with a wooden spoon. When all the flour is moistened, turn the mixture out onto a lightly floured surface and knead. In 5 minutes or so the dough will be very smooth. Cover with a dry towel and let rest for 30 minutes.

With a rolling pin, roll the dough from the center out, not quite to the edges, until it becomes a circle measuring about 12″ in diameter. It will be about ¼″ thick. Use a 2½″ biscuit cutter (or the top of a glass) to cut circles of dough. Roll out scraps and cut more circles until the dough has all been used. Wipe flour from your work surface.

Rub sesame oil over your work surface. Place one round of dough on the surface and pour sesame oil generously over it. Top with another round of dough and press down to seal and prevent slipping. Roll the two stacked pancakes until very, very thin, turning them over from time to time. They will be about 6″ in diameter.

Meanwhile, heat an ungreased skillet or griddle until hot. Cook the double pancake for about 30 seconds on one side and 10 seconds on the other side, taking care not to brown them. (They do not puff like chapatis or tortillas.) Flip the pancake out of the pan, separate the edges and pull apart. Continue cooking and separating the double pancakes until all are cooked (stack and set aside). If they are not to be served immediately, wrap in foil to prevent drying.

To serve, fold the pancakes in quarters as you would crêpes and overlap them on a serving plate. Just before serving, steam them for two minutes over boiling water to warm them through.

TO PREPARE IN ADVANCE: These pancakes freeze beautifully for months. Wrap them tightly for storage. Thaw before steaming.

PEKING SAUCE
See HOISIN SAUCE

PEPPER, FRAGRANT
See under PEPPERCORNS, SZECHUAN under PEPPERCORNS, OTHER in the HERBS, SPICES, AND SEASONING BLENDS section

PEPPERCORNS, SZECHUAN
See under PEPPERCORNS, OTHER in the HERBS, SPICES, AND SEASONING BLENDS section

PEA PODS
See SNOW PEAS

PEAS, SNOW
See SNOW PEAS

PEAS, SUGAR
See SNOW PEAS

PICKLES, CHINESE
CHINESE: *char quar kan*

There is an infinite variety of cans and jars of various vegetables such as cucumbers, turnips, cabbage, and ginger, pickled and seasoned with soy sauce. In China, these are commonly used as a seasoning, especially with the breakfast rice porridge, Congee.

STORAGE: Unopened, store on the pantry shelf; after opening, refrigerate for up to 6 months in a nonmetal container.

USE: Use as a seasoning for noodles and soups, or as a table relish.

PIGEON PEA
See under DAL, ARHAR

PINE NUTS, CHINESE TYPE
See under PINE NUT in THE FOODS OF EUROPE section

PLEATED SQUASH
See OKRA, CHINESE

PLUM DUCK
See DUCK, ROAST

PLUM SAUCE
OTHER: duck sauce

CHINESE: *so muey jeung*

This amber-colored sauce, available in cans and in bottles, resembles mango chutney in flavor and consistency. It is made from plums, apricots, or other fruits with the addition of chiles, vinegar, and sugar. Its flavor can be described as tangy-tart, sweet-sour, or sweet-hot, depending on the brand. It is often called Duck Sauce because it is so often served with duck.

STORAGE: It will keep indefinitely in the refrigerator in a glass container.

USE: It is used almost exclusively as a dipping sauce with egg rolls, meats, and poultry, and as a marinade/basting sauce for Plum Duck. It is sometimes used as a flavoring agent in cooking, to darken and blend a sauce. Add sugar if the sauce is too tart for your liking. It adds an intriguing flavor to salad dressings.

POMEGRANATES
See THE FOODS OF THE MIDDLE EAST section

POPPY SEEDS, WHITE
See HERBS, SPICES, AND SEASONING BLENDS section

PORK, BARBECUED ROAST
OTHER: Red Roast Pork

These small, deliciously flavored strips of pork shoulder, aromatically seasoned with Five Spice Powder and basted to a mahogany color, are sold in Chinese delis and barbecued-meat shops. Sliced thin they make a delicious snack or appetizer just as they are, but are also very useful as an ingredient in many dishes. We almost never pass up an opportunity to buy some to keep on hand in our freezer. Our recipe for it appears with FIVE SPICE POWDER.

STORAGE: Cut into small portions and wrap tightly to store in refrigerator for up to 5 days, or freeze for up to 4 months.

PREPARATION AND USE: Because it is pungently spiced, a little bit of this goes a long way. If used as an appetizer, allow approximately 2 ounces per person; if as a seasoning, only 1 ounce. The pork only needs warming up as it is already cooked. Slice in ¼" pieces to use as an ingredient in stir-fry vegetable dishes, combining with CHOY SUM (see CABBAGE, ORIENTAL), Chinese broccoli (see BROCCOLI, CHINESE), or LONG BEANS (see under BEANS).

Use to garnish a bowl of noodles in broth with thinly sliced scallion greens, or serve as a snack with or without a dipping sauce. It is a featured ingredient in Pork Fried Rice, and many Chow Mein recipes, and is an essential ingredient in Steamed Barbecued Pork Buns served as Dim Sum (Chinese snack foods).

We like it especially in a delicious noodle salad, the recipe for which follows.

SZECHUAN NOODLE SALAD

For 6 to 8 servings

This recipe, from Chinese-cooking authority Hugh Carpenter, has become one of our favorite dishes for buffet parties. It is ideal for picnics as well.

SZECHUAN DRESSING:
- 3 tablespoons red wine vinegar
- 2 tablespoons mushroom soy *or* heavy soy sauce
- 2 tablespoons minced fresh ginger
- 1½ tablespoons white sugar
- 1 teaspoon CHILI PASTE WITH GARLIC
- ½ teaspoon salt
- 2 tablespoons Chinese sesame oil

SALAD INGREDIENTS:
- 12 ounces fresh Chinese egg noodles (or any pasta of your choice)
- 3 cups mung bean sprouts, blanched
- 2 cups slivered barbecued pork *or* 1 cup small cooked shrimp and 1 cup slivered ham
- 2 red bell peppers, seeded and slivered
- 4 scallions, slivered, including part of the green stems
- ½ cup Chinese parsley (cilantro) leaves, firmly packed

To make dressing, combine all ingredients except sesame oil and stir to blend. Stir in sesame oil and set aside.

Cook the noodles (or pasta of your choice) until just tender. Rinse in colander under cold running water until cool. Drain well and transfer to a large bowl with the other salad ingredients. Pour the dressing over and toss to coat all ingredients.

Serve the salad at room temperature. Garnish with extra sprigs of Chinese parsley if desired.

TO PREPARE IN ADVANCE: The entire recipe can be prepared one day in advance. Refrigerate, but bring to room temperature before serving.

PORK, ROAST

CHINESE: *siew gee yuk*

These thick pieces of glazed roast pig with crackling skin seasoned with honey and spices are available by weight at Chinese barbecued-meat shops.

STORAGE: Refrigerate, tightly wrapped, for up to 5 days, or freeze for up to 4 months.

USE: Serve as an appetizer with dipping sauces such as OYSTER SAUCE or PLUM SAUCE. Dice to add to soups, or stir-fry with vegetables or seafood. It needs only brief heating because it is already cooked.

PRAWN POWDER
See SHRIMP, DRIED

PRESERVED VEGETABLES, CANTONESE
OTHER: Tientsin preserved vegetables
CHINESE: *chong choy*

This cured and salted celery cabbage or bok choy (see CABBAGE, ORIENTAL) is available in attractive small crocks or in cans. The leaves are rolled tightly and heavily seasoned with garlic and red pepper.

STORAGE: The unopened crock can be stored on the pantry shelf for 3 or 4 months because the contents are heavily salted. After opening, transfer to a glass jar with a tight-fitting lid to store in the refrigerator indefinitely.

PREPARATION AND USE: Rinse away excess salt before using. Add as a seasoning to soups and stir-fry dishes, especially those with beef or pork.

PRESERVED VEGETABLES, CHINESE
OTHER: Chinese sauerkraut, preserved cabbage, preserved winter vegetable
CHINESE: *hom choy, choan choy, mooey choy, do an choy* VIETNAMESE: *tan xai*

Various mixed vegetables are packed in brine and fermented to make Preserved Vegetables. They are sold in bottles or jars in Asian markets, and are usually dark in color from the addition of soy sauce.

254

STORAGE: Transfer to a tightly sealed glass jar to store in the refrigerator indefinitely.

PREPARATION AND USE: These vegetables are used as a table condiment. Small pieces add tang to soups and noodles. Rinse well, dry, and slice or dice. If using in a stir-fry dish, fry briefly in a dry pan to refresh them. They are often added to steamed dishes and to bowls of noodles in broth.

PRESERVED VEGETABLES, SZECHUAN

OTHER: Chinese preserved vegetable, preserved Szechuan cabbage

CHINESE: *jar choy*

These are knobby stems of mustard greens or kohlrabi preserved in salt with minced hot chiles. They are available in cans or jars.

STORAGE: After opening, they can be stored in a jar with a tight-fitting lid in the refrigerator indefinitely.

PREPARATION AND USE: Rinse off excess salt. Use, finely chopped, as a seasoning for salads, noodles, and other dishes, allowing 2 to 3 teaspoons per serving. In Singapore, it is combined with pork, celery cabbage, and rice flour noodles. It is often served as a snack with a drizzle of SESAME OIL. It is a common soup ingredient as in the following recipe.

PRESERVED VEGETABLE SOUP

4 cups clear chicken broth	For 4 servings
1 ounce CELLOPHANE NOODLES	
1 cup shredded cooked chicken *or* pork	
¼ cup finely shredded Szechuan preserved vegetables	
2 teaspoons light soy *or* mushroom soy sauce	
2 teaspoons sesame oil	

Bring the broth to a boil in a medium saucepan, remove from heat, and add the noodles. Cover and set aside while you prepare the rest of the ingredients.

Add the remaining ingredients to broth and noodles, return to heat, and simmer 2 minutes. Ladle into serving bowls and drizzle a little sesame oil over each bowl.

TO PREPARE IN ADVANCE: After cooling, this can be refrigerated for up to 2 days. Reheat to serve.

RADISH, WHITE

See DAIKON

RAMBUTAN

OTHER: *rampostan*

This fruit, native to Southeast Asia, which is only occasionally available in this country in Asian markets, is related to the litchi nut. It looks like an orange-red, warty chestnut, but the inside is soft and white, and sweetly delicate.

STORAGE: Store in the refrigerator, and eat as soon as possible.

PREPARATION AND USE: Cut the fruit open around the seed. The flesh clings to the seed and must be scraped away. Serve raw as part of a fruit salad or serve as a dessert or finger snack.

RAMEN

See under NOODLES, JAPANESE

RED GINGER

See GINGER, PRESERVED

RED GRAM

See under DAL, ARHAR

RED-IN-SNOW

OTHER: snow cabbage

CHINESE: *shut lay hug*

Red-in-Snow is a leafy green vegetable with red roots, available fresh during late fall, or salted in brine. The intriguing name comes from the fact that this vegetable grows so early in the spring that its roots are often visible in the yet unmelted snow. The taste is similar to broccoli.

STORAGE: Store in a paper bag inside a plastic bag in the refrigerator for up to a week. The salted form will keep indefinitely in a jar in the refrigerator.

PREPARATION AND USE: One pound serves 2 to 3, depending on its use. This is served as a main ingredient for vegetable stir-fry dishes, especially those containing lima beans or bamboo shoots; in soups; and is often combined with meat. The pickled form is crisp, and a delicious seasoning for meat dishes, especially pork.

RED ROAST PORK

See PORK, BARBECUED

RENKON

See LOTUS ROOT

RICE

Rice, because it is so easy to grow, is the primary food for most of Asia. It did, in fact, originate in Asia, and remains the most important part of every meal. Rice is itself the symbol of food so, when it is served, it is considered a good omen that there will always be food to eat. For the most part, Asians use white rice, not brown, but health-conscious Americans often substitute brown, and many macrobiotic Japanese restaurants serve brown rice.

STORAGE: Store all types of rice in an airtight container in a cool, dark place. Dry rice will easily keep for a year. Leftover cooked rice should be cooled, fluffed with a fork, and refrigerated. Use the next day in fried-rice dishes, or sprinkle with 1 tablespoon water per cup of rice to reheat slowly in a heavy saucepan or in the oven.

PREPARATION AND USE: Plan on approximately ½ cup raw rice (1½ cups cooked) per serving in Asian recipes, as Asians eat greater quantities than Americans. A rule for Americans is ⅓ cup raw rice (1 cup cooked) per serving. Different countries in Asia favor various types of rice and cooking methods. Following is a list of Asian types of rice and their special uses.

BASMATI RICE

OTHER: *bashmati* rice

This is a small-grained rice from India and Pakistan that has a fine texture and is very aromatic. It is considered the very best rice to use for Biriani, an Indian festival dish. It is available in some Asian and Middle Eastern markets. It requires less water in cooking than long-grain rice because it is always rinsed until the rinse water is no longer milky, and then soaked before cooking. As a general rule, soak 1 cup rice in 2½ cups water for 20 to 30 minutes, then drain it well. Melt 1 tablespoon butter in a heavy saucepan and sauté the rice gently to coat each grain with butter. Add 1¼ cups water and salt to taste, bring to a boil, cover, and simmer very slowly for 20 minutes. Let rest without removing the lid for 10 minutes before serving.

BROWN RICE

This is unmilled rice that has not had the bran layer removed by the miller. It is nutty in flavor and much more nutritious than white rice, but is not as popular with most cooks because it takes a good deal longer to cook and because the color is not quite so complementary to other cooked foods. It is available in most markets and health food stores in long-grain and short-grain varieties. It does not keep well and should be stored in the refrigerator.

As a general rule, brown rice takes three times as long to cook as white rice and uses twice as much water, though a quick-cooking brown rice will be found in most supermarkets. We like Madhur Jaffrey's method of cooking it, described in her new book, *World of the East Vegetarian Cooking,* which prevents brown rice from becoming too soft and mushy. Wash 1½ cups long-grain brown rice and drain it. Place it in a heavy, 2-quart saucepan (which has a tight-fitting lid) with 3 cups of water and let soak for one hour. Add ¾ teaspoon salt and bring to a boil; then cover, and lower the heat to a bare simmer, cooking for 35 minutes. Without lifting the lid, allow the rice to rest for 10 minutes before serving. You may wish to toss the cooked rice with a tablespoon or two of butter before serving.

GLUTINOUS (OR SWEET) RICE

OTHER: sweet rice, sticky rice, mochi rice, pearl rice

CHINESE: *naw may* INDONESIAN: *ketan* JAPANESE: *mochigome*
MALAYSIAN: *pulot*

This very white, short-grained rice is the starchiest of all rices and has a sweet, sticky consistency when cooked. It can be found in all Asian markets. (A brown glutinous rice can sometimes be found in health food stores and, like other kinds of brown rice, should be refrigerated for storage.) It is very popular in Asian cooking where it is made into all kinds of sweets and snacks. In Thailand, it is preferred to all other kinds of rice for general use, and is pressed into balls and used to scoop up food with the fingers of the right hand. It must be soaked or rinsed before cooking.

This type of rice is ideal for picnics and for those who like to cook rice ahead of time, because it doesn't harden on standing. Use 1½ cups raw rice for 4 servings. For general cooking purposes, rinse the rice and drain it well; then soak it for 2 hours in hot water or for 6 to 8 hours in cold water; drain it and rinse again. It can be cooked as other rice, but tends to become mushy if overcooked or cooked with too much water. Best results are obtained by either steaming the rice or cooking it in a double boiler. Place in a bamboo steamer and steam, covered, over boiling water for 20 minutes, or place in a double boiler with water to cover it by half an inch, and cook, covered, over boiling water for 20 minutes. Alternatively, it can be cooked in a heavy saucepan, using 1 part water to 1 part soaked rice, covered, over very low heat, for approximately 12 minutes. Salt is usually not added, but that depends on its use.

In China, glutinous rice is used primarily for desserts (such as Eight Precious Rice Pudding), to coat appetizer meat balls (such as Pearl Balls) and as an ingredient in poultry stuffings. To make Pearl Balls (rice-coated meatballs), soak the rice for 30 minutes. Roll the meatballs in the soaked rice, and then steam the meatballs for 45 minutes.

A Japanese festival dish, Sekihan, is made by steaming glutinous rice (soaked in the water from barely cooked AZUKI beans, see under BEANS) with the beans and garnishing with toasted sesame seeds. It is also used for various sweets, and rice-paste cakes—sticky, sweet, rice dumplings much favored by the Japanese. (See MOCHI.) A Vietnamese dish tops this rice with soybean sauce to serve with pork. In Laos, it is used almost exclusively. The Indonesian dish, Lemper, is made by spreading cooked glutinous rice over a banana leaf, filling with spicy chicken or pork, and wrapping into bundles to be steamed. Nasi Kunyit (glutinous yellow rice) combines it with turmeric, garlic, and coconut milk. In Thailand, the steamed rice is simmered with coconut milk and sugar to serve as a dessert or snack with fresh fruit.

RICE, LONG GRAIN

OTHER: Oriental rice, Texas patna

Long-grain white rice is the major rice served in China and in Chinese restaurants, and throughout most of Asia, for that matter.

As a general rule, use 1 cup long-grain rice to 1½ cups boiling water to make 2 to 3 servings of cooked rice for Asian meals where rice plays the predominant role. Unless using American packaged long-grain rice, pick over and rinse the rice very well with cold water before stirring it into boiling salted water. (In China, butter is never added to rice during the cooking. In America, ½ tablespoon of butter per cup of raw rice is often added to the cooking water.) Cook, covered, over low heat for 20 minutes. Turn off the heat and keep covered until serving time (up to 30 minutes). Excellent for use in making Fried Rice. In Singapore, the cooked rice is soaked in coconut milk to serve with many dishes.

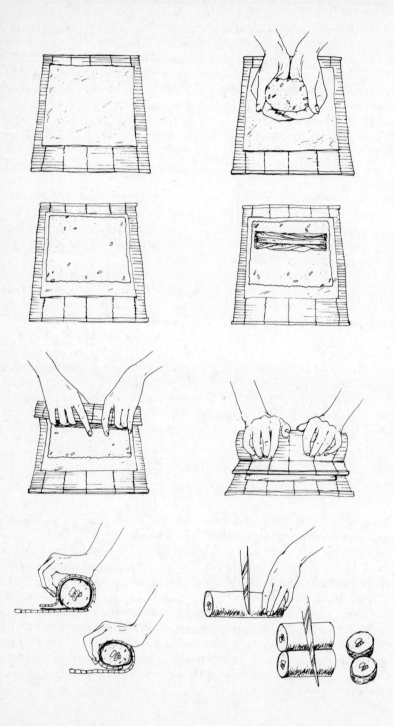

RICE, SHORT GRAIN

OTHER: *okome, shin mai* (newly harvested rice), oval-grain rice, Japanese rice
BRANDS: Cal-Rose rice, Blue Rose rice, Kokhuo Rose rice

This is the type of short-grain, medium-sticky rice most favored in Japan. When cooked, it is just clingy enough to be easily picked up with chopsticks. It can be purchased in cloth, paper, or plastic bags in oriental markets and in many supermarkets. Store in an airtight container in a cool, dry place for up to 6 months. Unlike most types of rice, short-grain rice eventually loses flavor on standing.

As a general rule, short-grain rice requires a bit less water than long-grain, so 1¼ cups water to 1 cup rice will suffice. Rinse rice very well, rubbing it between your hands until the rinsing water is no longer milky. Drain, and place in a heavy saucepan with cold water to cover (about ¾" above the rice level in the pan)—you can measure the water if you prefer. Bring to a boil; then cover and lower the heat to the lowest simmer and cook for 20 minutes. Without lifting the lid, allow the cooked rice to rest for 5 to 10 minutes.

It can be used to coat Pearl Balls (see GLUTINOUS (OR SWEET) RICE for directions). In Japan, the cooked rice is formed into balls to enclose a filling of fish, which are then rolled in AO NORI (see under SEAWEED, DRIED) or sesame seeds.

This rice is the type used for Sushi Rice. To make it, transfer rice immediately after it has finished simmering to a large, shallow baking sheet. Sprinkle with SUSHI-SU (2 tablespoons rice wine vinegar mixed with 1 to 2 tablespoons sugar, depending on how sweet you want the rice to be), toss and fan vigorously to hasten evaporation while the rice cools to room temperature. Place it in a covered bowl and use within two hours. A simpler version can be made as in the following recipe, and either can be used in the recipe for Cucumber Sushi Rolls that follows it.

CUCUMBER SUSHI ROLLS
(KAPPA-MAKI)

4 sheets NORI (see under SEAWEED, DRIED)   For 4 rolls
1 recipe Easy Sushi Rice
    Hand Vinegar, consisting of 1 teaspoon Japanese rice
      vinegar mixed with 3 tablespoons cold water
2 tablespoons WASABI, mixed to a paste with water
½ Japanese or hydroponic cucumber, cut in 3" sections and
      then into fine julienne strips
4 teaspoons toasted sesame seeds

TO SERVE:
> Japanese soy sauce
> Any remaining wasabi paste

It is easiest to use a bamboo sushi mat to make these, though a small kitchen towel can be used if necessary. Toast a sheet of nori by holding with tongs and waving over a gas flame for a few seconds until greenish and crisp. Place it, shiny side down, on the mat. Dip your fingers in Hand Vinegar and spread the rice, approximately ½" thick, over the seaweed, covering three-fourths of it, and leaving one-fourth (the part furthest from you) uncovered. Spread some wasabi paste in a strip across the center of the rice. Lay some cucumber strips on top and sprinkle lightly with toasted sesame seeds. Lift the closest edge of nori up and over the filling just to meet the other edge of nori beyond the far edge of the rice, using the mat to roll it very tightly. (This may take a bit of practice, but mistakes are edible.) Remove from the mat and use a very sharp slicing knife to cut in half crosswise. Cut each half in three pieces approximately 1" wide. Repeat until all rice and nori are used.

Stand the slices, cut side up and sides touching, on serving plates. Serve with Japanese soy sauce and wasabi paste for dipping.

TO PREPARE IN ADVANCE: Sushi rolls are best freshly made and eaten while the rice is still slightly warm. They can be left at room temperature or placed in the refrigerator for up to 12 hours, though the nori loses crispness on standing.

EASY SUSHI RICE

For 4 cups

The Japanese usually add the vinegar gradually to the seasoned cooked rice, fanning it continuously, to give the rice a lustrous appearance. (For that classic technique, and directions for making many varieties of sushi, see the Japanese cookbooks listed in our RECOMMENDED ETHNIC COOKBOOKS section.) This quick method has almost as good a result, the only difference being that the rice is a bit less shiny.

1½ cups Japanese short-grain rice
1½ cups water
¼ cup Japanese rice vinegar (SUSHI SU)
3 tablespoons sugar
2 tablespoons MIRIN or SAKE
2 teaspoons salt

Rinse rice in a strainer under cold water until the water runs clear; drain. Bring water to boil in heavy saucepan. Stir in rice, cover, and simmer over low heat for 15 minutes until the water has been absorbed. Stir in remaining ingredients, toss, and let stand, covered, for 15 minutes. The rice is now ready to use.

RICE CRUSTS, DRIED

CHINESE: *go bah*

These thin pieces of dried cooked rice are sold in plastic bags in Chinese grocery stores but they are invariably stale-tasting, and you would be better off making your own using a recipe in a Chinese cookbook.

STORAGE: They will keep indefinitely in an airtight container.

PREPARATION AND USE: These are used primarily to add the sizzle to Sizzling Rice Soup. Deep-fry the desired number of pieces for 10 seconds—they will triple in size. Immediately take them to the table and add them to hot soup, bracing yourself for steam and a delightful crackling sound.

SIZZLING RICE SOUP

RICE CRUSTS: For 8 servings
    Oil to coat a baking pan
1½ cups long-grain rice (regular, not converted)
2 cups water
    Oil for deep-frying (peanut oil preferred)

SOUP:
1 whole chicken breast, skinned, boned, and cut in ¼"
    strips *or* 12 ounces small raw shrimp
3 tablespoons cornstarch
2 tablespoons water
1 tablespoon light soy or mushroom soy sauce
6 cups clear chicken broth
    Optional: 3 dried Chinese or Japanese mushrooms,
    soaked, trimmed, and cut in fine shreds
3 scallions, thinly sliced, including part of the green
2 teaspoons sesame oil

Line a jelly-roll pan (or any shallow pan measuring approximately 10" × 15") with foil, and spread with oil. To make the rice crusts, rinse the rice well, drain, and spread on the baking pan, taking care that the grains of rice are touching each other. Pour 2 cups of cold water evenly over the rice, and let stand 30 minutes at room temperature.

263

Bake the rice at 350° for 30 minutes. Remove from the oven and, with the back of an oiled spoon, press the rice down firmly so the grains will stick together. Return to the oven, lower the heat to 300°, and continue baking, uncovered, for 1 more hour to dry the rice.

Cool slightly; then break into pieces approximately 3" by 3". (Some may still be damp.) Dry on racks, covered with a towel, overnight, or until completely dry.

To make the soup, mix the chicken or shrimp with 1 tablespoon of the cornstarch, coating it thoroughly and refrigerate for at least 15 minutes. (This will tenderize the meat.) While meat is tenderizing, start heating oil for frying the rice crusts in a deep saucepot or deep-fat fryer to 375–400°. Now combine the remaining cornstarch with water and soy sauce. In a large saucepan, heat the broth with the mushrooms to boiling point. Stir together the soy mixture and the chicken or shrimp, add to the simmering broth, and simmer 3 to 4 minutes, just until chicken or shrimp are cooked. Remove from the heat and add green onions and sesame oil. Keep warm, but do not boil.

At the last possible moment, and when oil has reached 375°–400°, fry the rice crusts, two at a time, for about 10 seconds on each side until puffed and browned. Drain on paper towels, take to the table, and immediately add to the soup (in tureen or individual serving bowls), which will cause the soup to steam and sizzle dramatically.

TO PREPARE IN ADVANCE: The soup can be reheated. The rice crusts can be stored in an airtight container for several days, or frozen. Thaw, uncovered, at room temperature until dry. Deep-fry just before serving.

RICE FLOUR

CHINESE: *doug may fun* (made from long-grain rice), *naw may fun* (made from glutinous rice) INDIAN: *chawal ka ata* JAPANESE: *joshinko* (made from short-grain rice), *shiratamako* and *mochiko* (made from cooked and uncooked glutinous rice, respectively)

These are very finely ground rice flours used for making all manner of sweets and confections, and used as thickeners. All are sold in Asian markets in 8- to 12-ounce containers. "Water-ground" rice flour is very fine-textured and very perishable.

STORAGE: Rice flours will keep indefinitely in an airtight container in a cool, dark place, but try to use them up within 3 months. If you buy one labeled "water-ground," it will have a very short life and should be used within a few days.

PREPARATION AND USE: *Joshinko* is used primarily to make confections. *Mochiko* is mixed with water to make MOCHI (rice cakes). Rice flours, which are soft and sticky when cooked, are used in the Orient in dough wrappers, pastries, and dessert soups. Those made with glutinous rice are especially fine to use as thickeners in Western-style desserts that are to be frozen because they will not separate like other thickeners such as cornstarch. Ground rice flour is used in southern India to make Dosas, crepe-like pancakes. In Sri Lanka, it is used to make Roti, a coconut flavored bread that is delicious with curries.

ROTIS

For 8 flat breads

This recipe has been adapted from Charmaine Solomon's *The Complete Asian Cookbook,* one of the finest books of authentic Asian recipes in existence. This is a Sinhalese version, popularly served for breakfast in that country. It is best made just before serving and is a fine accompaniment to Asian curries and rice dishes.

2 cups rice flour or ROTI FLOUR
½ cup grated fresh coconut or dried coconut
1 teaspoon salt
7 ounces water (about)
   GHEE or vegetable oil

In a medium mixing bowl, combine the flour, coconut, and salt. Add water to form a soft dough. Knead the dough into a ball, cover, and set aside for 30 minutes at room temperature.

Form the dough into 8 balls. Pat or roll each ball gently in a 5″–6″ circle. Heat a griddle or skillet with a light coating of GHEE or vegetable oil and cook in the same manner as tortillas, turning once, until lightly browned on both sides.

Serve warm.

RICE FLOUR NOODLES

See under NOODLES

RICE PAPER, VIETNAMESE

VIETNAMESE: *banh trang* or *cha gio*

A transparent dough made from rice flour and various other starches combined with water is used to make these very crisp, papery wrappers in Vietnam and other Southeast Asian countries. Their crosshatch pattern comes from being dried on bamboo mats. They can be found in many oriental markets, imported from Thailand or Vietnam. They are round or square and vary in size. The finest are very thin.

STORAGE: If tightly wrapped, they will keep indefinitely in a cool, dry place.

PREPARATION AND USE: Dampen the wrappers with cold water and set aside for a few minutes to soften. When soft and transparent, fill with food to be eaten by hand without further cooking, or with fillings to be deep-fried for crispy Vietnamese Spring Rolls. Any similar fillings, such as those for Philippine LUMPIA, or Hugh's Filling for Peking Pancakes (see under PEKING PANCAKES) can be used. Unlike Chinese-style spring rolls or egg rolls, these can be filled in the morning and refrigerated for several hours before cooking. For best results, place the sealed rolls in cool oil, then place over medium heat and cook for 20 to 30 minutes until they are crisp and golden. Drain well on paper towels.

RICE STICKS
See NOODLES, RICE FLOUR

RICE WAFERS
See SEMBEI

ROCK SUGAR
See SUGAR, ROCK

ROSE WATER OR ESSENCE
ARABIC: *ma ward*

Two types of rose-flavored liquids are available in Indian and Middle Eastern markets—rose water and rose essence. Both are made by distilling fresh rose petals, usually pink damask rose, but rose essence is highly concentrated. Both are used discreetly (better too little than too much). Many liquor stores and pharmacies carry rose water. Another product, called Rose Syrup, is imported from Singapore and sold in Asian markets in 8- to 16-ounce bottles. It consists of sugar, water, rose essence, and citric acid, comes in varying shades of pink, and is used in milk shakes and as a pancake topping. It should not be used as a substitute for the flavorings.

STORAGE: They will keep in a cool place indefinitely, though they lose strength on standing.

USE: There is a big difference in the strengths of these two products. A few drops of rose essence have the strength of a tablespoon of rose water. In America, these are often used to flavor blended drinks, but in Asia and the Middle East they are sprinkled over desserts and fresh fruit as a flavoring, and used as a flavoring in some baked goods, such as the Greek cookies, Kourabiedes.

This flavor is very often used in Indian and Sinhalese curried dishes, and an Indian dish, Yakni Pilau, consists of rice cooked with spices and rose water. A few drops of the essence flavors one layer of a jellied dessert served in Singapore, with the two other layers flavored one with vanilla, and the other with almond. In Morocco, it is a common flavoring for sliced oranges, which are then sprinkled with cinnamon. It is an important ingredient of Rahat Lokum, a dessert more commonly known as Turkish Delight. In Greece, it is added to Halva to make Halvas Me Anthonero.

ROSE WINE SPIRITS

This liqueur made from roses is available in Chinese wine stores.

STORAGE: It will keep indefinitely in the liquor cabinet.

PREPARATION AND USE: Used to add a rose aroma and flavoring to desserts, or simply as a liqueur.

ROTI FLOUR

This creamy, rather granular flour is less processed than our all-purpose flour. You will find it in Asian markets and in some health food stores.

STORAGE: As any flour.

USE: Roti flour is used in Asia to make many types of unleavened breads, such as Paratha. It is also used to make Roti, a popular bread served as an accompaniment to meals. Our recipe appears with RICE FLOUR.

SAFFRON

See HERBS, SPICES, AND SEASONING BLENDS section

SAKE

(SAH-keh)

OTHER: *nihon shu* (Japanese rice wine)

The word "sake" in Japan actually refers to all liquors. In the United States, it refers only to rice wine, which is often heated to serve as a beverage and also used extensively as a seasoning in cooking. The Japanese have found that it contains amino acids, which makes it an excellent meat tenderizer. It also removes excess saltiness and fish flavors from foods. It is available in most liquor stores and in those oriental markets that sell alcoholic beverages.

STORAGE: Fine sake does not keep longer than a year. After opening, store in the refrigerator in a tightly sealed container and enjoy as soon as possible.

PREPARATION AND USE: Sake is traditionally served warm in the wintertime as a beverage. We have a glazed pottery "sake set" that we particularly enjoy. The serving container is first set into a bowl of very hot water and then brought to the table where the warmed sake is poured into small, jigger-like cups. During the summer, it is more commonly served "on the rocks." When used in cooking, the alcohol is often burned off, just as it is with wines used in Western cooking, though a few minutes of simmering will do the job for you.

SAMBAL

This term refers to red-chili condiments and pastes used in the cuisines of Southeast Asia. It refers as well to the assortment of condiments served with Indonesian Rijsttafel (literally "rice table"). The kinds that are often found in Asian markets (and in Dutch markets, which are an excellent source of Indonesian ingredients) are sambal *oelek (ulek),* which is mostly chiles and salt, sometimes mixed with TAMARIND water, and can be used in place of Moroccan HARISSA (see THE FOODS OF THE MIDDLE EAST section), sambal *bajak,* which is similar except for the addition of dried shrimp and spices, and sambal *manis,* which is a sweeter and milder type. Some recipes suggest substituting pure Asian chili powder in equal measure.

STORAGE: After opening, store in the refrigerator indefinitely.

USE: Use as a seasoning in cooking and as a table condiment with Southeast Asian rice dishes. Sambal manis is often served with LUMPIA. Sambal oelek is used in Indonesian Saté Udang (skewered grilled prawns with garlic and JAGGERY). Sambal bajak is used in Indonesian Saté sauce for grilled skewered meats.

SANSHO

See PEPPERCORNS, SZECHUAN in HERBS, SPICES, AND
SEASONING BLENDS section

SAPODILLA

See THE FOODS OF LATIN AMERICA section

SATO IMO

See TARO ROOT

SATSUMA IMO

(SAH-tsoo-moh EE-moh)
OTHER: Japanese sweet potato

Sometimes available in Oriental produce markets, these red-skinned and orange-fleshed sweet potatoes are slightly bitter, and not as sweet as the more familiar sweet potato or yam. Any sweet potato or yam can be substituted.

STORAGE: They will keep for up to 2 weeks in a cool, dry spot.

PREPARATION AND USE: Bake without peeling to serve as a delicious accompaniment to almost any meal. Sliced, it is excellent for Tempura (deep-fried shrimp and vegetables). In Japan, as *yakimo,* it is traditionally baked on hot stones, and sold in the streets from carts during the wintertime. It is made into a puree and formed into chestnut-shapes to serve as a confection on New Year (for this raw slices are soaked in cold water for 24 hours to remove any trace of bitterness that would be undesirable in a sweet).

SAUERKRAUT, CHINESE

See PRESERVED VEGETABLES, CHINESE

SAUSAGE, CHINESE LIVER

CHINESE: *gum gun yuen*

Duck liver is added to pork liver to make a darker, less sweet, and stronger-flavored sausage than Chinese pork sausage (SEE SAUSAGE, CHINESE PORK). Liver sausage is used and stored in the same manner.

269

SAUSAGE, CHINESE PORK

OTHER: Cantonese sausage

CHINESE: *lop cheong*

This highly seasoned, sweet, smoky sausage comes 4″ to 6″ long, and is available in most Chinese meat markets where it is generally sold in pairs (there are approximately 4 pairs to a pound). It has a rather hard, brittle texture similar to Italian PEPPERONI (see under SAUSAGES, SEMI-DRY AND DRY in THE FOODS OF EUROPE section).

STORAGE: Tightly wrapped, it will keep for up to 1 month in the refrigerator or 6 months in the freezer.

PREPARATION AND USE: One sausage will serve 1 or 2, depending on how it is used. Wash well and either simmer or steam them for about 15 minutes until they are translucent in appearance. Quite often they are steamed right along with the rice, releasing their flavorful juices into those items as they cook. Cut in pieces to serve or to use in stir-fry or other dishes. Cooked ARROWROOT is often served with them instead of rice. In Malaysia, these sausages are steamed and thinly sliced to flavor a dish of fried rice noodles with pork, squid, prawns, and oyster sauce.

SCALLIONS, PICKLED

CHINESE: *kew tow* JAPANESE: *rakko*

These are the white bulbs of scallions, pickled in vinegar and sugar, available in jars of varying sizes.

STORAGE: They will keep indefinitely in the refrigerator.

USE: They are used to add flavor and texture to sweet-and-sour dishes and as a seasoning for bland foods. They are a very common table relish. Use to garnish salads and other dishes.

SCALLOPS, DRIED

CHINESE: *gong yew chew*

These amber-colored dried disks of scallops lend a strong and sweet fishy flavor to soups and vegetable dishes.

STORAGE: They will keep indefinitely in a jar on the pantry shelf.

PREPARATION AND USE: They must be soaked before using—in warm sherry or water for 8 hours or so. Then steam for 10 minutes to soften. Shred to add to soups and braised or stir-fry dishes.

SEA CUCUMBER
See BÊCHE DE MER

SEA SLUG
See BÊCHE DE MER

SEA URCHIN
See UNI

SEAWEED, DRIED

Seaweeds, of which there are many types, are widely used in Asian cooking. Dried varieties are sold in Asian markets and in many health food stores, usually in clear packets so the shopper can see what they look like. Following is an alphabetical listing of those commonly used in Asian recipes.

AO NORI
(AH-oh NOH-ree)

These flakes of a type of dried green seaweed are available in small bottles with shaker tops. They are an extremely rich source of iron. A powdered form, *ao noriko,* is also sold.

STORAGE: They will keep indefinitely in a cool, dry spot.

USE: They are most commonly used as a table condiment to sprinkle over noodle or rice dishes. The powdered form is often used as an herb seasoning and to flavor potato chips.

HAIR SEAWEED

CHINESE: *faht choy*

These fine strands of a dark purple marine plant resemble tangled hair—hence the name. They add an interesting texture to soups and other dishes, and are a traditional ingredient to serve for Chinese New Year, because the

Chinese ideograms of its name translate as "may you become rich." It is sold in Chinese markets and is very expensive.

STORAGE: It will keep indefinitely tightly wrapped on the pantry shelf.

PREPARATION AND USE: One-quarter cup is usually ample for 4 servings. Soak for 1 hour in warm water, or in equal parts water and dry sherry. Rinse very well in cold water and pull apart gently. Toss with oil and sherry to coat the strands. Let stand a few minutes. Rinse and drain again. Use as an unusual garnish for many dishes and soups. Add to vegetable dishes for intriguing texture.

Hijiki
(HEE-jee-kee)

These black, brittle, ½" strands of a type of seaweed are soaked and used as a vegetable. The strips are darker in color and wider than HAIR SEAWEED. Hijiki can be found in Japanese markets and health food stores. It has a strong, slightly anise flavor and a high calcium content.

STORAGE: It will keep in a cool, dark, dry place indefinitely. After opening, any unused portion can be stored in an airtight container for several months.

PREPARATION AND USE: Allow ¼ to ½ cup for 4 servings. Rinse in cool water, and then soak either overnight in cool water, or for 20 minutes in warm water. Swish it around with chopsticks and lift gently, leaving any grit at the bottom of the soaking pan. Rinse again, and then cook briefly in a small amount of seasoned broth. Use as a garnish or add to vegetable dishes. In Japan, Hijiki Nituke is cooked with fried bean curd and finely cut carrots and onions.

Jee Choy
OTHER: purple laver

Jee choy is made from a dark purple marine plant and is sold, dried in tissue-like sheets, measuring 7" to 8" square, in packages by weight. The Chinese name means "purple vegetable." It is the same type of seaweed as HAIR SEAWEED, but differently shaped. It has a tangy, slightly sweet flavor and is highly nutritious.

STORAGE: If tightly wrapped, it will keep indefinitely on the pantry shelf.

PREPARATION AND USE: Soak for 1 hour in cold water or 10 minutes in warm water. Rinse and squeeze dry. It is usually served in soups. At Mr. Chow's restaurants in New York and Beverly Hills, it is cut into strips, and then deep-fried and sprinkled with salt to serve as an appetizer.

KOMBU

(KOHM-boo)
OTHER: *konbu, kubu,* kelp, sea tangle

Kombu is dried folded sheets of kelp. It is available in Japanese markets and health food stores, in cellophane packages of varying sizes. It is used primarily along with KATSUO-BUSHI to make DASHI (fish stock). There are six main varieties, of which *Hidaka* konbu is considered the finest available.

STORAGE: The unopened package will keep indefinitely in a dry place. After opening, it will keep in an airtight container at room temperature for several months.

PREPARATION AND USE: One ounce of this makes 4 servings of dashi. Do not wash, but gently wipe away any surface powder. The surface can be lightly scored, but there is some debate among Japanese chefs over whether this is desirable. Our recipe for dashi uses kombu. After steeping the sheets of kelp to make dashi, save them in a plastic bag in the refrigerator to make rolls (as you would use flour tortillas to make Burritos) of cooked foods, such as beans, fish, etc.

Kombu is used for Sushi (vinegared rice dishes) and is sometimes pickled to serve as a relish. Fried, salted kombu is an excellent snack to go with beer or SAKE. In Japan, this has a myriad of uses and is even used as a kind of chewing gum.

NORI

(NOH-ri)
OTHER: *asakusa* nori, *sushinori,* roasted seaweed, *murasaki* nori, purple nori

These thin sheets of dark green or purplish dried seaweed are available in plastic packages or in cans. The sheets, which measure 7" by 8", resemble carbon paper. They may be packaged in cellophane, usually 10 sheets to a package, flat or folded. Some fancy more expensive brands come in tin boxes or canisters. Smaller sheets or strips, called "miniatures," are used as a garnish atop rice for breakfast or are crumbled to use as a seasoning. Packaged nori labeled *yakinori* is pre-toasted; that labeled *ajijsuke-nori* is seasoned with soy sauce.

STORAGE: After opening, store any unused sheets in the freezer or in an airtight container along with the moisture-absorbing granules with which it was originally packed. Freezing is the best method of storing this in order to preserve its delicate fragrance for a maximum period of time. Don't be a miser when using this, because its quality deteriorates on standing.

PREPARATION AND USE: The flavor will be enhanced if you take a few seconds to toast the shiny side of a sheet of nori just before use. Hold one corner with tongs and wave it over a gas flame for a few seconds until it becomes greenish and crisp. Nori is often used to wrap seasoned rice and vegetables to create Norimake-zushi, and to wrap MOCHI (rice balls) as a snack. It is also crumbled to make the seasoning called AO NORI.

SHIRATA KOMBU

(shee-RAH-tah KOHM-boo)
OTHER: translucent kelp

These thin, pale beige, silklike sheets of kelp that have a delicate taste of the sea are occasionally available in plastic packets in oriental markets. Shirata kombu is the core of the kelp that is left after KOMBU is shaved away. Usually the packages contain 5 sheets, individually wrapped.

STORAGE: After opening, it can be stored tightly wrapped in the refrigerator for up to a month.

PREPARATION AND USE: These sheets are used as a garnish for soups and rice dishes. Moistened with rice vinegar, they become delicious edible wrappings for rice or cooked foods. In Japan, they are often simmered in a sweet-sour sauce and used to decorate a fish-rice loaf known as Saba-Zushi, or they are finely shredded to serve on cooked rice.

WAKAME

(wah-KAH-meh)
OTHER: lobe leaf seaweed

These strands of dried seaweed, which are extremely high in nutrients with almost no calories, are sold in oriental markets and health food stores in 6" strips. When soaked, they turn bright green and slippery. They are highly prized for their flavor and texture.

STORAGE: They will keep indefinitely in a cool spot in an airtight container.

PREPARATION AND USE: Soak in warm water for 5 to 20 minutes, depending on the quality of the wakame, until soft. Cut away and discard any tough parts. Chop to use as a garnish in soups and in vinegared relishes. Do not cook these strands longer than a minute or so or they will lose some of their nutrients.

SEAWEED NOODLES

See NOODLES

SECOND BAMBOO

See BEAN CURD, DRIED STICKS

SEMBEI

(SEHM-beh)
OTHER: rice wafers, rice crackers

The term "sembei" covers a wide range of rice wafers (available in various shapes and sizes in oriental markets and many supermarkets) that are made with rice flour and egg, and flavored with various seasonings, such as sesame seeds, seaweed, or soy sauce. They are sweet or salty, depending on the seasoning and, except for the unseasoned variety, they contain a high amount of MONOSODIUM GLUTAMATE.

STORAGE: After opening, they can be stored in an airtight container on the pantry shelf indefinitely.

USE: Serve as a snack. Except for those without seasonings, these are not for people on low-sodium diets.

SESAME OIL

OTHER: sesame seed-flavored oil

CHINESE: *jee ma yo* INDIAN: *til* JAPANESE: *goma abura*

Sesame oil is amber-colored with a strong toasted-sesame-seed flavor. Do not confuse this product with clear sesame-seed oil, which is cold-pressed oil found in health food stores and supermarkets. Of the Chinese brands, Sona and Lucky brands are superior to the more widely available Dynasty brand found in many supermarkets. As a general rule, Japanese brands are lighter in flavor than the Chinese. There is also a chili-flavored sesame oil to be found in oriental markets, which is used as a table seasoning—combining these two flavors (sesame and chili) is a good idea because both are best when added after cooking is finished.

STORAGE: Sesame oil will keep in a cool pantry for up to 6 months; in the refrigerator indefinitely.

PREPARATION AND USE: Add just before serving to stir-fried vegetables, soups, and sauces. It is delicious in salad dressings. If heated, it loses its flavor and it burns easily.

SESAME SEEDS

See HERBS, SPICES, AND SEASONING BLENDS section

SESAME SEED PASTE

OTHER: sesame paste

This thick, golden paste, the solids left from the production of sesame-flavored oil, looks and tastes very much like peanut butter. In fact, peanut butter that has been thinned a bit with hot water and some sesame-flavored oil makes an excellent substitute. It is similar as well to TAHINI (see THE FOODS OF THE MIDDLE EAST section), which is made with untoasted sesame seeds, and is popular in Middle Eastern cooking and widely available in health food stores. The oriental type, because it is made with toasted seeds, is much stronger in flavor.

STORAGE: It will keep indefinitely in the refrigerator.

PREPARATION AND USE: If the paste is too solid to get out of the jar, heat the jar gently in a pan of hot water or in the microwave oven for a few seconds. It is usually diluted with hot water to use. It adds a wonderful flavor to cold chicken dishes, such as Chinese Hacked Chicken, and to salad dressings and noodles. It is used in Vietnam to make a dish which translates as Beef in Sesame Sauce.

To make your own sesame paste, grind toasted sesame seeds in an electric coffee mill or spice grinder, and then thin with a bit of sesame oil.

SEVEN SPICE SEASONING

OTHER: seven-spice pepper

JAPANESE: *hichimi togarashi, shichimi togarashi*

This Japanese seasoning blend of hot pepper, *sansho* (see SZECHUAN PEPPERCORNS under OTHER PEPPERCORNS in HERBS, SPICES, AND SEASONING BLENDS section) pepper, sesame seed, mustard seed, pepper, poppy, or hemp seed, and flakes of NORI (see SEAWEED, DRIED) along with powdered tangerine peel is available in small shaker bottles in Japanese markets. *Hichi* (seven) is a dialect pronunciation of *shichi* (seven).

STORAGE: Purchase only in small quantities, as this loses its aroma quickly on the pantry shelf.

USE: Use as a table condiment, especially on hot SOBA (buckwheat noodles), UDON (wheat flour noodles) and KISHIMEN (flat white noodles). (See NOODLES.)

SEVIYAN

See under NOODLES

SHARK'S FIN

CHINESE: *yu chee*

The threadlike, dried cartilage from the fin of shark is available loose or in cans imported from the South Seas. This bland-tasting delicacy is considered essential for formal Chinese dinners, especially weddings, because it contains vitamins that are supposed to aid health and virility. It is also high in calcium, and very expensive.

It is available with or without the rough outer black skin, and those of the finest quality are about 5″ long (the average length is 2″ to 3″). They must be soaked before using. A cleaned and processed kind, called "Shark's Fin Needles," is sold in sealed packages. As a general rule, you will need 4 times the amount of the kind with skin, and 2 times the amount without skin, as you will the processed type. Canned shark's fin is cleaned, but only partially prepared.

STORAGE: All types, unopened, will keep indefinitely on the pantry shelf.

PREPARATION AND USE: All meat and skin should be removed. If starting with the type with black skin, simmer it for 1½ hours, cool, and remove the skin. Now this type, and the kind that comes without skin, should be simmered for 1 to 2 hours in fresh water with a slice of ginger and a clove of garlic. Rinse, and when cool enough to handle, shred and rinse again.

Processed shark fin should be soaked for 30 minutes in cold water. Rinse this, and canned shark's fin, well before adding to dishes. It combines well with many dishes—soups, poultry stuffing, pork, "red-cooked" meats, crabmeat. Its most traditional use in in Shark's Fin Soup.

SHAOSING WINE

See WINE, RICE, CHINESE

277

SHICHIMI
See SEVEN SPICE SEASONING

SHINING NOODLES
See NOODLES, CELLOPHANE

SHIN MAI
See RICE, SHORT-GRAIN

SHIRATAKI
See NOODLES

SHIRATAMAKO
See RICE FLOUR

SHISO
(shee-SOH)
OTHER: perilla; beefsteak leaves (red variety)

JAPANESE: *ao-jiso* (green); *aka-jiso* (red)

The green variety of this aromatic leaf from a plant of the mint family is available in bunches in oriental produce markets all year in areas where it is cultivated. If it is difficult to find, you can order the seeds from nurseries that specialize in oriental vegetables (see SHOPPING SOURCES) and grow this very easily in your garden. The red variety, which has different uses, may be harder to find.

STORAGE: Wrapped in damp paper towels and stored inside a plastic bag in the crisper of the refrigerator, it will keep for up to a week. The aroma diminishes on standing, so use as soon as possible for full enjoyment.

USE: This green is used primarily as an aromatic garnish, as a Tempura (deep-fried shrimp and vegetable) ingredient, and the chopped leaves can be added to salads or served with raw seafood dishes, such as Sushi and Sashimi. The red is not as fragrant and is used primarily in making UMEBOSHI (pickled plums) and other pickles. The pickled leaves are used for wrapping foods, similarly to pickled vine leaves (see GRAPE LEAVES in THE FOODS OF THE MIDDLE EAST section) but they have a considerably different flavor.

SHOGA
See GINGER, PICKLED

SHOYU
See SOY SAUCE, JAPANESE

SHRIMP CHIPS
See KRUPEK

SHRIMP, DRIED
OTHER: dried prawns, prawn powder

CHINESE: *har may* INDONESIAN and MALAYSIAN: *udang kering*
IN LATIN AMERICA: *camarón seco, camarón molido* (if ground) THAI: *kung haeng*

These small, amber-pink, dried shellfish have a very strong fishy taste and, after soaking, are used as a flavoring in many dishes. They are sold in cellophane bags of varying sizes, and the color is the clue to freshness—don't buy gray ones, they are old. MALDIVE FISH are sometimes substituted.

STORAGE: They will keep for up to 6 months on the pantry shelf.

PREPARATION AND USE: They are used whole, chopped, or finely ground, in mortar and pestle or pulverized in blender. Soak for 10 minutes to 1 hour in warm sherry or water. Add to soups and many dishes where a seafood taste is desired, such as Indonesian Prawn, Eggplant and Coconut Milk Soup. It is essential to Burmese Balachaung, an assortment of condiments and chopped herbs to accompany rice, the most popular item of which is referred to as *tolee molee*. Dried shrimp combines especially well with bean curd, spinach, and eggplant, and is used in Latin American and African cooking as well.

SHRIMP EGGS
OTHER: *har gee*

Sold by the ounce, these dried, brownish-hued eggs add a delicate shrimp flavor to many dishes. They are stronger tasting than fresh shrimp, but not nearly as fishy as dried shrimp.

STORAGE: These can be stored indefinitely in a cool, dry spot, tightly sealed.

USE: These are used primarily to flavor soups and stir-fry dishes.

SHRIMP PASTE, CHINESE

OTHER: shrimp sauce

CHINESE: *hom har jeung*

Chinese shrimp paste is a grayish-pink, pourable sauce with a very strong and zesty shrimp taste. It is salty and is used only sparingly, usually with a bit of sugar. Its strong aroma lessens as the sauce is cooked.

STORAGE: It will keep indefinitely in the refrigerator.

USE: Use very small amounts to add a shrimp flavor to dishes containing fish, chicken, and pork. It combines well with bean curd, vegetables, and fried rice.

SHRIMP PASTE, SOUTHEAST ASIAN

BURMESE: *ngapi* INDONESIAN: *trasi* MALAYSIAN: *blacan, blachan, bagoong* or *bagoongalamang* THAI: *kapee* VIETNAMESE: *mam ruoc*

This pungent product, a very common ingredient in Malaysian, Indonesian, and Southeast Asian recipes, can be found in Asian markets in two forms: fresh (or liquid) and dried. The fresh is usually pink and sold in bottles or jars, which must be stored in the refrigerator. The dried, which is made from pulverized, salted, fermented shrimp, ranges in color from pink to gray, and is sold in cakes, slabs, or cans. Both have a very strong odor, which disappears completely in cooking. The dried form is never used uncooked.

STORAGE: The dried paste, tightly capped, can be stored in a cool, dry place for months. The fresh should be refrigerated after opening.

PREPARATION AND USE: This is a very popular ingredient in Southeast Asia and is used to add a shrimp flavor to many sauces. As a general rule, twice as much of the liquid type is used as the dried, so ½ teaspoon dried, or 1 teaspoon liquid will usually flavor dishes to serve 4 to 6. If these products are not available, you can substitute anchovy paste, using half as much as the dried shrimp paste called for in the recipe, but only one quarter the amount of fresh called for.

The dried type, which must be cooked, should be minced or crumbled. It is then either cooked with other spices or roasted separately (for 2 to 3 minutes in a sealed foil packet placed over a gas flame or under a broiler—the foil prevents the aroma from permeating the house) before adding it to cooked dishes.

In Vietnam, shrimp paste is almost always added to soups. In Indonesia, it is used in Nasi Uduk (rice cooked in coconut milk with garlic and spices) and Nasi Goreng (fried rice with shrimp and meat). In Malaysia, it is used in SAMBALS to serve with rice and curries. In Thailand, it flavors many dishes, such as Kapee Pla (shrimp paste sambal) and NAM PRIK.

SHRIMP SLICES

See KRUPEK

SHUNGIKU

See CHRYSANTHEMUM GREENS

SILK MELON

See OKRA, CHINESE

SILK SQUASH

See OKRA, CHINESE

SILVER EARS

See CLOUD EARS, under MUSHROOMS, DRIED

SNOW CABBAGE

See RED-IN-SNOW

SNOW PEAS

OTHER: sugar peas, Chinese pea pods, edible pod

CHINESE: *ho lon dow* FRENCH: *mange-tout* INDONESIAN: *kacang kapri* JAPANESE: *saya endo*

These bright green, flat pea pods with a crisp texture are eaten in their entirety, pods and all. They are available fresh in most supermarkets all year, but their price is lowest between May and September. The small ones are the choicest and they are almost invariably stir-fried. Frozen snow peas are a limp imitation of their fresh counterparts and should be used only when fresh are unavailable. Ordinary fresh peas, which have a parchmentlike, inedible lining inside their pods, are not a substitute. The new "sugar snap" pea, developed by Burpee, is a cross between the two types, and may be substituted in recipes.

STORAGE: These will keep fresh for up to 1 week if placed in a paper bag inside a plastic bag in the crisper portion of the refrigerator. They may also be refrigerated for the same length of time in a bowl of cold water if the water is changed from time to time.

PREPARATION AND USE: Break off tips and pull backward to remove the strings. Add to any stir-fry dishes. They cook very quickly, so take care not to overcook them or they will lose their crisp quality and become mushy.

SOBA

See under NOODLES

SOMEN

See under NOODLES

SOYBEAN CHEESE

See BEAN CURD, FERMENTED

SOYBEAN PASTE, JAPANESE

See MISO

SOY FLOUR

See KINAKO

SOY SAUCE, CHINESE

CHINESE: *she yo* or *sho yu* (table soy—*jew yo*, dark soy—*cho yo*, heavy soy or black soy—*see yau*, light soy—*shang cho*, thick soy or "soy jam"—*yewn she jeung*) FRENCH: *sauce piquante de soya* INDONESIAN: *ketjap anis* (See also KETJAP MANIS) ITALIAN: *salsa di soya* MALAYSIAN: *kichup* or *tauhu* SPANISH: *salsa de soya* THAI: *nam pla siiw*

Soy sauce is a fragrant and savory, salty brown liquid made from naturally fermented soybeans, wheat, yeast, and salt. In China, there are many different brews—shops there sell 40 or 50 types—and these imported brands are by far the best to be found in American markets. A number of synthetically fermented soy sauces have appeared recently. To avoid them, look for the words "naturally brewed" on the label.

There are basically only a few types. Light soy is pale and thin. Dark soy, often called "table soy" because it is found on the tables of Chinese restaurants, has caramel added. Heavy soy, or "black soy" as it is sometimes called, has molasses added. These last two are used interchangeably, according to the preference of the cook. One of our particular favorites is "Mushroom Soy" (called also "Sauce de soja aux champignons" on the Pearl River Bridge label), which is imported from China. It is flavored with mushrooms during the final stages of processing and is delightfully smooth. "Soy jam" is the pastelike sediment of soy sauce and is sold in cans in Chinese markets.

STORAGE: Soy has a high salt content so it can be stored indefinitely on the pantry shelf. Any low-sodium brands should be stored in the refrigerator.

USE: Recipes usually specify whether light or dark soy sauce should be used, and after that it's up to you. Soy sauce can be used in a variety of dishes at the same meal because it changes character with each kind of food. Use sparingly to heighten the flavor of almost any dish. If used in a large quantity it asserts its own unique flavor. The Chinese don't use it as a table condiment ever; in fact, that behavior is considered an insult to the chef. Soy jam is extremely salty and should be used only in the smallest quantities.

SOY SAUCE, INDONESIAN

INDONESIAN: *ketjap asin*

283

This is not the same as the Indonesian sweetened soy, KETJAP MANIS, but a basic soy sauce. Substitute either Chinese or Japanese dark soy when a recipe calls for this.

SOY SAUCE, JAPANESE

JAPANESE: *shoyu* (SHO-yu), light soy: *usu-kuchi shoyu* (very pale and salty), dark soy: *koi-kuchi shoyu*

Various densities of soy sauce are used in Japan as they are in China, though the Japanese varieties are generally milder and less salty. Yamasa is the most widely known imported brand. It is slightly less salty than Kikkoman, a widely distributed brand, which is brewed and packaged in Wisconsin.

STORAGE: It will keep indefinitely on the pantry shelf, though if you don't use much soy you will be wise to store an opened bottle in the refrigerator because it starts to oxidize after a few months at room temperature. The green-label Kikkoman brand, which is a low-sodium soy, must be stored in the refrigerator.

USE: Use Japanese soy in the same manner as Chinese: sparingly as a seasoning to heighten the flavor of almost any savory dish. If used in large quantity, it asserts its own unique flavor.

SOY SAUCE, TAMARI

Tamari-type soy is a delicious, thick, unrefined yet mellow soy sauce available in health food stores. Many assume it to be a Japanese product, but the Japanese people we have asked about it say it is virtually unknown in Japan. It has a unique flavor that we enjoy very much. A salt-free tamari is also available.

STORAGE: This must be stored in the refrigerator after opening.

USE: Tamari is used mostly as a dipping sauce and as a table condiment.

SPINACH, CHINESE
See AMARANTH

SPRING ROLL SKINS
See EGG ROLL WRAPPERS

SQUASH, BOTTLE

OTHER: bottle gourd

CHINESE: *foo loo gwa*

A green squash available fresh in Chinese markets in spring and summer that is shaped like a short, squat bottle or bowling pin. Look for firm, unblemished skin.

STORAGE: It can be stored in the refrigerator for 3 to 5 days.

PREPARATION AND USE: One squash will serve 4 to 6 as part of another dish. Peel and slice to use in soups and stir-fry dishes.

SQUASH, PLEATED

See CHINESE OKRA

SQUASH, SILK

See CHINESE OKRA

SQUID, DRIED

CHINESE: *yo yu*

This is a brown and whitish-colored dehydrated seafood sold in Chinese markets. It is very strong-flavored.

STORAGE: If tightly wrapped, it will keep indefinitely on the pantry shelf.

PREPARATION AND USE: Soak 24 hours in warm water, changing the water several times. Remove the black outer skin. Cut in half and cut away any internal organs and tentacles. Score the inside of the body in a grid pattern to make it roll up into cylinders as it cooks. Deep-fry or stir-fry with vegetables, simmer in soups, or serve in a sweet-and-sour sauce.

SU

See VINEGAR, RICE, JAPANESE

SUGAR, MALT

OTHER: genuine maltose, rice honey

JAPANESE: *ame, mizuame*

Malt sugar is a dark natural sweetener available in 1-pound crocks in Chinese grocery stores and in jars or cans in Japanese markets. One good brand is Tungoon. It is used in China to coat the skin of Peking Duck to help it brown. Honey makes an acceptable substitute.

STORAGE: It will keep indefinitely in a dry spot.

USE: Use not only for Peking Duck, but to add color to almost any meat for barbecuing. It is used in Japan to make taffy-like confections.

SUGAR PEAS
See SNOW PEAS

SUGAR, ROCK
CHINESE: *bing tong*

An amber-colored or clear crystallized sugar, similar to rock candy, that is used to give a high gloss to sauces. Brown sugar can be substituted.

STORAGE: Indefinitely in a jar on the pantry shelf.

PREPARATION AND USE: Crush between towels to measure in a measuring spoon. Use in teas, glazed sauces, and Chinese "red-cooked" dishes.

SUGAR, SLAB
OTHER: Chinese brown sugar

CHINESE: *wong tong*

This dark brown sugar is available in Chinese markets in slabs measuring about 3″ × 5″ × ½″, amounting to about ½ cup. It is a combination of brown sugar, white sugar, and honey. Brown sugar is an adequate substitute.

STORAGE: It can be stored indefinitely on the pantry shelf.

PREPARATION AND USE: Crush between towels to measure in a measuring spoon. Use in glazed sauces and to sweeten teas.

SUSHI SU

See VINEGAR, RICE, JAPANESE

SWALLOWS' NESTS

See BIRDS' NESTS

SWEET CUCUMBER

See MELON, TEA

SWEET POTATO, JAPANESE

See SATSUMA IMO

SWIM BLADDER, DRIED

OTHER: fish maw or fish tripe (both incorrect terms)

CHINESE: *yee tow*

This is the air sac with which a fish raises and lowers itself in the water. It is available dried in some Chinese markets, and is sold by weight. It is tan-colored, comes in curved pieces, and has a unique taste which is not at all fishy.

STORAGE: It will keep in an airtight container at room temperature for up to 2 months, and in the refrigerator indefinitely.

PREPARATION AND USE: When soaked, this expands to 3 times its original volume, so buy only one-third the bulk you need for a particular dish. Soak for 3 to 4 hours in a generous amount of cold water to cover. Drain and blot dry; then dice to use in soups or in stir-fry meat dishes. When it is deep-fried, it is very like an light, airy dumpling.

SZECHUAN BEAN PASTE

See BEAN SAUCE, HOT

SZECHUAN PEPPERCORNS

See under OTHER PEPPERCORNS in THE HERBS, SPICES, AND
SEASONING BLENDS section

TAKUAN

(TAH-koo-ahn)

A very popular Japanese pickle made from white radish, dyed yellow or
as is, available in oriental markets in bottles and cans, and in refrigerated tubs
or bags. It is named after its inventor, a Zen priest of the 17th century.

STORAGE: The kind with preservatives, which comprises most of that sold
in the United States, can be stored in the refrigerator for up to six months.

USE: Served as a side dish (or condiment, really) with any complete Japanese
meal, appearing with the rice and soup at the end of the dinner. Season it
with a few drops of Japanese soy sauce.

TAMARI

See SOY SAUCE, TAMARI

TAMARIND

OTHER: Indian date

FRENCH: *tamarin* INDIAN: *imli* INDONESIAN and MALAYSIAN:
asam ITALIAN: *tamarindo* LAOTIAN: *mal kham* IN LATIN
AMERICA: *tamarindo* SINHALESE (Sri Lanka): *siyambala* THAI: *som
ma kham* VIETNAMESE: *me*

Tamarind is a legume with large brown pods containing seeds. The pulp
around the seeds is very sour and is used as commonly in India as we use
lemon juice. Its rich, spicy flavor is familiar to most of us in the flavor of
WORCESTERSHIRE SAUCE (see THE FOODS OF EUROPE section). It is sold in
the pod, or dried in brick form (in which case the softer the better) or, more
conveniently, in jars of concentrated pulp, which contains seeds. There is also
an "instant" powder. Lemon juice is often substituted for it, at a ratio of 2
parts lemon juice for 1 part tamarind pulp, but there is a considerable difference in flavor. A sweetened tamarind syrup, called *asem toelen,* is sold in
Dutch or Indonesian grocery stores. It is used to make soft drinks and as a
syrup, and should not be used as a substitute.

STORAGE: The pods, powder, and unopened jars of pulp will keep indefinitely on the pantry shelf. The prepared pulp will keep for a week in the refrigerator. It also freezes very well, and is convenient for use if frozen until solid in ice cube trays, and then transferred to a plastic bag for freezer storage.

PREPARATION AND USE: Recipes sometimes call for the pulp, and sometimes for the soaking water. To use dried tamarind, break off a small piece (2 tablespoons or so), pour boiling water over it, and let soak for 10 to 30 minutes or longer until soft. If it is very dry and resists dissolving, heat it slightly. Alternatively, it can be pureed in a blender. After it is soft, use it as you would the bottled: mash it to soften it, and then strain out the seeds and fibers through a fine sieve or cheesecloth. Recipes will call for specific amounts of either the sieved pulp or the soaking liquid. It is used to add an acidic taste to all kinds of spicy relishes, chutneys, and curried dishes. Follow label directions for the powdered form.

It is used in many Asian dishes, such as Thai Fried Fish with Tamarind, Indonesian Fried Bean Curd with Peanuts, and is used with chiles in the making of sambal olek (see under SAMBAL).

TANGERINE PEEL, DRIED

CHINESE: *tsen pei* or *gom pei*

This is curled and wrinkled tangerine rind sold by the ounce in cellophane bags. It is used sparingly to add a spicy citrus taste to many stir-fry dishes. The older it is, the more expensive and highly prized. It is easy to make: simply sun dry your own tangerine rinds. If not available, substitute fresh tangerine, orange, or mandarin orange peel.

STORAGE: You can store it in a jar on the pantry shelf for decades!

PREPARATION AND USE: Soak for 20 to 30 minutes in cold water. Scrape away and discard any white portion or pith. Use sparingly to season soups, meat and poultry dishes, and as a garnish. It is usually left whole, and removed from the dish before serving.

TARO ROOT

OTHER: Japanese country potatoes, taro potatoes, albi

IN THE CARIBBEAN: *eddo, colocasia* CHINESE: *woo tow* JAPANESE: *sato imo* (SAH-toh EE-moh)

Taro root is a starchy, potato-like tuber of the arum family with a brown, hairy skin and gray-colored interior. It is grown in tropical areas and can be found in Asian vegetable markets. It is very closely related to the CASSAVA (see THE FOODS OF LATIN AMERICA section) with which it can be used interchangeably. Neither is a potato, but they are similar in consistency and appearance and both have nutlike flavors. The Hawaiians boil, mash, and ferment taro roots to make their well-known staple, poi. Buy them firm to the touch and without blemishes. Some varieties are **highly toxic unless thoroughly cooked.** The greens are called CALLALOO in the Caribbean (see THE FOODS OF LATIN AMERICA section).

STORAGE: Use as soon as possible. They can be stored for up to 3 weeks in the crisper of the refrigerator.

PREPARATION AND USE: Peel first, and then cook as you would any potato for a tender, delicate vegetable. In Japan, it often appears in stew-like dishes, such as Oden (fish hot pot). Taro can be stir-fried, braised, or steamed. In China, they are used to make steamed or dried taro cakes filled with meat, seafood and vegetables, or into sweet tea cakes. The leaves are eaten in India, usually stuffed, and in Japan, where they are usually cooked for 45 minutes to serve as a vegetable. The greens are an essential ingredient for callaloo soup in the Caribbean. In Hawaii, taro is cooked and pounded into a paste called *paiai*, which is then thinned with water to make one-, two-, or three-finger poi, with one-finger being the thickest because it is dense enough to lift to the mouth with one finger.

TEMPEH

(TEM-pay)

Tempeh is an ancient Indonesian food that has become as important to the people of parts of Southeast Asia as BEAN CURD is in Japan and China. It is a nearly perfect food, containing a high amount of protein and all the vitamins essential to a vegetarian diet, which is followed by many Asians. It looks like Rice Crispies pushed together into cakes measuring 5″ by 1″, which is the form in which it's sold. It is usually made from soybeans, but there are some made from other beans, from grains, and even from coconut, **which is best avoided because it can become toxic.** The beans or legumes are soaked, dried slightly, and injected with a culture. They are then packed into plastic bags and, within a day or so, a puffy white substance binds the beans together. Soybean tempeh is now widely available as a highly nutritious, no-cholesterol food in the refrigerator sections of Asian markets and health food stores. The tastes and textures vary widely depending upon the stage of fermentation.

STORAGE: Store in the refrigerator for up to 3 weeks, or keep frozen for up to 6 months.

PREPARATION AND USE: Allow 2 to 3 ounces of tempeh per serving. Thaw partially, if frozen, before cutting into cubes or sticks. Tempeh absorbs seasonings and most recipes specify that it be marinated before it is deep-fried and served as French fried potatoes, with any number of spicy dipping sauces. It can also be cubed to add to stews and soups, or stir-fried with various sauces, and requires only 10 minutes or so of cooking with other ingredients.

TEMPURA KO

(TEM-poora KOH)
OTHER NAME: low-gluten wheat flour

This is the preferred type of flour used to make Tempura batter, which coats shrimp and raw vegetables to be deep-fried. You will find it in small bags in Japanese markets.

STORAGE: As any flour.

USE: Follow directions on back of bag or box, but take care in measuring that the flour is neither too firmly nor too loosely packed.

TEMPURA

8–12	large raw shrimp, shelled	For 4 servings
6	scallops, *or* cubes of fresh fish of your choice	

Assorted vegetables—choose any of the following:
Fresh SHIITAKE mushrooms, *or* dried shiitake, soaked
  and blotted dry
Broccoli flowerets
White mushrooms, halved through the stems
Zucchini, sliced diagonally
SHISO leaves
Sliced yam
Fresh green beans, strings removed (blanch in salted
  water 5 minutes, and drain)
Mild white onion in ½″ slices

THE BATTER:
1 cup Tempura Ko *or* cake flour *or* ½ cup *each* all-
  purpose flour and cornstarch
1 teaspoon salt
¼ teaspoon baking soda
1 egg, beaten
1 cup ice water
Bowl of ice in which to place the bowl of batter

291

TO COOK:
Vegetable oil

TO SERVE:
TENTSUYU (dipping sauce)

To prepare the shrimp, cut along the vein from the head almost to the tail; lift out the vein. Rinse, blot dry, and arrange on a chilled platter with all the vegetables to be cooked.

To prepare the batter, mix the flour, salt, and soda in a mixing bowl. Add the egg and ice water, mixing lightly with chopsticks until blended, but leaving some lumps of flour. Set the bowl of batter into another bowl containing ice cubes to keep it well chilled.

Pour vegetable oil in a deep-fryer or wok to a depth of 3", or in an electric skillet to a depth of 1½". Heat to 360–375°. Using chopsticks (or tongs), dip one item at a time into the batter and place directly in the hot oil. It will puff almost instantly because of the change in temperature. Cook only a few items at a time, without crowding the pan, until golden, no more than a minute or two. Drain on a rack (some woks have a special draining rack attached); then serve immediately with tentsuyu. Continue dipping and cooking tempura until all batter is used, skimming any particles of batter from the top of the oil—save them to use as crispy croutons on salads and other dishes.

TEMPURA OIL

This is a commercial oil for cooking Tempura (deep-fried shrimp and vegetables), which is not as highly refined as vegetable oils. It is, at times, mixed with sesame oil for extra flavor. It is not necessary to buy this oil to make Tempura.

TENTSUYU

(TEN-tsoo-yoo)
OTHER: Tempura dipping sauce

Tentsuyu is a canned, concentrated sauce made of DASHI, MIRIN, and SOY SAUCE seasoned with ginger. It is the traditional accompaniment for Japanese Tempura (deep-fried shrimp and vegetables). This is a convenience item and is not as fine as homemade.

STORAGE: Canned tentsuyu will keep indefinitely on the pantry shelf. Freshly made sauce, or canned sauce after opening, can be stored for up to 3 days in the refrigerator.

PREPARATION AND USE: This is diluted with water to the desired strength. Shredded DAIKON is almost always added.

TEMPURA DIPPING SAUCE

1   cup double-strength DASHI   For 4 to 6 servings
⅓   cup MIRIN
⅓   cup Japanese soy sauce
½   cup shredded DAIKON
1   tablespoon grated fresh ginger

In a small saucepan, warm dashi, mirin, and soy sauce. Remove from heat; stir in daikon and ginger. Spoon into individual serving dishes.

TERIYAKI SOSU

(TEH-ri-YAH-kee SOH-soo)
OTHER: teriyaki sauce

Teriyaki Sosu is a glaze made of soy sauce and ginger, which is available bottled in supermarkets throughout the United States. Kikkoman brand is widely available in supermarkets. Various Japanese brands in liquid or powdered form are available in Japanese markets. Most domestic types contain garlic, but the Japanese, who invented it, do not usually add it.

STORAGE: The sauce will keep several months on the pantry shelf, and indefinitely in the refrigerator.

PREPARATION AND USE: Some cooks like to marinate flank steaks or other meats in the sauce for several hours before grilling. The leftover marinade is then simmered to serve as a sauce. Some Japanese cookbooks advise that it should be brushed on grilled meats only during the final half of the cooking time.

THOUSAND YEAR OLD EGGS

See EGGS, THOUSAND YEAR OLD

TIENTSIN PRESERVED VEGETABLES

See PRESERVED VEGETABLES, CANTONESE

TI LEAVES

The shiny, oblong leaves of the *ti* plant are used in Polynesia for wrapping foods to be steamed. They can be special-ordered from florists and range in size from 2″ to 6″ in width and up to 2′ in length. If not available, lotus or bamboo leaves can be substituted, or simply use foil or vegetable parchment.

STORAGE: If allowed to breathe in a paper bag or perforated plastic bag, ti leaves can be refrigerated for up to 2 months in the refrigerator.

PREPARATION AND USE: If fresh and green, do not dampen before using to wrap foods to be steamed. If dried, they must be soaked until pliable. These are used in Hawaii to wrap chicken for a steamed dish called Laulau, and are wrapped around fish in a Tahitian dish that is then cooked in CO-CONUT MILK. The food is removed from the leaves, which are not eaten.

TOFU

See BEAN CURD

TOGAN

See MELON, WINTER

TONKATSU SOSU

(tohn-KA-tsu SOH-soo)

Tonkatsu Sosu is a Western-inspired, dark, spicy sauce, not unlike A-1 sauce, used primarily for breaded fried foods, which is available in bottles in Japanese markets. It most often contains the following: catsup, worcestershire sauce, soy sauce, mustard and SAKE. Bull Dog, Kikkoman and Kagome are the brands most often found. There are two types: thin, which is more like Worchestershire sauce, and thick, which is more like A-1.

STORAGE: The thin type should be refrigerated. The thick can be stored indefinitely on the pantry shelf, though it loses flavor on standing.

USE: The Japanese use this only on *Tonkatsu* (breaded fried pork) and the sliced raw cabbage that is traditionally served with it.

TORORO IMO

See YAMA-NO-IMO

TREE EAR

See CLOUD EAR, under MUSHROOMS, DRIED

TREFOIL

See MITSUBA

TREPANG

See BÊCHE DE MER

TSUKEMONO

(TSOO-keh-MOH-noh)

"Tsukemono" is the common name for a variety of Japanese pickled vegetables. Many are available in jars on shelves or in the refrigerator sections of Japanese markets.

STORAGE: Refrigerate. Depending on the kind, this lasts anywhere from a few weeks to several months.

USE: Serve as a dish or condiment on a separate tiny plate. Delicious with cooked rice.

TURMERIC

See HERBS, SPICES, AND SEASONING BLENDS section

TURNIP, SALTED

OTHER: preserved turnip, preserved parsnip

CHINESE: *choy pin* or *chung choy*

This cured root vegetable with its strong odor and very salty, spicy taste, is moist and chewy. It is sold in plastic bags. Rinsed of excess salt, it is used as a flavoring agent in many dishes, including the breakfast rice porridge, Congee.

STORAGE: It will keep in a jar with a tight fitting lid on the pantry shelf indefinitely.

PREPARATION AND USE: Rinse and drain. Shred or chop fine to flavor soups and steamed meat or fish dishes.

UDON

See NOODLES

UMEBOSHI

(OO-meh-BOH-shee)
OTHER: pickled plums

These pink-colored pickled plums, which have been naturally tinted with a leaf called *aka-jiso* (red SHISO), are available in jars or plastic bags of varying sizes in Japanese markets and in health food stores. They are extremely salty. Any bright red ones have been artificially colored and are inferior. The Japanese have found these have curative qualities for stomach ailments. When added to gruel, they are, in fact, the Japanese mother's answer to chicken soup! A paste of pureed umeboshi, called *bainiku,* is now available in bottles or cans.

STORAGE: These can be stored in the refrigerator for several years, though it is best to enjoy them as soon as possible because they lose flavor on standing.

PREPARATION AND USE: Umeboshi have a very salty, sour taste, and are served mostly as a condiment with various rice dishes. Eat whole, as a pickle, or remove the pits and mash them to use as a tangy seasoning in vegetable dishes. The paste is used to add tang to dipping sauces. Umeboshi are as commonly eaten for breakfast, 1 per person, as we enjoy orange juice in the United States. They are also served after meals with a cup of green tea, to freshen the palate.

UMESHU

(oo-MEH-shoo)
OTHER: plum wine

Umeshu is a slightly sweet, syrupy plum liquor (not actually a wine) which is often served "on the rocks" as an aperitif. Takara is a widely-distributed brand found in supermarkets and liquor stores.

STORAGE: Because of the sugar content, this does not spoil easily even if kept on the pantry shelf for months.

PREPARATION AND USE: Serve "straight" or "on the rocks" as an unusual apéritif. It adds a distinct fragrance and subtle sweetness to salad dressings and to various cooked poultry dishes.

JAPANESE COUNTRY DRESSING

6   ounces sesame oil   For 2½ cups
3   ounces Japanese plum wine
3   ounces Japanese soy sauce
2   ounces Japanese rice vinegar
    Simple syrup of 5 tablespoons sugar and 3 ounces water,
      boiled until sugar is dissolved
1   tablespoon fresh grated ginger

Combine all ingredients in a screw-top jar. Shake well before tossing with salads of lettuce, carrot, DAIKON, shredded chicken.

TO PREPARE IN ADVANCE: This dressing will keep for up to a month in the refrigerator.

UNI
(OO-nee)
OTHER: sea urchin

DANISH: *sopindsvin* FRENCH: *oursin* GERMAN: *Seeigel* GREEK: *achinos* ICELANDIC: *igulker* ITALIAN: *riccio di mare* NORWEGIAN: *Krakebolle* PORTUGUESE: *ourico-do-mar* SPANISH: *erizo de mar* SWEDISH: *sjöborre* YUGOSLAVIAN: *morski jez*

The fine, delicate roe of sea urchin is considered a great delicacy in Japan. Fresh roe can be purchased in fine Japanese markets and in some fish markets. It takes the roe from five sea urchins to make one serving, so it is very expensive. A fermented paste made from the egg sacs of the sea urchin is called *uni-no-shiozuke*. It is available, seasoned with salt, in bottles in Japanese markets.

STORAGE: Refrigerate to use as soon as possible.

PREPARATION AND USE: Uni is often served as a Sushi (vinegared rice) ingredient. Both uni and the commercial paste can be used to season soy sauce for dipping Sashimi (raw fish). We have heard of it being combined with egg yolk to brush on seafood or poultry that is grilled, and also as a flavoring ingredient in the dressing for Sunomono, a shellfish salad. Spread on cucumber to serve as an appetizer. Or use as a condiment for cooked rice, along with NORI (see under SEAWEED, DRIED), egg, etc.

VARAK

OTHER: *vark*, silver leaf

These edible, gossamer-thin sheets of silver or gold leaf are used to garnish festival dishes and desserts in India. Nestled individually between two sheets of tissue paper, they can be purchased at considerable expense at Indian markets. Indians claim that varak is good for the liver and has aphrodisiac qualities.

STORAGE: The silver leaf will tarnish like any silver. Store it in an airtight container in a cool, dry place. We usually put a piece of charcoal or carbon paper in with it to absorb moisture and deter tarnishing even further. Pure gold leaf will not tarnish.

PREPARATION AND USE: This leaf is so fine that it really cannot be handled. To use, remove the top layer of tissue, and then turn the leaf over on top of the food to be garnished, lifting off the remaining tissue. It is used mostly on rice dishes, such as Cashew Rice, and on rice-based desserts.

VEGETARIAN MEAT SUBSTITUTES

OTHER: vegetarian steak, chicken, pork, etc.

CHINESE: *mein gon* or *mein jing*

High-protein meat substitutes made with wheat gluten are available in cans in Chinese markets and health food stores. Many varieties are available, including substitutes for abalone, chicken, duck, ham, and pork (which is colored red). They are formed into brownish, chewy patties (or "steaks") approximately 3″ round or square and ½″ thick. They are already cooked and seasoned. Read the labels to find out what other ingredients, preservatives, etc., are present.

STORAGE: After opening, they can be stored in plastic wrap in the refrigerator for up to 4 days.

PREPARATION AND USE: Cut into desired size to use as a meat substitute in many dishes. It needs very little cooking, so lends itself beautifully to stir-frying.

VERMICELLI

See NOODLES, CELLOPHANE

VERMICELLI, SOYBEAN
See HARUSAME under NOODLES, CELLOPHANE

VINEGAR, RICE, CHINESE
CHINESE: *ba cho*

There are three varieties of bottled Chinese rice vinegar: White or pale amber vinegar (*bok cho*), black vinegar (*jit cho*), and red vinegar (*hak mi cho*). Vinegar from Thailand is especially mild.

STORAGE: These vinegars will keep for 3 months on the pantry shelf; indefinitely in the refrigerator.

USE: The white is used in sweet-and-sour dishes and as a dressing for raw vegetables. The black is used as a dip or table condiment, or to darken sweet-and-sour dishes. The red is used primarily as a dip for boiled crab, spring rolls, and other oily snacks or Dim Sum (tea cakes). As a general rule, Chinese vinegar is not as strong as American white vinegar or wine vinegar, so use only half the amount of the American when substituting.

VINEGAR, RICE, JAPANESE
JAPANESE: *su* or *sushi-su*

Most supermarkets in the United States now carry several kinds of rice vinegars, which are lighter and sweeter than Western-style vinegars. Some contain MONOSODIUM GLUTAMATE, and are otherwise seasoned. Marukan is the most widely known brand. Most Japanese cooks prefer to create their own seasoned vinegar by combining rice wine vinegar and sugar to taste.

STORAGE: They will keep indefinitely on the pantry shelf.

USE: In Japan, rice vinegar is used in making Sunomono (literally "vinegared things"), which are served at every meal. It is added to water (2 teaspoons per quart) to soak vegetables that discolor when exposed to air. Delicious as a simple and low-calorie salad dressing any time. Sprinkle some over shredded cucumber and top with toasted sesame seeds for a delightful, crisp salad. We created this recipe after tasting a similar salad in Thai restaurants, where it was served as a relish in small dishes.

THAI CUCUMBER SALAD

1   long English (sometimes called "burpless")   For 4 servings
    cucumber, *or* 2 regular cucumbers
    Salt
¼   cup of minced Bermuda onion
2   tablespoons rice vinegar (or 1 tablespoon white vinegar
    and 1 tablespoon water mixed with 2 teaspoons sugar)
2   teaspoons minced fresh coriander (cilantro or Chinese
    parsley)

TO SERVE AND GARNISH:
2   tablespoons chopped peanuts

Note: If using an English cucumber, don't peel or seed it. If using regular cucumbers, peel, cut in half lengthwise, and remove seeds with the tip of a spoon.

Slice the cucumber in thin crosswise rounds. Place in a cheesecloth-lined mixing bowl, sprinkle with salt, and toss to coat it well; let stand for 15 minutes to 1 hour. Lift the cheesecloth to enclose the cucumbers and wring out all the excess liquid drawn out be the salt.
    Place the squeezed cucumbers in a serving bowl and toss with the remaining salad ingredients. Sprinkle the peanuts over the top.

TO PREPARE IN ADVANCE: This is best served within a few hours, but it can be refrigerated for serving within a day or two.

WAKAME

See under SEAWEED, DRIED

WASABI

(Wah-SAH-Bee)
OTHER: Japanese green horseradish

Fresh wasabi is rarely, if ever, available in the United States, but the powdered form of this pungent green horseradish is widely available in supermarkets and in all oriental markets. Anyone who has ever enjoyed Sushi (vinegared rice dishes) has noticed its assertive flavor and sinus-clearing effect. A paste form of wasabi is available in tubes. If you can ever get your hands on fresh wasabi, do so. Its complexity is incomparable. Regular HORSE-

RADISH (see THE HERBS, SPICES, AND SEASONING BLENDS section) is not a substitute.

STORAGE: Fresh wasabi should be refrigerated and used as soon as possible. The powdered form can be stored on the pantry shelf for years. After mixing with water, store the paste in the refrigerator.

PREPARATION AND USE: Peel fresh wasabi and cut out any eyes. Grate on a fine grater using a circular motion. Mix the powder with water to make a smooth paste; cover, and let stand for 10 minutes to allow the flavor to develop fully. It is served smeared under the fish in Sushi, as an accompaniment to Sashimi (raw fish) or Kamaboko (fish cake), usually as a flavoring for the Japanese SOY SAUCE that accompanies those dishes. It is also included in dipping sauce for cold SOBA noodles (see NOODLES).

WATER CHESTNUT

OTHER: caltrop

CHINESE: *ma tie, pi-tsi* FRENCH: *saligot* or *macre* GERMAN: *Wassernuss* ITALIAN: *frutto della castagna d'acqua* JAPANESE: *kuwai* MALAYSIAN: *mah tie* THAI: *kajup*

The tuber of a sedge, which is an aquatic plant grown in East Asian marshes. The taste is slightly sweet and the texture is delightfully crisp. Always available in cans, whole or sliced. Fresh, dark purple-skinned water chestnuts are only available from July to September in Chinese markets. They are covered with a tough brown peel—hence the Chinese name, "horse's hooves."

STORAGE: After opening canned water chestnuts, rinse them and store in cold water in the refrigerator. They will keep for up to 3 weeks if you remember to change the water every few days. Fresh water chestnuts will keep, unpeeled, in a cool place for up to a week. They become mushy if frozen.

PREPARATION AND USE: Peel fresh water chestnuts (a tedious job, but worth it) and put in water to prevent discoloration. In China, fresh water chestnuts are eaten raw like a fruit and are often candied like apples.

Fresh ones should be blanched before adding to various dishes. Cut up and cover with cold water in small saucepan. Bring to a boil, lower heat, and simmer for 2 minutes. (Alternatively, you may wish to cook them whole in boiling water for 15 minutes or so, and then cool slightly and peel.) Add whole, sliced or diced water chestnuts to dishes when a crisp texture, white color, and slightly sweet flavor is desired.

One Chinese dish called Lotus Flowers calls for balls made of chopped water chestnuts, prawns, and ginger to be deep-fried.

WATER CHESTNUT POWDER

OTHER: water chestnut flour

CHINESE: *ma tie fun*

This starch made from powdered dried water chestnuts is available in 4- to 8-ounce packages in Asian markets and health food stores. It is more expensive than most of the other starches.

STORAGE: Tightly sealed, it can be stored on the pantry shelf for up to 3 months.

PREPARATION AND USE: It is used to thicken sauces, giving them a shiny glaze, and to give a very desirable crispy coating to foods that are deep-fried. Use as you would CORNSTARCH as a binder of sauces by stirring it into a paste with cold water and adding it gradually to simmering liquids. To coat foods to be deep-fried, dredge them in the powder and let stand for at least 5 minutes before frying.

WATER LILY ROOT

See LOTUS ROOT

WATER SHIELD

See JUNSAI

WHEAT STARCH

CHINESE: *dong mein fun*

Wheat starch is wheat flour from which all gluten has been extracted. It is available in 1-pound sacks in Chinese grocery stores.

STORAGE: Tightly sealed, it will keep on the pantry shelf indefinitely.

USE: In China this is used to prepare completely transparent dumpling skins for Dim Sum (Chinese snack foods) which are often shell-shaped and contain shrimp filling.

WHITE FRUIT

See GINGKO NUT

WHITE FUNGUS

See CLOUD EARS, under MUSHROOMS, DRIED

WHITE MUSTARD CABBAGE

See BOK CHOY, under CABBAGE, ORIENTAL

WHITE RADISH

See DAIKON

WILD PEPPER

See PEPPERCORNS, SZECHUAN under PEPPERCORNS, OTHER in HERBS, SPICES, AND SEASONING BLENDS section

WINE BALL

See WINE, FERMENTED RICE

WINE, FERMENTED RICE

This is a Szechuan flavoring made from the combination of glutinous rice with a crushed yeast ball and a little water, which is allowed to stand until a light, sweet wine develops. The round white balls (referred to as "wine balls" or "yeast balls"), 1″ in diameter, are not widely available in the United States, but may be sought out and found in most Chinatowns. The fermented rice wine should be found as well. Should you not be able to find either of these ingredients, we have had good luck substituting cream sherry.

STORAGE: The yeast balls can be stored indefinitely in an airtight container. The fermented rice and wine will keep in the refrigerator indefinitely.

PREPARATION AND USE: To make fermented rice wine, soak 2 cups of glutinous rice (sweet rice) in cold water for 8 hours. Steam the rice as usual, and then rinse with warm water. Place in an earthenware crock or other nonmetal container, such as a glass jar. Crush one-quarter of a yeast ball with 2 teaspoons flour and stir it into the rice. Make a small indentation in the center of the rice and pour ½ cup cold water into it. Wrap the container completely in foil or other insulation that will prevent light from entering, and place it in a dark spot for several days, checking after the second day to see if wine has developed in the indentation. Transfer the wine to containers for refrigerator storage. Use as a flavorful cooking ingredient in Chinese Szechuan-style stir-fry dishes of all types, when a deep, wine flavor is desirable.

WINE, RICE, CHINESE

CHINESE: *huang chiu*

Chinese rice wine is primarily used as a marinade and seasoning. It is generally agreed that the best brand is Shaohsing. Dry sherry is an acceptable substitute.

STORAGE: It can be kept, refrigerated, for up to 6 months.

USE: Use in cooking as you would dry sherry to lend a wine flavor to dishes.

WINE, RICE, JAPANESE

See SAKE

WINTER MUSHROOMS

See BLACK OR "WINTER" MUSHROOMS under MUSHROOMS, DRIED

WON TON SKINS

See WON TON WRAPPERS

WON TON WRAPPERS

OTHER: *won ton* skins, Chinese-style alimentary paste

CHINESE: *won ton pi* JAPANESE: *gyoza* (round skins)

These sheets of pasta dough, made from flour, eggs, and salt, are available in Chinese markets and in the refrigerator sections of most supermarkets today. The sheets are dusted with a powdered starch to prevent them from sticking together, and are used to make filled dumplings, which can be cooked in a number of ways. Many forms are available: round, square, thick or thin.

Depending on the manufacturer, they will vary from 75 to 120 per pound. They can be used in place of fresh pasta to make Italian Ravioli and other stuffed pastas.

STORAGE: They will keep, refrigerated, for up to 1 week; frozen, unopened, for up to 6 months.

PREPARATION AND USE: These can be deep-fried, pan-fried (to make fried dumplings or "pot stickers"), steamed or boiled in soup. Place a small amount (½ teaspoon) filling on the won ton skin, moisten the edges of the skin with water, and pinch to seal. Use the thin ones for steamed dumplings, Shiu May, and the thick or thin, depending on personal preference, for Won Tons. They are sometimes fried unfilled and served with a dipping sauce (usually sweet-and-sour). They are also made into Won Ton Cookies by deep-frying and sprinkling with powdered sugar. Our favorite use, though, is in making fried dumplings called Pot Stickers.

POT STICKERS WITH SAUCE

For approximately 48 dumplings
or 8 appetizer servings

These fried dumplings are always served with their crusty bottoms facing upward, and are traditionally accompanied by a simple dipping sauce of white vinegar and CHILI PASTE WITH GARLIC, mixed by each diner at the table to his or her own liking. Our more elaborate dipping sauce is highly recommended.

DUMPLINGS:

- 1 10-ounce package won ton wrappers or *gyoza* (round Japanese skins)
- 8 ounces lean pork, ground
- 8 ounces raw shrimp, chopped
- ½ pound fresh water chestnuts, peeled and minced, *or* 1 (8-ounce) can water chestnuts, minced
- 3 scallions, minced
- 3 tablespoons light soy *or* mushroom soy sauce
- 3 tablespoons sherry *or shao hsing* (Chinese rice wine)
- 1 tablespoon cornstarch
- 2 teaspoons minced fresh ginger

FOR COOKING:

- 4 tablespoons peanut or vegetable oil
- 1 cup chicken broth or water

OPTIONAL DIPPING SAUCE:
¼ cup light soy sauce
1 tablespoon vinegar
1 teaspoon sugar
2 tablespoons chopped cilantro (see CORIANDER)
4 scallions, sliced
2 quarter-sized slices ginger, minced
1 tablespoon sesame oil
1 teaspoon "hot" CHILI OIL

To make the dumplings, combine all ingredients except wrappers in a bowl, mixing very well. If using square won ton skins, place a stack of 10 or 12 skins on your work surface, and use the top of a drinking glass, the diameter of which is close to the width of the square, turned upside down to mark a circle on the top of the stack. Use scissors to cut the stack of skins into circles. (This is not necessary if using round gyoza skins.)

Hold one of the round skins in your hand and place about 1 teaspoon filling in the center. Dip your finger in water and dampen the inside edge of the skin; then fold to make a small turnover, pleating the edge in three tucks as you work from one side to the other. This takes a bit of practice, but is very easy once you get the hang of it. Continue making dumplings until all the filling is used, placing them on a tray so sides do not touch.

To cook, fry no more than 12 to 14 at a time—you may wish to have two pans cooking at a time, depending on how many you are serving. Heat 1 tablespoon oil in a heavy skillet (nonstick preferred). Place the dumplings, seam side up, in the hot oil, not crowding the pan, and cook over medium heat for 5 to 7 minutes, until the bottoms are well-browned. Pour in ¼ cup broth and cover the pan. Reduce the heat to low and simmer for 5 minutes. Remove lid and cook until the broth has evaporated. Carefully loosen any dumplings that may have stuck to the pan with a spatula; then turn out, upside down, on a warm serving platter. Continue in this fashion until all dumplings are cooked.

To make the dipping sauce, stir the soy, vinegar, and sugar in a 1-cup measure, just until the sugar has dissolved. Alternatively, this mixture can be warmed in a small saucepan. Add the remaining ingredients. Pour into individual serving dishes.

Serve the Pot Stickers hot with the sauce at room temperature.

TO PREPARE IN ADVANCE: Uncooked dumplings can be refrigerated, taking care that their sides are not touching or they will stick together, for up to 24 hours. Or, they can be frozen on a cookie sheet and transferred to storage containers when solidly frozen. They need not be thawed before cooking, but will need to simmer 10 minutes, rather than 5, after adding the broth to the pan. The dipping sauce can be made up to 24 hours ahead and refrigerated, but should be brought to room temperature before serving.

WOOD EARS

See CLOUD EARS, under MUSHROOMS, DRIED

YAMA-NO-IMO

(yah-mah-no-EE-moh)
OTHER: mountain yam, glutinous yam

Literally, Yama-No-Imo means "yams of the mountains." There are several varieties of this tan-colored Japanese tuber, which looks a great deal like an old bone. It is like a potato in texture, but becomes viscous and slippery once grated, and is then called *tororoimo*. Most Westerners find its gluey texture takes some getting used to. It is purported to be exceptionally good for the digestion.

STORAGE: It will keep for up to a week in the crisper of the refrigerator.

PREPARATION AND USE: Peel and grate to serve as a raw seasoning. We suggest you **wear gloves when handling it, or peel it under cold running water,** as it can be irritating to sensitive skin. This is used primarily as a cold seasoning and topping for Noodles Tororo-Soba. Grate as a seasoning over rice or Sashimi (raw fish).

YAM CAKES

See KONNYAKU

YARD-LONG BEANS

See BEANS, LONG

YELLOW BEANS

See BEANS, SOYBEANS, DRIED

YOGURT

See THE FOODS OF THE MIDDLE EAST section

YOKAN

(YOH-Kahn)

Yokan is a popular Japanese confection made from AGAR gelatin and sugar. It often contains ground AZUKI paste, persimmons, KOMBU or CHESTNUTS (preserved). It is available in oriental markets in foil or plastic packages.

STORAGE: It will keep indefinitely in the refrigerator, but it is delicate and loses texture at room temperature.

USE: Serve as a snack or dessert with green tea. It is extremely sweet to most tastes.

THE FOODS
OF
EUROPE

AUSTRIA
BELGIUM
BULGARIA
CZECHOSLOVAKIA
DENMARK
FINLAND
FRANCE
GERMANY
HUNGARY
ICELAND
IRELAND
ITALY
LUXEMBOURG
THE
   NETHERLANDS
NORWAY
POLAND
PORTUGAL
ROMANIA
RUSSIA
SPAIN
SWEDEN
SWITZERLAND
UNITED KINGDOM
YUGOSLAVIA

COUNTRY KITCHENS

The first blending of ethnic European foods and dishes occurred in the 11th century. For over 200 years nine waves of crusaders carried and deposited newly acquired culinary techniques, dishes, and foods back and forth across the face of Europe. In this way, basic foods were introduced and either took firm root in their new country soil or were imported from their neighbors.

The true dishes of Europe are the country-style dishes built around what the soil can best produce, and some of these are so brilliantly good that they have become the refined dishes each nation displays as its highest form of culinary skill, as we shall see. Every cuisine can be divided into two basic styles: high and low. France proves to be no exception; in fact, its greatest pride is its polished *haute cuisine* (high cuisine) which is mirrored internationally as a standard of culinary excellence. France's other cuisine, which feeds the majority of its people, is known as *bourgeois* or provincial. While the chefs of the great restaurants of Paris are preparing Pressed Duck, Foie Gras Chaud, and Feuilleté de Fruits de Mer for their elite clientele, families in the north of France, taking advantage of Normandy's dairy herds and orchards, dine in their country kitchens on simpler, heartier fare, perhaps Poulet Vallée d'Auge, chicken stewed in sweet butter annointed with Calvados (an apple brandy) and finished with heavy cream. If the family is nearer the coast and mussels are fresh, they may have Moules à La Normande instead, made of a lavender and purple mollusk with orange flesh, bathed in a rich, creamy shallot sauce. In the east of France, typical dishes are wild game, stews, or Choucroute Garnie, a robust dish of sauerkraut cooked in bacon fat and

309

wine surrounded by pork chops, sausages, and smoked pork or goose. An unusual culinary fact is that, here in Alsace-Lorraine, cabbage, introduced in the time of the crusades, transplanted from Mediterranean Greece, has found a perfect environment, and today Alsatians preserve and consume more sauerkraut than their German neighbors across the Rhine. The provincial home-cooking of Southern France raised the unpretentious baked bean to international fame in Cassoulet, a dish of beans, pork, preserved goose, and sausage. Simpler fare would be Soupe de Poisson, a hearty fish and garlic soup. In completing our brief four-cornered tour of France we ended in the west on the Bay of Biscay where Chaudrée de Fouras, the granddaddy of America's clam chowder, was created and still thrives. It is a classic seafood, wine, and onion stew. Regardless of how gifted French cooks may be they, like all other European cooks, accommodate their cooking to what the land under foot best produces. The force of the land upon the character of a country's food can be seen easily again in Italy.

Except for the lowlands of northern Italy, there is little good pasturage. Consequently, the expense of raising cattle has prevented beef from becoming a nutritional staple. In the north, veal is the most common meat and has been since the crusades. The city of Milan, incidentally, claims to have proof that its Costoletta alla Milanese, a breaded veal cutlet invented before the crusades, was the original Wiener Schnitzel of Germany. In the south, where grazing land is sparse, the time-honored choice of meat is kid or lamb, either of which is pan-roasted with garlic, spices, and wine, or spitted and dressed with rosemary. In the north, Italians cook with butter; in the south, where there are few dairy herds, they cook with olive oil. In the north, rice and corn grow best and are the traditional staples, from which they make their famous Risotto alla Pilota (rice with sausage and cream), and Polenta (a thick cornmeal mush), whereas in the south, it is wheat and pasta.*

Just like the Italian and French, Scandinavian cuisine is shaped by what is available. The unplantable mountains of Norway have always forced its people to look toward the sea for food. And, of all the fish they catch, the herring is the most important. Depending upon the kitchen, it will be served salted, spiced, dried, smoked, fresh, pickled, or fried. Everywhere in Scandinavia herring is a staple food. Because of its long popularity, it has the traditional place of honor at Sweden's famous Smörgasbord (bread and butter table), which also includes other fish plates, cold meats, salads, hot dishes, and desserts. Denmark, a flat peninsular finger pointing at Norway and

---

*A word about pasta here to shed some light upon the romantic notion that Marco Polo brought it back to Italy as a gift from the Kublai Kahn. Northern China invented wheat pasta. It crossed the border to India, where it was called *sevika*, which means "thread." India gave it to the Arab traders, who called it *rishta*, also meaning "thread." And the Arabs were doing business with Venice long before Marco was born. The modern Italian word *spaghetti* is a derivation of an old Roman word meaning "string."

Sweden from northern Germany, is a prosperous farming nation that derives two-thirds of its national income from the sale of bacon, hams, dairy products, and sugar beets to European markets. The Danish cuisine has many things in common with its Scandinavian neighbors to the north, one of the more prominent being their Smörgasbord lunch. There is a notable variation though; the Danes prefer their Smörgasbord in the form of beautifully presented open-faced sandwiches. And when it comes to the dessert course, the extraordinary pastry of Denmark is in a league by itself, demonstrating the quality of their locally produced sugar, flour, and dairy products.

Germany is another haven for pastry lovers, but is also a delight for those who swear by meat and potatoes. An outstanding producer of food, Germany grows fodder for its large dairy industry, potatoes, rye, sugar beets, barley, and wheat. Forested areas provide game, and wild boar is still to be found on restaurant menus, as well as Hasenpfaeffer, a spicy rabbit stew. The Germans are enthusiastic eaters and revel in dishes with rich sauces, such as Sauerbraten (a marinated pot roast traditionally served with potato dumplings and stewed dried fruit), veal cutlets, or roast goose. This dish usually makes its appearance at midday for the main meal. The evening meal is usually a cold snack consisting of bread, butter, sliced cold sausage, and cheese.

Central and Eastern European kitchens also concoct hearty, spicy, heavy dishes, using similar ingredients—goose, duck, hare, and sausages—all generally served with sauerkraut. Typical of family fare in Poland is Bigos, a hunter's stew of rabbit, beef, or pork cooked with cabbage, mushrooms, tomatoes, sausage, and wine. Poland has Germany as its neighbor on the left, which may have influenced its "heavy cooking," and Russia to its right, which may be responsible for Poland's robust Barszcz, a beet soup. Bursting with nourishing tidbits such as cabbage, apples, beans, beef, and tomatoes, Barszcz is probably also dólloped with sour cream, just as Borscht is, served next door in Russia.

Russia is capable, weather permitting, of growing everything that its populace needs. Though some of this huge land is subtropical, most of it suffers subfreezing winters. To endure such hardships, its people require warming and hearty food. Russian kitchens respond with meat-filled dumplings, thick, dark pumpernickel bread, and buckwheat groats called Kasha. However, the predominant staple in bourgeois kitchens throughout frozen Russia is soup —basic soups, thick or thin, hot or cold—Borscht (beet soup), Shchi (cabbage soup), Ouha (fish consomme) or Solianka (a fish or meat soup garnished with cucumbers). Depending upon the time of year, the catch, and available produce, a light fish soup can be transformed into an entire, robustly satisfying meal. Fish, eel, flat-tailed sheep, and wild game supply most of their animal protein. Four-fifths of the land mass of Russia, in relation to North America, is located north of Moose Jaw, Saskatchewan, with a climate too severe to graze cattle; consequently, dairy products and beef are luxuries.

In the emerald green British Isles where roast beef is king, the prevailing winds are the stormy westerlies that buffet and soak Ireland, which deflects the winds and fans the showers over the rolling hills of England and Scotland. Because of this dependable moisture, the British Isles had some of the best pastureland in Europe until the Industrial Revolution saw pastoral scenes dissolve into smoking industrial landscapes. Today, England is no longer agriculturally self-sufficient, and must import the majority of her food. England had become famous, however, for her beef, pork, and lamb; Cheddar, Cheshire, and Stilton cheeses; Devonshire cream, spitted beef dripping into a pan of puffing Yorkshire pudding, potted meat and crab preserved in overabundant butter, and sideboards featuring the oak-smoked haddock dish, Finnan Haddie with eggs and cream sauce. There is no place in England that is more than 60 miles from the sea and, at one time, English oysters were the secret ingredient in Steak and Kidney Pie.

The same westerly winds that soak the British Isles cause a chronic shortage of water in Spain and Portugal. Because so much of this Iberian peninsula is sunny and dry, most of its agricultural products are drought-resistant crops, such as olives, garlic, onions, barley, oats, and rye. With water conservation and irrigation, citrus fruits from Valencia, on the Mediterranean, and also grapes from which they make their classic wines, do very well on Spanish soil. It seems natural enough that nations preoccupied with getting enough water would adopt liquid-based cuisines, and they do. Soups and stews are the foundation of both the Portuguese and Spanish diets, from the simple but aggressive Sopa de Ajo (garlic soup) to the lyrical Zarzuela de Mariscos, Andalusian (southern Spain's) shellfish stew. Another Andalusian specialty uses nearly every one of Spain's favorite pantry items in happy combination— croutons, garlic, wine vinegar, olive oil, green pepper, onion, tomatoes, cucumber, almonds, black pepper, and salt. When chopped, measured, and mixed, this combination becomes a chilled liquid salad or soup of international fame called Gazpacho.

As you thumb through the following pages of European ingredients, we know that you will be as overwhelmed as we were with their ethnic diversity. There is, in proportion to the amount of land, more here in Europe than in any other country or geographical area of the world.

ALMOND, BITTER

Bitter almonds are grown throughout the Mediterranean. They are toxic in their raw state; their aromatic flavor is the result of an enzyme reaction that also produces prussic acid. They are processed to flavor extracts, Amaretto liqueurs, and ORGEAT, a syrup used in beverages. A few are often added to "sweet" almonds in European recipes to obtain a stronger almond flavor, as is the addition of almond extract for the same reason. Even though their toxic effect is destroyed by heat, it is illegal to sell them as an ingredient in the United States. Oil of bitter almond is used a great deal in cosmetics and lotions for its scent, but is toxic if taken internally and is sold in pharmacies only by prescription.

The center kernels from the pits of apricots and peaches, available in health food stores, are very similar in flavor and appearance, and are used instead of bitter almonds in various commercial Amaretti confections. You can substitute either in European recipes calling for bitter almonds, but **take care to roast the pits before use, because they have the same toxic effect as bitter almonds.** Almond extract, available in every supermarket, approximates the flavor of the bitter almond, but is cloying if used in excess. We often use Amaretto liqueur in recipes calling for this flavor.

STORAGE: Blanched and toasted peach or apricot kernels will keep in the refrigerator or freezer indefinitely.

PREPARATION AND USE: Blanch peach or apricot kernels for 1 minute in boiling water; then blot dry and toast in a 250° oven for 10 to 15 minutes until slightly colored. They should be crushed before use. They can be used in combination with sweet almonds to make AMARETTI cookies, using approximately 1 teaspoon kernels to 1 cup sweet almonds. A few drops of almond extract will give a similar flavor. They are used also in stuffings for pork to add a subtle flavor, and in all kinds of confections. The addition of 3 or 4 of these kernels, crushed, to peach, cherry, or apricot preserves, along with a splash of KIRSCH creates a jam fit for the gods.

ALMOND OIL

FRENCH: *huile d'amande*

Almond oil imported from France has the flavor and aroma of lightly toasted almonds. Like HAZELNUT OIL and WALNUT OIL it is sold in 8- to 12-ounce cans. It is very expensive. The domestic almond oil sold in health food stores is very mild in flavor and is not a substitute.

STORAGE: Stored airtight in a cool spot, it will keep for up to 4 months, or in the refrigerator indefinitely.

USE: This oil is used primarily in cold dishes where the flavor will be very noticeable. Use 2 to 3 tablespoons of it to a cup of vegetable oil when making homemade mayonnaise, or use it with lemon or vinegar in a simple salad dressing. In Europe, it often flavored confections, and was used to oil baking pans for cookies. Though some modern recipes specify its use in sautéing fish or vegetables, its flavor is destroyed when it is heated, so it is best to drizzle it over a finished dish, such as Sole Amandine (fish sautéed with sliced almonds), when an extra almond flavor is desired.

ALMOND PASTE

Almond paste is made with blanched almonds, sugar, and glycerine, and is sometimes given extra flavor with almond extract, or other flavorings. It is coarser and less sweet than MARZIPAN. In France there are two basic types:

1. Pâte d'amandes crue—raw almond paste—basically almonds and sugar ground together; may contain a bit of egg white. When equal quantities almonds and sugar are used, the mixture is called "Tant pour Tant." This is complicated by the fact that Tant pour Tant can be made with almonds or hazelnuts, so they are sometimes differentiated on labels of cans by being called "Tant pour Tant Amandes" or "Tant pour Tant Noisettes." Used for making petits fours and some cakes.

2. Pâte d'amandes cuite—"cooked almond paste"—also called "pate d'amandes confiseur" or "candy-maker's almond paste". Made of cooked sugar (to hard-ball stage) combined with ground almonds. This is used as topping for cakes (rolled out), or to make different shapes in the same way as Marzipan.

The brands found in the United States supermarkets and gourmet specialty shops vary in sweetness and consistency. Stores that specialize in nuts often make their own brands, which are usually excellent but very expensive. Odense, Reese, and Red-E are brands that are widely available in plastic tubes or cans. Well-stocked health food stores have an excellent and inexpensive almond paste with no preservatives.

STORAGE: After opening, wrap airtight to store in the refrigerator for up to 6 months.

PREPARATION AND USE: Almond paste purchased in health food stores tends to dry around the edges, so pinch off and discard any hardened surfaces. If the almond paste seems too dry, it can be softened with a few drops of glycerine, available at pharmacies, which will keep it soft during storage, or with almond or vegetable oil or egg white. Almond paste is used a great deal in European pastry and is the basic ingredient of marzipan. It is finely crumbled to add to some cake batters to make them firm. Rolled out like pastry, it is layered with poundcake to make tiny cakes called Petits Fours, or used as a topping for English Fruitcake beneath the traditional Royal Icing. It is quite easy to make at home, especially with an electric food processor, as in the following recipe.

ALMOND PASTE

2 cups (about 10 ounces) blanched whole or slivered almonds	For about 3 cups
1½ cups powdered sugar	

2 egg whites
1 teaspoon almond extract
1 teaspoon ROSE WATER (optional)

Place the almonds in the container of an electric food processor with the steel blade. Process to a fine powder. Add the powdered sugar, egg whites, and extract. Process until smooth, stopping from time to time to scrape the sides of the bowl with a rubber spatula. Taste, and add rose water and more almond extract if desired. Turn out onto plastic wrap, form into a roll, wrap tightly, and refrigerate for at least 24 hours. Use in place of commercial almond paste in any recipe.

APPLE TART
WITH ALMOND FILLING

1 (12") tart pan with removable bottom,   For 8 to 10 servings
   lined with chilled, sweet tart pastry

ALMOND FILLING:
1 recipe Almond Paste
2 large eggs
6 Golden Delicious apples, or other juicy apples
3 tablespoons sweet (unsalted) butter
3 tablespoons sugar

GLAZE:
6 ounces apricot preserves
1 tablespoon lemon juice

Preheat the oven to 400° with the rack in the lowest possible position.
Beat together until smooth the almond paste and eggs; spread evenly in the chilled tart shell. Peel and core apples. Cut in half lengthwise, then in thin wedges. Arrange 1 row of apple slices around the edge of the tart shell, overlapping them closely. Arrange a second row in the same manner in the opposite direction. Arrange apple slices in the center as desired.
Dot the apples with the butter and sprinkle evenly with the sugar. Bake on the bottom rack of the oven for 1 hour. Meanwhile, prepare the glaze. Combine preserves and lemon juice in a blender or food processor and puree. Transfer to a small saucepan, and warm before brushing over the hot tart.

TO PREPARE IN ADVANCE: This is at its best the day it is baked. Warm slightly before serving if desired.

315

AMARETTI

Amaretti are exceptionally fine, crisp and airy macaroon *biscotti* (cookies) studded with sugar crystals. They are sold in attractive red and orange cans labeled *Amaretti di Saronno* under the brand name Lazzaroni in Italian markets and gourmet specialty shops throughout the United States. They are expensive, but worth the price in flavor. The ones labeled *amaretti* are paper-wrapped in pairs. *Amarettini* are tiny cookies with the same flavor, but without the paper wrapping.

STORAGE: Stored in their original tin, these will keep for several months at room temperature, but do eventually become stale.

PREPARATION AND USE: Delicious just as they are. The cookies can be crushed to make a crumb crust for cheesecake by mixing 1½ cups of crumbs with 6 tablespoons (¾ stick) melted unsalted butter. Sprinkle crumbs over custards, ice creams, or fresh fruit for dessert. We make a very simple mousse-like dessert as in the following recipe.

AMARETTO CREAM
WITH RASPBERRIES

½ basket fresh raspberries   For 8 servings
1 cup sour cream
3 tablespoons liquid brown sugar (Domino brand) *or* ⅓
   cup granulated dark brown sugar, firmly packed
3 tablespoons Amaretto liqueur
1 teaspoon vanilla extract
1 cup heavy (whipping) cream
4 double-wrapped Italian macaroons (Amaretti di Saronno
   Lazzaroni)

Variations: You may wish to substitute other fresh or frozen fruits for the raspberries—strawberries, seedless grapes, peaches, or just about any other seasonal fruit.

Set aside 10 or 12 of the raspberries to use as a garnish for the finished dessert. In a medium mixing bowl, combine the sour cream, brown sugar, Amaretto and vanilla. Stir lightly to combine. Whip the cream in a chilled bowl until it is stiff; fold it gently into the sour cream mixture along with the crumbled macarooms and the remaining berries.

Spoon the mixture into a serving bowl (clear glass is best), or individual serving dishes. Chill in the refrigerator for up to 4 hours, or in the freezer for up to 2 hours.

Garnish the top of the dessert with the reserved berries before serving.

TO PREPARE IN ADVANCE: This is best when assembled within 4 hours of serving, but can actually be frozen for several days. If very hard, soften in the refrigerator for an hour or so before serving.

ANCHOVY

FRENCH: *anchois* GERMAN: *Sardelle* ITALIAN: *accuigaoralice*
SPANISH: *boquerón, anchoa* SWEDISH: *anjovis*

These tiny salted fish are a very popular seasoning throughout Europe. They are available in every supermarket in 2-ounce cans, either as flat fillets or rolled around CAPERS (see HERBS, SPICES, AND SEASONING BLENDS section) and packed in oil. Fine Italian cooks generally prefer unfilleted anchovies packed in salt, which are available only in Italian markets, either in bulk or in 1- to 2-pound cans. Imported anchovies from Portugal packed in olive oil are particularly fine and are available in gourmet specialty shops. The Spanish type, *boquerónes,* are sold in boxes or loose in some European specialty shops, and are usually white from being cured in vinegar. Pureed anchovies are available in tubes as ANCHOVY PASTE.

STORAGE: Canned anchovies in oil will keep indefinitely on the pantry shelf. After opening, transfer to a nonmetal container to store in the refrigerator for up to 2 weeks.

PREPARATION AND USE: The supermarket variety of canned anchovy can be excessively salty, so it is a good idea to rinse them gently under cold water and drain on paper towels before use. To use the dried, salted type, rinse off the salt, and soak for 10 minutes or so until they can be cut open to remove the central bone.

Salade Niçoise, Caesar Salad, and Greek Salad are famous for their addition of anchovies. Whole fillets can be laid in strips over salads, marinated sweet peppers, or atop buttered bread to be toasted as a canapé. The fillets can be mashed as a seasoning for salad dressings, mayonnaise, and all types of sauces, in which they combine especially well with garlic. They flavor the popular warm, creamy Italian dip Bagna Cauda, which is served with raw vegetables, and flavor Roman-style artichokes, stuffed with breadcrumbs, chopped anchovies, and olive oil. Mashed anchovies flavor the sauce for Vitello Tonnato (veal with tuna and anchovy-flavored mayonnaise), and this dish is often garnished with anchovy-caper rolls. They are often batter-dipped and deep-fried to serve as a savory snack with drinks.

Anchovies are used in Austria and in the Scandinavian countries in countless salads and potato dishes, such as the popular Swedish casserole Janssons Frestelse (Jansson's Temptation). Two crossed anchovy fillets atop a fried egg are the classic garnish for the Austrian dish, Schnitzel à la Holstein. Rolled caper-stuffed anchovies make an attractive garnish for salads and pasta dishes.

317

ANCHOVY PASTE

BRITISH: anchovy essence

This paste of mashed anchovies and salt is sold in 2-ounce tubes in most supermarkets. It is a convenience item which is not quite as flavorful as freshly mashed anchovies. To make your own anchovy paste, rinse and mash the fillets. The British anchovy essence is often made by pounding with herbs.

STORAGE: Paste will keep for up to 6 months if tightly capped and stored in the refrigerator.

PREPARATION AND USE: As a general rule, 1 teaspoon anchovy paste equals 1 mashed anchovy fillet. Just a tiny amount added to sauces and salad dressings can lend an unidentifiable zest. It can be used as a substitute for *blachan* (see SHRIMP PASTE, SOUTHEAST ASIAN in THE FOODS OF ASIA section). Anchovy butter, for serving on grilled steaks or fish, can be made by combining softened butter with anchovy paste to taste, a bit of lemon juice, and Tabasco sauce. In Provençal cooking, mashed anchovies are mixed with a small amount of olive oil, garlic and a sprinkling of vinegar to make the classic Anchoïade, which is spread on small pieces of bread fried crisp in olive oil to serve as an appetizer. A Corsican version adds figs to the mixture. Anchovy paste combined with mashed garlic makes an excellent seasoning for deviled eggs and for mayonnaise to serve with cold seafood. It occasionally flavors pasta sauces such as Marinara, made with tomatoes and garlic, and Putanesca, a sauce of olive oil, garlic, chopped tomatoes, and capers.

To make a Roman-style sauce for 1 pound (2 to 3 servings) cooked broccoli or cauliflower, heat a clove of garlic in 3 tablespoons olive oil in a small skillet, mashing it slightly to give off its flavor. Before the garlic browns, discard it, and stir 2 teaspoons anchovy paste, ⅓ cup dry vermouth or white wine, and a sprinkling of pepper into the garlic-flavored oil. Simmer briefly and pour over the warm vegetable.

ANGELICA

An herb you are not likely to find fresh in any market, though it is grown a good deal in Europe. The celery-like stalks are candied and sold in stores that carry CANDIED FRUITS.

ARBORIO

See RICE, ITALIAN

ARUGULA

(ahr-OO-goo-lah)

BRITISH: rocket, rocket cress FRENCH: *roquette*

"Arugula" is the Italian name for a pungent, slightly peppery tasting salad green of the mustard family. It is highly favored in Italy and is often featured in salads in the Nouvelle Cuisine restaurants in the United States. It can be purchased in specialty produce markets, especially those catering to an Italian clientele. It can be grown easily from seed, but do not confuse it with "sweet rocket," also called *roquette,* which is a flowering plant. When purchased, usually with its roots, arugula should be young, bright green, and very fresh looking. DANDELION GREENS (see THE FOODS OF REGIONAL AMERICA section) make a good substitute.

STORAGE: Wash in cold water, wrap in dry paper towels, and store in a plastic bag in the refrigerator for up to 3 days.

PREPARATION AND USE: This is strong flavored and can have a bitter aftertaste, so it is best mixed with other, more mildly flavored salad greens. For this reason, 1 bunch will serve 6. Remove the tough outer leaves and cut off and discard the stems. Tear into bite-sized pieces. Arugula has a great affinity for olive oil.

BAR-LE-DUC, CONFITURE DE

(BAHR-luh-dyook)

This famous preserve, which originated in the town of the same name in Lorraine, France, consists of a sugar syrup containing whole white or red currants. It can be found in gourmet specialty shops and is very expensive because the currants are hand-seeded.

STORAGE: After opening, refrigerate for use within 3 months.

USE: This is sometimes called for as a topping for desserts or as a filling for pastries in French recipes.

BARLEY AND PEARL BARLEY

FRENCH: *orge, orge perlée* GERMAN: *Gerste, Perlgraupen* ITALIAN: *orzo, orzo perlato* SPANISH: *cebada, cebada perlada*

This cereal grain is available as "whole grain" or "pearl." The whole grain is "pearled" to remove the outer hull, and the whiter or more "pearled" it is the less nutrients are left. Pearl barley is available in most supermarkets, and can be found in three sizes: fine, medium, and coarse. The medium size is most often specified for general use in recipes. Natural-food stores carry whole-grain or "hulled" barley, as well as Scotch barley, which is coarsely ground. Barley flour, used in breads, is sold in health food stores and is most often made from pearl barley. It is possible to grind whole-grain barley or Scotch barley into a more nutritious flour.

STORAGE: It will keep up to a month in an airtight container in a cool place, and indefinitely in the refrigerator.

PREPARATION AND USE: Barley swells a great deal in cooking, so 1 cup is the usual amount specified to serve 4 or 6 as a side dish. To make a barley pilaf to accompany meat or vegetable dishes, sauté 1 cup medium barley and 1 minced onion in 3 tablespoons butter until golden; transfer to a casserole for oven baking. Add 1 cup diced mushrooms (either fresh, or dried ones that have been soaked) and 3 cups beef or chicken broth with ½ teaspoon salt and a sprinkling of pepper. Cover tightly and bake at 350° for 1 hour and 15 minutes, stirring two or three times, until the barley is tender and the liquid has been absorbed.

Barley is widely used in Europe in thick soups, such as lamb-based Scotch Broth, and is often combined with mushrooms to serve as a side dish. Barley is a staple of Jewish cuisine. A Polish soup, Krupnik, is made of barley with scraps of meat and mushrooms. Scandinavians make a barley flatbread with soaked whole barley, buttermilk, and barley flour. In Latvia, it is the primary starch, and is used to make Miezu Putra, a stew with onion, sausages, and smoked meats. In Asia, it is ground into flour with lentils and used to make bread. We almost always add at least ¼ cup of fine or medium barley to vegetable soup.

BEANS, DRIED

FRENCH: *haricots* or *haricots secs* GERMAN: *Bohnen* IN LATIN AMERICA: *habas* ITALIAN: *fagioli*

Dried beans are not as essential to the cuisines of Europe as they are in other areas of the world, but they are still a common food and used in many delicious ways. Precooked beans in cans are available in supermarkets and ethnic markets everywhere but, with the exception of chick-peas (garbanzos), they make a poor substitute for dried beans that have been cooked at home.

STORAGE: Dried beans can be stored in a dry place for years, though they lose flavor on standing. Cooked beans improve in flavor if, after they are cool, they are placed in their cooking liquid in the refrigerator for at least 24 hours. They can be stored there for up to 5 days and will improve even more if boiled every day or two, as their cooking liquid becomes thicker and more flavorful with each boiling. Cooked beans and their liquid freeze well, either combined or separately.

PREPARATION AND USE: As a general rule, beans triple in volume when cooked, so 1 cup of dried beans will yield approximately 3 cups of cooked beans. Wash well in cold water and pick over to remove any gravel and broken beans. There is controversy over whether it is necessary to soak beans. Most cookbooks (except Diana Kennedy's Mexican cookbooks) say to cover them with three times as much water as beans and soak overnight, or bring them to a boil and set aside for 1 hour, discard the soaking water, rinse the beans well, and start with fresh water. We tend to agree with Diana Kennedy—that if you soak beans and discard the soaking water, a lot of the flavor and nutrients are lost.

To cook a batch of beans, use a heavy pot that won't scorch on the bottom. For 4 to 6 servings, place 2 cups of dried beans, soaked or not, in a pot with 5 cups of water, 1 minced or whole onion, and some garlic if desired, but do *not* add salt, tomatoes, or other acid ingredients at this time. Adding a tablespoon or so of oil, some salt pork, or a ham bone will prevent the liquid from boiling over. Bring slowly to a boil, and let simmer for 10 minutes, skimming any foam that rises to the surface. Cover and simmer slowly for 1½ to 3 hours until tender. Older beans take longer to cook. Salt, tomatoes, etc., can be added to taste during the last half hour of cooking, but if added earlier have a tendency to toughen the beans.

BORLOTTI

OTHER: *saligia*

This popular Italian dried bean is pink with red speckles. It is very similar to the pinto bean, which can be substituted for it in recipes since it is seldom available in the United States. NAVY BEANS or GREAT NORTHERN BEANS (see under BEANS in THE FOODS OF REGIONAL AMERICA section) are also good substitutes.

USE: In Italy, Borlotti beans are used in many soups, including the famous Pasta e Fagioli, and minestrone. They are baked in stews and casseroles and served in cold antipasto salads, which we enjoy sprinkled with Gremolata (see INDEX).

CANNELLINI

OTHER: Tuscan beans, white kidney beans

Cannellini are a white variety of kidney bean with a fluffy texture. They are imported from Italy dried or precooked in cans and can be found in Italian markets. We have had excellent luck in substituting GREAT NORTHERN BEANS and even the slightly smaller NAVY BEANS (see under BEANS in THE FOODS OF REGIONAL AMERICA section) in Italian recipes calling for cannellini, and always prefer dried beans we cook at home to canned beans.

USE: These are used in the same soups as BORLOTTI BEANS, or are tossed with vinaigrette dressing to make a cold antipasto salad. One of our favorite family dishes is one that we adapted from a recipe in Guiliano Bugialli's book *The Fine Art of Italian Cooking* (Times Books).

SALSICCE E FAGIOLI (ITALIAN SAUSAGE AND BEAN CASSEROLE)

For 8 servings

Serve with Italian red wine and a simple salad of marinated roast peppers.

12 "sweet" or "hot" Italian link sausages
3 tablespoons olive oil
3 cloves garlic, minced
2 teaspoons crumbled dried sage leaves
2 (28-ounce) cans Progresso peeled, crushed tomatoes
6 cups cooked white beans (such as cannellini, great
   northern, navy)

In a heavy skillet over medium heat, sauté the sausages in the olive oil for 8 to 10 minutes, turning often to brown them evenly. Add the garlic and sage and continue cooking for 2 minutes; then stir in the tomatoes. Simmer for 20 minutes to thicken the sauce. Stir in the cooked beans and simmer slowly for 10 to 15 minutes, until thickened.

TO PREPARE IN ADVANCE: This can be refrigerated and reheated to serve the next day, though it will thicken considerably, and care must be taken not to scorch it when reheating.

CHICK-PEAS

See under BEANS in THE FOODS OF THE MIDDLE EAST section

FAVA BEANS, DRIED AND FRESH

See under BEANS in THE FOODS OF THE MIDDLE EAST section

FLAGEOLETS

GERMAN: *Flageolett* SPANISH: *judía verde*

Flageolets are small, pale green, kidney-shaped beans with an exceptionally fine, delicate flavor, imported from France. They are available in gourmet specialty shops either dried in 1-pound boxes or precooked in 15-ounce cans. Both are quite expensive. There is no real substitute, but other beans are often used in their place.

PREPARATION AND USE: Two cups of canned flageolets, which are precooked and require only gentle heating, will serve 4. One cup of dried flageolets will serve 4, as they double in size during cooking. Dried flageolets are usually not soaked before use unless they are more than a year old, in which case they should be soaked as any dried bean.

To cook 1 cup, rinse and place in a heavy saucepan with 4 cups of water, a BOUQUET GARNI (see HERBS, SPICES, AND SEASONING BLENDS section, under SEASONING BLENDS), and a whole onion. Simmer, very slowly, covered, for 1½ to 2 hours until tender, adding boiling water if necessary if the water boils away. Add salt toward the end of cooking time. The beans can then be drained, but reserve the flavorful broth for soups or sauces.

In France, the cooked beans are often combined with sautéed minced onions and cream to accompany all kinds of meats and fowl, or are served with sausages added as a one-dish meal. They are occasionally used in place of white beans in the French dish called Estouffat from the province of Languedoc. They are particularly delicious with lamb, especially when heated just before serving in the pan juices, as in the following recipe.

FLAGEOLETS

1 box (2 cups) dried flageolets, cooked	For 6 to 8 servings

1   box (2 cups) dried flageolets, cooked   For 6 to 8 servings
      as described above in chicken broth rather than water
1   clove garlic, minced
3   tablespoons drippings from roast leg of lamb or broiled
      lamb chops
¼   teaspoon freshly grated lemon peel
      Salt and pepper, to taste
2   tablespoons minced chervil or parsley

Drain flageolets, reserving liquid for other uses. In a heavy saucepan, sauté the garlic briefly in the drippings. Add the cooked flageolets, mixing lightly. Season to taste with lemon peel, salt and pepper. Stir in fresh chervil or parsley. Serve with roast lamb or lamb chops.

GARBANZO

See under BEANS, in THE FOODS OF THE MIDDLE EAST section

LENTIL

OTHER: champagne or blond lentil

FRENCH: *lentille* GERMAN: *Linse* ITALIAN: *lenticchia* SPANISH: *lentega*

There are two European varieties of this small, delicious legume—one with tan skin with yellow flesh, and the other a tiny green bean called *lentille verte du Puy,* which has a slightly more pungent flavor. The former are available in most supermarkets; the latter, which are very expensive, may sometimes be found in gourmet specialty stores.

PREPARATION AND USE: Lentils never need soaking and, because they are smaller, they cook much more quickly than other beans. Pick them over carefully to remove gravel or grit and wash them well. Cover with 3 times their volume of water and simmer 20 minutes if you wish them to remain whole, or up to 35 minutes if you wish to puree.

One thinks of the tan lentils as part of a rich Bavarian lentil soup, flavored with a ham bone. In Germany, they are cooked with oxtails and potatoes in a dish called Sahn-Lensen mit Ochsenschwantz. In Italy, they are often cooked with sausages or made into soup flavored with herbs, to be eaten hot or cold. They are often served with ZAMPONE (see SAUSAGES, FRESH) on New Year's Day in the same manner as American Southerners eat black-eyed peas, in the belief that they bring good luck. In France, they are cooked with salt pork for Petit Salé aux Lentilles, and in Spain they are often combined with rice.

In the Middle East, they are cooked into porridge to be served hot or cold with a sprinkling of garlic and olive oil and eaten at any time of day. They are also cooked with BULGHUR (see THE FOODS OF THE MIDDLE EAST section), rice, or vegetables, but always with olive oil. Lentils pureed with cooked potatoes and cream make an excellent accompaniment to many meals.

The tiny green variety is considered a great delicacy and is used primarily as a salad, dressed with vinaigrette, to be part of a tray of *hors-d'oeuvres variés*.

BELGIAN ENDIVE

OTHER: French endive, witloof chicory

BRITISH: chicory FLEMISH: *witloof* FRENCH: *chicon, endive*

Endive is a small, compact, creamy white variety of chicory. It is grown underground, where it forms itself into a head that is dovetailed with yellow-toned tips. It was discovered by a horticulturist in Brussels, and most of the world's supply is still imported from there. It is available in fine produce markets and many supermarkets from September to May and is always very expensive but, fortunately, because there is no waste, a single head can be stretched creatively into several servings. Look for heads that are firm and crisp, and avoid any that are soft or discolored.

STORAGE: This vegetable becomes more and more bitter in flavor the longer it is exposed to light. Store tightly wrapped in the refrigerator for use within a few days.

PREPARATION AND USE: One head will serve 1 as a vegetable, 4 as part of a salad or as an appetizer dipper. Remove any wilted outer leaves and cut off the base. If it is to be served raw, taste it to see if it is bitter, and, if so, blanch it by placing it in a colander and pouring boiling water over it. They can be cooked whole, halved, or sliced in simmering salted water. Whole heads require 20 minutes of cooking, halves, 12 minutes, and sliced only 5.

We see this vegetable used in more and more interesting ways. The leaves, crisped in ice water, make imaginative holders for appetizer fillings, caviar, etc. Marcella Hazan, Italian-cookbook author, combines them in a salad with CRANBERRY BEANS (see under BEANS in THE FOODS OF REGIONAL AMERICA section). In classic French cuisine they are braised in butter and flavorful broth for 20 to 30 minutes, then covered with Bechamel sauce and grated cheese and gratinéed under the broiler. In Belgian cooking they are very often combined with ham, or wrapped in thin slices of ham to be served with various sauces. They are also a delightfully crisp addition to salads, in which they are often combined with apples, HEARTS OF PALM (see THE FOODS OF LATIN AMERICA section) or walnuts, as in the following recipe.

BELGIAN ENDIVE
WALNUT SALAD

2 heads Belgian endive   For 4 servings
4 white mushrooms

DRESSING:
1 small shallot, minced
1 teaspoon Dijon mustard
1 tablespoon white wine vinegar (can be tarragon-flavored)
1 tablespoon fresh lemon juice
¼ cup "extra-virgin" olive oil
¼ cup vegetable oil
1 tablespoon heavy (whipping) cream

TO SERVE:
2 teaspoons minced parsley
2 tablespoons chopped walnuts

Rinse endive, trim ends, and cut in lengthwise slivers. Place in salad bowl. Slice mushrooms as thin as possible through the stems and place on top of endive.

To make the dressing, whisk together the shallot and mustard in a small mixing bowl. Add the vinegar and lemon juice. Gradually add the oils, whisking constantly, followed by the cream. Pour the dressing over the salad and toss gently just until coated. Serve on salad plates, topping each serving with minced parsley and chopped walnuts.

TO PREPARE IN ADVANCE: The dressing will keep refrigerated for up to 3 days. Combine salad ingredients several hours ahead, cover with plastic wrap, and chill. For best flavor, bring dressing to room temperature. Toss just before serving.

BOUILLON

(boo-YOHN)

"Bouillon" is the French term for broth made from meat or poultry and assorted vegetables cooked in water. When clarified, it becomes CONSOMMÉ. ("Stock," on the other hand is made from bones.) Bouillons are available in cans, either regular strength or condensed, but they are generally over-salted and metallic tasting. It is so easy to make stock that it is truly a shame to discard any kind of meat or poultry bones and not make your own.

STORAGE: Bouillon will keep up to 1 week if tightly covered in the refrigerator if you simmer it for 5 minutes every 3 days to destroy any bacteria. It freezes beautifully for up to a year.

PREPARATION AND USE: Bouillon is the base for most soups and sauces. It can be used as a poaching liquid for vegetables, a process which only improves both the liquid and the vegetables. Following is a basic recipe.

BASIC BOUILLON

For 2 to 3 quarts

It is not really necessary to have a recipe to make bouillon, as the term applies to any liquid in which meat and vegetables have been cooked. The following amounts are simply a guideline.

2   chickens, whole or cut up, *or* 2–3 pounds poultry or
        beef, cut in 1½" to 2" pieces
4   carrots, cut in 1" chunks
4   stalks celery with leafy tops, cut in 1" chunks
1   onion, quartered
      The stems from 1 bunch parsley
1   teaspoon salt
8–10 whole black peppercorns

Combine all ingredients in a large stockpot. Add cold water to cover by 1". Bring to a boil and then lower the heat to a gentle simmer. Skim any foam that rises to the surface during the first 10 minutes of cooking. Cover and simmer for 45 minutes for fresh chicken (at which point it will be fully cooked and may be used for any desired purpose), or 2 hours for beef. Remove from heat and strain into a large bowl through a colander lined with several layers of rinsed cheesecloth or a clean kitchen towel. Let stand for 5 minutes until the fat rises to the top. Skim and discard the fat. Taste and correct seasonings. The cooked meat is never wasted, but served warm or cold with a Mustard Mayonnaise, or tossed with a basic Vinaigrette to become part of a salad.

BOUILLON CUBES AND GRANULES

Bouillon cubes and granules, as well as "stock bases" marketed by the various spice companies are available in beef, chicken, and various vegetable flavors. They are available in all supermarkets and gourmet specialty shops and vary considerably in flavor. They tend to be salty and contain MONO-SODIUM GLUTAMATE (see THE FOODS OF ASIA section), which is a chemical we avoid. They have no nutritional value. The finest brands are European imports, such as Leibig and Knorr-Swiss, which are widely available in cubes or granules.

STORAGE: After opening, these are best stored in the refrigerator.

PREPARATION: Follow directions on package.

BOUQUET GARNI
See HERBS, SPICES, AND SEASONING BLENDS section, under
SEASONING BLENDS

BOVRIL

Bovril is the trade name for a liquid beef concentrate from England. It is available in many supermarkets and gourmet specialty shops in 5.2-ounce jars.

STORAGE: Because of its high salt content, it can be stored on the pantry shelf indefinitely.

USE: Bovril is a seasoning base used to flavor soups, sauces, and stews, and to make a hearty "beef tea" as a snack. It is salty, so use sparingly.

BUCKWHEAT AND BUCKWHEAT GROATS
OTHER: beechwheat, brank, Saracen corn

DUTCH: *boek-weit* FRENCH: *sarrasin* GERMAN: *Buchweizen*
ITALIAN: *grano saraceno* RUSSIAN: *kasha* SPANISH: *trigo negro*

Buckwheat is the seed of a plant native to Russia, which is treated like a cereal. It is sold in health food stores and European markets as groats (whole grains), grits (ground groats in varying degrees of fineness), and as flour. These products have usually been toasted to intensify their flavors.

Kasha is the Russian term for braised buckwheat groat. It may occasionally refer to other grains, such as BULGHUR (see THE FOODS OF THE MIDDLE EAST section) and SEMOLINA, but kasha usually refers to braised buckwheat. It is a very popular food in Russian, Polish, and European Jewish cuisines.

The flavor is strongly nutlike and the texture is crunchy. Wolff's, a brand of buckwheat groats labeled "kasha," is sold in 1-pound boxes.

STORAGE: Buckwheat can be stored, like other grains, in an airtight jar in a cool place for up to a year.

USE: Buckwheat flour is most commonly used in the United States to make buckwheat pancakes. It is used to make thin crêpes known as Galletes de Sarrasin in the French province of Brittany. The flour is used in Russia for filled dumplings called Vareniki, to make mush, and in the making of Blini, pancakes traditionally served with caviar and sour cream. The fine grain of buckwheat grits is cooked into a porridge called Black Polenta in Europe, where it is eaten for breakfast.

Groats are often mixed with meat to make meatballs. But by far the most popular use of buckwheat is in the making of kasha, a pilaf-like dish. To make kasha, allow approximately ¼ cup of whole or coarse buckwheat groats per person for most recipes. For 4 servings, place 1 cup of the grain in a heavy pan with 1 lightly beaten egg, and stir over medium heat until the egg is cooked and dry. This step keeps the grains separate when cooked. Add 4 tablespoons (½ stick) butter and 2 cups broth or water, ¾ teaspoon salt, and a sprinkling of pepper. Cover, and simmer over very low heat for about 15 minutes until the liquid has been absorbed. Seasonings such as minced onion, butter, or chicken fat are usually added, as well as mushrooms, toasted walnuts or pine nuts, and even curry powder, depending on the meat with which it will be served.

When tender, kasha is fluffed to serve as a starch in place of potatoes, or to use as a base for many other dishes: casseroles, stuffings for fish or chicken, and even a stuffing for meatballs. To make Kasha Varnishkas, a dish popular with Russian and Polish Jews, combine ½ pound BOW-TIE noodles, cooked (see under PASTA), and 1 minced onion browned in butter with the cooked kasha. Cooked kasha makes a hearty stuffing for vegetables like cabbage and green peppers, and for turnovers called Pirozhki in Russia and Piroshki in Poland, and is an excellent accompaniment to lamb and duck. It is a superb bread ingredient.

BÜNDERFLEISCH

OTHER SWISS NAMES: *bundnerteller, bindenfleish*

This is a salt-cured and air-dried beef from the canton of Grisons in the Swiss Alps. It is BILTONG (see THE FOODS OF AFRICA section) or JERKY (see THE FOODS OF REGIONAL AMERICA section) risen to epicurean heights. It is imported in small quantities and is available only occasionally in gourmet specialty shops. One type is lightly smoked.

STORAGE: Wrap tightly to store in the refrigerator for up to a month.

PREPARATION AND USE: This is usually served as PROSCIUTTO (see under HAM), thinly sliced as an appetizer. It can also be scraped or flaked and served with a light oil and vinegar dressing, or used as an elegantly flavored chipped beef.

CALVADOS

(KAHL-vah-dohs)

Calvados is a very dry apple brandy distilled from apple cider. The quality can vary widely (it must be well-aged to be good and come from the Vallée d'Auge in Normandy). It is available in fine liquor stores and is quite expensive. American applejack, which is widely available and much less expensive, can be substituted in most recipes with not much discernible difference in flavor, though some experts disagree on this point.

STORAGE: It will keep indefinitely at room temperature.

USE: This is a very common ingredient in the dishes of Normandy in France, where it is often combined with cream in a sauce for chicken, pheasant, veal, or pork. It is considered essential in the famous dish, Tripes à la Mode de Caen. Use it in place of brandy whenever a slight apple flavor would be desirable. We like it in chicken liver pâté and use it to flame an apple-filled omelette.

CANDIED FRUIT

OTHER: glacé fruit

All kinds of fruits are candied: cherries, pineapple, oranges, lemons, citron, and the stalks of an herb known as angelica. The very best ones can be purchased in shops that specialize in candied fruits. Avoid the mixed-fruit supermarket variety, which is laden with preservatives.

STORAGE: Store in a cool, dark place for up to 2 months, or freeze for indefinite storage.

PREPARATION AND USE: The supermarket variety can be improved greatly by marinating it in brandy, liqueur, or *eau de vie* [clear fruit brandy, such as framboise (raspberry) or KIRSCH], for an hour or so before it is used. Blot dry before use.

These types of fruits are used throughout Europe in all sorts of fancy pastries and puddings. Angelica, which is green, is primarily cut into decorations for breads and cakes.

330

CAPERS

See HERBS, SPICES, AND SEASONING BLENDS section

CARDOON

FRENCH: *cardon* GERMAN: *Kardone* ITALIAN: *cardone* SPANISH: *cardo silvestre*

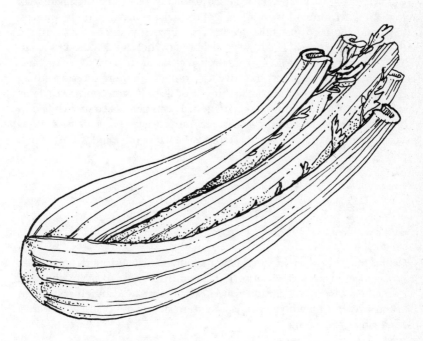

Cardoon is a Mediterranean plant of the artichoke family (a thistle). It resembles celery in appearance and has an artichoke-celery flavor. The small tender ones found in Italy are seldom found here unless cultivated in home gardens. Those found in specialty produce shops tend to be large and somewhat bitter. The best substitutes are CELERY ROOT or celery, though there is a substantial difference in flavor.

STORAGE: Rinse well, wrap in paper towels and store in a plastic bag in the refrigerator for up to a week.

PREPARATION AND USE: There is a good deal of waste, so buy 2 pounds to yield 1½ pounds of edible vegetable for 4 servings. Remove any wilted outer stalks, any stringy parts, and the fluffy top. If very large, the cardoon will probably be bitter, so you would be wise to use only the tender stalks, or to blanch the larger stalks for a minute or two in salted water. Cardoon discolors on standing, so if not using cut pieces immediately, place them in water to which a teaspoon or so of lemon juice or vinegar, or a pinch of granulated vitamin C (ascorbic acid), has been added. In fact, adding any of these to the water in which the cardoon is cooked will help to preserve the white color. They will, depending on the amount, require 45 minutes or so of simmering to become tender.

Cooked, diced cardoon can be added to salads, or can be the main salad ingredient when dressed with a vinaigrette. Italians prefer it dipped in egg batter and deep-fried just until tender. The French cover cooked cardoon with Béchamel sauce, sprinkle with cheese, and heat under the broiler to serve it au gratin, or puree it with Béchamel sauce to serve as a vegetable with any kind of roast meat. In Provençal cooking, they are topped with an anchovy sauce for a traditional Christmas Eve dish. It is a versatile vegetable that lends itself to all kinds of preparation. It can be cooked and chilled in a vinegar marinade to serve à la Grecque, pureed with potatoes to serve as an accompaniment to most any meat, or tossed with butter and white truffles.

CAUL

OTHER: net fat

CHINESE: *mong yo* FRENCH: *crépine*

Caul is the white, lacy-looking, fatty membrane that surrounds an animal's stomach. Beef or pork caul can be purchased from some specialty butchers, but you'd be wise to call ahead to check whether it's available. If you live in a city that has a Chinatown, caul is easy to track down, because it is widely used in Chinese cooking.

STORAGE: Wrapped airtight, it will keep in the refrigerator for up to 3 days, or in the freezer for up to 6 months.

PREPARATION AND USE: Caul is stiff and tears easily, so soak it in room temperature salted water for 15 minutes or so to soften it before unfolding. Cut it to the desired size.

Many French recipes specify the use of caul as a lining for pâtés and *terrines* (meat or game cooked in earthenware dishes) because it gives an attractive appearance. It is also used as a casing for various *charcuterie* (pork butchery) items such as CRÉPINETTES (flat sausages without skins—see under SAU-SAGES, FRESH), in which case the caul is cut into 5″ squares and used to wrap any sausage filling or forcemeat. In China, it is used primarily as a wrapping for foods to be deep-fried.

CELERY ROOT

OTHER: celeriac, celery knob, turnip-rooted celery

FRENCH: *céleri-rave* GERMAN: *Knollensellerie* ITALIAN: *sedano rapa*
SPANISH: *apio-nabo*

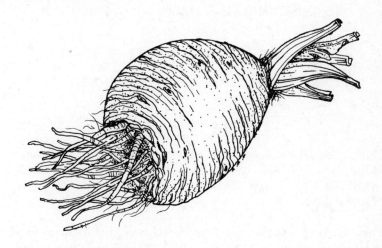

This type of celery is grown only for its large, delicious, knobby brown root. Its flavor has been described as a cross between celery and walnuts. It is available in produce markets during the fall and winter months. Buy medium-sized, smooth ones, as they are the tastiest and the easiest to peel.

STORAGE: Store in a paper bag inside a plastic bag in the refrigerator for up to 5 days.

PREPARATION AND USE: One celery root, measuring 3″ to 4″ in diameter will serve 2 in most recipes. The skin must be peeled to reveal the white flesh. (If not using the root immediately, drop it into cold water to which you have added a teaspoon or so of lemon juice, vinegar, or a pinch of granulated vitamin C to prevent darkening.)

Celery root can be eaten raw if it is young and tender, cut in thin strips and tossed simply with a mustard-flavored mayonnaise to make Céleri Rémoulade, this last variation being one of the most popular *hors-d'oeuvres* in France. After marinating in vinaigrette dressing for several hours, it can be tossed with other salad ingredients. Celery root makes a tasty addition to soups, stews, and Asian stir-fry dishes. It can also be cooked to serve as a vegetable. Simmer whole, without peeling, for 5 to 10 minutes, until tender.

Then peel, slice, and toss with butter, or puree the root with an equivalent amount of cooked potato to make a delicious accompaniment to almost any main course.

CÈPE

See MUSHROOMS, DRIED OR CANNED

CHANTERELLE

See MUSHROOMS, DRIED OR CANNED

CHEESE

DANISH: *ost* DUTCH: *kaas* FINNISH: *juusto* FRENCH: *fromage* GERMAN, AUSTRIAN, SWISS: *Käse* ITALIAN: *formaggio* POLISH: *ser* PORTUGUESE: *queijo* RUMANIAN: *brînză* RUSSIAN: *syr* YUGOSLAVIAN: *sir*

There are over 300 classified European cheeses, a bewildering array of names for the consumer. All are made from the milk of various animals. A number of books have been written on the subject that describe the manufacture of all the different kinds.

For this book, which deals with ingredients, we limit ourselves to cheeses used in cooking. First, we divide them into six categories to provide information on storage and use. Then, we list specific cheeses alphabetically within their categories with country of origin, description of taste and texture, and recommendations for their use.

Some cheeses are more suitable for cooking than others, depending on how smoothly they melt and how they combine with other foods. Cheese has long been used as a primary ingredient in such European dishes as Welsh Rarebit, soufflés, fondues, and in fillings for quiche. Adding cheese to Béchamel sauce (a basic cream sauce) turns it into Mornay Sauce. Cheese cannot tolerate high temperatures so it is best to grate or chop it and add to soups and sauces just before serving, stirring just until the cheese is melted. Many semi-firm cheeses adapt well to being breaded and deep-fried, as in the classic Mozzarella Fritta.

As a general rule when buying cheese to be grated, buy twice the grated amount called for (this will be a cup measurement, but it works out). For example, for 1 cup grated cheese, buy ¼ pound solid; for 4 cups grated, buy 1 pound solid. Fresh cheeses, such as cottage cheese and ricotta, being very moist, are exactly equal, so 8 ounces equals 1 cup.

The very finest quality cheeses can be purchased in cheese shops, gourmet specialty shops, and many fine supermarkets. In a cheese or other specialty shop you needn't be embarrassed to ask for a taste of a certain cheese before purchasing it because it is difficult to tell by its look whether a cheese is exactly ripe or past its prime. The usually more limited varieties of plastic-wrapped cheeses sold in supermarkets cannot be tasted, but are generally of good quality because of rapid turnover. Check the package carefully to make sure it is sealed and that the cheese seems moist. Dark edges indicate drying.

Following are our own classifications of cheese. We have included information on *Chèvres* (French goat cheeses) because there is a current interest in them, and they are being specified more and more as an ingredient.

SOFT, UNRIPENED CHEESES

This category includes most of the fresh cheeses: cottage cheese, cream cheese, Neufchâtel, and ricotta.

STORAGE: These are very perishable, so should be refrigerated, tightly wrapped, for use as soon as possible (within 2 weeks). Cream cheese can be frozen, but Neufchâtel, having more moisture and less butterfat, does not freeze well at all.

USE: Serve as fresh as possible and slightly chilled. Curd cheeses, such as ricotta, are often used in cooking, in such dishes as Lasagne, Gnocchi, Ravioli Nudi (pasta filling without pasta), and in many cheesecake recipes. Cream cheese is often used to make appetizer spreads, as a dessert with fresh berries or tart preserves, and in many cheesecakes and cake icings.

Gervais: A well-known make of **Petit-suisse.** This is an expensive French version of fresh cream cheese. You will find it in 4-ounce foil packages. It is rich and tangy, and is often salted and peppered to serve as an appetizer spread, or sweetened and flavored to serve for dessert.

Mascarpone: A fresh Italian "double cream" (meaning it has more than 60 percent butterfat) cheese that resembles clotted cream and has a fine, buttery flavor. The taste is similar to a combination of our domestic cream cheese and sour cream, which can serve as a substitute if mascarpone is not available. It is sold only in fine cheese shops and gourmet specialty shops and is extremely perishable, so plan to use it as soon as possible. Taste it if possible before purchase to ensure that it is fresh. It is superb as a dessert cheese as it is (we like it with berries and other fresh fruit), but is sometimes flavored with sweet flavorings such as liqueurs or candied fruits. With savory seasonings such as anchovies or mustard it is served as an antipasto.

Neufchâtel: A French cream cheese, which is lower in butterfat (and therefore in calories) and contains more water than our commercial cream cheese.

Because of this it has a shorter shelf life and does not freeze well. It can be used in the same manner as cream cheese—as a dessert and as a base for dips and spreads. The Swiss version is **Neuchâtel.**

Petit Swiss (Petit-suisse): See GERVAIS.

Ricotta: A fresh, fluffy Italian cheese made from the whey of cheeses such as mozzarella, provolone and, in this country, from Cheddar and Swiss. Literally translated, "ricotta" means twice cooked, and it is so named because it is made by cooking the whey from a previously cooked cheese, or cooking the whey twice. It is not even considered a cheese in Italy. It resembles cottage cheese in appearance and texture, but not in flavor. Domestic ricotta made with partially skimmed milk is more like the true Italian ricotta. If using the domestic type made with whole milk in Italian recipes, dry it by placing it between two paper towels for a few minutes, or let it drip in a cheesecloth bag for an hour or so to drain off some of the water. This fresh cheese is extremely perishable, so make sure it is snowy white when you buy it; yellowing indicates spoilage.

Fresh ricotta is an important ingredient in some recipes for Lasagne, and is used to make ricotta GNOCCHI and fillings for pasta such as a ravioli and cannelloni. As a dessert ingredient, it is sweetened, mixed with candied fruit and layered with spongecake and liqueur to make the classic Cassata, used for cheesecake and, flavored, to use as a dessert filling for the crisp, deep-fried pastry tube, Cannoli. A dried type of salty ricotta, sold only in Italian delis, is sliceable.

SOFT, RIPENED CHEESES

This category includes surface-ripened cheeses such as French Brie and Camembert and the Danish Crèma Dania, as well as the rich and buttery "double crèmes" (which contain more than 60 percent butterfat) and "triple crèmes" (which contain 75 percent). Of the high-butterfat types, only Boursin is listed because it is often used in appetizer and quiche recipes. Boursault, L'Explorateur, and other "triple crèmes" are not listed here because they are too rich for cooking, but they remain our favorite dessert cheeses.

STORAGE: Once cut, surface-ripened cheeses stop ripening. A perfectly ripened Brie or Camembert, which has just been purchased for serving on the same day, should be covered and kept in a cool spot until ready to serve. For longer storage, wrap tightly in plastic wrap, overwrap with foil, and store in the coldest part of the refrigerator for use as soon as possible (within a few days). If surface mold forms, cut it away. We have successfully frozen these cheeses for up to 2 months. They should be thawed slowly in the refrigerator.

USE: These are seldom used in cooking, but we mention those few in the alphabetical listings that are occasionally called for in recipes. The crusts of surface-ripened cheeses can be eaten, not cut away, unless specified in particular recipes, or if they are overly strong. The following cheeses are called for in recipes for cheese puffs, cheesecakes, and various snack crackers to make from leftover cheese. They can be baked *en croûte* in puff pastry and served hot, cut like a pie, for luncheon or supper accompanied by red wine and fruit.

Boursin: A white, creamy French cheese, which is either flavored with garlic and herbs *(Boursin à l'ail et au fines herbes),* or coated with cracked black pepper *(Boursin au poivre).* It is usually served as a spread with crackers (we like it on bagels), but makes an interesting topping for cooked vegetables or grilled meats. Less expensive domestic imitations, such as Rondelé, are not as good as the original. We use these cheeses to fill mushroom caps which we bake at 400° just until the cheese is bubbly, and then serve warm as an appetizer. The herb and garlic version gives a tart garlic flavor to the following appetizer recipe.

SPINACH PÂTÉ

For up to 24 servings

Serve this bright green loaf warm, or at room temperature; as an appetizer spread for crackers, or sliced as a vegetable accompaniment to simple entrées.

  Butter or shortening to grease the baking pan
3 pounds fresh spinach, washed, and center ribs removed, *or*
    3 (10-ounce) packages frozen chopped spinach, thawed
4 tablespoons (½ stick) butter
1 medium onion, chopped
1 stalk celery, diced
2 large eggs
⅔ cup (5–6 ounces) BOURSIN-style cheese
¾ cup dry breadcrumbs
½ cup grated Parmesan cheese
1 teaspoon salt
½ teaspoon freshly grated nutmeg
¼ teaspoon ground black pepper

TO GARNISH AND SERVE:
    Carrot or pimiento strips
    Crackers (optional)

Grease a terrine or glass loaf pan (approximately 7½″ × 3½″) with butter or solid shortening. Line the pan with waxed paper or parchment paper and coat the paper with butter or shortening. Preheat oven to 400°.

If using fresh spinach, cook it until wilted in only the water that clings to the leaves; drain, chop fine, and cool. Squeeze all excess moisture from the cooked, or thawed frozen, spinach with your hands.

Melt butter in a large skillet. Sauté the onion and celery until the onion is transparent but not browned. Remove from heat.

In the container of an electric blender or food processor fitted with the steel chopping blade, combine the eggs and Boursin-style cheese and process until smooth. Add the remaining ingredients along with the drained spinach. Process until the mixture is pureed. (If using a blender, stop the motor several times to push the mixture into the blades with a rubber spatula.)

Turn the mixture into the prepared pan. Cover with buttered waxed paper, followed by the lid or a piece of aluminum foil. This will prevent the top from developing a crust.

Bake for 50 to 65 minutes, until the center feels firm to the touch. Cool. Turn out of the pan onto a serving dish. Garnish the top of the loaf with strips of carrot or pimiento. Serve with crackers, if desired.

TO PREPARE IN ADVANCE: This keeps well, but loses its bright green color as it stands. It will keep in the refrigerator for up to 5 days or frozen, for up to 1 month. Bring to room temperature before serving.

Brie: Golden, soft, surface-ripened French cheese with a white or tan edible crust. It should be purchased either in whole rounds measuring at least 10″ in diameter, or cut from such rounds. The center should be creamy and evenly golden. Avoid any in small boxes. Brie is best purchased between October and April. "Brie de Meaux" and "Brie de Melun" are considered very fine. When buying a round, open the wrapper and smell the crust; there should be no ammonia odor. It should feel a bit firm. Once cut, it stops ripening.

Brie is traditionally served with bread or unseasoned crackers, such as water biscuits or Bremner wafers, before or after meals, but can also be encased in puff pastry (see PASTRY, PUFF) and served warm. It is elegantly served when topped with nuts and baked in a quiche dish until it has melted—it becomes runny like a fine Fondue, and is served as a dip for bread cubes or firm crackers. Brie can be frozen successfully due to its high butterfat content. Leftover Brie can be scraped of its crust and used to make Brie wafers, a snack cracker baked with sesame seeds to serve as an appetizer and accompaniment to soups, as in the following recipe.

Sesame Brie Wafers

8 ounces Brie, skin removed	For about 50 wafers
4 ounces (1 stick) butter	
1 cup all-purpose flour	
½ teaspoon cayenne (ground red pepper)	
½ teaspoon celery salt	
½ cup sesame seeds, toasted in a skillet until golden	

In a food processor or electric mixer, combine the Brie and butter. If very firm, let soften for a few minutes, then blend until thoroughly combined. Add the remaining ingredients, except sesame seeds, and mix until the dough is very smooth.

Divide the dough in half and place each half on a separate piece of waxed paper. Use the paper to help you form each portion into a long roll about 1″ in diameter. Overwrap with foil and refrigerate overnight.

Preheat the oven to 400°. Using a serrated knife, cut the chilled rolls into crosswise slices ¼″ thick. Press one side of each into sesame seeds and place, seed-coated side up, on a cookie sheet. Bake 8 to 10 minutes, until golden. Serve warm or at room temperature, as an appetizer or an accompaniment to soups.

TO PREPARE IN ADVANCE: The unbaked dough can be frozen. The baked wafer can be stored for up to 3 days in airtight tins.

Camembert: A French surface-ripened cheese more highly revered in France than the milder Brie. It is best purchased between January and April and only in whole rounds. When perfectly ripe it has a white crust and should be buttery, but not runny. Avoid any that looks shrunken. Quality of Camembert varies enormously, even in France. It can be quite strongly flavored and is seldom used in cooking, though it can be used for the same purposes as Brie. We like to coat chilled wedges of Camembert with egg and fresh bread crumbs and brown them quickly in butter to serve as a surprising flavor contrast with a lightly dressed green salad.

Crema Dania: Sometimes called **Crema Danica,** this is a rich and creamy, soft-ripened Danish cheese sold in butter-shaped bars with a thin waxy skin. It is similar to Brie and can be used in the same ways, but most often serves as a dessert cheese. Avoid any with an ammonia odor.

Semi-Soft Cheeses

This category includes smooth, buttery textured cheeses, and the *pasta filata* ("plastic" or hand-stretched and kneaded) types.

STORAGE: Wrap tightly in plastic wrap and overwrap with foil to store in the refrigerator up to 3 months. These cheeses, even if cut, continue to age and become stronger in flavor the longer they are kept. Rub cut surfaces with butter or dip in hot paraffin for longer storage. Surface mold doesn't harm the cheese underneath, but should be cut away. Freezing is not recommended because it alters the texture and melting quality.

USE: Though many of these are excellent snacking cheeses, a number in this category are widely used in cooking for their smooth melting qualities.

Bel Paese: Literally "beautiful country," this mildly robust, slightly sweet Italian cheese is one of the world's most popular table cheeses. Be warned that the imported and the domestic have similar wrappings—the map is the clue. The Italian import has a map of Italy; the domestic has a map of North and South America. The domestic cheese is sometimes superior. This is a fine cheese for snacking and picnicking any time, superb in sandwiches, and can be used as a flavorful substitute for mozzarella in recipes. Cubed, it adds a special spark to all kinds of salads. Thinly sliced, it makes a flavorful last-minute topping for chicken or veal cutlets, if heated only until melted. Cheese-topped croutons, Crostini, are made in Italy.

Bonbel: The French brand name for an exported type of Saint Paulin, a bland, semi-soft, buttery cheese, which is mild when young but becomes quite strong as it ages. Slice to use in sandwiches or cut in julienne strips for salads.

Caciocavallo: The Italian name means "cheese on horseback" because, in its traditional shape, this cheese resembles saddlebags. It is actually shaped more like a flask and is tied with a cord as is the more familiar PROVOLONE. This is a cow's milk cheese of the *pasta filata* type, which is stretched and shaped by hand. It has a natural smoky flavor and, when young, has a texture somewhat like a very flaky CHEDDAR (or KASSERI—see THE FOODS OF THE MIDDLE EAST section, under CHEESE), and is often served warm as an appetizer like the latter. When aged, it has a sharper flavor and becomes hard enough to grate and use as a seasoning cheese in all manner of cooked dishes and sauces. It is often used in baked pasta casseroles.

Esrom: A Danish semi-soft, surface-ripened, golden cheese, sometimes called **Danish Port-Salut,** because it somewhat resembles the French cheese in flavor. It is buttery and bland when young, but when aged is quite pungent in flavor, more like German TILSIT. It is available in bricks, and may be flavored with various herbs, spices such as caraway, or black pepper. It has a very distinctive flavor and should be used judiciously, depending on its strength of flavor, in cooking as a seasoning in sauces and quiches, or sprinkled over cooked vegetables.

Leyden: A Dutch cheese flavored with seeds of caraway or cumin, or both. It is semi-soft and spicy. It is usually served as an appetizer with beer, but is often grated over salads and sauerkraut. It can be blended with half its volume of sweet butter, shaped into balls, and rolled in pumpernickel bread crumbs to make Cheese "Truffles" to serve as an appetizer.

Mozzarella: Sometimes called "pizza cheese" this is the delicious *pasta filata* or plastic-type cheese that melts into long stringy strands. Of our domestic brands, the type made with partially skimmed milk is closest to the Italian. It is used in making Veal Parmigiana, now on the menus of many American restaurants, and in the fried sandwich seasoned with anchovy called Mozzarella in Carrozza. Mozzarella di bufala, the finest Italian mozzarella available, is made from the milk of water buffalos. It is sold packed in water, is very soft, and is served primarily as a table cheese, or as an appetizer drizzled with olive oil and fresh herbs to serve on bread. Mozzarella "affumicata" is a lightly smoked version that is excellent in salads or grated as a topping for Pizza Rustica, or can be drizzled with the finest olive oil and sprinkled with cracked black pepper to serve as an antipasto or salad. "Scamorza" is a very expensive dried mozzarella-like cheese (sometimes lightly smoked), which is highly prized, and is usually drizzled with olive oil in the same manner as "affumicata."

When mozzarella is breaded and fried to serve hot with well-seasoned tomato sauce it becomes a succulent first course, as in the following recipe.

MOZZARELLA MARINARA

4 (⅜″ thick) slices from a brick of whole-milk   For 4 servings
   mozzarella (available at Italian delis)
   Approximately ½ cup milk
   Approximately ½ cup flour
   Approximately 1 cup dry bread crumbs, plain or seasoned
1 cup olive oil (or ½ cup *each* vegetable oil and olive oil)
   Optional: 8 anchovy fillets, drained

MARINARA SAUCE:
2 cloves garlic, minced
¼ cup olive oil
2 tablespoons minced parsley
1 tablespoon chopped fresh basil *or* 1 teaspoon dried basil, crumbled
2 pounds ripe tomatoes, peeled, seeded, and coarsely chopped *or* 1 (28-ounce) can crushed tomatoes in tomato puree (Progresso brand)
½ cup dry vermouth *or* ⅔ cup dry white wine
1 strip fresh lemon peel
1 teaspoon salt

Dip the cheese slices in milk, then in flour, then in milk again, and finally in bread crumbs. Be sure all surfaces of the cheese are completely coated. Place in the refrigerator for at least 30 minutes while you make the sauce.

To make the sauce, sauté the garlic in the olive oil in a heavy skillet. Add remaining sauce ingredients and simmer over medium-low heat, stirring often, for about 30 minutes, until thick.

Have warm serving plates waiting in the oven. Heat the oil(s) in a heavy (preferably nonstick) skillet. Brown the coated cheese, about 30 seconds on each side, removing them from the skillet before they become runny. Drain on paper towels.

Place a few spoonfuls of warm sauce on each plate, top with fried cheese, followed by more sauce. If desired, top each serving with two crossed anchovies.

TO PREPARE IN ADVANCE: The sauce will keep refrigerated for up to 4 days or, frozen, up to 4 months. Coat the cheese in the morning, place in the refrigerator, and fry just before serving.

Port-Salut or **Port-du-Salut:** A French cheese invented by Trappist monks, which is widely served as a table cheese, and is highly regarded for its creamy flavor. It is seldom used in cooking but occasionally used in sandwiches, baked pastries, or as a flavoring for eggs.

Provolone: A cow's milk *pasta filata* or plastic-type kneaded cheese, very popular in Italy where it is often formed into the shapes of little pigs, pears, or sausages, and then bound with a cord to hang and ripen. It comes smoked and unsmoked. Smoked is "provolone affumicato." Young provolone, aged only a few months, is called "dolce"; it makes a fine sandwich and snack cheese, especially when served with salami, or sautéed in butter to serve like KASSERI (see THE FOODS OF THE MIDDLE EAST section, under CHEESE). Older cheese, aged up to six months, is called "piccante"; it has a real bite to it and is too strong to be eaten in a sandwich or with fruit. The domestic type is really not at all like true Italian provolone, being much blander and far less complex. Provolone is used a good deal in Italian cooking, in sauces, casseroles, and as part of an antipasto platter.

Saint Paulin: See Bonbel.

Taleggio: A very rich, semi-soft, straw-colored northern Italian cheese that ranges, depending on age, from mild to quite pungent. You will find it in flat squarish blocks covered with wax or with a rosy rind. The center may be very soft and pasty. It is made from cow's milk and ages very quickly, darkening as it does so. It can be substituted for mozzarella, lending much more flavor to a dish, but is really best as a fine table cheese served with salad, or as a dessert with grapes. We like it tossed with roasted and peeled red peppers for an antipasto salad.

FIRM AND SEMI-FIRM CHEESES

This category comprises a large number of excellent cooking cheeses.

STORAGE: Firm cheeses have the longest storage life, with some Cheddars and Swiss types keeping up to 9 months. Coat the cut edges with butter or hot paraffin to prevent drying and surface mold, wrap tightly in plastic and overwrap with foil, and store in the bottom of the refrigerator. Alternatively, rub the cut surface with the dull side of a knife to partially seal the surface before wrapping. These cheeses freeze well for up to 2 months. Wrap pieces (not whole wheels) tightly and freeze very quickly to 0°. Thaw very slowly in the refrigerator or they are apt to become crumbly. Leftover grated cheeses of this classification store well in the freezer for a month or longer and are handy to sprinkle, without thawing, over casseroles, soups, or omelets.

USE: These cheeses are widely used as ingredients because they melt smoothly and lend robust flavor to many European dishes.

Appenzeller or Appenzell: A golden Swiss-type cheese that is creamy and tangy from being marinated in cider or spiced white wine before it is aged. It usually has a brown rind, small holes, and is a bit crumbly. It can be very strong in flavor if aged, so you would be wise to taste it before purchasing to see if it suits your own preference. It gives a fine fruity flavor to casseroles and sauces, and is often combined with other Swiss types, such as EMMEN-THALER and GRUYÈRE. It can be used in Swiss Fondue and is excellent in Scalloped Potatoes, allowing 1 ounce (¼ cup) of the grated cheese per potato. We add chunks of it to potato salad.

Asiago: A straw-colored, waxlike Italian cheese. It has a rich, sweet and salty flavor that is very pleasant, whether the cheese is young and served as a table cheese with fruit for dessert, or aged to use for grating. It is often grated into sauces and melts very easily. That labeled "Asiago d'Allevio" is sharp yet smooth, and is used for grating; "Asiago grasso di Monte" or "Asiago pressato" has a mellow, slightly sweet flavor and is served primarily as a dessert cheese. The Italian stuffed beef roll, Bracciola, often combines this cheese with mozzarella. We like Asiago with baked eggplant, and sprinkled over Mediterranean-style vegetable dishes.

Bellelay: Also called **Tête de Moines** (or monk's head), this is a pungent semi-soft Swiss-type cheese similar to Gruyère. It is wrapped in bark and ages very well and can be kept for 3 to 4 years. It is imported only in limited quantities.

Caerphilly: A fresh, rather salty, white Welsh Cheddar-type cheese made of buttermilk. It is best purchased in late summer. It doesn't keep well, so store it wrapped in a damp cloth and overwrapped with foil, and use it up quickly.

It is especially good crumbled into salads and, as it melts well, is often used to add tang to cheese sauces and casseroles.

Cheddar: A large family of firm, flavorful cheeses that originated in England. Cheddar is infinitely suited to cooking and is the essential ingredient in such dishes as Welsh Rarebit and Macaroni and Cheese, and is even used in cheesecake. One dish that has become very popular because it is so tasty and easy to make is Cheese Strata, which can feature any of these firm cheeses.

Cheshire: One of the oldest and most popular English Cheddars, flavored by the salty marsh grass on which Cheshire cows graze. A "red" (actually orange) version is colored with ANNATTO (see ACHIOTE SEED in THE FOODS OF LATIN AMERICA section), and a "white" type is yellow. Authentic Cheshire has a "CCC" mark stenciled on the outer rind. It is somewhat crumbly and ranges from mild to sharp depending on age, and is an excellent cheese to use whenever Cheddar is specified.

Derby or **Derbyshire:** This is an English cheese similar to Cheddar but moister and milder in flavor. It is not a great example of English cheese, and is more interesting in its other form (see SAGE DERBY).

Double Gloucester: A rich, orange-colored English Cheddar, one of England's finest cheeses. The English enjoy it in sandwiches, or wrapped in lettuce leaves to be served with pickles or jam. It is excellent for use in cooking whenever Cheddar is specified but, because it is expensive, you may wish to substitute a good American Cheddar.

Dunlop: This Scotch cheese, a bit moister and milder than Cheddar, is considered one of the finest of all cheeses for grilling because it softens and browns without melting. It is imported only in limited quantities. Look for creamy color and thin skin, and taste a bit to make sure it's not over-aged and bitter.

Edam: Named for the port in The Netherlands where it originated, this is a flattened-ball-shaped cheese with a red or silver covering of wax. A whole one weighs about 30 ounces, and the government seal of The Netherlands is stamped directly onto the cheese beneath the wax coating. It differs from GOUDA in that it is made with partially skimmed milk, and is therefore firmer. It will range from semi-soft to firm and has a mild to strong nutty flavor. Domestic versions are seldom aged so are usually milder than imported ones. It is often served as a snack with beer, but can be sliced for sandwiches and used to season sauces and casseroles.

To make an appetizer known as Stuffed Edam, the top is cut off and the center of the cheese scooped out to leave a ½" shell. A filling is made by mashing the cheese from the center and adding various seasonings, such as chopped shallots, white wine, mustard, paprika, and caraway seeds, and is then mounded back into the original container and served as a spread with crackers. Grated Edam is excellent to use sprinkled over cooked vegetables or sprinkled into a cream sauce flavored with fennel or caraway to serve over steamed broccoli or cabbage. A Filipino recipe for sweet rolls specifies it, as do various recipes throughout Latin America, where local versions of Edam are made.

Emmenthaler or **Emmenthal:** The original Swiss cheese, golden with large holes, or "eyes," and a sweet nutlike flavor. It is exported to all countries in wheels weighing 150 to 200 pounds. **Emmenthal** is a French version. Look for moist, buttery holes and the word "Switzerland" stenciled on the outer rind. This type of cheese grates and melts beautifully, especially if well-aged, so it is widely used in soufflés, Swiss Fondues (usually in combination with Gruyère or Appenzeller), sauces, and casseroles besides being used in the more traditional ways as a table cheese and sandwich filling. Cut in fine julienne strips and dressed with a creamy dressing it becomes a salad. The rich fried French ham-and-cheese sandwich, Croque Monsieur, is usually made with this or Gruyère, which is similar, though a bit firmer and stronger-flavored, and can be substituted for Emmenthaler in recipes.

Fontina: There are two types, Italian and Scandinavian. The Italian type has a mild nutty flavor but strong aroma, and somewhat resembles Gruyère. "Fontina Val d'Aosta," from an area near the Piedmont region of Italy, has, according to legend, the slightly earthy taste of white truffle because the local cows may graze near those delicacies. Look for light brown rind with a purple trademark stamped on it to indicate authentic Italian fontina. Fontina with a red rind is from Denmark and is softer textured and stronger-flavored than the Italian. It is a popular sandwich cheese, and may also flavor sauces and casseroles. Either kind can be used in recipes that specify mozzarella. An aged fontina melts easily and is essential to the Italian version of fondue called Fonduta, which is served with toast triangles and, during the fall, is topped with finely shaved, fresh white truffles, which are optional in the following recipe.

FONDUTA

For 4 servings

Serve Fonduta as an appetizer or fireside supper with crusty Italian bread for dipping, or over toast. It can also be served as a sauce over Polenta.

1¼   pounds Fontina Val d'Aosta
1   teaspoon cornstarch
⅔   cup milk or half-and-half
3   egg yolks, at room temperature
    Salt and white pepper
1   small fresh white truffle (optional)

Cut the greyish rind from cheese, and discard. Cut cheese in ½″ dice. If serving as a dip, have ready a warm serving bowl, or individual warm ramekins, and bread with which to serve.

In a heavy saucepan, combine the cornstarch and milk or half-and-half. Stir to combine. Add the cheese and whisk constantly over medium-low heat just until the cheese has melted, about 5 minutes. It will be a bit stringy at this point. Remove from the heat.

In a small mixing bowl, whisk the yolks until light. Stir about ¼ cup of the cheese mixture into the yolks to warm them, then pour the yolk mixture into the saucepan. Cook over lowest heat, whisking until smooth and creamy. Add salt and white pepper to taste.

Pour immediately into warm bowl(s). Top with freshly grated white truffle and serve immediately.

Gjetost: This is the national cheese of Norway and very popular in Scandinavian countries. It is a caramel-colored cow's and goat's milk cheese with a slightly sweet flavor. The color is caused by the milk sugar caramelizing during cooking. It combines well with eggs and is often grated over egg dishes or used as an omelet filling. Grated, it can be melted slowly into a sour-cream sauce to serve over veal or chicken. A sauce for roast venison is made by melting this cheese into the pan drippings along with currant jelly and cream. It makes an excellent filling, for sandwiches with pumpernickel and other dark breads, and for baked apples.

Gouda: A yellow Dutch cheese, higher in fat and a bit softer than Edam. It is coated with wax, and is mild and creamy when young, but when aged becomes quite sharp. There are small versions, often covered with red wax called "baby" Gouda. Domestic ones are never aged and have a mild nutlike taste. An aged version flavored with herbs is called "Pompadour." In Holland, Gouda is used to make a fondue type of dish called Kaasdop, which is served with new potatoes and rye bread. It is often sprinkled into hot potato soup or over vegetables. It can, like mozzarella, be breaded and fried to serve with a squeeze of lemon juice and a sprinkling of capers.

Groviera: This is the Italian version of GRUYÈRE, and is generally quite good.

Gruyère: A mild, nutlike, cream-colored Swiss-type cheese with smaller holes than EMMENTHALER and a higher butterfat content. It is one of the finest of all cheeses for cooking, having a bit more bite than Emmenthaler. It is usually a bit firmer and has a harder rind. The true Swiss import is widely available, as well as a French version, which tends to be less sweet. Beware of "processed" Gruyère cheese sold in many supermarkets—it barely resembles the real thing. Gruyère is superb for cooking and very commonly used in French onion soup, sauces, souffleés and salads, and is often used in the making of Swiss Fondue, because it melts smoothly and evenly if well aged. It is often sprinkled as a topping over German Spätzle (noodle dumplings). It is essential in Gougère, a crusty baked ring of savory cream-puff dough, served with a fine red Burgundy.

Jarlsberg: This Norwegian Swiss-style cheese has a slightly sweeter and milder flavor than EMMENTHALER. It can be used in any recipe that specifies Swiss cheese and adds an excellent flavor to sauces and salads. We often use it in quiches and *frittatas,* as in the following recipe.

FRESH VEGETABLE FRITTATA

For 6 to 8 servings

Frittata is an Italian dish, a sort of crustless quiche. This version, not Italian, is our own improvisation. Serve it warm or at room temperature, for breakfast, brunch, supper, or a picnic. It is easiest to julienne or slice the vegetables and grate the cheeses with an electric food processor.

¾	cup sour cream
10	eggs
2	tablespoons minced parsley or chervil
1	tablespoon minced fresh dill, *or* 1 teaspoon dried dill weed
1¼	teaspoon salt
¼	teaspoon ground black pepper
1	good dash of cayenne (ground red pepper)
2	leeks, white part only, split lengthwise and cleaned, then chopped
2–3	medium zucchini, cut in julienne strips
5	medium-sized fresh mushrooms, sliced
1	large carrot, grated
2	tablespoons butter or margarine
¼	pound Jarlsberg, Gruyère, or natural Swiss cheese, grated
¼	cup grated Parmesan

TO GARNISH AND SERVE:

2	Italian pear tomatoes or 6 cherry tomatoes, sliced
1	tablespoon minced parsley or chervil

Mix the sour cream in a mixing bowl with a whisk until smooth. Beat in the eggs, one at a time, followed by the parsley, dill, salt, pepper, and cayenne. Set aside.

If using an electric food processor to chop or slice the vegetables, proceed in the following manner and place them in a mixing bowl. Cut the leeks into 1″ crosswise pieces and process in the work bowl of a food processor using the steel blade until finely chopped. Cut the zucchini into julienne strips, either by slicing with the slicing blade, then stacking the slices upright in the feed tube and slicing again, or by using the julienne or French fry blades available with some food processors. Slice the mushrooms, using the slicing blade, by stacking them on their sides in the feed tube. Grate the carrots, using the shredding blade, by stacking them on their sides in the feed tube and using a light up-and-down motion on the pusher while the motor is running.

Preheat the oven to 375°. Melt the butter in a 8″–10″ ovenproof skillet or au gratin pan. Stir in the vegetables and cook, covered, for 5 minutes. Pour in the egg mixture and remove from the heat. Distribute the grated cheeses evenly over the top. (Parmesan can be "grated" by cutting it into 1″ cubes and processing 1 cup of cubes at a time with the steel blade.)

Bake for 20 to 30 minutes, just until set in the center. Garnish the top with sliced tomatoes and minced parsley or chervil. Serve directly from the baking dish.

TO PREPARE IN ADVANCE: This will keep at room temperature for up to 6 hours. Reheat to serve, or serve at room temperature.

Kashkavàl: A Rumanian and Bulgarian semi-hard, yellowish table cheese made from sheep's milk. The Bulgarian tends to be more delicate and less salty than the Rumanian. It has a slightly sour but very pleasant taste that makes it a fine sandwich cheese. It can be used in the same way as KASSERI (see THE FOODS OF THE MIDDLE EAST section, under CHEESE) to make the flaming appetizer Saganaki. It is used a great deal in Central European potato and cornmeal dishes. PROVOLONE or imported MUENSTER can usually be substituted for it.

Kuminost: Also called **Nökkelost.** This is a Norwegian semi-firm cheese spiced with caraway, cumin, and clove. In Norway, it is often served as an appetizer with aquavit, but is also grated to sprinkle over salads and sauerkraut and in potato dishes, soups, and omelets. It is also used to flavor quiches and casseroles. Slices can be melted over roast pork just before slicing and serving.

Leicester: A moist, orange-colored, Cheddar-type cheese that melts beautifully. It has a flaky texture, which makes it difficult to slice but easy to grate. Avoid any with white edges because it may indicate bitterness. This cheese doesn't age well.

Manchego: This is Spain's most famous cheese and is golden, rich, and mellow. If labeled "curado" it is aged up to 3 months; "viejo" is aged longer. These are semi-firm and very buttery, and can be used in the same manner as mozzarella in casseroles and as a topping for various Spanish appetizers (*tapas*).

Muenster, also spelled **Munster:** When purchasing this cheese, look for the country of origin. The original Muenster was created in France and is creamy, with an orange rind and a strong flavor. The German version, Münster, tends to be a bit milder than the French. Our domestic versions tend to be a bit rubbery and bland. FONTINA can be substituted. All can be sliced to serve in sandwiches and are excellent melting cheeses and can be used to flavor sauces and casseroles.

Nökkelost: See KUMINOST

Raclette: The national dish of Switzerland is not Cheese Fondue, but Raclette, which is made by placing half a wheel of raclette cheese in front of a roaring fireplace until the surface melts, and then scraping the melted part onto warm plates to serve with small boiled red potatoes, pickled onions, and sweet gherkins or CORNICHONS. It is important to use the true raclette cheese for making it. An easier version can be made by melting the sliced cheese on individual ovenproof dishes. The cheese can be used the way any SWISS cheese is used in soups and sauces.

Sage Derby: DERBY or DERBYSHIRE cheese to which sage leaves have been added to create a marbled appearance and fine herby flavor. It is usually found in cheese shops at Christmastime. Serve as an appetizer, or cube it to add to salads.

Samsoe: The Danish national cheese, which is mild and nutlike in flavor and has irregular small holes. It is a superb sandwich cheese and can be used as one would Edam or Swiss-type cheeses in salads, sauces, and cooked dishes. It makes an excellent Cheese Fondue when substituted for EMMENTHALER in Swiss Fondue, with aquavit substituting for the usual required amount of KIRSCH. Cut in small dice or fine julienne strips, it is a flavorful addition to salads, especially those containing beets and sweet pickles.

Swiss: A generic term for Switzerland-style cheese with large holes and nutty flavor. Examples are EMMENTHALER and GRUYÈRE, but the term is used for all cheeses of this type. Aged Swiss cheeses melt much more smoothly than young ones. These are excellent salad cheeses.

Tilsit: A cheese descended from Dutch GOUDA, which can range from mild to very strong in flavor. It is medium-firm and has many small holes. It is often used to flavor egg dishes, and the milder types can flavor sauces and cooked dishes. A sprinkling of grated Tilsit does wonders for hot potato pancakes.

Tybo: A cream-colored SAMSOE type of cheese availiable in loaves. It has a fine, smooth flavor, somewhat milder than Samsoe, and is excellent on sandwiches and in sauces and cooked dishes. One variety is flavored with caraway seeds.

Wensleydale: There are two types of this English cheese from Yorkshire. "White" is young and tangy, like a fine flaky Cheddar, and is the perfect cheese to serve with apple pie. "Blue" Wensleydale is the same cheese that has been inoculated with a special mold to become similar to STILTON, but creamier and usually milder in flavor. It, like the other blue-veined cheeses, adds a special tang to savory dishes, salads, appetizers, etc.

"BLUE" CHEESES

These pungent cheeses are streaked with blue or green mold and have been helped along in their aging process with an inoculation of penicillin culture.

STORAGE: Store cut pieces in a nonmetal container, or wrapped airtight in plastic, in the coldest part of the refrigerator for up to 3 weeks. Whole cheeses, wrapped in a damp cloth and overwrapped with foil, will keep for months if they are rewrapped carefully each time they are opened.

PREPARATION AND USE: Serve at room temperature as a snack or with fruit and a robust red wine or vintage port. These cheeses make delicious sauces when spread over grilled steaks or hamburgers and allowed to melt slowly. Crumble them into salads, salad dressings, and omelets. Use them to flavor appetizer mousses. They are especially compatible with walnuts.

Danablu, sometimes called **Danish Blue:** This is a cow's milk cheese from Denmark that ranks high among the world's blue-veined cheeses. It is white with blue-green veins, salty, and very tangy. It is used like other "blues," and in salads for Scandinavian Smörgasbords.

Gorgonzola: A superb Italian cow's milk cheese with greenish-gold veins. It is named for the town near Milan, Italy, where it originated. It is a bit milder and creamier than blue-veined cheeses from other countries. Another version called "Gorgonzola dolce" or "Dolcelatte" is very mild and sweet and is served as a dessert cheese, but is difficult to find in the United States except in the elaborate, and very expensive, new cheese "tortas" in which layers of it are alternated with layers of fresh basil and pine nuts to make a cake-like creation, which is sold in cheese shops and gourmet specialty shops to serve as an antipasto or dessert.

Use Gorgonzola as you would any blue-veined cheese. It is particularly suited to salad dressings, or being served on its own with apples, pears, and even peaches for dessert. We like to melt it in crisp potato skins as a snack, or combine it with an equal amount of softened cream cheese, which we mix in a food processor or electric mixer until very smooth and serve as an appetizer spread with thin crackers or Scandinavian flatbread.

Roquefort: The oldest cheese of France and perhaps the most widely known cheese in the world. This is a luxurious blue-veined cheese made of sheep's milk with a very pungent, salty flavor. Its name is strictly protected and may be used only for the cheese aged in the limestone caverns of Mount Cambalou, near the town of Roquefort. That which is exported to America is slightly milder than that produced for European consumption. Look for a red sheep on its foil wrapper. It is often the most piquant of the blue cheeses, and some people mix it with a bit of butter if they find the taste too strong, or use a bit less than the recipe specifies and substitute heavy cream for the remainder.

Roquefort is one of the great flavors in salad dressings, and we prefer it mashed with a Mustard Vinaigrette to toss with greens rather than in the ordinary sour cream-based dressing so popular in American restaurants. It can be crumbled over potato salad, cooked vegetables, and egg dishes. It can be used as a flavoring like other blue-veined cheeses, and as a filling for omelets and tiny appetizer pastries, but is superb on its own with a fine sauterne or an aged port. It is delicious in soufflés.

Stilton: England's royal blue-veined cheese with a very sharp, rich flavor. It is dryer and firmer than other "blues," and yellower in color. It melts smoothly like a Cheddar, and makes a piquant addition to sauces, salads, and cooked dishes. Because of its fine melting quality it is an excellent candidate for quiche fillings, cheese sauces, and even a Stilton Rarebit.

HARD, GRATING CHEESES

These are hard, strong-flavored cheeses classified in Italy as *grana,* made up of tiny crystals suspended in the paste, which are ideal for grating.

STORAGE: Whole pieces, tightly wrapped in plastic wrap and overwrapped with foil, keep for months in the refrigerator if the cut edges are rubbed with butter or dipped in melted paraffin. Alternatively, they can be wrapped in damp cheesecloth and overwrapped with foil to keep them moist. They must be carefully rewrapped each time they are opened. These cheeses continue to ripen as they age and become stronger flavored. They freeze better than other types.

PREPARATION AND USE: Parmesan is often used as a table cheese, but the others are usually grated and used sparingly as a seasoning for pasta dishes, casseroles, soups, and sauces. They should be grated as near to serving time as possible because their flavor dissipates rapidly. Many of these cheeses are so hard that they tend to break the grating disc of electric food processors, so should be cut into cubes to chop, one cupful at a time in a blender, or food processor fitted with the chopping blade.

Parmigiano: Known to most of us as **Parmesan** cheese, this is the finest type of *grana* cheese. It is an essential ingredient in both Italian and French cooking. The very best, and most imitated, imported brand is Parmigiano-Reggiano—its name is stamped on the rind. It has a slightly salty, piquant flavor, which makes it one of the best cheeses for seasoning in cooking. It is best to buy it from a whole wheel in a cheese shop or Italian deli. Look for pale yellow color and a mild flavor (ask to taste it)! It ages better than almost any other cheese and is not exported until two years old. Remove the rind before grating. If grating it in a food processor, cut into ½" cubes and chop them with the steel blade rather than with the grating disc, which will break when such a hard cheese is pressed too vigorously against it. The rind is hopeless to grate. Marcella Hazan, author of several fine Italian cookbooks, says to save the rind to use in soups. Parmigiano can be stored, tightly wrapped, in the refrigerator for weeks, but we prefer storing it in the freezer to prevent its drying out. That labeled "Giovanne" is young, and is used as a table cheese. That which is aged three years is termed "Stravecchio"; four to five years, "Tipico."

Parmesan can be served as a table cheese accompanied by a fine red wine, or grated over pasta and salads. It is ideal for cooking because it almost never turns stringy, and is used as a seasoning in many cooked dishes such as Eggplant or Veal Parmigiana. Italians add it to many dishes, not just Fettucine Alfredo, and have even created a version of Fonduta based on it (see recipe following FONTINA under FIRM AND SEMI-FIRM CHEESES). It functions as a topping for almost any casserole, turning brown and crusty in the baking. The French very often combine it in dishes with their own version of Gruyère, adding it to Mornay sauce, soufflés, Beignets (cheese fritters) and sprinkle it over their gratinéed dishes. We add it to the crusts for quiches, as in the following recipe.

QUICHE PRINTANIÈRE

PARMESAN CRUST: For 8 servings
1¾ cups all purpose flour*
 ¼ cup freshly grated Parmesan
 ½ teaspoon salt
 4 ounces (1 stick) sweet (unsalted) butter, frozen or well
      chilled
 ¼ cup solid shortening (Crisco), well chilled
 ¼ cup ice water
 2 teaspoons Dijon mustard

FILLING:

    1   (6-ounce) jar marinated artichoke hearts (Progresso or
          Cara Mia brand)
    2   small ripe but firm tomatoes (Italian pear-shaped
          preferred)
    6   ounces fresh mushrooms
    2   large leeks
    1   tablespoon butter
    1   clove garlic
   ¼   cup grated Parmesan
    4   ounces Gruyère or Swiss-style cheese, grated
    4   large eggs
    1   cup light cream (half-and-half)
   ½   teaspoon salt
   ¼   teaspoon freshly ground black pepper
 2–3   teaspoons melted butter
    1   tablespoon minced parsley

*****Note:** "Instant blending" flour (Wondra) makes an especially light and flaky crust.

To make the crust, place the flour, ¼ cup Parmesan and salt in a bowl. Using a pastry blender or two knives, cut the butter and shortening into the flour until the butter is the size of corn kernels. Sprinkle the ice water over the mixture, tossing until moistened. Turn out onto a strip of plastic wrap and press into a round patty of dough. (This whole process can be done in seconds in a food processor with on-and-off bursts—do not process to a ball, though, or the pastry will be tough.) Wrap the rather soft dough in plastic wrap and refrigerate for at least 30 minutes before rolling to firm it and relax the gluten in the flour.

Roll the dough (a well-floured pastry cloth available in cookware shops makes the job easier) to about 3/16" thick. Use the pastry to line a 12" tart pan, trimming the dough to ½" beyond the edge of the pan. Fold the edges in, building up a rim of pastry above the edge of the pan. Place on a baking sheet for ease of handling. To prevent shrinkage, line the inside of the pastry with parchment or foil and fill with raw beans (which are stored in a jar to use over and over again for this purpose). Bake at 350° for 20 minutes. Remove beans and paper, prick the dough all over with the tines of a fork, and brush the surface of the pastry with the mustard. Return the pastry shell to the oven to bake 10 minutes longer. Cool. (Partially baking the crust in this manner makes it extra crisp.)

Meanwhile, prepare the filling. Drain the artichoke hearts of all marinade and blot with paper towels; chop into ½" pieces. (Reserve the marinade, if desired, for use in marinating other cooked vegetables, or as a salad dressing.)

353

Slice tomatoes crosswise, ¼″ thick, sprinkle with salt, and drain on paper towels for at least 15 minutes to draw out excess liquid. Cut the mushrooms into thick slices through the stems. Cut away the green tops of the leeks and pare a thin slice from the root end. Cut the white parts of the leeks in half lengthwise, rinse if necessary to remove any grit, and cut in ½″ crosswise sections.

Melt the butter in a skillet and sauté the leek and garlic briefly until wilted. Add the mushroom slices with a light sprinkling of salt. Cook, uncovered, over medium-high heat, until most of the liquid from the mushrooms has cooked away.

Sprinkle the ¼ cup grated Parmesan over the bottom of the pastry. Arrange the artichoke hearts and grated Gruyère over them. In a mixing bowl, beat the eggs lightly; then add the half-and-half, ½ teaspoon salt, and ¼ teaspoon black pepper. Pour this custard slowly over the ingredients in the crust. Arrange the drained tomato slices evenly over the top.

Bake in the center of a 375° oven for 30 minutes, or until a knife inserted 1″ from the center of the quiche comes out clean. Remove from the oven and brush the top with melted butter. Sprinkle with minced parsley. Cool 10 minutes before slicing. Serve warm.

TO PREPARE IN ADVANCE: This is best fresh from the oven. Bake the crust in the morning and leave at room temperature. The vegetables can be prepared several hours ahead and left at room temperture. Fill and bake just before serving.

Pecorino: A generic name for *grana* (hard, grating) cheeses made from sheep's milk, which are saltier than Parmigiano. Among the aged ones that are grated and used much like Parmigiano are Romano (or Roman), which is Italy's oldest cheese and considered the best of this type, Sardo (Sardinian— more pungent than Romano), Siciliano (Sicilian), and Toscano (Tuscan). These are generally whiter in color than the golden-hued Parmigiano and have a sharper taste and more pungent aroma. You may find some variations such as "Pecorino Pepato" from Sicily, which contains whole peppercorns. When purchased, these cheeses should be hard and dry.

Serve them when they're young as a table cheese with robust-flavored foods such as sausages, Mediterranean olives, and coarse bread. Or use them in cooking when you wish a sharper flavor than Parmigiano. Many Southern Italians prefer this type of cheese to Parmigiano, but they are seldom used in northern Italy and only in combination with Parmigiano. Some Italian delis sell a Pecorino type and Parmigiano grated together, though we prefer to grate them ourselves and know what we are getting. Using both types in a traditional Lasagne recipe makes the dish more complex and robust.

Romano: See PECORINO. In addition to the commonly found Romano made of sheep's milk, there is a goat's milk version called "Caprino Romano," which is extremely sharp, and a "Vacchino Romano," which is mild.

Sapsago: A hard, dry, green cheese from Switzerland flavored with powdered leaves of meliot, a bluish clover. It has a distinct, earthy flavor and a slight scent of hay, and is used primarily for grating and flavoring cream soups and egg dishes. Added judiciously to a cream sauce it complements cooked shrimp.

Sardo: See PECORINO

Sbrinz: A hard Swiss grating cheese similar to Parmigiano. When young, it is called **Spalen** and is served as a table cheese and in cooked dishes. Aged, it is also served as a table cheese, or grated to use in place of Parmigiano.

Sicilano: See PECORINO

Toscano: See PECORINO

GOAT AND SHEEP CHEESES

This category includes the tangy, brine-cured goat and sheep cheeses, as well as the soft French goat cheeses classified as Chèvres, available in the United States and imported from France, usually in log, pyramid, or round shapes, and sometimes coated with ashes, herbs, or strands of straw. All have an earthy, rather tart taste. These salty, brine-cured cheeses have long been important ingredients in Central Europe and the Middle East. Though Chèvres were once obscure, there are now over 70 types to choose from. However, we shall not list them in this book because they are seldom used as ingredients. All are mild-flavored when young, but become stronger tasting as they age. Novices would be wise to start by tasting the younger types first.

STORAGE: Brined cheeses, such as Feta, can be stored in salt water (or milk, if you wish to rid it of saltiness) to cover it completely. They will keep for months, but become stronger-flavored and firmer the longer they are stored. Chèvres are perishable, so should be tightly wrapped in plastic wrap to store in the coldest part of the refrigerator for up to 2 weeks.

PREPARATION AND USE: The salty flavor of the brined cheeses make them ideal for tangy additions to all kinds of savory dishes, from pastry fillings to salads.

Rounds of goat cheese can be marinated in olive oil with chopped fresh herbs for an hour or so and served with crusty French bread. Alice Waters, owner of the Chez Panisse restaurant in Berkeley, California, coats rounds of goat cheese with olive oil and fresh bread crumbs and then bakes the rounds until warm and golden to serve as an accompaniment to a lightly dressed salad. Richard Olney, French-cooking authority, cuts goat cheese that has passed its prime into cubes and wraps them in fresh vine leaves (see GRAPE LEAVES in THE FOODS OF THE MIDDLE EAST section), brushes them with olive oil and bakes them until soft.

We see these goat and sheep cheeses appearing in recipes more and more often, especially for quiches.

Banon or **Le Banon:** One of the best of small goat's milk cheeses, wrapped in a chestnut leaf that has been dipped in cognac or *eau de vie* (clear fruit brandy), and then tied with raffia. A true French Banon has a label indicating it was shipped through Marseilles. It is milder in flavor than most Chèvres. It is sometimes made with sheep's or cow's milk.

Boule de Périgord: A mild, but expensive, Chèvres studded with pieces of black truffle.

Bryndza or **Brynza:** A salty, white Rumanian cheese, which is popular in Hungary and Czechoslovakia, is made of sheep's or cow's milk and cured in brine in the same manner as FETA, but is usually creamier and smoother in texture. It is used as a topping for the Rumanian cornmeal dish called Mamaliga. In Hungary, soft Bryndza is mixed with herbs and spices to make Liptauer Cheese served as a spread.

Bucheron: One of the best known French Chèvres and widely available. It will be found rolled in ashes or herbs.

Chèvre Valençay: Sometimes called **Pyramide** as a flat-topped pyramid is the shape it comes in, is a French goat cheese with a greyish, powdery, edible crust. It is usually served with unseasoned crackers or crusty bread and fruit. Crumbled, it can add a tart flavor to cheese sauces and casseroles.

Feta: A white brined cheese originally from Greece, but now made in quantity in the Balkans, Germany, and Denmark. Danish feta cheeses tend to be harsh-flavored, but those made in Bulgaria and Germany are usually milder and creamier than the Greek. **Telemes,** the name for feta in Northern Greece, is imported and should not be confused with American Teleme, which is bland and buttery. Crumble it in salads, add it to stews, and use it in fillings with FILO PASTRY (see THE FOODS OF THE MIDDLE EAST section). It is served with all Greek meals as a table cheese accompanied by Mediterranean olives and crusty bread.

For a delicious appetizer, heat 8 ounces feta, cut in ½" thick slices, in a heat-proof dish with 2 tablespoons melted butter until the cheese is bubbling. Sprinkle cracked pepper and fresh lemon juice over the top and serve very hot with crusty bread.

A simple Central European salad can be quickly made as in the following recipe.

SERBIAN SALAD

1	tablespoon red wine vinegar	For 6 servings
1	tablespoon olive oil	
1½	teaspoons chopped fresh oregano *or* ½ teaspoon dried, crumbled	
	Freshly ground black pepper, to taste	
5–6	ripe tomatoes	
1	large green bell pepper, seeded and diced	
4	scallions, very thinly sliced	
2–4	ounces feta cheese, crumbled	

Combine vinegar, olive oil, oregano, and pepper. (Salt is unnecessary because the feta is salty.)

Cut the tomatoes in half crosswise; squeeze over the sink to discard the seeds. Dice the tomatoes fine and place in a shallow serving dish with the bell pepper and scallions. Drizzle the dressing over the vegetables and toss lightly. Crumble the feta evenly over the salad. Serve at room temperature for best flavor.

TO PREPARE IN ADVANCE: This should be assembled within 2 hours of serving.

Montrachet: A medium-mild Chèvre. It is sold in 3- or 11-ounce logs, and has usually been rolled in salted ashes, which gives it a grey coating.

Sainte Maure: A strong-flavored French Chèvre which is considered one of the best. It is sold in a long 10-ounce cylinder. The farm-made version is characterized by a grey coating and a straw running through the center.

Telemes: See FETA

CHESTNUTS

FRENCH: *marron, châtaigne* GERMAN: *Edelkastanie* ITALIAN: *castagna, marrone* SPANISH: *castaña, marrona*

Chestnuts are widely used in European cooking. They are sweet and starchy, and are the only nut that must be cooked in some manner before being eaten. Chestnuts are available to us in three forms: fresh, canned, and dried.

FRESH CHESTNUTS

Fresh chestnuts are imported in several very similar varieties and can be found in produce markets only during the winter months. Care must be

357

taken in purchasing them because they can easily be spoiled on the inside without showing any sign of it on their outer husks. Look for glossy, unblemished nuts. They should feel firm, solid, and heavy for their size.

STORAGE: Fresh unshelled nuts will keep up to a week in a cool place. After peeling and cooking, store tightly covered in the refrigerator for up to 3 days.

PREPARATION AND USE: One pound of unshelled nuts will yield about ¾ pound of shelled nuts, which is enough for 2 to 3 servings. Before cooking, the chestnut shell must be slashed to prevent its bursting during the cooking. The usual method of doing this is to cut a cross in the flat side of the shell with a sharp paring knife. To roast, place them in a pan in a 400° oven for about 20 minutes until they feel soft, or roast them in a perforated tin, or in a chestnut-roasting pan (available from cookware shops) over an open fire, shaking the pan often for even cooking. Peel and eat.

For use in recipes, it is necessary to peel the chestnuts. After cutting the cross, place them in a pan and cover with cold water. Bring to a boil and let simmer gently for 3 to 4 minutes. Remove the pan from the heat, but leave the chestnuts in the hot water. Remove a few chestnuts at a time and use a pointed knife to loosen the shell, and then peel it off. Most of the inner membrane will still adhere to the nut, but can be dealt with once all the chestnuts have been shelled. Leave the chestnuts in the hot water until you are ready to peel the membrane and, if the water cools, bring it to a boil again. When all have been shelled, heat them in vegetable oil in a skillet, stirring, until the membrane is crisp. Then rub each nut between paper towels to remove all the remaining membrane, which in some varieties can be tenacious and must be even further coaxed off with a paring knife. Alternatively, they can be roasted at 350° for 8 minutes, or deep-fried for 2 minutes, then peeled. After peeling, the chestnuts should be cooked gently just until they are tender in broth or milk, according to your recipe. Take care not to overcook them or they will crumble.

Chestnuts are most often roasted in the United States to eat by a cozy fire, but are widely used in Europe as a vegetable, where they are braised to serve as a flavorful garnish for veal dishes, combined with other vegetables such as brussels sprouts, onions, and mushrooms to serve as a side dish, or are pureed to accompany pork or game dishes. In France, they make an elegant soup, Potage de Marrons, and are used in all manner of elegant dessert gâteaux (cakes). Chestnut puree is used in dessert crêpes and flavored with cognac. In Germany, whole ones are cooked with red cabbage. In Italy, they are often braised in consommé with prosciutto and sherry. A whimsical Italian dessert is named Monte Bianco after a mountain in the Italian Alps. It consists of a mound of pureed chestnuts flavored with chocolate and rum, which is topped with a cap of whipped cream "snow." An Italian confection is made by coating chestnuts with cocoa to resemble black truffles. In Spain, chestnuts flavor ice cream and confections. Chestnuts have long been popular in Greece, where they are used in puddings and stuffings and are often flavored with anise. In Asia, they are mashed to flavor pastries and stuffings, and are added whole to stir-fry dishes.

Canned Chestnuts

Canned chestnuts are imported primarily from France, produced by the same company that originated and began marketing them in the 19th century, Clement Faugier. Those imported from Hungary tend to be slightly less sweet than the French brand. Following is a list of the types of canned chestnuts to be found in gourmet specialty shops, with suggestions for their use.

Marrons Entiers Naturel: Whole chestnuts packed in water, available in 10- and 20½-ounce cans from Clement Faugier. These are excellent, almost as good as cooked fresh chestnuts, and are used primarily as a garnish for main dishes, for braising with other vegetables, and in stuffings.

Puree de Marrons Naturel: An unsweetened chestnut puree in 15-ounce cans under the Clement Faugier label. This is used in sauces, soups, and as a base for desserts. The Gerbaud brand from Switzerland is available in 8- or 31-ounce cans from Paprikas Weiss (see SHOPPING SOURCES) and is thick enough to press through a ricer into spaghetti-like strands, which can be heaped in serving dishes, sprinkled with rum, and topped with whipped cream for a very easy dessert.

Crème de Marrons: A sweetened puree available in 17-ounce cans (or in 2¾-ounce tubes packaged by Sabaton) used exclusively as an ingredient in desserts, and as a topping.

Marrons Glacés: Whole chestnuts candied in a vanilla-flavored syrup, available in tins and jars of various sizes from Clement Faugier and others. These are expensive. They are used to garnish desserts or are rolled in sugar to serve as confections. (For a less expensive substitute, see CHESTNUTS, PRESERVED in THE FOODS OF ASIA section.)

Marrons Débris: Chestnut pieces in vanilla syrup available in 7-ounce cans from Clement Faugier. They have the flavor, but neither the perfect appearance nor the high price of Marrons Glacés.

Dried Chestnuts

Dried chestnuts are sold in Italian markets as *secchieli,* and in Chinese markets as *loot jee.* They are already peeled and skinned, but lose some of their flavor in the drying process, so should be used only when fresh ones are unavailable. They have a mild smoky taste.

STORAGE: They will keep in an airtight container in a cool place for up to 2 months, or in the refrigerator or freezer indefinitely. After cooking, they should be covered tightly to store in the refrigerator for up to 3 days.

PREPARATION AND USE: Dried chestnuts must be reconstituted before use. Wash well, then soak for 6 to 8 hours in cold water, or quick-soak by bringing them to a boil in a generous amount of water and setting aside for 1 hour. Remove any small clinging remnants of skin. To cook the chestnuts, bring to a simmer and cook to the desired degree of tenderness (chewy to serve whole, or very soft if they are to be mashed), which may take from 1 to 2 hours. When drained, they are used in the same manner as cooked fresh or canned whole chestnuts.

CHESTNUT FLOUR

ITALIAN: *farina dolce*

Chestnut flour is available in Italian markets and in health food stores.

STORAGE: It is quite perishable and should be stored in the refrigerator for use within a month of purchase.

USE: Chestnut flour is used to thicken Italian sauces and to make various breads, puddings, cakes, and Polenta (mush). A Corsican chestnut porridge made with olive oil is called Ferinana; a sweet version is called Brilloli.

CHOCOLATE

Although chocolate is native to Mexico, Europe has taken it to its heights. Whole books have been written on chocolate and the processes involved in its manufacture, but we will concern ourselves in this book only with the use of it as an ingredient. There is a vast assortment of chocolates available and they vary enormously in taste. We recommend that you seek out some of the less familiar brands, which can be found in gourmet specialty shops or purchased through mail-order (see SHOPPING SOURCES), and make taste comparisons. We'll wager that the chocolate you have been using will no longer be your preferred brand. And, as an ingredient, the finer the flavor used in a recipe, the better the result. Be sure to read labels and avoid anything labeled "artificial" chocolate—it contains no chocolate and, in our opinion, tastes terrible. The words "chocolate flavored" on a label mean that the item contains less than the U.S. Food and Drug Administration standard requirements for chocolate. Following are categories of chocolate used in recipes, along with some of our preferred brands.

STORAGE: Chocolate can be stored, wrapped airtight, in a cool place for up to 4 months. If stored in the refrigerator it will "sweat" as it comes to room temperature and will be likely to lump when melted. If exposed to too much air or heat during storage, the surface will develop pale spots or a covering called "bloom." This is harmless and does not indicate spoilage.

PREPARATION AND USE: To melt chocolate, place it in a *dry* double boiler top over *warm* water. Chopping it will speed the melting and make overheating less likely. Stir constantly just until melted and remove from the heat. It can also be melted in a microwave oven, right in its parchment wrapper, allowing 1 minute per ounce on "high" power. Looks are deceiving when chocolate is melted in the microwave because the chocolate retains its solid shape until it is stirred, so take care that you don't overheat it with this method. If chocolate lumps or "tightens" during melting, it is either because it had a drop or two of moisture in it or because it was exposed to too much heat. Stir in 1 teaspoon solid vegetable shortening per ounce of chocolate to reliquify it.

Chocolate is used in every imaginable kind of European dessert—gâteaux (cakes), mousses, éclairs, soufflés, ad infinitum, from France's Mousse au Chocolat, Germany's Black Forest Torte, Austria's Sacher-torte, Swiss Chocolate Fondue, to Hungarian Rhapsody. It flavors hot beverages, cookies, and confections of all description, and is a surprising ingredient in Mexico's national dish Mole Poblano de Guajolote (turkey in a spicy dark sauce).

BITTERSWEET CHOCOLATE

A wide variety of bittersweet chocolates, which contain more chocolate liquor than other chocolates, is available. Excellent brands include Tobler Tradition Bittersweet Chocolate (Switzerland), Lindt Excellence Bittersweet Chocolate (Switzerland), Guittard French Vanilla (U.S.A.), Feodora Edel Bitter (Germany), Perugina Luisa (Italy), and other too numerous to mention. Some labeled "extra-bittersweet" are less sweet or more sweet, depending on the brand. As a general rule, this type of chocolate is interchangeable in recipes with sweet and semisweet types.

COATING CHOCOLATE

Coating chocolate, often called "couverture," is real or imitation chocolate and is excellent for making decorations and for dipping cookies. It is often used in bakeries but is not easily found by the average consumer. It can be purchased in 10-pound bars through wholesale bakery supply houses and in some gourmet specialty shops. Excellent brands are Stoelwerk's Royal York Coating and Semper Swedish Coating Chocolate.

COCOA

We refer here to the pure, unsweetened powder and not to the various cocoa "mixes" available. When the cocoa butter is pressed out of the pure chocolate liquor, a dry cake is formed, which is then pulverized into a powder called cocoa. Cocoas vary in fat content from 14 percent to 25 percent. If treated with an alkalai during the processing, the cocoa is darker and mellower in flavor, and this type of cocoa is referred to as "Dutched" or "Dutch-style," which will appear on the label. Hershey's cocoa is available in all supermarkets. Exemplary imported brands are Droste and Van Houton.

DIETETIC CHOCOLATE

This is not low-calorie chocolate as one might assume by the name, but a chocolate that has been sweetened with sorbitol or mannitol instead of sugar. It is intended for use by diabetics and others who are on sugar-restricted diets. Because of the drying effect these other sweeteners have on the chocolate, extra fat is often added to these products making them actually higher in calories than the real thing. We think they taste awful.

MILK CHOCOLATE

Milk chocolate is only about 10 percent chocolate liquor, but that liquor comes from the strongest-flavored beans, so it can hold its own when combined with milk, sugar, and flavorings. It is available, with and without nuts, in all supermarkets in candy bar form, in morsels, and in "kisses." Hershey's Golden Almond Bar is our favorite widely distributed milk chocolate. Lesser-known brands are Droste Milk Chocolate (Holland), Lindt Chocolate "au lait" (Switzerland), and Cadbury Milk Chocolate (England). Milk chocolate is seldom used in cooking, but we have seen it specified in pies.

SEMISWEET AND SWEET CHOCOLATE

The terms "semisweet" and "sweet" give clues to the relative sweetness of these chocolates. Sweet and semisweet chocolate are similar to bittersweet chocolate but may, by U.S. Food and Drug Administration rules, contain only half as much chocolate liquor. This type of chocolate is found in every supermarket. Baker's semisweet chocolate comes in 8-ounce boxes of individually wrapped 1-ounce squares, which are grooved so they can be easily split into ½-ounce pieces. Baker's German's (it's German chocolate all right, and is used in German Chocolate Cake, but it was first made by a Mr. German) sweet chocolate comes in a 4-ounce bar that looks like a candy bar.

Hershey's special dark sweet chocolate comes in 1.2-, 3.5-, and 8-ounce candy bar shapes in red wrappers. As a general rule, the bars are the best buy. Less common brands that are worth seeking out include Zaanland Semi Sweet Chocolate (Holland), Sarotti Halb-Bitter Chocolate (Germany), Lanvin Special Pâtisserie (pastry-making) Chocolate (France), Droste Semisweet Chocolate (Holland). We especially like this type of chocolate in a soufflé, as in the following recipe.

CHOCOLATE SOUFFLÉ

For 4 to 6 servings

The idea for a flourless soufflé came to us from Jacques Pépin.

Butter and sugar to coat a 6-cup soufflé dish, or 4
   individual 1½-cup soufflé dishes
4 ounces Hershey's dark sweet chocolate
1 ounce (1 square) unsweetened chocolate
½ cup milk
2 teaspoons vanilla extract
2 teaspoons instant coffee powder or granules
4 large eggs, at room temperature
2 additional egg whites, at room temperature
¼ teaspoon cream of tartar
¼ cup granulated sugar

TO SERVE:
Powdered sugar
Sweetened whipped cream or vanilla ice cream

Butter and sugar the inside of the soufflé dish(es). Place on a cookie sheet for ease of handling. Preheat the oven to 375°.

Melt the chocolates in a heavy saucepan with the milk, vanilla, and coffee, stirring constantly. As soon as the mixture is smooth, remove from the heat. Let cool slightly; then beat in yolks with a whisk. Pour into a large mixing bowl.

Using a hand whisk or electric mixer with whisk attachment, beat the egg whites with the cream of tartar until they form soft peaks, just to the point at which they do not slide when the bowl is tilted. Gradually beat in sugar, one tablespoonful at a time, to create a meringue.

Fold ⅓ of the whites thoroughly into the chocolate mixture to lighten it. Gently but thoroughly fold in the remaining whites. Turn the mixture into the prepared dish(es), smoothing the tops with a rubber spatula.

Bake at 375° for approximately 30 minutes for the large soufflé, 12 minutes for individual soufflés. Remove from the oven and sprinkle sieved powdered sugar over the tops. Serve immediately with whipped cream or ice cream.

TO PREPARE IN ADVANCE: The soufflé, except for beating and folding in whites, can be made in the morning. Press plastic wrap into the surface to prevent a skin from forming and set aside at room temperature. Beat whites, fold into chocolate mixture, and bake just before serving.

UNSWEETENED CHOCOLATE

Sometimes called "bitter" or "baking" chocolate, this is hardened chocolate liquor, which contains no sugar, but may contain vanilla or vanillin, which will appear on the label as "natural (or artificial) flavor." The only available brands are Baker's, Hershey, and Wilbur. Hershey is the stronger tasting and most granular of the three, Baker's is the mildest and smoothest. They are packed in 8-ounce boxes of paper-wrapped 1-ounce squares, which are easily divided into ½-ounce portions. Any "pre-melted" chocolate sold in packets is a chocolate-flavored liquid, not real chocolate. The following cake is rich and chocolaty, like a gooey brownie.

FUDGE WALNUT TORTE

For 12 large slices or
24 small slices

The center of this torte should be soft and fudgy like a gooey brownie, so be careful not to overbake it.

CAKE:
      Shortening to grease the pan
 5 ounces (5 squares) unsweetened chocolate
2½ sticks (10 ounces) unsalted (sweet) butter
 5 large eggs
2½ cups sugar
1¼ cups unsifted all-purpose flour
1½ tablespoons Myers' dark Jamaican rum
 2 teaspoons vanilla
¼ teaspoon salt
 2 cups diced pecans

ICING:
 5 ounces semisweet or bittersweet chocolate
 1 ounce (1 square) unsweetened chocolate
½ stick (2 ounces) unsalted butter
 1 tablespoon light corn syrup
24 large, perfect pecan halves

Preheat the oven to 350°. Grease a 9″ springform pan or a 9″ round cake tin with shortening. Cut a circle of foil or parchment paper to fit the bottom of the pan, place inside, and grease that.

To make the cake, melt the chocolate with the butter over low heat in a heavy-bottomed saucepan taking care not to scorch the chocolate. Set aside.

Place the eggs in a large mixing bowl with the sugar and beat with a whisk just until blended and smooth—do not overbeat. Stir in the chocolate mixture. Add the flour, rum, vanilla, and salt and mix just until blended. Fold in the diced pecans.

Pour the batter into the prepared pan. Place on a heavy baking sheet for ease of handling and bake for 60 to 75 minutes until the center is just firm. Cool in the pan for 15 minutes; then turn upside-down on a rack to cool, removing the foil or parchment. Cool completely before icing.

To make the icing, combine the ingredients (except pecans) in a heavy-bottomed saucepan and stir over low heat just until melted and smooth. Cool about 10 minutes or until of spreading consistency, then spread evenly over the cake, top and sides. (This will be easier to do if you place the cake on a lazy susan with waxed paper under the cake to catch the dripping icing.) Place the pecan halves in a circle around the top of the cake.

This dessert is very rich. We recommend cutting it into thin slices (a single pecan on the top of each piece). Sweetened whipped cream flavored with vanilla or dark rum can be served as an accompaniment.

TO PREPARE IN ADVANCE: May be stored, covered, at room temperature for up to 3 days, or frozen for up to 2 months. If freezing, it is best to do so before icing. If the iced cake is to be frozen, freeze it unwrapped until the icing is very solid, then wrap carefully to prevent marring the icing.

WHITE CHOCOLATE

This is not chocolate at all because it contains no chocolate liquor. It is made with cocoa butter, sugar, vanillin, and other flavorings, and tastes like a very sweet, mild milk chocolate. It has become a status ingredient in recent years, being used for dipping strawberries and making mousses and cakes. Fine brands are Tobler Narcisse, Lindt Blancor, and Toblerone Blanc.

CHUFA

OTHER: rush nut, nut rass, earthnut, earth almond, tiger nut

"Chufa" is the Spanish name for a grass-like stalk cultivated for its small tubers, which can be eaten like peanuts. Dried chufa tubers can be found in Spanish and some Latin American markets. They are small and knobby and covered with a brown skin. Oddly enough, shriveled ones have a chestnutlike taste, more pleasant, sweeter than fresh ones.

STORAGE: They will keep indefinitely in an airtight container in a cool place.

PREPARATION AND USE: These are eaten raw or roasted by the poorer people of Europe, but by far the most popular use of these tubers is to make a drink called Horchata de Chufa, popular in Spain and parts of the Yucatán. To make 4 servings, 1 pound tubers are lightly toasted, and then soaked for 2 to 3 hours in 1 quart water to cover, along with sugar to taste and a bit of cinnamon. They are then mashed or pureed in a blender, allowed to stand a few hours longer, and strained through cheesecloth. The resulting drink is very bland and tastes rather like almond milk. It is served as a refreshment.

CIUBRITSA

(Chew-BREET-sah)

A Bulgarian herb resembling TARRAGON, for which it can be substituted after being pulverized. It is not available in this country as far as we know, nor are seeds available.

USE: Bulgarians combine this herb with salt and cayenne to make a dip for bread, or to sprinkle over yogurt. It is also cooked with beans and paprika in the dish, Fassoul Yahnia, and is served fresh in the leaf salads that country enjoys so much.

COD, SALTED AND DRIED

OTHER: salt cod

FRENCH: *morue* GREEK: *bakaliaros* ITALIAN: *baccala*
PORTUGUESE: *bacalhau* SPANISH: *bacalao*

Dried salted cod has an important history in all the areas of the Mediterranean. It can be purchased in Italian, Latin American, and Asian markets. A whole fish has a broad triangular shape, but pieces of varying sizes can be purchased. Look for white flesh with black skin attached, rather than yellow flesh, which is an indication of age.

STORAGE: Tightly wrapped in a cool dry place indefinitely, though it loses flavor and requires lengthier soaking the longer it stands.

PREPARATION AND USE: Salt cod is always soaked in fresh water before use, the length of the soaking depending upon age and method of cure. If it is in large pieces, break it up and put it in a bowl with a generous amount of cold water. Change the water every 3 or 4 hours for 24 to 48 hours until the fish softens. (The longer the soaking period, the milder the flavor.) Place in fresh water, skin side up, with a bay leaf, and bring to a simmer, taking care not to boil it or it will toughen. Let poach at a bare simmer, spooning off the scum from the surface, for about 10 minutes, until it flakes easily when pierced with a knife. Drain, reserving the poaching liquid if your recipe calls for it. Scrape off the fatty skin and remove any exposed bones with your fingers. It is now ready to use in recipes.

This has been an important Lenten ingredient for so long and in so many countries that there are hundreds of methods of preparation. The French make their famous Brandade de Morue by pounding it to a paste with olive oil, milk, and garlic and mounding it into a domeshape to be served with fried bread. This same dish is sometimes flavored with chopped truffles sautéed in butter. In Vicenza, Italy, it is baked with anchovies, onions, and white wine to serve with Polenta (a cornmeal mush). In Spain it is most commonly prepared *à la vizcaína*, layered and baked with tomatoes, onions, and red peppers. Other famous Spanish preparations are Bacalao en Salsa Verde and Bacalao Ligado. Portuguese-style indicates the use of tomatoes, onions, potatoes, and olive oil. This fish is loved by the Portuguese, both rich and poor, who have devised more than 100 recipes for its use in their country alone. It is an ingredient far from the Mediterranean in the original New England Boiled Dinner.

CONFIT DE CANARD
See CONFIT D'OIE

CONFIT D'OIE
OTHER: salted spiced preserved goose

Confit d'oie is made of goose pieces that have been salted, then cooked in goose fat with spices and herbs. The meat is packed in the cooking fat, which serves as a preservative. Most often this is made in the home, but it can be found in cans in gourmet specialty shops. Confit de Canard is duck preserved in the same manner and used in the same way.

STORAGE: Store in the refrigerator for up to 3 months, or in the freezer indefinitely.

PREPARATION AND USE: An elegant way to serve this is in small portions with white beans that have been cooked with onion and garlic and then pureed. This is a traditional ingredient of Cassoulet, the famous stew

367

of beans, pork, duck, and sausages which three separate towns in the Languedoc region of France claim as an original dish. Its ingredients vary slightly depending on its point of origin. Cassoulet can be made without confit d'oie, of course, and usually is in this country. But, for traditionalists, here is our recipe for making the ingredient.

CONFIT D'OIE

For 1 goose

This may seem like a great deal of work (and it is) but, besides the flavorful goose itself, you'll get delicious cracklings, and a lot of tasty fat that can be used for sautéing.

1 goose (8–11 pounds), thawed if frozen
7 pounds of goose or pork fat, including the excess fat from
the goose itself

SPICE MIXTURE:
3 tablespoons salt
4 teaspoons ground white pepper
1 teaspoon ground ginger
1 teaspoon ground nutmeg
1 teaspoon dried thyme, crumbled
1 teaspoon crumbled bay leaf
½ teaspoon ground allspice *or* clove

Rinse goose and dry well; reserve giblets for another purpose. Cut the goose into small serving pieces with poultry shears. Pull away any large pieces of fat to use as part of the required fat; refrigerate.

Combine the salt and spices and rub thoroughly into the pieces of goose. Cover tightly and leave at room temperature for 24 hours.

The next day, cut all the fat to be used into ½" pieces and place in a large stock pot with 1 cup of water. Cover the pot loosely and place over low heat so the fat melts slowly. This will take about an hour. Place a candy thermometer in the fat. You will notice a crackling sound when it reaches 212°. Scoop out any crisp cracklings with a slotted spoon and drain on paper towels, to use over salads, baked potatoes, and cooked vegetables.

Wipe the goose with paper towels. Lower the heat under the fat until the thermometer registers 200°–205°. Place the pieces of goose, one piece at a time, in the fat (it will spatter) and cook, maintaining this temperature for 1½ hours, at which time the goose will be cooked and very tender. Lift the pieces of goose from the fat and cool. Continue cooking the fat for 10 minutes after the goose has been removed to evaporate any juices.

To serve, add the pieces of goose to casseroles, or cut from the bones and dice to add to Lentil Soup or other bean dishes, sautéed vegetables, and other preparations that would benefit from this spicy flavor accent.

TO PREPARE IN ADVANCE: The pieces of goose will keep, completely covered with the fat in which they were cooked, in a deep container in the refrigerator for up to 6 months, or in the freezer indefinitely. Alternatively, the pieces of goose can be tightly wrapped for freezer storage and the fat frozen separately.

CONSOMMÉ

"Consommé" is the French term for BOUILLON that has been clarified. When it is reduced over heat to concentrate the flavor it is called *consommé double*. Consommé Madrilene is flavored with tomato. Canned consommé is available in all supermarkets, but is a poor substitute for homemade. Crosse and Blackwell is a good English brand.

STORAGE: Consommé can be stored in the refrigerator in a nonmetal container for up to 2 weeks if it is boiled every 4 or 5 days to destroy any bacteria.

PREPARATION AND USE: To clarify 3 cups bouillon, chill it first so all fat can be lifted from the surface. Beat 2 egg whites in a medium saucepan until they are foamy. Add 2 crushed egg shells and the bouillon. (Other seasonings such as parsley stems, leek, chopped tomato, or herbs may be added as desired.) Bring just to a boil stirring, then stop stirring, lower the heat and let simmer slowly without actively bubbling for 10 minutes. Line a colander with a clean kitchen towel or several layers of cheesecloth that have been rinsed in cold water and thoroughly wrung out. Set the colander over a pan into which the consommé can drip. Pour the mixture gently into the colander and allow it to filter through undisturbed or it will be cloudy.

Consommé is the base for all clear soups and aspics. Bouillon is used whenever clarity is not necessary. Consommé Madrilène is served either hot or chilled, in which case it is jellied and can make a delicious first course topped with a dollop of sour cream or CRÈME FRAÎCHE, caviar, and a sprinkling of freshly snipped chives.

CORNICHONS

Cornichons are tiny French gherkins pickled in vinegar, and are available in fancy food shops in bulk or in jars of varying sizes. They are often combined in jars with tiny pickled onions and branches of tarragon.

STORAGE: If covered with their original pickling liquid, these will keep for up to 6 months in the refrigerator without losing crispness.

PREPARATION AND USE: Cornichons are traditionally served with meat pâtés and *terrines* (foods cooked in earthenware dishes) because their tart pungency cuts the richness of these fatty dishes. They are also served with the Swiss national dish, Raclette (cheese melted in front of a fire and scraped onto serving plates). They may be cut lengthwise into fan shapes to garnish meat platters and salads.

CORNMEAL

See POLENTA in this section, or CORNMEAL in THE FOODS OF REGIONAL AMERICA section

CRÈME FRAÎCHE

This is the naturally thick, slightly sour-tasting cream of France that is a staple of the French kitchen. It is much appreciated for its nutlike flavor. It is thicker than our heavy cream but has a similar butterfat content, and paler in color than DEVONSHIRE CREAM, but not as thick. Imported, refrigerated crème fraîche is now sold at exorbitant prices at gourmet specialty shops and some supermarkets. We give instructions for making a reasonable facsimile below.

STORAGE: Store for up to 2 weeks in a covered container in the refrigerator.

PREPARATION AND USE: You can produce a close facsimile by stirring 1 tablespoon of "starter" (buttermilk, sour cream, or yogurt) into 1 cup raw (unpasteurized) whipping cream, which is available in most dairy markets and health food stores. Allow it to stand in a warm place for 8 hours or longer until thickened, stir, and place in the refrigerator, where it will continue to thicken on standing. This has a very similar flavor to crème fraîche but thins out to cream consistency when cooked. We prefer making it with buttermilk because it doesn't curdle when cooked, as it does when made with sour cream or yogurt. In France, crème fraîche is used in sauces and soups, and is spooned, as is, over fresh fruit, especially the tiny FRAISE DE BOIS.

The real crème fraîche retains its thickness and does not curdle when cooked.

CROUTONS

These are fried cubes or slices of bread, plain or seasoned. Avoid the cardboard cylinders of "salad croutons" found in supermarkets because they are stale-tasting and usually laden with preservatives. Freshly made ones may be found in French markets, but they are easily made at home from bread that is past its peak of freshness.

STORAGE: Freshly made croutons can be stored in an airtight tin in a cool place for up to 2 weeks.

PREPARATION AND USE: Salad croutons, made by frying small cubes of French bread (or rye or wheat bread) in butter or olive oil until they are crisp, are a crunchy ingredient to add to salads and sprinkled over casseroles, soups, and dishes to be browned under the broiler. They are traditional in the cold Spanish vegetable soup, Gazpacho, as a garnish for pureed vegetables, and in scrambled eggs. A Russian egg dish combines them in a flat, baked omelet with scallions and Parmesan cheese. Fried, crustless bread slices are another type of crouton, used as a base for tournedos of beef, and often spread with pâté. In Italy, these are covered with cheese and baked in the oven, to make Crostini. A popular French country appetizer is croutons made from thin slices of French bread—*baguettes* or *flutes*—which have been prepared as in the following recipe. They make a delicious snack or soup accompaniment served either warm or at room temperature.

FRENCH BREAD CROUTONS

Makes about 50 slices

A loaf ("flute") of French bread, about 14" long
1 stick (4 ounces) butter or margarine, melted
Fresh herbs, salt and pepper, *or* any mixed dried herb blend, to taste

Slice bread into ¼" crosswise or diagonal slices. Dip one side of each slice in melted butter, place in a single layer on cookie sheets. Sprinkle lightly with seasonings. Bake at 350° for 7 to 10 minutes until crisp and golden brown.

Serve warm or at room temperature, as a snack or accompaniment to soups or salads.

TO PREPARE IN ADVANCE: These will stay fresh in an airtight tin for up to 2 weeks.

CURRANTS

FRENCH: *cassis* (black currants), *grosseiles* (red or white currants)

We refer here not to the tiny, dried, raisin-like zante grape called currants, but to the red, white, or black berries from a wild bush grown in northern Europe. They are available fresh only during July and August in specialty produce markets, but are widely used in preserves (see BAR-LE-DUC) and jellies. They are also used to make a sweet syrup called Crème de Cassis, which may or may not contain alcohol and which is sold in liquor stores. The berries can be purchased in jars in gourmet specialty shops packed in light syrup. An exemplary brand is Globus from Poland.

STORAGE: Fresh currants should be refrigerated unwashed in a plastic bag for use as soon as possible (within a few days). Or spread them on a baking sheet and freeze them. When solid, transfer to an airtight container and keep frozen for up to 2 months.

USE: These are used primarily for making jellies or jams, but are superb when substituted for blueberries in muffins and breads. Red currant jelly is a very common ingredient in French cooking, melted into Sauce Espagnole for game, and melted as a glaze for tarts. In England, currant jelly flavors Cumberland Sauce along with port wine, and lemon and orange juice, which is served with cold meats and game. In Scandinavia, currant jelly flavors red cabbage, a creamy sauce for poultry, and dessert puddings. In Denmark it is spooned into baked apple halves that surround roast goose on Christmas Eve.

DEVONSHIRE CREAM

OTHER: clotted cream

A very thick, yellow cream made in England by heating milk that has a thick layer of cream on top, which has separated from the milk naturally (the milk has not been homogenized). When cool, the crust and its underlying layer of thick cream is lifted off. It is imported in very small quantities and sold in the finest gourmet specialty shops at great expense. An adequate substitute is softened cream cheese, the finest quality available in a cheese shop. It is similar to EISHTA (see THE FOODS OF THE MIDDLE EAST section).

STORAGE: Store in the refrigerator for use as soon as possible (within a week).

USE: In England, Devonshire cream is used primarily as a topping for fruit and desserts. It is so thick that it is often spread like butter over warm bread to be eaten with preserves. It serves as a filling for a traditional Cornish roll called a Split. It is not used in sauces or soups, or heated for any other use.

EGGPLANT

BRITISH: *aubergine* FRENCH: *aubergine* GERMAN: *Eierfrucht*
ITALIAN: *melanzana* POLISH: *baklazany* RUMANIAN: *vinete*
RUSSIAN: *baklazhany* SPANISH: *berenjena*

For general information and preparation, see THE FOODS OF THE MIDDLE EAST section.

USE: Eggplants are used abundantly in European cooking and combine beautifully with other late-summer produce such as tomatoes, onions, peppers, and Mediterranean herbs. A Rumanian method of preparing it is to bake it until tender, then stuff with sautéed onions. Russian "Caviar," a spicy eggplant relish, is called Ikra Iz Baklazhanov in Russian and Srpski Ajvar in Serbian. A Spanish vegetable stew, Pisto, which combines it with ham, sweet red peppers, garlic, mushrooms, and artichokes, is served hot or cold. In Italy it is combined with tomatoes to make a pasta sauce and Eggplant Parmigiana. In Sicily, eggplants are the basis for the delicious antipasto, Caponata. Best known of all French eggplant dishes is Ratatouille Niçoise, a stew of tomatoes, eggplant, onion, garlic, zucchini, peppers, and herbs.

RATATOUILLE NIÇOISE

For 12 (1-cup) servings

In our version, fresh vegetables are not overcooked and each retains its own identity. This should be made a day before serving so the flavors have time to blend.

½ cup fruity olive oil
1 medium onion, minced
2 cloves garlic, minced
1 tablespoon chopped fresh oregano *or* 1 teaspoon dried oregano, crumbled
1 tablespoon chopped fresh basil *or* 1 teaspoon dried basil, crumbled
1 bay leaf
4 pounds fresh ripe tomatoes, peeled, seeded, and diced *or* 2 (28-ounce) cans whole tomatoes and their liquid, *or* crushed tomatoes
1¼ cups dry white wine
1 teaspoon salt
A good sprinkling of black pepper or cayenne (ground red pepper), to taste
4 medium zucchini, cut crosswise in ¼" slices
4 red bell peppers (seeds and membranes removed), cut in ½" strips
2 green bell peppers (seeds and membranes removed), cut in ½" strips
2 medium eggplants, *or* 8 small eggplants, diced
¼ cup minced parsley

TO GARNISH AND SERVE:
   Lemon wedges, if the dish is served cold

   Heat the olive oil in a large, heavy (not iron) pot. Sauté the onion until just beginning to brown. Add the garlic, herbs, and bay leaf, and sauté briefly. Stir in the tomatoes, breaking them up with a spoon. Add the wine and simmer, uncovered, for 30 minutes. Add 1 teaspoon salt and black pepper or cayenne, and taste for seasoning.

   Add the zucchini, peppers, eggplant, and parsley to the sauce. Simmer, covered, for 15 minutes. Then remove cover, stir gently, and simmer slowly until the vegetables are just tender. Stir only if necessary, and very gently, taking care not to crush the vegetables. Taste and correct the seasoning and discard the bay leaf. Cool and refrigerate.

   Serve at room temperature with lemon wedges, or reheat gently over low heat.

TO PREPARE IN ADVANCE: Prepare at least one day in advance. This will keep for up to 5 days in the refrigerator in a nonmetal container. It loses much of its texture if frozen.

ENDIVE

See BELGIAN ENDIVE

ÉPICES FINES

See HERBS, SPICES, AND SEASONING BLENDS section, under
SEASONING BLENDS

ESCARGOT

(ess-kar-GOH)

ENGLISH: snail GERMAN: *Schnecke* ITALIAN: *chiocciola, lumaca*
SPANISH: *caracol*

"Escargot" is the French term for an edible land snail. Canned Burgundian escargots are available in 7-ounce cans in gourmet specialty stores everywhere today. Taiwan now produces 75 percent of the world's supply, much of which is sent to France for packaging and exportation. The reusable shells are so expensive to sterilize to U.S. Food and Drug Administration requirements that most canned escargots are now sold in this country without them. Cookware shops sell ceramic shells that work very nicely. Some fancy-food shops now sell frozen escargots in their shells with their traditional seasoning butter, ready to pop in the oven.

STORAGE: Canned escargots can be stored for up to 1 year on the pantry shelf. Once opened, they can be stored in a nonmetal container in the refrigerator for up to 3 days; frozen, for up to 4 months.

PREPARATION AND USE: For most recipes, allow 6 to 12 escargots per serving. Drain the escargots and rinse them very well. Blanch them in boiling water for 30 seconds. If they are to be served in their shells, place them in their shells along with whatever seasonings or sauce will be baked with them. Place them in snail dishes called *escargotières,* available in specialty cookware shops, or on a bed of rock salt to hold them steady. They require only 10 to 12 minutes in a 350° oven to become piping hot. To eat snails, use a special snail pincer to hold the shell steady while you lift out the snail with a small fork.

In France, and throughout the world, Escargots à la Bourguignonne are considered a great delicacy when prepared with garlic-flavored butter and heated in their shells to serve with plenty of warm French bread to mop up the juices. Other regions of France have their own special versions, such as the Gascony sauce called L'aillada, which contains olive oil and leeks as well as garlic, and the Languedoc version with Aïoli (garlic mayonnaise). In Corsica, they are chopped and mixed with spinach, minced anchovies, and lemon to be served in *coquilles* (scallop shells). They can also be marinated in vinaigrette to serve with a Rémoulade sauce, or be cooked in a quiche. A recent trend is to serve escargots in mushroom caps instead of in shells. We know of no one who is more creative in the kitchen than award-winning Chef Richard Wing, who taught us to make an appetizer of escargots in the following manner:

ESCARGOTS IN PASTA SHELLS

48	canned French escargots (snails)	For 4 to 6 servings
48	large pasta shells (CONCHIGLIE or LUMACHE—see PASTA)	
1–2	medium zucchini, very thinly sliced	

SAUCE:

4	ounces (1 stick) butter, melted
2	cloves garlic, mashed or minced
1	tablespoon green bell pepper, minced
1	tablespoon scallion, minced
2	tablespoons tomato paste or tomato puree
1	teaspoon parsley, finely chopped
1	teaspoon peanut butter
1	teaspoon Dijon mustard
4	drops Tabasco sauce
½	cup dry white wine
	Salt and pepper to taste

Rinse the escargots very well; then blanch in boiling water for 30 seconds, or deep-fry in oil for 10 seconds; drain and dry on paper towels. This freshens and firms them. Cook the pasta shells according to package directions just until barely tender, rinse with cold water, and drain. Blanch the zucchini slices in simmering water for a few seconds and drain.

Combine the sauce ingredients in a saucepan over moderate heat, stirring constantly until the sauce starts to bubble. Stir in the escargots and simmer slowly for 5 minutes.

Place a slice of blanched zucchini in each indentation of special serving dishes called *escargotières* (or place on a bed of rock salt in large, ovenproof baking dish, side by side). Stuff each pasta shell with an escargot and place on top of a zucchini slice. Top each pasta shell with another zucchini slice and spoon any remaining sauce over the tops.

Ten minutes before serving, bake at 350° for 8 to 10 minutes, until the sauce is bubbling. Serve with chilled white wine and French bread to mop up the juices.

TO PREPARE IN ADVANCE: Prepare in the morning except for final baking. Leave, covered, at room temperature, and bake just before serving.

FARFEL

See EGG BARLEY under PASTA

FARINA DOLCE

See CHESTNUT FLOUR

FENNEL, FLORENTINE

OTHER: Florence fennel, sweet fennel, Roman fennel

FRENCH: *fenouil* GERMAN: *Fenchel* ITALIAN: *finocchio* SPANISH: *hinojo*

We refer here to the bulbous vegetable, not the herb and its dried seed described in THE HERBS, SPICES, AND SEASONING BLENDS section. Fennel is a delicately licorice-flavored plant with a round base made up of broad celerylike leaf stalks. In fact it looks like fat, squat celery. The ends of the stalks have feathery foliage that looks a great deal like dill. You will find it in Italian markets and specialty produce markets throughout the winter and in early spring. In the West, at least, many supermarkets carry it. Look for crisp, very pale greenish-white, unblemished bulbs with outer stalks at least 9″ long.

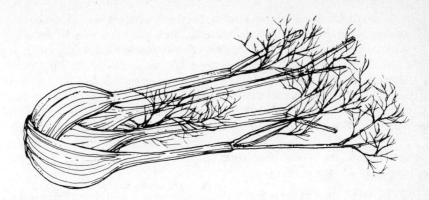

STORAGE: Store in a paper bag inside a plastic bag in the refrigerator for use within 4 days.

PREPARATION AND USE: For most purposes, 1 bulb will serve 2. To use raw, remove any tough outer stalks and trim away the base. It can be cut crosswise into slices, or with the grain into long strips, as preferred. Raw fennel stalks can be used in the same manner as celery as an appetizer, or can be sliced as a salad ingredient. To cook fennel, it should be halved or quartered lengthwise, depending on its size, and then poached in water or broth to cover for 4 to 5 minutes, just until tender when pierced with a knife. Any recipe for cooked celery heart can be adapted to this vegetable. Cooked fennel can be drained and seasoned as desired with melted butter, a topping of Mornay sauce, or a sprinkling of Parmesan to serve as a vegetable. It can be dipped in a Parmesan cheese batter and deep-fried, or placed in a vinaigrette to marinate overnight to be served as a salad. It has a special affinity for seafood.

FILO PASTRY
See THE FOODS OF THE MIDDLE EAST section, and STRUDEL LEAVES in this section

FINES HERBES
See HERBS, SPICES, AND SEASONING BLENDS section, under SEASONING BLENDS

FINNAN HADDIE
OTHER: finnan haddock, smoked haddock

Finnan haddie is named for Findon, Scotland, where it was discovered by accident when fire swept an area where haddock had been hung to dry. The "smoked" golden brown fish were tasted and a new food was born. It is exported to the United States from Scotland, but is also produced in New England. You will find this in well-stocked supermarkets and fish markets everywhere, and it is usually filleted but still attached to the backbone. It can vary greatly in quality, from moist and mild, to fibrous and sour. Press it to make sure it is soft. The golden color is often a result of a dye used in the curing process, and not from smoking. Nowadays, cod is often substituted for haddock, the world population of which is on the decline. The best portion is a center cut.

STORAGE: Store in the refrigerator for use within 3 days. Freezing changes the texture, but it can be frozen for up to 3 months, if necessary.

PREPARATION AND USE: One pound of smoked haddock will serve 2 or 3. Soak for 30 minutes in warm water to rid it of excess salt and soften it. Usually there are a few bones, so feel it carefully and remove them and any skin. The classic Scottish method of preparation, and the way we often prepare it for breakfast, is to poach it slowly in milk for 10 minutes, basting it often, and then serve it with pats of sweet butter to melt slowly over the top.

It always takes well to the addition of cream, and is delicious in a cold appetizer mousse in place of the omnipresent cooked salmon. In Scotland, it is often topped with a poached egg. In the English dish, Kedgeree, it is combined with rice, cream, and hard-cooked eggs, with just a touch of curry powder and saffron.

FLOWERS, CRYSTALLIZED

Violets, rose petals or tiny rosebuds, lilacs, mimosa, or mint leaves that have been dipped into a sugar syrup of an exact temperature are thereby "crystallized" (preserved) for use as dessert decorations. They are available in fancy-food shops in small round boxes that are either decorated with floral designs, which make them look like minature hat boxes, or made of clear plastic through which the crystallized flowers can be seen. They are imported from France and are quite expensive. A few baker's supply houses and fine food stores sell them loose, by weight.

STORAGE: Sealed airtight in a cool, dry place, they will keep indefinitely.

USE: The violets and lilacs are the most popular because of their purple color, which provides an attractive contrast with chocolate desserts of all descriptions. They are also used on wedding cakes. They are edible, but have almost no flavor.

FOIE GRAS

Literally "fat liver," this French term refers to the liver of a goose or duck which has been fattened by forcefeeding to have an abnormally large liver. The animals are allowed no exercise at all, and though critics complain that it is cruel treatment, the farmers who raise them claim they enjoy it. The best fresh goose liver is from Alsace and Southwestern France. You will find it only through a specialty shop, from which it may be ordered by mail, during the Christmas season. You will pay dearly for it. Duck liver is not considered as great a delicacy as the goose liver. Fine fresh foie gras is creamy pink. There are several types of canned foie gras, imported from France, Austria, Hungary and Germany, which may be purchased in fancy food shops. They are listed here in descending order of quality. (Because foie gras is often specified as an ingredient we are discussing it here. Jewish chopped chicken liver and Scandinavian pâtés are prepared foods, so are not described in this book.)

Foie Gras Naturel en Bloc: The finest canned quality of goose liver which must contain 80% goose liver. It comes in oval cans of varying sizes, from 5 ounces to 28 ounces. It is expensive. Exemplary brands are Edouard Artzner and Rougie.

Block de Foie Gras: This is a combination of the finest quality foie gras mixed with lesser quality. If labeled "truffé" it is studded with chopped truffles. It is sold in a trapezoid-shaped cans ranging in size from 5 to 15 ounces and is almost as expensive as fois gras naturel.

The following are prepared items, seldom used as ingredients because they melt easily.

Puree de Foie Gras: Sold in cans of varying sizes. By French law this must contain 75% foie gras of any quality.

Mousse or (pate) de Foie Gras: A mixture of pork, eggs and some fois gras, with very little taste of goose liver. It is sold in 3-ounce tins.

STORAGE: Fresh prepared foie gras should be kept chilled for use within a few days. Canned foie gras, once opened, can be stored tightly wrapped in plastic wrap for up to 4 days in the refrigerator. It can be frozen but the smooth texture will suffer.

PREPARATION AND USE: Fine foie gras is traditionally served chilled, in thin slices or curls, at the beginning of a meal with thinly sliced toast and an excellent wine. Allow 2 ounces per serving. It is also prepared en gelée (encased in clear aspic), or baked inside pastry cases. It is classically used in

France as a thinly sliced garnish atop such famous preparations as Tournedos Rossini (medallions of beef topped with a lightly sautéed medallion of foie gras, chopped truffle and truffle-flavored Sauce Espagnole). It was traditionally used instead of Duxelle (mushroom forcemeat) for Beef Wellington. The finest foie gras does not melt when heated, but the lesser quality canned versions do, and are added to some French sauces.

FRAISES DES BOIS

These tiny wild strawberries are considered a great dessert delicacy in France when topped with CRÈME FRAÎCHE. They are sometimes found in mountain areas of the United States and can, only very rarely, be found in fancy-food shops at great cost. There are, however, French brands of preserves featuring this fruit, and also a fruit brandy (*eau de vie*). Small strawberries can be substituted.

STORAGE: Store unwashed in a paper bag in the refrigerator to enjoy as soon as possible.

USE: It would be anathema to serve fresh ones any way but *au naturel* as part of a fruit plate for salad, or on their own for dessert with crème fraîche.

GELATIN, LEAF

OTHER: gelatine

FRANCE: *gélatine* GERMAN: *Gallert* ITALIAN: *gelatina* SPANISH: *genciana*

Most of the gelatin sold in the United States is the powdered type and comes in boxes of packets, each packet containing ¼ ounce (1 tablespoon) of powdered gelatin. This is a convenient and commendable product. Many French chefs prefer leaf gelatin, however, which is not only expensive, but must be sought out in fancy-food shops and bakery supply houses, where it is usually sold with instructions for use. Look for clear, not yellowed, sheets. In our opinion it is not worth the uncertainty and we see no reason to buy it when the powdered type is so consistent in quality.

STORAGE: Wrapped airtight, leaf gelatin will keep indefinitely in a cool place, though it will eventually decline in quality.

PREPARATION AND USE: Unlike the powdered product, this tends to vary in setting power, so follow package directions. Usually 3 sheets of gelatin are approximately equivalent to 1 envelope powdered gelatin. Place the sheets of gelatin in cold water to cover and let soak for 10 to 20 minutes until very supple. Lift out of the water and place in a small heavy saucepan with a tablespoon of water and stir over very low heat just until the sheets have dissolved, or add to very hot liquid that is part of recipe (consommé, custard, etc.)

This can be used in any recipe, sweet or savory, calling for gelatin.

GÉNOISE

(zhay-NWAHZ)

This is a classic, plain French sponge cake, which we have decided to list here even though it is a prepared item because it is often used as a basis for creating other desserts, especially an infinite number of other fancy cakes (*gâteaux*). Génoise, made from flour, eggs, sugar, butter, and sometimes vanilla, and sometimes flavored with cocoa, is not particularly difficult to make at home, though it takes some practice to master. Even Julia Child prefers to purchase plain génoise at a fine French bakery in order to save her energy for more creative cooking. It is somewhat dry with many holes, so it is capable of absorbing a great deal of flavorful syrup.

STORAGE: Plain génoise, tightly wrapped, freezes beautifully for up to 6 months.

USE: The cake is usually sliced in thin, even layers, soaked with a liqueur-laden sugar syrup until it is extremely moist, and then layered with preserves or mocha or chocolate-buttercream icing to create all manner of delights. Fine French cookbooks, especially those dealing with pastry, will give you all kinds of creative ideas.

GIROLLE

See CHANTERELLE, under MUSHROOMS

GLACE DE VIANDE

(GLAHS da vee-AHND)
OTHER: meat glaze, meat extract

True glace de viande is beef or veal stock that has been simmered until reduced to a thick glaze, so that a small amount gives a highly condensed flavor of the original. Some fancy-food shops have quality glaces de viande available frozen. Often they have caramel added (made from sugar) to give a rich brown color. B.V. brand, manufactured by Wilson, BOVRIL, and MAR-MITE (a yeast extract), are often used in recipes when the product is specified.

They contain a few flavor ingredients other than beef extract, but are generally good products, and can be used in the same manner as homemade glace de viande. Restaurant supply houses carry soup bases of chicken, beef, ham, and lobster. Always read labels to avoid chemicals and preservatives.

STORAGE: Because they are highly condensed and quite salty, these will keep for up to 1 year in the refrigerator.

PREPARATION AND USE: To make glace de viande, boil stock until it has reduced to a thick sauce. When cool, it will be pastelike in consistency, and highly condensed, so stir only a small amount at a time into dishes that require richer flavor, and take care to simmer the dish long enough for the glace to melt and distribute evenly before checking the taste. We add this to soups, stews, sauces, and vegetable dishes when a richer meat flavor is desirable. Some glaces de viande are used to make broth and have directions for doing so on the label.

GNOCCHI

(NYOH-kee)

These Italian dumplings, made in many varieties, are used as a base for prepared dishes. They may be made of ricotta cheese, cornmeal, and even pumpkin, and formed into small pillow shapes or balls, and are often rolled in flour with the tines of a fork to give them a grooved surface. Because many types are now available in the frozen food sections of gourmet specialty markets, we have decided to describe them here. There is even a gnocchi-shaped noodle (see CAVATELLI, under PASTA). Fine French and Austrian gnocchi are made with *pâte à choux* (cream puff pastry), piped into rounds to be poached in water, then drained and baked with Mornay sauce, and recipes for these may be found in French cookbooks. Following is a brief description of prepared Italian gnocchi you are likely to find. Follow package directions for thawing and cooking.

Gnocchi alla Romano: Made from a thick semolina and egg batter seasoned with nutmeg, cut into small shapes, and baked in the oven with butter and grated Parmesan.

Gnocchi di Patate: Made of mashed potatoes, bits of ham, eggs, and Parmesan, these are usually rolled into balls, poached in water until they rise to the surface, then drained to be served with tomato sauce, PESTO, chicken liver sauce, or simply butter and Parmesan.

Gnocchi di Ricotta: Made of ricotta, flour, and eggs, these are usually poached to be served with butter and Parmesan, a tomato sauce, or PESTO.

Gnocchi Verdi: Spinach is added to gnocchi di ricotta, and these are usually served baked simply with butter and Parmesan. They are sometimes called Ravioli Nudi, and are a delicious example of the height to which gnocchi can ascend.

GOLDEN SYRUP

OTHER: refiner's sugar

This is a very popular English product sold in 1-pound jars in gourmet specialty shops under the brand name of Lyle's. It is a lightly carmelized, amber-colored syrup of refined cane sugar. It should not be difficult to find, but a reasonable facsimile can be made for use in recipes by combining 1 part dark corn syrup with 5 parts light corn syrup. Equal amounts of honey, CANE SYRUP or unsulphured MOLASSES (see THE FOODS OF REGIONAL AMERICA section) can be substituted with considerable difference in flavor, but similar sweetness.

STORAGE: Tightly capped, it will keep indefinitely in a cool dark place.

USE: In England, this is a traditional accompaniment for suet pudding and is as important to the British as maple syrup is to Americans. It is used as an ingredient in many English desserts, but also as a spread for bread, a topping for pancakes, a glaze for ham, and is drizzled over broiled grapefruit and cereals.

GRAPESEED OIL

FRENCH: *huile de pépins de raisins*

Grapeseed oil, imported from France or Switzerland, and sometimes flavored with HERBES DE PROVENCE (see HERBS, under SEASONING BLENDS in the HERBS, SPICES, AND SEASONING BLENDS section) is available in some gourmet specialty shops. It is extracted from the seeds of grapes and is very expensive. Peanut oil can be substituted.

STORAGE: It will keep indefinitely in a cool dark place.

USE: This is the favored oil for cooking meat in Fondue Bourguignonne, a Swiss specialty in which meat is skewered and cooked by each diner at the table until the meat is brown, and then dipped into any of an assortment of sauces, such as Béarnaise, Horseradish, Mustard Mayonnaise, Curry.

GRENADINE

(GREN-ah-deen *or* gren-ah-DEEN)

There are two types of French grenadine both of which are red, sweet, and syrupy. One contains alcohol and the other does not, and both are available in liquor stores. At one time, both were made from the juice of pomegranates, but now are made from several different fruits, under secret formulas. French POMEGRANATE JUICE (see THE FOODS OF THE MIDDLE EAST section) can be substituted, but is more tart. Unsweetened grape juice can be substituted with some difference in flavor and color.

STORAGE: Grenadine that contains alcohol can be stored indefinitely at room temperature. Refrigerate the nonalcoholic type after opening.

PREPARATION AND USE: Both are used as a flavoring for cocktails, a sauce for dessert, and in cooking to add a sweet-tart flavor and red color. We use it as a glaze for roast pork.

GUANCIALE

(gwahn-CHAH-lay)

Guanciale is cured (but not smoked) pork jowl, much esteemed in Italy as the flavoring for Pasta Carbonara. You are very unlikely to find it in the United States, but you can substitute PANCETTA with excellent results. Some Italian cookbooks translate it as bacon, but it is not smoky tasting, and a better substitute is lean salt pork that has been well blanched.

STORAGE: Store guanciale, tightly wrapped, in the refrigerator for up to 3 weeks, or in the freezer for up to 6 months.

PREPARATION AND USE: Allow 2 ounces per serving as a flavoring ingredient in pasta sauces and in the cooking of beans. Use in any recipe suitable for pancetta.

HAM

FRENCH: *jambon* GERMAN: *Schinken* ITALIAN: *prosciutto*
NORWEGIAN: *skinke* POLISH: *szynca* ROMANIAN: *sunca*
SPANISH: *jamón*

Ham refers to the hind leg of a pig that has been cured, and sometimes smoked. The curing is always done with salt, either rubbed into the ham or made into a brine. The term is sometimes incorrectly applied to pork shoulder.

There is, at the time of this writing, an embargo on the importation of raw pork products, so you will probably find only domestic or Canadian versions of the following hams in gourmet specialty shops and ethnic delis. None requires cooking.

STORAGE: Store tightly wrapped in the refrigerator for up to 1 week. The texture is adversely affected by freezing.

PREPARATION AND USE: Most of the following are usually served thinly sliced as an appetizer. Cooking toughens them, so when they are used as a flavoring in heated dishes, care should be taken not to heat them long. Specific dishes are listed here with PROSCIUTTO, the term usually used when referring to European-style dry-cured ham. In Switzerland, ham is used in veal or chicken cutlets "Cordon Bleu," in which the pounded cutlet meat is stuffed with Swiss-type cheese and a slice of ham, and then breaded and sautéed.

The following recipe demonstrates how these hams are used to flavor dishes without overcooking.

TRUFFLE-STUFFED VEAL CHOPS

For 4 servings

This is another treasured recipe from Penny Birnbaum.

4   veal chops, 1″ thick
4   thin slices (2″ by 2″) FONTINA cheese
1   small TRUFFLE, cut in 8 slices
4   thin slices raw cured ham (proscuitto, parma, bayonne)
    Salt and freshly ground black pepper
¼   cup clarified butter*
2   large shallots, minced
8   mushrooms, quartered
½   teaspoon fresh rosemary *or* ¼ teaspoon dried rosemary,
    minced
¼   cup cognac or brandy
¼   cup sweet vermouth, Madeira, or sherry
1   cup Sauce Espangnole (see SAUCES, FRENCH)
½   cup heavy (whipping) cream

*Note: Clarified butter is simply butter from which the milk solids have been removed. It is the same thing as GHEE except that it is not cooked. To make it, melt butter in a small saucepan over very low heat, or in a glass measuring cup in a microwave oven. Let stand, undisturbed, for 5 minutes to allow the solids to settle. Skim any milk solids from the top with a spoon; then carefully pour the clear butter into another container, leaving the rest of the milk solids in the bottom of the pan or cup. This butter oil does not spoil as does plain butter, and can stand a much higher cooking temperature without burning, so it is better for sautéing. Some cooks use equal parts of butter and oil in its place for sautéing.

Make an incision 3″ wide and almost to the bone in the side of each chop, forming a pocket, in the same manner as you would for stuffed pork chops.

Enclose 1 piece cheese and 2 thin slices truffle in each slice of ham and insert in the pocket. Sprinkle the chops lightly with salt and freshly ground black pepper.

In a heavy sauté pan, brown the chops in the clarified butter, turning to color evenly on both sides, until they are done, 8 to 10 minutes. Remove from the pan and keep warm on a platter or on serving plates in a 150° oven. To the drippings in the pan add the shallots, followed by the mushrooms and rosemary. Stir for 1 minute. Add the brandy and the vermouth, Madeira, or sherry to the pan, and simmer until the liquid has almost totally evaporated. Stir in the Sauce Espangnole, simmer 3 to 4 minutes to thicken; then pour in the cream, and simmer a minute or two longer.

Spoon the sauce over the chops and serve immediately.

TO PREPARE IN ADVANCE: The chops can be browned, but not fully cooked, several hours before serving. Finish the sauce up to, but not including, the addition of the cream. When ready to serve, place the chops in the sauce and simmer just until tender. Remove chops, simmer sauce, uncovered, until thickened to the desired consistency; then add cream as above.

Bayonne: A cured, lightly smoked ham originally from a French town of the same name. The color is more golden than rose-hued. It can be found in French *charcuteries* (pork butcher shops) and gourmet specialty shops. It is usually eaten as is in the manner of PROSCIUTTO, but is occasionally used as a flavoring in the same manner as prosciutto, though it toughens when cooked.

Canned Hams: Excellent boneless hams are imported from Denmark, Holland, and Poland. Unless labeled "sterilized" they should be stored in the refrigerator, even before opening. Krakus is a brand of Polish ham that has been widely advertised as having less fat than other canned hams. We have purchased these several times and, though they are indeed lean and look impressive, they lack the fine smoky flavor we enjoy. PRAGUE and YORK hams are occasionally available canned.

Capocollo: Not really a ham because it is from the shoulder of the pig. This cured pork product is a specialty of Parma, Italy. It is sold in many Italian delis and is used in sandwiches with provolone cheese and browned onions.

Culatello: An exceptionally fine Italian raw ham that has been cured and aged in wine. Domestic versions can be found only rarely in fine Italian markets and gourmet specialty shops and are quite expensive. It is served raw, very thinly sliced, as an appetizer.

Parma: The true PROSCIUTTO, named for the town where it originated. Most supermarkets have refrigerated plastic packages of thinly sliced Parma ham, usually made domestically. The supermarket variety is not as fine as the kind you will find in an Italian deli, but can be used for the same purposes as prosciutto—in cooking, or served with figs or melon as an antipasto. Giuliano Bugialli, Italian-cooking authority, refers to the Parma from Langhirano as a "dessert" prosciutto.

Prague Ham: (Prazska Sunka): A Czechoslovakian ham that is cured and smoked. It is very popular in France and other European countries for its fine flavor. If raw, it must be cooked (see HAM in THE FOODS OF REGIONAL AMERICA section). A canned type is occasionally found.

Presunto: A fine quality cured and smoked Portuguese ham, similar to prosciutto *cotto* (see PROSCIUTTO). Domestic versions can be found occasionally in gourmet meat markets. In Portugal, it is often cooked with white beans, or fresh favas (see under BEANS, in THE FOODS OF THE MIDDLE EAST section).

Prosciutto: The Italian word for ham. This has become a generic term for PARMA hams. There are two types. Prosciutto *crudo* is a superb raw ham, air-dried with salt and seasonings, and Prosciutto *cotto*, which is cooked, is almost as good and much less expensive. If several types are available, ask for a small taste of each. Both raw and cooked types of prosciutto are best eaten as is, served as an elegant first course or antipasto, draped over wedges of fresh honeydew melon, cantaloupe, or figs. Cooking toughens it, so if using it as an ingredient in a heated dish, take care not to cook it long. It, and similar hams, are specified as ingredients in a filling for Cannelloni and other pastas, in soufflés, and as a topping for sautéed veal with FONTINA cheese (see CHEESE, FIRM AND SEMI-FIRM). In Bologna, it flavors the famous Salsa Bolognese. In Rome, it is a classic flavoring for cooked peas.

The rind of prosciutto, used to flavor soups such as Pasta e Fagioli, is called *contenna*, and is blanched before use. Salt pork can be substituted for this.

Serrano: A Spanish type of raw cured ham similar to PROSCIUTTO, but sweeter. It tends to be tougher than other hams of the same type because it is made from leaner pork. It is cured by soaking in wine for several months, and then coated with a paste of olive oil and paprika and hung to dry for several months longer. Domestic versions can be found in Spanish and Latin American markets. It is served in the same manner as PROSCIUTTO, or in sandwiches.

Westphalian: An exceptionally fine, lightly smoked, rather hard ham made from pigs that feed on acorns from Westphalia's oak forest, giving it a dark brown color. It is then cured and smoked over juniper branches. Look for it in German delis and gourmet meat markets. It can be thinly sliced to serve in the same manner as prosciutto, but is most commonly served in Germany as part of a ham platter, atop leaves of butter lettuce and pumpernickel bread.

York: This most famous of English hams, pale pink and mild, may be the most difficult to find.

HAZELNUT OIL

FRENCH: *huile de noisettes*

Hazelnut oil, imported from France in 8- to 17-ounce cans, has the flavor and aroma of roasted hazelnuts. It is found in gourmet specialty shops and is expensive, about the same price as the finest "extra-virgin" OLIVE OIL.

STORAGE: After opening, store in a cool place for up to 6 months. It can be refrigerated if you plan to keep it longer, but should be brought to room temperature to reliquify before use.

PREPARATION AND USE: This is a strongly flavored oil that is usually used as a flavoring in combination with lighter oils. Use a teaspoon or two of it in recipes for hazelnut cookies or when sautéing fish. Blend 1 or 2 teaspoons of it into a cup of mayonnaise, add 1 tablespoon chopped roasted hazelnuts, and you have an easy and exotic dip for spears of BELGIAN ENDIVE. Add a few drops to recipes for chicken salad, to oil-and-vinegar dressings, or in the cavity of an avocado. We add a few drops of it to a cream sauce for spinach fettucine, which we sprinkle with toasted nuts. It adds a deep nut flavor to the following chocolate chip cookies recipe.

CHOCOLATE CHIP HAZELNUT COOKIES

½ cup shelled hazelnuts (filberts)   For approximately 3 dozen
8 ounces (2 sticks) butter, softened
1 tablespoon hazelnut oil
1 cup powdered sugar
1 teaspoon pure vanilla extract
   Salt
2¼ cups all-purpose flour
1 (6-ounce) package semi-sweet chocolate morsels
   Additional powdered sugar in a shaker or sieve, to
     sprinkle over the baked cookies

Toast the hazelnuts on a baking sheet in a preheated 350° oven for 15 minutes, stirring once or twice. Transfer the nuts to a towel and, while still warm, rub off any of the dark outer skin that comes off easily. Chop coarsely. Oil a cookie sheet with 1 teaspoon of the hazelnut oil.

In a large mixing bowl, beat together until very creamy the butter, the remaining 2 teaspoons hazelnut oil, and the powdered sugar. Add the salt, vanilla, and flour. Mix in the chocolate pieces and chopped nuts. Break off pieces of dough and roll into 1″ balls. Place 2″ apart on the prepared baking sheet and flatten, using the bottom of a drinking glass or the tines of a fork, to about ⅜″ thickness. Bake at 350° for 15 minutes.

Sprinkle with additional powdered sugar while still warm.

TO PREPARE IN ADVANCE: These will keep in an airtight tin for up to a week or, frozen, for up to 4 months.

HEAD CHEESE
See under SAUSAGE, COOKED

HERBES DE PROVENCE

A blend of herbs typical of the cooking of southern France, which is imported into this country in small clay crocks. We once emptied the crock onto our kitchen table and separated the contents into piles of different herbs so that we could approximate the mixture in our own kitchen.

STORAGE: Store as any dried herb for use within one year.

PREPARATION AND USE: To make ½ cup of mixed herbs that closely resembles the original, combine in a small bowl the following dried herbs: 3 tablespoons *each* marjoram, thyme, and summer savory, 1 tablespoon sweet basil, 1½ teaspoons crumbled rosemary, ½ teaspoon *each* crumbled sage and fennel seed, and ¼ teaspoon dried lavender. Crumble between your fingers to sprinkle over meat or poultry before roasting, and use to season stuffings and vegetables. Try the following recipe for Tomato Herb Mustard, which is a good accompaniment for ham or cold cuts.

TOMATO-HERB MUSTARD

1   (8-ounce) jar Poupon Dijon mustard   For about 1¾ cups
6   tablespoons (3 ounces) tomato paste
½   cup Herbs of Provence (purchased, or homemade, using
     our recipe)
1   tablespoon mustard seeds, crushed
1½ teaspoons paprika

Combine all ingredients in a jar. Refrigerate for at least a week to allow the flavor to develop.

TO PREPARE IN ADVANCE: This will keep indefinitely in the refrigerator, though the herb flavor becomes stronger as it stands.

HEARTS OF PALM

See THE FOODS OF LATIN AMERICA section

HERRING

FINNISH: *silli* FRENCH: *hareng* GERMAN: *Hering* ITALIAN: *aringa* NORWEGIAN: *sild* SPANISH: *arenque* SWEDISH: *sill*

Herring has a history of being the most widely eaten seafood of northern Europe. We will not concern ourselves with fresh herring in this book, nor with the many varieties of prepared herring, as they cannot be considered ingredients, but only with the types of salt and canned herring available in ethnic markets. Small herrings are very often canned to be labeled sardines, which are actually small pilchards, fish of the herring family.

KIPPERED OR SMOKED HERRING

These dried, split herring, sometimes called "kippers," are air-dried and cold-smoked. They are usually dotted with butter and broiled to serve as part of the traditional English breakfast. "Bloaters" are slightly fatter because they are not gutted before they are given the same treatment. Smoked herring are sold filleted, by the pound, in plastic packages and in cans in many markets, but freshly prepared ones can occasionally be found in fine fish markets, where they are apt to be fresher and milder. The best are copper-colored from having been smoked over oak chips. Avoid any that are very dry or have a strong odor. Check the label of any packaged ones for preservatives.

STORAGE: Refrigerate, and use within a few days.

PREPARATION AND USE: If serving whole, allow 1 to 2 per serving, depending on their size. They are best when soaked for an hour or longer in milk or wine to remove excess smoky flavor. They are very often marinated in olive oil with sliced onions and carrots to serve cold. To serve warm, they require only heating, and can be baked with a drizzling of butter (and a sprinkling of WORCESTERSHIRE), sautéed or broiled with butter, or poached in milk to serve with scrambled eggs. Take care not to heat them too long or they will become dry. They are also well suited to being warmed in a cream sauce to serve in pastry cases or over split English muffins. They can be soaked in lemon juice for 6 to 8 hours in the refrigerator, and then drained and sliced to serve like smoked salmon. The Scots usually coat them with oatmeal before frying. They are very often a part of Scandinavian Smörgasbord, prepared in many ways.

SALT HERRING

Salt-cured or brined herring have long been a staple of the European diet. They can be found in some European markets packed in brine. The best ones are from Holland and Germany, and are sold from 10-pound kegs in European delis. Fresh herring can be "salted" by removing the scales and gutting them, then soaking in a brine of salt and water (strong enough to float a raw egg) for 12 hours. Drain, dry, and pack into a glass container between layers of coarse salt with peppercorns and bay leaf if desired. Cover tightly and store in a cool place, checking often to make sure they are thoroughly covered with the brining liquid that is created by the salt. Prepared salt herring, already soaked and pickled, are available in jars and cans in many guises, marinated in wine, sour cream, or mushroom sauce.

STORAGE: Salt herring in brine can be kept in a cool place or in the refrigerator indefinitely if always covered with pickling brine. Prepared herring, once opened, should be refrigerated for use within a week.

PREPARATION AND USE: Salt herring should be soaked in cold water for at least 24 hours, changing the water several times. Once soaked, they can be prepared like fresh herring in any recipe, but will have a saltier flavor. Blot dry, fillet them, and remove the skin or not depending on the recipe you are using. Any remaining bones can be picked out with tweezers, though this step is unnecessary if the herring are to be pickled, because the marinade will dissolve them. They do not require cooking, and are most often marinated for 1 to 4 days.

Salt herring are very important to Scandinavian Smörgasbord, at which they appear in a staggering number of preparations. In Finland, they are pureed with mashed potatoes into fish balls called Sillipyörykät, or marinated with onions and dill to make Sudlasilli, garnished with hard-cooked eggs. Glassblower's Herring, Glasmästarsill, is a Swedish preparation of salt herring marinated in a jar with vegetables, spices such as mustard seed and ginger, and a sweet-and-sour pickling liquid.

Salt herring, especially in the United States, are cut up to be placed in a sour cream and onion sauce (which we like especially if slices of apple and a bit of curry flavoring are added), are pickled in vinegar with pickling spices, or are wrapped around a stuffing of dill pickle and onion and covered with a spicy vinegar to make Rollmops, a German preparation, which is marinated for four days and is then usually served with a sour cream sauce. Dutch

Maatjes herring is made with fresh herring from the first catch of the season, which is lightly cured with salt and sugar and eaten without cooking. The Germans soak salt herring in milk, and then coat with eggs and crumbs to deep-fry in a dish called Gebratene Heringe.

JERUSALEM ARTICHOKE

See THE FOODS OF REGIONAL AMERICA section

KASHA

See BUCKWHEAT AND BUCKWHEAT GROATS

KIRSCH

OTHER: *kirschwasser*

This clear fruit brandy *(eau de vie),* which is made from crushed cherries and their kernels in France, Germany and Switzerland, is available in all well-stocked liquor stores.

STORAGE: It will keep indefinitely if tightly capped and stored in a cool place.

USE: Kirsch, more than any other clear fruit brandy, is called for in recipes. It is widely used in pastry recipes and sprinkled over cold fruit for a simple dessert. It is a traditional ingredient of the Swiss Fondue Neuchâteloise, and in Alsatian sauerkraut dishes, and is essential to Germany's elaborate Black Forest Cherry Torte.

LAVENDER

See HERBS, SPICES, AND SEASONING BLENDS section

LEEK

FRENCH: *poireau* GERMAN: *Lauch* ITALIAN: *porro* SPANISH: *puerro*

Leeks are of the onion family and look like giant thick scallions with ridged leaves. They are plentiful in France, where they are often referred to as "poor man's asparagus." They are expensive in the United States, where they are available only in fine supermarkets and produce markets. Their flavor is more subtle than that of other members of the onion family and they are well worth their price for the fine flavor they add to soups. Look for young ones that are mostly white, and avoid any that have tough center cores or wilted leaves. If they are to be cooked whole, buy them as equal in size as possible.

STORAGE: Store unwashed in a plastic bag in the refrigerator for up to 4 days.

PREPARATION AND USE: Usually only the white part is used in recipes (to avoid adding any color), but the most tender green part is edible as well. Leeks must be carefully cleaned because their layers hold sand and soil. Trim off the tough green top and either discard it or use it for flavoring BOUILLON. Remove any dried outer layers. Trim away a thin slice from the root end. If the leek is to be chopped for a recipe, cut it in half lengthwise. Riffle it as you would a deck of cards to see where any sand may be lurking, then riffle it again under cold running water to rinse the sand away. If the leek is to be cooked whole, leave 2″ of base intact, but quarter the remainder lengthwise, and rinse thoroughly between the layers.

If the leeks are very young and tender they can be sliced or slivered and added raw to salads. When cooked whole, they are tied together to hold their shape and braised or poached lightly in stock just until they are tender, drained, and cooled in a vinaigrette or served as they are with butter. A Romanian recipe marinates cooked leeks in a sweet-and-sour tomato sauce, and a Niçoise version marinates them in olive oil, tomatoes, and garlic. In France, they are, like celery root, sometimes served with a mustard-flavored mayonnaise as part of a selection of *hors-d'oeuvres variés*. Famous dishes that use leeks as an essential ingredient are Scotch Cock-a-leekie (stewing hen cooked with leeks and garnished with cooked prunes), Belgian Waterzooi (creamy chicken or fish stew), and Swedish Färsrulader (leek-stuffed veal roulades).

To use leeks in soups, cut halved leeks crosswise into thin slices and steam them in butter in a covered soup pot until they are limp, then add the BOUILLON and other ingredients called for in the soup recipe. One of the most famous soups based on leeks is Vichyssoise, made with pureed cooked leeks and potatoes, chicken stock, cream, and a sprinkling of chives. It is usually served cold. Potage Parmentier is similar to Vichyssoise, but the green part of the leek is used along with a larger quantity of potatoes and the soup is not pureed. It is served hot as is the very similar Romanian Ciorba. Leeks add a special flavor to all kinds of creamed vegetable soups, as in the following recipe.

BASIC CREAM
OF VEGETABLE SOUP

2 tablespoons butter	For 8 servings

2 tablespoons butter

4 cups any vegetables,* cleaned, peeled if necessary, and
     chopped

1 large leek, halved, cleaned, and thinly sliced

2 ribs celery, chopped

¼ teaspoon salt

2 quarts well-seasoned chicken broth

1 pound baking potatoes, peeled and diced

¼ cup minced parsley (optional)

1 tablespoon chopped fresh herbs of your choice *or* ¾ to 1
     teaspoon dried herbs, crumbled

1 cup heavy cream
    Salt and white pepper to taste
    Optional: freshly grated nutmeg to taste

*Note: Suggested vegetables are broccoli, cauliflower, mushrooms, summer squash, sorrel, spinach, watercress.

Melt the butter in a large, heavy Dutch oven or soup pot and sauté the chopped vegetables of your choice with the leek, celery, and salt over medium heat for a minute or so. Cover and cook over low heat for 5 minutes. Add the broth and potato, bring to a boil, cover, and simmer very slowly for 20 minutes. Add the parsley and herbs and simmer, uncovered, 10 minutes longer.

Ladle 3 cups of soup or so at a time into the container of an electric blender. Blend on "high" until smooth, and pour into a heavy saucepan. Add the cream and season to taste with salt, white pepper, and freshly grated nutmeg if desired. (Season more assertively if the soup is to be served cold.) Bring just to a simmer; remove from the heat.

Serve hot or chilled.

TO PREPARE IN ADVANCE: This will keep in the refrigerator for up to 3 days. Reheat, without boiling, in a heavy saucepan over medium heat, stirring often. The soup can be frozen for up to 3 months; thaw completely and process in an electric blender until very smooth before reheating or serving cold.

LEMON CURD

Lemon curd is a smooth, lemony spread made from lemon juice, eggs, and sugar. An English product, it is available in European markets and specialty food shops in jars.

STORAGE: After opening, it can be stored in the refrigerator for up to 3 months.

PREPARATION AND USE: This is most often used as a spread for bread, but also serves as a filling for tarts or miniature pastries. It is easy to make at home, and a real cinch if you have a microwave oven.

LINGONBERRY

OTHER: crowberry

German: *preiselbeeren*

This is a small, wild variety of cranberry that grows in Scandinavia, Russia, Canada, and Maine. Fresh ones are not sold commercially. Swedish lingonberry preserves are available in 10-ounce jars in European markets and gourmet specialty shops. Cranberries can be substituted in recipes specifying fresh lingonberries.

STORAGE: After opening, preserves can be stored in the refrigerator indefinitely.

USE: In the Scandinavian countries, lingonberries are made into sweet sauces, which are served with Swedish pancakes, omelets and puddings. In Finland, they make a popular sweet fruit soup called Mehukeitto, which is served hot or cold. They are delicious as a filling for French crêpes and make an excellent relish to serve with ham, turkey, or other meats with which cranberries might be served.

LOX

See SALMON, SMOKED

MADEIRA

FRENCH: *madère* GERMAN: *Maderawein* ITALIAN: *vino di Madera*
SPANISH: *vino de Madera*

There are several types of this wine, which is fortified with cane spirit and is a product of the Portuguese-owned island of Madeira. The three that are eminently suited for cooking are Sercial, which is nutty-flavored and very dry, Verdelho, which is medium-dry, and Rainwater, a blend aimed primarily at the American market, which is medium-dry. Two others, Bual and Malmsey, are sweeter and, though they are often served with soups or desserts, are almost never used in recipes.

STORAGE: Capped tightly, Madeira will keep in a cool place for up to 6 months.

PREPARATION AND USE: French cooking makes use of Madeira in flavoring Sauce Espagnole (or basic brown sauce) to make Sauce Madère. This is traditionally served with beef or ham, and mushrooms or truffles are often added. It is equally good with poultry, sweetbreads, or kidneys.

To make it, use approximately ¼ cup of the wine to 1 cup of your favorite rich brown sauce. Simmer the wine first (with minced shallots, if desired) in a small saucepan until it has reduced to ¼ of its original volume—the pan can be almost dry, but take care not to scorch it. Then add the brown sauce and heat to serve.

MARMITE

Marmite is the brand name of a dark-colored brewer's yeast extract flavored with salt, carrots, onions, and spices. It is an English product from the makers of Bovril and is available in gourmet specialty shops and in health food stores in 5-ounce jars. It is a rich source of vitamin B .

STORAGE: Refrigerated after opening it will keep indefinitely.

PREPARATION AND USE: This contains no meat, but ¼ teaspoon can add a rich, meaty flavor to 4 cups of soup or stew. It is often spread very thinly as is, or mixed with butter or margarine, on toast to eat as a snack.

MARRON

See CHESTNUT

MARSALA

Marsala is a fortified Sicilian wine, as widely used in Italian cooking as MADEIRA is in France. The best-known label is Florio, and it can be found in Italian markets and fine liquor stores everywhere. The various types include *all'ouvo* (with egg) and *mandorla* (almond-flavored). It ranges from somewhat dry to sweet.

STORAGE: Like MADEIRA, this has a long shelf life and will keep indefinitely in a cool place if tightly sealed.

USE: Used primarily in northern Italian cooking, this is an essential ingredient for Zabaglione, the sweet frothy pudding whipped up tableside in fancy restaurants from egg yolks, sugar, and Marsala as the sole ingredients. The making of Zabaglione requires constant attention and a special pan, but it is versatile in that it can be spooned over fresh fruit or puddings as a sauce, or cooled and folded into whipped cream to be served as a mousse. In making Zabaglione, any type of Marsala can be used—dry, sweet, or flavored. For most cooking, though, a dry one is preferred. Zabaglione made with dry Marsala and no sugar can serve as a sauce for game birds. The drier Marsalas are often used in veal dishes such as Scaloppini de Vitello al Marsala, and chicken dishes such as Pollo alla Cacciatora. It combines well with game, and chicken livers as well, but is seldom used in fish dishes.

MARZIPAN

FRENCH: *massepain* ITALIAN: *marzapane* SPANISH: *marzapán*

Marzipan is a paste of blanched almonds, sugar, and egg white which is smoother and sweeter than ALMOND PASTE. It is sometimes flavored with vanilla, orange peel, or other flavorings. You will find it in European markets and gourmet specialty shops in cans or plastic tubes. The Odense brand, imported from Denmark in a 7-ounce plastic tube, is a good brand that is widely distributed. Rose essence is usually added to it when making Greek and Middle Eastern recipes.

STORAGE: After opening, wrap airtight to store in the refrigerator for up to 6 months.

USE: A very common flavoring ingredient for cake icings and confections, used in the same manner as almond paste. Exquisite candies, shaped and colored to look like various fruits, are very popular at holiday time. Roses and other flowers are fashioned from marzipan to use as cake decorations. Such confections are sometimes baked briefly to dry the outside surface. Marzipan or almond paste is used as a filling for Swedish Lucia Buns and many European pastries, including French croissants. Small cookies made in France are called *massepains*.

MATZO

See THE FOODS OF THE MIDDLE EAST section

MOSTARDA

OTHER: *mostarda di frutta*

This Italian fruit relish is made from various whole fruits preserved in a syrup of mustard oil and various spices. It may contain pears, cherries, figs, plums, and apricots. It is available at gourmet specialty shops in jars of varying sizes, but in Italy it is sold from the barrel.

STORAGE: After opening, store in the refrigerator for use within a month.

USE: This is served, much like cranberry relish, with cold meats such as ham, tongue, and turkey. We like it with cold salmon or lobster.

MUSHROOMS

DANISH AND SWEDISH: *svamp* FRENCH: *champignons* GERMAN: *Pilz* ITALIAN: *funghi secchi* (dried) POLISH: *grzyby* (wild), *grzyby suche* (wild dried), *pieczarki* (cultivated) RUMANIAN: *ciuperci* RUSSIAN: *griby* SPANISH: *hongos* SWEDISH: *champijons* (cultivated)

Following is a list of European mushrooms available in gourmet specialty shops and through mail-order sources. Fresh European types are seldom sold commercially. Dried mushrooms are, for the most part, imported from Poland, and are excellent because their flavor is actually intensified in the drying process. They have a delicious musky, almost smoky flavor that is unlike any fresh mushroom. We have found it impossible to remove all the sand-like debris contained in the mushrooms and have learned to accept it as a special character of this delicacy. See also TRUFFLES. The fresh, cultivated "field" mushroom is called *champignon de Paris* or *champignon de couche* in France.

STORAGE: Dried mushrooms should be stored in an airtight container in a cool spot or in the refrigerator, and will have the finest flavor if used within a year. They may develop an odor if not tightly sealed but that does not indicate spoilage, and the odor will disappear in cooking. Unopened canned mushrooms can be stored for a year; after opening, they will keep in the refrigerator for up to a week.

PREPARATION AND USE: Dried European mushrooms need to be rinsed well and, even then, you are very likely to find some sand still lurking. We have convinced ourselves that it is part of their charm. We have not had this problem with dried oriental mushrooms. Soak dried mushrooms for 10 to 90 minutes in hot water or stock, depending on their size and age. (Some cooks prefer to soak them for 8 hours or longer in cold water, saying that they retain more flavor with this method.) Squeeze out excess moisture from the soaked mushrooms, rinse well, and cut away any woody stem before using. Usually the soaking liquid, poured through several layers of rinsed cheesecloth to rid it of any grit, is used in the recipe for additional flavor. Save any trimmings and soaking liquid (if not otherwise used) to add flavor to stocks, soups, and sauces.

The following recipe is suitable for any of the mushrooms listed below.

CROÛTE AUX CHAMPIGNONS

For 6 servings

A delicious and rich luncheon dish, or a first course for a dinner menu that features a very simple entrée, such as rack of lamb with buttered vegetables.

6 baked puff pastry shells (patty shells or *vol-au-vents*), homemade or purchased from a bakery
   Minced parsley or chervil to garnish

MUSHROOM FILLING:

1 pound fresh white mushrooms, cleaned and quartered through the stem *or* 1 to 2 ounces dried wild mushrooms*
3 large shallots, minced
4 tablespoons (½ stick) butter
4 teaspoons "instant-blending" flour (Wondra), or regular all-purpose flour
1½ cups heavy (whipping) cream
1 scant teaspoon salt
1 good dash of ground red pepper (cayenne)
⅓ cup dry sherry or Madeira, *or* equal parts cognac and dry sherry
2 teaspoons cold butter

***Note:** Soak dried mushrooms according to directions in the following listings. Strain the soaking liquid and simmer until condensed to utilize as an addition to the sauce.

To make the filling, sauté the mushrooms and shallots in the butter in a large, heavy skillet, stirring often for about 2 minutes. Sprinkle the flour evenly over the mushrooms and stir to blend it. Pour in the cream, salt, and cayenne and stir over medium heat until it begins to bubble. Simmer 3 to 4 minutes until the sauce has thickened and reduced to the desired consistency. Add the sherry or Madeira and simmer briefly to evaporate any of the raw alcohol taste. Remove from the heat; taste, and correct the seasoning. Whisk in the cold butter to finish the sauce and give it a glazed appearance.

To serve, warm the pastry shells in a 350° oven for 5 to 7 minutes to restore crispness. Spoon the hot mushroom filling into the shells. Sprinkle with parsley or chervil and serve immediately.

TO PREPARE IN ADVANCE: The mushroom filling can be made the day before serving except for the final addition of butter. Press plastic wrap into the surface to prevent a skin from forming, and refrigerate. Reheat very gently in a heavy skillet or double boiler.

CÈPE

OTHER: *cep*

LATIN: *Boletus edulis* ITALIAN: *porcini*

These highly prized large-capped brown mushrooms often grow beneath chestnut trees. They are available dried in European markets and gourmet specialty stores by the ounce, and often labeled by their Italian name, *porcini*. Look for large, light-colored ones and avoid any that are crumbly. Italian cookbook author, Giuliano Bugialli recommends the Italian Folci brand as being particularly fragrant. These mushrooms are expensive, but only about one-fourth the cost of MOREL mushrooms and are well worth the investment for their earthy fragrance. The whole caps usually cost twice as much as the sliced. These can be stored for up to 2 years without losing too much flavor.

PREPARATION AND USE: One ounce of dried cèpes will serve 4 to 6 in most recipes for soup, sauce, or stew. Soak these in very hot water for about 20 minutes until softened; squeeze and rinse. Strain the soaking liquid through several layers of fine cloth to rid it of sand.

These provide a superb woodsy flavor and aroma to stuffings, soups, and sauces. In Provence, France, they are sautéed in olive oil, and then topped with chopped onion, garlic, and bread crumbs just before serving. They are used in soufflés, quiches, and all manner of creamy sauces. In Poland, they are used in Bigos, or Hunter's Stew, the national dish of game, assorted sausages, and sauerkraut or cabbage; in Barszcz Wigilijny (Christmas Eve beet soup); and Uszka (tiny ear-shaped dumplings filled with mushrooms). They are used in Hungary, Russia, and Poland in Barley Soup, often in combination with potatoes, sour cream, and dill. A popular German sauce made with these and sour cream is called Schwammerlosse. In Italy, they are sautéed with onion and garlic in butter and olive oil; then their own soaking liquid is added and thickened with flour or roux to make a sauce called Salsa de Funghi to be served with poultry, veal, or pasta.

They are superb when added to fish dishes, and are often cooked with anchovy and lemon to be served on slices of fried bread. They are at their full glory in a delicate, creamy Risotto. Our recipe is adapted from one of cookbook author, Marcella Hazan's.

RISOTTO CON FUNGHI SECCHI

For 6 servings

This is traditionally served as a first course before a simple entree such as sautéed veal.

1   ounce dried cèpes or *porcini* mushrooms
1   quart clear beef or chicken broth
4   tablespoons (½ stick) butter
3   tablespoons vegetable oil
1   large shallot, minced
2   cups Arborio rice (see RICE, ITALIAN)
¼   cup freshly grated Parmesan cheese
   Freshly ground pepper

TO SERVE:
Freshly grated Parmesan cheese

Soak the mushrooms in 2 cups hot water for 30 minutes. Strain through paper towels, reserving the liquid. Rinse the mushrooms and soak again in 2 more cups hot water for 15 minutes, and strain again. Rinse well under cold water. Chop fine.

In a 3-quart saucepan combine the liquid from soaking the mushrooms with the broth. Bring to a slow simmer. Have a 4-ounce ladle next to the pot.

Melt half the butter with the oil in a very heavy pot of at least 3-quart capacity. Sauté the shallot briefly; then add the rice and stir to coat it well. (A wooden spoon is best from this point on, as it won't get hot.) Add a ladleful of the simmering broth mixture and stir for a minute or two until the liquid is absorbed. Add more simmering broth mixture to the rice each time the rice dries out, stirring frequently to prevent sticking. Continue in this manner for about 10 minutes, at which time add the mushrooms. Continue adding the broth mixture until the rice is creamy and nearly tender—it should give some resistance to the bite. Stir in the grated Parmesan and the remaining butter. Add black pepper to taste, and salt if needed, and serve immediately, with extra grated cheese to be passed at the table.

TO PREPARE IN ADVANCE: The risotto can be cooked halfway, to the point where the mushrooms are to be added, and then spread thin on a cold baking sheet. Leave at room temperature for up to 4 hours. To finish the cooking, return to the saucepan, add the mushrooms, and cook, adding simmering broth as above. It will not be necessary to add all the broth for the rice to become tender if prepared in this manner.

CHANTERELLE

OTHER: *girolle*

ITALIAN: *fungo gallinaccio* or *fungo finferlo* LATIN: *Cantharellus cibarius*

Chanterelles are trumpet-shaped, yellow-orange mushrooms with rather frilly caps and little stems that grow wild in France. They can be purchased in European markets and gourmet specialty shops either dried or canned.

The canned ones are not recommended as the mushrooms lose much of their flavor and texture in the process. If dried are not available, substitute CÈPE mushrooms, or one of the Asian varieties of dried mushrooms, such as SHIITAKE or BLACK MUSHROOMS, which are considerably different in color. (See MUSHROOMS, DRIED, in THE FOODS OF ASIA section.)

PREPARATION AND USE: Chanterelles have a fine, though delicate, flavor and a rather spongy texture. They will become tough if overcooked, so you would be wise to add them near the end of the cooking time, or sauté them separately to use as a garnish for many French dishes, such as Suprême de Volaille Poulette (boned chicken breast with a creamy, nutmeg-flavored sauce and mushrooms). They can be served as a main ingredient in a simple sauce of garlic and butter on toast, or with cream and shallots to serve *sous cloche* (under glass), or as a filling for Tartelettes. Use in any recipe calling for cultivated muchrooms, but take care not to overcook.

MOREL

FRENCH: *morille* GERMAN: *Morchel* ITALIAN: *morchella* LATIN: *Morchella esculenta* or *M. vulgaris* SPANISH: *colmenilla*

Morels have tall conical caps rather than flat or dome-shaped tops and are crinkly in appearance, like accordians. They are available either dried or bottled in European markets and specialty shops and are usually the most expensive of all. Look for small ones with dark caps.

PREPARATION AND USE: One ounce will be enough for 4 to 6 servings. Soak them for 20 minutes in boiling water, rinse well, and cut in half lengthwise. Wash several times, and soak again in warm water to allow any remaining sand to fall out. Lift carefully, rinse again, and they are ready to use.

They are usually added to a sauce just before it is finished and only warmed through. These are strong in flavor and can be used in combination with cultivated mushrooms to add a depth of flavor to many dishes. They can be used in all recipes that call for CÈPE mushrooms. They are often used as a flavoring in soups, sauces, potatoes, and scrambled eggs. Many cooks prefer them over any others in *Coq au Vin* (chicken stewed in red wine).

MUSTARD

FRENCH: *moutarde*

Mustard seed and powdered mustard are discussed in the HERBS, SPICES, AND SEASONING BLENDS section. We deal here with the various European prepared mustards to be found in gourmet specialty shops and European markets. All are prepared from a combination of white or yellow mustard seed both of which have distinct flavors, and brown mustard seed, which adds pungency. They are mixed with vinegar or wine; and various flavorings, such as sugar, horseradish, and spices, are added. They come in a variety of containers: tubes, crocks, jars, even coffee mugs.

STORAGE: Prepared mustard, once opened, keeps its optimum flavor longer if stored in the refrigerator, and is best used within 6 months, but can never actually go bad.

USE: Prepared mustard is used directly from the jar as a spread or an ingredient, and it has the same binding effect on mayonnaise as powdered mustard. It, too, may be flavored with any of the aforementioned seasonings, or you can create your own blend.

Following are listings of representative mustards from European countries and more specific uses for them.

DUTCH MUSTARD

Dutch mustards, available in jars and crocks of various sizes in European markets, are generally strong-flavored and tart.

ENGLISH MUSTARD

The finest dry mustard, Colman's, is an English product (see HERBS, SPICES, AND SEASONING BLENDS section). It is available wherever spices are sold, and has recently appeared on the market in a jar as a pungent prepared mustard. Other English prepared mustards are usually rather sweet. Savora is an example, but is not widely available in this country. Crabtree and Evelyn's various grainy mustards are much more bland than French and German types. Mustard is a common flavoring for such dishes as Welsh Rarebit, and Cumberland Sauce to serve with game.

FRENCH MUSTARD

France gives us a wide selection of quality mustards. The name of the city of Dijon has become a generic term for a type of mustard produced there. Dijon mustard, based on white wine, is a basic ingredient of vinaigrettes, mayonnaises, and sauces. Grey Poupon (made in the United States) is a widely distributed brand, and is the one most often specified in French recipes. When added to a sauce of reduced cream and shallots it makes a spicy accompaniment to grilled steaks, kidneys, and pork. Other well-known and fine quality brands are Amora and Maille.

Bordeaux mustard, not commonly found, is darker and earthier and complements spicier dishes, such as sausages.

Coarse-grained mustards, which contain crushed mustard seeds, are very good with pâtés, sausages, and peasant-style dishes, such as Choucroute Garni (sauerkraut with assorted meats and sausages). The Pommery brand, sold in variously colored stoneware jars, boasts several kinds of Moutarde de Meaux: grainy; with peppercorns; and "extra strong," all sold in 9- to 17½-ounce crocks.

There are varieties of flavored mustards being newly imported from France that have green peppercorns, lemon, tomato, and various herbs added. They are considered a condiment and are not intended for use in recipes. They are usually expensive and we urge you to make your own, beginning with a good Dijon-style mustard and adding whatever flavor suits the dish with which it will be served.

The use of mustard in cooking is demonstrated in the following recipe.

CHICKEN SUPRÊMES IN MUSTARD CREAM

For 4 servings

This has a flavor of the French countryside, especially if you use the coarsely seeded type of French mustard called Moutarde de Meaux. Again, we've applied a Chinese technique of marinating the chicken before cooking to make it superbly tender and succulent.

2 whole chicken breasts, skinned and boned
1 tablespoon cornstarch
1 egg white
1 teaspoon sherry or white wine
¾ teaspoon salt
½ stick (4 tablespoons) butter
2 large shallots
1 cup dry white wine, dry vermouth, or champagne
1 cup heavy (whipping) cream
⅓ cup Moutarde de Meaux (or other coarse-textured
     mustard)

TO GARNISH AND SERVE:
Sprigs of fresh watercress

Remove the tendons and trim the chicken breasts neatly. This part of the chicken is called the *suprême*.

In a glass pie plate or other shallow dish, combine the cornstarch, egg white, sherry or wine, and salt, beating with a fork until well combined. Marinate the chicken breasts in this mixture for at least 20 minutes or for up to 2 hours, turning them over from time to time.

Within 20 minutes of serving, melt the butter in a medium-sized heavy skillet and add the chicken breasts and the shallots. Sauté chicken breasts briefly on each side. (Take care not to scorch the shallots as they burn easily.) Add the wine or champagne, cover the skillet, and cook gently for 10 minutes.

Remove the chicken with tongs and keep warm. Boil the cooking liquid over high heat until it has reduced to about ⅓ of its original volume. Stir in the cream and simmer, uncovered, for about 5 minutes until it reaches a sauce consistency. Lower the heat under the pan and whisk in the mustard. Bring to a simmer, but do not let it boil hard or the sauce may separate.

Taste, and correct the seasoning. Transfer to warm serving plates or platter. Garnish with sprigs of fresh watercress and serve immediately.

TO PREPARE IN ADVANCE: Bone and prepare the chicken the day before and wrap tightly for refrigerator storage. Marinage no longer than 2 hours and cook just before serving.

GERMAN AND BAVARIAN MUSTARDS

There are many German mustards, but the ones most often imported to this country are generally rather dark, musty, and strong-flavored. Imported Düsseldorfer Senf is extra hot and good. Inglehoffer is a domestic brand of this type. German mustards are excellent accompaniments to sausages and sauerkraut.

SCANDINAVIAN MUSTARD

Smooth and sweet, these are often flavored with dill to complement the various dishes served on a Smörgasbord, and on open-face sandwiches. An example is Konditeri. German-style mustard is used in Sweden to make Gravlaxsås, a sweet, dill-flavored sauce that accompanies GRAVLAX, salt-cured salmon.

NOODLES

See PASTA

OLIVE, EUROPEAN

FRENCH: *olive* GERMAN: *Olive* ITALIAN: *oliva, uliva* SPANISH: *oliva, aceituna*

Olives are native to the Mediterranean, with Spain and Italy competing to be the largest producer. Olives are either green (picked before they have ripened) or black (allowed to ripen on the tree). The green *manzanilla* olive of Spain, sometimes called a "Spanish" olive, is a small variety widely cultivated in the United States, and often stuffed. The *Sevillana* or "Queen's olive" is a very large variety of green olive also widely cultivated in the United States. Mediterranean-style olives which look shriveled and have a distinctly different flavor from our usual domestic type of olive, can be found in gourmet specialty shops and ethnic markets, in brine or coated with oil, and those sold in bulk are much finer than those that are bottled and canned. Greek olives (see OLIVES, MIDDLE EASTERN, in THE FOODS OF THE MIDDLE EAST section) are often easier to find, are excellent, and can be substituted. California black and green olives, found in every supermarket, are plump and smooth-skinned and are less pungent than Mediterranean-style olives. Following this entry are some of the Mediterranean-style olives you are most likely to find, and specific suggestions for their use.

STORAGE: Bottled or canned olives, once opened, should be stored in a nonmetal container in the refrigerator. Depending on their type and the strength of the brining solution, they will keep well for a week to 6 months, but grow softer the longer they have been stored. Loose olives can be stored up to a month in their original brine in the refrigerator. If white film forms on the surface, it should be wiped away. If loose olives become soft, they are spoiled and should be discarded.

PREPARATION AND USE: Green olives are used mostly as a garnish and flavoring, but are often stuffed with almonds, anchovies, capers, pimiento, and other savories. Black, or "ripe" olives, packed in brine or oil, may be mild, or dry and shriveled with a smoky taste. In Italy, as in Middle Eastern countries, they are very popular as an appetizer *(antipasto),* and green olives are popular as an ingredient in uncooked pasta sauces. In Sicily, green olives are stuffed, breaded, and deep-fried as an appetizer. In France, especially in Provence, green olives are enjoyed plain or stuffed with capers, anchovies, etc., as an appetizer, but are also used in the making of stews as are black olives. In Spain, green olives are often cooked with tomatoes, onions, and almonds in a sauce used for chicken.

OLIVES CASSÉES

Olives cassées are broken and brined green olives often flavored with fennel and orange rind, that are a specialty of Nice.

USE: Popular as an antipasto, but often cooked as a garnish for game birds.

OLIVES NIÇOISES

These tiny Provençal olives, ranging from brown to purple to black, have been cured in brine and then packed in olive oil with HERBES DE PROVENCE (see HERBS, SPICES, AND SEASONING BLENDS section, under SEASONING BLENDS). They are available in jars, sometimes labeled "olives noires de Niçe," and they have not been pitted. Gourmet specialty shops have them packed in large canning jars, which make attractive serving containers. Substitute oil-packed olives from Italy or Greece, but remove the pits.

USE: These are used primarily as a garnish for salads, or placed on the table as an accompaniment to meals. They are cooked as well, in some French stews.

OLIVES FARCIES

Olives farcies are green olives that have been stuffed with capers or anchovies (or both), almonds, and the ubiquitous pimiento. They are available in Mediterranean markets packed in brine or in olive oil.

USE: Stuffed olives tend to be very salty. They are served primarily as an appetizer or as an accompaniment to cocktails. Pimiento-stuffed olives are often sliced to use as a colorful garnish.

OLIVES PIQUÉES

Olives piquées are shriveled black olives that have been salted to draw out their juices, and then packed in olive oil with seasoning. These are occasionally found in Mediterranean delis. They are used in the same dishes as Niçoise olives with some difference in flavor. They often garnish Pissaladière, an onion tart garnished like an Italian Pizza, which is a specialty of Nice, and flavor Tapenade, the name for a tuna-based Provençal dip, spread, and sauce. If you have purchased dry, oil-packed black olives, such as the Moroccan type, which are bitter or too strongly flavored for your taste, simmer them for 5 to 10 minutes and drain before use.

OLIVE OIL

FRENCH: *huile d'olive* ITALIAN: *olio di oliva* SPANISH: *aceite de oliva*

The consumer has many qualities of olive oil to choose from. Most favored among fine cooks is the dark green, fruity oil from the first pressing of the olives, called "extra-virgin" or "fine-virgin." These superior-quality olive oils are imported from France or Italy. They are available only in gourmet specialty shops and fine Mediterranean markets, and are very expensive. Guiliano Bugialli, Italian-cooking expert, says that Goya, a Spanish brand, is closest to the fine Tuscan oil he favors. Marcella Hazan, Italian cookbook author, recommends highly the fruity oil from Sicily called *Madre Sicilia* or *Due Sicilie*. Of lesser quality is "pure" olive oil, from the second pressing of the olives, which is lighter in color and blander in flavor than "virgin." This is the best kind to use for most cooking purposes. Examples of this type of oil are Bertolli and Berio, Italian brands that are available in supermarkets almost everywhere. Mediterranean markets will also have excellent oils of this type from Italy, Spain, and Greece. They each have a slightly different taste, so we suggest that you buy small quantities of several brands to taste for yourself. Olive oil, like wine, should be chosen by personal preference. Avoid any so-called "imported" olive oil with no indication of the country of origin.

STORAGE: Light is harmful to olive oil so always store it in a cool, dark place. We decant our fine oil into a green glass, fish-shaped Italian wine bottle with a cork, which looks festive in our kitchen, but also prevents spoilage from ultraviolet rays. Stored properly, fine olive oils will keep for a year, but if you are a miser with your olive oil, go against the advice of experts and store it in the refrigerator. It will become cloudy, but will clear as it comes to room temperature; the flavor will be intact and you will not have to worry about having rancid oil.

PREPARATION AND USE: Olive oil is not recommended for frying because it has a low-smoke point. The finest "virgin" oil is used solely in cold dishes, or is poured over hot dishes just before seving so that the rich flavor can be fully savored. Use the finest oil in dishes that feature it as a major ingredient, especially in salads and simple pastas, such as Aglio e Olio (literally "garlic and oil"). Use lesser quality oils in robust dishes where the flavor will be dominated by other ingredients. In Italy, olive oil is very often served as a table condiment for diners to pour over salads and other dishes.

Olive oil is especially delicious with summer foods: tomatoes, onions, garlic, basil, and other fresh herbs. It is used in cooked dishes such as Caponata (tomato-eggplant relish with capers), Ratatouille (Mediterranean vegetable stew), Bagna Cauda (warm garlicky anchovy dip for vegetables, popular in Italy and southern France), Paëlla (saffron rice garnished with chicken and seafood), and in Mediterranean dishes too numerous to mention. It is the primary cooking oil of Greece and much of the Middle East.

ORANGE, SEVILLE

OTHER: bitter orange, sour orange

FRENCH: *bigarade* SPANISH: *naranja agria*

Seville oranges have a tough, dark red-orange skin and are widely grown in the Mediterranean and Caribbean areas. They are inedible when raw, but have a splendid flavor when cooked. This is the type of orange used in making the finest orange-flavored liqueurs such as Grand Marnier, Cointreau, and Curaçao. Fresh ones can occasionally be found in specialty produce markets and in Caribbean and Korean markets during January and February, but they are generally unavailable. Ask the produce manager of your supermarket if they can be ordered. They may not be stocked simply because there is not much demand. Diana Kennedy makes a Mock Seville Orange Juice, which

THE FOODS OF EUROPE

she terms a "slightly inadequate substitute" for use in recipes that call for it by combining 3 tablespoons orange juice, 3 tablespoons grapefruit juice, 2 tablespoons lemon juice, and 1 teaspoon finely grated grapefruit rind. This yields ½ cup.

STORAGE: Seville oranges can be stored in a paper bag in the lowest part of the refrigerator for up to 3 weeks. For longer storage, squeeze the oranges and place the juice in a nonmetal container along with some of the finely grated peel (zest) and store in the freezer for a year or longer.

USE: The English consider marmalade made from Seville oranges to be the finest of all, and they import large quantities of these oranges for that purpose. The French, when they can find them, use the finely grated rind (zest) and juice of this orange to flavor their rich brown Sauce Bigarade, which is served with duck. In southern France, they also dry the peel to use in a BOUQUET GARNI by stripping off just the outer peel and leaving it to dry for three days in an airy place. The oranges are widely used in meat and poultry dishes in the Caribbean and the Yucatán, in such dishes as Pollo en Pibil (chicken cooked in a banana leaf), and JÍCAMA (see THE FOODS OF LATIN AMERICA section) Salad with CILANTRO (see CORIANDER, in the HERBS, SPICES, AND SEASONING BLENDS section).

ORGEAT

(ohr-ZHA)

FRENCH: *sirop d'orgeat*

This sweet, opaque syrup flavored with sweet and bitter almonds is available in well-stocked liquor stores. It contains no alcohol.

STORAGE: After opening, it will keep indefinitely stored in a cool place.

USE: This is used to add an almond flavor to beverages and dessert sauces, and is the secret ingredient in tropical punches and cocktails such as Mai Tais.

PANCETTA

(pahn-CHET-ah)

Pancetta is an Italian bacon (not smoked), seasoned with pepper and rolled tightly into a sausage shape. When unrolled, it is about ¼" thick and a mixture of fat and lean. Buy it in an Italian deli where there is a good turnover of goods because, if it is stored too long, it can become rancid. If you cannot find a source for it, substitute salt pork into which you have pressed some cracked black pepper, and don't bother to blanch out the salt because pancetta is salty.

STORAGE: It is best to store this in the freezer if you have no immediate use for it, though it will keep in the refrigerator for up to 3 weeks.

PREPARATION AND USE: Because GUANCIALE (cured pork jowl), the traditional flavoring ingredient of Carbonara Sauce, is not available in this country, we use pancetta instead. It is combined with tomatoes and rosemary in an uncooked pasta sauce. We prefer it cooked as a flavoring ingredient for meat sauces and vegetables, as in the following recipe.

BAKED PEAS WITH PANCETTA

For 8 servings

These cook in the oven right in their serving dish.

2   cloves garlic, peeled
2   tablespoons olive oil
¼   cup pancetta, diced in ¼" cubes
2   (10-ounce) packages frozen tiny peas, frozen or thawed
2   tablespoons minced parsley
    Salt and pepper to taste

In a casserole, sauté the garlic in the oil until browned. Remove and discard the garlic. Sauté the pancetta for a minute or so and remove the pan from the heat. Let cool.

Add the peas to the casserole, breaking up any solid lumps if frozen. Cover tightly (using foil under lid if lid is not secure) and bake at 375° for 45 minutes if peas are frozen; for 15 to 20 minutes if thawed. Stir in the parsley and the salt and pepper; serve immediately.

TO PREPARE IN ADVANCE: If your casserole is a freezer-to-oven type, the peas can be placed in the baking dish with the oil and pancetta, and stored in the freezer until ready to bake.

PASTA

"Pasta," which is the Italian word for paste, has become a generic term for all varieties of spaghetti, macaroni, and noodles but, according to U.S. Government standards, spaghetti and macaroni products are not required to contain eggs, whereas "noodles" must contain 5.5 percent egg solids. Cookbooks list over 500 varieties of pasta *fresca* (fresh pasta) and pasta *secca* (dried pasta) which are, in many cases, whimsically named by the Italians. In addition, many of the traditional shapes will have the Italian terms *rigati* and *riccie* tacked onto their names. These refer to texture. *Rigati* denotes "grooved" pasta and *riccie* denotes pasta with a ruffled edge.

Gourmet delis throughout the United States are now carrying fresh pasta, so that those who don't enjoy making it or don't wish to pay restaurant prices can enjoy it at home. You will find it available in colors ranging from red to orange to green depending on which pureed vegetable is used to color the dough. Dried pasta is found everywhere, but the imported De Cecco brand, available in various shapes and sizes, is very widely distributed and is excellent.

Chinese EGG ROLL WRAPPERS, and the smaller WON TON skins, can be used as fresh pasta dough for making small shaped and filled pastas at home. They are available in Asian markets and many supermarkets in the refrigerator sections. (See THE FOODS OF ASIA section for general information.)

STORAGE: Fresh pasta should be refrigerated and used as soon as possible. It can be frozen for up to 2 weeks; it becomes brittle if frozen longer. Dry pasta will keep in a cool, dry place for months.

PREPARATION AND USE: One pound of dried pasta serves 6. One pound of fresh pasta serves 4. To cook pasta, use at least 6 quarts of boiling water, 2 tablespoons of salt, and a tablespoon of oil (to prevent the water from boiling over) for each 1 pound of dried pasta or 2 pounds of fresh pasta. The water should be boiling fiercely. (At high altitudes, add 1 teaspoon baking soda per 1 gallon of water for a faster boil.) Add the pasta slowly so that the boiling temperature is maintained. Spaghetti and long noodles can be added to the water as if playing a game of pick-up-sticks—when released they fall in all directions.

Test the pasta often for doneness. The time it takes to cook will vary according to thickness of the pasta and whether it is fresh or dried. It should always be cooked *al dente*, literally "to the tooth," or firm. This will take less than a minute for fresh pasta, 5 to 10 minutes for dried. When almost done, drain immediately into a colander. (It will continue to cook just a bit.) It is not necessary to rinse pasta if you have used sufficient water. Drain well and return it to the empty cooking pot with a lump of butter or a drizzling of olive oil and toss lightly to coat it. (It can, of course, be tossed with your chosen sauce at this point, but the addition of butter or oil will prevent the pasta from sticking together if it must stand for any length of time.)

We have tried every conceivable way to cook pasta in advance. We even tried undercooking it considerably, but in vain. There is no way to keep cooked pasta firm and fresh-tasting for any length of time. Leftover pasta can, of course, be reheated, and often is in restaurants, but the firm texture is lost.

To use EGG ROLL WRAPPERS or WON TON skins (see THE FOODS OF ASIA section), wipe off their coating of cornstarch with a dry towel and follow directions for filled pastas found in Italian cookbooks.

In Germany, egg noodles (*Nudeln*) are very popular and are almost always homemade. They may be tossed with butter or bacon fat to serve, or may be further seasoned according to the dish they accompany with paprika, poppy seeds, dill, pieces of ham or crisp bacon, sour cream, or cottage cheese. Thin noodles are used in soups, and all sizes are molded into rings to be filled with stews. Sweet noodle puddings are served as desserts or as accompaniments to meats served with sweet sauces, such as ham or tongue. In Poland, pasta dough is stuffed with sausage or sauerkraut to make Pierogi to serve in broth. In Czechoslovakia, noodles (*holvshki*) are often tossed with chopped cooked cabbage and bacon drippings.

In Hungary, pasta squares (*metélt*) are often served and can be approximated by cutting fresh or dried 1″ wide noodles into squares. They are often seasoned with paprika and tossed with cooked new potatoes and sautéed onions to accompany roast meats. These or fresh egg noodles (*galuska*) are a "must" with Gulyas (goulash), the famous Hunter's Stew.

Russians eat tiny stuffed noodles, similar to but smaller than Italian ravioli, called Pelemeni. A stuffed turnover of dough often with a sweet filling, served as a dessert, is called Vareniki.

Scandinavian countries serve noodles with their delicate meatballs coated in creamy dill sauce.

In European and American Jewish cooking, noodles are used to make Kugel (noodle pudding) to serve on Sabbath and holidays. These usually contain ingredients such as dried apricots, raisins, chopped apples, nuts, and sugar, and flavorings such as vanilla, lemon peel, and cinnamon. Kugel contains cottage cheese, cream cheese, or sour cream, only for the holiday of Shavuot or Pentecost.

In France, noodles (*nouilles*) are especially important in the regional cooking of Alsace and Provence. Fresh herbs are sometimes added to the noodle dough. They may topped with sauces, as in Italy, or accompany stews, roast lamb, and pork. In Nice, they are topped with a mixture of chopped ham, fresh herbs, and garlic, which has been barely warmed in fruity olive oil. Or they may be tossed with garlic and several kinds of cheeses.

And in Italy, plain noodles are occasionally served in place of Risotto Milanese, the traditional accompaniment to Osso Bucco, veal shanks braised in tomato sauce with a topping of lemon peel, garlic, and parsley, and in our simple version using cubed veal, which we call Veal Stew alla Milanaise. But usually they are sauced with cream and cheese, with cooked or uncooked tomato sauces, or simply with olive oil and garlic.

As a general rule, meat sauces are served with the shaped pastas, such as shells and gnocchi, which capture the pieces of meat or sausage for easier eating. The long, smooth types are used for thinner sauces, which cling.

Following are brief descriptions of some of the shapes you will find.

Agnolotti: Half-moon shaped turnovers stuffed with meat or vegetable filling, sometimes available frozen in Italian specialty markets. They are traditionally tossed with butter and grated Parmigiano, or used in soups, like dumplings.

Bows or **Bow-Ties:** See FARFALLE

Bucatini: This hollow spaghetti is sometimes called *perciatelli* (or "pierced"). It is available in dried form in most Italian delis. It is often served "all'Amatriciana," with a sauce of tomatoes, GUANCIALE or PANCETTA and grated *pecorino romano* (see CHEESE, PECORINO).

Cannelloni: Flat squares of fresh pasta which are rolled around a stuffing, and then sauced and baked. There is a tubular shape of dried cannelloni, which is more an American invention than Italian. It would be preferable to use lacy French *crêpes* or EGG ROLL WRAPPERS if fresh pasta squares are not available (see THE FOODS OF ASIA section).

Capelli d'Angelo: The literal meaning of the name is "angel hair." This is very thin, fresh or dried, pasta often found on the menu of fine restaurants. It is at its best in a rich meat broth with a sprinkling of freshly grated Parmigiano.

Cappelletti: The name means "little hats." These are stuffed fresh pasta, similar to ravioli, with a filling of veal, pork, or ham. They are sometimes available frozen in Italian specialty markets. They are served in soups, tossed with butter and Parmigiano, or with a simple tomato sauce.

Cavatelli: This is a rippled pasta shell sometimes called "gnocchi" by pasta manufacturers. It is available in a dried form in most Italian delis and makes an interesting alternative to the more popular grooved "shell." We like it with a chicken liver and tomato sauce as in the following recipe.

CAVATELLI CARUSO

CARUSO SAUCE: For 2 to 4 servings
- 2 tablespoons butter
- 2 tablespoons olive oil
- 8 medium-sized fresh mushrooms, quartered
- 1 small clove garlic, minced or pressed
- 1 large shallot, minced
- ½ pound chicken livers, cleaned and cut into quarters
- 2 ripe tomatoes, skinned, seeded, and diced, *or* 1 cup
      canned crushed tomatoes
- ¾ cup dry white wine *or* ⅔ cup dry vermouth
- 1 teaspoon coarse Kosher salt (or ¾ teaspoon regular salt)
- ½ teaspoon fresh rosemary, *or* ¼ teaspoon dried rosemary, crushed
- ½ teaspoon ground black pepper

TO SERVE AND GARNISH:

12 ounces dried cavatelli *or* other pasta shape of your choice,
     cooked according to package directions
 1 tablespoon butter
 2 tablespoons minced fresh parsley
     Freshly grated Parmesan

To make the sauce, heat the butter and oil in a large skillet over medium heat. Add the mushrooms, garlic, and shallot, and sauté for 2 to 3 minutes, stirring often. Add the chicken livers and sauté 2 to 3 minutes longer. Stir in the remaining sauce ingredients and bring to a simmer. Cover the pan and cook slowly for 10 minutes.

Cook the cavatelli according to package directions. Drain and return to the cooking pot with butter and parsley, tossing to coat thoroughly. Divide the pasta among warm serving plates. Spoon sauce into the center of each mound of cavatelli. Pass freshly grated Parmesan at the table.

TO PREPARE IN ADVANCE: The sauce will keep well in the refrigerator for up to 3 days or in the freezer for a month. Reheat gently just until warm, adding water to thin if the sauce seems dry.

Conchiglie: The name means "conch" or "sea shells." The ridged type with which most of us are familiar are called conchiglie *rigate*. The small cavity of this and the other shell-shaped pastas, such as CAVATELLI, are ideal for trapping meat, pieces of vegetables, or sauces. Large shells are usually stuffed; the tiny ones used in soup. This pasta is also called *maruzze*.

Ditali: The name means "thimbles." This is actually a macaroni, which is cut shorter than the elbow macaroni with which we are all familiar. It is sometimes called "salad macaroni" and is used in salads and soups.

Egg Barley: Also called Farfel, this is a Hungarian-style noodle shaped like grains of barley. It is sold in supermarkets and Jewish food stores. Streits is one widely distributed brand. The "fine" is used in soup, the "coarse" as ORZO for which it can be substituted. It is often toasted before use to intensify its flavor, and this can be done at home by spreading it in a baking pan, placing it in a 350° oven for 15 to 20 minutes, and shaking the pan from time to time to brown it evenly. It is cooked like any pasta, just until tender, and then tossed with butter or SCHMALTZ (see under CHICKEN FAT in THE FOODS OF REGIONAL AMERICA section) and seasonings. Milton Williams, one of Los Angeles' finest caterers, makes a soufflé with this, as in the following recipe.

BARLEY SOUFFLÉ

For 10 to 12 servings

This is a sturdy soufflé to serve as a starch with roasts, steaks, or other plain meats.

- 7 ounces egg barley, cooked according to package directions, and drained
- ½ pound butter, softened
- 3 ounces cream cheese
- 1 pint (2 cups) sour cream
- 6 large eggs, separated, at room temperature
- 3 tablespoons fresh lemon juice
- 2 teaspoons sugar
- 1¼ teaspoons salt (use your favorite seasoning salt if desired)
- ¼ teaspoon freshly ground black pepper
- 1 additional teaspoon lemon juice, for beating the egg whites

Butter a 2½- to 3-quart soufflé dish or two 5- to 6-cup soufflé dishes. Preheat the oven to 375°. Cook barley according to package directions.

In a large mixing bowl, whisk the butter and cream cheese until smooth. Whisk in the sour cream, yolks, lemon juice, sugar, and seasonings. (The mixture will look like waffle batter at this point.) Stir in the cooked, drained barley and set aside.

In the grease-free bowl of an electric mixer, beat the whites with the 1 teaspoon lemon juice until they form soft peaks, at the point where they still do not slide when the bowl is tilted. Fold half of the beaten whites thoroughly into the barley mixture. Carefully fold in the remaining whites. Pour into the prepared soufflé dish.

Bake in the center of the oven for 20 minutes; then lower the heat and bake 30 to 40 minutes longer. (If using the two smaller soufflé dishes, bake 10 minutes at 375°; then lower the heat and bake about 20 minutes longer.) Serve at once.

TO PREPARE IN ADVANCE: Soufflés should be served immediately as they collapse soon after leaving the oven. This has more body than most, and can even be reheated for late arrivals.

Elbow: Any of the tubular pastas may be cut into 1″ to 2″ lengths to form small semicircles. They are widely used in baked casseroles, such as Greek Patstitsio, and Macaroni and Cheese.

Farfel: See EGG BARLEY

415

Farfalle: These are "butterflies" that look like bows. *Farfallone* are the largest; *farfallette* are small; and the smallest are *farfalline*. Large ones are often served sauced; the smaller ones are served in soups. They are used in Kasha Varnishkas (see BUCKWHEAT and BUCKWHEAT GROATS).

Fettuccine: "Small ribbons," the Roman term for egg noodles, usually about ³⁄₈" wide, available fresh or dried. These can substitute for noodles in any recipe. In Italy, fettuccine is served with many sauces: creamy, as in Fettuccine all'Alfredo, or with a sauce of Gorgonzola; buttery, as in Fettuccine col Rosmarino with garlic and rosemary; or with "white" or "red" clam sauce. We like spinach fettuccine served with a walnut cream sauce.

Fide: A very fine German egg noodle.

Fideos: Very fine Spanish noodles similar to fine VERMICELLI. They are often cooked and then fried to serve with vegetables in Spain. In Mexico, they are used to make Sopa Seca ("dry soup").

Fusille: Cookscrew-shaped "twists," often called *rotini* or "spirals." This pasta shape is good with thick, creamy sauces, but not with fluid or oil-based sauces. We created the following sauce especially for this pasta.

CREAMY CLAM SAUCE
FOR PASTA

20	medium-sized fresh clams, scrubbed and soaked For 4 servings for 2 hours in cold water
2	cups water
1	tablespoon butter
2	cups rich fish *fumet* or substitute*
1	(8-ounce) bottle clam juice (or liquid from steaming the fresh clams)
½	cup vermouth or ⅔ cup dry white wine
2	cups heavy (whipping) cream
2	egg yolks, at room temperature
2	to 3 teaspoons fresh lemon juice Salt and ground red pepper (cayenne), to taste

TO GARNISH AND SERVE:

12	ounces fusille, or other shaped pasta of your choice, cooked *al dente*
2	teaspoons fresh snipped chives or Chinese garlic chives (see CHIVES, CHINESE)

***Note:** Fish *fumet* (concentrated broth) is easily made with lean fish trimmings obtained without charge from the fish markets if you make a purchase.

A quick substitute can be made from 1 cup bottled clam juice, 1 cup clear chicken broth, and ⅓ cup white wine or ¼ cup dry vermouth, which should be simmered uncovered for 5 to 10 minutes to evaporate the alcohol in the wine.

Bring water to a boil for cooking the pasta according to package directions.

Steam the clams in a heavy pot with 2 cups water for 10 minutes or so until they all open. (Do not lift the lid for the first 6 minutes or the steam will escape.) Meanwhile make the sauce.

Sauté the shallots briefly in the butter in a heavy saucepan. Add the *fumet*, clam juice and vermouth. (When the clams have opened, strain their broth and set the clams aside, covered with foil to stay warm.) Boil the mixture over high heat until it has reduced in volume to about ¾ cup. Stir in the cream and simmer slowly for 5 minutes. During this time, cook the pasta according to package directions.

To finish the sauce, stir a bit of the hot fumet mixture into the two beaten egg yolks to heat them slowly, lower the heat under the saucepan to the lowest possible setting, then stir the yolk mixture into the remaining fumet mixture whisking constantly until thickened. Do not let the sauce boil or it will curdle. Remove from the heat. Stir in the lemon juice, and salt and cayenne to taste.

Spoon the sauce over the drained pasta on warm plates. Top with the clams in their open shells and sprinkle with chives. Serve immediately.

TO PREPARE IN ADVANCE: The sauce can be made ahead of time if you opt for bottled clam juice over the broth obtained by steaming the clams. If so, freeze that broth for use next time you make this. The sauce can be reheated in a double boiler or in a microwave oven if care is taken not to overheat and curdle the sauce.

Galuska: Hungarian term for fresh egg noodles.

Gemelli: These "twins" look like a rope of twisted spaghetti.

Gnocchi: See under separate entry, GNOCCHI

Holvshki: Czechoslovakian term for egg noodles.

Lasagne: Wide strips of pasta which are layered in casseroles with meat or vegetable fillings, usually with Salsa Balsamella and Bolognese sauce. In the United States, Lasagne is traditionally made with a Tomato-Sausage sauce. The dried form available in all supermarkets is thick with ruffled edges. We think it is much too thick. The pleasure of making one's own pasta is truly evident when cutting lengths of very thin fresh pasta dough in strips to fit the pan and not having to cook the pasta before layering it with the fillings.

Linguine: The name, which means "little tongues," refers to the tapered edges of this long, narrow pasta. It is widely available in its dried form. It is often served with "white" or "red" clam sauce, with PESTO, or with broccoli and cream sauce, as in the following recipe.

LINGUINE WITH BROCCOLI

	For 4 servings
2 tablespoons butter	
1 small onion, minced	
1 large bunch broccoli, flowers and small tender stems only, finely chopped	
2 cups heavy (whipping) cream	
1 teaspoon salt	
Freshly grated nutmeg, to taste	
Cayenne (ground red pepper), to taste	
12 ounces dried linguine, cooked according to package directions	
¼–½ cup freshly grated Parmesan cheese	

In a heavy medium-sized sauté pan, melt the butter and sauté the onion until transparent. Add the broccoli, toss with the butter and onion. Cover and cook slowly for 3 to 4 minutes. Remove the lid and pour in the cream. Cook uncovered, about 5 minutes, until the cream has thickened to a sauce consistency. Season to taste with salt, freshly grated nutmeg, and cayenne.

Drain the pasta and toss immediately with the hot sauce. Serve with freshly grated Parmesan cheese.

TO PREPARE IN ADVANCE: Best when freshly made, but can be covered and set aside for up to 2 hours; then reheated to serve.

Lumache: A variety of shell-shaped pasta, more dome-like than CONCHIGLIE. *Lumachine* are "small snails."

Macaroni: See MACCHERONI

Maccheroni: This is the Italian spelling of macaroni. The -*ini* suffix indicates "small" macaroni; the -*oni* indicates "large." A very tiny variety is called *maccheroncelli*. That which is labeled *lisci* is smooth; *rigati* is ridged. This type of small, hollow pasta is popular in southern Italy with tomato sauce. The large size is combined in Maccheroni al Forno with tomato sauce, mushrooms, grated Parmigiano, and Salsa Balsamella to be baked in a casserole in the oven. Small macaroni is often baked in a Timbale (mold) like a custard to serve as a starch with meals.

Mafalda or **Mafalde:** A broad noodle with both edges rippled. It looks like a narrower form of the dried LASAGNE noodles.

Manestra: Greek rice-like pasta similar to ORZO.

Manicotti: The name means literally "small muff," and in Italy often refers to small, stuffed pasta like CAPPELLETTI. However, the shape seen throughout the United States is a giant ridged tube of pasta, about 1″ in diameter larger than dried CANNELLONI. The ends are usually cut on the diagonal. It is an American invention not appreciated in Italy. It is usually parboiled for 5 minutes, stuffed with cheese or veal filling, and then baked with a meat, tomato, or cream sauce.

Maruzze: See CONCHIGLIE

Metélt: Hungarian pasta squares, which can be approximated by cutting fresh or dried 1″ wide noodles into squares. They are often seasoned with paprika and tossed with cooked new potatoes and sautéed onions to accompany Gulyas and other stews.

Mostaccioli: "Small mustaches," which are the same thing as *penne* (quills). These are straight tubes with diagonally cut ends. We are fond of this pasta with many types of smooth sauces.

Noodles: A generic name for ribbon-like pasta. "Noodles" refers to all types and sizes of dried egg noodles sold in all supermarkets and ethnic markets in varying widths from narrow to extra-wide. According to U.S. Government regulations, they must contain at least 5.5 percent egg solids. (Pasta products not designated "noodles" need not contain eggs.)

Nouilles: French term for noodles.

Nudeln: German term for noodles.

Occhi di Lupo: Large tubes called "wolf eyes" that look like giant MACCHERONI, and can be stuffed like CANNELLONI or MANICOTTI.

Orzo: The name of this rice-shaped pasta means "barley." We enjoy it served in place of rice, especially when tossed with butter and grated Parmigiano.

Pastini: This term covers a large variety of tiny pastas that are served in soups. Examples are *anellini* ("little rings"), *stellini* ("little stars"), *acini* ("peppercorns"), *funghini* ("little mushrooms"), *tubetti* ("tiny tubes").

Penne: See MOSTACCIOLI

Ravioli: Stuffed pasta "pillows," available frozen in Italian delis and gourmet specialty shops. Fillings consist of meat, vegetables, cheese or combinations of these. They are served with a thin tomato sauce and grated Parmigiano, or with butter or meat sauce. One can purchase for some home pasta machines attachments for making these from two strips of pasta dough.

Rigatoni: Very large, grooved pasta tubes, almost as large as MANICOTTI, but shorter and with straight-cut ends, which hold together beautifully in baked dishes, even if overcooked. This is hearty fare. One famous dish, Rigatoni Ripieni, consists of this pasta stuffed with tuna and ricotta cheese and baked with a creamy Parmigiano sauce.

Rotelle: "Small wheels," a variation of the corkscrew-shaped FUSILLE, often served with tomato or tomato and sausage sauce. Occasionally this refers as well to the wheel-shaped RUOTE DI CARRO pasta.

Rotini: See FUSILLE

Ruote di Carro: "Cartwheels," a wheel-shaped pasta that is very popular in southern Italy. Sometimes called simply **Ruote.**

Shells: See CONCHIGLIE

Spaghetti: Literally "strings." **Spaghettini** is a smaller version. In Venice, it is called *bigoli.* This is the most commonly sauced pasta in Italy, though Marcella Hazan, Italian-cooking authority, says it is rarely if ever served with a meat sauce (that distinction falls to TAGLIATELLE) and *never* with meatballs. One of the easiest and most popular ways to serve it is with a simple sauce of olive oil in which chopped garlic and mashed anchovies have been sautéed.

Spirals: See FUSILLE

Tagliatelle: The Bolognese term for a ribbon-shaped egg noodle like FET-TUCCINE, but generally wider and not as thick. It varies in width from ¼" to ¾". It is a specialty of Bologna and is traditionally served with meat sauces. When made of both egg and spinach pasta, it becomes Paglia e Fieno, "straw and hay."

Tarhonya: Hungarian egg noodles shaped like grains of barley. They are traditionally browned in lard with minced onions and paprika to serve with meat dishes. (See EGG BARLEY.)

Tortellini: A small, ring-shaped, stuffed pasta, rounder and smaller than CAPPELLETTI, which is sometimes whimsically referred to as "Venus's navel." It is widely available frozen with a variety of fillings. It is usually filled with veal or chicken, and seasoned with nutmeg. It is served in clear broth (see CONSOMMÉ), as in Tortellini in Brodo, or with a rich creamy Alfredo-style sauce flavored with nutmeg. It is sometimes filled with ricotta cheese and parsley and served with a tomato sauce.

Tubettini: Tiny tubes used in soup.

Vermicelli: Literally "little worms." This is the southern Italian name for SPAGHETTI. In the United States, the term refers to very thin, dried spaghettini.

Ziti: Literally "bridegrooms." This is a tubular pasta available in several variations: *rigati* (grooved), *tagliati* (cut), to name a few. It is often served baked with cheese or, as in Modena, with turkey, mushrooms, and sour cream, in a dish called Ziti con Petto di Tacchino.

PASTRY, PUFF

FRENCH: *pâte feuilletée*

An exceptionally fine French pastry dough is made by wrapping cold butter inside cold dough, and then rolling it out and folding it several times. When baked, it puffs to several times its original height and separates into many layers of crisp, buttery pastry, giving a "thousand leaf" effect. Making the pastry the classic way is arduous and tricky, and even making the so-called Mock Puff Pastry requires a good amount of practice and skill. Fortunately the unbaked dough can be purchased from fine French pastry shops by the pound, though this may require advance ordering. There is at least one brand of commercial puff pastry available frozen in supermarkets throughout the United States. It is, however, made with vegetable shortening instead of butter, so it lacks the desired flavor. Excellent directions for making the classic version of Mock Puff Pastry appear in Volume II of *Mastering the Art of French Cooking,* by Julia Child and Simone Beck. We prefer to buy prepared dough from a fine French bakery.

STORAGE: Wrapped airtight with plastic wrap, then overwrapped with foil, the dough should be refrigerated for use within a few days. It freezes beautifully for up to a year, and should be thawed slowly in the refrigerator for 24 hours.

PREPARATION AND USE: Two pounds will make 2 average entrée recipes, 16 patty shells, or 1 or 2 large vol-au-vents. The trimmings are not wasted as they can be cut into small squares or rectangles to make appetizers called Feuilletés or Bouchées (tiny patty shells to be filled with savory or sweet fillings), patty shells, and vol-au-vents (large oval or round patty shells to be filled with creamed seafood, ham, or poultry), as well as elaborate pastries, like Napoleons. So much can be done with it—from creating small bite-sized appetizer turnovers filled with ham or Roquefort cheese, to an elaborate version of leek and cream-filled Flamische. The trick to making this dough puff as much as possible is to have it well chilled before placing it in a very hot oven. Consult French cookbooks and pastry books for more ideas. A perfectly ripened whole Brie cheese can be wrapped in it to bake and serve as a main course.

PERNOD

(pehr-NOH)

Pernod is a yellowish, anise-flavored liqueur, similar to absinthe, but made without wormwood. It is named for the family who first produced absinthe. It is available in all well-stocked liquor stores.

STORAGE: It will keep indefinitely at room temperature.

USE: This is often specified in French recipes to add a mild licorice flavor to fish stews and soups. It should be used judiciously for its flavor can be overpowering. It is often the secret ingredient in French bouillabaisse, and in Oysters Rockefeller, a New Orleans creation, though whether it was used by the creator of the recipe, Antoine Alciatore of Antoine's restaurant, shall remain a secret.

PESTO

OTHER: *pesto alla Genovese, battuto alla Genovese*

One of Italy's most outstanding sauces is an uncooked paste of fresh sweet basil, *grana* cheese (such as Parmigiano, Romano, or Sardo), garlic, nuts (pine nuts or walnuts), and the finest olive oil. It is a specialty of Genoa, dating back to the time of Virgil. Pesto is available in the frozen-food sections of Italian delis and some supermarkets all year, and can be excellent. The canned or bottled type, which is not refrigerated, is not recommended because the flavor suffers greatly in the canning process.

STORAGE: Store fresh or frozen Pesto in the freezer for a year or longer. It is most convenient to freeze it in small quantities so only the required amount need be thawed.

PREPARATION AND USE: Pesto is not cooked. One cup of room-temperature Pesto will serve 4 when tossed with hot, drained pasta. It is also served as a condiment with soups such as minestrone, as a pizza topping, and even as a spread for toasted, buttered rolls. It makes an excellent seasoning for cooked vegetables, scrambled eggs, and baked potatoes. Combining ¼ cup of Pesto with ¾ cup of mayonnaise makes the best dip for freshly cooked shrimp imaginable. We use it as a quick seasoning sauce for freshly cooked vegetables such as green beans or thinly sliced zucchini.

Fresh basil is available in supermarkets during the summer, and is one of the easiest herbs to grow. We suggest you use it to make the following recipe.

PESTO

For 2 cups or 8 servings

This is traditionally made in a marble mortar, but is much more easily made in an electric food processor.

  2   cups firmly packed fresh basil leaves (no substitute)
  ½   cup parsley, leaves only
  ½   cup "extra-virgin" olive oil
  ¼   cup long slender pine nuts *or* walnuts
  2   cloves garlic, peeled
1¼   teaspoons salt
  ¾   cup freshly grated Parmesan cheese (up to half this
        amount can be Romano if desired)
  4   tablespoons (½ stick) butter, at room temperature

TO SERVE:
  1   pound dried pasta, any shape

Combine the basil, parsley, olive oil, pine nuts, garlic, and salt in the container of a blender or food processor. Process at high speed, stopping the motor occasionally to scrape down the sides of the container with a rubber spatula. When well blended, add the grated cheese and blend only a second or two to mix. Add the soft butter; blend only for a second or two longer. Do not overblend or you will lose the crumbly texture of the Parmesan.

Serve Pesto on hot drained pasta after thining it with about a tablespoon of the water in which pasta was cooked. Toss to coat evenly and serve immediately.

Use also as a flavoring for soups, cooked vegetables, and Pesto Mayonnaise, which can be used as a dip for shellfish or raw vegetables, or as a dressing for chicken or seafood salad.

TO PREPARE IN ADVANCE: Freeze Pesto (before the addition of grated cheese and butter) in small jars. To thaw, set the jar in warm water, stirring until softened; then proceed as directed. Leftover Pesto can be refrigerated for up to a week or frozen for up to 3 months.

PINE NUT

OTHER: Indian nut, pigñon nut, pinocchio

FRENCH: *pignon* GERMAN: *Piniennuss* ITALIAN: *pignolo* LATIN: *Pinus Pinea* SPANISH: *piñon*

There are two kinds of tiny cream-colored pine kernels that are widely used in cooking. (See also PIÑON NUT in THE FOODS OF REGIONAL AMERICA section for more information.) The most prized is the Portuguese type, which is from the parasol-shaped stone pine tree that grows throughout the Mediterranean. These are long and slender nuts that are oily and have a delicate pine taste. They are widely used in the cooking of Europe and the Middle East. They are available here in Mediterranean markets and health food stores and are always very expensive. Another pine nut is the Chinese type, which is broader at one end than the other. It is available in the same stores as well as in Asian markets and is always 30 to 50 percent less expensive than the Portuguese type. It has a much stronger, almost turpentine, flavor and is not nearly as highly prized.

STORAGE: Both types are oily and become rancid very quickly. Wrap tightly and store in a cool place, or the refrigerator, for use as soon as possible. We always freeze those we won't be using right away, though some cooks claim that freezing changes their texture.

PREPARATION AND USE: Both types can be used in dishes without cooking, but their flavor is greatly enhanced when roasted until golden. Spread them on a baking sheet and toast at 350° for 8 to 10 minutes.

Pine nuts have a great affinity for spinach, eggplant, and roast peppers. In Italy, these are a traditional ingredient in PESTO. They are also used a great deal in stuffings, sauces of all description, and desserts. In Spain and Portugal, they are cooked with Bacalao (COD, SALTED AND DRIED) along with raisins in a tomato sauce, in chicken dishes, Paella, and in a great number of sweet dishes. The Middle East uses them in pilafs, stuffed vine leaves, and sweet puddings. The Chinese use them in chicken dishes, and they are featured in a Korean dish called "Steamboat."

POLENTA

"Polenta" is an Italian term for a type of cornmeal that is a staple starch in northern Italy. It is sold in Italian markets in fine and coarse grinds. American cornmeal can be substituted. White water-ground CORNMEAL (see THE FOODS OF REGIONAL AMERICA section) can be substituted in equal measure. If using regular yellow cornmeal, use 1⅓ cups for each 1 cup polenta specified in a recipe. (The term can also apply to other flours and meals.)

STORAGE: The primary polenta dish is a type of mush, which is served topped with cheese, tomato sauce, and sausages, or even with sweet sauces. It is used to make Roman Gnocchi, and a Romanian dish called Mamaliga, and is eaten in place of bread with most soups and stews, and often layered with cheese and sour cream.

POPPY-SEED FILLING

This is a sweetened paste of poppy seeds available in 12-ounce cans in European and Jewish markets and gourmet specialty shops.

STORAGE: After opening, transfer contents to a nonmetal container and store, tightly covered, in the refrigerator. It will keep for up to a month.

USE: This is used as a filling for strudel and various pastries in Germany and Hungary, and for the Jewish three-cornered pastry, Hamantaschen.

POTATO STARCH

OTHER: potato flour, fecula

FRENCH: *fécule de pommes de terre* NORWEGIAN: *potetmel*

This is a starch-like flour obtained from grinding dried potatoes. It can be found in health food stores, European markets, and in many supermarkets.

STORAGE: Store in an airtight container in a cool place for up to 6 months.

PREPARATION AND USE: It is blended to a paste with water like other starches (cornstarch, arrowroot, etc.) and stirred into simmering liquids, becoming translucent and lending a glossiness to the liquid as it thickens it. Like other starches, it should not be cooked much after it has done its job because it breaks down and loses its binding power if overheated.

Potato starch gives a pleasant potato taste to the liquids in which it is used, and is especially good for creamed soups. It is often used in European cooking, and in Jewish cooking especially, in cakes and as a thickener for soups and sauces. It is especially recommended for those on a gluten-free diet.

PRALIN

OTHER: praline paste

OTHER FRENCH: *praliné*

Pralin is a sweet powder or paste made of sugar that has been caramelized and mixed with toasted almonds or hazelnuts, and then finely ground. It is usually homemade, but can be purchased in some gourmet specialty shops, cake supply shops, or through mail-order sources.

STORAGE: Stored in an airtight container in the freezer, it will keep for up to a year.

PREPARATION AND USE: Pralin is a very common ingredient in French pastry creations, used to flavor buttercream icings, custards, and mousses. It is sprinkled over custards, ice cream, or cakes. It is not difficult to make.

PRALIN

1½ cups almonds, filberts, walnuts, or pecans,   For 2 cups
     with or without skins
1½ cups granulated sugar
     Oil to coat a baking sheet

There are two ways to make pralin. The nuts can be toasted and stirred into caramelized sugar, or the untoasted nuts can be caramelized along with the sugar. Both methods work equally well: the first is safer, the second quicker.

Method 1: Spread the nuts on a baking sheet and bake at 350° for 20 minutes, stirring from time to time, until they are toasted and browned. Set aside. In a heavy, 3-quart saucepan, combine the sugar with ¼ cup cold water. Place over medium-high heat and bring to a boil without stirring. Cook without stirring, but swirl the pan by the handle from time to time, until the syrup is dark golden and caramelized. Remove from the heat, stir in the nuts to coat them completely, then turn out onto an oiled baking sheet.

Method 2: Combine sugar and nuts in a heavy saucepan. Cook over very low heat, stirring constantly, until the sugar turns dark golden. Turn out onto an oiled baking sheet.

When cool, break into small pieces. Depending on use, the pralin may be ground to a powder in an electric food processor or blender, or coarsely crushed by placing inside a plastic bag and pressing with a rolling pin.

PRALIN CREAM

For 4 servings

Pralin Cream is a quick dessert which is, perhaps, the easiest way to use pralin.

1½ cups heavy (whipping) cream
½ to ¾ cup powdered pralin, to taste

Beat the cream in a chilled bowl with chilled beaters just until it holds a soft shape. Use a large rubber spatula to fold the pralin gently into the cream. Spoon into dessert dishes. Serve with fresh fruit if desired.

TO PREPARE IN ADVANCE: Refrigerate up to 4 hours before serving.

PRESERVES

There are great varieties of jams, jellies, marmalades and "butters" to be found in European markets. These include preserved Cloudberries or Lingonberries from Sweden; Rose Petal Jelly, Morello Cherry Jam, and Chestnut Spread from France; Seville Orange Marmalade and Ginger Marmalade from England; Prune Lekvar and Apricot Butter from Hungary. They are now found in all gourmet specialty shops.

STORAGE: After opening, they can be stored in the refrigerator for 6 months or longer. Sugar is a natural preservative, and all of these items contain a good deal of sugar.

USE: All kinds of cakes and cookies are made using these preserves as a filling.

PROSCIUTTO
See HAM

PUFF PASTRY
See PASTRY, PUFF

PUMPERNICKEL
OTHER: Westphalian rye bread

See also SCHWARTZBRÖT. Pumpernickel is a coarse, dark bread made of rye flour, which has been allowed to rise and cook very slowly so that the natural sugar in the flour darkens and sweetens the bread evenly. Purchase it freshly made from a European bakery. The original German Pumpernickel was made of 100 percent rye flour, but most sold in the United States contains whole wheat flour and cornmeal. Flavorings such as chocolate, beer, and spices or orange peel are often added, and potatoes are a very common ingredient to make the bread moist. There is a widely available, non-yeast type of pumpernickel that you will find in loaves in the refrigerator sections of supermarkets.

STORAGE: Bread that isn't to be used right away is best stored in the freezer. If pre-sliced, it is easy to separate and thaws almost instantly.

PREPARATION AND USE: Pumpernickel is often used in stuffings and as an accompaniment to sausages and cheeses. The small, thin slices are ideal for serving with appetizer spreads such as Liptauer Cheese. This type of bread is traditional for Scandinavian open-faced sandwiches, which are often accompanied by a sweet, dill-flavored mustard sauce. A German dessert called Götterspeise is made by folding ½ cup each of pumpernickel crumbs and grated sweet chocolate into 2 cups sweetened and flavored whipped cream to make 4 servings.

QUATRE ÉPICES

See HERBS, SPICES, AND SEASONING BLENDS section, under
SEASONING BLENDS

RAPE

OTHER: broccoli rabe

FRENCH and SPANISH: *colza* GERMAN: *Raps* ITALIAN: *colza,
brocoletti di rapa*

Rape is a very sharp-flavored green, a relative of cabbage and somewhat similar to turnip greens. In the United States, it is used primarily as animal fodder and tends to be more strongly flavored than the kind found in the markets of Italy. You will find it only in specialty produce markets where there is a large Italian population. Look for fresh looking leaves and tiny yellow buds. Its seeds are the source of rapeseed oil, which is sometimes used as a cooking oil in Europe and the Middle East, but which nutritionists claim is harmful to health.

STORAGE: Rinse, shake dry, and wrap in a paper towel to store in a plastic bag in the crisper of the refrigerator for up to 4 days.

PREPARATION AND USE: To cook, remove any roots and tough ribs and soak in cold water for 30 to 60 minutes. Drain and press out excess water; then chop coarsely and sauté in olive oil, seasoned with cooked minced onion or garlic. Cover and steam slowly for just a few minutes until tender. A final sprinkling of grated Parmigiano will do no harm at all. Any that is left over can be dressed with vinaigrette to serve as a salad the next day. The flavor borders on bitter so this requires assertive seasoning. The tiny, broccoli-like flowers can be removed to sauté with garlic, tomato, and fresh herbs to serve separately as a vegetable, or to toss with warm, cooked pasta.

428

RICE, ITALIAN

ITALIAN: *arborio* or *vialone*

Arborio has become a generic name for the pearly rice grown in the Po Valley of northern Italy. It is named for the village in the humid rice-growing Piedmont region where it is grown. It is shorter and rounder than American short-grain rice, and is the preferred rice to use in all Italian cooking. Specialty food shops and Italian markets always have it. Second choice is *vialone,* which is slightly smaller.

STORAGE: It will keep, stored in an airtight container in a cool, dry place, for a year or longer.

PREPARATION AND USE: Arborio can be cooked in the same manner as other types of rice, but is at its finest when prepared as Risotto. To prepare this way, it is cooked briefly in butter or oil with flavorings; then simmering broth is added, little by little, and it is stirred almost constantly for 20 minutes or longer until the rice is tender and very creamy. It is always served with freshly grated Parmigiano.

Fine Italian cookbooks have recipes for Risotto in many variations. For instance, the famous Risotto alla Milanese is flavored and colored with saffron, but other common additions are seafood, Marsala, beef marrow, chicken livers, ham or mortadella, and dried mushrooms (a recipe for the last appears under MUSHROOMS, CÈPE). We love this dish because we can prepare it from whatever broth and bits of leftovers and garden herbs we have on hand. We have made Risotto with other kinds of rice, but it lacks the velvety, creamy quality that makes the dish so special. This type of rice is used in many Italian desserts, such as Budini di Riso (baked rice cakes) and Ciambella di Frutta (rice ring filled with wine-marinated fruit), and is a common ingredient in Italian soups. It can be boiled like other rices (see RICE, in THE FOODS OF ASIA section for general information).

ROSE HIPS

DANISH: *hyben* GERMAN: *Haggebutten* SWEDISH: *nypon*

These tart, red, bulbous fruits of the dog rose are available, dried, in health food stores and in some German and Scandinavian markets. In America, they are usually processed into vitamin C tablets, or used for tea, but in Europe they are used fresh or dried in cooking.

STORAGE: In an airtight container in a dark place these keep well for up to 6 months, but lose flavor on standing.

PREPARATION AND USE: In Denmark and in Germany, these are mostly made into preserves to be served with meat or game. Because the rose hips are low in pectin, apple is usually cooked with them. They are also used to flavor sauces and soups. A cold Danish soup called Hybensuppe, served as a first course or as a dessert, is made by soaking 8 ounces (about 2 cups) of dried rose hips in 6 cups water overnight. The juice is then strained, simmered, and thickened with 1½ tablespoons cornstarch and sweetened to taste with honey. It is then chilled and served with whipped cream and toasted almonds. A hot soup, Hagebuttensuppe, popular in Germany, is made in the same manner but is spiced with cinnamon, cloves, and white wine.

RYE

FINNISH: *ruis* FRENCH: *seigle* GERMAN: *Roggen* ITALIAN: *segala* SPANISH: *centeno* SWEDISH: *rag*

Rye, a grass cultivated for its cereal grain, is native to Europe, and provided for many years the primary grain used in European bread making. Rye groats (whole grain) and grits (coarse, medium, or finely cracked grain) are sold in health food stores. Pure rye flour is grey in color, and may be labeled "light" or "dark"—the light has been sifted and some of the bran has been removed, making it less nutritious. Widely distributed brands found on supermarket shelves are Fisher, Pillsbury, and Stone Buhr. Rye is also used in the making of rye whiskey and a Russian alcoholic drink called *kvass*. Pepperidge Farm makes a sprouted rye bread that is nationally distributed. In the west, Good Stuff Bakeries makes a Natural Sourdough Rye Bread and Rolls, as well as Pumpernickel Bread and Rolls. There is Cream of Rye cereal, and a rolled rye, which is similar to oatmeal.

STORAGE: Whole or cracked rye, or rye flour can be stored in an airtight container in a cool place for up to a year.

PREPARATION AND USE: Coarsely cracked rye can be prepared in exactly the same way as Kasha (see BUCKWHEAT AND BUCKWHEAT GROATS), to serve as an accompaniment to meat or vegetable dishes. For cereal, allow ½ cup of uncooked cereal and 1 cup liquid (milk or water) per serving. Bring the liquid to a simmer with a pinch of salt, stir in the cereal, reduce heat and cook without stirring until tender, about 20 minutes. Harvest time is celebrated in Finland with bowls of rye porridge called Ruispuuro.

Rye bread is *the* bread to serve with German and Central European sausages, and with hearty Russian stews and soups. Swedish Limpa (known as Vörtlimpor), a rye bread that is almost cakelike, containing candied orange peel and anise, is traditionally served at Christmas. Rye flour is used not only for PUMPERNICKEL and rye breads, but to make superb rye dumplings, which are steamed on top of sauerkraut as in the following recipe.

RYE BREAD DUMPLINGS

For about 12 slices or 6 servings

Other breads, white or wheat, can be substituted.

4 tablespoons (½ stick) butter
3 cups of ½" cubes of light rye bread that has been trimmed
  of crusts
¼ cup minced onion
⅔ cup all-purpose flour
2 tablespoons minced parsley
½ teaspoon salt
⅓ cup milk

Melt 3 tablespoons of the butter in a heavy skillet. Add the bread cubes and toss them with the butter, stirring until toasted. Remove from the pan.

Add the remaining butter and sauté the onions in the same skillet until they are transparent and just beginning to brown. Place in a mixing bowl, sprinkle with the flour, and toss to combine. Stir in the parsley, salt, and milk. Mix until smooth; then lightly but thoroughly mix in the toasted bread cubes. Let stand 30 minutes.

Divide the dough in half and form into 2 rolls, each about 6" long and 2" in diameter. Place in a skillet half filled with gently simmering water and poach for 30 minutes, turning them over once. Drain on paper towels. Cut into ½" slices to accompany soups or stews.

SALMON, CURED

FINNISH: *riimisuolainen lohi* NORWEGIAN: *gravlaks* SWEDISH: *gravlax* or *gravad laks*

This salmon, which has been cured with salt, sugar, and dill, can be purchased in Scandinavian delis, where it is usually called by its Swedish name, Gravlax. It is a Swedish specialty and one of the finest of Scandinavian delicacies. It is easy to make whenever fresh salmon is available. In Norway, it is traditional to add a bit of cognac to the cure.

STORAGE: Refrigerated, it will keep for up to a week.

PREPARATION AND USE: Gravlax is served as part of a Smörgasbord, on Scandinavian open-faced sandwiches, or as an appetizer with chilled aquavit, almost always accompanied by a sweet, dill-flavored mustard sauce, and toast triangles. When served as a main course, a crisp cucumber salad accompanies it along with boiled potatoes, Swedish Limpa Bread, and sweet

431

butter. The skin from the cured salmon is traditionally sautéed and served as a side dish with the Gravlax. Cut in serving pieces, the cured salmon is often barbecued over a wood fire in individual aluminum-foil packages, which are left open so the fish will develop a slightly smoky flavor. We like it raw or barbecued, thinly sliced, as a filling for miniature crêpes made in a Swedish pancake *(plätt)* pan. When fine fresh salmon is available, we hope you will make the following recipe.

GRAVLAX AND GRAVLAX SÅS

GRAVLAX: For 8 or more servings

2–3	pounds center-cut salmon fillets with skin
½	cup sugar
¼	cup coarse (Kosher) salt
⅓	cup coarsley chopped fresh dill
2	teaspoons crushed white peppercorns

GRAVLAX SÅS:

½	cup dark, spicy mustard (such as Gulden's or one of the German brands)
2	teaspoons dry mustard
⅓	cup sugar
¼	cup wine vinegar, red or white
½	cup vegetable oil
3–4	tablespoons finely chopped fresh dill

Remove any bones and wipe salmon dry with paper towels. Combine the sugar and salt in a small bowl; rub about one-fourth of this mixture into the salmon pieces. Sprinkle one-fourth of the mixture over the bottom of a porcelain or glass dish and top with one of the salmon fillets, skin-side down. Sprinkle with the dill, peppercorns, and most of the remaining sugar-salt mixture. Top with the second fillet, skin-side up, followed by the remaining sugar and salt.

Cover the fish with a piece of plastic wrap and weight down with a plate or dish on which a heavy can or saucepan has been placed. Refrigerate for 6 hours, and then pour off the accumulated juices from the dish. Return to the refrigerator, still weighted, for at least 48 hours for the curing process to be completed.

To serve, cut into very thin diagonal slices across the grain, freeing it from the skin. (The skin is traditionally sautéed in butter and rolled up to serve as a garnish.) Arrange the slices of Gravlax on a large serving board or on individual dishes. Serve with toast points or thinly sliced dark bread, sliced cucumbers, and the Gravalax Sås.

To make the sauce, whisk together the two mustards in a small mixing bowl. Beat in the sugar and vinegar and then, very gradually, beat in the oil, a few drops at a time, until all has been ac ded and the sauce has the consistency of mayonnaise. Stir in the dill.

TO PREPARE IN ADVANCE: The salmon will keep for up to 2 weeks in the refrigerator. The sauce can be refrigerated as well—if it separates on standing, whisk or shake vigorously until recombined.

SALMON, SMOKED

FRENCH: *saumon fumé* NORWEGIAN: *royktlaks* RUSSIAN: *kopchennaya losos*

The very finest smoked salmon comes from Scotland, and is known as Scotch Salmon, with that from Nova Scotia, Denmark, and Norway being very close in quality. It is raw, but cured with salt and lightly smoked, which gives it a rosy, translucent appearance and a delicate taste of wood and ocean. These fine varieties are available in gourmet specialty shops, and they are very expensive.

Lox, a Jewish specialty, is smoked salmon that has been soaked in a brine containing sugar. It is sold in delicatessens and in many supermarkets. It is saltier than the Scotch smoked salmon. The cut from the underpart of the salmon is called "belly lox," and is fatter, saltier, and less expensive than the choice center cut. Lox "trimmings" are sold for use in recipes; they have excellent flavor but poor appearance.

STORAGE: Smoked salmon or lox should be wrapped airtight for refrigerator storage of up to a week, or can be kept for up to 6 months if sliced and stored in a jar of peanut oil in the refrigerator. Freezing changes the texture.

PREPARATION AND USE: Usually thinly sliced as an elegant appetizer, allowing about 3 ounces per person, this should be served as simply as possible. Slice thin, but not so thin that it falls apart. The slices are overlapped on a serving platter and served with cracked pepper and lemon wedges. Usually the fine French *nonpareille* capers are served, or other condiments such as finely minced onion, chopped hard-cooked egg, and olive oil. Lox is traditionally served with cream cheese and bagels. In Scandinavia, smoked salmon is an important part of Smörgasbords.

In cooking, smoked salmon is used in recipes for mousse or as a quiche or omelet filling. An easy pâté-like spread is made by combining 12 ounces of smoked salmon (trimmings are fine) with 8 ounces sweet butter and 1 tablespoon lemon juice in a food processor fitted with the steel blade. Puree until smooth, transfer to a serving container, and top with a layer of sour cream and a sprinkling of black caviar, fresh dill, or capers. We sometimes add 6 ounces of thinly sliced smoked salmon to 4 servings of Fettuccine Alfredo just before serving.

SALTPETER

OTHER: potassium nitrate, Prague powder

Saltpeter is a chemical used in brines for hams and bacon and is added to sausages and luncheon meats for the sole purpose of preserving a pink color. It is specified in most sausage recipes, and is sold in pharmacies in powdered form. Sausages made without it are grey or brown.

STORAGE: It will keep indefinitely in an airtight container on the pantry shelf. If exposed to humidity, it will lump.

PREPARATION AND USE: The usual amount to use in making sausages is ¼ teaspoon of the powder to 6 cups of combined meat and fat. This is a chemical that is best used in small quantities because too much will toughen meat. It can be omitted from recipes with no effect upon taste or quality, but will have a considerable effect on color.

SAUCES, FRENCH

"Saucier" is a trade name for a line of basic sauces sold frozen in gourmet specialty shops and some supermarkets. They are made of natural ingredients, are quite good and are, naturally, expensive. They are convenient, though for busy cooks. At least three types are available: Beef with Tomatoes (which substitutes in recipes for basic brown sauce, or Demi-Glace and Sauce Espagnole), Bordelaise (brown sauce with wine and mushrooms), and Fish with Lobster. Such basic sauces are also easy to make at home, and recipes are found in any French cookbook.

STORAGE: If frozen, they should be used within 3 or 4 months. Defrost in the refrigerator. If leftover sauce is to be refrozen, add some water to thin it and simmer it for 5 minutes first to destroy any bacteria.

PREPARATION AND USE: These are not salted, so will probably taste bland. They are not intended to be used as they are, but to be the base for other sauces, which are usually made at the last minute from whatever pan juices are created by the cooking of meat, fowl, or seafood. For instance, Steak au Poivre Vert can be created very easily by sautéing 2 individual steaks in clarified butter in a skillet to the desired degree of doneness, then removing them to a warm platter and stirring a few chopped shallots into the pan drippings, adding healthy splashes of brandy and Burgundy, and cooking over high heat until the liquid has almost evaporated. Stirring 1 cup of basic brown sauce (Beef with Tomatoes) into the pan with 2 teaspoons of green peppercorns and heating through finishes the preparation, except for a final taste for seasoning and the addition of 1 teaspoon cold butter stirred in after the pan is removed from the heat to give the sauce a lovely glaze. The whole process doesn't take more than 10 minutes, so one can see what a convenience it is to have such sauces on hand. The Bordelaise sauce is used in the same way for beef, chicken, or veal dishes. The Fish with Lobster sauce acts as a base for other fish sauces, and also as a base for stews such as Bouillabaise. The following is a very quick version of brown sauce made with canned broth rather than the traditional browned veal bones.

QUICK BASIC BROWN SAUCE

For 1 quart

This is not a finished sauce, but an ingredient to use when Brown Sauce or Sauce Espagnole is specified in a recipe.

¼ pound (1 stick) butter
1 large onion, finely diced
2 medium carrots, scraped and finely diced
¼ cup chopped parsley (leaves or stems)
1 large clove garlic, smashed with the side of a knife
1 teaspoon chopped fresh thyme *or* ¼ teaspoon dried, crumbled
½ cup all-purpose flour
3 (10¾-ounce) cans condensed beef broth or bouillon, *or* 1 quart homemade beef broth
3 cups water
1 cup mixed wines (we use ¼ cup sherry or Madeira, ⅓ cup chablis, and a red Burgundy to make 1 cup)
1 bay leaf
1 stalk celery
2 tablespoons tomato paste
1 whole clove
½ teaspoon beef extract *or* 1½ teaspoons Maggi seasoning
Black pepper to taste

Melt the butter in a heavy, 4-quart saucepan. Add the next five ingredients and cook, stirring often, until they start to brown. Stir in the flour, and continue cooking, stirring often, until the mixture (or roux) turns a pale tan color. (Be careful not to scorch the flour or it will not thicken the sauce properly.) Stir in the remaining ingredients. Bring to a boil; then lower the heat and simmer gently, uncovered, for 40 minutes, stirring occasionally. Strain.

TO PREPARE IN ADVANCE: When cool, freeze in ice-cube trays, and then transfer the frozen cubes to plastic bags for freezer storage. Any required amount can then be quickly thawed.

SAUERKRAUT

FRENCH: *choucroute* GERMAN: *Sauerkraut* ITALIAN: *salcrautte* SPANISH: *chucruta*

Sauerkraut is shredded cabbage that has been salted with pickling salt (and sometimes with flavorings such as caraway or juniper berries) and allowed to ferment in its own juice. Though known as a German specialty, it may have originated either in China or Ancient Rome, where salting-preserving of vegetables for winter use was a common practice. Sauerkraut is sold in supermarkets and ethnic markets in bottles, cans, and sometimes in plastic bags. German markets have imported wine-simmered sauerkraut in cans. Kraut is sold from barrels in some ethnic markets, and homemade versions are sold in delicatessens. Homemade sauerkraut takes about three weeks to stop bubbling, indicating that it has finished the fermentation process.

STORAGE: Because it's pickled, kraut keeps for a long time. It can be stored in its original liquid in a nonmetal container in the refrigerator for a month or longer.

PREPARATION AND USE: Allow about 32 ounces sauerkraut for 4 servings. Sauerkraut can be served raw as a pickle relish, but is usually cooked. Always taste before cooking. If it is too salty, rinse in a strainer or soak in cold water for 10 to 15 minutes, then drain. Kraut is best when it is moist, but not soupy. Sauté kraut (purchased in bulk or in a bag) briefly in a stainless or enamel saucepan in a bit of fat, and then simmer, covered, with broth or white wine just to cover for 10 to 20 minutes until tender. Bottled or canned kraut is usually precooked (read the label) and needs only be simmered for 5 to 10 minutes in broth or wine. We often add applesauce to the cooking liquid, which gives it a mellow sweetness, but all kinds of seasonings can be tossed in as well: bacon drippings, onion, garlic, bay leaf. In Hungary, cooked kraut is sauced with a mixture of sour cream, flour, and a pinch of sugar.

Sauerkraut is a German specialty often served as a garnish or vegetable with sausages and other meats and with potatoes or dumplings, though we are told that more is consumed in France than in Germany. The French make a splendid dish called Choucroute Garnie, which takes kraut to its highest glory. A famous Polish dish, Bigos (Hunter's Stew), also contains a variety of meats and sausages. We like it especially with a creamy sauce as in the following recipe.

SZÉKELY GULYÁS

1	pound sauerkraut, fresh, canned, or packaged	For 4 servings
2	pounds lean, boneless pork, cut in 1″ cubes	
2	tablespoons rendered pork fat	
1	large onion, minced	
1	clove garlic, minced	
2	tablespoons sweet Hungarian paprika	
3	cups chicken or beef broth	
2	teaspoons caraway seeds	
1	ripe tomato, peeled, seeded, and pureed *or* ½ cup canned tomato puree	
1	cup sour cream	
1	tablespoon cornstarch	
1–2	tablespoons fresh lemon juice, to taste	

Rinse the sauerkraut well under cold running water. Taste, and if too salty, soak for 10 to 15 minutes in cold water. Drain well. Trim fat from the pork and cook the fat in a heavy (not iron) stew pot over medium heat until melted. Discard all but 2 tablespoons of the fat.

Sauté the onions in the fat until they are transparent. Add the garlic and paprika and cook for a few seconds longer; then add 1 cup of the broth, and caraway seeds. Stir in the pork cubes and then distribute the rinsed sauerkraut evenly over the pork. Stir the tomato puree into the remaining broth and pour over the sauerkraut. Bring to a simmer; then reduce the heat to very low, cover, and simmer very slowly for 1 hour, or until the pork is tender. Check the amount of liquid in the pot once or twice toward the end of the cooking time to make sure there is enough, adding water if necessary.

Combine the sour cream and cornstarch in a mixing bowl, whisking until well blended. Stir into the pot over very low heat, whisking just until thickened. Do not boil. Remove from heat and add lemon juice. Taste, and add salt and pepper if needed.

Serve in deep plates, with additional sour cream to garnish if desired.

TO PREPARE IN ADVANCE: This can be refrigerated for up to 3 days. Reheat very gently in a double boiler or microwave oven.

SAUSAGE

FINNISH: *makkara* FRENCH: *saucisse, saucisson* GERMAN: *Würst*
HUNGARIAN: *kolbasz* ITALIAN: *salsiccia* POLISH: *sosiski* RUSSIAN:
kolbasa, saussiska (smoked) SPANISH and PORTUGUESE: *salchicha*

An entire book could be written on this fascinating subject. Sausages, which are a completely prepared food, often become ingredients in other dishes. For that reason, we wish to clarify the subject as much as possible by describing the main types of sausages, how to store them, and some general uses, and then give an alphabetical listing within the types of those you are likely to find in ethnic markets, and their specific uses.

Virtually all sausages sold in the United States have been made in the United States or Canada. The government, in an effort to control the incidence of food-related illnesses, does not permit importation of pork products from Europe unless they have been prepared to conform to strict import codes.

The finest sausages are to be purchased in ethnic markets, such as French *charcuteries* (pork butcher shops), German delis, and fine sausage shops. Those found in supermarkets are usually much lower in quality, though some brands, such as Usinger, which is made in Milwaukee, are exceptionally fine and widely distributed. Because they vary so much from one sausage-maker to the next, seek out and taste unusual sausages. The only way to know them is to taste and compare. Sausage making is not an exact science, so be flexible when you shop, allowing for variations in size and seasonings. Jane Grigson's book, *The Art of Making Sausages, Pâtés, and Other Charcuterie* (Knopf, 1968), is the only book on basic sausage making, and gives excellent instructions for this surprisingly simple craft.

All ingredients must be listed on the labels of packaged sausages. SALT-PETER, an additive that preserves a rosy color, is not at all necessary to quality and taste so, if you find a sausage shop that does not use it and you don't mind the greyer than usual color, feel safe in buying.

All Kosher sausage products are made without pork, according to strict Jewish dietary law. Not all the listed types adapt well to the restrictions, but excellent Kosher SALAMI, KNACKWÜRST, and FRANKFURTERS are available in many supermarkets. Other types can be found in Kosher markets.

There are really only three basic types of sausage: fresh, cooked, and dried (either semi-dried or completely dried). Within the types, some may be cured or smoked or both, depending on the maker. Fresh sausage must be cooked before serving either warm or cold. The cooked and dried varieties can usually be eaten cold, but often benefit from warming.

FRESH SAUSAGE

Fresh sausage is made of raw meat—pork, beef, veal, chicken, rabbit, lamb—combined with seasonings (such as onion, garlic, herbs, and spices), extenders (such as cereals) or binders (such as bread crumbs or eggs). They may or may not be enclosed in edible SAUSAGE CASINGS. Fresh sausage is occasionally smoked for added flavor but is still not considered cooked. Examples of fresh sausage are breakfast patties and Italian link sausages.

STORAGE: Refrigerate fresh sausage for use within 3 days; fresh-smoked for use within a week. Freeze either for up to 6 months. Thaw before cooking.

PREPARATION: Allow approximately 4 ounces of fresh sausage per person. All raw, uncured sausages made of pork must be thoroughly cooked. Some fresh sausages, such as Italian links and chorizos, are often removed from their casings to become ingredients in sauces or stuffings. To sauté small patties or links, place in a skillet with ¼ cup of liquid (water, wine, beer, cider, etc.) as specified in the recipe, cover, and simmer for 5 to 10 minutes; then remove the lid and continue cooking, turning often, until the water has cooked away and the sausages are evenly browned. Larger links require longer cooking to be sure they are cooked through. They can be simmered until no pink shows in the center, or they can be simmered until partially cooked and then browned in a skillet. For a crusty skin on link sausages, pat dry after the initial simmering, dredge in flour, and then brown in butter or drippings. Some tender link sausages, such as WEISSWÜRST, which contains eggs, should be steamed over boiling water for 20 to 30 minutes, depending on their size.

Bauernwürst: Literally " peasant sausage." This is a German sausage similar to the frankfurter, but coarser and spicier, often containing whole mustard seeds. It can be found, cooked or uncooked, in German delis. Steam or simmer, and then fry in drippings, or broil, until browned. Serve with sauerkraut.

Bockwürst: A fresh, finger-size, whitish sausage very popular in Germany in the spring during the bock beer festival. It is made with veal (sometimes with pork added), delicately seasoned with chives, parsley, and nutmeg. It must be cooked and is usually pan-fried to serve hot with mashed potatoes or sauerkraut, accompanied by bock beer. It also makes a fine breakfast sausage. Berliner bockwürst is a red smoked and cooked version that is as popular a street food in Berlin as our hot dog is in the United States, and is steamed and accompanied by sauerkraut and mustard.

Chipolata: Though the name is Italian, this small, coarse-textured, spicy pork sausage is French and is available from *charcuteries* (pork butchers). They are 2″ to 3″ long, and are flavored with thyme, chives, red pepper flakes, nutmeg, cloves, and coriander. In France, they are pan-fried to garnish roasts and poultry, or may be grilled or poached in white wine to serve with potatoes. They may also be cooked with onions, tomatoes, and garlic and served with crusty bread. There is no really adequate substitute.

Chorizo: A sausage made of lightly smoked pork meat and fat, highly seasoned with garlic, red pepper, ground coriander, cumin, and paprika, and often containing red wine. The "Spanish-type," used in European recipes, and the "Mexican-type," will be found described under CHORIZO in THE FOODS OF LATIN AMERICA section. Chorizo can be found in Spanish and Latin American markets, sold in links about ¾" in diameter and 8" long. Chorizo, canned in lard, is imported from Spain. The usual supermarket variety, especially in California, contains unsavory items such as lymph nodes and salivary glands, and becomes a soupy mass when you fry it. Look for firm, semi-dry types. In Portugal, it is called Chourico; in France, Chorizo or Saucisse d'Espagne.

Chorizo is sometimes removed from the casing and added as a flavoring to soups and stews. The firmer type of whole sausages are often grilled to serve with cooked garbanzos (chick-peas) or black beans, and are used as an ingredient in one-dish meals, such as Paella. In Fabada Asturiana, it is combined with MORCILLA (see COOKED SAUSAGE), salt pork, ham, and fava beans to make a soup. LINGUIÇA (see SEMI-DRY AND DRY SAUSAGE) can be substituted without much difference in flavor. Other smoked, highly spiced sausages, such as COTECHINO or KIELBASA (see SEMI-DRY AND DRY SAUSAGE) can be substituted, but there will be a big difference in flavor.

Chourico: See CHORIZO

Cotechino: A large Italian-style pork sausage, seasoned similarly to ITALIAN LINK sausage, which is the Italian version of the French Saucisson à l'Ail. It is sold raw in Italy to be pricked and poached gently for several hours, allowing approximately 1 hour per pound. A partially cured and cooked version is the type you are most likely to find in Italian delis and fine sausage shops. It requires only 30 to 45 mintues of gentle poaching. It is an excellent sausage to serve hot with pureed lentils or hot potato salad, in Cassoulet (the famous French dish of meat and beans) and in Saucisson en Brioche (sausage in pastry).

Cotechino is traditionally an ingredient of Bollito Misto (mixed boiled meats), which is a dish much more exciting than the name implies, as it contains an assortment of beef, chicken, tongue, and veal cooked in a savory broth and served with a garlic-and-anchovy-flavored olive oil sauce called Salsa Verde.

Crépinette: Think of this as a sausage without skin. It is a French sausage, fresh or cooked, usually made of seasoned pork combined with various seasonings, which has been wrapped in CAUL instead of being placed in SAUSAGE

SKIN. It is usually flattened into round or oval shapes, and can be purchased only in fine French *charcuteries* (pork butcher shops). If cooked, it can be eaten cold.

For those interested in learning sausage making, this is a sausage that is easy to make. Raw crépinettes are brushed with melted butter and coated with bread crumbs to be sautéed in butter or broiled on a rack for 10 minutes on each side. They are generally served with mashed potatoes, and sometimes accompanied by a flavorful brown sauce. In Bordeaux, they are traditionally served with raw oysters on the half-shell.

Italian Link: Two varieties of fresh pork sausages are widely available in supermarkets and Italian delis and lend themselves to all kinds of Italian preparations. Both are seasoned with garlic, fennel seeds, and wine, but the "hot" variety has red pepper added, and the "sweet" only a bit of ground black pepper. There are usually 10 to 12 in a pound.

If making these at home, pork casings are the right size to use (see SAUSAGE CASINGS).

Removed from their casings and crumbled, they become a sauce ingredient—we use a combination of the two to make a sauce for cooked pasta and Lasagne—and pizza topping. To serve them in their casings, it is best to parboil them for a minute or so in water, and then pan-fry or grill them. They are often cooked with bell peppers to make Sausage and Peppers, which is served as is, atop pasta, or with Italian cornmeal Polenta. They can be skewered with red and green bell peppers between them to be grilled and served as a stuffing for Italian sandwich rolls. We sauté them with tomatoes and sage to serve with cooked cannellini beans—a recipe for this dish appears under BEANS, CANNELLINI. We like them especially when cooked with chicken as in the following recipe.

CHICKEN LENORE

4–6 sweet Italian Link sausages,   For 4 to 6 servings
    cut in 1″ pieces
  1 chicken, cut in serving pieces *or* 3 whole chicken
    breasts, split
  4 garlic cloves, minced
  1 bay leaf
  4 ounces dry red wine
  1 pound fresh tomatoes, peeled, seeded, and diced, *or* a
    16-ounce can crushed tomatoes in tomato puree
  8 medium mushrooms, quartered through the stems
  1 green bell pepper, seeded and diced
  1 tablespoon chopped fresh oregano *or* 1 teaspoon dried,
    crumbled

441

In a heavy sauté pan, brown the sausage and the chicken pieces. Add the garlic, bay leaf, and wine. Cover and simmer for 15 minutes. Add the remaining ingredients, cover, and simmer over low heat for 20 minutes longer, until the chicken is tender when pierced with a fork.

TO PREPARE IN ADVANCE: Cool and refrigerate for up to 3 days. Reheat just until hot.

Salsiccia: This is the Italian word for sausage, equivalent to the French word, *saucisse*. It refers to small fresh sausages meant for cooking and eating hot. There are hundreds of varieties in Italy, usually named for the province of origin. Examples are Casalinga ("homestyle"), garlic-and-pepper-flavored pork sausage found only in Italy, either homemade or in shops, and Luganeghe, a pork sausage from the lake district of northern Italy. ITALIAN LINK can be substituted in Italian recipes. Salsiccia Secca refers to a dry sausage, SALAME (see SEMI-DRY AND DRY SAUSAGE). Italian delis will have domestically made sausages of this type, most of which are meant to be eaten cooked in the manner of Italian link sausages.

Toulouse: A small, fresh, coarse-textured French pork sausage. These usually weigh about 4 ounces each. Braise or pan-fry, or remove from casings and use to flavor stuffings. Whole, they are superb served with lentils or beans.

Weisswürst: Similiar to BRATWÜRST (see COOKED SAUSAGE), this small "white sausage" is made with veal, cream, and eggs. It is a specialty of Munich and is usually served for Oktoberfest with rye rolls and sweet mustard, accompanied by pretzels and beer. It is steamed and the casing is removed as it is eaten. The meat, after steaming, can be cut up to serve in soups or stews, to resemble light veal dumplings.

Zampone: A northern Italian pork sausage whose casing is the boned foot of a pig. It is a fresh sausage, available only in specialty Italian delis, that requires slow simmering. It is then sliced to serve with cooked beans in the manner of COTECHINO, or as a part of the Bollito Misto platter described with that listing.

COOKED SAUSAGE

Cooked sausages are completely cooked and, like fresh sausages, may be smoked as well. They needn't be cooked further for serving, but they usually are because the flavor is best when hot.

STORAGE: Refrigerate, tightly wrapped, for use within 2 weeks, or freeze for up to 6 months. Thaw before cooking. Alternatively, they can be covered with rendered lard, put in jars, and stored at room temperature for a year or longer, and the flavor and texture will be better than if refrigerated or frozen.

PREPARATION: These are fully cooked so they can be served as they are at room temperature, but they're usually much more flavorful if heated—by simmering, steaming, sautéing, or grilling.

In Germany, these and semi-dry sausages (see the following category) are served hot or cold, with the usual accompaniments of potato salad (cold with cold sausage, hot with hot), or sauerkraut, and beer. Often a selection of sausages is served accompanied by bread, mustard, and pickles. In France, as in Germany, sausages are served with sauerkraut *(choucroute),* but are often baked inside mustard-brushed brioche dough to make a superb and hearty "sandwich" called Saucisse in Brioche. Saucisses au Vin Blanc is a dish of sausages cooked in white wine with brown sauce.

In Russia, Saussiski v Tomate is smoked sausage simmered in tomato sauce. In Finland, thick sausages are slit deeply, brushed with mustard, and stuffed with sautéed onions to be baked with a tomato sauce to make the dish called Paistettu Makkara. The Polish dish, Sosika à la Sierputowski, is simply sausages with a warm mustard sauce. Korhelyleves is a Hungarian sauerkraut soup with sausages and sour cream.

Andouille: A French sausage, 2″ to 3″ in diameter, made of tripe or threaded layers of CHITTERLING (see THE FOODS OF REGIONAL AMERICA section) seasoned with CAYENNE, lots of black pepper and QUATRES ÉPICES (see HERBS, SPICES, AND SEASONING BLENDS section), which is a specialty of Normandy. Fresh sausage is simmered in white wine and then smoked, which gives it a blackish, lumpy appearance. It can be found in fine French *charcuteries* (pork butcher shops). The interior is very dark, and attractively marbled with white fat. It is most often thinly sliced to serve at room temperature as an appetizer, but is also cut in ¼″ slices and sautéed in butter or drippings just long enough to warm, and is then served with mashed potatoes.

Andouillette: A smaller version (1″ or less in diameter) of the tripe or chitterling sausage, ANDOUILLE, which is cooked, but usually not smoked. They are often pressed into squarish cylinders, covered with fat, and wrapped in paper. They are found in French *charcuteries* (pork butcher shops), and are quite expensive, so they are often cut in ½″ pieces to be sautéed before becoming part of an omelet. To serve whole, cut a few slits in the skin, sauté or grill, and serve like andouille with mashed or sautéed potatoes, or with sauerkraut. They differ considerably from the CREOLE Acadian sausage of the same name (see under SAUSAGES in THE FOODS OF REGIONAL AMERICA section).

Arles: See SALAME

Baloney: See BOLOGNA

Bangers: A generic term for various British sausages.

Black Pudding: Sometimes called "blood pudding." British term for BLOOD SAUSAGE. In Scotland, lamb instead of pork is occasionally used. An Irish type, Drisheen, is large and very highly prized. These sausages are usually fried in bacon fat and served with sautéed apple rings or potatoes, and slices of bacon. A Russian type, Palten, is served with brown butter, and the Finnish version, Veripalttu, is eaten with cranberry sauce.

Blood Sausage: The American term for dark-colored sausages made with pork blood and various meats and spices, including coriander. The cooked type, which are all you are likely to find, is usually served thinly sliced at room temperature, but can be heated. Small ones can be sautéed in butter or bacon drippings, turning often, for 3 to 5 minutes. The uncooked type is simmered, and then sliced and browned. It is served in the same manner as the British BLACK PUDDING, German BLUTWÜRST, French BOUDIN BLANC, and Spanish MORCILLA.

Blutwürst: German version of BLOOD SAUSAGE, usually made of pork and bacon fat and seasoned with marjoram and allspice. It is served cold with bread and potato salad, or broiled or fried to serve with potatoes and apple sauce. A large ring is best braised: brown in a skillet in butter or bacon drippings, add 1 cup liquid (water, wine, or stock) and simmer, covered, for 10 to 30 minutes, depending on whether it has been precooked. Serve with mashed potatoes or sauerkraut. A variation, **blut zungenwürst,** contains large pieces of pickled tongue and is dried to be eaten raw, as part of a cold-cut platter. It can be sliced, dredged in flour, and browned briefly on each side in butter or bacon drippings. **Berliner blutwürst** is a smoked version containing cubes of bacon, which is usually just warmed (to prevent toughening), either by placing in very hot water for 20 minutes or gently browning in butter or bacon fat, and is traditionally served with cranberry sauce.

Bologna: There are several types of bologna (commonly called **baloney** by Americans) to be found in delicatessens besides the pre-sliced sandwich rounds found in every supermarket. It is a lightly smoked, pinkish, cooked sausage named for the Italian town in which it was created. The American version is milder than the Italian, and is spiced with garlic, sage, salt, and pepper. It comes in large rounds or rectangles, and is usually made of a combination of pork and beef. Recent additions are turkey and chicken types. Veal bologna is very delicate. Kosher bologna is made with beef. **Chub** is a combination of beef, pork, and bacon and is especially smooth-textured. **Schinkenwürst** is a German ham bologna.

Bologna is usually served as a cold cut or in sandwiches. Occasionally it is cooked, but is most tender if served at room temperature. Small pieces can be added to salads and soups. The English often fry slices for breakfast.

Boudin Blanc: A creamy cooked sausage made in France of minced pork or veal and chicken or rabbit, combined with cream, eggs, fresh bread crumbs, onions, and spices, including mace and white pepper. Usually it is 1" to 1½" in diameter and 6" to 12" long. This type of sausage is very expensive and will be found only in French *charcuteries* (pork butcher shops) and sausage shops. It can be made at home from recipes found in French cookbooks. It is precooked, and usually brushed with butter and broiled just until heated through, to be served with mashed potatoes.

Boudin Noir: French BLOOD SAUSAGE, usually glossy and black in appearance. It usually contains cream, onion, and ÉPICES FINES (see HERBS, SPICES, AND SEASONING BLENDS section, under SEASONING BLENDS). It is generally more highly spiced than German or American versions. It is seasoned differently in various parts of France and may contain apples, chestnuts, garlic, spinach, herbs, or garlic. It will be found only in French *charcuteries* (pork butcher shops) or fine sausage shops, and is served like other blood sausage, either hot with sautéed potatoes, or cold as an hors d'oeuvre or sandwich ingredient.

Bratwürst: Literally "frying" sausage, this is a plump German pork (or occasionally partially veal) sausage, sold in links, either fresh or precooked. It is whitish in color and may be flavored with nutmeg or mace, sage, coriander or caraway, and lemon juice. It is usually 1" to 1½" in diameter and 4" to 6" long, and may be fine or coarse in texture. It is popular in Germany and Switzerland. If fresh, it must be cooked, and is often simmered in beer and then broiled or fried until browned and served with sauerkraut and pan-fried or hashed-brown potatoes. The Usinger brand, made in Milwaukee and widely available, is precooked and needs only warming. There is a smoked version of this sausage, which is larger and is steamed to serve hot or cold.

Braunschweiger: A creamy smoked liverwurst named for Brunswick, West Germany, its town of origin. It is served cold as a spread for sandwiches, bread, or crackers, much like a smooth pâté.

Chub: See BOLOGNA

Frankfurters: Originally a German sausage named for Frankfurt, its town of origin, this has become a generic term for the ubiquitous hot dog, or **weiner,** as it is called in Vienna. Frankfurters vary in size from miniature "cocktail " types (24 to a pound) to "foot-long" (4 to a pound), but the most common come 8 to 10 to a pound. They are made of pork, beef, chicken, or turkey. "Beef franks," by law, contain beef, seasonings, and preservatives, but no binders (bread crumbs or eggs). "Meat franks" may contain a combination of beef and pork with seasonings, but no binders. Those labeled "frankfurter" may contain a certain percentage of binders. "Kosher franks" are made of beef and are usually highly seasoned. All are precooked, but taste best when served hot, either poached or grilled or coated with cornmeal batter to make "Corn-Dogs."

In Germany, they are served like other sausages, either hot with sauerkraut or hot potato salad, or cold with cold potato salad. A German soup, Bohnensuppe, contains kidney beans, turnips, and sliced frankfurters. They are also used to make Wurstgulyas, a goulash made with paprika, caraway seeds, and sour cream.

Gasleverkorv: See LIVER SAUSAGE

Head Cheese: Small chunks of meat from a hog's head and tongue cooked in a gelatinous broth which, when cooled, holds the pieces suspended, like a fine aspic. It is usually flavored with sage and summer savory, salt and pepper, and occasionally juniper berries and pistachios. It may contain meat from the feet of the animal to give extra gelatin to the broth. It is eaten, thinly sliced, at room temperature. This is at its finest served during the summertime accompanied by a simple vinaigrette sauce. It is widely available, in German delis, and in some supermarkets. (In France, the broth is not added to the final product.)

Knackwürst: Fat sausages, also called **Knockwürst** and **Knoblauch,** 1½" to 2" in diameter and 6" to 8" long. They are very similar in flavor to FRANKFURTERS, but thicker and often more highly seasoned with garlic. Usually 4 will weigh 1 pound. They can be substituted for hot dogs and are often served with sauerkraut. Already cooked, they require only heating through by poaching for 10 minutes or so, or splitting and pan-frying. In Germany, they are often cooked with pork chops to serve with sautéed potatoes, and are used sliced in potato salad.

Knoblauch: See KNACKWÜRST

Leberkäse: Literally "liver cheese." This is a smooth and delicate German liver pâté flavored with onion, garlic, bacon fat, and eggs, which is nearly always served hot. It is sliced from ½" to 1" thick and then steamed for 20 to 30 minutes to serve with rye bread. Alternatively, it can be sautéed with sliced onions in a heavy (preferably nonstick) skillet over very low heat for about 5 minutes on each side, just until heated through, and should be carefully turned with a pancake turner to prevent its falling apart. It is occasionally served at room temperature.

Liver Sausage or **Liverwürst:** There are as many types of creamy liver sausages as there are makers. It is a ready-to-eat sausage, made of liver (usually pork, but sometimes beef or goose), which may or may not be smoked, and is seasoned in many different ways. Most are very smooth and rich, like a pâté, and are highly seasoned. American liverwurst is generally not smoked— German liverwurst is. Examples of German liverwurst are BRAUN-

SCHWEIGER, **Trufflewürst** (with truffles), **Sardellenwürst** (with anchovies). A French Strasbourg version is made of goose liver and contains pistachio nuts.

Liver sausage is usually served at room temperature as part of a plate of cold cuts, as a sandwich filling, or as a spread for rye bread or crackers. Firm types can be heated like LEBERKÄSE, and served with cabbage. A Swedish version called **Gasleverkorv** is used in making Swedish black-bean soup.

Lyonnaise: See SALAME

Mettwürst: Sometimes called **Teewürst** or **Schmierwürst,** this German sausage is bright red, very rich, spreadable, thoroughly smoked and cured, and made of beef and pork flavored with coriander and pepper. It is not cooked in the making, but can be eaten as is as a spread for bread. It is never served hot.

Morcilla: This Spanish type of blood sausage is called **Murcela** in Portugal. It can be found in Spanish and Latin American markets, and there are variations: the Andalusian contains marjoram, rice, and almonds; the Portuguese is flavored with cumin. BLOOD SAUSAGE from other countries can be substituted with some variation in flavor. In Spain, it is used in the dish called Fabada, described with LINGUIÇA (see SEMI-DRY AND DRY SAUSAGE), and also flavors an appetizer *(tapa)* made of simmered tripe, CHORIZO (see FRESH SAUSAGE), wine, leeks, paprika, and cloves. In Portugal, it appears in Rojões com Murcela à Beira Alta (pork and sausage platter).

Murcela: See MORCILLA

Pudding: A British term for some sausages, such as BLACK PUDDING.

Sanguinaccio: Italian term for BLOOD SAUSAGE.

Sardellenwürst: See LIVER SAUSAGE

Saucisse: A French generic term for a small sausage, often individually named for the locale where it is made. The German frankfurter is an example, but the term covers a wide variety of fresh, cooked, or cured sausages to be found in French *charcuteries* (pork butcher shops). Saucisse de Strasbourg is nearly identical to KNACKWÜRST and FRANKFURTER. Saucisse de Toulouse is made of coarsely ground pork, and one fancy type, Saucisse au Champagne, is made of finely ground pork with champagne and truffles. These are used in Saucisson en Brioche (sausage rolls) and Friandises (puff pastry sausage rolls), and as an ingredient in such regional dishes as Cassoulet (bean and meat stew) and Choucroute Garnie (sauerkraut garnished with meats). In the dish Saucisses au Vin Blanc, these sausages are poached in white wine with herbs, especially sage.

Schinkenwürst: See BOLOGNA

Schmierwürst: See METTWÜRST

Sibiu: See SALAME

Sülze: A German sausage very similar to HEAD CHEESE, but made of meat from pig or calf feet combined with chopped vegetables and pickles, molded in a more tart-flavored meat aspic. **Sylte** is the Danish name.

Sylte: See SÜLZE

Teewürst: See LIVER SAUSAGE

Tesi Szalami: See SALAME

Thuringer: A German term referring to the Thuringia region of central Germany. It is attached to the names of different types of sausages: to a fresh (occasionally "scalded") sausage, to CERVELAT (see SEMI-DRY AND DRY SAUSAGE) and to a type of BLUTWÜRST. The fresh, a pork and veal combination is flavored with coriander, celery seed, and ginger. If not labeled "scalded," it should be braised or simmered until no pink shows in the center and then browned in butter. The semi-dry (cervelat) type is mildly flavored with coriander and is rather soft. Both are delicious in Cassoulet or served with potatoes or beans.

Trufflewürst: See LIVER SAUSAGE

Wiener: A term that means "from Vienna."

Wienerwürst: The Austrian name for FRANKFURTER.

SEMI-DRY AND DRY SAUSAGE

Semi-dry sausages, usually made with partially cured meats, have been smoked long enough to remove at least 20 percent of their moisture. They are often referred to as "summer" sausage because, in the days before refrigeration, they could be kept for a period of time without spoiling. Examples of this type are kielbasa and most cervelat.

"Dry" sausages are cured or smoked sausages that have been dried for 1 to 6 months to remove more of their moisture. This process must be done carefully to prevent shriveling. These tend to be the spiciest sausages of all, and are usually more expensive than fresh or cooked sausages. Examples of this type are salami and pepperoni. In Germany, dry sausages are called *Dauerwürst*; in France, *saucissons secs*; in Italy, *salsiccia secca*.

STORAGE: This type of sausage can be stored at room temperature for 2 or 3 days, which makes it handy to take along when hiking or on long car trips. To preserve its quality, it is best to store it in the refrigerator (for up to 3 weeks), or freeze it (for up to 6 months). Alternatively, it can be stored in jars, covered with rendered lard, at room temperature for a year or longer, and the flavor and texture will be better than if refrigerated or frozen.

PREPARATION AND USE: Semi-dry and dry sausages are very often eaten as snacks—sliced and served with cheese and bread. They are often heated as well, in the same types of dishes as those mentioned in the preceding classification. The highly spiced varieties often become a garnish for cooked dishes such as pizza, or are added in small amounts as a flavoring to stuffings, salads, soups, and vegetables. They often make up part of an antipasto assortment.

Bierwürst: Literally "beer sausage," the name derives from the fact that this used to be made with meat that had been marinated in beer. It is a SALAME type of sausage, very strongly flavored with garlic, that is found only in German sausage shops. It is usually served cold, thinly sliced, as part of a cold cut platter, or is sliced as a sandwich filling with rye bread. Beer is the traditional accompaniment.

Butifara: A rather coarse, highly seasoned Spanish pork sausage, often flavored with nutmeg and cloves. As it is seldom available, substitute CHIPOLATA (see FRESH SAUSAGE) or LONGANIZA.

Cervelas sometimes called **saveloy:** A French semi-dry sausage, approximately 1½" in diameter and 8" to 12" long, weighing close to a pound. It is made with pork and garlic, and is usually poached to serve hot with mustard or horseradish sauce, and potato salad. It can be sliced to serve cold as an appetizer. Substitute other semi-dry sausages, such as SAUCISSON or KIELBASA.

Cervelat: A general name for a variety of Central European smoked semi-dry or "summer" sausages, made of pork or beef. Cervelats are similar to mild SALAMI, but finer textured and moister. They are often smoked but seldom contain garlic. Like salami, they are usually served thinly sliced at room temperature with coarse bread. Examples of this type of sausage are TOURISTENWÜRST (German), GÖTEBORG (Swedish), LANDJÄGER (Swiss), and MORTADELLA (Italian). These sausages can be diced to add as a flavoring to cooked beans, Macaroni and Cheese, cooked vegetables such as spinach or green beans, poultry stuffings, scrambled eggs, and cheese soufflés.

Frizzes or **Frizzie:** An Italian SALAME type of dry sausage, heavily seasoned with garlic. Two types are sold in Italian markets, both flavored with anise. The "hot" is corded with red string, the "sweet" with blue. These are usually snack salame, to be sliced and served with bread and cheese, or as part of an antipasto assortment. They are used to garnish pizza or, cut in small dice, to flavor stuffings, salads, and pasta dishes.

Göteborg: A large Swedish CERVELAT type of coarse-textured sausage flavored with cardamom, and smoked and air-dried. It is a snack sausage, usually sliced to serve with bread and mustard.

Gothaer: A German CERVELAT type of sausage that is made of finely chopped pork. It is almost never cooked, and functions as a snack or sandwich sausage.

Kielbasa: The Polish word for sausage, of which there are over 70 kinds in Poland. In America, the terms "kielbasa" and "Polish sausage" have come to refer to the highly seasoned, smoked, semi-dry garlic-flavored sausage that is sold in 1" to 2" thick rings weighing a pound or more in many supermarkets. It is made of pork, often in combination with beef or veal, and is always flavored with garlic, and other seasonings such as black pepper, paprika, marjoram, and savory.

This type of sausage can be eaten cold with horseradish or mustard sauce, but is at its best when warmed. It is often simmered in beer or broth to serve with red cabbage, sauerkraut, beans, or lentils. It is an excellent sausage to use whenever "garlic" sausage is specified, and often used in French recipes for Saucisson en Broiche (sausage baked in crust). Small pieces add interest to casseroles. James Beard simmers slices of kielbasa in red wine with minced shallots to skewer and serve warm as appetizers. We like it sautéed with red and green peppers to serve with mashed potatoes. In Poland it is cooked with beef and bacon and served with a paprika and sour cream sauce, and is a traditional ingredient in Bigos, the Polish Hunter's Stew, with dried mushrooms, various other meats, sauerkraut, and wine.

Landjäger: (Literally "hunter.") These are dried Swiss CERVELAT type of sausages, sold in pairs. They are smoked, hard, rectangular shaped sausages which are usually eaten raw at room temperature as a snacking or sandwich sausage. Occasionally they are used to season casseroles, soufflés and sliced potatoes cooked in cream.

Linguiça: A Portuguese sausage similar to CHORIZO (see FRESH SAUSAGE), but milder and slimmer, about ½" in diameter. Its strong garlic flavor enhances casseroles, soups, and stews. It will be found in both Spanish and Latin American markets because it is a popular type of sausage in Brazil, appearing in their national dish, Fiejoada. In Portugal, it is used in many dishes, including Caldo Verde with potatoes and kale, which is traditionally served with a sweet bread called Broa and vinho verde (green wine). In restaurants in Portugal, linguiça is often grilled on small skewers at the table for an appetizer. It is also popular in Hawaii where there is a large Portuguese population.

Longaniza: A Spanish oven-dried sausage, milder than CHORIZO (see FRESH SAUSAGE), which is flavored with garlic and oregano. It is similar to LINGUICA, and the two may be used interchangeably.

Mortadella: Bologna's famous pork sausage, the original of what Americans call baloney. It is smooth and delicately flavored, larded with cubes of fat and sometimes studded with black peppercorns. In Italy, it is often 18″ in diameter and is classified as a CERVELAT because it is briefly air-dried. The original is never imported except for a canned, cooked version, which is not at all like the real thing. A domestic mortadella, usually 6″ to 9″ in diameter and strongly flavored with garlic, is available. It should be eaten thinly sliced, but be sure to slice it at least ⅛″ thick because it is a tender sausage that can fall apart. In Italy, it is used in some stuffings for pasta and other cooked dishes, and is sometimes wrapped around bread sticks to serve cold as an antipasto.

Pepperoni: A dried Italian-style sausage made of beef or pork and highly seasoned with black and red peppers. It is popular in America as a spicy topping for pizza, though it is usually served in Italy in paper-thin slices as an appetizer.

Polish Sausage: This term has become synonymous with KIELBASA.

Salame or, plural, **Salami:** This term has become almost interchangeable with CERVELAT in referring to a spiced sausage made of uncooked cured pork or beef, combined with seasonings, and air-dried. As a general rule, though, salami are usually coarser, spicier, and a bit drier, and are not smoked. Unlike Cervelat, they are usually spiced with garlic. Italian examples include Genoa salami, very dry, rich, and flavorful, with garlic and whole white peppercorns, Cotto ("cooked") salami, dark, garlic-flavored, and studded with black peppercorns, FRIZZES and PEPPERONI. Some of our Italian-domestic varieties are Alesandri and Alpino. In Italy, whole salami have tags attached: the letter "S" indicating only pork has been used, and "SB" indicating that beef or veal has been added.

Italy, Germany, Yugoslavia, Hungary, and France all make this spicy beef or pork sausage with different seasonings. You will find them studded with pistachios, peppercorns, coriander seeds, depending on the type. French versions include Arles, a coarse Provençal sausage corded with crisscrossed strings, and Lyonnaise, an all-pork type. Hungary makes a red paprika-flavored salami called Tesi Szalami. A Rumanian version, Sibiu, is flavored with white pepper and is slightly sweet. Kosher salamis are all beef.

You can have salami sliced in the stores where you buy them, but they will retain their full flavor if sliced just before use. They are primarily a snacking sausage, served as part of an antipasto platter or as a sandwich filling, but small bits are sometimes added to cooked dishes, such as pasta, as a flavor accent. We like to make a simple appetizer by filling thin slices of salame with cream cheese that has been mixed with scallions, and either rolling them into tubes or folding them in half-moon shapes. All types of salami are superb in sandwiches with mustard and dill pickles.

451

Saucisse d'Espagne: See CHORIZO

Saucisson: A French term for a medium to large sausage, flavored with QUATRES ÉPICES (see HERBS, SPICES, AND SEASONING BLENDS, under SEASONING BLENDS) and other spices. They can be eaten cold as an appetizer, or poached to serve with sautéed potatoes or sauerkraut. Saucisson *à l'ail* is garlic sausage, for which KIELBASA can be substituted. Saucissions *fumés* are smoked types, and saucissons *secs* are dried and similar to SALAME.

Saveloy: See CERVELAS

Touristenwürst: A German type of CERVELAT sausage, which is soft-textured, and sold in a large ring. Literally translated, the name means, "sausage made of tourists."

Würst: The German term for all types of sausage.

Würstchen: Small sausage like FRANKFURTERS (see under COOKED SAUSAGE).

Zungenwürst: See BLUTWÜRST, under COOKED SAUSAGE

SAUSAGE CASINGS

Small pork, beef, or sheep intestines are carefully cleaned and preserved in brine or salt to make sausage casings. They can be purchased from specialty butchers or sausage shops and come in sets that look like wet spaghetti. Beef casings are the largest, 2½″ to 3″ in diameter; pork casings measure 1½″ to 2″ in diameter; and sheep casings are 1″ in diameter. These intestine casings, as well as some membranes from other parts of the animal, are used throughout Europe. Buy the size appropriate to the size of sausage to be made rather than matching the casing to the types of meat used in the filling. Synthetic casings, made of plastic or hydrocellulose, are also sold, but not all are edible, so those are usually peeled off the sausages before eating. If casings are unavailable, washed cheesecloth, cut 3″ longer and twice the circumference of the sausage you wish to make can be substituted. It must, of course, be removed before serving.

STORAGE: Layered in salt in a nonmetal container, these will keep for up to 6 months in the refrigerator.

PREPARATION AND USE: Cut into 6′ (six-foot) lengths and soak in cold water with a bit of vinegar added for at least an hour, or overnight. Lift from the water, cut into 2′ lengths and place one end of the casing over your kitchen faucet so that cold water can run through the intestine to rinse out all the remaining salt brine. It is now ready to fill, using the sausage stuffing attachment to an electric meat grinder, a pastry bag, or other sausage making apparatus. Do not fill too tightly or they will burst when heated, even if the sausages are pricked before cooking. Most homemade sausages are hung in a cool place for 1 to 2 days to allow the flavors to develop.

SCHWARTZBRÖT

OTHER: black bread

"Schwartzbröt" is the German word for black bread—a very dark, Russian-style rye bread. In northern and Central Europe, this is a generic term for a very black type of PUMPERNICKEL. It is much darker in color, and often sweeter in flavor from the addition of molasses than the Westphalian type of rye bread (see PUMPERNICKEL). It can be purchased at some bakeries, and is sold in small rectangular loaves in the refrigerator sections of most supermarkets.

STORAGE: Bread that isn't to be used right away is best stored in the freezer. If pre-sliced, it is easy to separate and thaws almost instantly.

USE: In Germany, Schwarzbröt-Rahmsuppe is made by simmering crumbled bread in stock with caraway seeds, pureeing it, and then adding sour cream. This bread is made into a dessert, Schwarzbröt-Gewürztorte, by soaking crumbs in wine and then combining with egg yolks, candied fruit, and spices, folding in beaten egg whites and baking like a cake. It is then split, sprinkled with liqueur and layered with marmalade filling.

Cube and fry black bread for CROUTONS to use in salads or as a topping for casseroles and cooked vegetables. Soak to make dumplings as in our recipe with the PUMPERNICKEL entry.

SECCHIELI

See CHESTNUTS, DRIED

SEMOLINA

FRENCH: *semoule* GERMAN: *Griessmehl* ITALIAN: *semolino*
SPANISH: *semolino*

Do not confuse this with our domestic breakfast cereal of the same name. It is a flour made from the hard, coarse, endosperm portion of durum wheat that is sifted away during processing. It is an amber-colored granular flour available in fine, medium, and coarse grinds in Italian, Middle Eastern, and East Indian markets, and in health food stores. It is sometimes labeled "farina," which is confusing because that Italian term could apply to any type of flour. The semolina found in Italian markets is either medium or very fine grind, and deeper in color than that found in health food stores. According to Madhur Jaffrey, Indian-cooking authority, regular cream of wheat can be used as a substitute in some Indian recipes.

STORAGE: In an airtight container in a cool place it will keep indefinitely.

PREPARATION AND USE: Recipes specify which grind of semolina to use, but coarse and fine can be substituted with only slight change in texture. The finest grind is the preferred flour to use in making fresh pasta because it requires less kneading than coarser grinds. The resulting pasta is firmer and more golden than that made from ordinary wheat flour. It is also excellent for Roman Gnocchi, pizza, and other Italian dishes and, in Czech potato dumplings called Bramborové Knedlíky, it is used in place of or in combination with wheat flour. The coarse grind is used primarily as a breakfast cereal, and is cooked with 3½ parts water to 1 part semolina for approximately 30 minutes.

Semolina is used in the Middle East to make the granules known as COUS COUS (though other grains may be used) and, in India, for Dosas (yogurt pancakes), Pani Puri (semolina wafers), and for Upama (a spicy cereal served for breakfast with fresh coriander and coconut chutney in southern India). In Burma, a semolina pudding is made with coconut milk and sesame seeds, which is cut like a cake, and in Sri Lanka it is used in the making of Love Cake, flavored with rose water, cashews, and spices, traditionally served on birthdays.

SHALLOT

OTHER: Bombay onion

FRENCH: *échalote* GERMAN: *Schalotte* ITALIAN: *scalogno* POLISH: *cebulka* SPANISH: *chalote* or *cebolleta*

Shallots are small members of the onion family that are more flavorful, mellow, and digestible than its other members. They have a very subtle garlic flavor and grow in bulbs or clusters of cloves, much like garlic, but have reddish-brown papery skin covering a pale lavender interior. There is a "grey" variety, less often seen, which is supposed to be even more flavorful then the "red." Shallots are available in many fine supermarkets throughout the United States because of our great interest in French cooking, in which they are a primary sauce ingredient. They are always expensive.

When purchasing fresh ones, look for those that are large and firm. Most growers now cultivate large shallots because they are so much easier to peel than small ones. Freeze-dried chopped shallots are available on supermarket spice shelves, but they are not as tasty as the fresh ones and must be reconstituted before use.

In England and Australia, scallions (green onions) are referred to as shallots.

STORAGE: Kept in a cool, dry place in a basket where air can circulate around them, shallots will last for a month or longer. If you use a great many shallots, you may find it handy to make use of a restaurant trick—mince a cupful or so at a time and place in a jar with a tablespoon or so of oil to coat them and prevent their drying out. Then store in the refrigerator (for a month or longer), measuring out the required amount as needed, and avoiding last-minute peeling and chopping. Freeze-dried shallots can be stored on the pantry shelf for up to 6 months, but they lose flavor on standing.

PREPARATION AND USE: When a recipe calls for one shallot, it means the whole bulb or approximately 2 tablespoons minced shallots. Four shallots are equivalent to 1 medium onion in size. Freeze-dried shallots need to be reconstituted in water according to package instructions. In preparing sauces, shallots should be sautéed briefly in butter or pan drippings before adding the rest of the sauce ingredients to bring out their full flavor. They scorch easily, though, so they should be carefully watched during this procedure.

Shallots are very commonly used in Balinese cooking because they grow there in great abundance. Shallots have a special affinity for wine and are particularly suited to sauces for delicate foods such as chicken, veal, and fish. They are essential to Sauce Béarnaise and, because of their natural emulsifying action, are often part of the very popular Beurre Blanc sauce served in Nouvelle Cuisine restaurants. This basic type of sauce takes only minutes to make with a little practice and is superb with fish. Here is how Jean Troisgros, famous French chef, taught us to make it.

FILLETS DE SOLE TROISGROS

For 6 first-course servings
or 3 main-course servings

 3 medium carrots, minced or very thinly sliced
 4 medium shallots, peeled and minced
 1 stalk celery, including the leaves, minced
    Optional: 1 teaspoon minced fresh herbs
 6 medium fillets of sole
1¼ cups dry white wine (Chef Troisgros used a Pinot
    Chardonnay)
 8 ounces (2 sticks) sweet (unsalted) butter, cut in ½" cubes
    and chilled
    Salt and white pepper, to taste
    Minced parsley or chervil, to garnish

455

In a large skillet, combine the carrots, shallots, celery and optional herbs. Add ½ cup water. Bring to a simmer, cover the pan, and cook slowly for 2 minutes—the vegetables should remain crisp. Fold the sole fillets in half (end to end), skin-side (shiny side) in, and place them on the vegetables in the pan. Pour the wine over the fillets and bring to a simmer. Cover tightly and cook very slowly for 5 minutes, just until fillets are easily flaked with a fork. Using a slotted spoon, gently lift the fish and vegetables from the broth to a warm serving platter, leaving as much of the broth in the pan as possible. Cover the fish loosely with foil to stay warm while you make the sauce.

Boil the broth over high heat, pouring any poaching liquid from the platter back into the pan, until it has condensed to about ⅓ cup. Add half the chilled butter cubes, whisking constantly, until melted into the sauce. Without letting the sauce boil, add the remaining butter, and continue whisking until just melted. (The acidity of the poaching liquid creates a liaison with the butter, making a smooth creamy sauce similar in consistency to a thin hollandaise.) Remove the pan from the heat and season the sauce to taste with salt and white pepper.

Blot any liquid from the platter of fish which would thin the sauce. Pour the sauce over the warm fish fillets, garnish with parsley or chervil, and serve immediately.

SNAIL

See ESCARGOT

SPICE PARISIENNE

See ÉPICES FINES in the HERBS, SPICES, AND SEASONING
BLENDS section, under SEASONING BLENDS

SORREL

OTHER: sourgrass, dock, patience

DUTCH: *zuring* FRENCH: *oseille* GERMAN: *Sauerampfer* ITALIAN: *sauro* POLISH: *szczaw* SPANISH: *acedera* YIDDISH: *schav* or *chav*

Sorrel is a green that looks a good deal like spinach but with paler green, arrowhead-shaped leaves. It tastes like sour spinach. It is sold in bunches in produce markets and fine supermarkets all year, but its peak season is during the summer months. Look for young, tender, crisp leaves. The finest, and mildest, variety is called French sorrel. It is available preserved in jars in European or Jewish markets labeled under the Yiddish name of *schav* or *chav*.

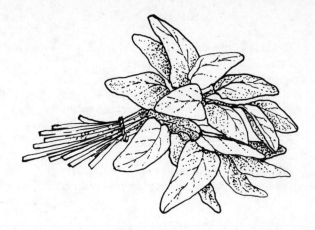

It is extremely easy to grow in the garden, or even in pots in the house, and will survive drastic neglect.

STORAGE: Rinse fresh sorrel and shake it dry; then wrap in dry paper towels and store in a plastic bag in the refrigerator for up to 4 days. The bottled type, after opening, can be stored for 3 to 4 days in the refrigerator.

PREPARATION AND USE: Cut away and discard the stems and center ribs and rinse well. The leaves can be cooked whole, like spinach, or can be cut crosswise into fine strips, called *chiffonnade*. Sorrel wilts quickly, so it should be cooked briefly, like tender spinach, in just the water that clings to the leaves and just until it is tender. As a general rule, 6 to 8 ounces of sorrel is the right amount to buy per serving if it is served by itself as a vegetable but, because it turns rather grey when cooked, it is often combined with an equal amount of spinach or other greens that keep their color.

Very tender leaves are used in salads in combination with other greens. The French use it as a flavoring herb with veal, poultry, and fish, and usually prepare it simply as a vegetable with a seasoning of butter or a bit of CRÈME FRAÎCHE or sour cream.

Sorrel is widely used in Poland as a vegetable and as an ingredient in soups and sauces. As a vegetable, it is usually pureed and combined with sour cream and a bit of sugar, but may be combined with egg yolks. A Polish sauce, Sos Szezawiowy, is made with chicken stock, flour, sorrel, and sour cream. It is commonly served with egg dishes, veal, and beef. The Dutch usually don't puree sorrel, but combine cooked leaves with butter and raisins. In England, it is cooked and pureed with butter, lemon, and brown gravy to serve as a sauce for roast goose.

In general, sorrel enhances cream soups and adds a new dimension of taste to the following French sauce, which goes beautifully with fish or chicken.

457

SORREL SAUCE

2 large SHALLOTS, minced   For 4 to 6 servings
1 tablespoon butter
½ cup dry vermouth *or* ⅔ cup dry white wine
4 cups fish or chicken bouillon
1½ cups CRÈME FRAÎCHE or heavy (whipping) cream
4 cups sorrel leaves (about 4 ounces), veins removed and
      cut crosswise into fine shreds
2 tablespoons butter, chilled
      A few drops of lemon juice, to taste
      Salt and white pepper *or* cayenne (ground red pepper), to
      taste

In a heavy skillet, sauté the shallots in the butter, just until transparent. Add the vermouth or wine and broth and boil over high heat until the liquid has reduced to a condensed and syrupy glaze. Add the crème fraîche or cream and cook 2–3 minutes until thickened to the desired sauce consistency.

Add the shredded sorrel leaves and simmer 15 seconds or so; then lower the heat, and whisk in the cold butter just until melted. Remove from the heat and season to taste with lemon juice, salt, and pepper.

TO PREPARE IN ADVANCE: Make up to, but do not include, the addition of the sorrel leaves; cover with plastic wrap to prevent a skin from forming, and refrigerate. Add sorrel, butter, and seasonings just before serving.

STRUDEL LEAVES

OTHER: strudel sheets

GERMAN: *Strudelteig*

Strudel leaves are almost identical to FILO PASTRY (see THE FOODS OF THE MIDDLE EAST section), from which they are a direct descendant, except that the sheets of papery strudel dough may be slightly thicker, and the dough usually has some egg added to it. The sheets are usually larger than filo leaves, anywhere from 17″ × 24″ to 36″ × 36″. You will find this dough in boxes of 4 sheets, to make 2 or 4 individual strudels, in gourmet specialty shops and in European markets in the refrigerator or freezer sections. It is not sold by the pound like filo. Filo dough can be substituted with almost identical results; in fact, the Strudelhaus brand of strudel dough we have found commercially available contains no egg, so it is virtually the same dough as filo. Directions for making strudel dough will be found in German and Austrian cookbooks, but it is tricky and requires long kneading and a deft hand.

STORAGE: If refrigerated when purchased it can be stored unopened in the refrigerator for up to 3 weeks, or frozen. If frozen, thaw overnight in the refrigerator. Plan to use the whole package for a variety of dishes. Once thawed, it is best not to refreeze because the sheets may stick together. If for some reason you decide not to use the whole package at one time, roll it up carefully inside its plastic cover and place inside a damp towel. Store in the refrigerator for use within a few days.

PREPARATION AND USE: Strudelen (the plural of strudel) are horse-shoe-shaped filled pastries popular in Bavaria and Hungary because they are inexpensive and make convenient dishes for Lent. They are filled with savory fillings, such as fish or cabbage, or with sweet fillings of apples, cottage cheese, poppy seeds, jam and coconut, or cherries. The average strudel serves 12 and requires approximately 4 cups of filling. Because the sheets vary in size and thickness according to the manufacturer, follow directions on the box for the amount of filling to use. If substituting especially thin filo, you may wish to use several more buttered layers than specified in the recipe.

The dough is placed on a clean cloth and brushed completely with melted butter. It is then usually sprinkled with bread crumbs and topped with a second sheet of dough, which is also buttered. (Up to 4 layers may be required in a recipe.) Half the sheet is now covered with about 1 cup of fine bread crumbs to within 2″ of the edges. The chosen filling is evenly distributed over the crumbs, and drizzled with 2 to 3 tablespoons of melted butter. The top and side margins of the dough (the 2″ of dough at the top and sides not covered with crumbs or filling) are folded in over the filling. The strudel is rolled up tightly by lifting the cloth and holding it taut with both hands. The roll is then eased onto a buttered baking sheet and curved into a horseshoe shape. It is brushed with butter and baked in a 350° oven for about 45 minutes, during which time it is brushed with butter two or three times. Sometimes recipes specify that a little milk or cream be poured over it during the last 20 mintues of cooking (this is absorbed by the dough). It is served warm or at room temperature. Sweet-filled strudels are often served with whipped cream.

SUGAR, EUROPEAN TERMS

The following sugars are mentioned in European recipes. They are listed here with explanations and suggested substitutes.

Castor Sugar, also **Caster Sugar:** British sugar is coarser than that in the United States, but their castor sugar is exactly like our granulated.

Sucre Glace: The French term for confectioners' (powdered or 10 X) sugar.

Sucre en Poudre: The French term for granulated sugar.

Sucre Semoule: The traditional definition for a coarse grind of sugar called "preserving sugar," often used in making preserves in Europe. It does not burn as easily as other grinds, so requires less stirring. It is seldom seen in the United States. Granulated sugar can be substituted.

TOMATOES

DUTCH: *tomaat* FRENCH: *tomate* GERMAN: *Tomate* GREEK: *domate* ITALIAN: *pomodoro* POLISH: *pomodory* SPANISH AND PORTUGUESE: *tomate* TURKISH: *dómátiz*

Tomatoes are the fruit of a vine of the nightshade family, native to South America. They were brought into popularity in Europe, specifically Italy.

The finest fresh tomatoes are vine-ripened but, unless home grown or purchased from a country roadside stand, they are nearly impossible to find. Because most fresh tomatoes found in supermarkets are picked green and are turned red by a dose of ethylene gas in the truck as they are being transported to market, they have no odor and very little flavor. Tomatoes are sold in supermarkets all year, with their peak season during May, June, and July. Varieties include the huge "beefsteak" tomatoes, "salad" tomatoes, pear-shaped Italian "plum" tomatoes, and yellow or red "cherry" tomatoes. When purchasing, look for those that are already ripe. In the West, Mexican tomatoes with more flavor are available, but import laws restrict them to 2″ or less in diameter. We have found the most flavorful supermarket tomatoes to be Italian plum and cherry (or "egg") tomatoes. We grow our own tomatoes during the summer for use in salads, sauces, and for stuffing, but usually use canned tomatoes for general cooking purposes.

STORAGE: Fresh tomatoes should not be refrigerated unless they are becoming overripe. Place firm tomatoes in a warm spot in the kitchen, such as on a sunny windowsill, and they will improve in flavor and soften. Once ripe, they should be used, but can be placed in the refrigerator for 2 to 3 days.

PREPARATION AND USE: The usual serving is 1 plum tomato per serving, or 4 ounces. Tomatoes are sliced horizontally or chopped to use in salads and relishes without peeling. If they are to be stuffed, they are usually cut in half and their seeds squeezed out, but the skin is usually left on. For sauces, soups, stews, and many other dishes, it is usually necessary to peel them. There are two simple ways. Spear with a folk and hold over a gas flame, turning it, until the skin splits. This is the quickest method if you have only a few tomatoes to peel. Alternatively, drop the tomatoes into boiling water for 30 to 45 seconds. Let cool; then peel. Either way the skin slips off easily.

Tomatoes can be stewed, pan-fried, stuffed, grilled and simmered in soups and sauces. It was Italy that took them to culinary heights with pasta sauces, pizza, and preparations too numerous to mention. In France, tomatoes are an essential ingredient in many dishes especially in those followed by the terms *Niçoise, Provençale, Portugaise, Languedocienne.* In Spain, they are usually stewed with olive oil to make a sauce, or a base for the national dish, Paella, and are essential to the cold soup-salad, Gazpacho. In Germany, they are used in Tomaten Zwiebelsalat (marinated tomato and onion salad), are stuffed with rice or cheese, and are the base for tomato sauce (Tomatensosse) made with bacon fat to be served with noodles. In France and Poland, tomatoes are often stuffed with meat or vegetables and rice to be baked. In Greece, tomatoes are stuffed with eggplant, grated cheese, and eggs in a dish called Domates Yemistes Me Melitzanes. In Mexican cooking, they are much used in Salsas (table sauces), guacamole (avocado spread), and many stewed dishes and beans. In the United States, red or green tomatoes are often sprinkled with brown sugar and fried in bacon fat to be served with cream gravy. But we like fresh tomatoes *au naturel,* in a simple salad with an herb dressing.

TOMATOES WITH FRESH BASIL DRESSING

For 4 servings

4 ounces whole-milk mozzarella cheese, very thinly sliced
2 large ripe tomatoes, sliced ¼″ thick
 Optional: 1 tablespoon freshly grated Parmesan cheese

DRESSING:
3 tablespoons "extra-virgin" olive oil
1 tablespoon red wine vinegar
1 clove garlic, peeled
1 tablespoon minced fresh basil
⅛ teaspoon salt
 Freshly ground black pepper

Alternate slices of tomatoes and cheese, overlapping, on individual serving plates or a small platter. Combine dressing ingredients in electric blender or mixing bowl and blend well. Spoon the dressing over the tomatoes and cheese and serve immediately.

TO PREPARE IN ADVANCE: The dressing can be stored in a jar in the refrigerator for up to a week. For best flavor, bring all ingredients to room temperature before serving.

CANNED TOMATOES

ITALIAN: *pomodori pelati*

Canned tomatoes are often the cook's best bet. More and more, because of the poor quality of supermarket tomatoes, we find ourselves relying on canned tomatoes for preparations that will be cooked, and many cooking experts appear to be doing the same. Their flavor is often far superior, and they are very convenient. There is a difference between types and brands of canned tomatoes. Several brands of Italian pear-shaped "plum" tomatoes are imported and are now sold in many supermarkets as well as in Italian markets. They have a flavor closer to that of Italian tomatoes than our domestic brands. Giuliano Bugialli recommends the San Marzano brands of Cirio, Vitelli, and Progresso. The latter should have the words "imported from Italy" on the can, because some Progresso tomatoes come from Argentina. We like the Progresso "peeled crushed tomatoes with added puree" sold in 28-ounce cans, and use it interchangeably in most recipes in place of "peeled whole tomatoes with their liquid" called for in most recipes. Read the labels of canned tomatoes to avoid added acid, calcium salts, or sugar.

STORAGE: After opening, canned tomatoes can be stored in a nonmetal container in the refrigerator for up to 4 days.

PREPARATION AND USE: Substitute canned tomatoes for fresh, pound for pound. A 28-ounce can yields 3½ cups.

TOMATO PASTE

ITALIAN: *concentrato doppio di pomodoro*

It is a great convenience that tomato paste, imported from Italy, is now available in toothpaste-like tubes, for those times when you need just a dab. The Cirio brand can be found in Italian markets and gourmet specialty shops. Avoid any that has baking soda listed as an ingredient on the label. Contadina is an excellent domestic brand available in cans.

STORAGE: After opening, tomato paste in tubes can be stored in the refrigerator indefinitely. Canned tomato paste should be transfered to a non-metal container and covered with oil to prevent drying. It can be refrigerated up to 2 weeks or frozen indefinitely.

USE: Use as any domestic tomato paste. A small dab may be all a sauce needs to lift the flavor. Tomato paste is highly concentrated in flavor, so it is used to add a strong tomato flavor, and some thickness, to sauces, soups, and stews.

TRUFFLES

FRENCH: *truffe* GERMAN: *Trüffel* ITALIAN: *tartufo* POLISH: *trufle* SPANISH: *criadilla de tierra*

These round, pungently flavored underground fungi are the most expensive cooking ingredient in the world. They range in size from as small as a marble to as large as an orange, and have an aromatic and really indescribable flavor somewhat like wild mushrooms. They are just beginning to be successfully cultivated. (The term "truffle" can also refer to a European chocolate confection, which is not dealt with in this book because it is not an ingredient.)

The finest black truffles are found in the French region of Perigord and in Umbria, Italy. They also grow in Poland, England, North Africa, and in parts of the United States, but these are not considered anywhere nearly as fine in flavor or aroma. They are dug up, by specially trained pigs or dogs, from around the base of oak trees during December and January. West German scientists have recently speculated that pigs are attracted to truffles because they contain a compound similar to a chemical sex attractant found in pigs.

The black truffle, which has a strong aroma but subtle flavor, is the most favored in French Haute Cuisine. They are much used, sliced or diced, as elegant garnishes for many dishes. Fresh black truffles can be found in fancy food shops at exorbitant prices from December through February. They have a much more pungent flavor and aroma than canned truffles. Canned black truffles cannot be compared to fresh and we would never buy them. If you absolutely cannot obtain fresh, they are available canned in gourmet specialty shops in several forms:

"Peeled": The finest quality, large and round with no holes. A 7-ounce can contains a single truffle, which just about fills the can.

"Brushed": Less perfect in color and shape than "peeled."

Truffle Pieces or "Peelings": The poorest quality.

Truffle Paste: Comes in a 1-ounce tube. This is usually spread on toast or used as a flavoring in sauces.

"Trufflettes": Imitation black truffles made from egg yolks and sherry. Reasonably convincing to use as a garnish, and about one-sixth the price of canned truffles, but still very expensive.

The white, or cream-colored, truffles of the Piedmont region of Italy are a more highly prized fungi in Italy than the black truffles of France. Fresh white truffles tend to be even more expensive than the black. They are in season for only a few weeks, from late October to early December, during which time, it is rumored, they sell for $750 a pound and are difficult to get even at that price. Fortunately, a little bit goes a long way. They have a much more pungent, garlicky flavor than black truffles. White truffles suffer greatly in the canning process and cannot be compared to the fresh. They are sold in small tins and also in paste form. We don't consider any form of canned white truffles worth the price.

STORAGE: In Europe, fresh truffles are often wrapped and stored in a basket of eggs or in a bag of rice so their aroma will permeate those ingredients. Fresh truffles should be tightly wrapped in plastic wrap, overwrapped with foil, and stored in the refrigerator for use within a few days. Some experts recommend covering them with Madeira or sherry in a nonmetal container to keep them moist. They can also be frozen quite successfully. Canned ones, after opening, should be stored in their liquid (or Madeira or sherry) in the same manner as fresh.

PREPARATION AND USE: Wash fresh truffles very gently. Peel carefully, so as to waste nothing, and reserve the peel to flavor broths or sauces. If using canned truffles, be sure to save any juice to use for flavoring sauces or soups. Black truffles can be cooked slightly, but are best added at the very end of the cooking time. Canned ones are already cooked, but the same rule applies. White truffles are almost never cooked, but are most often just shaved over a hot dish on the way to the table. One truffle would be ample for any recipe for 4 servings. Be sure to use a light hand with herbs and other seasonings when adding truffles to a dish so their delicate flavor will be noticeable.

Black truffles are often sliced and cut in decorative shapes to use as a garnish. Minced, they are added to pâtés, stuffings, scrambled eggs, potato salad or to sauces such as the classic Sauce Périgueux. The French dish, Poularde Demi-Deuil (literally "chicken in half mourning"), has slices of truffles slipped under the skin, and minced truffles in the stuffing.

White truffles are used in Italy to make Fonduta con Tartufi, a fondue-like dish. They are also shaved over hot pasta that has been coated with a light, non-cheesy cream sauce—one of the most deeply satisfying dishes we've ever shared. In Turin, Italy, a simple Risotto garnished with shaved white truffle, called Riso in Bianco con Tartuffi Bianchi, is a great specialty.

VERMOUTH

FRENCH: *vermouth, vermout* GERMAN: *Wermut* ITALIAN and SPANISH: *vermut*

Vermouth is a fortified wine of Italian descent. There are two types: white, and sweet, which is a dark red color. Both are widely used as ingredients in cocktails, but the white is often specified as a substitute for white wine in recipes, because it is flavored with a variety of herbs. We recommend using only the driest types, such as Noilly-Prat from France, as a cooking ingredient because Italian brands tend to be sweeter, and domestic brands vary so much in flavor.

STORAGE: For storage of more than 2 weeks, place in the refrigerator after opening.

USE: White vermouth can be substituted for white wine in most recipes and, because it is stronger in flavor, a bit less should usually be used.

VESIGA

OTHER RUSSIAN: *viziga*

"Vesiga" is a Russian term for the gelatinous marrow from the backbone of the great sturgeon. Fresh, it is a ropelike substance. In some places, such as New York City, it may be purchased in a dried form in gourmet specialty shops. It has a very bland, chewy texture when cooked, and is considered a delicacy.

STORAGE: Fresh vesiga should be stored in the refrigerator for use within 1 or 2 days; or frozen. Dried vesiga can be stored in an airtight container in a cool place for up to 6 months, though it loses quality on standing.

PREPARATION AND USE: Buy 8 ounces of fresh vesiga, or 4 ounces of the dried form to make about 1½ cups of a chopped, translucent, chewy aspic to use as an ingredient in Russian recipes. Fresh vesiga should be rinsed in cold water and split to be thoroughly cleaned. Dried vesiga should be soaked in water to cover for 3 hours. Either should then be simmered in lightly salted water for 2 to 4 hours, taking care that the water in which it cooks doesn't boil away. Drain, discard any clinging meat, and chop and use as specified in Russian recipes, as a chopped aspic-like garnish for cold fish presentations, or to serve in a clear fish broth.

The original Russian recipe for Kulebyaka, or Coulibiac as it is more commonly called in America, specified that fresh vesiga be mixed with the bulghur, rice, or kasha that makes up the filling. It seldom appears in recipes today and may certainly be omitted from any recipe that calls for it.

VINEGAR

FRENCH: *vinaigre* GERMAN: *Essig* ITALIAN: *aceto* SPANISH: *vinagre*

When it comes to imported vinegars, the interested cook has a wide selection to choose from. The wine vinegars of France, especially those from the vicinity of Orléans, are especially fine. The Dessaux Fils brand, widely distributed and sold in fine supermarkets and gourmet specialty shops, is available in two types: white-wine vinegar flavored with tarragon, or red-wine vinegar, both in 34-ounce bottles. Of our domestic supermarket brands, Spice Island and Four Monks most resemble fine French wine vinegars. White "champagne" vinegar is also sold, imported from Reims, or domestically made by Regina. Sherry wine vinegar from Spain or France, often used by top French chefs, has a distinct, rich sherry taste, and has often been aged 25 years or more. The dark, syrupy Italian Balsamico vinegar is slightly sweet (from the natural sweetness of the grapes used in its making), and has a very mellow flavor from being aged, sometimes for many years, in vats made of different woods. England has its beer and malt vinegars, which are amber colored, and slightly bitter. Scandinavian, German, and central European vinegars are not much imported.

There is a new line of French vinegars flavored with such items as garlic, raspberries, and even green peppercorns, which are sold in gourmet specialty shops and are always expensive. We suggest that you start with a fine wine vinegar, such as Dessaux Fils, and flavor your own with whatever you choose: fresh herbs, shallot, mint, raspberries, etc.

STORAGE: Stored in a cool, dark place, vinegar will keep for up to 6 months. If you are a miser with vinegar, store it in the refrigerator. If a film develops on the surface, it will not harm the vinegar or you, but should be strained off for aesthetic reasons. If the film is moldy, toss the vinegar out.

PREPARATION AND USE: Save herb vinegars and the more unusual vinegars for salads, sauces, and dishes where their taste will be evident. To make your own herb-flavored vinegars, start with 12 ounces of good red- or white-wine vinegar. Place 2 cups of fresh herb leaves, rinsed and patted dry, in a clean, wide-mouthed, 1-quart jar. Bring the vinegar to a boil in a saucepan and pour over the herbs. Let cool to room temperature uncovered; then cover with a lid and set in a cool place for 2 weeks, turning the jar often to mix. Strain and pour into clean bottles to store like any vinegar.

Red and white vinegars are basically interchangeable in recipes unless the color of red vinegar would affect a pale sauce. Sherry vinegar is strong-flavored, and one-third less of it should be used when substituting for wine vinegars. The Italian Balsamico vinegar is dark and syrupy and makes a salad dressing straight from the bottle for sliced tomatoes and leafy greens. Malt vinegar is always served in England with Fish and Chips and can be sprinkled over cooked greens or used in place of cider vinegar in any recipe.

Throughout Russia and much of Europe, vinegar is used as an important ingredient in cooked foods to give them a slightly sour flavor; examples are sauerbraten and horseradish sauces that accompany most meat, poultry, and fish dishes in Germany and Central Europe. It is used a great deal in soups, such as Lentil Soup, Onion Soup, and Polish Chlodnik. The Scandinavian countries make good use of strong white vinegar and sugar combined to flavor all kinds of Smörgasbord dishes, from herring to salads. In France, it is used in all manner of sauces, from brown sauce to serve with meat or game, to mayonnaise, to Beurre Noir (brown butter with vinegar and capers) served with eggs. It is the essential ingredient in Vinaigrette sauce served as a salad dressing or used as a marinade for cold vegetables. Following is our favorite recipe for that practical sauce.

SHALLOT VINAIGRETTE

For 3 cups

This is a delicious French dressing to keep on hand for use as a basic salad dressing, adding herbs at the last minute according to the ingredients of the salad. It is superb for marinating leftover vegetables to serve as a cold salad the next day.

1 cup red wine vinegar
2 tablespoons Dijon-style mustard
2 large shallots, minced
1 clove garlic, minced or pressed
1 tablespoon coarse salt
1 teaspoon Worcestershire sauce
¼ teaspoon ground black pepper
1½ cups light-flavored salad oil, such as sunflower or
    safflower
½ cup fine quality olive oil

In a 1-quart glass jar combine all ingredients except oils. Shake well to blend. Add the oils and shake again.

For best flavor, pour out the required amount of dressing into a bowl 10 minutes or so before serving. Add herbs if desired and let the dressing rest at room temperature to warm it slightly and develop the flavors of the herbs. Tarragon is one of our favorite additions; as is basil when tomatoes are one of the salad ingredients.

PREPARATION AND USE: This will keep for a month or longer in the refrigerator. Salad dressings taste best if they are not overly chilled at serving time.

RASPBERRY VINEGAR

For about 2 cups

This old-time ingredient has recently been made popular again by restaurants that feature "Nouvelle Cuisine." We have sampled various commercial brands, most of which taste as if they had been flavored with an extract, and found them not to our liking. In making our own, we tested the recipe with and without sugar and found we prefer it with.

1 pound (2 small baskets or 2½ cups) fresh red raspberries
⅓ cup sugar (optional)
2 cups Dessaux Fils red wine vinegar, or other fine quality
    red or white wine vinegar

Combine ingredients in glass, ceramic, or stainless double boiler. Bring the water in the bottom of the double boiler to a simmer and cook ingredients, uncovered, for 10 minutes.

Transfer to a container with a lid for refrigerator storage. Chill for 3 weeks. Strain out berries and press pulp.

TO PREPARE IN ADVANCE: After straining, this can be stored in the refrigerator indefinitely.

WALNUT OIL

FRENCH: *huile de noix* GERMAN: *Nüssol* ITALIAN: *olio di noce*

Walnut oil imported from France is richly flavored with walnuts. It is sold in gourmet specialty shops in cans or bottles of various sizes and is very expensive. Its flavor is subtle in comparison to HAZELNUT OIL. The walnut oil sold in health food stores is much less expensive, but bland in comparision.

STORAGE: Once opened, it can be stored in a cool place for up to 6 months. We always store it in the refrigerator.

PREPARATION AND USE: The subtle flavor of walnut oil is destroyed by heat, so use this only in simple cold dishes in which the subtle flavor will be apparent. The French use walnut oil primarily for dressing salads to which it gives a superb nutty flavor. It is used to make CROUTONS, and in the making of mayonnaise to dress potato salad tossed with walnut halves or spooned over cooked and cooled asparagus. We like it best in a simple oil and lemon dressing (2 parts oil to 1 part lemon) for a salad of spinach or watercress with walnuts, or used in place of olive oil in cold pasta sauces.

WORCESTERSHIRE SAUCE

Invented by chemists Lea and Perrins during the reign of Queen Victoria, this has become one of the world's most popular condiments and ingredients. The exact components are kept secret, but the Lea & Perrins label lists vinegar, molasses, sugar, anchovies, tamarind, onions, garlic, shallots, and spices. The original is sold in every supermarket, along with some domestic imitations.

STORAGE: It can be stored indefinitely on the pantry shelf, though it can get an oxidized flavor if stored for more than 6 months.

PREPARATION AND USE: Worcestershire has become a popular steak sauce and table condiment, but it is also used to give a blast of flavor to many soups, sauces, stews, and salads. It adds a spark to French Soupe à l'Oignon. It is a "must" for Caesar Salad (romaine lettuce dressed with lemon, Worcestershire, coddled egg, garlic, mashed anchovy, and freshly grated Parmigiano cheese), which was invented in Tijuana, Mexico, but is now an American classic. It has a special affinity for cheese and is essential to many English cheese dishes, such as Welsh Rarebit, as in the following recipe.

WELSH RAREBIT

3 cups (12 ounces) Cheddar cheese, For 4 servings
such as CHESHIRE or CAERPHILLY
2 tablespoons butter
½ cup ale, beer, or milk
2 teaspoons Worcestershire sauce
½ teaspoon powdered English mustard
Salt and cayenne (ground red pepper) to taste

TO SERVE:
8 slices bread or 4 English muffins, split, toasted, and
buttered, or browned in bacon drippings.

Grate or chop the cheese fine and allow it to come to room temperature.
Rarebit can be made in a very heavy saucepan, if you are careful not to overheat it. It is safer to make it in a double boiler, where it can stay warm until serving, or make it quickly in a glass bowl in a microwave oven. Heat all ingredients, except cheese, just to a simmer. Place over hot, not simmering, water, or lowest possible heat, and stir in the cheese, a handful at a time. Heat gently, stirring constantly, just until melted and smooth, taking care not to let the mixture boil. (If using the microwave, heat in 10-second periods, whisking between each one.) As soon as smooth, remove from the heat. Taste, and correct seasoning.
Spoon over toast or English muffins on warm plates, and serve immediately.

ZEST

FRENCH: *zeste*

Zest is simply the outer peel of citrus fruit. The zest of oranges and lemons are the most often specified in French recipes, and a special gadget called a zester (*zesteur* in French), which removes this outer peel in long, thin strips, is available in cookware shops. (Be sure to get a sharp one or it is a waste of money!) Many recipes call for grated peel, so it is a good idea to get in the habit of saving the peel from whatever citrus fruit you may be juicing so you will have it on hand when needed. Whole or grated citrus peel is sold dried in the spice sections of many markets, but it lacks the aromatic scent and full flavor of fresh.

STORAGE: Wrapped tightly, this can be stored in the freezer for up to a year.

PREPARATION AND USE: Zest can be removed from citrus fruit in several ways. It can be removed using a fine hand-grater or pared off with a vegetable peeler and then cut into fine strips or minced as required. We find it easiest to use a special zester. It should be held at a 45-degree angle on the skin of a thick-skinned orange or lemon, and pulled downward, using the thumb for leverage. Long strips of zest are often used as a decorative garnish in dishes that feature citrus flavors, such as Canard à l'Orange. If finely "grated" rind is called for in a recipe, simply use a sharp chef's knife to chop the zest into fine pieces.

Strips of zest can be cooked in butter and sugar for use as a decoration for desserts, and even meat dishes, such as veal or chicken. It is made in the following manner.

CARAMELIZED LEMON ZEST

Zest of 2 lemons	For ¼ cup

2 tablespoons sweet (unsalted butter)
1 teaspoon sugar

Remove the zest from the lemon with a zester (or use a swivel-blade vegetable peeler; then cut the peel into very fine julienne strips).

Melt the butter in a small heavy skillet. Add the zest and sugar and cook over very low heat, stirring with a wooden spoon, until the sugar has melted, Drain the zest on paper towels.

Serve as a garnish on desserts or on sautéed veal or chicken dishes.

PREPARATION AND USE: This can be stored in a covered jar in the refrigerator for up to a week. Warm in a skillet before serving.

ZWIEBACK

Literally, "zwieback" means twice baked, and this crisp, slightly sweet German cracker has been cooked twice: first the loaf of bread is baked, and then slices of that bread are toasted until very dry. They look like pieces of firm, dried toast. Zwieback is available in most supermarkets.

STORAGE: After opening, transfer to an airtight container for storage of up to 2 months.

USE: It is used in making a German rice pudding called Zwiebackmus. A dessert pudding, Appleschoteltje, made with baked apples, meringue, and zwiebach crumbs, is popular in Holland and France. The syrup-soaked Greek nut cake, Revani, sometimes has zwieback crumbs added to the batter.

The primary use in this country seems to be as a long-lasting snack for teething babies. We think this makes the best of all possible crusts for cheese-cake. To make it, crumble the crackers into the container of a blender or electric food processor and process until powdered. Mix 1 cup crumbs with 3 tablespoons soft butter, 2 tablespoons sugar, and ½ teaspoon ground cinnamon, and press into the bottom of a 9″ or 10″ springform pan. Bake 10 minutes at 350°. Use with any cheesecake filling, baked or unbaked.

THE FOODS
OF
LATIN AMERICA

ARGENTINA
BAHAMAS
BERMUDA
BOLIVIA
BRAZIL
BRITISH
  HONDURAS
CARIBBEAN
  DEPENDENCIES
CHILE
COLOMBIA
COSTA RICA
CUBA
DOMINICAN
  REPUBLIC
ECUADOR
EL SALVADOR
GUATEMALA
HAITI
HONDURAS
MEXICO
NICARAGUA
PANAMA
PARAGUAY
PERU
THE GUIANAS
URUGUAY
VENEZUELA
WEST INDIES

A KALEIDOSCOPE OF CUISINES

The discovery of the Americas and the islands of the Caribbean nudged the culinary world out of the Dark Ages. The sheer vitality and diversity of their produce inspired Old World kitchens and quickly became indispensable to every cuisine.

The Spanish took with them on their expeditions their traditional diet of wheat bread, olive oil, rice, onion, garlic, and wine, but they returned with infinitely more. They found an enormous variety of new vegetables and fruits, including among them chile, peppers, beans, potatoes, sweet potatoes, and squash not to mention chocolate, vanilla, and turkey, all of which have been incorporated into Western cuisines. On the other hand, the influence of Spanish-Portuguese exploration upon this area was also felt, and made the cuisines so uniformly similar that we feel our Latin American section should include the Caribbean, Mexico, and Central as well as South America.

Acting as a huge magnet, the shores of Latin America have accommodated wave upon wave of ethnic groups to its pure American Indian culture. Argentina is a good example, as its population is a mixture of Italians, French, English, Germans, Spanish, and native Indians and, as if by consent of the ethnic majority, the cuisine preference is about 60 percent Italian–native Indian. The Germans and the Italians have together introduced a wide variety of sausages, and the French, an atmosphere of Paris, with breakfasts of hot coffee and hot milk, a substantial lunch at noon, tea at 5:30, and dinner between 10:00 p.m. and 2:00 a.m.

The markets have for sale all of the temperate zone's fruits and vegetables that North Americans are acquainted with, plus a few of the more unusual,

473

such as the *cardoon*, a vegetable relative of the artichoke family. Trout, game, and seafood are abundantly available, but Argentineans are, first and foremost, beef eaters, as reflected in such favored dishes as Carne Asado (broiled beef ribs), which they baste and serve with an aromatic spicy sauce, and stuffed beef roll, which they call Matambre. If one dish could be selected as representative of national taste, it would have to be Carbonada Criolla, a meaty vegetable soup, which is often served in a giant, hollowed-out squash, accompanied perhaps by Risotto with Peas.

It was the Spanish who introduced beef and pork to Argentina, but it was the native Indian as kitchen help (conquistadores did little work) who blended the new with the old and developed lasting culinary innovations, such as their spicy vegetable, beef, and pork-stuffed corn husks called Humitas. Here the native influence is easily apparent as it is also in their Maté (borrowed from neighboring Paraguay), a drink of crushed evergreen leaves steeped in boiling water, traditionally served in a hollow gourd and sipped through a silver straw.

Argentina's western neighbor, Chile, shares the same cultural heritage; however, there is no one predominant cuisine. It is a nation on a huge seafood binge, delighting in fish soups and stews, such as Chupe de Mariscos, a seafood chowder, often spicy. One dish Chile has in common with Argentina is Empanadas, turnovers that are filled with meat, onion, eggs, olives, or whatever looks good to the cook that day. In many ways, this reminds one of Cornish Pasties, though smaller. Perhaps Empanadas de Crema, miniature half-moon cream pies, are empanadas at their improvisational best. They are seen everywhere in Chile. These small Argentinean pies show up again in Brazil, as Empadinhas de Camaroes, unsweetened pies with a shrimp filling.

We find an entirely different kaleidoscope of cultures in Brazil, and the cooking here is not Italian–native Indian, but Portuguese–native Indian. Brazil's immigrants have been drawn mainly to the area south of Rio, where you will find settlers from Germany, Italy, Austria, Switzerland, Poland, Russia, and the single largest Japanese colony outside Japan. Here, literally a world apart from the fierce Amazon Jungle in the northwest, is a gourmet's paradise, where absolutely everything known to please the palate can be found, including limitless variations of fresh seafood from 5,000 miles of Atlantic coastline, tropical and subtropical fruits of all kinds (some unknown outside of Brazil), wine, cheese, truly extraordinary coffee, and the Brazilian white-lightening rum called *cachaca*. Brazilians have in common with the majority of South Americans a love of black beans and rice. They are, in fact, the basis of their national dish, Feijoada, (pronounced fay-ZHWAH-dah), a dish that is a fairly good introduction to the diet of this country because it's neither too spicy nor too rich. It is made with a variety of meats, including dried beef, *manioc* meal, and slices of orange, and is traditionally served in the major cities of Brazil on Saturdays. We recommend it as an excellent buffet dish—one serving consists of a sausage, a pork chop, rice and beans, onion rings, bananas, and a slice or two of orange! Another favorite dish is Camaroes a Bahiana, which is shrimp in a highly spiced, thick tomato sauce served with rice.

Colombia, at the northern tip of the Andes, has two separate cuisines: the *sierra* (mountain) and the *tierra caliente* (tropical). In modern Colombia, these two cuisines occasionally blend. A good example is the popular Ajiaco, a delicious chicken and potato soup served with buttery avocados or slices of corn on the cob. Colombia is settled only on the narrow region that lies between the low foothills of the Andes and the coast of the Caribbean to the north, and Panama and the Pacific on the west. The most popular dish is a fish stew called Fancocho, which many Europeans have compared to bouillabaisse. Another traditional dish is Puchero Santa Fereno, a combination of broiled chicken, brisket of beef flavored with port wine, plus pumpkin and vegetables. Arroz con Pollo, literally chicken with rice and, of course, Tamales, spicy meat pies steamed in banana leaves, are not only nutritious but tasty.

Not far from Colombia are the islands of the Caribbean, the first land to be seen in the New World, and sugar cane, an ideal crop, was introduced there early. To develop sugar plantations, colonists arrived from half a dozen countries, and slaves by the hundreds of thousands were brought from Africa. This tapestry of cultures, Spanish, English, French, Dutch, African, and native Carib Indian, have left the cooking world an interesting inheritance. After colonization, each island seemed content enough to live with and develop what it had. And what they all had in common was the sea, the native Indian culture, and a healthy sprinkling of early Spanish–Portuguese influence.

An island-hopping overview of some of the better-known culinary innovations includes conch, a great favorite in the Bahamas. There are, among these 700 islands, dozens of variations on its use, such as cracked conch, which is dipped in batter and deep-fried, or conch chowder (stewed with vegetables), and even a conch salad. Another local specialty of the Bahamas is green turtle pie, which is simply turtle meat baked in a pastry shell.

In Barbados, some of the more exotic specialties are coconut bread, Coo-Coo, which is a type of cornmeal pudding similar to West Africa's Fufu, curried goat, and Jug-Jug, a mixture of corn, peas, and ground meat, which is a traditional Christmas dish.

In Bermuda, perhaps lobster is the most popular dish but, running a close second, is cassava pie, made of seasoned pork, chicken or beef, thickened with cassava flour.

Of all the islands in the Caribbean, Cuba is the most Spanish in background and preference. The most popular shellfish is *langostino,* a fresh-water prawn. And, served everywhere, you find that staple of the Caribbean, black beans and rice, called Moros y Christianos (Moors and Christians). In Cuba, however, the rice is flavored with saffron. As for meat, pork is king, and the favorite for holiday fare is suckling pig.

In Dominica, aside from the normally wide range of tropical fruits, there is what the natives call mountain chicken, *crapaud*, which is, in fact, a large island frog. On Granada, the specialty is avocado ice cream. French Guadeloupe entices its visitors with such specialties as Colombo, meat served in a saffron sauce, or Accras, seafood that is fried and wonderfully seasoned with herbs.

Pork, beef, and lamb are well liked in the islands of the Caribbean, but red meat seems to be of little importance to the people, whose everyday diet is primarily seafood and vegetables. The food of French Martinique is sophisticatedly French, embracing haute cuisine, but there is a Creole inventiveness that asserts itself, especially with the seafoods, in the stuffed crabs, and in the island's deep-fried Plantains Stuffed with Beef.

Puerto Rico, like Cuba, reflects the heavy influence of Spain on its food, one of its favorite dishes being Paella, made with a variety of seafood and Spanish sausage called *chorizo*. Another of their popular foods, which is used as a snack, is Tostones, made of thin deep-fried slices of plantain, a starchy fruit of the banana family that is not sweet, and is always cooked. More often, plantains are used as a vegetable, with a taste somewhere between a banana and a potato.

In Trinidad, take your pick of cuisines—English, American, French, Chinese, Indian, or Creole. This is also the home of stuffed crab backs, miniature oysters, and Angostura Bitters.

The Virgin Islands offer up their version of a type of soup made with greens called *callaloo*. Another specialty is Herring Gundy, a salad.

The Caribbean Sea is held captive by these islands on the east and by Central America to the west. There is, however, a substantial difference in the cuisines of these two Caribbean areas. Whereas the islands represent a happy scramble of international fare, the countries to the west, between North and South America, are influenced by a heavy native Indian–Spanish heritage, and their cuisines are only minor variations on the overwhelmingly heavy cadence of Mexican cuisine immediately to their north.

The Mexico conquered by Hernando Cortes consisted of countless independent villages, scattered about and nestled into fertile, and almost inaccessible valleys, with little or no intercommunication or commerce. The end result of Cortes's invasion was a unification of the country and the opening up of conduits of cultural communication, through which flowed a stream of Mediterranean onions, garlic, wheat, and oil.

If asked to point out the major difference between Spanish cooking and Mexican–Indian cooking, we could safely say it was the difference between frying and boiling. In pre-Spanish Mexico, cooking fats and oils were not used. The native Indian methods of cooking were boiling, broiling, or steaming. Frying was a gift from the Old World to the New, and was a direct result of the introduction of Spanish swine. Today, over half of all the food prepared in Mexico is fried in some way. Fried chunks of succulent pork, called Carnitas, Tacos, and fried pork skins called Chicharrón are a few examples. Some of the more sophisticated villages adapted quickly to the new Spanish foods, innovatively modifying them into many fine dishes. For example, instead of making corn tortillas, they made Spanish flour tortillas. Onions were quickly mixed with their tomato–chile sauces. Pork and kid *(cabrito)*, as well as beef, instantly created hundreds of new variations in their diets.

The unique decentralization of Mexican valley, or "pocket," culture, helped to preserve the best of pre-Spanish cooking. And the best that could be done in their clay pots was to stew. Mexico's most outstanding dishes always were delicious thick sauces over generous nuggets of vegetables and meats, such as Pollo en Pipián, chicken bathed in a sauce thickened with ground roasted pumpkin seeds.

The foundation, then, of Mexican cooking, is its diversity of sauces. Mexico's national holiday dish is Mole Poblano de Guajolote, turkey in Pueblan sauce. The word *mole* comes from the Aztec word *molli,* which means a liquid mixture containing chile. In the rural areas of Mexico, some kitchens still use a three-legged stone mortar and pestle called the *molcajete* to grind and prepare their *moles. Mole* can also be bought in paste or powdered form at local native markets.

Lest our discussion frighten the chile-wary cook, we must admit that not all sauces contain chile. In fact, not all Mexicans like chiles, and those who do use their own combinations, with their own preferred degree of hotness.

The cuisine of modern Mexico is unified, and regional produce is well distributed; however, local specialties are based upon the raw materials that flourish in that region only. For example, in northern Mexico, where the weather is hot and dry, wheat and cattle thrive and, consequently, they play a large part in northern Mexico's cuisine. Examples of this region's food are its variety of cheeses and flour tortillas. Central Mexico, which was the home of corn and the center of Aztec culture, developed such classic dishes as corn tortillas and Tamales, corn dough stuffed and steamed in corn husks or banana leaves. Southern Mexico is hot and moist and naturally produces tropical fruits and vegetables in abundance. Here we find one of the most individualistic of all of Mexico's regional cuisines, the Yucatecan or Mayan, where the food is often a bright orange color, the natural result of using a favorite rusty-red seed, *achiote* (annatto), which is typically used in Pollo Pibil, chicken pieces marinated in a spicy *achiote* paste called *recado colorado,* and then wrapped in banana leaves and steamed in a pit.

Food is important socially as well to the Mexican people and street eating is a national pastime, a way of life, with vendors selling everything from Tacos and Burritos to sweets *(dulces)* such as candied sweet potato *(camote),* sweet breads and ices, nuts and hulled pumpkin seeds, which are piled for sale neatly on the ground. There are very few children or adults, either playing or working, who don't have something tucked in pocket or purse for sustenance until their next meal.

The following pages will lead you more deeply into the cuisines of the New World, whose ingredients are satisfyingly earthy, and oftentimes unusual. Here we find vegetables and fruits that are becoming more and more widely available, ingredients that were once considered too exotic for innovative use.

ACHIOTE CONDIMENTADO

See RECADO COLORADO

ACHIOTE SEED

(ah-chee-OH-tay)
OTHER: butter coloring, *annatto, urucú, biji* (a round variety), *achuete, roucou*

IN THE PHILIPPINES: *atchuete*

Achiote is the rusty-red seed of the tropical *annatto* tree, available whole or ground in 1-ounce bags in Latin American, East Indian, and Spanish markets. Take care that those you buy have a bright color; brown ones are too old. The powdered form is often called "butter coloring" in the United States, where it is commonly used to color not only butter but also cheddar cheese, margarine, and smoked fish. The flavor is slightly musky and the seeds are used primarily for color—in oil in the Caribbean, in a blended spice paste called RECADO COLORADO in the Yucatán. Achiote is occasionally available in paste form, which saves the soaking and grinding procedures described below. It is a natural product that can be used safely without concern.

STORAGE: The seeds may be stored indefinitely in a tightly covered jar in a cool, dry place. Coloring oil made with the seeds, as described below, should be stored in the refrigerator for use within 3 months.

PREPARATION AND USE: Achiote is used primarily to lend rice or other foods with which it is cooked a bright, saffron yellow color. Especially in Caribbean cooking, the seeds are used to color cooking oil or lard which is then called *aciete* or *manteca de achiote* or *annatto*. To make it, heat 2 parts oil or lard with 1 part seeds in a heavy saucepan or skillet over medium-low heat for 5 to 10 minutes until the oil is bright orange. Remove as soon as the oil starts to lighten in color or both the flavor and the color will be lost.

Cool and store in a jar in the refrigerator to use as you would any fat in cooking.

For most Mexican recipes the seeds are ground. If you have an electric coffee/spice mill, they are easily powdered. If they are to be ground in an electric blender, which won't produce nearly as fine a powder, they must be soaked before grinding, and, if the seeds are very hard, they should be simmered in water to cover for 2 to 3 minutes and allowed to stand until cool. Achiote powder, when added to the water in which rice is cooked, adds its yellow-orange color (similar to saffron) as well as a curious, slightly musky flavor. The powder is often used, like paprika, to coat meats before roasting.

In the Yucatán, achiote is ground with other spices into various seasoning pastes, used in dishes such as Pollo Pibil (chicken in banana leaves) and Adobo sauces, which may be purchased in local markets. See RECADO COLORADO for an example. In Jamaica, the oil is used to color Stamp and Go (codfish cakes). In Peru, it is used in Chancho Adobado (pork in orange and lemon sauce with sweet potatoes) and Ají de Gallina (chicken in spicy nut sauce). In Colombia, the oil is added to the dough for a Tamale-like dish steamed in banana leaves called Hallacas Centrales. In the Philippines, it is used in various chicken dishes and in Kari-Kari (beef and vegetable stew). A simple yellow rice is made in the Yucatán.

ACITRÓN

(ah-see-TROHN)
OTHER: *biznaga*

Acitrón, a pale yellow, candied cushion cactus *(echinocactus grandis),* adds little flavor but interesting texture to many Mexican dishes. It is sold in 1" bars in Mexican markets. Candied pineapple or other bland candied fruits make acceptable substitutes.

STORAGE: Tightly wrapped in the refrigerator, it will keep indefinitely, though if very moist it can mold. It turns sugary within 2 months at room temperature.

USE: This is eaten as is for a simple sweet, or is chopped to flavor Picadillo (spicy meat hash used as a stuffing for chiles or Tacos), or desserts. The usual amount is ¼ cup finely diced acitrón to 1 pound meat or to 4 cups of dessert, when a texture contrast is desired.

ADOBO DE ACHIOTE

See RECADO COLORADO

AJI

See CHILES

AKEE

OTHER: *ackee, achee,* vegetable brains

This is an exotic red fruit with three compartments which, when ripe, expand and burst to reveal three seeds that look like black chestnuts, but which are inedible. Beneath them, the flesh of the fruit looks and tastes a great deal like scrambled eggs. Akee was introduced to Jamaica by Captain Bligh, who brought it from West Africa in 1793, and its popularity is confined to that island. Because certain parts of the fruit are highly toxic if underripe, it is just as well that it is available in Caribbean markets in the United States only in cans, packed in water.

STORAGE: After opening, the unused portion can be stored in its original liquid in the refrigerator for up to 3 days.

USE: An 18-ounce can, drained, yields about 1 cup of akee, the equivalent of the edible portion of 2 dozen akees. This is usually enough for 4 servings when combined with other ingredients.

Though a fruit, this is most often treated as a vegetable. In Jamaica, it is cooked with salted codfish, chiles, and onion to make the national dish, Saltfish and Akee. It has a bland taste, and is often combined with meat and cheese for au gratin and curried dishes, or is sieved and sweetened to make a dessert soufflé.

ANGOSTURA

This bitter bark of a South American tree is used as a flavoring agent but is most commonly known in the form of aromatic liquid "bitters" of the same name, which is available in most liquor stores.

STORAGE: The bitters will keep indefinitely on the pantry shelf.

USE: Use a few drops as a flavor enhancer for cocktails and for Caribbean stewed dishes.

ANNATTO

See ACHIOTE SEED

ARROWROOT

OTHER: *arracacha*, arrowroot starch

FRENCH: arrowroot GERMAN: *Pfeiwurz* ITALIAN: *maranta* or *tubero edule* SPANISH: *arrurruz*

Arrowroot is a rhizome that is made into the finest and easiest to digest of all starches. It is used for thickening sauces and lending a glossy appearance to them without leaving any starchy taste. It is preferable to cornstarch because of its very neutral flavor and because it lends such a beautiful glaze to sauces. It is quite a bit more expensive, however. Natural-food advocates favor it as a thickening agent also. The majority of the world's supply is exported from St. Vincent Island in the British West Indies. You will find it in most supermarkets in the spice section, and it is widely available (and considerably less expensive) in Asian and Caribbean markets.

The root is occasionally eaten in the Caribbean as a starchy vegetable, as it is in China. See ARROWROOT in THE FOODS OF ASIA section for preparation.

STORAGE: If stored airtight in a cool, dry place, it will keep indefinitely.

PREPARATION AND USE: Arrowroot is used to thicken sauces, and as an ingredient in cakes and cookies. It has a stronger thickening power than cornstarch. To thicken 1 cup liquid, use 1 teaspoon arrowroot powder per each 1½ teaspoons cornstarch, or 1 tablespoon of flour called for in a recipe. Make a paste of 1 part powder to 2 parts cold water. Stir gradually into boiling soups or sauces. Once thickened, sauces should not be boiled for more than a few seconds, as any starch will break down and lose its thickening power when overcooked.

On St. Vincent, it is used to thicken a custard of evaporated milk, sugar, and eggs, served over fresh fruit.

ATE

(AH-tay)

Ate is a firm, jamlike paste made from various fruits. *Guayabate,* for instance, is made from guavas; *membrillate* from *membrillo* (quince), and *ate de mango* from mangoes. The most famous ates are from Morelia in the state of Michoacán, Mexico. You will find them in Latin American and gourmet specialty shops. An excellent basic recipe may be found in *The Complete Book of Mexican Cooking* by Elisabeth Lambert Ortiz (Bantam Books).

STORAGE: After opening, wrap the unused portion tightly in plastic and

481

keep in a cool, dry place (for up to a month), or store in the refrigerator and it will keep indefinitely. Take care that it does not dry out.

USE: These pastes are sliced to serve with crackers and mild cheese such as Chihuahua (see QUESO DE CHIHUAHUA, under CHEESE), Monterey Jack, or cream cheese for dessert.

AVOCADO

OTHER: alligator pear, love fruit

FRENCH: *avocat, poire d'avocat* GERMAN: *Advocatbirne* SPANISH: *aguacate* (ah-wah-KAH-tay)

This buttery fruit of a tropical and subtropical tree is often treated as a vegetable. Two of the finest American varieties are the Haas, bumpy-skinned and black, available in summer, and the Fuerte, one of the smooth-skinned green types, available in winter. There are numerous larger varieties, found especially among those from Florida, which tend to be much less flavorsome and more watery in texture. Calavo is a California brand, not a variety of avocado. Easterners tell us that the best ones they find are from California.

STORAGE: All avocados are picked when unripe, so you will be wise to buy them several days before they are needed to allow time for ripening. A very hard avocado will take up to 5 days to ripen. If you are in a rush to ripen them, place them in a paper bag or fruit ripener with a ripe tomato or banana. To slow down ripening, store in the refrigerator. If using only half an avocado, leave the pit in the unused portion, brush the cut area with lemon juice, and cover tightly with plastic wrap for refrigerator storage of up to 3 days.

PREPARATION AND USE: For most uses, allow 1 avocado for 2 servings. To cut half-shells, use a stainless knife to cut lengthwise around the avocado pit; then twist the halves to separate. Remove the seed by whacking it sharply with the blade of your knife and twisting slightly—it will lift right out. To slice or dice, place the peeled halves cavity side down on a cutting board. Diced or sliced, avocados make a delightful garnish for many salads, sandwiches, and Latin American dishes of all descriptions. Rings of avocado make an attractive garnish—to make them, cut the avocado in crosswise slices before peeling; then peel the rings.

In Mexico, guacamole, a mixture of mashed avocado, onion, tomato, CIL-ANTRO (see CORIANDER, in the HERBS, SPICES, AND SEASONING BLENDS section), chiles, and salt is almost as common as Salsa Cruda, the spicy tomato sauce served on every table. Guacamole or avocado slices garnish everything from Huevos Rancheros to Tostadas. In northern Mexico, avocado is mashed and used as a spread, which is why it is known as Mantequilla de Pobre ("poor man's butter"). In Cuba, an Avocado Sauce is made to serve with red snapper. In Mexico and in Venezuela, slices of avocado are placed in a bowl into which hot soup is ladled. We have even found recipes for Avocado Mousse and Avocado Pie.

We have seen avocado halves, "fruit on the half shell," used in such a myriad of intriguing ways recently—as a first course, with the cavity created by the removal of the pit filled with a vinaigrette, or even a warm dressing of equal portions catsup, Worcestershire sauce, and butter. Halves can be filled with seafood or chicken salads to serve as a light main course or with ice cream or guava jelly to serve as a dessert. Cream of Avocado Soup served in the shell is a specialty of Bernard's restaurant in the Biltmore Hotel in Los Angeles.

AVOCADO LEAVES

Diana Kennedy, renowned Mexican-cooking authority, says that the leaves of avocado trees are toasted and ground to lend an anise–hazelnut flavor to many dishes in the region south of Mexico City and Puebla. They are seldom available in markets but, if you are fortunate enough to have an avocado tree, you have a ready supply. Some trees yield leaves with almost no taste at all, so experiment until you find some that are flavorful.

STORAGE: Fresh avocado leaves can be dried in your kitchen or wherever air circulates freely. Alternatively, they can be dried in a turned-off oven for approximately 2 days. When dry, wrap airtight and put in a cool place for storage of up to 6 months.

PREPARATION AND USE: Toast the leaves for a minute or so in a dry skillet or on a *comal* (tortilla griddle) to bring out their flavor. Use as you would a bay leaf to season a slow-simmered stew, or grind fine to sprinkle on bean dishes. They are often used as a flavoring in PIPIÁN dishes (stews thickened with nuts or seeds).

AZAFRÁN

OTHER: Mexican saffron

Mexican "saffron" is not the same thing as the very expensive European or Asian SAFFRON (see HERBS, SPICES, AND SEASONING BLENDS section). The threads come from the stigmas of the large orange flowers of the safflower plant, the same plant whose seeds yield safflower oil. Azafrán is commonly found in 1-ounce bags in Latin American markets, but can be purchased in bulk at herb shops.

STORAGE: Store as you would the expensive saffron, in a cool dark place, for use within a few months.

USE: This is used in larger amounts than saffron, but in the same manner, to give rice a deep yellow "saffron" tint. Use 1 tablespoon of Mexican saffron for ¼ teaspoon of true saffron. The flavor is slightly less sweet than true saffron, so you may wish to add a bit of sugar to taste. A similar color is achieved with ACHIOTE SEED.

BACALAO

OTHER: salt codfish

FRENCH: *morue*

Salted codfish, and often other types of fish, are popular ingredients on many of the Caribbean islands. For general information, see COD, SALTED AND DRIED in THE FOODS OF EUROPE section.

STORAGE: It will keep indefinitely in a cool, dry place.

PREPARATION AND USE: Soak the bacalao in cold water to cover for at least 2 hours, or longer if it is especially salty. Drain and rinse it well. Pour boiling water over it and allow it to stand for 5 to 10 minutes to remove more of the salty flavor and to make it soft enough to remove any bones. Bone; then use as directed in the recipe. As a general rule, 8 ounces will be ample for a recipe to serve 3 or 4. In the Caribbean, this ingredient is used in many ways: in salads and fritters, with AKEE as the national dish of Jamaica, and marinated to serve as a side dish.

BANANA LEAVES

SPANISH: *hojas de plátano*

Banana leaves are often used in Mexico, the Caribbean, Central America, and Southeast Asia in place of corn husks or foil to wrap Tamales (corn dough filled with meat or sweet mixtures) or other foods to be steamed. They are easiest to find in Latin American markets at Christmas and Easter when these foods are traditional holiday fare. (Of course, if you have a banana tree, you have your own supply.) Dried, in packages, they often look disreputable at best. TI LEAVES (see THE FOODS OF ASIA section) can be substituted. Oiled parchment paper, or foil, can also be substituted, but with much sacrifice of appearance and flavor.

STORAGE: Wrap tightly in foil and store in the crisper of the refrigerator for use within 3 months, or for as long as you like in the freezer. Thaw before using.

PREPARATION AND USE: If a white surface mold has developed during storage, simply wipe it off. Rinse and dry well before using. Cut away and discard the center vein and cut the leaf into 8″ to 12″ squares along the veins of the leaf. Warm briefly over a gas flame, or pour boiling water over the leaves in a colander, to make them pliable. Use to wrap foods to be steamed. An overwrapping of foil is usually recommended to prevent leaking. The steamed food is served in the leaf, but the leaf is not eaten.

A popular Yucatecan dish is Pollo Pibil, chicken marinated in a paste of sour orange juice, spices, and achiote paste, and then steamed in a banana leaf. In Colombia and Venezuela, the leaves enclose elaborate Tamale-like creations called Hallacas Centrales, with a filling of chicken, pork, raisins, olives, and capers, which are then overwrapped with paper and tied with string. In Sri Lanka, banana leaves are used to wrap curries and various sambals to make individual servings of a festival dish called Lampries. In Indonesia, they wrap spiced fish to be charcoal-grilled and, in Bali, they wrap a troutlike fish, Ikan Pepes.

BAY RUM BERRIES
See HERBS, SPICES, AND SEASONING BLENDS section

BEANS, DRIED
DOMINICAN REPUBLIC and PUERTO RICO: *habichuelas* FRENCH CARIBBEAN: *pois* SPANISH: *frijoles* (free-HOH-lehs)

Technically the word "pulse" is more accurate than the word "bean," but we will use the word "bean" to describe any seed from the pod of a leguminous plant, and this will apply to all beans, peas, lentils, etc.

It would be difficult to imagine a complete Latin American meal without beans because they are such an important staple food in that area. In Mexico and other tropical places, they are usually not soaked overnight before cooking as is the tendency in the United States because, in a warm climate, they begin to ferment in the soaking water unless refrigerated.

STORAGE: Dried beans can be stored in a dry place for years, though the fresher they are, the better their flavor. Beans that are more than a year old take longer to cook. Cooked beans improve in flavor if, when cool, they are placed in the refrigerator for at least 24 hours. They can be kept for up to 5 days in the refrigerator if they are boiled for 10 minutes every third day—

the cooking liquid becomes thicker and more flavorful with each boiling. Cooked beans also freeze well, but it is best to freeze beans and liquid separately.

PREPARATION AND USE: As a general rule, beans triple in volume when cooked, so 1 cup of dried beans will yield approximately 2½ to 3 cups of cooked beans. Wash well in cold water and pick over to remove any gravel. It is not absolutely necessary to soak beans, although almost all cookbooks (except Diana Kennedy's) say to soak them, and many cooks feel it is important, too. Soaking can be done in two ways: overnight in cold water, or for 1 hour in water in which they have been boiled for 2 minutes. With either method, use approximately three times as much water as beans. There is disagreement over whether to discard the soaking water, rinse the beans, and start with fresh water, or to use the soaking water to cook the beans. Some experts say the soaking water contains nutrients; others that it interferes with the utilization of proteins.

To make 6 servings, place 1 pound of dried beans, soaked or not, in a heavy pot with 8 cups of water, 1 minced or whole onion, a ham hock or garlic, as desired, but *no salt*. (Mexican cooks often add a sprig of EPAZOTE, 1 or 2 SERRANO chiles (see under CHILES, FRESH), and 2 tablespoons lard.) Simmer slowly for 1½ to 3 hours until tender. Salt may be added to taste during the last ½ hour of cooking but, if added earlier, it is believed to toughen the beans. When served from the pot with some of their cooking liquid, they are called Frijoles de la Olla. The cooking broth is often used as a base for various soups.

To make basic "refried" beans or FRIJOLES REFRITOS (the "re" prefix does not mean "again," but is an emphatic description meaning "well-fried"), use pinto, pink, or black beans cooked as described above. Heat ¾ cup bacon drippings, lard, or butter in a very heavy skillet (cast iron is ideal). Place some of the cooked beans with their liquid in the pan and mash thoroughly. Keep adding liquid and beans and mashing until all beans and liquid have been used. Stir constantly to prevent scorching. "Refried" beans are often served with crumbled cheese (QUESO BLANCO, see under CHEESE) and radish roses to garnish, with wedges of fried tortilla to use as scoops.

BLACK BEANS

OTHER: turtle beans, black turtle beans, Mexican black beans, soup beans

SPANISH: *frijoles negros* (free-HOH-lehs NEH-grohs)

These small, flat, charcoal-colored beans with a white spot are less than ½″ in length. These have a delicious meaty flavor and are the most popular bean in the Caribbean and in southern Mexico.

486

USE: Mexican cooks swear by EPAZOTE in the pot.

A Yucatecan specialty is Panuchos—thick corn tortillas filled with black beans, fried or hard-cooked egg, and topped with shredded chicken, onion rings, and cheese. In the Caribbean, black beans are served with white rice in a dish called Moros y Christianos (Moors and Christians). Black beans are traditional in the Brazilian national dish, Feijoada Completa, which is garnished with a large variety of cooked meats and sprinkled with *farofa* (toasted *manioc* meal, see CASSAVA MEAL).

Black beans are excellent soup beans and have an affinity for sherry. We think they are the most elegant of all dried beans because of their attractive color, which contrasts so beautifully with garnishes such as sour cream, avocado, purple onion, sliced lemon, hard-cooked egg, chopped chiles, cooked rice, or diced tomato. We like them so well that we often serve a simple black bean soup, flavored with a bit of epazote, for casual Sunday afternoon parties. We provide clay dishes of assorted condiments and a small cruet of sherry for guests to help themselves. Here is our recipe for the soup and the condiments.

SOPA DE FRIJOL NEGRO (Black Bean Soup)

2   cups dried black beans, rinsed and soaked in 6 cups cold water
2   large onions, chopped
6   cloves garlic, minced
1   green bell pepper (seeds and veins removed), diced
¼   cup bacon drippings, lard, or cubed salt pork
    Some sprigs of fresh EPAZOTE *or* 1 teaspoon dried
1   teaspoon ground cumin
3   to 4 cups beef or chicken broth
½   cup Madeira or sherry

For 10 to 12 servings

CONDIMENTS: (Use any or all)
    Wedges of lime
    Minced mild white onion
    Chopped fresh coriander (cilantro or Chinese parsley)
    Salsa Cruda (see RECIPE INDEX)
    Hard-cooked egg, minced

Place the beans and their soaking liquid in a large, heavy soup pot with all the remaining ingredients except the broth and the Madeira or sherry. Bring to a boil; then lower the heat and simmer very slowly for 2 to 3 hours until the beans are very tender, adding boiling water if necessary to keep the mixture from scorching. Drain the beans, reserving their cooking liquid and returning it to the cooking pot. Puree the beans, 1 to 2 cups at a time in a blender or electric food processor, and add them to the liquid. (Some beans may be left whole, if desired, for texture.) Add broth to thin the soup to the desired consistency. Simmer 10 minutes; then add the Madeira or sherry and remove from the heat. Transfer to a warm tureen or soup bowls, and serve immediately with condiments, which diners can serve themselves.

TO PREPARE IN ADVANCE: This can be stored in refrigerator for up to 4 days or in the freezer for up to 6 months. Reheat gently in a heavy saucepan.

PINK BEANS
OTHER: *rosadas,* Mexican red beans, chili beans

These are oval, pinkish-tan beans with a flavor very similar to PINTO BEANS, with which they can be used interchangeably in recipes. They are available all year in most supermarkets.

USE: These are the most commonly served cooked beans in Mexico—they accompany most meals, and are used to make "refried" beans, Frijoles Refritos, and "chili" beans. They are pureed for use as a sauce for Enchiladas, and are also added to stews and combined with rice.

PINTO BEANS
OTHER: *frijoles pintos*

Pinto beans are a pale pinkish-tan color, speckled with brown spots. They have a rather meaty flavor and the same mealy texture as PINK BEANS, with which they are interchangeable.

USE: The spots disappear in cooking, but there is no loss of flavor. They appear in soups, Chile con Carne, American southwestern-style Barbecue Beans and, in Mexico, are often flavored with beer or tequila, to make Frijoles Borrachos.

BIGARADE
See ORANGE, SEVILLE, in THE FOODS OF EUROPE section

BIZNAGA
See ACITRÓN

BRAZIL NUT

OTHER: para nut, cream nut

FRENCH: *noix de Brésil* GERMAN: *Paranuss* ITALIAN: *noce del Brasile* SPANISH: *nuez del Brasil*

Brazil nuts are large, triangular nuts available in most supermarkets, either in their shells, or blanched and shelled, but with some of their skin left on. Their shells are very hard and difficult to remove, so you would be wise to buy them shelled from a reliable source where there is a large turnover (they lose flavor quickly after being shelled). Brazil nuts come from large trees that grow along the Amazon River in Brazil, and most of what we see in markets is exported from there. Their oil is often used in Brazil as a flavorful substitute for olive oil.

STORAGE: We store these nuts, like most nuts, in the freezer to preserve their flavor as long as possible, though they may lose a bit of their crispness.

PREPARATION AND USE: To bring out their flavor, toast them in a 350° oven for about 15 minutes until golden. They are most often salted to serve as snacks. For desserts, they are often sliced, which is made easier if they are soaked for 30 minutes or so to soften them.

In Brazil, they are used in Pato Com Molho de Laranja (duck in orange sauce). They are often used to garnish vegetables such as broccoli and other greens, and are ground as a stuffing for avocados.

BREADFRUIT

FRENCH: *fruit à pain* ITALIAN: *frutto del albero del pane* SPANISH: *fruta del árbol del pan*

This is a large green fruit, related to the JACKFRUIT (see THE FOODS OF ASIA section). It was brought to the West Indies from Tahiti by Captain Bligh, who was commissioned in 1787 by King George III of England to do so. It has become a staple food in the West Indies and in Brazil. You will sometimes find fresh breadfruit in Latin American markets. There are several varieties, but most are 8″ to 10″ in diameter, look like bumpy green grapefruits, and have a bland, whitish, bread-like center. They are also available in 26-ounce cans.

STORAGE: Whole breadfruit will keep for weeks in a cool place.

PREPARATION AND USE: Breadfruit must be cooked to be edible. One breadfruit, weighing about 2 pounds, or a 26-ounce can, will be ample for 6 servings. To serve as a vegetable side dish, peel fresh breadfruit and cut out the core, or drain canned breadfruit. Cook with desired seasonings in water to cover for about 15 minutes until tender, drain, and mash with butter to the consistency of mashed potatoes. They have a starchy taste that makes them an excellent substitute for potatoes, rice, or CASSAVA, and are often used as a soup ingredient or are made into balls and filled with the Jamaican dish, Saltfish and Akee.

In Barbados, breadfruit are made into a molded paste called Coo-Coo (the Caribbean version of African Fufu). In Grenada, they are made into a version of Vichyssoise, and in Martinique are made into a dish called Pudding au Fruit de Pain. Sometimes a dish is made by baking a whole breadfruit in foil, scooping out the center, combining it with meat or fish, and returning it to the shell for serving.

BRIONNE

See CHAYOTE

CAJETA

(kah-HET-tah)

OTHER: *leche quemada, dulce de leche, manjar blanco,* caramel candy

The word "cajeta" means, literally, little box, but cajeta, here, means a thick, golden, opaque honeylike paste used as a spread, a specialty of the small town of Celaya in the state of Guanajuato in central Mexico. It is named after the box in which it has been traditionally packed. There are many fruit- and nut-flavored variations, but the original is a simple combination of goat's milk, sugar, vanilla, and cinnamon cooked until thick and caramelized. You may find both domestic and imported types sold in jars in Mexican markets. Excellent recipes can be found in *Mexican Cookery,* by Barbara Hansen (H.P. Books), and in *The Cuisines of Mexico,* by Diana Kennedy (Harper & Row).

STORAGE: Cajeta can be stored indefinitely in an airtight container in a cool place.

USE: This is usually served just as it is for dessert, but is sometimes spooned over ice cream as a sauce, spread on toast, used as a pastry filling, or rolled in chopped nuts to make a confection.

CALABAZA

(cah-la-BAH-za)

OTHER: *crescentia cujete,* calabazilla, West Indian pumpkin, green pumpkin

Calabaza is a yellow-skinned, squashlike, winter vegetable with orange-yellow flesh that has a delicate, pumpkinlike flavor. Do not confuse with *calabacita,* which is the Spanish word for zucchini. Calabazas are round or oblong and can be found in Latin American produce markets, usually by the piece. Hubbard or butternut squash can be substituted. The blossoms from the vine *(flores de calabaza)* are often cooked (see SQUASH BLOSSOM).

STORAGE: Whole calabazas can be kept for months in a cool place. If cut, pieces should be stored in the refrigerator for use within a few days.

PREPARATION AND USE: One pound usually serves 4 to 6 in a recipe for soup or stew. Cook as you would any pumpkin or winter squash, and use as a vegetable, or in soups or desserts, such as pudding or pie.

This is a very popular vegetable in Argentina where it is used in fritters and puddings, and in an elaborate beef stew presentation called Carbonada Criolla, in which 6 servings of stew are baked in the shell of a 10-pound calabaza. In Martinique, it is used in a dish called Colobo de Giraumon in which it is mashed with onion, bacon, tomatoes, garlic, cloves, and curry powder.

CALABAZILLA

See CALABAZA

CALCIUM HYDROXIDE

See SLAKED LIME in THE FOODS OF REGIONAL AMERICA
section

CALLALOO GREENS

OTHER: taro greens, elephant ears, *calaloo, callilu, callau*

CHINESE: *hin choi* INDIAN: *bhaji* JAPANESE: *hiyu*

This name refers not to one, but to two different plants, which are used interchangeably, and also to a famous Caribbean soup. One of the plants is the MALANGA, which has large green leaves shaped like elephant ears. The other plant is AMARANTH or Chinese spinach (see THE FOODS OF ASIA section), which has small green leaves. You can find both of them in Asian and Latin American markets. Spinach or Swiss chard can be substituted for either. Cans of callaloo are sometimes labeled "chopped spinach in brine" in Caribbean markets.

STORAGE: Callaloo greens can be stored in a paper bag inside a plastic bag in the refrigerator for up to a week. Once opened, the canned greens can be stored in a nonmetal container in the refrigerator for up to 4 days.

USE: Callaloo soup is popular in Trinidad, Jamaica, Haiti, and other Caribbean islands. It is often served with rice or a smooth paste of cooked plantains called Coo-Coo. Each island has its own version, but okra is always used, giving the dish a slippery texture, disliked by many. Here is ours, made as they serve it in Trinidad.

CALLALOO SOUP

1	pound callaloo greens, spinach, or Swiss chard	For 6 servings
	or 1 pound canned callaloo greens, drained	
4	ounces salt pork, finely diced	
1	bunch scallions, finely chopped	
2	cloves garlic, minced	
1½	teaspoons fresh thyme, or ½ teaspoon dried thyme, crumbled	
5	cups well-seasoned chicken or fish stock	
8	ounces small fresh okra *or* a 10-ounce package frozen okra, thawed	
1	cup COCONUT MILK	
6	small crab claws, *or* 8 ounces cooked crabmeat	
	PICKAPEPPA SAUCE *or* Tabasco Sauce, to taste	
	Salt and freshly ground black pepper	

Rinse the greens, remove stems, and drain. In a heavy pot of at least 4-quart capacity, sauté the salt pork until lightly browned and partially rendered. Stir in the scallions, garlic, and thyme, and cook briefly. Add the greens and the broth, bring to a boil, and simmer slowly for 30 minutes. Add the okra and simmer 10 minutes longer. Transfer the mixture to a blender and puree it, or beat it vigorously with a whisk until it is relatively smooth. (The soup may be made ahead of time to this point.)

Add the coconut milk and crab and simmer only until the crab is hot. Season to taste with Pickapeppa or Tabasco, salt and pepper. Serve in soup bowls, apportioning one crab claw or piece of crab per serving. Serve extra hot sauce as a table condiment.

CAMARÓN SECO

(kahm-ah-ROHN SEH-koh)
OTHER: dried shrimp

CHINESE: *har may* INDONESIAN AND MALAYSIAN: *udang kering*
THAI: *kung haeng*

Small dried shrimp are available in 1-ounce packets in Latin American and Asian markets. The most flavorful have shell and tail still on. Avoid any that are powdered or pale in color. For general information, see SHRIMP, DRIED in THE FOODS OF ASIA section.

STORAGE: Can be kept up to 6 months in an airtight container in a cool place.

PREPARATION AND USE: For best flavor, these should be toasted in a dry skillet for 1 to 2 minutes before use. Those with heads and shells must be cleaned. Place in water to cover and simmer for 5 minutes. Let cool in the broth for a few minutes; then drain, reserving the broth, and remove heads, tails, and shells. Those that have been shelled before they were dried can be soaked for 5 minutes in warm sherry or water to freshen them and improve their flavor. Use both shrimp and broth as a flavoring in soups, sauces, and recipes in which a strong shrimp flavor is desirable.

In Mexico, they are used to make shrimp fritters served as a Lenten dish. In Brazil, they flavor a Bahian dish made with fish and shrimp called Vatapá, and Carurú de Camarão (shrimp and okra with peanuts). In Trinidad, they flavor a Filipino-inspired dish, Pancit (noodles fried with shrimp and tossed with a multitude of chopped vegetables).

CANE SYRUP, PURE

See THE FOODS OF REGIONAL AMERICA section

CARDOON

See THE FOODS OF EUROPE section

CARNE SECA

(KAR-neh SEH-kah)
OTHER: dried beef

IN BRAZIL: *tasajo* or *charqui* IN MEXICO: *tasajo*

Carne seca is lean beef that has been salted and sun-dried. It is available in some Latin American markets, and by mail-order from Casa Monejo (see SHOPPING SOURCES). It is similar to BILTONG (see THE FOODS OF AFRICA section). The name *charqui* has been corrupted by Americans to JERKY (see THE FOODS OF REGIONAL AMERICA section).

STORAGE: It will keep indefinitely in an airtight container in a cool, dry place.

PREPARATION AND USE: Eight ounces is sufficient for 8 to 10 servings. It is soaked for 6 to 8 hours and then drained before use. In northern Mexico, it is served as an appetizer, and is also used as a flavoring in soups and rice dishes. This is an essential ingredient in Feijoada Completa, the national dish of Brazil, for which it is simmered for 30 minutes in water to cover, and then sliced, to be served as part of a large array of cooked meats with black beans and various condiments.

CASSAREEP

This is a dark brown West Indian condiment made by squeezing the juice from grated bitter CASSAVA, which is then simmered with brown sugar and spices until syrupy. (The cassava pulp is reserved for use in other recipes.) It is available bottled in Caribbean markets. Its flavor is both bitter and sweet.

STORAGE: It will keep indefinitely in a cool place. Refrigerate after opening.

USE: This is an essential ingredient in West Indian Pepperpot (meat stew of oxtails, beef or pork, and chicken, served with rice), popular in Trinidad, St. Kitts, and Barbados.

CASSAVA

OTHER: *manioc, oca, oka, oxalis root*

IN BRAZIL: *aipim, macaxeira* (sweet cassava) FRENCH: *cassave* or *manioc* GERMAN: *Maniok* ITALIAN: *manioca* SPANISH: *mandioca* (bitter cassava), *yuca* (sweet cassava)

Cassava, the tuber of a tropical plant, is 8″ to 10″ long and approximately 2″ in diameter and has a tough brown skin. It is the source of commercial TAPIOCA, but is used primarily as a bland starchy vegetable in many tropical areas. There are many varieties, but only two types: bitter, **which is poisonous unless cooked;** and sweet. It is available all year in Latin American markets, fresh or frozen.

Grated raw cassava is very often squeezed of its juice, which is then boiled to make CASSAREEP (the uncooked juice is poisonous). The grated cassava that is left is often pressed into an iron skillet, sprinkled with coconut and

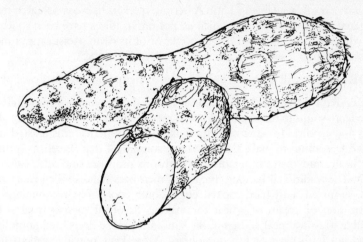

brown sugar, topped with more grated cassava, and baked at 350° for 20 minutes, to be served as a flat cake called Cassava Bread. If the grated cassava is sun-dried, it becomes CASSAVA MEAL.

STORAGE: Refrigerate fresh cassava for use within a few days, as the flesh discolors on standing. Frozen cassava can be kept frozen for up to 4 months.

PREPARATION AND USE: Cassava can be cooked to serve as a starchy vegetable in place of potatoes or rice. An average root will serve 3 to 4. **Be sure to cook it thoroughly.** First, peel and wash it; then cut it into 2″ pieces and boil it in salted water for 1 hour or longer. It will be soft and fibrous when tender. (Directions on packages of frozen cassava say to boil for 30 to 45 minutes, in water to cover to which salt and lemon juice have been added, until it is tender.) Drain; then remove center "ropes" and mash or dice to serve simply, seasoned with butter, or to add to soups or stews. Cassava is sometimes thinly sliced, rinsed, dried, and deep-fried to serve as an appetizer. To make the Cuban dish Brazo Gitano de Yuca, it is mashed and mixed with butter, eggs, and flour to make a dough, which is then patted flat and rolled around a meat stuffing, and baked.

CASSAVA FLOUR

See TAPIOCA

CASSAVA MEAL

OTHER: *manioc* meal, *farinha de mandioca*

FRENCH: *farine de manioc* IN THE FRENCH CARIBBEAN: *farine*

Cassava meal, available in Latin American markets, is a coarse starch made of grated bitter cassava from which all poisonous juices have been squeezed and which is then sun-dried. It has no flavor of its own. Moist cassava meal, pressed through a sieve to form round pellets, is TAPIOCA.

STORAGE: It will keep indefinitely in an airtight container in a cool place.

PREPARATION AND USE: Cassava meal is often mixed with water and stirred into soups to thicken them, and is used in the making of many Brazilian cakes and candies. In parts of Central and South America, it is toasted with fat and seasonings to make Farofa, a table condiment that Brazilians sprinkle over beans and many other dishes to absorb moisture and add a toasted flavor. The traditional Farofa served with their national dish, Feijoada Completa, is mixed with hard-cooked eggs. Some cookbooks recommend the substitution of cream of wheat for making Farofa if cassava meal is not available. Cassava meal is used in St. Vincent to make deep-fried dumplings served hot with meat or fish dumplings. A breakfast porridge called Angú de Farinha de Mandioca is made in Brazil. To make 4 servings, add 1½ cups cassava meal gradually to 4½ cups boiling water while stirring constantly. Cook for 10 minutes, stirring constantly; add salt to taste.

CECI

See CHICK-PEAS, under BEANS, in THE FOODS OF THE MIDDLE EAST section

CHAYOTE

(cha-YOH-tay)
OTHER: christophine, *chuchu,* mango squash, vegetable pear, *mirleton* (Louisiana), *pepinello*

AUSTRALIAN: *choko* IN BRAZIL: *xuxu* BRITISH: *cho-cho*
FRENCH: *brionne*

This pear-shaped, pale- to dark-green tropical squash is available year 'round in Chinese or Latin American markets, and in many supermarkets in the western and southern United States. It has a delicate flavor and firm, almost crisp, flesh. These elegant squash measure 3″ to 8″ in length and have either smooth or corrugated skins. Select the smallest, and those that are the darkest green for best flavor and texture. The peel and soft seed of young *chayote* are edible.

STORAGE: Unwrapped, they will keep for up to 3 weeks in the refrigerator.

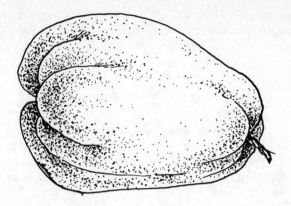

PREPARATION AND USE: One average chayote weighs 1 pound and will serve 2 to 3. Scrape away any soft spines. Peel because the skin can cause a gaseous feeling. Dice the flesh and the soft seed into the desired size and simmer in salted water for 10 minutes or so, just until tender. Drain and toss with butter and seasonings.

Chayotes can be substituted in recipes for any tender squash; served as a vegetable, buttered or seasoned; or stuffed to serve as a main course. Cookbooks on Cajun or New Orleans cooking have many recipes for stuffing mirletons or "vegetable pears," as they are called there. They should be simmered whole for 45 minutes or so depending on age, until fork tender; then split, and the centers scooped out and mixed with bread crumbs, cheese, and seasonings, and returned to their shells to bake at 350° for 20 minutes. In Mexico, chayotes are often cooked with sugar and nuts to serve as a dessert. In Martinique, they are stuffed with sautéed onion and Parmigiano cheese in a dish called Christophine au Gratin, or are marinated in a vinaigrette sauce.

Chayotes are very easy to grow. Simply plant one from the market in your garden during the spring. Put it in the ground on a slant, with the stem end slightly exposed, water well, and you will soon have a vigorous vine that will bear up to 3 dozen chayotes. The asparaguslike shoots are edible as are the leaves and sweet-potato-like roots.

CHEESES, LATIN AMERICAN

Latin American cheeses, called *quesos* in Spanish, are not much exported, but some are copied domestically, and others can be replaced in recipes by

American substitutes. We refer you to Diana Kennedy's comprehensive article on the subject of Mexican cheeses in the February 1982 issue of *Cuisine* magazine.

QUESO AÑEJO

(KAY-soh ah-NYEH-ho)

The name of this crumbly, rather salty, white cheese means "aged." It is sharper in flavor than other Mexican cheeses, which makes it a popular flavoring for spicy dishes. Substitute Argentinean Sardo, Parmigiano, or FETA (see CHEESE, GOAT AND SHEEP, in THE FOODS OF EUROPE section), which is much sharper.

STORAGE: Tightly wrapped in plastic wrap, it will keep in refrigerator for up to 2 weeks.

PREPARATION AND USE: Crumble small quantities of this rather dry cheese over Enchiladas, salads, and *antojitos* (snacks), such as Sopas (filled rounds of corn dough). It is often used with peeled green chiles as a filling for flour tortillas, which are deep-fried, and as a filling for Enchiladas. This cheese only softens when heated and does not melt into stringy ropes as do other cheeses, such as Monterey Jack (see under CHEESES, in FOODS OF REGIONAL AMERICA section).

QUESO ASADERO

(KAY-soh ah-sah-THER-oh)

The name means "fit for roasting" because the cheese melts so smoothly and evenly. This white, whole-milk cheese can be found packaged in two ways: in braided loaves, or sliced in thin rounds and packaged like tortillas. It has a mild flavor, slightly more acid than mozzarella. Monterey Jack, provolone, mozzarella, or our domestic muenster, all of which have excellent melting qualities, can be substituted.

STORAGE: Wrapped tightly in plastic wrap, it can be stored in the refrigerator for up to 3 months.

PREPARATION AND USE: Place grated or thinly sliced cheese between 2 flour tortillas, heat on a griddle, and cut into sixths to make a delicious Quesadilla, to serve with Salsa Fresca and guacamole as a snack. This is an excellent cheese for stuffing chiles for Chiles Rellenos de Queso, or Tacos de Queso. Slices of this cheese can be used to wrap Ceviche (fish marinated in lime juice with cilantro), which is then served with Guacamole Sauce to become Ensalada de Queso Asadero. In Mexico, it is often melted in a pan over coals to serve as a sort of appetizer Fondue. Sprinkled with PILONCILLO and nuts, it serves as dessert.

QUESO BLANCO

(KAY-so BLAHN-ko)
OTHER: white cheese, *queso tipo cotijo, queso fresco, queso de metate*

IN EL SALVADOR and VENEZUELA: *queso de presno* IN PUERTO RICO: *queso de Puna*

The most common Latin American cheese, generally available in Latin American markets and some supermarkets, is a moist, unripened "ranch style" white cheese made from partly skimmed milk. It is fresh, mild, and slightly salty. It may vary in consistency from soft (like cottage cheese) to firm and crumbly. If not available, substitute a moist type of Farmer cheese, a dry cottage cheese mixed with a bit of salt, or mild FETA cheese (see under CHEESE, GOAT AND SHEEP, in THE FOODS OF EUROPE section).

STORAGE: If fresh when purchased this will keep, tightly wrapped in the refrigerator, for up to 2 weeks.

USE: The firm, crumbly version of this cheese does not melt as readily as mozzarella, Monterey Jack, or muenster. It is often crumbled or grated over hot Enchiladas, Tacos, or Refried Beans just before serving. It is used as a stuffing for Chiles Rellenos, and can be folded inside warm tortillas along with cooked NOPAL. It can be sprinkled into soups, such as Sopa Ranchera, made with POBLANO chiles (see under CHILES) and SQUASH BLOSSOMS. In Peru, it is essential to Ocopa Arrequipeña (potatoes with peanuts, chiles, and cheese sauce).

QUESO DE BOLA

(KAY-so deh BOH-yah)
OTHER: Edam (manufactured in Latin America)

Queso de bola is a ball-shaped, ripened, whole-milk cheese, a specialty of Chiapas, Mexico. Its shape and nutty flavor resemble those of Edam, which is manufactured in Mexico and usually substitutes for it.

STORAGE: If stored in its original paraffin coating, this keeps well for a month or more in the refrigerator.

PREPARATION AND USE: Queso de bola (or Edam) is served primarily as a table cheese, cut in wedges, with bread or crackers. Large ones (3½ to 4 pounds) are sometimes hollowed out to leave a ½" shell and then stuffed with various fillings combined with some of the scooped-out cheese, and baked. In Curaçao, this dish is called Keshy Yena Coe Carne if stuffed with meat; Keshy Yena Coe Cabaron if stuffed with shrimp. The secret of making it is to soak the cheese shell in cold water for an hour before filling. It is then filled, and baked in a casserole at 350° for 30 minutes, transferred to a serving dish, and cut in wedges to make 8 portions. Excellent recipes for several versions appear in *The Complete Book of Caribbean Cooking*, by Elisabeth Lambert Ortiz (M. Evans and Company).

QUESO DE CHIHUAHUA

(KAY-soh deh chee-HWAH-wa)

Chihuahua cheese originated in the Mennonite communities in the state of Chihuahua in northern Mexico. It is imported into the United States and can often be found in Mexican markets. It has a fine, creamy flavor, which reminds us of a cross between Monterey Jack and a mild Cheddar. It may be porous in appearance with many small holes. Monterey Jack or a mild muenster are our preferred substitutes.

STORAGE: Wrapped tightly in plastic wrap and stored in the refrigerator, it will keep for up to 3 months. Cut away any surface mold as you would from Cheddar, Swiss, and other cheeses.

PREPARATION AND USE: This is the cheese used in Mexico as Americans use a large selection of cheeses with fine melting qualities: Monterey Jack, mozzarella, domestic muenster, mild Cheddar, Swiss, etc. It is used for stuffing chiles for Chiles Rellenos, over dishes to be *gratinéed,* and is often melted for a Fondue, topped with cooked, crumbled chorizo for dipping *tostaditas* (crisp tortilla chips). Thin slices garnish Caldo de Queso (broth with mild chiles, potatoes, and tomatoes). Grated chihuahua is sprinkled over beans in a popular dish called Molletes—hollowed-out French rolls (*bolillos*) filled with FRIJOLES REFRITOS (refried beans), to bake and serve hot with fresh Salsa.

QUESO DE CREMA

(KAY-soh deh KREHM-ah)

This is a rich fresh cheese made of milk and cream popular in Cuba, El Salvador, and parts of South America. It is not available here. A fine cream cheese is the best substitute.

STORAGE: It can be stored tightly wrapped in plastic wrap for up to a month in the refrigerator.

USE: Especially popular in Cuba to serve as a substitute for butter. In Mexico, cubed cream cheese is sprinkled over cooked NOPAL, which has been seasoned with chiles and EPAZOTE (see HERBS, SPICES, AND SEASONING BLENDS section), and heated just until warm. It is used in making a version of Chile con Queso using TOMATILLO, garlic, green chiles, and cilantro (see CORIANDER, in the HERBS, SPICES, AND SEASONING BLENDS section). This type of cheese is also used for the nut sauce that tops the meat-stuffed poblano chiles decorated with pomegranate seeds, Chiles en Nogada. Following is our version from the town of San Miguel de Allende, in Guanajuato, where we once lived.

CHILES EN NOGADA

For 10 to 12 servings
as one of several dishes

This dish, which features the colors of the Mexican flag, is traditionally served on patriotic holidays, specifically the 16th of September, Mexican Independence Day, when fresh pomegranates are in season. We advise purchasing extra chiles, so any that tear badly during the peeling need not be used.

14 fresh CHILES POBLANOS, peeled, slit down one side, and carefully seeded
1 tablespoon vegetable oil
1 teaspoon vinegar
2 teaspoons grated onion

PICADILLO FILLING:
2 pounds coarsely ground lean pork or beef
2 medium onions, minced
2 cloves garlic, minced
2 pounds ripe tomatoes, peeled, seeded, and chopped *or* a 28-ounce can crushed tomatoes
1 cup raisins, soaked in ⅓ cup dry sherry for at least 20 minutes
¾ cup toasted PINE NUTS or slivered almonds
¼ teaspoon ground cinnamon
Pinch of ground cloves
Salt and pepper, to taste

SAUCE:
1 pound queso de crema *or* cream cheese, softened
1 cup milk, or more as needed
1 clove garlic, crushed
½ teaspoon salt
1 cup shelled walnuts *or* pecans

TO SERVE AND GARNISH:
½ cup fresh POMEGRANATE seeds*
  Sprigs of fresh coriander (cilantro or Chinese parsley)

***Note:** Fresh pomegranates are in season from late September through November. Chopped pimiento or bottled spiced crab apples can be used as a color substitute, but with a good deal of difference in flavor.

Place the prepared chiles in a glass dish, sprinkle with the oil, vinegar, and grated onion, and leave at room temperature while you make the filling.

Cook the meat in a skillet with the onion and garlic, breaking it up with the back of a spoon. When it has lost all its pink color, stir in the tomatoes, raisins, nuts, cinnamon, and cloves. Simmer slowly for 5 minutes. Taste, and add salt and pepper as needed. (This will be served at room temperature, so add a bit more seasoning than you think it needs.)

Combine the sauce ingredients and blend one-half of the mixture at a time in a blender or electric food processor. Thin with additional milk if necessary.

To serve, place the picadillo filling (slightly warm or at room temperature) inside the marinated chiles. Arrange them 1″ apart on a large platter. Spoon the sauce over the center of the platter of filled chiles, leaving some of the chiles exposed. Sprinkle pomegranate seeds (or substitute) over the top. Garnish the platter with sprigs of fresh coriander.

TO PREPARE IN ADVANCE: The meat filling can be refrigerated for up to 3 days, or frozen for up to 3 months. Heat in a saucepan just until warm before filling the chiles. The sauce can be refrigerated for up to 3 days, but bring to room temperature before spooning it over the chiles.

QUESO ENCHILADO

(KAY-soh ehn-chee-LAH-thoh)

This is AÑEJO cheese that has been covered with powdered chili.

STORAGE: As AÑEJO.

USE: Use as an appetizer or table cheese or as a substitute for QUESO AÑEJO.

QUESO FRESCO

See QUESO BLANCO

QUESO PANELA

(KAY-soh pahn-EHL-ah)
OTHER: *tuma*

This fresh, semi-soft cheese, made from whole or partly skimmed milk, is shaped like a small, ridged basket, and usually weighs 8 ounces. It is slightly salty, and rubbery in consistency. You will find it in varying qualities in Latin American and Middle Eastern markets. Substitute Monterey Jack, QUESO BLANCO, QUESO DE CHIHUAHUA, or a very mild FETA (see CHEESE, GOAT AND SHEEP, in THE FOODS OF EUROPE section).

STORAGE: Wrapped tightly in plastic wrap, it will keep for up to a week in the refrigerator.

PREPARATION AND USE: This is a mild cheese which, if of good quality, goes well with crispy rolls as a table cheese with meals, and with fruit pastes (see ATE) for dessert. It is often used in making Quesadillas (tortillas heated with a cheese filling), and is especially good with cooked NOPALES.

QUESO DE PRENSO
See QUESO BLANCO

QUESO DEL PAÍS
(KAY-soh dehl pah-EES)
OTHER: *queso de la tierra*

IN COLOMBIA: *queso estera*

The name means, literally, "native cheese." This is a fresh, white Puerto Rican cheese, usually eaten very fresh when it resembles cottage cheese, which can substitute in recipes for it. When cured, it becomes semi-soft and slightly bitter. Domestic substitutes would be Monterey Jack or a mild domestic muenster.

USE: In Puerto Rico, this is the primary cooking cheese, and is used specifically in Pastelitos de Queso (cheese turnovers).

QUESO RANCHERO
(KAY-soh rahn-CHEHR-oh)
OTHER: *ranchero seco*

Queso Ranchero is a dry, salty cheese. A domestic version is made in Los Angeles and sold in Latin American markets throughout the United States. Substitute QUESO AÑEJO, or Argentinean or Italian Sardo or Romano.

STORAGE: Tightly wrapped in the refrigerator or freezer, it will keep for months.

USE: Use as you would any sharp-flavored grating cheese. In Mexico, it is used primarily to top *antojitos* (appetizers).

QUESO SARDO
(KAY-soh SAHR-doh)

This is Argentina's version of the salty, rather sharp-flavored Romano-type cheese used for grating. It was originally made in Sardinia from sheep's milk, but is now commonly made from cow's milk. See ROMANO under CHEESE, HARD GRATING, in THE FOODS OF EUROPE section for general information.

CHERIMOYA
(cher-eh-MOY-ya)
OTHER: chirimoya, sherbet fruit, custard apple

Cherimoya is a green subtropical fruit originally from the highlands of Ecuador and Peru. It is heart-shaped, covered with thumbprint-like indentations, and has a creamy white flesh that tastes something like vanilla ice cream mixed with a bit of strawberry, pineapple, and banana. Cherimoyas are now cultivated in California, as well as being imported, and are in season from November through May. They are expensive because the trees produce very little fruit naturally, and require pollination by hand in order to develop a crop that takes 8 to 10 months to mature and must be tree-ripened. Choose them with an even green color; brown color and cracks at the stem end indicate that the fruit is overripe. A ripe fruit will yield to pressure.

STORAGE: If hard, let ripen at room temperature. Ripe cherimoyas do not keep well. Store in the refrigerator and use as soon as possible.

PREPARATION AND USE: Surely the most sensible use for this fruit is to eat it as is, removing the multitude of large seeds as you go. The diced fruit can be added to fruit salads. In a restaurant in Mexico, we enjoyed a gorgeous molded dessert that derived its delicate flavor from this fruit, but when we attempted to duplicate it we were discouraged by the tedious task of removing all the seeds.

CHICHARRÓN
(chee-chah-RROHN)

Chicharrón (we are told that the word is properly used only in singular form) are crisp sheets of deep-fried pork skin used as a nibble and as an ingredient. They are made from fresh pork skins that have been briefly air-dried and then fried twice in lard heated to two temperatures, the first about 325°, the second about 375°, in much the same manner as Pommes Soufflées, the puffed potato slices made famous by Parisian restaurants. Because of this special treatment, they puff and turn into honeycombed cracklings. They are nearly impossible to make at home, but are available in Latin American markets in bags, much like our potato chips. The best ones are freshly made and those in bags often taste stale. Chicharrón are heavy—a little goes a long way.

STORAGE: Store in airtight containers to use as soon as possible.

PREPARATION AND USE: Seasoned with salt, these are Mexico's national nibble. They are usually served with a squeeze of lime or bitter orange juice and chili powder as a snack. They make fine appetizer dippers with guacamole or with salsas. They are often stewed with TOMATILLO(S), fresh chiles, and CILANTRO (see CORIANDER in the HERBS, SPICES, AND SEASONING BLENDS section) to make Chicharrón en Chile, used as a filling for tacos.

CHICK-PEAS

See under BEANS in THE FOODS OF THE MIDDLE EAST section

CHILES

Chiles are native to Latin America, where they were used as a flavoring and a natural preservative long before the arrival of the conquistadores. They are of the *capsicum* family, not "peppers" at all, but were called that originally because Columbus was seeking that spice of the East Indies, and chiles have a spicy pungency. (The name "pepper" seems to have stuck with sweet chiles, which can be found unders PEPPERS, SWEET.) Some experts declare that the word "pepper" should never be used with chiles, whereas others, such as Phil Villa, the chile breeder for Ortega, feels that chiles should properly be called peppers.

There are over 100 classified varieties of chiles in the countries of Mexico, Central and South America, and the Caribbean, so it is not surprising that there is considerable confusion about which one is which. To add to the confusion, they cross-pollinate very easily, creating an incredible number of varieties. Even chiles on the same plant can vary from mild to hot. Our research has shown that many of the chiles are identified differently by different experts in the United States and Mexico.

It is a fact that chiles range in size from ⅛″ to 8″ in length. A general rule, though not infallible, is that the smaller the chiles, the hotter they are. Their colors go from green to yellow to orange to red as they ripen. To describe "hot" chiles, we prefer the Spanish term *picante* (pee-KAHN-tay) to describe the degree of hotness. Most of the heat is in the seeds and the membranes, which can be removed to make chiles less *picante*.

FRESH CHILES

When you buy fresh chiles, make sure they are plump and smooth. They are sold in many supermarkets in the West and Southwest, but the best ones can be found in large produce markets where there is a large Mexican population.

STORAGE: Chiles keep well, though they lose flavor on standing. Store them for up to 3 weeks in the refrigerator wrapped in paper towels. Do not store them in plastic or they will sweat and spoil very rapidly. They can be frozen, but not very successfully. We prefer to freeze the larger ones after we have charred them, but before peeling, in order to retain maximum flavor. Wrap them separately in plastic wrap lest they stick together, or put them in small individual sandwich bags. To use, simply thaw, peel, seed, and devein them.

PREPARATION AND USE: All chiles should be handled with care because they contain a chemical irritant (*capsaicin*) that can cause **discomfort, or even a painful rash** in those who are highly sensitive. You will be wise to **wear rubber gloves** when handling them until you determine your degree of sensitivity. To remove the peel from chiles it is necessary to char the skin, either in direct flame, on a rack over an electric burner, or under the broiler, turning often to brown the skin evenly. They are then placed inside a clean towel or plastic bag where they will steam for a few minutes, separating the flesh from the skin. Peel by scraping off the skin with the back of a knife on a flat surface or by rubbing under cold running water. Most of the "hotness" is in the membranes and seeds, so make as small a slit in the side of the chili as possible to remove those carefully if you wish a milder flavor. **Be sure to wash your hands after handling them and take care not to rub your eyes or any delicate membranes while you are handling them. Rinse eyes immediately with warm water if you do touch them accidentally.**

As the chile is opened, you will be able to tell by the smell if it is especially hot. Chiles that are too *picante* can be soaked after they are peeled in a solution of vinegar and water or salted water for 20 to 30 minutes to tone down the flavor. Chiles that are to be stuffed should have their seeds and veins carefully removed through a very small opening, without removing the stems and retaining as much of their original shape as possible. Those that are to be cut into strips (*rajas*) don't require such careful handling.

ANAHEIM CHILE
See CHILE VERDE

CALIFORNIA CHILE
See CHILE VERDE

CHILE CAYENNE
(CHEE-leh kah-YEHN)

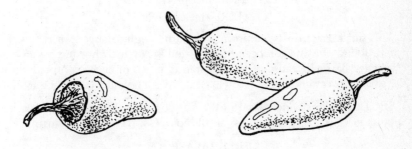

Available, often on strings, in Latin American as well as Asian markets, this Asian chile is green, slender, and about 3″ long. It is quite hot. It can be used sparingly in place of fresh JALAPEÑO and SERRANO chiles.

PREPARATION AND USE: You will be wise to cut out and rinse away some of the membrane and seeds. These are widely used in Yucatecan cooking, in flavoring refried black beans, and are pickled with onion rings to serve as a condiment.

CHILE GÜERO
(CHEE-leh GWEHR-oh)
OTHER: *x-cat-ik* (in the Yucatán)

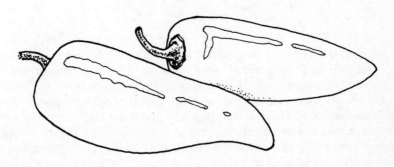

There are several varieties of this pale yellow, literally "blonde," mild to very hot chile available fresh in Latin American markets and many supermarkets in the West and Southwest.

PREPARATION AND USE: These can be diced and used without peeling to add spiciness to guacamole, and used whole in many stewed dishes. When used in sauces, such as Salsa de Chile Güero, they are usually simmered for 15 minutes and then peeled. The seeds are usually used as well.

CHILE HABANERO
(CHEE-leh ah-bah-NEH-ro)
OTHER: Havana chile

This small, lantern-shaped green chile turns bright orange as it ripens. It will be found only in Caribbean markets, and is extremely hot and has a very distinctive flavor. Because of its appearance, it can often be confused with the smaller sweet *aji* pepper (see PEPPERS, SWEET), which is not hot at all.

USE: This chile is widely used in the Caribbean. In Yucatecan cooking, it appears in Lomitos (pork pieces) and Frijoles Coladas (sieved beans).

CHILE JALAPEÑO
(CHEE-leh ha-lah-PEH-Nyoh)
OTHER: *chile cuaresmeño* (or Lenten chile)
IN VERACRUZ: *chile huachinango*

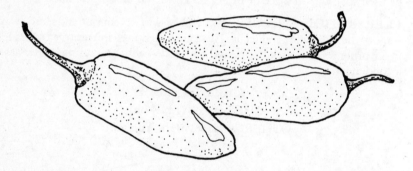

Jalapeño is a bright- to dark-green, sometimes greenish-black, extremely hot chile, about 2″ long and ¾″ wide, available fresh in supermarkets nationwide. Some experts say that the jalapeño and the *cuaresmeño* (not found in the United States) are not the same chile, but for cooking purposes they are interchangeable. They can be successfully frozen just like SERRANO chiles, for which they can be substituted, though jalapeños have a slightly soapier taste. Canned jalapeños (packed in water, not pickled) can be used when fresh are not available. Ortega is a widely distributed brand of canned chiles.

USE: These are the traditional chiles to use when preparing Mexico's most famous fish dish, Huachinango Veracruzana, with garlic, onions, tomatoes, stuffed olives, and capers. They also flavor Huevos con Camarones (eggs with shrimp) and Salsa Ranchera (a chile-tomato sauce with onions and garlic served as a table sauce).

CHILE POBLANO
(CHEE-leh poh-BLAH-no)
OTHER: *chile para rellenar, chile ancho* (fresh)

This very dark, blackish-green, tapered chile with a triangular shape is the fresh form of the ANCHO chile (see DRIED CHILES). It is very common in Mexico, especially in the region of Puebla for which it is named, but is not widely available in the United States except in large cities and Mexican communities. Poblanos are somewhat similar in taste to the green bell pepper, only spicer. The peak of their season is summer and early fall. Substitute Ortega mild green chiles for canned poblano chiles and California (or Anaheim) chiles for fresh poblanos if they are not available, but those chiles lack the poblano's rich flavor.

PREPARATION AND USE: These are *the* chiles to use to make Chiles Rellenos. A cheese stuffing is traditional for *chiles rellenos,* whereas a *picadillo* (spicy ground meat and raisin stuffing) is used to make a festive dish served on St. Augustine's Day called Chiles en Nogada, which is topped with a walnut and cream cheese sauce and decorated with pomegranate seeds (our recipe appears with QUESO DE CREMA, under CHEESES, LATIN AMERICAN). If they are stuffed to serve unbaked they are usually soaked in salt water for an hour after peeling, to soften them. If particularly thick skinned, they are simmered for a minute or so before soaking. These chiles are used as well in making Arroz Verde (green rice), and to fill Tacos de Queso (cheese tacos). They are particularly flavorful in soup, as in the following recipe.

SOPA DE CHILES POBLANOS

8 medium chiles poblanos   For 8 servings
1 tablespoon butter
1 medium onion, minced
1 small clove garlic, minced
1 sprig fresh EPAZOTE, *or* a pinch of dried epazote
8 cups chicken broth
   Salt to taste
1½ cups fresh corn kernels or a 10-ounce package frozen
      white or yellow corn

TO GARNISH AND SERVE:
½ cup sour cream
1 ripe tomato, seeded and diced *or* ¼ cup slivered almonds,
      toasted

Char and peel the poblanos as described in the general directions for chiles. Chop them fine. In a 3- to 4-quart heavy saucepan, melt the butter and sauté the onions with the chopped chiles, garlic, and epazote until the onions are nearly transparent. Transfer to the container of a blender or electric food processor and puree, adding some of the chicken broth to keep the mixture moving through the blades. Return to the saucepan, add the remaining chicken broth, and simmer, covered, for 15 minutes. Season to taste with salt. Add the corn and simmer 10 minutes longer, or until the corn is tender.

Serve hot, topping each serving with a small dollop of sour cream and a sprinkling of diced tomatoes or slivered almonds.

TO PREPARE IN ADVANCE: This can be stored in refrigerator for up to 3 days or in the freezer for up to 4 months. Reheat gently to serve.

CHILE SERRANO
(CHEE-leh seh-RRAH-no)

These small, tapering, bright green, hot and very savory chiles are always available in Mexican communities. As they ripen, they turn orange and then red. JALAPEÑOS, which are larger and have a slightly soapier taste, can be substituted.

STORAGE: They keep well for up to 2 weeks if wrapped in paper towels (not plastic) in the crisper portion of the refrigerator. If you wish to freeze

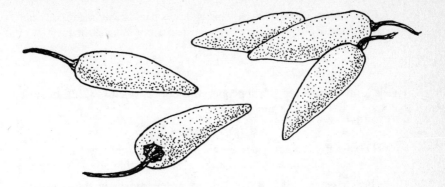

them, simmer them in water to cover for 5 minutes; then drain and freeze 3 or 4 to a plastic bag. If frozen without this blanching process they lose their wonderful spicy flavor.

USE: These chiles are often pickled to serve as a very hot table relish. They season all manner of Mexican dishes such as Chilaquiles (our recipe appears under TORTILLAS, CORN). These are the chiles we prefer when making guacamole. They are used in many spicy Mexican sauces, such as the following recipe for an uncooked condiment sauce called Salsa Cruda.

SALSA CRUDA

1 clove garlic, minced or pressed   For about 3 cups
6 ripe tomatoes, peeled, seeded, and diced
½ mild white onion, minced
2 tablespoons minced fresh coriander leaves (cilantro or
      Chinese parsley)
2 chiles serranos, seeded and minced*
1½ teaspoons salt
¼ teaspoon sugar

*Note: If serrano chiles are not available, substitute jalapeños, fresh or canned, or 4 small fresh yellow chiles. Wear rubber gloves when handling chiles in case your skin may be sensitive.

If making by hand, simply combine all ingredients. If making in a food processor, chop the peeled garlic first in a *dry* processor bowl using the steel blade. Add the remaining ingredients and process in on-off bursts until the mixture is of a chunky sauce consistency. Do not process until smooth or the sauce will be too runny.

Serve with Mexican meals or as a dip for fried tortilla chips (*tostaditas*).

TO PREPARE IN ADVANCE: This is best when freshly made, but can be stored for up to 3 days in the refrigerator in a nonmetal container.

CHILE VALENCIANO
(CHEE-leh vah-lehn-see-AH-no)

This is really a sweet green bell pepper. It is not classified as a chile because it is not spicy hot (see PEPPERS, SWEET).

CHILE VERDE
OTHER: mild green chiles, Anaheim chile, Fresno chile, mild California chile, mild New Mexico chile

These bright green chiles, 4" to 8" long, are abundant in the West and Southwest in summer and fall. The fresh New Mexico variety is darker green and more slender than the others. Mild green chiles are widely available canned, in which case they are labeled "roasted and peeled" and come either whole or diced. The Ortega brand of canned green chiles are of this variety, which makes them the most common chile available in America. They are sold in most supermarkets in 4- or 7-ounce cans, and vary from mild to mildly hot.

PREPARATION AND USE: Canned diced chiles contain seeds so they are always hotter than the canned whole chiles, which are often slit and rinsed of seeds and membranes before use. These chiles are widely used in dishes where a mild chile flavor is desirable, from Chile con Queso (chile-cheese dip for tortilla chips) to Carne con Chile Verde (beef with green chiles).

YELLOW CHILES

There are many varieties of yellow chiles available fresh in supermarkets across the country. Varieties include: yellow wax, Hungarian or Armenian wax, floral gem, banana pepper, *caribe*. They are easily confused with GÜERO, and it is nearly impossible to know the degree of hotness without tasting them, so one has to take one's chances when buying them.

CANNED CHILES

Several popular varieties of chiles are available in cans—plain, pickled, or in sauce.

Mild Green Chiles: Plain chiles to be used as cooking ingredients are always peeled before canning and the finest ones will say "roasted and peeled." Ortega is an excellent brand that is widely available in supermarkets and Latin American markets. Rinse brine from canned chiles thoroughly before adding them to a recipe. If you choose, rinse away all the seeds to make them milder in flavor. They can be stored, after opening, in their brine in a covered, nonmetal container in the refrigerator for up to a week.

Chiles Jalapeños: Whole or diced are available packed in brine. Use only if fresh are not available as they lose flavor and color in the canning process; and take care to rise away the brine.

Chiles Serranos or **Jalapeños "en Escabeche":** These small hot chiles, available in cans or jars, are pickled whole, or sliced, with bits of carrot, onion, and other seasonings. They are a very common table condiment throughout Mexico and can be found in many American supermarkets. We have often seen pickled whole ones served as an appetizer or snack *(antojito)* during Lent, stuffed with cheese or fish. Different brands vary in "hotness."

Chiles Chipotles en Vinagre or **Adobo:** These are smoked jalapeños that have been either pickled or sauced. Do not substitute for dried chiles chipotles in recipes because the flavor is altered considerably by these sauces. Either type can be used in Tinga Poblano (shredded spiced pork), and both are used as a filling for Tacos in Puebla, Mexico.

Yellow Chiles: Pickled and bottled yellow chiles are available in the markets of many nationalities. They vary from mild to hot, and are used in dishes mostly for appearance.

DRIED CHILES

We are always enchanted by the sight of strings of dried red chiles, called *ristras,* hanging in kitchens of our own Southwest. Tiny dried red chiles are available in most supermarkets, but for a wide selection you will either have to find a well-stocked Mexican market or order by mail. You will be wise to study pictures of the different kinds so you can identify them, and even send a sample when ordering by mail because they are often mislabeled in markets.

STORAGE: We sent away for a wreath of chiles to bedeck our front door for Christmas one year and learned a fairly expensive lesson. When we went to the box in our garage the following year to get the wreath it was alive with tiny creatures that live on chiles. And we should have known better because we have been telling our students for years to store all red spices such as chili powder, paprika, ground red pepper, etc., in the refrigerator for that very reason. Dried chiles can be stored in a cool dry place for up to 2 months, but they deteriorate quickly, especially if they are not in perfect condition to start with, so it is better to use them up rather than keep them too long and have to toss them out. They can be stored in a tightly closed container in the refrigerator for a longer time, but their appearance will suffer a bit.

PREPARATION AND USE: Dried chiles are prepared differently for different recipes. The tiny ones are usually crumbled into sauces or over cooked dishes as a seasoning. Large ones are toasted, soaked, and stuffed, or made into either a pulp or a powder. Wipe away any surface dust with a damp cloth. If they are dry and stiff, toast them for 3 to 4 minutes on a griddle or in a dry skillet to soften them, taking care not to give them a bitter flavor by scorching them. After they are cool you can grind them, removing the seeds or not as your recipe or taste dictates. They are most easily ground in an electric coffee/spice mill. Follow the directions in the recipe you are using. The most common way of using them is to remove the stems and then slit the sides to remove the seeds and veins. To make most sauces, a pulp is made by soaking chiles, toasted or not, depending on the recipe, in hot water (approximately 1 cup boiling water for 6 chiles) for 20 minutes until soft. The chiles are then pureed, a few at a time, with their soaking liquid in the blender, with care being taken not to overprocess, as the mixture should be a bit chunky.

CHILE ANCHO
(CHEE-leh AHN-choh)
OTHER: Mexican chile (along with *pasilla* chiles) as a generic name

Ancho, the most commonly used dried chile in Mexico, is the deep mahogany-colored dried form of the popular POBLANO chile. Its name refers to the "broad" triangular shape. It is approximately 4½" long and 3" wide and has a wrinkled appearance. It is rich, full-flavored, and slightly hot. It is often labeled Pasilla Ancho in the western United States.

PREPARATION AND USE: This chile is almost always soaked and ground to become an ingredient in cooked sauces. It is used in making Adobo, a marinade of chiles, vinegar, garlic, and oregano, used to marinate (and in some areas of Mexico to preserve without refrigeration) meat and chicken. It is added to corn MASA to make a chile-flavored dough for making Quesadillas (cheese-filled tortillas), and other *antojitos* (appetizers) such as Totopos. It is a common flavoring for Mancha Manteles (a pork stew, literally "tablecloth stainer") along with MULATO and PASILLA chiles. It is commonly used to make RED CHILE SAUCE, MEXICAN, as in the following recipe.

RED CHILE SAUCE

12 dried New Mexico or California chiles (about 4 ounces)	For about 3 cups
2 dried CHILES ANCHO	
3 cups hot water	
2 cloves garlic, pressed	
1 teaspoon salt	

1½ teaspoons chopped fresh oregano *or* ½ teaspoon dried
oregano, crumbled
½ teaspoon ground cumin
¼ cup lard or vegetable oil
2 tablespoons flour
2–3 teaspoons vinegar, to taste

Rinse and dry the chiles. Heat briefly on griddle or in skillet to soften them; remove stem, seeds, and veins. (Take care not to scorch the chiles as you warm them or they will taste bitter.) Tear into pieces and place in a medium saucepan. Add 3 cups water and bring just to a simmer. Remove from heat and let stand for 1 hour. Drain and reserve soaking liquid.

Place ⅓ to ½ the chiles in the container of a blender or electric food processor with the garlic, salt, oregano, cumin, and just enough of the soaking liquid to keep the mixture moving through the blades. Process until pureed and pour into the soaking liquid. Continue until all the chiles have been pureed. Strain the mixture through a medium strainer, pressing and discarding any pulp left in the strainer. Measure and add water if necessary to make 4 cups of liquid.

In a medium skillet, cook the lard or oil and the flour until the flour is lightly toasted. Add the strained chili puree and simmer, stirring often, for 5 minutes. Add vinegar, and season with salt and pepper to taste.

The sauce can be used as an enchilada sauce, or as a table sauce for Tacos, Tostadas, or as a dip for fried tortillas.

TO PREPARE IN ADVANCE: This can be stored in the refrigerator for up to 4 days, or in the freezer for up to 4 months.

CHILE DE ÁRBOL
(CHEE-leh deh AHR-bohl)
OTHER: *pico de pajaro*

This small, bright scarlet, extremely hot chile, available in Latin American markets, is slender and about 2″ long. Other small, hot dried chiles, such as CHILE JAPONÉS, can be substituted.

CHILE CASCABEL
(CHEE-leh kah-skah-BEL)

Chile cascabel is a round chili, approximately 1″ in diameter that looks like a dried cherry tomato. Its name means "rattle" because the seeds make a rattle-like noise when shaken about in the pod. This is mildly hot with a slightly nutty flavor. It is not one of the easiest chiles to find, but can be ordered by mail.

PREPARATION AND USE: This is an excellent chili for condiment sauces. Some of the seeds are usually used.

515

CHILE CHIPOTLE
(CHEE-leh chee-POH-tleh)
OTHER: *chilpotle, chipocle*

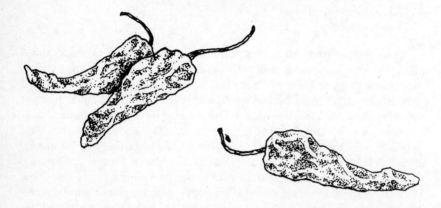

Chipotle is a hot chili with a unique smoky flavor. Mature red jalapeños are dried and smoked, making them dark brownish-red, plump, and twisted. They are very hot and have a distinct flavor that is wonderful for seasoning soups and stews. You will find these chiles, dried, in Latin American markets. They are also found canned, in vinegar, or in red Adobo sauce, but the canned ones should not be substituted for the dried as they have an entirely different flavor.

PREPARATION AND USE: Use sparingly, as they are strong in flavor. If not crisp, they are toasted lightly before use. They are commonly used in a table sauce, Salsa de Chipotle, in combination with cooked TOMATILLOS, garlic, and cilantro (see CORIANDER, in the HERBS, SPICES, AND SEASONING BLENDS section), to serve with Tostadas, Panuchos, Sopas Secas (dry soups) and Tacos. They are used to make Tinga, a Puebla-style shredded meat or chicken dish similar to Ropa Vieja. They flavor cooked pork or CHORIZO, and are mixed with grated cooked potato to serve as a Taco filling with avocado and raw onion rings.

CHILE GUAJILLO
(CHEE-leh gwah-HEE-yoh)
OTHER: *chile travieso*

This very dark brownish-red chili with a shiny smooth, tough skin is quite easy to recognize. It is usually about 4″ long and 1″ wide. It is extremely hot and flavorful and is used in both cooked dishes and table sauces. Because the skin is so tough, it needs to be soaked longer than other chiles.

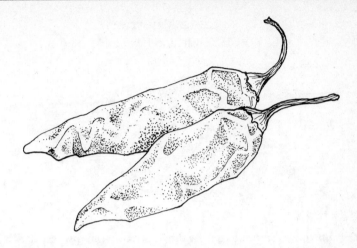

USE: These extremely flavorful chiles are especially suited to condiment sauces. They often flavor dishes with rabbit, and are used in the popular Chilaquiles (strips of corn tortilla cooked in a spicy sauce).

CHILE JAPONÉS
(CHEE-leh zhah-poh-NEHS)
OTHER: *serrano seco, chile puya*

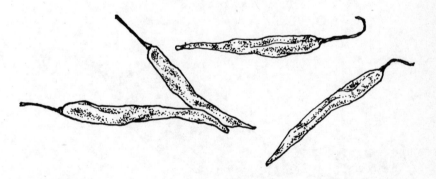

A small, slender dried chile, not as brightly colored as the CHILE DE ÁRBOL, very commonly found in Latin American and Asian markets. It can be substituted for either the dried cayenne chile or the dried serrano. It is extremely hot.

USE: This is often used with TOMATILLOS and garlic to make a table sauce, Salsa de Chile Japonés.

517

CHILE MULATO
(CHEE-leh moo-LAH-toh)

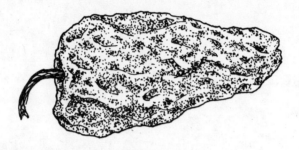

It is sometimes difficult to tell the difference between this very dark, almost black, dried chile and the CHILE ANCHO with which it is often combined in cooking. The best method is to hold them up to the light—reddish color is ancho, brown is mulato. The mulato is also smoother, tougher, and slightly sweeter than the ancho, but the flavors are somewhat similar.

USE: Like the ancho, it is usually cooked in sauces, such as MOLE, and in RED CHILE SAUCE, MEXICAN, and Enchilada Sauce.

CHILE PASILLA
(CHEE-leh pah-SEE-yah)
OTHER: *chile negro,* dried *chile chilaca*

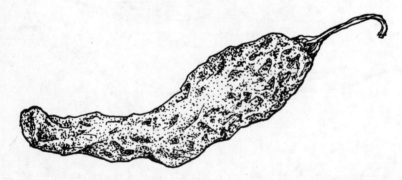

In our California markets we see two types of pasillas, the chubby, dark red "chile pasilla ancho" and the "pasilla negro de Mexico." The latter is a long wrinkled brownish-black chile with a round tip, and that is the one to look for when a recipe specifies *chiles pasillas.* It is more pungent but less flavorful than the ancho or mulato chile. The seeds are extremely hot, but the flesh of this chile is fairly mild with a slightly smoky taste.

518

PREPARATION AND USE: The pasilla is often used in both cooked dishes and table sauces. It is often specified in Mexican pork dishes, such as Chile Macho de Puerco (pork in hot chile sauce), and Tapado de Cerdo (smothered pork). These chiles can be made into a condiment by toasting them in hot oil in a skillet, turning often to prevent burning, until they puff up and become crisp. When cool, the stems and "hot" seeds may be discarded. The chile is then crumbled to sprinkle as a seasoning in soups and stews.

CHILE PEQUIN
(CHEE-leh pay-KEEN)

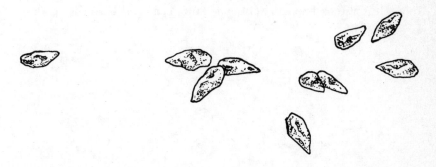

This is a tiny, tapered, bright red dried chile, available in some supermarkets in jars or cellophane packets. These are very hot.

PREPARATION AND USE: They must be crushed before use. If not available, substitute an equal amount of ground red pepper (cayenne) or twice as much CHILE TEPÍN. Two pequin chiles equal ½ teaspoon ground red pepper. They are often used in Pozole (meat and hominy stew).

CHILE DE RISTRA
(CHEE-leh deh REE-strah)
OTHER: dried New Mexico chile, dried Anaheim chile, dried California chile, *chile de la Tierra, chile colorado*

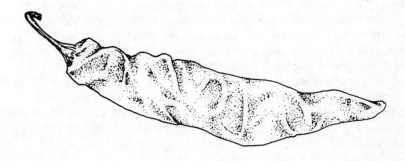

Several varieties of these mild, red, dried chiles are used commonly in the southwest of the United States for cooking and for decorations—for decorating, they are tied together with strings and hung from ceiling beams. They are a dark reddish-brown, 5″ to 6″ long, and about 1½″ wide. The New Mexico variety is slightly hotter than the California. They are not nearly as flavorful as other dried chiles, such as ANCHO and PASILLA, but are sometimes confused with (and labeled) GUAJILLOS, which are extremely hot and flavorful.

USE: This is the chile commonly used to make Salsa de Chile Colorado, or Enchilada Sauce, usually used in combination with dried anchos and pasilla chiles. It is also traditional in Carne de Puerco en Chile Colorado (pork in red chile sauce).

CHILE TEPÍN
(CHEE-leh tay-PEEN)

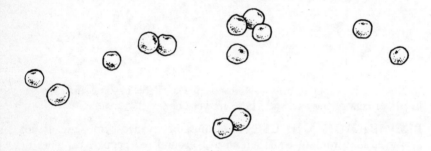

This is a tiny round red chile with a flavor similar to CHILE PEQUIN. Cayenne (ground red pepper) can be substituted: 4 tepín chiles equal ½ teaspoon cayenne. Or substitute 2 tepín chiles for each CHILE PEQUIN.

POWDERED CHILES

Many types of chiles are available in powdered form in Latin American markets. You can make your own from any dried chile. Among those powders we have seen in markets are *chile mole* (mixed with spices similar to "chili powder" found in supermarkets), *pimentón dulce* (sweet paprika), ancho (brick red), mild California (medium red and very mild), New Mexico (medium red, hotter than California), pasilla (dark red), chile de arbol (light orange, very hot), and *quebrado* (labeled "very hot"). The commercial type of "chili powder" packaged by the large spice companies and available in every supermarket has a variety of added seasonings such as garlic, ground cumin, and oregano, which would drastically change the flavor of an authentic Mexican recipe.

To make powdered chiles, grind the dried chiles (after toasting them lightly and seeding them) in a blender or spice grinder/coffee mill. As a general rule, 1 tablespoon of powder equals 1 whole dried ancho, mulato, New Mexico, California, or pasilla chile called for in a recipe. The hotter types should be used sparingly—½ to 1 teaspoon or so for 4 servings for starters.

CHOCOLATE, MEXICAN

Mexican chocolate is rich, sweetened chocolate flavored with cinnamon, almonds, and vanilla and comes in flat round cakes. The most commonly found brand, Ibarra, is sold in cylindrical, red and yellow 570-gram (20-ounce) boxes. The texture is much grainier than Americans are used to. Each 3.3-ounce cake is marked to be easily broken into eighths. Substitute 3 ounces sweet chocolate (such as Hershey's dark sweet chocolate in a red wrapper) plus ½ teaspoon ground cinnamon and a dash each of almond extract and Mexican or domestic vanilla extract added to the liquid in the recipe if Mexican chocolate is not available.

STORAGE: If tightly wrapped in plastic wrap or foil, it will keep indefinitely in a cool place.

PREPARATION AND USE: Mexican chocolate is an ingredient in the famous Mole Poblano (chicken or turkey in a chili-nut sauce), but it is most often whipped with hot water or milk to make hot chocolate to serve with *pan dulce* (sweet rolls). To make one serving of the traditional Mexican chocolate drink, heat 1 cup water or milk and add ¼ cake of chocolate. When dissolved, beat with whisk (or *molinillo*, a special wooden utensil used especially for this) until the mixture froths on the top. The flavor of Mexican chocolate is not appreciated by all, so experiment with it gradually.

CHIRIMOYA

See CHERIMOYA

CHORIZO

(choh-REE-zoh)
OTHER: Mexican sausage, Spanish sausage

Latin American, Caribbean, and Spanish markets carry many varieties of this garlicky, spicy sausage, as do many supermarkets in the United States. Mexican chorizo is often made with fresh pork and is usually air-dried and quite crumbly; Spanish chorizo is made with smoked pork and formed into firm sausages that are much more easily sliced than the Mexican. The Mexican type is usually more sharply flavored, but that depends on the maker.

Chorizo contains a combination of dried red chiles, oregano, ground cumin and cloves, paprika and vinegar. This sausage, available in links of various sizes either fresh or canned in lard, must be cooked. Occasionally a 10″ dried version, called *estilo Cantimpalos*, is found in markets, which is excellent. Most Mexican cookbooks contain recipes for making your own chorizo, which is a good idea considering not only how enormously they vary in flavor and consistency, but also the poor quality of the chorizos usually found in supermarkets, especially in Southern California. One cup of homemade chorizo equals ½ pound of purchased chorizo.

STORAGE: They can be refrigerated for up to 2 weeks, or frozen indefinitely.

PREPARATION AND USE: The Spanish-style chorizos can be cooked in their casings and are often grilled slowly over charcoal until they are cooked through. For most recipes using any type of chorizo, though, one is required to remove the casing and either slice or crumble the filling into a heavy skillet and then fry slowly to render out the fat, taking care not to over-brown because the spices can burn. West Coast versions of the Mexican type often turn into a soupy mass when cooked.

Chorizo is often used with cheese as a filling for Enchiladas. One of the most common dishes using chorizo is Chorizo and Eggs, in which 2 beaten eggs are scrambled with 2 ounces of cooked chorizo and its rendered fat, to make 1 serving. It is used in the Philippines as well, specifically in a stuffing for rolled beef in a dish called Pochero, a version of French Pot au Feu with chick-peas and vegetables. Any type of chorizo can be used as a flavoring in Paul's recipe for beans.

CHORIZO CHILI BEANS

3   cups dried PINTO BEANS *or* PINK   For approximately 16 servings
    BEANS, cooked and drained, but
    with liquid reserved
6   knobs chorizo (approximately ¾ pound)
3   pounds lean ground beef
1   onion, finely diced
1   green bell pepper, seeded and finely diced
1   clove garlic, minced
1   (19-ounce) can RED CHILE SAUCE (Chile Las Palmas) or 2
    cups homemade
2   pounds ripe tomatoes, peeled and diced *or* a 28-ounce can
    peeled whole or crushed tomatoes with their liquid
1   tablespoon chopped fresh oregano *or* 1 teaspoon dried,
    crumbled

Remove the chorizos from their casings and place in a clay bean pot (olla), large kettle, or Dutch oven. Add the ground beef and cook, breaking meat up with the back of a spoon until it is crumbly and has lost its pink color. Add the onion, bell pepper, and garlic and sauté for 5 minutes. Add the Red Chile Sauce and tomatoes. Simmer slowly for 2 hours.

Add the cooked beans to the sauce, along with enough reserved bean liquid to make a thin stew. Stir in the oregano and simmer slowly, uncovered, for 20 minutes or so, until thickened to your liking. Taste, and add salt and pepper as needed.

Serve with rice as a main course, or as an accompaniment to other Mexican dishes.

TO PREPARE IN ADVANCE: This can be stored in the refrigerator for up to 4 days, or frozen for up to 3 months.

CHRISTOPHINE

See CHAYOTE

CHUCHU

See CHAYOTE

CHUFA

See THE FOODS OF EUROPE section

COCONUT

See THE FOODS OF ASIA section

COMINO

See CUMIN in HERBS, SPICES, AND SEASONING BLENDS section

CORIANDER, FRESH

See HERBS, SPICES, AND SEASONING BLENDS section

CORIANDRO

See CORIANDER, FRESH in HERBS, SPICES, AND SEASONING
BLENDS section

CORN, DRIED

OTHER: dry, white field corn

SPANISH: *maíz desgranado*

Dried corn is made into a special cornmeal called MASA, which is used to make corn tortillas, tamales, etc. It is a tedious process in which the corn is boiled and then soaked with slaked lime (calcium hydroxide) for several hours until the skins of the kernels loosen. The corn is cooled, and then rubbed between the palms to remove all the skins. The skinless kernels are called *nixtamal,* and they are ground fine to make masa. (We do not recommend doing this at home.) The resulting meal has an entirely different flavor from ordinary cornmeal because of the lime used in the processing. Fresh masa can be purchased in Latin American markets and in *tortillerías*. Dried masa (masa *harina*) can be purchased in 5-pound sacks in many supermarkets.

CORN HUSKS, DRIED

Dried, beige-colored corn husks are sold in packages by weight, ready to use for wrapping Tamales, one of the most famous of all Mexican prepared dishes, traditionally served only on festive occasions because they take so long to make. If you wish to make your own dried corn husks, remove husks from fresh corn, cut off the ends, and flatten husks out. Hang to dry in a sunny window, or in a clean, airy spot indoors. Parchment paper and foil make acceptable substitutes, but lack the flavor and authentic appearance of corn husks.

STORAGE: If wrapped airtight, they can be stored indefinitely in a dry place. If moisture is present, the husks will mold and be unusable.

PREPARATION AND USE: Cover dried husks with hot water and let soak for 1 to 2 hours until soft and pliable. Remove any silk; rinse, and pat dry. Tear some of the husks into strips to use as ties for the Tamales after they are wrapped so they will keep their shape while they are steamed. MASA is spread on the corn husks and filled with seasoned meat, or even a sweet mixture of raisins and nuts; then all is folded up inside the husks, tied with a strip of corn husk, and steamed until the dough is firm. In making the sweet type, the masa is often colored in pastel hues. The meat-filled type accompany plain roast meat or poultry, or any Mexican menu.

CULANTRO

See CORIANDER, in the HERBS, SPICES, AND SEASONING
BLENDS section

CUMIN

See HERBS, SPICES, AND SEASONING BLENDS section

DENDE OIL

See PALM OIL in THE FOODS OF AFRICA section

DJON DJON

These are tiny black mushrooms, available only in Haiti, that give off their black color into cooked dishes. Dried European mushrooms have a very similar taste and can be substituted in Haitian recipes. Dried Asian mushrooms are not as similar in flavor, and would be the second choice.

EPAZOTE

(ehp-ah-ZOH-teh)
OTHER: *pazote* (Spain), goosefoot, Jerusalem oak pazote (California),
Mexican tea, pigweed, wormseed

LATIN: *Chenopodium ambrosioides*

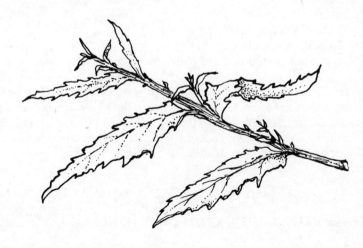

There are, as you may have noticed by the "other" names, many varieties of this pungent herb, which grows wild in places all over the United States. You may well find it growing in your own backyard. It is sometimes available dried, almost never fresh, in Latin American markets. We have found it nearly impossible to locate commercially, but have found that our favorite California supplier of fresh herbs, Taylor Herb Gardens, has made plantlings available and seeds can be purchased from a supplier in Texas. (See SHOPPING SOURCES). It is especially favored in the cooking of the Yucatán peninsula. Diana Kennedy, in all three of her Mexican cookbooks, says she uses it often because she is quite fond of it. It is, along with a number of other herbs, such as MINT, OREGANO and CUMIN, a *carminative,* meaning that it reduces the gas associated with beans. Like fresh coriander, the taste for epazote is usually an acquired one. If found in a market, a small bunch of fresh epazote will consist of approximately 8 sprigs.

STORAGE: Store as any fresh or dried herb.

USE: This is very often used in small quantities to flavor black bean soup or other mixtures containing beans, because of its flavor and carminative qualities. It is, in fact, unthinkable to Mexicans to cook black beans without it. One tablespoon of fresh, or 1 teaspoon dried, epazote is sufficient for 4 to 6 servings in most recipes. It is also used in Green Pumpkinseed Sauce for Papadzules (tortillas filled with hard-cooked egg).

QUESADILLAS WITH EPAZOTE

This is a recipe from Barbara Hansen, author of *Mexican Cookery* (H.P. Books), who warns not to use too much epazote, as it is strongly flavored. She makes these quesadillas quickly in a microwave oven.

PER SERVING:
1　corn or flour tortilla
1　or 2 thin slices Monterey Jack cheese
1　or 2 small sprigs epazote
　　Optional: a few thin strips of peeled green chili

Lay the cheese, epazote, and green chili strips on a tortilla. Roll up or fold in half like a turnover to enclose them and wrap the tortilla in a paper towel. Microwave on "medium-high" for 20 to 30 seconds to warm the tortilla and melt the cheese. Alternatively, cook the folded tortilla on a griddle, turning once or twice until hot. Serve with Salsa if desired.

FAVA BEANS

See under BEANS in THE FOODS OF THE MIDDLE EAST section

FIDEOS
(fee-DEH-yohs)

Fideos are coils of very fine noodles and can be found in Latin American markets. VERMICELLI or other fine pastas such as CAPPELLETTI (see PASTA in THE FOODS OF EUROPE section) can be substituted.

STORAGE: Store in a cool, dry place indefinitely.

PREPARATION AND USE: Fideos are used in Mexican soups *(sopas aguadas)* and the very popular "dry soups" *(sopas secas)*, in which there is very little liquid. This type of pasta is cooked in an entirely different manner in Mexico than elsewhere. Sopa Seca de Fideos is made by frying the dry noodles in fat until they are browned. Then broth, tomatoes, and seasonings are added and the whole is cooked, stirring often, for about 20 minutes until the noodles are very soft and the liquid almost completely evaporated. This type of soup is usually served between the "wet" soup and the main course at *comida,* the main meal of the day, served about two o'clock.

FLOR DE CALABAZA
See SQUASH BLOSSOM

FLOUR, TORTILLA
See MASA HARINA

FRESADILLA
See TOMATILLO

FRIJOLES
See BEANS, DRIED

FRIJOLES REFRITOS
(free-HOH-lehs reh-FREE-tohs)
OTHER: "refried" beans

Prepared refried beans, made from pinto or pink beans, are available in 17- and 29-ounce cans in supermarkets all over America. The Rosarita brand is one that is widely distributed. The canned version is very convenient and quite good, but not as good as homemade. It is very easy to make this dish from any type of cooked beans; directions can be found under BEANS, DRIED.

STORAGE: Once opened, these can be stored in a nonmetal container in the refrigerator for up to a week, or frozen for an indefinite period.

PREPARATION AND USE: Refried beans are served as an accompaniment to many Mexican meals and are used as an ingredient in Tostadas, Burritos, Huevos Rancheros, etc. To serve as a starchy accompaniment, reheat in a buttered dish until hot, topping with grated cheese during the last few minutes of cooking. We like to season them with melted bacon drippings, garlic, and diced green chiles to taste, to serve as a chafing dish bean dip with *tostaditas* (wedges of crisp-fried corn tortillas) for dipping. A more elaborate appetizer can be made in the following manner.

NACHO APPETIZER PLATTER

For 12 to 16 appetizer servings

Our method of serving this is less messy than the traditional.

BEAN DIP:
2   tablespoons bacon drippings
1   clove garlic, minced
1   (29-ounce) can refried beans *or* 3½ cups homemade
       refried beans
6   ounces sharp Cheddar cheese, grated
3   fresh CHILES POBLANOS, or 5 Anaheim chiles, roasted,
       peeled, seeded, and diced, *or* 1 (7-ounce) can diced
       green chiles
     Salt to taste

TOSTADITAS (OR TOTOPOS):
2   dozen corn tortillas
     Oil for frying

TO GARNISH AND SERVE:
2   ounces sharp Cheddar, shredded
4   scallions, thinly sliced
1   cup guacamole (see AVOCADO)
1   cup Salsa Cruda (see CHILE SERRANO)
1   cup dairy sour cream
     Optional: 1–2 tablespoons minced fresh coriander
       (cilantro or Chinese parsley)

To make the bean dip, heat the bacon drippings in a heavy saucepan or skillet. Sauté the garlic briefly; then stir in the beans, Cheddar, and chiles. Cook, stirring constantly, over very low heat to prevent scorching, just until the cheese is melted. Remove from heat and season to taste with salt. Place in a shallow 9″ or 10″ round baking dish, such as a glass pie plate or ceramic quiche dish.

To make the tostaditas, cut the corn tortillas into sixths or eighths and dry for several hours at room temperature. (This process may be speeded up by placing them in a 200° oven for about 20 minutes, stirring from time to time.) Heat 1 cup oil in a skillet or wok and fry the tortilla pieces, a few at a time, until they are crisp and golden. Lift out with a slotted spoon and drain on paper towels. Add more oil to the pan as needed until all are fried.

Twenty to 30 minutes before serving, top the bean dip with shredded Cheddar and bake at 350° until bubbling. Place on a serving dish or in a basket that is at least 2″ larger in diameter than the bean-dip dish. Surround with the tostaditas. Sprinkle sliced scallions over the dip. Top with dollops of guacamole, salsa cruda, and sour cream. Sprinkle with chopped cilantro and serve immediately.

TO PREPARE IN ADVANCE: The bean dip can be refrigerated for up to 4 days, or frozen. Tostaditas will keep several days in an airtight container— we keep them in a brown grocery bag, stapling the top closed.

FRUTA BOMBA

See PAPAYA

GARBANZOS

See CHICK-PEAS, under BEANS, in THE FOODS OF THE MIDDLE EAST section

GOOSEFOOT

See EPAZOTE

GRANADILLA

(grah-nah-DEE-yah)
OTHER: passion fruit, purple granadilla

"Granadilla" is the Spanish name for passion fruit which, in all its varieties, is sweet and aromatic. Colors of skin and the jelly-like flesh vary greatly depending on the variety of this oval tropical fruit. One type has a very wrinkled purple skin with orange flesh. In Mexico, the most popular variety is the yellow granadilla, which has a yellow-orange skin and grayish flesh. You will find them in Latin American markets in the fall. They are ripe when the skin yields to gentle pressure. Passion fruit juice (usually sweetened with sugar) is widely available in cans or bottles in supermarkets and health food stores.

STORAGE: Once ripe, they will keep in the refrigerator for up to 3 days.

PREPARATION AND USE: The flavor on its own can be cloying, so mix it sparingly with other fruits or fruit juices. The multitude of edible seeds are nearly impossible to remove. Cut in half, sprinkle with lemon or lime juice, and eat out of your hand, seeds and all. The hard skin is not eaten. You may wish to sieve the pulp in an attempt to remove the seeds, and then add the juice to a combination of other fruit juices for a delightful tropical drink, but it is much easier to buy the commercially bottled or canned juice.

GREEN CHILE SALSA

Green chile salsa, one of the most common canned Mexican-style food products, now found on the shelves of almost every supermarket, is a combination of tomatoes, onions, and mild green chiles. Many shoppers expect it to be green because of the name, but find it is a red, tomato-based sauce to which green chiles have been added. It is a commercial version of the table sauces served with every meal in Mexico. It has a mild spiciness that makes it versatile as a cooking ingredient. The Herdez brand, imported from Mexico, contains a bit of cilantro and is generally spicier than the more commonly found Ortega and Las Palmas brands.

STORAGE: Once opened, it can be stored in the refrigerator in a nonmetal container for up to a week.

PREPARATION AND USE: Warmed, right from the can, this makes an excellent sauce for a cheese omelet. We use it to add flavor to shredded beef Ropa Vieja, which can be served as a Mexican dish on its own, or as a filling for flour tortillas in making Burritos.

ROPA VIEJA

For up to 16 servings,
depending on use

Mexicans often use whimsical names for dishes. This one means "old clothes," and is supposedly so named because it looks rather like dingy rags.

4–5 pounds boneless beef pot roast, cut in 2″ slabs with the
   grain*
  2 large onions, finely chopped
  2 cloves garlic, minced
  ¾ teaspoon ground cumin
 28 ounces Ortega Green Chile Salsa or 3½ cups
   homemade
   Salt and pepper to taste

*Note: We used to use brisket of beef when that cut was inexpensive, and left it in one piece to cook. Now we use whatever is the least expensive type of pot roast.

Place the pot roast slabs (do not trim all fat) in a kettle with onion, garlic, and cumin and water to cover. Bring to a boil; then cover and simmer slowly for 3 to 4 hours, until the meat is very tender when pierced with a fork. Remove from the heat, lift out the meat onto a plate, and let cool until it can be shredded with the fingers. After shredding, return it to the broth, stir in the Green Chile Salsa, and simmer, uncovered, until most of the liquid has evaporated. Season with salt and pepper to taste.

TO PREPARE IN ADVANCE: This will keep in the refrigerator for up to 4 days or in the freezer for up to a month. Thaw if frozen, and reheat slowly in a heavy saucepan, adding a bit of water if the mixture becomes too dry.

GREEN PUMPKIN

See CALABAZA

GREEN TOMATO, MEXICAN

See TOMATILLO

GUANÁBANA

(gwahn-AH-bahn-ah)
OTHER: soursop, *annona*

FRENCH: *corossol*

Guanábana is a very large tropical fruit with a dark green, spine- or wart-covered rind. The flesh varies from white to pink to yellow-orange. This fruit is often the size of a football, does not travel well, and is seldom available fresh in the United States. The juice or "nectar," available canned in Latin American markets, has a flavor much like that of pears. The unsweetened pulp, which has a consistency rather like that of cotton, is occasionally available frozen in Caribbean markets.

STORAGE: After opening, the nectar can be stored in a nonmetal container in the refrigerator for up to a week. Fresh fruit, sealed in plastic wrap, can be stored in the refrigerator for up to 5 days.

PREPARATION AND USE: Often used to make drinks, jellies, and conserves, especially in Cuba. The pulp or nectar makes delicious frozen sherbets when combined with half its quantity of whipping cream, sweetened to taste with simple syrup (equal parts sugar and water boiled until the sugar has dissolved), and frozen in an ice cream freezer. (Lacking a commercial freezer, simply place the mixture in a mixing bowl in the freezer, and remember to whip it several times while it is setting to give it a light consistency.)

GUAVA

FRENCH: *goyave* ITALIAN: *guaiva* PORTUGUESE: *gioaba*
SPANISH: *guayaba*

Guava is a fruit of the myrtle family that grows wild all year in Mexico and is now cultivated in Florida and California. It is a very popular fruit—sweet, aromatic, high in vitamin C, and found in many varieties including pineapple guava, and strawberry guava from Brazil. The outer skin colors range from yellow to red-purple to black. The granular flesh, studded in the center with small seeds, ranges in color from white to salmon to red. If it is to be eaten raw, the guava should be ripe enough that the skin yields to light pressure. If it is to be cooked (in jellies or preserves), the flesh should feel quite firm. You will also find canned guava "shells" (peeled and seeded halves) in 34-ounce cans in Latin American markets (the Clemente Jacques brand is the best we've found), as well as the popular paste, GUAYABATE (see ATE), guava nectar, and guava jelly.

STORAGE: The ripe fruit keeps well. Ripen at room temperature until the skin yields to light pressure; then it can be refrigerated for up to a week. After opening, canned shells or nectar can be stored in a nonmetal container for up to 4 days.

PREPARATION AND USE: To eat raw, cut guava in half lengthwise; then slice to enjoy it as is or with a mixture of other fruits. The seeds are usually eaten as they are said to be good for elimination. To make guava "shells," halve and peel the guavas and poach them in a simple syrup just until they are tender; then cool and scrape out the center seeds. The halves can be filled with sweet mixtures to bake as a dessert, or can be used as a pie filling with their juices thickened with arrowroot, tapioca, or cornstarch. Guava makes superb jellies, preserves (dark red ones are considered finest), and a marvelous pancake syrup. Guayabate is very popular in Mexico and in the Caribbean as a dessert with mild cheese.

HEARTS OF PALM

OTHER: palm heart, swamp cabbage

FRENCH: *chou palmiste* SPANISH: *palmito*

This very delicious and expensive vegetable is the ivory-colored interior of a palm tree, usually the cabbage palmetto, the official state tree of Florida. Small trees must be chopped down in order to obtain the heart, which explains why this is such an expensive item. It is available fresh only in Florida and some tropical countries, but can be found, packed in water, in 10- or 30-ounce cans in fancy-food stores across America. Hearts of palm look like pure white asparagus stalks of various diameters. The flavor is reminiscent of artichoke, the texture is silky and tender.

STORAGE: Fresh can be stored, tightly wrapped, in the refrigerator for up to 5 days, though it may darken on standing. Once opened, the canned hearts can be transferred to a nonmetal container and stored in their own juice for up to 10 days.

PREPARATION AND USE: Raw hearts of palm are shucked to reveal the edible center, and may be thinly sliced and eaten raw like cabbage. They must be cooked to use in recipes that call for canned ones. Peel and cook in unsalted water until tender, about 10 minutes. Let cool.

Hearts of palm make a very elegant salad ingredient sliced into rounds. Or slice lengthwise to serve with a vinaigrette or mayonnaise. When served warm, they are usually seasoned with lemon butter. In Martinique, they are covered with Béchamel sauce and grated cheese and browned under the broiler. Brazil's elaborate Cuscuz de Galinha, a dish of molded steamed chicken, cornmeal, and vegetables, is garnished with hard-cooked eggs, oranges, and sliced rounds of hearts of palm.

INDIAN NUT

See PIÑON NUT in THE FOODS OF REGIONAL AMERICA section

JAMAICA
(hah-MĪK-ah)
OTHER: *flor de jamaica, rosella* (Jamaica), sorrel (Caribbean)

Jamaica is a dark red variety of hibiscus flower available dried in Latin American, and some Middle Eastern and Asian markets.

STORAGE: It will keep indefinitely in a cool, dry place.

PREPARATION AND USE: The flowers are steeped to obtain a pink, almost cranberry-flavored liquid, which is then strained, sweetened to taste, and flavored with lime to serve over ice as an iced tea-like drink that is very popular with children. To make 8 servings, pour 4 cups boiling water over 1 cup of dried jamaica flowers combined with ¼ cup sugar and let stand and cool for 2 hours. Strain, pressing liquid from flowers; add 4 cups cold water and 2 tablespoons fresh lime juice. Serve over ice. In Trinidad, it is often fermented, and then rum is added to make a cocktail.

JERUSALEM OAK PAZOTE
See EPAZOTE

JÍCAMA
(HEE-kah-mah)

Jícama is a tropical root vegetable of the morning glory vine that looks very much like a brown-skinned turnip. But there the resemblance ends, for the crisp white flesh tastes like a delicious cross between an apple and a water chestnut. This vegetable is as important to Mexicans as the potato is to Americans. Jícama is found in many supermarkets nowadays where it is sold whole or in pieces, with plastic wrap covering the cut surfaces.

STORAGE: Whole jícama or large pieces will keep for 1 to 2 weeks in the refrigerator. Store small cut pieces in cold water to cover to retain crispness and prevent drying.

PREPARATION AND USE: One pound will serve 3 to 4 for most uses. Mexicans eat jícama as a snack, sliced and seasoned with a sprinkling of lime juice and powdered chile. It is also used in a popular Mexican salad called Pico de Gallo (rooster's beak), with diced fresh orange and powdered chile.

Peeled and cut into large sticks, jícama can be served as an hors d'oeuvre with your favorite dip. Jícama makes an excellent substitute for water chestnuts in Chinese cooking because it has a similar color and crispness, which is not lost in cooking, and is much less expensive. Add, after dicing, to fruit salads, soups, stews, and many dishes that would be enhanced by a crisp texture. It is ideal to use instead of turnips for making vegetable "daisies" because it does not discolor when exposed to air. A simple salad that goes equally well with Latin American dishes as it does with Asian dishes is made as follows:

JÍCAMA SALAD WITH CILANTRO

For 4 to 6 servings

This is an easy-to-make and refreshing salad to serve with any highly spiced meal.

1   pound jícama, peeled
3   tablespoons fresh lemon juice
1   tablespoon fresh coriander (cilantro or Chinese parsley) leaves, tightly packed

Cut jícama in fine julienne strips, or grate on a medium grater or in the food processor. Place in a serving bowl.

In the container of an electric blender, combine the lemon juice and fresh coriander and process until blended. Pour this dressing over the jícama and toss to coat evenly.

Serve chilled, as an accompaniment to Mexican or Southeast Asian dishes.

TO PREPARE IN ADVANCE: Cover tightly and refrigerate for up to 8 hours.

LARD

SPANISH: *manteca de cerdo*

For general information, see LARD in THE FOODS OF ASIA section. Lard has had a history as a popular cooking fat in Mexico, where it was always used in making flour tortillas and in tamale dough. As it increases in price, vegetable oils are replacing it in popularity. Some cooks have an aversion to the idea of lard and its heavy "barnyard" taste; others swear by it for making flaky pie crusts. Commercial purified lard, sold in rectangular boxes, is full of preservatives. Buy lard instead from a reliable butcher or render your own (directions in THE FOODS OF ASIA section).

LONGANIZA

(Lawn-gah-NEE-zah)

This is a Spanish type of sausage, made with lean pork, garlic, oregano, and paprika, that is milder than CHORIZO. It is long, not tied in links, and will be found in Latin American and Spanish markets. See SAUSAGES in THE FOODS OF EUROPE section for general information.

STORAGE: It will keep in the refrigerator for up to a month or in the freezer indefinitely.

PREPARATION AND USE: Substitute longaniza for chorizo when a milder taste is desired. Longaniza can be charcoal-grilled in the same manner as Spanish-style chorizo. In the Caribbean, it is usually skinned and coarsely chopped to use as an ingredient in such dishes as Sancocho de Frijoles (a bean stew from the Dominican Republic) and Sancocho de Gandules (Pigeon Pea Stew with calabaza and yams).

MALANGA

(mah-LAHN-gah)
OTHER: *dasheen, tannia yautía,* new *cocoyam, yuca*

Malanga, a tropical tuber with brown skin and white to lavender flesh, is very important to the cooking of the Caribbean. It is starchier than our domestic potato and has a nutlike flavor. Those found in markets in the United States usually weigh 1 to 2 pounds. There is a good deal of confusion over these and the tubers of the CASSAVA, and TARO ROOT (see THE FOODS OF ASIA section), but that needn't concern us much because all are very similar in taste and in use. The arrow-shaped leaves of the plant are called CALLALOO GREENS.

STORAGE: These will keep for a month or longer in a cool spot.

PREPARATION AND USE: One average malanga serves 2 to 4. Peel and boil or bake to use as a substitute in any potato recipe. If to be baked, parboil for 30 minutes, then bake at 375° for 1½ hours. If to be boiled, peel and cut in 1″ dice and simmer in water to cover for about 45 minutes until tender. Small ones are served like new potatoes. In the Dominican Republic, the flesh is grated to make yam cakes, in the same manner as potato pancakes. These are often used in stews along with sweet potatoes, yams, and taro, as in the following recipe for a Puerto Rican beef and vegetable stew.

SANCOCHO

For 8 servings

More a soup than a stew, this is served in bowls.

1½ pounds lean beef stew meat, cut in 1" cubes
½ pound lean boneless pork, cut in ¾" cubes
2 medium onions, chopped
4 cloves garlic, minced
3 ripe tomatoes, peeled and chopped *or* a 16-ounce can
     peeled whole tomatoes
2 red bell peppers (seeds and membranes removed),
     chopped
1 green bell pepper (seeds and membranes removed),
     chopped
2 teaspoons salt
2 small, fresh chiles serranos, seeded and diced
1 bay leaf
1 pound malanga, peeled and cut in 1" chunks
1 pound TARO ROOT, peeled and cut in 1" chunks
1 pound sweet potato (or "yam"), peeled and cut in 1½"
     chunks
1 pound pumpkin, peeled and cut in 1" chunks
2 ears fresh or frozen corn, husked and cut in 1" crosswise
     sections
1 ripe PLANTAIN, peeled and cut in ½" crosswise sections
1 tablespoon lime juice, or more to taste
1 tablespoon chopped fresh coriander (cilantro or Chinese
     parsley)
1 tablespoon chopped fresh oregano, or
1 teaspoon dried oregano, crumbled

In a large stew pot or Dutch oven, combine the meats, onion, garlic, tomatoes, and peppers. Add water to cover by 1"–2". Bring to a boil and simmer, uncovered, for 10 minutes, skimming any foam that rises to the surface.

Partially cover the pot and simmer over low heat for 1 hour. Add the malanga, sweet potato, coriander and oregano, and simmer approximately 30 minutes longer until the meat and vegetables are tender. Toss the pieces of plantain with the lime juice and add both to the pot along with the corn and pumpkin. Simmer about 10 minutes longer, until the corn is tender. Taste for seasoning, adding salt and pepper as desired.

Serve in large soup bowls.

TO PREPARE IN ADVANCE: This is best freshly cooked when vegetables are still slightly firm. It may be cooled, refrigerated up to 4 days, and reheated for serving. The pumpkin disintegrates on standing and thickens the soup to a stew-like consistency.

MANGO

(MAYN-go)

This delectable tropical fruit, native to India, comes in many types. The most commonly found has yellow and pink skin and bright orange flesh, and is in season from May through September. The large, flat, tenacious seed is difficult to remove from the soft juicy meat, so ingenious ways of cutting this fruit have been devised. Green mangoes (except for a few rare types) are not ripe; yellow ones are. For those to be eaten raw, look for tinges of yellow and pink developing on the smooth skin. Ripe ones should have a strong fragrance and feel slightly soft to gentle pressure. There are several varieties including tear-shaped ones and round ones. Because they can vary so much in flavor, and because they are expensive, you would be wise to buy one and taste it before purchasing a quantity of them. Canned mangoes in syrup can be found in Latin American grocery stores.

STORAGE: After ripening at room temperature, they can be stored in the refrigerator for up to 3 days. Once opened, canned mangoes can be stored in a nonmetal container in their own syrup in the refrigerator for up to 4 days.

PREPARATION AND USE: One medium mango will serve 1 or 2 and will yield approximately 1 cup of pulp. For easy serving, cut lengthwise next to the flat seed. Use a dull table knife with a rounded point to make crisscross grids in the flesh without cutting through the skin. Press the center skin of each half to open the grids outward. The cubes of mango, which now protrude, can be lifted off with a fork. A mango cut in this manner can be used as a garnish, as an accompaniment to many meals, as a salad, or as a dessert.

Chef Michel Stroot makes a Mango Cream from fresh mangoes for guests at the Golden Door Health Spa in Southern California. Into the container of an electric blender he places the flesh of 1 or 2 mangos with 1½ cups of low-fat yogurt, 2 tablespoons honey, and 1 tablespoon lemon juice. He purees the mixture and pours it into small serving dishes, garnishing each serving with a thin slice of bright green peeled kiwi. This mixture can be served chilled or frozen.

Green mangoes are used to make chutneys, relishes, and beverages and, in the Caribbean, the seed is roasted and the inner kernel eaten. (See THE

FOODS OF ASIA section for additional information.) A dramatic dessert can be made by heating canned mangoes with their syrup and a bit of cinnamon and nutmeg in a chafing dish and then flaming them with a bit of tequila to spoon over servings of vanilla ice cream, as in the following recipe.

FLAMING MANGO TOPPING
FOR ICE CREAM

For 6 servings

Betty Kempe, owner of the Villa Santa Monica in San Miguel de Allende, Mexico, serves this as a flamboyant dessert to her hotel guests. It couldn't be simpler or more delicious.

1 (1-pound, 12-ounce) can sliced mangoes in syrup
¼ teaspoon ground cinnamon
  A sprinkling of freshly grated nutmeg
1–1½ quarts vanilla ice cream
⅓ cup tequila

Pour the mangoes and their syrup in the top of a chafing dish or other skillet from which you can serve a flaming sauce. Break up the mango pieces with a spoon into bite-sized morsels. Sprinkle on the cinnamon and nutmeg, bring to a simmer, and cook slowly for a few minutes to thicken the syrup. Meanwhile, spoon servings of ice cream into bowls.

Just before serving, lower the lights in the dining room, warm the tequila in a ladle, ignite with a match, and pour it over the warm mangoes. When the flames die, spoon the mangoes and sauce over the servings of ice cream.

TO PREPARE IN ADVANCE: Servings of ice cream can be waiting in the freezer. Heat and flame the mangoes just before serving.

MANGO SQUASH

See CHAYOTE

MANZANILLA

(mahn-zah-NEE-ya)
OTHER: chamomile

These dried flowers are used to brew chamomile tea used as a remedy to calm the stomach.

MASA, FRESH
(MAH-sah)

Both tortillas and Tamales are made with this moist corn dough, which is made from dry corn that has been soaked in slaked lime (calcium hydroxide). Fresh masa is available in some Mexican markets and, by advance order, in some Mexican restaurants. Masa used to make tamales (masa *para tamal*) usually has all hulls removed and is beaten with lard until very fluffy. It is sold in some supermarkets in the West and Southwest of the United States, and can be purchased from *tortillerias,* where it is usually necessary to buy a large quantity.

STORAGE: This does not keep well, so buy it as needed, or freeze it for up to a month. It can be refrigerated for use within a day or two.

PREPARATION AND USE: Half a pound (8 ounces) of masa will make 12 to 16 corn tortillas. To make tortillas, roll a piece of masa with your hands into a ball the size of a walnut. Place a small plastic bag (sandwich size) on the bottom of an open tortilla press. Position the ball slightly off center, toward the hinge, and top it with another plastic bag. Press. Peel the top plastic bag carefully from the pressed tortilla and lay the tortilla on a hot griddle. As it warms, the second plastic bag can be easily lifted off. In a minute or so, when the tortilla begins to look dry around the edges, turn it over to cook on the second side. When lightly colored, turn it back to the first side, and let cook briefly, during which time it will probably puff. Place in a napkin inside a basket or large plastic bag while you continue making the rest of the tortillas. This process becomes very easy and automatic with practice, and you will develop a rhythm of pressing tortillas and flipping those that are cooking on the griddle. Stacking newly cooked tortillas as they are made keeps them warm and moist. Serve as soon as possible.

To make tamales, fresh masa is beaten with lard until it is very light and fluffy. It is then spread on damp CORN HUSKS or BANANA LEAVES, covered with a sweet or savory filling, and then all is wrapped and tied. Tamales are steamed for 45 minutes to an hour until the dough is cooked. In Mexico, they are almost never served with a sauce, though it is a common practice to serve them with a red chile sauce in the United States.

MASA HARINA
(MAH-sa ah-RREE-nah)
OTHER: corn tortilla flour, instant masa

Masa harina is flour of specially prepared corn which, with the addition of water, makes a dough very similar to fresh masa. The Quaker brand is widely available throughout the United States. Never substitute cornmeal for this ingredient—it is an entirely different product and will make a stiff and brittle approximation of a tortilla.

STORAGE: Tightly covered in a cool place this will keep for up to 3 months, or indefinitely in the refrigerator or freezer.

PREPARATION AND USE: For the equivalent of 8 ounces fresh masa, or enough to make 12 to 16 corn tortillas, combine 2 cups of masa harina with 1¼ to 1½ cups of warm water. The dough should cling together but not be too wet. Let rest for 20 minutes before making tortillas (as directed under MASA, FRESH).

Corn masa and flour masa are both used in making Chalupas (small, filled, "canoe"-shaped appetizers) and other antojitos (appetizers). This product makes an excellent thickener to use in place of flour for Chile con Carne, and other chile-based sauces.

MASA TRIGO

(MAH-sa TREE-goh)

Masa Trigo is an "instant" flour tortilla mix made by Quaker and sold in supermarkets in various metropolitan areas and in the West and Southwest of the United States. It is a mixture of wheat flour, lard, leavening, and salt.

STORAGE: Tightly covered, it will keep in a cool place for up to 3 months, or indefinitely in the refrigerator or freezer.

PREPARATION AND USE: To make flour tortillas, mix 2 cups of Masa Trigo with ½ cup or more of warm water to make a pliable dough. Knead until smooth; cover with a towel and allow to rest for 20 minutes. Shape into 12 balls and roll each out on a lightly floured surface to form a circle measuring approximately 6″ in diameter. Place on a hot griddle and cook 1 or 2 minutes per side until lightly browned.

Flour tortillas are filled with cheese and heated on a griddle to make Quesadillas; used to wrap meat or beans to make Burritos or Chimichangas (deep-fried Burritos); deep-fried as a base for Tostadas; and used in countless other ways as the "bread" of northern Mexico. They can be made at home without commercial Masa Trigo—our recipe appears with TORTILLAS, FLOUR.

MELON, TREE

See PAPAYA

MEXICAN TEA

See EPAZOTE

MIRLETON

See CHAYOTE

MOLE

(MOH-leh)

The word *mole* indicates any sauce made with chiles, which can be, but is not necessarily, "hot." There are as many variations in Mexico of such sauces as there are curries in India. Probably the most familiar is the traditional Mole Poblano from Puebla, which is an elaborate, spicy red sauce served on holidays, and containing chiles, spices, ground seeds and nuts, and unsweetened chocolate. When served with turkey, it is Mexico's national dish, Mole de Guajolote. There are also green *moles* made of tomatillos, cilantro, green chiles, ground pumpkin seeds, and nuts. As in making a curry sauce, the ingredients are ground to a paste and then cooked in fat for a few minutes to blend the flavors. Various commercial mole pastes and powders for making them are available in Mexican markets in 8- or 18-ounce jars or 3-ounce cans. Excellent recipes for several kinds of moles appear in *Mexican Cookery* by Barbara Hansen (H.P. Books).

STORAGE: Once prepared, mole sauces should be refrigerated and will keep for up to 3 days or, if frozen, for up to 3 months, though they will lose some of their spiciness when frozen.

PREPARATION AND USE: Mole sauce is used to bind cooked meat or poultry in order to make a mole dish. The sauce is often thinned with some of the broth from cooking the meat. The commercial paste should be used as directed on the bottle to use as a sauce in mole dishes or as a sauce for Enchiladas.

NARANJA AGRIA

See ORANGE, SEVILLE in THE FOODS OF EUROPE section

NIXTAMAL

See under CORN, DRIED

NOPAL

See NOPALES

NOPALES

(noh-PAH-lehs)

OTHER: nopal cactus, prickly pear cactus, tuna (the fruit) *nopalitos* (when cut in small pieces)

The leaves or "paddles" of nopal or prickly pear cactus have a slight green-bean flavor. Nopales are available all year in several forms in Mexican markets: fresh (whole or chopped), cooked, or canned. When buying fresh nopales, look for the smallest and palest because they are the most tender. Buying bags of those that are already diced is a great convenience. The deli sections of large Mexican markets have precooked nopales in their cooking liquid, which is also a convenience. The canned type, *nopalitos tiernos al natural,* is diced or in strips, packed in water. *Nopalitos en vinagre,* which are diced and pickled in vinegar, should not be used in place of fresh.

STORAGE: Fresh cactus can be stored for a few days in the refrigerator, but should be used as soon as possible. Either canned type should be transferred to a nonmetal container and stored in its own juice in the refrigerator; the pickled pieces will keep indefinitely, but those canned in water will keep only a week or so.

PREPARATION AND USE: One pound of nopales will serve 6 to 8 in most recipes, and make enough filling for 12 tacos. To prepare fresh cactus, hold it with tongs while you scrape away the spines with a sharp knife. It is not necessary to peel it. Cut in small pieces (less than ½" dice) and simmer in salted water to cover in a covered pan for 5 to 10 minutes. Remove the cover and simmer until the cactus is tender and most of the liquid has cooked away. It will remain somewhat firm even when tender. Cactus gives off a slippery secretion much like okra. If you wish to rid it of the slippery substance, blanch it for 5 minutes in boiling salted water, then rinse it well in a colander, cover with a damp towel, and let stand for about 30 minutes, allowing the substance to drip away. Then simmer in salted water until just tender. Rinse canned *nopalitos* well. Season as desired to serve as a vegetable by itself, in combination with scrambled eggs, or use as an ingredient to add to soups. We enjoy *nopalitos* particularly as part of a salad, as in the following recipe.

ENSALADA DE NOPALITOS

For 6 servings

This makes a tasty accompaniment to many Mexican meals.

1 (16- to 20-ounce) jar nopalitos
3 to 4 scallions, sliced thin
3 ripe tomatoes, seeded and chopped
1–2 tablespoons chopped fresh coriander (cilantro or Chinese parsley)
. 2 teaspoons vegetable oil
2 teaspoons vinegar
½ teaspoon salt
1 CHILE SERRANO, seeded and minced

Rinse the nopalitos thoroughly in a strainer under cold running water; blot dry on paper towels. Combine with remaining ingredients in a serving bowl and chill for 30 minutes before serving.

TO PREPARE IN ADVANCE: This will keep in the refrigerator for up to 3 days.

ORANGE, SEVILLE

See THE FOODS OF EUROPE section

PALM OIL

See THE FOODS OF AFRICA section

PANOCHA

See PILONCILLO

PAPAYA

OTHER: pawpaw (mistakenly—see THE FOODS OF REGIONAL AMERICA section), tree melon

CUBA: *fruta bomba* DOMINICAN REPUBLIC: *lechosa* FRENCH: *papaye* GERMAN: *Melonenfrucht* ITALIAN: *papaia*

The Mexican variety of this tropical fruit, which can weigh in excess of 10 pounds, is larger and less sweet than the Hawaiian. The Hawaiian is much more readily available nationwide, and can be used in Mexican recipes. It is extremely digestible—in fact, an enzyme from the papaya is the main ingredient in commercial meat tenderizers. The height of the season is in May and June. Look for blemish-free fruit that yields to slight pressure and has yellow coloring developing in the green skin. If they are to be cooked, buy them underripe. Handle papayas gently because they are easily bruised.

STORAGE: Ripen at room temperature in a dark place. They will then keep refrigerated for a day or two. They do not keep well after ripening.

PREPARATION AND USE: Serve halves or smaller pieces of ripe papaya with a squeeze of lime for a first course or light dessert. Or fill as you would an avocado with chicken or seafood salads. The seeds are edible and have a peppery taste. Use a few of them as a garnish or in a salad dressing. Unripe papayas are often used to make chutneys and relishes, or are cooked in a cream sauce to serve as a vegetable side dish in the Caribbean. In Mexico, they are commonly made into soft drinks, conserves, and confections *(dulces)*.

Marion Cunningham, editor of the widely acclaimed 12th edition of the *Fannie Farmer Cookbook,* likes to serve warm, pickled papaya as a side dish to a poultry main course. She instructs, "Make a simple syrup by simmering together 1½ cups sugar and 1 cup water until the sugar is dissolved. Add 1 underripe papaya, diced, and its seeds and 2 teaspoons pickling spices (available in the spice sections of supermarkets). Simmer 15 minutes, remove from heat and let stand for an hour or more. Serve warm or at room temperature."

PARSLEY, CHINESE

See CORIANDER, in the HERBS, SPICES, AND SEASONING BLENDS section

PASSION FRUIT

See GRANADILLA

PAW PAW

See THE FOODS OF REGIONAL AMERICA section

PAZOTE

See EPAZOTE

PEA, BLACK-EYED

See BLACK-EYED PEA, in THE FOODS OF AFRICA section

PEANUT

See GROUNDNUT in THE FOODS OF AFRICA section

PEPITAS

(peh-PEE-tahs)
OTHER: pumpkin seeds

With or without their white hulls, pumpkin seeds and the seeds of similar squash are a popular ingredient in Mexican cooking. The delicately flavored, thin, dark green kernels removed from the center of the flat white seeds are available salted and roasted in jars in most supermarkets, at premium prices. Unsalted, raw seeds, with or without hulls, can be found in health- or natural-food stores.

STORAGE: Store in the refrigerator because they turn rancid rapidly.

PREPARATION AND USE: Either roasted or raw, these make delicious snacks. We often saw street vendors in Mexico with small piles of pepitas or other squash seeds around them for sale by the handful. In Mexico, many types of squash seeds, hulled or otherwise, are roasted and ground to flavor and thicken sauces for popular dishes such as Pollo en Pipián, which always contains these seeds. They are essential to the Yucatecan dish, Papadzules (enchiladas stuffed with hard-cooked egg with pumpkin seed sauce), and the oil squeezed from the seeds is used there as a garnish as well.

The flavor of pumpkin seeds is very complementary to avocados. We often serve them whole, roasted in butter, with or without the addition of chili powder. (The husks have no real flavor, but eating the seeds whole saves the tedious process of hulling, and the hulls contain fiber, so roasted whole seeds make an excellent quick snack while carving the annual pumpkin.) To roast them, melt 3 tablespoons butter in a large heavy skillet. Stir in 12 ounces pepitas, hulled, or well washed and dried if fresh with hulls still on, and cook, stirring, over medium heat until they turn golden. (You will hear a popping sound as they cook—that's normal.) Season with 1 teaspoon chili powder (optional) and with coarse salt and garlic salt, or both, to taste. Serve warm or at room temperature.

PEPPERS, SWEET

OTHER: bell pepper, green pepper, globe pepper, pimiento (red), *"chile"* *valenciano*

Columbus, in his search for spices, found an entirely different type of pepper from the one he was seeking when he discovered the New World. Both sweet "peppers" and chiles originated in Mexico, but their use spread so rapidly though the world's cuisines that it was assumed they were also native to India and other lands. Sweet peppers and chiles are of the *capsicum* family, and are unrelated to the *piper nigrum* family, for which they were named for their "peppery" taste. Some are long and thin and others are wide and fat. They are green when ripe, but turn red and become sweeter as they continue to ripen. Some Italian varieties are yellow or yellow-green and one sweet Caribbean variety *(aji)* is tiny, red, and lantern-shaped but these varieties are seldom found in the United States. Sweet "bell" peppers are in season all year, with their peak season during the summer, but the red ones, commonly called pimientos, are most easily found during the fall. When purchased, sweet peppers should be firm and shiny with smooth skins. Avoid any that are soft or wrinkled.

STORAGE: Refrigerated in a paper bag, they will keep for up to 5 days.

PREPARATION AND USE: For stuffed "bell" peppers, allow 1 per serving; for other recipes, ½ medium pepper per serving. For most uses—in soups, stews, and salads, for example—peppers are halved, seeded, and then diced. If they are to be stuffed, the top is cut off and discarded along with the seeds, and the hollowed-out shells are then blanched for 1 minute in boiling water and allowed to drain and cool, upside down. For many Italian recipes, and for marinated peppers, they are charred and peeled in the same manner as fresh chiles, to be dressed with vinegar and oil.

PICKAPEPPA SAUCE

This is the brand name of a Jamaican chili-pepper sauce widely distributed in the United States in 5-ounce bottles. It is a spicy, hot and sweet sauce with a tomato-tamarind-mango base. A second type, labeled "hot pepper sauce," much hotter and thinner in consistency, is occasionally found as well. The latter is similar to TABASCO SAUCE (see THE FOODS OF REGIONAL AMERICA section), which can be substituted for it.

STORAGE: It will keep indefinitely on the pantry shelf even after opening.

USE: It is a table condiment. In the southern United States, the thick sauce is often used to coat a brick of cream cheese to serve as a quick appetizer spread with crackers. We think it is one of the finest of all "steak sauces."

PIGEON PEA
See THE FOODS OF AFRICA section

PIGÑOLA
See PIÑON NUT in THE FOODS OF REGIONAL AMERICA section

PIGWEED
See EPAZOTE

PILONCILLO
(pee-lohn-SEE-yo)
OTHER: *panocha, panella* (Colombia)

Piloncillo is a dark brown unrefined sugar with a molasses-like taste used to sweeten coffee or desserts. It is available in Latin American markets in hard cones of varying sizes, or ground, in small cellophane packets. If not available, substitute dark brown sugar or JAGGERY (see THE FOODS OF ASIA section) in equivalent amounts.

STORAGE: Tightly wrapped, it will keep indefinitely on the pantry shelf.

PREPARATION AND USE: The cone-shaped sugar must usually be grated or shaved with a knife or vegetable peeler into a powder before using. Pack firmly as you would brown sugar for measuring. This step is not necessary if it is to be used in a syrup, as it melts in cooking. It is used in a Mexican dessert, Capirotada, made of cubed bread cooked with nuts (pine nuts or almonds), cheese, raisins, cinnamon, and cloves.

PIÑON NUT
See THE FOODS OF REGIONAL AMERICA section, and under PINE NUT in THE FOODS OF EUROPE section

PINK BEANS
See BEANS

PINTO BEANS

See BEANS

PIPIÁN

(pee-PYAHN)

This popular variation of a MOLE (sauce with chiles) is spicy and thickened with either ground pumpkin seeds or sesame seeds. Recipes for several versions appear in *The Complete Book of Mexican Cooking* by Elisabeth Lambert Ortiz (M. Evans & Co.). A commercial powder or paste for making it is available in 3-ounce cans in Latin American markets, and is quite good for a convenience item. The La Victoria brand contains chili powder, bread crumbs, sunflower seeds, peanut butter, and garlic powder.

STORAGE: Store the powder as any spice. Once prepared, Pipián sauces should be refrigerated and will keep up to 3 days or, if frozen, for up to 3 months, though they will lose some of their spiciness if frozen.

PREPARATION AND USE: A quick version, Pipián Rápido, can be made by combining the contents of a 10-ounce can of Mexican RED CHILI SAUCE with 2 teaspoons of smooth peanut butter and salt to taste, for 2 to 3 servings. Three ounces of the commercial powder is added to 3 cups broth from cooking 4 servings of chicken and simmered 3 to 4 minutes until thickened.

PLANTAIN

OTHER: cooking banana, Adam's fig

FRENCH: *banane* SPANISH: *plátano, plátano macho* (a large variety)

The yellow type of plantain is a huge, thick-skinned triangular fruit of the banana family. There are many varieties of this starchy fruit, ranging in color from green to yellow to red to black, which is as popularly served in some tropical countries as potatoes are in the United States. It can be found in Latin American markets. The plantain has a mild, almost squash-like flavor. **It must be cooked to be edible.** Ripe ones are black-skinned and yield to soft pressure. Green plantains, which are firm and harder to peel, ripen very quickly at room temperature. If ripe plantains are not available, substitute green unripe bananas, and cook a shorter time than directed.

STORAGE: Unlike bananas, the plantain can be stored after it is ripe in the refrigerator, wrapped in plastic, for up to 3 days.

PREPARATION AND USE: Peel, and remove all the fibrous strings. This is very easy to do when plantains are ripe but, if green, make one lengthwise incision and three incisions around the diameter, one in the center and one an inch from each end, to facilitate removal of the tenacious skin. They are often halved lengthwise and sautéed in oil until golden on both sides to serve as a side dish. They may also be roasted in the skin—make a lengthwise cut in one side to prevent bursting, rub with oil or butter, and roast at 350° for 30 to 45 minutes, until tender when pierced.

In the Caribbean, plantains are most commonly sliced and deep-fried like potato chips to make Tostones de Plátano, which when well prepared are crispy outside and creamy inside. Chunks of raw *plátano* are often added to soups and stews, and their starchiness thickens these dishes slightly. In Mexico, they are fried and mashed with onions and tomatoes to serve as a side dish with seafood, and in Veracruz they are often served with rice. In Puerto Rico, lengthwise slices are sautéed; then the two ends are fastened together to form rings, which are filled with a meat mixture, and then deep-fried. In Colombia and Venezuela, they are made into cinnamon-spiced cakes, Tortas de Plátano, which are served as a starchy side dish with the main course.

POZOLE

See HOMINY in THE FOODS OF REGIONAL AMERICA section

PRICKLY PEAR CACTUS

See NOPALES

PUMPKIN SEEDS

See PEPITAS

QUINCE

See THE FOODS OF THE MIDDLE EAST section

RECADO COLORADO

OTHER: *recado rojo, achiote condimentado*

This is a seasoning paste used in Yucatecan cooking, commonly sold in markets in the Yucatán, and occasionally sold in well-stocked Mexican markets. Because it contains ACHIOTE SEED(S), it gives a bright orange color to foods with which it is cooked.

STORAGE: It can be stored in the refrigerator for up to a week.

PREPARATION AND USE: To make ¼ cup (4 tablespoons) recado colorado, combine 1 tablespoon crushed achiote seeds (or sweet paprika or mild powdered chile, if the seeds are not available), 2 peeled cloves of garlic, ½ teaspoon ground cumin, ½ teaspoon crumbled oregano, 3 allspice berries, 2 teaspoons salt, and 2 tablespoons lime or lemon juice or white vinegar in the container of an electric blender. Grind until smooth.

This paste is rubbed into meat or chicken in such dishes as Cochinta Pibil (barbecued pork), and Pollo Pibil (chicken steamed in a banana leaf), allowing 2 to 3 teaspoons of the paste per serving. It is used in the sauce of a Yucatecan version of tamale pie called Mucbil-Pollo.

RED BEANS

See BEANS, PINK

RED CHILI SAUCE, MEXICAN

This is not the same thing at all as the popular chili sauce sold next to the catsup bottles in every supermarket. This is a canned sauce made from the pureed pulp of dried red chiles and cooked with various spices. It is a convenience item used in many Mexican "enchilada" sauces and other dishes. Las Palmas is the most popular brand, and it is sold in 10- and 19-ounce cans.

STORAGE: After opening, it will keep in a nonmetal container in the refrigerator for up to a week.

PREPARATION AND USE: This product can be a time-saver because it saves toasting, soaking, and pureeing dried red chiles and also the time it takes to seek out the chiles, but it lacks the nuances of flavor present in the many varieties of dried red chiles that one would use in a homemade sauce. It is very commonly used by Mexican-Americans to make dishes such as Chilaquiles and Enchiladas.

RED KIDNEY BEANS

See BEANS, KIDNEY, in THE FOODS OF REGIONAL AMERICA section

REFRIED BEANS

See FRIJOLES REFRITOS

ROSADAS

See BEANS, DRIED, PINK

RUM, JAMAICAN

Often recipes specify "dark Jamaican rum." The most widely distributed brand, and our favorite rum to use in desserts, is Myers'.

STORAGE: Store indefinitely at room temperature.

USE: Use whenever dark rum is specified in dessert recipes. We also add a bit to cooked black-beans.

SAFFRON, MEXICAN

See AZAFRÁN

SALSA JALAPEÑA

(SAHL-sah ah-lah-PEHN-yah)

Two general types of this convenience product are available in jars in many supermarkets. One is red, made with tomatoes or ripe (red) jalapeño chiles; one is green, made with TOMATILLOS. Both are hot, or *picante*. La Victoria produces several varieties of this sauce with different names—Salsa Ranchera, Salsa Victoria, Salsa Picante, to name a few. Their "hotness" is cleverly indicated by a picture of a thermometer on the left side of the label.

STORAGE: Refrigerated after opening, it will keep indefinitely.

USE: These sauces are used as table condiments to serve with all kinds of Mexican dishes from breakfast omelets to vegetables and rice, to Tacos.

SALT COD

See COD, SALTED AND DRIED in THE FOODS OF EUROPE
section

SAPODILLA

OTHER: *zapote, chiku, chicozapote*

FRENCH: *sapotille* ITALIAN: *sapota*

This is the fruit of a large, tropical evergreen tree that grows wild in Mexico, the Caribbean, and Central America, and is now cultivated throughout the tropical countries of the world. The tree is the source of *chicle,* which is the basis for chewing gum. The fruit of the tree resembles a potato, but has a rough cream colored skin with tinges of orange and flesh that is green when unripe, but turns orange, red, or yellow as it ripens and develops a sweet, bland taste. It is grainy-textured and moist, but not juicy. It is very unlikely that you will find this in markets but, if you do, choose fruit that is free of bruises.

STORAGE: Ripen at room temperature. It will then keep, refrigerated, for up to 6 weeks.

PREPARATION AND USE: The unripe, green-fleshed fruit is inedible. Use an apple corer to remove the center core with its large black seeds from ripe sapodilla. Eat as is, combine with other fruits for salads or desserts, or make into jams in combination with other fruits. The skin is not eaten.

SAUSAGE, MEXICAN

See CHORIZO

SAUSAGE, SPANISH

See CHORIZO and LONGANIZA

SHADDOCK

OTHER: *pomelo*

Shaddock is a very large, yellow or brown, thick-skinned citrus fruit that is an early ancestor of the grapefruit. Its reddish flesh has a rather pungent, thirst-quenching flavor resembling that of blackberries, only slightly more sour. It can be found in some Latin American markets and stores that specialize in exotic produce. It is named for the Captain Shaddock who introduced it to the Caribbean islands from the East Indies during the 17th century. It is believed that the shaddock, when crossed with an orange, gave birth to the grapefruit.

STORAGE: Ripe fruit can be stored for up to a week in the refrigerator.

USE: In Caribbean cooking, the shaddock is used in salads, especially with pork. It is also used in Thailand and Southeast Asia.

SHRIMP, DRIED
See CAMARÓN SECO

SLAKED LIME (CALCIUM HYDROXIDE)
See THE FOODS OF REGIONAL AMERICA section

SOUP BEANS
See BEANS, DRIED, BLACK

SOUR ORANGE
See ORANGE, SEVILLE in THE FOODS OF EUROPE section

SOURSOP
See GUANÁBANA

SPANISH BEANS
See BEANS, CHICK-PEAS in THE FOODS OF THE MIDDLE EAST section

SQUASH BLOSSOM
OTHER: *flor de calabaza*

Male and female blossoms grow on all plants of the squash family and this may be exciting for the squash plant but there is no need for us to differentiate when using them in cooking. Fresh blossoms are sometimes available by the bunch in Latin American, Filipino, and Italian produce markets during the summer and early fall. Depending on the variety of squash (calabaza or pumpkin), 25 to 40 blossoms will weigh about a pound, enough for 10 to 12 servings.

STORAGE: Buy just before using, or store in the refrigerator for use as soon as possible.

PREPARATION AND USE: Remove the stems and the long sepals. In Mexico they are chopped to use as a soup ingredient for Sopa de Flor de Calabaza, or are sautéed with onion, garlic, and mild chiles to serve as a vegetable dish. They are chopped and sautéed with EPAZOTE to scramble with eggs to make Huevos con Flor de Calabaza. We especially enjoy these as an appetizer when dipped into a beer batter and fried until golden.

SUGAR, BARBADOS

Barbados sugar is a fine quality brown sugar cultivated in Barbados with a bit of a rum flavor. It is sometimes found in specialty markets and natural-food stores.

STORAGE: It will keep indefinitely in the refrigerator.

USE: It can be substituted for dark brown sugar in any recipe.

SWAMP CABBAGE

See HEARTS OF PALM

TAMARIND

See THE FOODS OF ASIA section

TAPIOCA

OTHER: tapioca starch

CHINESE: *gun fun*

Tapioca is an easily digestible starchy food obtained from the bitter CAS-SAVA. It is widely available in pearl-like balls and as a floury starch. Tapioca starch or "flour" found in Asian markets and health food stores is very waxlike in texture.

STORAGE: It will keep indefinitely on the pantry shelf.

PREPARATION AND USE: The pearl-like balls are often used in soups in the same manner as barley or pasta, or are made into tapioca puddings, flavored with cream or with wine in South America. The starch makes an excellent thickening agent, and is used in the same manner as cornstarch or arrowroot, for sauces and pie fillings.

TARO ROOT

See THE FOODS OF ASIA section

TOMATE, TOMATE DE CÁSCARA, TOMATE VERDE

See TOMATILLO

TOMATILLO

(tohm-ah-TEE-yoh)

OTHER: *tomate* (or *tomatito*) *verde, mil tomate,* Mexican green tomato, *tomate de cáscara, fresadilla*

CANNED ARE LABELED: *"tomatitos verdes, pelados"; "tomatillos enteros"*

The tomatillo, a close relative of the husk tomato and ground cherry, looks like a small green tomato with a thin, parchment-like husk. Unlike those relatives, the real tomatillo actually fills the papery husk. Tomatillos have a very distinctive, slightly apple-like flavor, which develops as they cook. You will find them available fresh or canned in many supermarkets and in Latin American markets.

STORAGE: Fresh tomatillos can be stored in a paper, not plastic, bag in the crisper section of the refrigerator for up to 3 weeks. They are usually used while green though they turn yellow when fully ripe. Once opened, the canned will keep stored in a nonmetal container in the refrigerator for up to 5 days.

PREPARATION AND USE: Unlike red tomatoes, these are never eaten raw. One pound of raw tomatillos equals 1 cup cooked. To prepare fresh tomatillos for any use, remove the husks, rinse, and place in a heavy saucepan with water to barely cover. Simmer for about 10 minutes until they are just tender when pierced. Do not overcook or they will burst and spill their flavor into the cooking liquid. Drain and puree in an electric blender or food processor with a bit of their cooking liquid. Diana Kennedy, Mexican-cooking authority, recommends that canned tomatillos be pureed in the blender, adding ⅓ cup water and a pinch of sugar for every cupful.

These are best known as the base of Salsa Verde, or green taco sauce, in which they are combined with chiles. Mexican cooks also toast them on a *comal* (griddle) while still in their skins until they are soft and brown, removing their husks before using them as an ingredient in guacamole, soups, or as a vegetable with cream cheese. We are especially fond of the Chile Verde recipe which follows.

CHILE VERDE

For 8 to 10 servings

This recipe was given to us by Rue Pine, an instructor of Mexican cooking at UCLA. It is a delicious pork and green chile stew, perfect for filling warm flour tortillas to make Burritos. We often serve it as one of two main dishes at a Mexican dinner, with condiments such as sour cream, scallions, grated cheese.

4–6	fresh green CHILES VERDES or CHILES POBLANOS, *or* a 7-ounce can whole green chiles
1–2	tablespoons rendered pork fat or bacon drippings
3½	pounds lean boneless pork, cut in ¾" cubes
1	medium onion, diced
1	large clove garlic, pressed or minced
¼	cup flour
1	(10-ounce) can green tomato sauce *(salsa de tomatillo)*
1	(13-ounce) can whole tomatillos *(tomatillos enteros)*, drained
1	cup strong chicken or beef broth
½	teaspoon dried oregano, rubbed between the palms of your hands
	Salt to taste

WARNING: Wear rubber gloves when handling chiles if your skin is sensitive. Do not touch your eyes while working with them; if you do so, rinse eyes thoroughly with water.

If fresh chiles are to be used, they must be peeled. Spear each with a long-handled fork and hold close to an open flame (or under broiler), turning often, until the skin is evenly black and charred. Place the chiles in a plastic or paper bag for 10 to 15 minutes—during this time they will steam and release the skin. Peel off the skin, and discard the seeds and membrane. Cut into strips. If canned chiles are to be used, remove the seeds and membrane and cut chiles in strips.

Heat the rendered pork fat or bacon drippings in a large heavy pot. Add pork, a few pieces at a time, turning until pieces have been seared on all sides. (Do not crowd the meat during this step or it will *stew* in its juices instead of browning.) Remove the meat with a slotted spoon to another container, and continue until all the meat has been seared. Add the onion and garlic to the drippings and cook, stirring until the onion is transparent. Stir in the flour and cook until bubbly. Return the pork to the pot with all remaining ingredients. Partially cover the pan and cook for 1 to 1½ hours until the pork is very tender.

TO PREPARE IN ADVANCE: Like most stews, this tastes even better the second day. It freezes well for up to 4 months.

TORTILLAS, CORN
(tor-TEE-yahs)

This, the "bread" of central and southern Mexico, is a thin cake made of corn flour that is quickly baked on a *comal* (griddle). More than anything else in Mexico, we miss the delicious, almost paper-thin tortillas that were hand-patted by women in the marketplace who cooked them over small coal-heated pieces of iron and then slipped them into baskets lined with snowy embroidered linens. The aroma was sublime. They cost only one *peso* (then 8¢) for 40! We have never tasted corn tortillas that compared with those; even though we have found others handmade, they have always seemed thick and crude when we remembered those of San Miguel de Allende. Machine-made tortillas are quite good though, and are available in most parts of the United States in supermarkets and tortillerías. Canned ones are dismal. Crêpes made with MASA HARINA make an interesting and quite delicate substitute. (To make fresh corn tortillas, see MASA, FRESH.)

STORAGE: Wrapped airtight in plastic wrap, they will keep in the refrigerator for up to 3 days, though the sooner consumed the more delicious they are. They can be frozen; thaw before using.

PREPARATION AND USE: Most often tortillas are served warm with meals as a bread. To keep them warm, wrap in paper towels, then in a damp towel, and then in foil—all this to prevent drying—and put in a warm (200°) oven where they will keep for up to 3 hours. Leftover tortillas can be re-warmed individually over direct gas flame, or can be rewarmed in foil-wrapped packets in stacks of 6 or less in a low oven. To freshen and reheat slightly dried tortillas, dampen both sides with your hands, which you've dipped in water, and heat in a dry skillet or on a griddle until they are pliable. Leftover tortillas should *never* be tossed out!

Corn tortillas are wrapped around fillings to make Enchiladas, Tacos, Flautas (small rolled tacos served with guacamole sauce). Sonora-style Enchiladas are stacked with filling between them instead of rolled individually. Stale tortillas can be cut in sixths or eighths to make *tostaditas* or *totopos,* which are oven-baked or deep-fried until crisp to serve as dippers for guacamole, refried beans, and fresh Salsas, or cut into strips to use in Chilaquiles, a breakfast dish that contains stale tortilla strips and a spicy sauce, as in the following recipe.

CHILAQUILES

1 dozen corn tortillas	For 8 servings

    Oil for frying

12 ounces grated QUESO DE CHIHUAHUA or Monterey Jack
    cheese
1 white onion, finely diced

SAUCE:
2 tablespoons oil or lard
1 medium onion, minced
1 clove garlic
2⅓ cups homemade RED CHILI SAUCE *or* 1 (19-ounce) can
    Chile Las Palmas
3 CHILES JALAPEÑOS *or* SERRANOS, seeded and minced
½ teaspoon ground cumin
    Pinch ground oregano

TO SERVE:
1 cup QUESO·BLANCO, crumbled, or 2 cups sour cream
    Fresh coriander to garnish

Cut the tortillas in sixths and, if fresh, dry at room temperature for an hour or longer. Heat ¾″ of oil in a wok or skillet, and fry the tortillas, a few at a time, until golden and crisp. Drain well on paper towels. Cool.

To make the sauce, heat the oil or lard in a skillet and sauté the onion and garlic until the onion is transparent. Stir in the chili sauce, chiles, cumin, and oregano. Simmer slowly for 10 minutes. Taste for seasoning, adding salt and pepper as needed.

Place a layer of fried tortillas in a 3-quart shallow casserole. Sprinkle with grated cheese and chopped white onion. Continue layering until all the tortillas, cheese, and onion have been used, ending with a layer of cheese.

Pour the sauce evenly over the top of the casserole. Bake at 350° for 40 minutes, or until bubbling. Remove from oven, top with crumbled queso blanco or dollops of sour cream, and sprinkle with chopped fresh coriander.

TO PREPARE IN ADVANCE: This is best when freshly baked. The sauce can be prepared ahead and even frozen. Assemble casserole without sauce in the morning and leave at room temperature. Pour the sauce over it just before baking.

TORTILLAS, FLOUR

OTHER: *tortillas de harina*

In northern Mexico the traditional "bread" is the flour tortilla made of flour, salt, lard, and warm water. Unlike corn tortillas, they are rolled with a rolling pin rather than being patted. They are rolled very thin, usually to 6″ to 8″ in diameter, though often larger, and are cooked briefly on both sides on a griddle. They taste much more like bread than corn tortillas. An instant mix for making them is called MASA TRIGO.

STORAGE: These freeze beautifully, so whenever we see especially nice ones on our travels, we buy stacks and stacks to store in our freezer. They keep, if tightly wrapped in plastic, in the refrigerator for up to 4 days.

PREPARATION AND USE: Flour tortillas are used to make the popular Burritos (little burros) found these days in fast-food restaurants throughout the United States, as well as Chimichangas (deep-fried Burritos filled with beans, rice, cheese, and meat). An easy dish we enjoy often is Quesadillas, simple sandwiches of flour tortillas with a filling of any kind of melted cheese, served with guacamole, and a fresh Salsa for dipping. Barbara Hansen, Mexican-cooking authority, makes them quickly in a microwave oven—her recipe appears with EPAZOTE. Some recipes for flour tortillas specify the addition of baking powder, but we prefer them made without leavening and with more lard than most recipes specify. We make them as follows:

FLOUR TORTILLAS

4   cups sifted all-purpose flour   For about 18 (8″) tortillas
2   teaspoons salt
½   cup lard or solid vegetable shortening
½   cup or more warm water

Combine the flour and salt in a large mixing bowl. Add the lard or shortening, mixing it into the flour with your hands. Add the water and mix thoroughly, kneading the dough for 2 to 3 minutes until smooth and well blended, adding more warm water if the dough is too stiff. Cover with a towel and set aside for at least an hour at room temperature.

Knead the dough briefly. Pull off an egg-sized piece of dough and roll into a ball. Press to flatten; then, on a lightly floured board, roll out with a rolling pin as thin as possible, keeping it as round as you can. (This takes practice, so don't be upset if your early attempts are oddly shaped—they taste just as good as symmetrical ones.) Place on a hot griddle (comal) for 15 seconds or so until lightly browned, then turn to brown the second side lightly. (It is important not to have the griddle too hot or the tortilla will brown quickly and not have time to cook.) The tortilla may puff as it cooks. If it does, press down on it with the back of a spatula or spoon. When done, remove from the griddle and keep warm in a plastic bag, or in a serving basket lined with a towel, as you continue making tortillas until all the dough has been used. Serve warm.

TO PREPARE IN ADVANCE: Tortillas can be stored in a sealed plastic bag in the refrigerator for up to 5 days, or they can be frozen. To reheat, place on griddle or hot skillet, turning several times, until warmed through, or reheat, covered, in a microwave oven.

TUNA

OTHER: prickly pear, Indian fig, Barbary fig, cactus pear

ISRAELI: *sabra* ITALIAN: *fico d'India*

The fruit of the prickly pear cactus varies in shape, color, and sweetness. We have seen them range from yellow to bright red. The stiff rind, covered with spines, encloses a moist, granular, seed-studded meat. Buy them in season from October through January in Latin American and Mediterranean markets, and in some supermarkets in the West and Southwest. Look for small ones that are firm, but not rock-hard. Often the spines will have been removed.

STORAGE: Ripen at room temperature. They will then keep in the refrigerator for up to 3 days.

PREPARATION AND USE: Buy 1 or 2 per serving. Rinse them, holding them with tongs to protect your hands from the soft spines. Use a sharp knife to cut off the ends, and then cut lengthwise to open the fruit and lift out the pulp with a spoon. Some recipes will tell you to burn away the spines over a gas flame, but that is way too much bother and not at all necessary. Discard the seeds. The pulp makes a delicious salad or dessert with a sprinkling of lime juice and some sweetened whipped cream.

TURTLE BEANS

See BEANS, DRIED, BLACK

UGLI FRUIT

Ugli fruit is a hybrid cross of grapefruit, orange, and tangerine, called "ugli" because of its bumpy appearance. This is a popular fruit in Jamaica, and is available in exotic-produce markets during the winter. Its flavor is more reminiscent of orange than it is of grapefruit, and it is slightly sweeter than both. When ripe, the skin has tinges of orange.

STORAGE: It will keep for up to a week in the refrigerator.

PREPARATION AND USE: The loose skin is easily peeled away. It has only a few seeds and is most commonly eaten in the hand. It may be used like oranges or grapefruit in salads, sherbets, etc.

VEGETABLE PEAR

See CHAYOTE

VERDOLAGA

See PURSLANE in THE FOODS OF THE MIDDLE EAST section

WEST INDIAN PUMPKIN

See CALABAZA

WILD MARJORAM

See OREGANO in the HERBS, SPICES, AND SEASONING BLENDS section

WORMSEED

See EPAZOTE

YAM

See THE FOODS OF AFRICA section

YARD-LONG BEANS

See BEANS, LONG in THE FOODS OF ASIA section

THE FOODS
OF THE
MIDDLE EAST

AFGHANISTAN
ALGERIA
ARABIAN
  PENINSULA
EGYPT
IRAN
IRAQ
ISRAEL
JORDAN
LEBANON
LIBYA
MOROCCO
SYRIA
TUNISIA

CARAVANSARIES

Before recorded history, the Arabs were transporting on the caravan roads of the Middle East such wares as jewels, incense, perfumes, metals, dyes, rare woods, oils, ivory, silk—and spices and other foods. At dusk, they would stop and settle for the night in walled caravansaries, preparing mèals over common fires and entertaining themselves and local merchants with stories of travel and strange delights. The thirteen countries listed here all share the same basic food products, from which they have established their cuisines. It is as if the Arabs had planted seeds everywhere they went, from China in the East to Spain in the West. Their caravan trade routes traced the Mediterranean coastline of North Africa as well, all the way to the Atlantic, through the Strait of Gibraltar.

The land-bridge called the "fertile crescent," which includes Iran, Iraq, Israel, Jordan, Lebanon, Syria, and Turkey, has been used since the beginning of time as the major trade route for Asian silk and spice caravans connecting the East with the West. Along this trade route, foods and their methods of preparation were interblended, and cultural boundaries were crossed. The caravan routes were highways of information, from age-old Asia to awakening Europe, and the countries through which these lazy serpentine caravans passed were among the first to be culinarily developed. An even swifter, more powerful influence intervened for a time to help cross-pollinate the foods of the Middle East: the carrying of the word of Mohammed out of the Arabian desert. Within a hundred years, the fierce desert armies of Mohammed had successfully conquered lands from China to Spain, intermingling cultures and cuisines every step of the way.

As an example, the Kabsah, made with seafood or meat, is the national dish of Saudi Arabia. This dish traveled to Spain with Mohammed's armies a thousand years ago and it is today the famous Valencian Paella.

Iran and Turkey, both parts of this fertile crescent and crossed by the caravan-highways from the East, developed cuisines rich and heavy with spices, especially saffron, and rice. Iran's cuisine is based on long-grain rice, appearing in such dishes as Shirin Polo, sweet rice served with chicken breasts, sliced almonds, and orange peel, and in Chelo-kebab, cubes of lamb served over rice, which is their national dish. Everywhere in the Middle East Shish-kebab (cubes of marinated lamb, skewered and charcoal grilled) is celebrated—from Israel, Iraq, Iran, Syria, Jordan, North Africa to Turkey, where it is proclaimed the national dish. *Kebab,* in Turkish, means "chunks of mutton," and *sis* (prounounced SHISH) means "skewered on a sword." Another outstanding Turkish dish is called Dolmas, and is made of cabbage, eggplant, or green peppers hollowed out and stuffed with aromatic, spicy rice, and served cold in olive oil, or stuffed with meat and rice and offered hot. Lamb and kid are specialties, as is Ayran, a yogurt drink; black barley bread; Kadaif, shredded dough pastry; Doner Kebab, lamb roasted on a vertical spit, similar to the Israeli and Lebanese Schwarma, and to the Grecian Gyro.

Muslim Turkey invaded Greece and occupied it for a hundred years. Although today Greeks are Christians, their cuisine remains primarily Arabic, as does their choice of staples—lemons, olives and olive oil, pine nuts, eggplant, garlic, tomatoes, yogurt, and lamb. These staples are the basis of Arabic-Middle Eastern cooking as well as that of Greece. We should not find it unusual, then, that these staples are used in similar combinations in the two countries, producing similar dishes, such as Dolmathes, the stuffed grape leaves of Greece, and the Dolmas of Turkey. Baklava, feta cheese, skewered lamb—these are Greek. They are also native to all of the Middle East. This is not to imply that the Greeks have no individuality. They have, and they take great pride in their Tyropites (filo and feta cheese pie), their Avgolemono (egg, lemon, and chicken soup) and Moussaka (eggplant and ground lamb casserole). In Greece, lamb is used for practically all meat dishes, preferably broiled, roasted, or stewed. Pork was forbidden by Greece's early Muslim conquerors and, continuing to today, throughout these islands lamb is the overwhelming choice, as it is in North Africa's Maghreb.

The Mediterranean area was a rich avenue of trade for the Muslim Arabs, especially along the coasts of northern and eastern Africa. At the top of the Sahara Desert, in the far northwest corner of the African continent, there is an unexpected range of towering green mountains, the Atlas Mountains. Their existence prevents the cool, moist air and rain of the Atlantic from reaching the valley floor of the world's largest wasteland, the Sahara. The story is not all bad, though. The good is that this trapped moisture rolls back down the gradual green slopes on the windward side of these mountains on its journey back to the sea, and forms a natural irrigation system. This green desert miracle is known as the Maghreb, and includes Morocco, Algeria, and Tunisia.

Cous Cous, the national dish of the Maghreb, is a steamed wheat semolina, lamb, and vegetable stew. It was created first in Morocco, but today Cous Cous is as standard throughout the Arab world as fried chicken is in our South. However, each area's Cous Cous has its own distinguishing touches. In Morocco, for example, there is the subtle, heady touch of saffron. Algerians thicken and flavor theirs with a puree of tomato. The Tunisians, with their love of red pepper, make theirs fiery hot.

Another Moroccan favorite, which comes from the native quarter known as the Casbah is the Tagine, an exotic, sweet and spicy stew, usually composed of meat, poultry or fish, raisins, prunes, dates, almonds, and honey. Bstilla, a pigeon pie, is also a favorite Moroccan dish. More than a pie, it is a mélange of exotic ingredients arranged between layers of thin, filo-like dough, with spices, sugars, poultry, and sliced, roasted almonds, generously topped with powdered sugar and artfully dusted with cinnamon in exotic North African designs.

The northeast coast of Africa was extremely important to the Arabs for transporting not only spices, but slaves, frankincense and myrrh, along what was known as the Incense Road. This road began and ended in Egypt and the kitchens of Egypt were well supplied indeed. Though the Muslim world controlled the spice trade for centuries, and Cairo had its choice of over 200 of the world's aromatics in its spice bazaars, the majority of Egypt's dishes are not over-spiced. Sometimes, of course, they can be fiery, but more often they consist of subtle, bland, and flavorful mixtures, the making of which often remains a kitchen secret.

Egyptian foods are Arabic as well. Their Cous Cous dish, when used as a standard main course, has a rich brown sauce made aromatic with onions and coriander, plus a mysterious ingredient we've discovered to be mastic, an anise-tasting resinous gum brought from the Isles of Greece. The Egyptian cook also uses steamed semolina cous cous as a sweet dessert by adding sugar and a topping of peanuts.

If there were one dish more popular than all the others in Egypt—a national dish—it would be a brown bean and egg dish called Ful Mesdames: small brown fava beans, slow-simmered and seasoned with garlic, lemon, and salt, served in a soup bowl and garnished with hard-boiled eggs, drizzled with olive oil and a sprinkling of parsley. Tamiya is another national treat: patties of deep-fried crushed fava beans, spiced with garlic, red pepper, onions, coriander, and parsley. This is the Egyptian version of Felafel, the street food of Israel.

Israelis have adopted into their new home the foods and delicacies of all the lands of their exile, and have incorporated the cooking secrets and techniques of practically every nation on earth. In addition, from a once unpromising area, now irrigated, come citrus fruits, figs, dates, melons, grapes, and almonds. And from Israel's desert come quince, clementines, pomegranates, loquats, guava, and the unusual custard apple, sold by street vendors in Tel Aviv, from beds of shaved ice, to be eaten like boiled eggs with a plastic spoon. Due to Israel's open immigration policy, this "Paris of the East" cooks in over fifty cuisines, and in each of these "cuisine communities" can be found the dishes familiar to Jewish homes back in their native lands.

It would be difficult to completely separate and classify the intermingled cuisines of these Middle Eastern countries that have been, literally, the crossroads of the world. However, the constant movement on the caravan-highways has finally slowed, and these mobile cuisines have settled down and have assumed national identities.

As you wander through these pages of Middle Eastern ingredients, you'll find among them the foods that fed the courts of Cleopatra, as well as the foods of the ancient storytellers of the Caravansaries.

AMARDEEN

See QAMARADIN

ANISE

See HERBS, SPICES, AND SEASONING BLENDS section

ANISE-FLAVORED LIQUEURS

Clear anise-flavored liqueurs distilled from grapes, dates, and other fruits are the most popular aperitifs served in the Middle East, where they are often homemade. The most commonly found are Ouzo, Arak and Raki. One of the more obscure is Mahya, an anise-flavored fig brandy brewed by the Jews in the high Atlas Mountains in Morocco.

STORAGE: These will keep indefinitely at room temperature.

USE: These liqueurs are most often served straight, with a water chaser. If served over ice or diluted with water, as most tourists prefer, they turn milky. Because these liqueurs are very strong they are always served with something to eat, most often with *mezze*, an assortment of olives, nuts, and other foods to nibble on. They are occasionally used as ingredients in cooking, most often in fish stews and in the preparation of liver.

ARAK

See ANISE-FLAVORED LIQUEURS

BAMIYA

See OKRA

BAMIES or BAMYA

See OKRA

BASTEKA

OTHER: *bastehk,* "shoe leather"

Basteka is a mixture of grape juice and cornstarch that has been dried into ¼″ thick pliable sheets. They are available in Armenian and other Middle Eastern markets.

STORAGE: They will keep indefinitely in a cool, dry place.

PREPARATION AND USE: Basteka is most commonly eaten as a quick, nourishing snack. It is often wrapped around walnuts or almonds to make a sweetmeat.

BASTOURMA

OTHER: Turkish "bacon"

SYRIAN: *gadîd*

Bastourma is Armenian sun-dried beef (sometimes lamb is used in the Middle East), which has been seasoned with garlic and cumin and coated with "hot" paprika, salt, and pepper. It is dark brown and very, very lean, and is sometimes referred to as "Turkish bacon" because the Turks, as Muslims, do not eat pork. This can be found in Middle Eastern delis, where it is thinly sliced to order, like PASTRAMI (see THE FOODS OF REGIONAL AMERICA) or PROSCUITTO (see under HAM in THE FOODS OF EUROPE section).

STORAGE: It will keep for up to a month if tightly wrapped in the refrigerator.

PREPARATION AND USE: This is most often served as a *mezze* (appetizer). If slicing this at home, scrape away excess spice coating before slicing. Our Lebanese friends, Julie and Jim Nassraway, who own a Middle Eastern market and bakery in Los Angeles, use it to make one of our favorite sandwiches, which they call "Armenian Delight." Freshly baked PITA BREAD is cut open and the inside is spread generously with LABNI (yogurt cheese—see under CHEESES). The sandwich is then filled with thinly sliced bastourma and *pepperoncini* (mild Italian pickled peppers).

BEANS

(See BEANS, DRIED in THE FOODS OF LATIN AMERICA section
for general information.)

Chick-peas, fava beans, and lentils are the primary beans of the Middle East. They are an important source of protein and are often served cold for breakfast seasoned with olive oil and garlic. A few others such as lupini are used less often. All of the following are available dried or canned in Middle Eastern markets. When purchasing dried beans, look for uniform color and size. Canned beans are not much of a bargain in cost, nutrition, or taste. They often have chemicals added to preserve their color, so are best avoided. If you do buy canned, we suggest Progresso, a widely distributed brand of canned beans.

STORAGE: We store dried beans in glass jars on our pantry shelf because we enjoy looking at the many varieties. They keep for years in a cool, dry spot, though they do lose some of their flavor on standing, and will require longer cooking to become tender. Canned beans, after opening, can be stored in the refrigerator in their original liquid for at least a week.

CHICK-PEAS

ARAB: *hummus* or *hommos* GREEK: *revithia* INDIAN: *channa*
ITALIAN: *ceci* PORTUGUESE: *grão* SPANISH: *garbanzos*

Pale yellow chick-peas (sometimes labeled *garbanzo* beans) are available, dry or canned, in supermarkets nationwide. In Middle Eastern markets, you will also find toasted and salted chick-peas, which are served as a snack or added to dishes with very little cooking required.

PREPARATION AND USE: Before cooking dried chick-peas it is best to soak them for at least 8 hours in water. (If the water where you live is particularly "hard," it will be helpful to add ¼ teaspoon of soda to the water.) As a general rule, 1 cup of dried chick-peas will yield 3 cups of cooked, and a 20-ounce can contains approximately 2 cups when drained. Depending on their size, they will be tender when simmered for 30 to 60 minutes, but don't worry, over-cooking will do them no harm. Canned chick-peas are almost as good as freshly cooked, and no apologies will be necessary if you decide to use them. They are already cooked so they require only warming, unless they are to be used in soups, in which case they must be pressed through a sieve to remove their skins.

Chick-peas lend their earthy flavor to a huge variety of stew recipes, from Spanish Cocido to the similar Filipino Puchero, made with chicken, pork, and CHORIZOS (see THE FOODS OF LATIN AMERICA). But nowhere are they more popular than in the Middle East, especially in the form of HUMMUS, the ubiquitous chick-pea spread, sauce, and dip. In Morocco, they are cooked in Tagines (stews), and COUS COUS dishes. In Israel, they are ground and combined with bulghur wheat to make highly seasoned fritters called Felafel, exactly like the Egyptian fava bean fritter called Tamiya which, when stuffed into pocket bread with cucumber and tomato relish, is a popular street food in many Middle Eastern cities. Felafel also make excellent appetizers on toothpicks. This recipe comes from our editor, Janice Gallagher, who has a passion for spicy foods.

FELAFEL

FILLING: For 30 pieces or 6 servings
- ½ pound (1 cup) dried chick-peas
- 3 tablespoons BULGHUR or cracked wheat
- 2 tablespoons flour
- 2 cloves garlic, minced or pressed
- 1 teaspoon ground cumin
- 1 teaspoon salt
- ⅛ teaspoon crushed red chiles
- ⅛ teaspoon ground coriander
- Oil for deep-frying

CUCUMBER-TOMATO RELISH:
- 3 medium, ripe tomatoes, seeded and finely diced
- 1 medium cucumber, peeled, seeded, and finely diced
- 1 green bell pepper, seeded and finely diced
- ¼ cup minced parsley or fresh coriander
- Salt and black pepper to taste

TAHINI DRESSING:
- ¾ cup TAHINI
- ¾ cup lemon juice
- 2 cloves garlic
- 2 tablespoons fruity olive oil
- 2 tablespoons minced parsley
- ½ teaspoon salt
- ¼ teaspoon ground red pepper (cayenne)

TO SERVE:
> PITA BREAD or steamed COUS COUS
> PISTACHIO NUTS (optional)

Soak the chick-peas in water to cover overnight. Soak the bulghur or cracked wheat in water to cover for 1 hour. Drain both and either grind twice through the fine blade of a meat grinder or process in an electric food processor with the steel blade until the mixture is finely ground. Transfer to a mixing bowl and add the seasonings. Wet your hands and form the mixture into 30 balls, approximately 1″ in diameter. (A melon ball utensil can be used.)

To make the Cucumber-Tomato Relish, combine the ingredients in a serving bowl, stir, and season to taste. To make the tahini sauce, combine the ingredients in an electric blender or mixing bowl and mix until smooth. If too thick, thin with water.

Heat oil for deep-frying to 375°. Fry the chick-pea balls, a few at a time, until golden brown. Drain on paper towels and serve hot in pockets of pita bread or on top of cooked cous cous, with cucumber-tomato relish and tahini sauce, and a sprinkling of pistachio nuts if desired.

TO PREPARE IN ADVANCE: The chick-pea balls can be refrigerated before frying, covered with a damp cloth, for up to 24 hours. Fry just before serving. The relish and the dressing are best freshly made and served at room temperature.

FAVA BEANS

OTHER: *bob,* broad beans, horse beans, Windsor beans, shell beans

ARAB: *fool, foul, fuls* ARMENIAN: *paghlah* FRENCH: *fèves* GERMAN: *Saubohnen* GREEK: *fava* (fresh), *koukia* (dried) IN MOROCCO: *byesar* SPANISH: *haba*

Fresh green fava beans, which look like large limas, as well as large and small dark brown or white ones, dried or canned, are one of the most popular foods in the Middle East. Fresh ones can be found in Italian markets and some supermarkets during the spring. Removed from their pods, they are often found in the frozen food sections of Middle Eastern markets, where you will also find the small dark brown or white ones, dried and canned. The fresh and the dried are not similar in flavor, and one type should not be substituted for the other in recipes.

PREPARATION AND USE: To prepare fresh favas, buy ¾ pound per serving. Remove them from their pods and rinse well. **Never serve them in their pods because some people have a severe allergic reaction to the**

furry lining of the pods. They are often served raw, with only a bit of salt for dipping. For most uses, however, cook fresh or frozen favas in salted water to cover just until tender, which will take only a few minutes if they are young and fresh, or up to 15 minutes if they are older. If the beans are not young, their skins must be slipped off after they are cooked. Fresh favas can be substituted for less flavorful LIMA BEANS (see under BEANS in THE FOODS OF REGIONAL AMERICA section) in any recipe. They are an excellent soup ingredient and vegetable side dish, seasoned simply with butter or cream and herbs, lemon, or a bit of meat such as PANCETTA (see THE FOODS OF EUROPE section) or LONGANIZA (see THE FOODS OF LATIN AMERICA section). In France they are often used in salads, or cooked, flavored with SAVORY (see HERBS, SPICES, AND SEASONING BLENDS section).

Dried favas must be soaked for 8 hours in cold water, or for 1 hour in hot water, and then peeled of their tough skin and cooked until tender. Salt should be added only during the last half hour of cooking. If the skin is tough and is not removed, it must be slipped off before the beans can be eaten. Canned beans are already cooked and need only seasoning—usually olive oil, garlic, and lemon but, as we've said, they do not have the flavor of fresh beans and should not be substituted for them.

When dried white favas (usually sold skinned) are cooked and made into a puree called Ful Nabed or Byesar, similar to the chick-pea HUMMUS, they make a popular spread or dip for bread. Pureed and seasoned, they are combined with fava bean flour and formed into fritters called Tamiya, which are exactly like the chick-pea Felafel. The small dark brown ones are cooked and seasoned to make a dish called Fuls Mesdames, traditionally served with Hamine Eggs, which are boiled for up to 6 hours with onion skins, resulting in tan-colored eggs with very creamy yolks. You will find all sorts of recipes using fresh and dried favas in Middle Eastern cookbooks.

LENTILS

ARABIC: *ads majroosh* or *adas* ARMENIAN: *vosp* GREEK: *faki* (also refers to soup)

The Egyptian or Syrian red lentil and the larger European grey-green lentil are the most popular types in the Middle East. They are a very important staple source of protein. You will find several types in supermarkets, natural-food stores, and Middle Eastern markets, including a quick-cooking type.

PREPARATION AND USE: As a general rule, 1 heaping cup of lentils weighs approximately 1 pound and will yield 2¾ cups of cooked lentils. Pick them over carefully and wash them. Depending on their variety and age, they need only 20 to 40 minutes to cook without presoaking. To serve as a side dish, they should be cooked only until just tender, but if to be pureed for soups or other recipes, they should be cooked longer until they, are easily mashed. (The variety of red lentils that are split cook much faster than those that are whole.)

In Morocco, lentils are cooked in soups, such as Harira. The Greeks enjoy them cooked with square noodles and garnished with fried onion in a dish called Faki Me Pasta, and the Armenians combine them with bulghur wheat in pilafs. Most popular of all is lentil soup, under many names. A lentil salad, made by dressing freshly cooked lentils with a vinaigrette dressing while they are still hot and then tossing them lightly with chopped scallions and to-matoes, is one of the best ways we know to serve them.

LUPINI BEANS

Lupini beans, found dried or canned in Middle Eastern markets, look like small white fava beans, but are actually members of the pea family. They are not particularly prized.

USE: In some countries, these are roasted to use as a coffee substitute, but they are most often served as snacks, roasted and salted like peanuts.

BHARAT

An aromatic mixture of 1 part ground dried rosebuds (available at fine spice stores) and 2 parts ground cinnamon called for in Tunisian recipes.

STORAGE: Store in the refrigerator for use within a month.

USE: In Tunisia, this is often a seasoning for sweet lamb Tagines (stews) that feature fruits.

BOTARGO

OTHER: *batarekh, botarega, batrakh*

FRENCH: *poutargue* ITALIAN: *bottarga* JAPANESE: *karasumi*
SPANISH: *huevos de mújol*

Botargo is the salted, dried, pair of roe from grey mullet in its original membrane, dried, pressed into a flat sausage shape, and dipped in wax, available in some Middle Eastern and Italian delis. It may vary in color from amber to orange to brown and is an expensive delicacy. You can buy it whole, sliced, or packed in oil. Other roes, from tuna or other fish, may be sold under the same name, but are generally much larger. The Greek TARAMA, sold in Greek markets, is moister and comes packed in jars, but is virtually the same thing.

TO SERVE:

8 rounds of PITA BREAD (pocket bread) *or* 1 small head
   Romaine lettuce, trimmed and chilled
   Optional: 1–2 cups LABNI

Note: Some cooks like to add chopped cucumber. If you do, sprinkle the chopped cucumber with salt and set aside for at least 30 minutes to draw out some of the water (which, if not removed, would make the Tabooli soggy). Wring out in cheesecloth before adding.
   Place the bulghur wheat in a small mixing bowl with the water or chicken broth. Let stand at least 30 minutes while you prepare the other ingredients.
   Drain any excess liquid from the wheat and place in a large mixing bowl. Toss with the remaining ingredients until well mixed. Taste for seasoning, and add salt and pepper if needed.
   Serve in a bowl surrounded by halved rounds of Pita bread or leaves of Romaine. Diners can serve themselves by placing the salad in the Pita or rolling it in the lettuce leaves. Labni can be served as a spread if desired.

TO PREPARE IN ADVANCE: This will keep, covered, in a nonmetal container in the refrigerator for up to 4 days.

CAROB

OTHER: St. John's bread, locust bean

FRENCH: *caroube* GERMAN: *Johannisbrot* ITALIAN: *carruba*
SPANISH: *algarroba*

This is the pod from a tree native to Syria that is said to have sustained St. John the Baptist in the wilderness. It is harvested in the fall and dried to use primarily for cattle fodder. The dried pods are eaten by children in the Mediterranean as a sort of candy bar. Carob seeds are sold in health food stores in the United States to eat as a sweet out-of-hand snack, much like raisins. Carob chips can be purchased in 6-ounce bags in supermarkets and health food stores for use in place of chocolate chips. Carob powder or "flour," available in health food stores, is used as a substitute for cocoa. It contains no caffeine, as chocolate does, and is naturally sweet in flavor.

STORAGE: The powder can be stored in an airtight container in a cool place indefinitely. The moist seeds should be stored in the refrigerator.

PREPARATION AND USE: Carob is purported to be a substitute for chocolate, but it is not completely satisfactory for that purpose due to its bland flavor. As a chocolate substitute, we were given a formula of 3 tablespoons carob powder mixed with 2 tablespoons water or milk as being equivalent to 1 square of bittersweet chocolate. It is naturally sweet and therefore not a suitable substitute for bitter chocolate.

Carob powder is used in Mediterranean cooking in cakes, puddings, and ice cream. It is also considered extremely soothing to the digestion, and is often made into a drink with water or milk, sweetened to taste with honey. Books on health food cookery, such as those published by Rodale, have recipes for many kinds of desserts using carob.

CHEESES

Following is a brief description of cheeses called for in Middle Eastern recipes. Most are fresh and perishable. Some will be found in Greek or other Middle Eastern grocery stores, and substitutes are recommended for others. Most are served as appetizers, but many find their way into recipes to add a special tang and, in some cases, even thicken stews. They are almost totally overlooked by authors of books on cheese.

DOMIATI

This is an Egyptian cheese made from cow's milk, and brined, very similar to FETA. It is not presently available in the United States. Substitute a mild feta.

FETA

This most popular of Greek cheeses, eaten daily by Greeks, is made from goat's or sheep's milk and is the most reasonably priced of all imported Greek cheeses. It is pure white, and salty from being cured and stored in salt water and whey. You will find authentic imported Greek and Bulgarian feta in Greek delis. The Greek is a bit firmer and saltier. Other countries such as Italy and Yugoslavia export most of what is found in stores in the States. If in doubt as to its quality, always ask to taste it first. Danish feta is made from cow's milk and is usually crumbly and less mellow. When possible, it is always best to buy feta moist from a tub of whey; that found wrapped in plastic packages in supermarkets is inferior.

STORAGE: Fresh cheeses are meant to be consumed as fresh as possible, though it is possible to store feta submerged in salt water in a covered jar in the refrigerator for months. (In Greece, an olive is place in the brine in which feta is to be stored—it should float.) Feta becomes sharper and saltier the longer it stands.

PREPARATION AND USE: If you wish to draw out some of the salt, rinse the feta with water or soak it in milk for an hour or longer. Sliced feta is served as a table cheese with every Greek meal. It is commonly served as an appetizer with olives, but is also used extensively in cooking—as a filling for Bourekia (cheese-filled pastries), in salads, crumbled over sliced tomatoes, and in stews such as Stifatho. It flavors omelets, soufflés, and even biscuits called Biskotakia Me Feta. You can make these biscuits at home by adding ½ cup of crumbled feta and ½ teaspoon of sugar (to offset its sharp flavor) to 2 cups of flour in an ordinary biscuit recipe to yield 16 biscuits.

GOUTA

Gouta is a soft, fresh Tunisian goat's cheese, which is not imported at this time. It is somewhat similar to a very mild, creamy FETA, which may be substituted for it.

HALOUMI

Haloumi is a whole milk, *pasta filata* (cheese that melts into long strands) type of cheese, similar to MOZZARELLA (see under CHEESE, SEMI-SOFT, in THE FOODS OF EUROPE section) but cured in brine like FETA. It is sold sealed in plastic packages, usually flavored with mint, in many Middle Eastern markets.

STORAGE: In its original wrapper this can be refrigerated for months, (look for the date stamped on the package), and actually improves with age. After opening, leftover cheese, tightly wrapped in plastic wrap, will keep for up to 2 months in the refrigerator.

USE: Serve as a table cheese, or in any manner that you would use mozzarella, i.e., breaded and fried as an appetizer, as a filling for stuffed pastas, or in layered casserole recipes. Cubed, it makes a very tasty addition to salads, and can be sautéed in butter, like KASSERI. In Cyprus, where it originated, it is used to make Flaounes Kypriotikes (mint-flavored cheese tarts).

KASSERI

This firm, golden colored Greek sheep's milk cheese with a sharp buttery flavor is available in Greek delis. It is softer in texture and milder in flavor than KEFALOTYRI. An American version, similar to a sharp, salty Cheddar, is made in Wisconsin, but is not as flavorful as the imported.

STORAGE: Wrapped tightly in plastic wrap in the refrigerator, it will keep for up to a month. It will become harder and stronger in flavor as it stands.

PREPARATION AND USE: This cheese is most often served at room temperature with warm bread and a full-bodied red wine. It is also used in various Greek stew recipes, and is often grated to use as one would Parmesan.

In Greek restaurants, it is often sautéed in butter, or broiled with a squeeze of lemon juice, to make a delicious appetizer called Saganaki, which is then flamed dramatically with brandy at the table, as in the following recipe.

SAGANAKI

For 4 servings

This can be served as an appetizer, or as an entrée for luncheon or supper accompanied by a green salad, Greek olives, and a glass of wine, white or red.

12–16 ounces Kasseri or KEFALOTIRI cheese, cut in 3- to 4-
        ounce slices, approximately ½" thick
  ⅓ cup flour
  ¼ pound (1 stick) butter
  1 lemon, cut in half
     Brandy or cognac

Dip cheese slices in water, blot dry, and dust lightly with flour. Place in the freezer for at least 15 minutes before cooking.

The slices of cheese can be fried all at once in a large skillet, or individually in a chafing dish or small skillet at the table. Have warm serving plates waiting.

Melt the butter and sauté the pieces of cheese for approximately 30 seconds on each side, until just beginning to melt. Sprinkle each with a generous squeeze of lemon juice. Heat brandy or cognac in a ladle, ignite, and pour over the cheese. When flames die, serve immediately, accompanied by crusty bread.

TO PREPARE IN ADVANCE: Place floured cheese slices in freezer several hours ahead of time. Fry just before serving.

KATSCHKAWALJ

This is a hard, salty *pasta filata* (cheese that melts into long strands) type of sheep's milk cheese very like the Romanian KASHKAVÀL (see CHEESE, FIRM AND SEMI-FIRM, in THE FOODS OF EUROPE section), which is much easier to find and makes a very acceptable substitute.

STORAGE: This is salted and cured, so it will keep considerably longer than other firm cheeses. It will keep wrapped tightly in plastic wrap in the refrigerator for up to 3 months.

USE: This is a common table cheese in the area that used to be Macedonia, but is now divided between Greece, Yugoslavia, and Bulgaria. Cookbook author, Paula Wolfert, tells us she has a friend in Salonika who grills cubes of it on a brochette (skewer).

KEFALOTIRI

OTHER: *kefalotyri*

This is a hard, pale yellow, grating cheese, the Greek version of Parmesan, which derives its name from the fact that it is shaped like a head (*kefali*). It has a fine nutty flavor. Romano or Parmesan can be substituted.

STORAGE: As this is a hard cheese, it can be frozen, tightly wrapped in plastic wrap for up to 6 months. It can be refrigerated for up to 3 months.

PREPARATION AND USE: This grates easily and is delicious on pasta dishes (Greek meat sauces for pasta are usually quite thick and contain a dash of cinnamon), in meat casseroles, poultry stuffings, and omelets, and sprinkled over pilafs. It is also used to coat patties of leftover mashed potatoes, which are fried to make Patatokeftedes and served with a topping of yogurt. It may be used in place of KASSERI to make Saganaki. Moussaka and other Middle Eastern eggplant creations, such as Hunkar Begendi (literally "the king liked it"), an elaborate Turkish lamb and eggplant casserole, are enhanced by it.

KOPANISTI

Kopanisti is a Greek blue-mold cheese imported in jars and available at Greek delis. It has a very sharp, peppery taste. Roquefort or other blue cheeses can be substituted (see CHEESE, "BLUE," in THE FOODS OF EUROPE section) with some difference in flavor.

STORAGE: It will keep for up to a month in an airtight container in the refrigerator.

USE: This is a popular appetizer spread in Greece, but is also used in salad dressings, mashed, with vinegar and oil.

LABNI

OTHER: *lebna, labanee*

Labni is a fresh Lebanese cheese made of yogurt that has been salted and allowed to drain in a cheesecloth bag for 8 hours or longer until it has thickened to a soft cream cheese consistency. It can be purchased in many Middle Eastern markets, but is very easy to make at home. It has a very sour yogurt taste that complements many spicy dishes.

STORAGE: It will keep for up to a month in a nonmetal container in the refrigerator.

PREPARATION AND USE: To make labni, line a mixing bowl with 2 layers of well-rinsed cheesecloth. Place 2 quarts of plain yogurt in the bowl and stir in 1 tablespoon of salt until it is well combined. Bring together the edges of the cheesecloth and tie it into a bag to hang from your kitchen faucet. Let drain overnight; then unwrap and transfer to a container for refrigerator storage. Serve chilled.

This is commonly served with Middle Eastern meals as a *mezze* (appetizer) spread on flat bread, as a side dish, or to use in pita sandwiches or on crackers. It is often flavored with herbs such as basil, marjoram, garlic, or fresh coriander when served as an appetizer spread. In some Arab countries, it is rolled into small balls and stored in olive oil to cover; then sprinkled with oregano or paprika to eat as a snack (as Chèvre is sometimes treated in France). We like it spread inside pita bread pockets to be stuffed with Tabooli (bulghur salad).

MIZITHRA

OTHER: *mitzithra, myzithra, mezithra*

There are two types of this cheese. The most commonly found is the greyish, semi-soft, salty type exported from Greece or Italy, which is sold in Middle Eastern markets. The other type, *hlori mizithra*, is a soft, fresh cheese made from the whey of feta, and is similar to fresh RICOTTA (see CHEESES, SOFT UNRIPENED, in THE FOODS OF EUROPE section). It is seldom exported, but is occasionally found in Greek markets.

STORAGE: The hard type may be stored, tightly wrapped in plastic wrap in the refrigerator for up to 3 weeks. Refrigerate the fresh type for use as soon as possible, within a few days.

USE: The hard type is often grated with a fork to serve over pasta or is served simply as a table cheese. The soft version, *hlori mizithra*, is popular used in Greek pies, both sweet and savory. Substitute cottage cheese or ordinary ricotta for it in recipes.

PEYNIR

"Peynir" is the Turkish word for cheese. When used in cookbooks, it applies to a cheese that is bland when fresh, but that becomes saltier and firmer as it ages. It is not imported. A mild FETA can be substituted.

STRING CHEESE

OTHER: Armenian string cheese

String cheese is a *pasta filata* type of cheese (it melts into long strands) and is sold in logs in most Western supermarkets in the United States. It has a similar melting quality to MOZZARELLA (see CHEESE, SEMI-SOFT, in THE FOODS OF EUROPE section), but is a good deal saltier.

STORAGE: It will keep for up to a month in the refrigerator if tightly wrapped in plastic wrap. After shredding, it can be stored in the refrigerator, tightly covered, for up to 3 days.

PREPARATION AND USE: The intriguing thing about this cheese is that it can be pulled apart and separated into fine threads. It is used primarily as a snacking or picnic cheese, but makes an excellent garnish for many salads and vegetable dishes.

TULUM

Tulum is a sharp-flavored Turkish sheep's milk cheese sold in sheepskin bags. It is not imported, but is similar in flavor to a sharp FETA, which can substitute for it in recipes. Roquefort and Danablu are second choices as substitutes.

TUMA

This fresh cheese is available in Lebanese and Armenian markets. It is very similar to PANELA (see CHEESE, QUESO PANELA, in THE FOODS OF LATIN AMERICA section) and is used in the same ways.

CHERRIES, SOUR

OTHER: *morello* cherries

IRANIAN: *albaloo* ITALIAN: *marasco*

These dark, sour cherries, used in the making of Maraschino liqueur, are seldom available fresh, but are easily found canned whole in syrup (Krakus brand is 33 ounces), made into preserves, or made into a sweetened syrup in 12- or 16-ounce bottles. This is an extremely popular flavor in the Middle East. Dried sour cherries are sometimes available in Greek markets. A wild-cherry preserve called *visino glyko* is sold in Greek markets.

STORAGE: After opening, store like any preserve in the refrigerator; it will keep indefinitely. Dried cherries may be stored up to a year in a cool, dry place.

PREPARATION AND USE: The preserve is often served as is for dessert topped with cream, or is stirred into water to make a sweet beverage. The syrup is used to flavor sauces, sweet or savory. Dried sour cherries must be soaked for 24 to 36 hours; then drained and pitted. In Iran, they are often cooked along with rice and chicken or lamb in a dish called Pollo. To make dried sour cherries into a preserve, simmer the cherries, after they are soft, in a sugar syrup flavored with lemon to cover until they are tender; then lift out and pack into jars. Simmer the syrup until it is thickened, then pour over the cherries and store as you would the commercial product.

CHICK-PEAS

See under BEANS

CITRON

FRENCH: *cédrat* GERMAN: *Zitron* IRAQI: *debdeb* ITALIAN: *cedro* SPANISH: *cidra*

Citron is a thick candied citrus peel with a slightly resinous taste. The fresh fruit, which looks like a quince, dates back to the time when it grew in the Hanging Gardens of Babylon. It is made into various liqueurs, *kitrinos* and *cedratine,* in the Middle East and Europe. A preserve made of it can often be found in Greek markets. It is always best to buy all types of candied fruits in specialty shops or through mail-order houses where you know they are freshly made without preservatives. (See SHOPPING SOURCES.)

STORAGE: The finest quality, made without preservatives, is best stored in the freezer for maximum freshness. The ordinary supermarket variety is loaded with preservatives but will, nevertheless, develop a stale taste on standing.

USE: Dice to use as a flavoring in desserts, fruitcakes, and various Middle Eastern confections. In Morocco, it is used to flavor olives. In the Arab countries, it is used along with nuts as a filling for dates, and is folded into a cold custard called Mouhallabiyya. The Arabs also make it into a jam called Roubb al-Kabbâb.

In Italy, it is used in a fruitcake-like confection, Siennese Panforte, and as a flavoring in Cannoli (tubes of fried pastry filled with ricotta cheese and pieces of candied fruit and chocolate). In England, it is an ingredient with currants in Hot Cross Buns, traditionally eaten on Good Friday.

CORIANDER

See HERBS, SPICES, AND SEASONING BLENDS section

COUS COUS

Cous cous is a fine pellet made from semolina flour, available in several sizes in all Middle Eastern and some European markets, health food stores, and some supermarkets, in bulk or packaged. The most commonly found type is a fine-grain cous cous used in the Moroccan dish of the same name. The various sizes of cous cous can be used interchangeably. There is an Armenian version, called *mougrabeya*, which is quite large and an Israeli type, which is toasted. (There is even an "instant" or quick-cooking version, which should be avoided.)

STORAGE: Stored airtight in a cool, dark place, this will keep for years.

PREPARATION AND USE: Unless you simply can't be bothered with being authentic, ignore the directions on the box. Cous cous must be specially handled in order to have each grain come out plump and separate. Ideally, it is steamed, usually above the stew with which it will be served, in a steamer called a *couscousière*.

Rinse the cous cous in a strainer with cold water. Rub it between your palms to separate the grains; then spread in a shallow pan and let rest for 10 to 15 minutes until plumped. Meanwhile, line the top of a steamer or a colander with cheesecloth to prevent the pellets from falling through large holes (a *couscousière* doesn't require lining). Place the cous cous in the chosen container over simmering water, and cook, *uncovered,* for 30 minutes. Transfer to a bowl, sprinkle with salted water to separate the grains, and then rub the grains with oiled hands to separate them further. (This can be done ahead to this point—simply set aside.) Thirty minutes before serving, finish steaming the cous cous, uncovered, for another 30 minutes.

Cous cous is served as one would rice or other grains, but is most widely known for being made into a dish of the same name, which contains lamb or chicken with various vegetables and a large variety of spices. It is the national dish of Morocco, Tunisia, and Algeria, traditionally served for Friday lunch. It is usually served with HARISSA. In Egypt, cous cous is often sprinkled with sugar and nuts to serve as a sweet dish.

CRACKED WHEAT

See BULGHUR WHEAT

DATE

ARABIC: *ajwi* or *balah* FRENCH: *datte* GERMAN: *Dattel* ITALIAN: *dattero* SPANISH: *dátil*

Honey dates, the shiny, sweet brown fruit of the date palm, are one of nature's most delicious sources of natural energy. There are over 30 varieties in northern Africa. Most dates found in the United States are grown in California, and are available in supermarkets and health food stores all year, but 75 percent of the world's supply is grown in Iraq. The most common variety is the Deglet Noor, native to the Sahara.

Dates are sold either fresh or dried, but it is not easy to tell the difference. The supermarket varieties are dried. Unless ordering by mail from one of the fine date packagers, or purchasing in a health food store, read the label on the package to be sure there are no preservatives. There are several outstanding, less familiar varieties, such as the caramel-tasting Barhi and the luscious giant Medjool, which we hope you will sample through mail-order sources (see SHOPPING SOURCES).

STORAGE: Wrapped airtight, dates will keep indefinitely in the refrigerator. They have a tendency to absorb odors and flavors of other foods, so make sure the package they are in is sealed. If surface crystals form, simply wipe them off with a damp paper towel.

PREPARATION AND USE: Unless you have purchased pitted dates, remove the long slender seed from the center of each. Dates are often used in Middle Eastern cooking, not only in salads and desserts but in delicious stews of lamb or chicken along with nuts and other sweet fruits. They are often served just as they are, or stuffed with nuts or MARZIPAN (see THE FOODS OF EUROPE section) and rolled in sugar or dipped in syrup as a simple dessert. In Baghdad, they are served with a TAHINI dip. Many Moroccan Tagines (stews) are enhanced by the addition of dates, as is rice pilaf to be served with fish or game. Dates and a bowl of cold buttermilk are traditionally served with Harira Soup at the nightfall breaking of the Ramadan fast in southern Morocco.

Their sweet, slightly smoky flavor is especially suited to experimentation in the kitchen. We like them stuffed with flavorful sausage and baked to serve as an appetizer on toothpicks, or stuffed with coconut or dried apricots to serve at room temperature, and we often chop them to use as a bread, muffin, or chutney ingredient.

DIBS

OTHER: *dibis*

"Dibs" is an Arabic term for sweetened carob-bean or date syrup available in Lebanese and other Middle Eastern markets. In the Middle East, it is usually homemade in large quantities for year-round use.

STORAGE: Refrigerated after opening, it will keep indefinitely.

PREPARATION AND USE: The Lebanese mix 4 parts of this with 1 part TAHINI to serve for breakfast as a dip with Arabic bread. In Iran, it is mixed with melted butter and sprinkled with walnuts to serve with bread. Iraqis use date syrup to flavor soups and salads. It is also used as a sweetener for teas and many dishes.

DIOUL

See WARKA

EGGPLANT

ARABIC and LEBANESE: *batinjan* ARMENIAN: *patlijan* GREEK: *melitzanes* TURKISH: *patlican*

Eggplant is a neglected vegetable in the United States, but one of the most popular vegetables of the Middle East where it is cooked in every conceivable way—sautéed, stuffed, mashed, pickled. Fresh eggplant, both the large pear-shaped type and the smaller Japanese type, are available in produce markets most of the year. Pick firm, shiny, tight-skinned ones that feel heavy for their size. The small ones are preferred for two reasons: they have fewer seeds and they soak up less oil in cooking. Dried eggplant, especially for winter use, is available in most Middle Eastern markets, as well as tiny pickled eggplants in jars.

STORAGE: Refrigerate fresh eggplant in a plastic bag for use as soon as possible. Dried eggplant can be kept in an airtight container at room temperature indefinitely. Pickled eggplant should be refrigerated after opening for use within a month.

PREPARATION AND USE: Eggplants that must be peeled for certain recipes are charred over an open fire. Use a gas flame or slide them under the broiler; when cool, the skin is easily removed. This vegetable can absorb an incredible amount of oil in cooking, so we like to treat it in a special way if it is to be sliced and fried for a recipe. Cut large ones in ½" crosswise slices, cut small ones in half lengthwise, and sprinkle the cut portions generously with salt. Set aside for 20 minutes and let it rid itself of excess moisture. Blot dry (the salt drips away with the liquid) with paper towels and then brush lightly with olive oil (flavored with garlic, if suitable for the recipe). Bake at 400° for 10 to 15 minutes, or place under the broiler, turning once, until well browned. We place this on top of pasta before topping with tomato sauce, but it also lends itself to many other uses after this treatment. Dried eggplant should be soaked until soft, and then cooked or layered in casseroles

585

as desired. Pickled eggplant, especially popular in Lebanon, makes a welcome addition to an appetizer tray.

All kinds of eggplant recipes such as "poor man's caviar" abound in Middle Eastern cookbooks. In Afghanistan, as in many Middle Eastern countries, the most popular way of serving it is in a dish called Buraunee Baunjaun, which is sautéed eggplant topped with a sauce of yogurt and garlic. In Egypt, slices are often baked with a sweet tomato topping. Pureed eggplant, seasoned with TAHINI, lemon, and garlic becomes the popular cold dip, Baba Ganoosh; seasoned with cooked eggs and sesame oil, it becomes the Israeli "mock liver," another popular cold dip. Greeks enjoy it stuffed to make Yemises, in fritters called Tyanites, and made into a sweet spicy preserve called Melitzanes Glyko, which is served as a condiment with roast meats. But Greeks enjoy it most of all in their famous Moussaka, layered with lamb and topped with cheese custard. Many Turkish and other Middle Eastern recipes team it with lamb. The Turkish dish, Imam Bayildi (literally "the priest fainted"), presumably got its name from the amount of olive oil used in the preparation—it was either too rich for the Imam's blood or his pocketbook, depending on which tale you believe. This is how we make it.

IMAM BAYILDI

1 medium, or 2 small, eggplants   For 4 servings
2 teaspoons salt
½ cup olive oil
1 large onion, minced
2 cloves garlic, minced
3 ripe tomatoes, peeled and seeded
⅛ teaspoon black pepper
   Minced parsley, to garnish

Cut eggplant(s) in half lengthwise, but do not peel. Score the cut edges in a crisscross pattern and sprinkle each half with ¼ teaspoon salt. Set aside for 1 hour at room temperature. Press the liquid out of the eggplants with paper towels. Scoop out the centers of the eggplant halves leaving ½″ shells. Dice the scooped-out eggplant into ½″ cubes. Brush the rims of the eggplant shells with olive oil.

Heat ⅓ cup of the olive oil in a heavy skillet or sauté pan. Sauté the onion and garlic until the onion is transparent. Add the tomatoes and sauté 5 minutes; remove from heat. In a separate skillet, brown the cubes of eggplant in the remaining olive oil and add to the tomato mixture. Add the remaining 1½ teaspoons salt, and the pepper. Place the eggplant shells in an oiled baking dish large enough to hold them without crowding. Fill the shells with the tomato mixture. Bake at 350° for 30 minutes. Serve warm or cold.

TO PREPARE IN ADVANCE: Prepare in the morning; leave at room temperature or chill. Serve at room temperature or slightly warm.

EISHTA

OTHER: clotted cream

TURKISH and YUGOSLAVIAN: *kaymak*

You won't find this in markets, but you will find it called for in Egyptian recipes. It is a luxurious thick cream stripped in rolls from the top of buffalo milk. Substitute a fine quality cream cheese that has been softened several hours at room temperature.

USE: It is often spooned as a topping over the sweet syrup-drenched desserts so popular in the Middle East.

FARINA

"Farina" is the Italian term for flour, and has become a generic term for any ground grain. In Middle Eastern cooking, however, it refers to ground white wheat or "cream of wheat." Substitute regular, not "quick cooking," cream of wheat, sold in any supermarket.

STORAGE: In an airtight container on the pantry shelf it will keep indefinitely.

PREPARATION AND USE: Farina is used in many Middle Eastern desserts. An Afghan pudding, Halwau-E-Aurd-E-Sujee, contains farina, pistachios, almonds, and rosewater, and it is used in the Israeli walnut cake, Karidopita. Our Greek friend, Ann Pappas, gave us her recipe for one version of the popular Greek nut cake, Ravani, which is drenched in syrup, as are most Middle Eastern desserts.

RAVANI

Butter and flour for baking pans   For 24 servings
1 dozen eggs, separated, and at room temperature
1 cup sugar
½ cup farina *or* regular cream of wheat
2½ teaspoons baking powder
Freshly grated rind from 3 oranges and 3 lemons
1 pound blanched, slivered almonds, toasted until golden, and finely ground
2 teaspoons pure vanilla extract
1 teaspoon lemon juice

SYRUP:
- 3 cups sugar
- 1½ cups water
- 1 stick cinnamon
- 1 teaspoon lemon juice

Butter and flour an 18″ × 12″ baking pan or two 13″ × 9″ pans.

Place the egg whites in the large grease-free bowl of an electric mixer, preferably one with a whisk attachment. Place the yolks with the sugar in a large mixing bowl, and beat together until pale yellow. Beat in the farina, baking powder, and grated rinds, followed by the ground almonds and vanilla.

Beat the egg whites with the lemon juice until they hold stiff peaks. Fold half of the beaten whites into the batter thoroughly. Fold in the remaining whites gently, but thoroughly. Turn the batter into the prepared pan(s), smooth the top gently, and bake for 30 to 40 minutes.

Meanwhile, prepare the syrup and let it cool. Combine syrup ingredients in a small saucepan and simmer for 10 minutes. Remove from the heat and set aside.

When the cake is done, remove it from the oven. Using a skewer, poke holes, 1″ apart, in the top of the cake(s). Gently pour the cooled syrup over the hot cake(s). Cool before cutting into 3″ squares. Serve with sweetened whipped cream, if desired.

TO PREPARE IN ADVANCE: This stays moist because of the syrup in it. Wrap airtight to store at room temperature for up to 3 days, or in the freezer for up to 3 months. Bring to room temperature before serving.

FELAFEL MIX

This is an "instant" mix for making Felafel (highly spiced ground chickpea and wheat fritters), a popular food sold by street vendors in the Middle East, New York City, and rapidly becoming popular in large cities throughout the United States.

STORAGE: It will keep indefinitely on the pantry shelf. Refrigerate after opening.

PREPARATION AND USE: The mix needs only to be combined with water, formed into balls, and deep-fried. The balls can be served warm as an appetizer, but are most often placed in PITA BREAD to be topped with the likes of cucumbers, tomatoes, and TAHINI sauce to create what is sometimes called the "Israeli hot dog." The recipe for Felafel "from scratch" appears under BEANS, CHICK-PEAS.

FIGS, SMYRNA

These sweet, chewy, golden dried figs, originally from Izmir on Turkey's Aegean coast, are now cultivated in California and are available in Middle Eastern markets and health food stores. The California Smyrna is called Calimyrna. They are considered the finest type of dried fig and have a fine, nutty flavor. Those that are imported often have a bay leaf packed with them to ward off weevils. They should feel a bit soft and have a fresh aroma.

STORAGE: If tightly wrapped, they will keep indefinitely in the refrigerator.

PREPARATION AND USE: Remove any pieces of rush used to hang the figs while they dry. Serve as a dessert, as is, or stuffed with nuts or CITRON to make a sweetmeat. They can be used in place of dried apricots in any recipe. We like them drizzled with honey and baked to serve warm with whipped cream. In some Middle Eastern and European recipes they are combined with fennel to make stuffings for lamb and poultry. They are the very best figs to use in making a traditional English Figgy Pudding, as in the following recipe.

FIGGY PUDDING

Shortening to grease an 8-cup	For 12 to 16 servings
steamed-pudding mold and lid	
Sugar to coat the inside of the mold	

1   pound dried Smyrna figs, stemmed
2   cups milk
1½ cups cake flour
1   tablespoon baking powder
1   teaspoon ground cinnamon
1   teaspoon freshly grated nutmeg
1   teaspoon coarse salt
12 ounces sweet (unsalted) butter
1   cup sugar
3   large eggs
1¾ cups fresh bread crumbs
2   tablespoons freshly grated orange rind

RUM HARD SAUCE:
2   cups powdered sugar
¼   pound (1 stick) soft butter
2–3 tablespoons Myers' dark Jamaican rum

Grease the inside of an 8-cup steamed-pudding mold and its lid with shortening; then dust with granulated sugar; set aside.

Remove the stems from the figs and chop the figs finely. Place in a heavy saucepan with the milk and bring to a boil. Lower the heat and simmer, stirring often, for 20 minutes. Remove from heat and cool.

Sift together onto a long sheet of waxed paper the flour, baking powder, spices, and salt. In the large bowl of an electric mixer, beat the butter and sugar until very creamy. Beat in the eggs, one at a time, beating very well after each addition, and stopping the motor from time to time to scrape the sides of the bowl with a rubber spatula. Beat in the bread crumbs and orange rind. Add the fig mixture alternately with the flour mixture, beating very well after each addition. Spoon the pudding mixture into the mold, and tie the lid on with string to hold it tightly during the cooking.

Place the mold in a large kettle on a rack or trivet to hold it off the bottom. Pour in boiling water to half the depth of the mold and cover the kettle tightly. Bring to a boil, lower the heat to keep the water simmering, and steam the pudding for 2 hours. Keep the water boiling gently during the cooking time, adding more boiling water as necessary. Remove from the kettle and let cool, *without removing the lid,* for 30 minutes.

To make the Rum Hard Sauce, sift the powdered sugar through a kitchen strainer at least 5 times. (It is too light to fall through a sifter—this sounds tedious, but it makes an especially fluffy sauce.) Beat the butter until very soft in an electric mixer; then beat in the powdered sugar and rum, and continue beating until very light.

Cut the string, remove the lid, and invert the pudding onto a serving dish. Serve warm with room temperature Rum Hard Sauce.

TO PREPARE IN ADVANCE: Figgy Pudding can be made weeks in advance. Wrap in cheesecloth that has been soaked in cognac, brandy, or rum, and wrap it tightly in foil and store in the refrigerator. It can be reheated in the oven (rewrap in foil after removing the cheesecloth) or re-steamed in its mold. Either way, allow about 20 minutes. The Rum Hard Sauce is at its best if served the day it is made, though it can be made ahead of time for convenience. Store at room temperature for up to 3 days, or in the refrigerator for up to 2 weeks.

FILO PASTRY

(FEE-loh)
OTHER: *fila, phyllo, phylla, fillo*

TURKISH: *yufka*

Filo is the Greek word for leaf, and refers as well to a tissue-paper thin pastry that can be found either refrigerated or frozen in gourmet specialty shops, Middle Eastern markets, and in many supermarkets in 1-pound boxes. Each box will contain approximately 24 sheets (leaves) of dough that measure

9″ × 13″ to 16″ × 18″, depending on the manufacturer. It is almost identical to STRUDEL LEAVES (see THE FOODS OF EUROPE section), which usually contains eggs and tends to be a bit thicker. Both are very difficult to make at home. Sometimes boxes are numbered to denote the thickness of the dough, with #1 being the thickest and #4 the thinnest. Brands vary greatly, so find one you can trust and stick with it. We have had good luck with Long Beach brand on the West Coast. Though not the same as WARKA (Tunisian *malsouqua* and Algerian *dioul*), the pastry used in Morocco to make Bstilla, cinnamon-flavored chicken in pastry, and a Tunisian pastry called Brik, it is often substituted for it, because warka is not sold commercially in the United States.

STORAGE: If refrigerated when purchased, it can be stored unopened in the refrigerator for up to 3 weeks, or frozen. If frozen, thaw overnight in the refrigerator. Plan to use the whole package within a few days for a variety of dishes to be frozen for future use because the unused leaves dry out quickly. Once thawed, it is best not to refreeze because the sheets may stick together. If, for some reason, you decide not to use the whole package at one time, roll it up carefully inside its plastic cover and place inside a damp towel. Store in the refrigerator for use within a few days' time.

PREPARATION AND USE: Filo to be used to make tiny individual appetizers or to line baking or pie pans must be handled carefully but rapidly in the following manner:

Remove the filo from the refrigerator an hour or so before you plan to use it. Have all your filling ingredients ready before you open the plastic bag surrounding the pastry inside the box. Remove the dough and unfold it; then lay it on a flat surface where you have plenty of space to work. Place a piece of plastic over the sheets of dough (we use a new waste basket liner) and top that with a damp towel to weight it down. This will prevent air from reaching the dough and drying it out, but take care not to let the damp towel touch the dough.

To make tiny appetizers, triangular or rolled, remove one sheet of dough at a time and lay it on a dry kitchen towel on your work surface. Lightly sprinkle the entire surface with melted butter, margarine, olive oil, or corn oil, as directed in the recipe. Paula Wolfert, expert on Mediterranean cooking, tells us that everyone uses too much oil or butter on filo, so don't overdo.

For triangular-shaped puffs, cut the sheet of dough into 3 widthwise strips (about 4″ × 12″). Fold each strip in half lengthwise, buttered side in, and then brush the top with oil or butter. Place a teaspoonful of filling (which should always contain some egg so the filling will puff in the oven) on the bottom of each folded-over strip. Fold as you would a flag (see illustration) to the end of the strip and seal to create triangular-shaped pastries with several layers of dough. Brush with oil or butter to seal and prevent drying.

To make rolls, cut each sheet into 3 lengthwise strips after sprinkling with

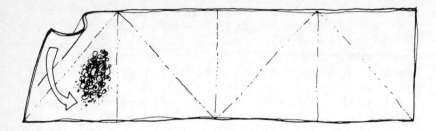

butter or oil. Place about 1½ teaspoons of filling on the end of each strip of dough, ½" in from each side. Fold in the edges along the length of the strip and brush with butter. Roll up to enclose the filling, and brush the tops to prevent drying.

If making ahead, freeze them, preferably unbaked, on a baking sheet until solid; then transfer to a plastic bag for freezer storage. When ready to serve, bake, seam-side down, without thawing, in a pre-heated 375° oven for 15 minutes or until golden brown and puffed. Cool slightly before serving.

SPINACH FILLING FOR FILO

For about 36 appetizers
or 1 (9") pie

This is enough filling for ½ pound (12 sheets) commercial filo pastry. Double the recipe if desired, or make another filling, in order to use up the entire 1-pound package.

2   pounds fresh spinach, washed, stems removed, and chopped, *or* 2 (10-ounce) packages frozen chopped spinach, thawed
2   tablespoons fruity olive oil
2   medium onions, minced
1   bunch scallions, finely chopped
8   ounces FETA cheese, crumbled
2   tablespoons minced fresh dill, *or* mint
½   teaspoon salt
¼   teaspoon freshly grated nutmeg
¼   teaspoon ground black pepper
3   eggs, beaten

If using fresh spinach, cook it with only the water that clings to the leaves, and just until wilted. Drain, cool slightly, squeeze out liquid, and chop fine. If using thawed frozen spinach, squeeze out all excess liquid. Set aside.

In a heavy skillet, sauté the onion and scallions in the olive oil just until the onion is nearly transparent. Stir in the spinach and cook, stirring often, until all excess moisture has evaporated. Remove from heat and mix in the remaining ingredients in the order listed.

FETA FILLING

For about 36 appetizers

Filling for ½ pound (12 sheets) commercial filo. Double the recipe or make another filling in order to use up the entire 1-pound package of dough.

    4 ounces FETA cheese, crumbled
    3 ounces cream cheese
    1 large egg
    ¼ cup minced parsley
    ⅛ teaspoon freshly grated nutmeg
       Dash of cayenne or white pepper

Combine ingredients in the bowl of an electric mixer or food processor and process until creamy.

CHINESE CHICKEN FILLING

For approximately 36 appetizers

Not at all Middle Eastern, but an example of how any savory mixture can be used as a filling for filo appetizers.

    ¼ cup light soy sauce
    ¼ cup sherry or *shao hsing* (Chinese rice wine)
    1 teaspoon sugar (rock sugar preferred)
    2 tablespoons Chinese OYSTER SAUCE
    2 points star anise, *or* ⅛ teaspoon FIVE SPICE POWDER
    3 quarter-size slices fresh ginger root
    1 clove garlic, minced or pressed
    2 whole chicken breasts, split and boned
       Filo pastry (12 sheets, cut in squares, to make triangles)

In a small saucepan, combine the soy, wine, sugar, oyster sauce, star anise or Five Spice Powder, ginger, and garlic. Simmer, uncovered, for 5 minutes. Add chicken breasts and bring to a boil. Cover the pan, lower the heat, and simmer very gently for 15 minutes, turning the chicken once to color evenly with the glazing sauce. Remove from heat and cool to room temperature.

Dice the chicken fine and return it to the sauce. Use chicken pieces and sauce as a filling for filo triangles.

When it comes to lining baking or pie pans, filo is a great dough to experiment with. Six to 8 sheets, buttered or oiled, can be stacked and pinched or folded in around the edges to make a pie shell for just about any recipe. Excess dough is never trimmed as is pie crust. Use it for single- or double-crust pies of any ethnic variety, sweet or savory, and to add interest to your favorite quiche recipe. Rectangular pans for casserole-type dishes or desserts are usually lined with 10 leaves, filled and baked at 350° for 30 to 40 minutes, and then allowed to rest at least 5 minutes before cutting.

In Morocco, WARKA is baked into a complex pie of pigeon or chicken, eggs, onions, almonds, sugar, and cinnamon, which is called Bstilla, and is indescribably delicious. In Tunisia, *malsouqua* is used to make Brik, a filled triangular pastry that is deep-fried and, in Algeria, *dioul* pastries are shaped like cigars and filled with fish purees or ground lamb.

The Greeks make a filling of cheese or spinach for their tiny triangular pastries called Tyropite to serve as appetizers, or use filo to line pans for pies such as the feta and spinach filled Spanakopita. Baklava, that diamond-shaped, many-layered, nut-filled pastry drenched with cinnamon-flavored syrup, is one of the most popular of all Middle Eastern desserts. Various shapes of small pastries are filled with meat or cheese in Turkey to serve as appetizers, and even for breakfast.

FIREEK

See BULGHUR WHEAT

GRAPE LEAVES

OTHER: vine leaves

ARMENIAN: *derev* FRENCH: *feuille de vigne* GERMAN: *Rebenblatt*
GREEK: *yalantzi* ITALIAN: *foglia di vite* SPANISH: *pámpano*

Grape vine leaves, bottled or canned in brine, are available in 8- and 16-ounce jars in all Middle Eastern markets. The 16-ounce jar contains 40 to 50 leaves. California leaves are more tender than imported ones. One pound of fresh leaves when prepared for stuffing is equivalent to the number in a 16-ounce bottle.

STORAGE: Once opened, these can be stored in a nonmetal container in their original brine in the refrigerator indefinitely.

594

PREPARATION AND USE: Canned leaves must be carefully separated to prevent tearing. Rinse them well to rid them of the strong brine taste. To prepare fresh leaves, wash them well and then steam for 30 to 60 seconds and use like canned leaves. Place shiny-side down and place your chosen filling toward the large end of the leaf. Fold in the sides and roll up. Place, seam-side down, in a baking pan and follow directions in your recipe.

Grape leaves, widely used throughout the Middle East, are wrapped around a stuffing, usually a rice mixture; then cooked, cooled, and served cold as an appetizer with lemon wedges, or warm with a Greek Egg-Lemon sauce called Avgolemono. Stuffed grape or vine leaves are called Dolmades, and in Greece they are filled with lemon- and dill-flavored rice; the Turkish version usually contains rice, a bit of meat, and some raisins and nuts. The Lebanese flavor the filling with mint and serve it with a yogurt dip.

GUAVA

See THE FOODS OF LATIN AMERICA section

HARISSA

Harissa is a fiery Tunisian seasoning sauce or paste available in bottles or cans in Levantine and some Middle Eastern markets. It is made of dried red chiles, garlic, olive oil, and occasionally caraway seeds. In Morocco, harissa is simply red pepper, salt, and oil, and does not contain caraway seeds. SAMBAL *oelek,* an Indonesian condiment (see THE FOODS OF ASIA section), makes a perfect substitute according to Paula Wolfert, expert on Moroccan cuisine. She says the commerical harissa pastes are awful and that she never uses them.

STORAGE: Harissa may be stored up to 2 months in the refrigerator. Every time you spoon some out of the jar, make sure any newly exposed surface is covered with oil.

PREPARATION AND USE: In Fez, and in most Moroccan tourist hotels, harissa is used in the preparation of the national dish of Morocco, Cous Cous. (In Rabat, however, Cous Cous is more commonly a sweet dish, made with onions, raisins, and lamb.) Harissa is usually mixed with lemon, cumin, and fresh coriander to season some of the broth left from cooking the lamb used in Cous Cous, thus creating a delicious, fiery condiment to serve with that dish. It is sometimes thinned with lemon juice and olive oil to serve as a table condiment, or as a dressing for salads. A homemade version is made as follows.

HARISSA

For 1 cup

This Harissa can be used in place of Sambal Oelek in Indonesian recipes, though that product uses tamarind liquid or vinegar for the tart flavor in place of lemon.

1   cup dried red chiles, including seeds (approximately 1
      ounce), crumbled
2   teaspoons salt
    Fresh lemon juice or vinegar
    Olive oil

Note: One clove of garlic can be added to the mixture if desired. Paula Wolfert, author of *Couscous and Other Good Food From Morocco* (Harper & Row), tells us that Harissa does not contain caraway seeds, as many books indicate.

Place the chiles in a small saucepan with water just to cover and bring to a simmer. Remove from the heat and set aside for 1 hour. Drain, and place chiles in electric blender. Add the salt, and just enough lemon juice to keep the mixture moving through the blades as it is pureed to a paste. Transfer to a small glass jar for refrigerator storage, smooth the top, and pour sufficient oil over the top to prevent air from touching the surface.

HONEY

Honey is very commonly used throughout the Middle East to sweeten not only desserts, but various North African Tagines (stews). Middle Eastern honeys are not often imported, but you may find Mount Hymettus honey in a Greek market. It is made by bees that feed on the tiny purple thyme flowers and is highly prized for its rather medicinal thyme flavor.

STORAGE: It will keep indefinitely on the pantry shelf.

PREPARATION AND USE: Honey is often used in syrups for desserts such as Baklava, and Melopita, a honey cheese pie made with the soft type of MIZITHRA (see CHEESES). Thyme-flavored honey is not really suited to Greek desserts and is seldom used for them, but this type of honey is used in Morocco for both desserts and Tagines.

HUMMUS

Hummus is a creamy sauce of ground chick-peas seasoned with lemon juice, garlic, and olive oil, which is used as a dip, sauce, and spread in Israel, the Arab countries, and in Turkey. When combined with TAHINI (sesame seed paste) it is called Hummus Bi Tahina. Both versions are available in all Middle Eastern markets, freshly made or in bottles or cans. It is very easy to make from dried or canned CHICK-PEAS (see under BEANS).

STORAGE: After opening, it can be stored in the refrigerator for up to a week, or frozen for longer storage.

PREPARATION AND USE: This is most often served simply as a dip for PITA BREAD or crackers, or spooned over Felafel (chick-pea fritters, see recipe under BEANS, CHICK-PEA). It serves as a basic sauce for many foods, including lamb dishes, cooked vegetables, such as eggplant and cauliflower, and with grains, such as COUS COUS and BULGHUR WHEAT. In Israel, it is often enriched with mashed avocado.

HUMMUS BI TAHINA

2 cups chick-peas, freshly cooked or canned,   For 3 cups
   with their liquid
⅔ cup fresh lemon juice
⅔ cup TAHINI (sesame seed paste)
3 cloves garlic
½ teaspoon salt, or more to taste
¼ teaspoon freshly ground black pepper
¼ teaspoon cayenne (ground red pepper)
¼ teaspoon sweet or hot paprika
   Optional: 2–3 tablespoons minced fresh herbs, such as
   coriander or dill, *or* ¼ teaspoon ground cumin

TO SERVE:
1 tablespoon olive oil
½ teaspoon paprika
1–2 teaspoons minced fresh parsley, *or* fresh POMEGRANATE
   seeds

Drain chick-peas, reserving liquid (and 1 tablespoon whole chick-peas for garnish). Combine ingredients in container of electric food processor or blender and puree until very smooth and the consistency of mayonnaise. Thin if necessary with reserved liquid from chick-peas.

Transfer to a serving dish, spreading it evenly. Mix together olive oil and paprika, and drizzle over the top. Garnish with reserved chick-peas and a sprinkling of parsley or pomegranate seeds. Serve as a dip for PITA BREAD or sesame crackers.

TO PREPARE IN ADVANCE: This can be stored in the refrigerator for up to 3 days.

KADAIFI PASTRY

OTHER: *kataifi, konafa, kadaif, cadaif*

ARABIC: *burma, knafi*

Sold by the pound in the refrigerator or frozen-food sections of Greek and other Middle Eastern specialty markets, this pastry is made by pouring a flour and water batter through a perforated tin onto a hot griddle and then sweeping it off almost immediately before it has time to color. The pastry, which is threadlike in appearance, remains soft. It is easier to work with than FILO PASTRY because one doesn't need to worry so much about its drying out. Nut-filled rolls made with this pastry are often sold in Greek bakeries and markets. One of our Lebanese cookbooks recommends that regular shredded wheat, which has been crushed, but not soaked, be substituted if kadaifi is not available.

STORAGE: Store in the refrigerator for use as soon as possible.

PREPARATION AND USE: This is used only in sweet dishes. The Greeks make an excellent pastry using this dough. They make a filling of ground walnuts, sugar, eggs, spices, rose or orange-flower water, and butter, form it into rolls, and wrap the rolls in kadaifi. The secret is that a *cold* syrup is poured over the *hot* rolls after baking, as it is for Baklava. In Lebanon and Turkey, as well as in Greece, the dough, generously rubbed with butter, is pressed into a buttered pan and then spread with the same nut mixture, or a custard filling, and topped with more dough. It is generously buttered and baked and doused with cold syrup; then cooled and cut into squares. This type of pastry absorbs great quantities of butter during cooking, so take care that all exposed surfaces are generously brushed.

KISHK

OTHER: *kishik*

Kishk is a staple food in Lebanon and Syria, traditionally made by the whole family during the summer for winter use. It is a mixture of *laban* (yogurt) combined with bulghur wheat and salt that is allowed to ferment for nine days, and then dried on rooftops. It is then rubbed between the palms of the hands to make a powder with the texture of cornmeal and used as a seasoning and thickening agent. Fortunately, it is available by the ounce in most Middle Eastern markets.

STORAGE: Store like any flour. It will keep indefinitely in a cool, dry place.

PREPARATION AND USE: The most common way of using this is to make a soup or porridge by adding it to some oil in which onion or garlic has cooked, cooking it for a few minutes, and then adding water until it reaches the desired consistency. Our Lebanese friends say that they add it to many dishes where a tart, yogurt taste is desirable, as in sauces for one type of Kibbi (lamb and seasonings formed into small oval meatballs), and cabbage. To use it to thicken stews, soups, or sauces, cook 1 cup kishk with 2 tablespoons butter or other fat over very low heat for 3 to 4 minutes, stirring often, to make a roux. Add gradually to the liquid to be thickened until the desired soup or sauce consistency is reached. This amount will thicken approximately 8 cups of liquid to a creamy sauce consistency. (Leftover roux made with kishk can be frozen.) Kishk is salty, so take care in adding salt to any dish to which it is added.

LAHVOSH

OTHER: Armenian cracker bread

This round, crisp, cracker-like bread made of wheat flour, yeast, malt, and sesame seeds, is served with many meals in the Middle East. It is available in varying diameters, and is sold in paper bags in many Middle Eastern markets, and in supermarkets in large metropolitan areas.

STORAGE: It can be stored, airtight, for up to a month.

PREPARATION AND USE: Though this is most traditionally broken into pieces to serve as an accompaniment to many meals, it can be used in the making of a large sandwich roll, as in the following recipe.

LAHVOSH SANDWICH ROLL

1 roll makes 6 sandwiches

This recipe uses large rounds of lahvosh, which measure approximately 15″ in diameter and are usually sold in 15-ounce packages containing 3 rounds.

1   (5-ounce) round of lahvosh (cracker bread)
    Water to dampen the bread

FILLINGS: (Use any or all of these ingredients)

- 8 ounces softened cream cheese or butter, *or* 1 cup mayonnaise
- 2 tablespoons mustard (optional)
  Fresh herbs, minced, *or* herb seasoning of your choice
  Salt and pepper
- 6 ounces ham, roast lamb, beef, or salami, sliced as thinly as possible
- 1 small Bermuda onion, very thinly sliced
- 1–2 cups shredded lettuce

Dampen the lahvosh by holding it under cold running water; then place it between two damp towels. In 20 minutes or so it will have softened.

Gently spread the top of the bread with cream cheese, butter, or mayonnaise, and optional mustard. Sprinkle generously with herbs or herb seasoning, salt and pepper. Arrange the meat evenly over the bread. Top with onion and lettuce, taking care not to make the filling too thick. Roll up the bread into a tight cylinder shape enclosing the filling.

Cut into 6 crosswise slices to make sandwich rolls. Serve immediately or let dry briefly at room temperature to firm the outside of the lahvosh and make the sandwiches easier to handle.

TO PREPARE IN ADVANCE: As with most any sandwich, this is best made within a few hours of serving, so the vegetables retain their crispness. The whole roll can be wrapped in plastic wrap or foil to carry to a picnic and cut at the site.

LA KAMA

This is a recipe adapted from a recipe in Paula Wolfert's cookbook, *Couscous and Other Good Foods From Morocco*. Combine in an empty spice bottle 3 parts *each* of ground black pepper, ground ginger, and ground turmeric, 2 parts ground cinnamon, and 1 part freshly grated nutmeg.

STORAGE: Stored in a cool, dark place, it will keep for up to 3 months.

USE: This is used in Tangier where it is used instead of RAS EL HANOUT to season Tagines and Harira soup.

LAKERTHA

OTHER: *lakerda*

Lakertha is the name of a popular Greek pickled fish, usually mackerel, tuna *(tunny)*, or bonito *(palamida)*, available in jars or cans in Greek markets.

STORAGE: After opening, transfer with its brine to a nonmetal container and refrigerate; it will keep for up to a week.

PREPARATION AND USE: Drain of liquid and slice thin, as you would smoked salmon, to serve as an appetizer with slices of lemon.

LAVENDER

See HERBS, SPICES, AND SEASONING BLENDS section

LEMONS, PICKLED

ARABIC: *lamoun makbouss*

These are not the same as the salted, preserved lemons of Morocco (see LEMONS, PRESERVED), but are more like a condiment to serve with Middle Eastern meals. They turn orange in the pickling because paprika is added. Some Middle Eastern markets make their own, or sell a commercial variety in jars, but they can be easily made by a process we adapted from Claudia Roden's *A Book of Middle Eastern Foods*. Cut lemons into ½″ slices and freeze them on a baking sheet overnight. The next morning, place them in a colander and sprinkle them heavily with salt. Allow them to drain in the colander for up to 8 hours. When soft, arrange them in layers in a glass refrigerator container sprinkling each layer with paprika. When all the lemons are in the jar, cover them with vegetable oil. Close the jar and set aside at room temperature for 3 to 4 days.

STORAGE: Refrigerate. They will keep indefinitely.

USE: Serve as a condiment with Middle Eastern dishes. They add a pretty orange color and tangy flavor to many meals. The olive oil in which they were preserved can be used as a seasoning in salads and relishes.

LEMONS, PRESERVED

IN MOROCCO: *msir*

These are essential to many Moroccan Tagines (stews), in dishes such as Chicken with Lemons and Olives, and in salads, but are seldom available in the United States unless you have a North African market nearby. However, they are easy to make—except for the long wait. The following recipe is an adaptation of Paula Wolfert's method, found in her *Couscous and Other Good Foods From Morocco* (Harper & Row).

Use Meyer lemons if available, and wash them well to remove any wax or insecticide spray. Cut 5 or 6 lemons lengthwise to within ½″ of their stem ends to open them. Sprinkle their pulp heavily with salt (we use kosher salt) and press them back into their original lemon shape. Pack them into a sterilized, pint-sized canning jar, sprinkling salt generously between each layer and pushing the lemons down to fit in the jar. Add *fresh-squeezed* lemon juice to cover the lemons by ½-inch, leaving some air space at the top of the jar, seal the jar tightly, and set in a warm place in your kitchen—where you will remember to shake it daily for 30 days! The lemons plump after a week and it is necessary to add more fresh lemon juice to keep them covered. In 30 days, the lemons are ready to use in Moroccan recipes.

An alternative method told to us by Michel Ohayon, owner of Koutoubia Restaurant in Los Angeles, is to pour ¼-inch layer of oil over the lemons and their liquid to keep out air. The oil makes shaking unnecessary and prevents any white film or mold from developing.

STORAGE: These can be stored for up to a year in a cool place, though they may develop a white film, which needs only to be rinsed off. They can, of course, be refrigerated after they have finished curing, but be sure to keep them submerged in the lemon juice. If they begin to smell like furniture polish, throw them out.

PREPARATION AND USE: For sanitary reasons do not put your fingers in the brine. Remove a lemon from the brine with a clean instrument, and rinse it well to rid it of excess salt before using in North African recipes. The salted lemon pickling liquid can be used over and over and a sprinkling of it can add a special tang to salad dressings, Bloody Marys, etc. They are used whole or quartered according to the recipe, and the pulp is sometimes scraped away and discarded. They are commonly used to flavor Lemon Chicken Tagine, many versions of which appear in Moroccan cookbooks.

LENTISK

See MASTIC

LIMES, DRIED

Whole, brownish, dried limes are available in Middle Eastern markets. They have a delightful aroma. You can make your own by boiling fresh limes in salt water to cover for 5 minutes and then allowing them to dry in the sun until they are hard.

STORAGE: They will keep indefinitely in an airtight container in a cool place, but they eventually lose their fragrance on standing.

PREPARATION AND USE: Iranians use these when cooking rice and in other dishes to produce a sharp, tart flavor. They are washed; then halved to remove the seeds; then simmered with other ingredients in stews and rice dishes. One or 2 dried limes are generally used to season 4 servings.

LOQUAT

See THE FOODS OF ASIA section

MAHLEB

OTHER: *mahlab, mahlepi*

This Persian spice, available in Middle Eastern markets, is the ground seed of a wild, cherry-type fruit. It was originally used in perfumes and medicines.

STORAGE: As any ground spice.

USE: Mahleb gives an intriguing fruit flavor to breads, cookies, and sweet pastries. The usual amount used is ½ to 1 teaspoon of ground mahleb to 2 cups of flour, depending on whether other spices are specified. If it is not available, you can grind together and substitute the following in equal measure: 2 inches stick cinnamon, 3 cloves, and 1 bay leaf.

MALSOUQUA PASTRY

See WARKA

MASTIC

ARABIC: *mistki* or *mustica* GERMAN: *Mastix* GREEK: *mastiha*
IRAQI: *Al mastaki* ITALIAN: *mastice, lentischio* IN MOROCCO: *mska*
SPANISH: *almáciga, mastice, lentisco*

This is not flavorless *gum arabic*, as some cookbooks would have you believe, but a sweet, slightly licorice-flavored resin of the lentisk (or similar) bush of the *Pistacia* genus, which grows on the island of Chios and in other areas of the Mediterranean. It is a highly prized flavoring throughout the Middle East, and you will find it in small, clear or amber-colored, pebble-like crystals in Middle Eastern markets where it is sold by the ounce. A Greek liqueur, Masticha, made only on the island of Chios, is flavored with this, and is served over ice as an aperitif. Small packets are sold by Athens' street

603

vendors to chew as gum. Medicines are flavored with it as well. There is no substitute.

STORAGE: It will keep indefinitely in a cool, dry place.

PREPARATION AND USE: The crystals must be pulverized into a powder before they can be used, sparingly, to flavor desserts such as Rahat Lokum (Turkish Delight), Loukoumi (a Greek version of Turkish Delight), puddings, almond paste, cookies, cakes, and candies. One-quarter teaspoon of pulverized mastic is the usual amount for 4 dessert servings. In Greece, it flavors a sweet, porridge-like fruit soup called Heelo, which is cooked with dried apricots and spices. Our Lebanese friends tell us they remember an ice cream made of milk flavored with SAHLAB and mastic, which had a gummy, almost elastic, consistency. In Morocco, it flavors ALMOND PASTE (see THE FOODS OF EUROPE section) and a Tagine made with chicken and onions, and it is the hard to identify, "secret" ingredient in some Cous Cous dishes.

MATZO

OTHER: *matsoh, matzot, matzoh*

Matzo is a thin, crisp, unleavened cracker that was made originally of only two ingredients, wheat flour and water, with no other seasonings. It is the unleavened bread of the Bible, created by the Israelites who, in their flight from Egypt, did not have time to let their bread ferment. It is used by Jews as a special part of their Passover celebration and has become very popular as a cracker year 'round. It is readily available in supermarkets, salted or unsalted, and even flavored with onion. There is also an "egg" matzo to which egg has been added.

STORAGE: These will keep indefinitely in an airtight container.

PREPARATION AND USE: Although most commonly used as a snack cracker, it is also made into a popular breakfast dish known as Matzo Brei, in which the matzo is broken into pieces, soaked in water, and then mixed with eggs and fried. It forms the basis of several fruit desserts, and is used to make MATZO MEAL.

MATZO MEAL

Matzo meal is MATZO that has been ground into a meal. It is available, usually in "fine" or "medium" grind, in most supermarkets and in all Jewish food stores.

STORAGE: It will keep indefinitely in an airtight container in a cool place.

USE: The fine grind is used in making gefüllte fish, pancakes, potato dishes, and Passover desserts. The medium grind is most commonly used to make matzo balls (dumplings) called Knaidlach, and for breading foods to be fried.

MULOUKIA

OTHER: *melokhia, muloukhie, milookhiyya*, Spanish sorrel

Muloukia is a green leafy vegetable that looks a great deal like spinach and is one of the most commonly eaten foods in Egypt. It has a bland, slightly astringent taste. You will rarely find it fresh, but you will find it dried, or packed in brine in 24-ounce cans, in Middle Eastern markets. Fresh sorrel or spinach can be substituted, but will have a different flavor.

STORAGE: As any herb.

PREPARATION AND USE: Two ounces of dried muloukia is equivalent to 1 pound of fresh, and is sufficient to flavor 5 cups of soup. Soak the dried leaves for 20 minutes in warm water to which you have added a bit of lemon juice. This is most often added gradually to soups flavored with garlic and ground coriander, in which case the leaves are crumbled before soaking to add a viscous quality, much like okra, or it is cooked like spinach into a puree served as an accompaniment to rice and other dishes.

NOODLES

Following are some of the dried noodles that may be called for in Middle Eastern recipes. Most are available in Middle Eastern markets and substitutes are recommended for others.

Fide: A fine Greek noodle used primarily in soups.

Manestra: Greek rice-shaped pasta, similar to ORZO.

Orzo: Pasta shaped like a cantaloupe seed, which is often served with meat or cheese sauce. In Greece, it is often cooked in the pan juices from roast lamb in place of potatoes, and is sprinkled with grated KEFALOTIRI (see under CHEESES) before serving.

Sheriya: A thin, 1" long noodle commonly served in Morocco. It is cooked exactly like COUS COUS to use in meat dishes and desserts. Substitute spaghettini (see SPAGHETTI) or VERMICELLI (see under PASTA in THE FOODS OF EUROPE section) and cut into 1" lengths.

Trahana: A Greek noodle made with yogurt or buttermilk. The dough is rubbed between the palms of the hand to form oatmeal-like flakes, which are usually cooked in broth to make a porridge. It is available, dried, in Greek markets.

STORAGE: See under PASTA in THE FOODS OF EUROPE section.

OIL

Various kinds of oil are used in the Middle East for cooking and deep-frying, usually corn, cottonseed, or nut oils. OLIVE OIL (see THE FOODS OF EUROPE section), which is plentiful, is almost always used for dishes that will be served at room temperature, and for frying fish. There is a tendency to use a great deal more oil in recipes than Americans are used to, so you may wish to use your own discretion when following recipes from Middle Eastern cookbooks. Special cooking oils made from butter that has been boiled and clarified, much like Indian GHEE (see THE FOODS OF ASIA section), are called SÂMNA and SMEN. The latter is often flavored with herbs.

OKRA, DRIED

ARABIC: *bamiya, bamieh* GREEK: *bamies* TURKISH: *bamya*

General information on fresh OKRA will be found in THE FOODS OF AFRICA section.

Okra is a common vegetable in the Middle East, but its mucilaginous texture is not appreciated there. In Middle Eastern markets, you will find tiny dried okra hanging on strings. They are used in the cooking of Greece, Turkey, and the Levant. Dried okra do not have the mucilaginous quality of fresh, canned, or frozen okra, so they will not thicken the dishes to which they are added.

STORAGE: Dried okra can be stored for up to 6 months in an airtight container on the pantry shelf, though they eventually lose flavor.

PREPARATION AND USE: One cup of dried okra is sufficient for 4 servings in most recipes. Boil in salted water until they are tender. They are already scraped, so they need only be blotted dry. Sauté or add to a sauce with meat.

Okra is often combined in the Middle East with lemon and lots of garlic. A Turkish dish, Katalu, is a vegetable mélange very similar to French Ratatouille, except for the addition of okra. In Greece, okra cooked in olive oil with tomatoes and onions is called Bamies Me Domates, and is usually served as a separate course. (If fresh okra is used for the latter, it is usually soaked for several hours in vinegar to rid it of its slippery quality.)

OLIVES

ARABIC: *zeitoun* GREEK: *ellies*

In the Middle East, olives are almost always served with meals, just as they are, or part of a *mezze* (appetizer) table. For the most part, only the countries of North Africa (Morocco, Algeria, and Tunisia) use them in cooking, but few Middle Eastern meals would be considered complete without them. (They are often used in cooking in Europe, see OLIVE, EUROPEAN, in THE FOODS OF EUROPE section.) Various green olives, which are picked unripe, and black olives, which are tree-ripened, are sold in bulk, or occasionally bottled, in Middle Eastern markets. Following is a brief description of those you are likely to find.

STORAGE: Loose olives can be stored for up to a month in their original brine in the refrigerator. Depending on their type and the strength of the brining solution, they will keep well for a week to 6 months, but grow softer the longer they are stored. If a white film forms on the surface, it should be wiped away. If the olives have become quite soft it means they are spoiled and should be discarded.

BLACK or FRENCH/MOROCCAN

These are small, wrinkled black olives with a bitter flavor that have been cured in salt. In Morocco, they are often served covered with HARISSA. We are told that the Progresso brand of canned black olives is imported from Morocco.

GREEK JUMBO

This is a large olive, similar to the KALAMATA, but softer and larger.

GREEN CRACKED

These are unripe olives (*Agrinon* and *Nafpiou* are Greek varieties) that have been brined several times to rid them of bitterness. To serve as a *mezze* (appetizer), pit them and marinate, if desired, in lemon juice, garlic, and herbs for several hours before serving. To use them in cooking, rinse to remove excess brine and then add them to stews and Tagines, especially with chicken. Medium-sized Spanish or California olives are not adequate substitutes.

KALAMATA

This is a medium-sized, purple-black Greek olive with an oblong shape and pointed ends. The flesh alongside the pit is often slit to allow the flavorings in the brine in which they have been cured to penetrate more easily. They are cured in vinegar and are the finest eating olive of the Mediterranean—juicy, slightly firm, and delicious. They are always in "Greek" salad, with FETA (see under CHEESES), tomatoes, and cucumbers. Kalamata olives are seldom used in cooking, but they add an especially delicious flavor to the following stew from a recipe in Mary Wilde's *The Best of Ethnic Home Cooking*.

PAPOU'S GREEK STEW

¼ cup imported olive oil
2 pounds lean lamb or beef stew meat
6–7 cloves of garlic, peeled
2 medium-sized yellow onions, peeled and quartered
Salt and pepper
1 cup dry red wine
6 ounces canned tomato paste
2 cups water or stock
1 bay leaf
1 teaspoon ground cinnamon
Peel of 1 orange or tangerine, fresh or dried
4 red-skinned potatoes, quartered
1 bunch of young carrots, scraped and cut into chunks
5–6 stalks of celery, cleaned and cut diagonally into chunks
½ pound fresh, mature green beans, with ends and
strings removed, cut in half
¼ pound Kalamata olives

Heat the olive oil in a large heavy kettle. Add the lamb and brown on all sides (10 to 15 minutes). Add the garlic, onion, and a little salt and pepper, and cook until the onion and garlic are soft. (If you don't want to eat the whole garlic buds when the stew is done, remove them. Many Greeks prefer to eat the whole cooked cloves and consider them to be very healthful and strengthening. Garlic does become sweeter the longer it is cooked—still, it's an acquired taste.) Add the wine, tomato paste, water or stock, bay leaf, cinnamon, and orange or tangerine peel. Stir with a long wooden spoon to blend and let the meat simmer slowly with the spices for about an hour or until the lamb is tender. Add the potatoes, carrots, and celery and simmer for about 15 minutes. Then add the green beans and simmer, covered, for 15 minutes until the vegetables are tender but not too soft. Add the olives and cover. Remove from the heat and allow to stand for at least an hour. Reheat just before serving. Remove the bay leaf and citrus peel and serve the stew in deep, wide dishes. Offer a tossed green salad and good bread for dunking, as well as chunks of FETA cheese and a jug of deep red wine.

TO PREPARE IN ADVANCE: This stew is at its best when made several hours (or even a day) ahead.

RIPE OLIVES

There are many types of vinegared ripe olives, including the KALAMATA and the Greek Royal Victoria. In most cases, they are brownish, purplish, or black, though a few are green in color. American black olives are cured differently and are nearly flavorless in comparison, so are not recommended as substitutes in Middle Eastern recipes.

ORANGE-FLOWER WATER

OTHER: orange blossom water, orange blossom essence

ARABIC: *mazahir* FRENCH: *eau de fleur d'orange* IRAQI: *ma'keddah*
IN MOROCCO: *zhaar*

Orange-flower water is used in Moroccan and Middle Eastern cooking and is often distilled in the home from fresh orange blossoms. It can be found in well-stocked liquor stores, in pharmacies, and in Middle Eastern and Indian markets. That imported from Lebanon is less expensive and often has chemicals added or is simply a combination of orange oil and water. The French, though expensive, is more aromatic than our domestic brands.

STORAGE: It will keep indefinitely on the pantry shelf, but loses strength on standing.

USE: In Morocco, this is often used to perfume the water poured over your hands to rinse them after a meal and it is used to flavor Cous Cous in some homes. Throughout the Middle East, it is a flavoring for drinks, cookies, almond pastries, and many custard desserts, specifically Muhallabia and Baklava. In the United States, it is an ingredient in various "fizz" drinks, such as a Ramos Gin Fizz.

PEKMEZ

OTHER: black honey

This is the Arabic term for a molasses made from grapes, similar to blackstrap molasses. It can be found in Middle Eastern markets.

STORAGE: It will keep indefinitely on the pantry shelf.

USE: This is used primarily as a sweetener for tea.

PINE NUT

OTHER: *snobore, snoober,* pine kernel

TURKISH: *fustek*

General information on the PINE NUT will be found in THE FOODS OF EUROPE section. In the Middle East, the long slender type is used extensively in pilafs, stuffings, fillings for vine leaves, and in jam and desserts. They should be lightly toasted to bring out their flavor before using in recipes.

PISTACHIO NUT

OTHER: green almond

Pistachios, native to the Levant, are small nuts in tiny clam-like shells. The inner kernels are pale green in color, except in Syria where they are yellow. Pistachios are expensive because they must be hand-sorted to obtain the open ones, but those purchased in bulk in Mediterranean and Middle Eastern grocery stores are much less expensive than those found in supermarkets. Health food stores are also a good source of supply, especially for unsalted pistachios. Avoid those that are dyed red.

STORAGE: These keep better than most nuts, but are best stored in the refrigerator or freezer unless they will be used up within a month.

PREPARATION AND USE: These are most commonly shelled and eaten in the hand as a snack, especially as a *mezze* (appetizer) with one of the anise-flavored liqueurs, such as Ouzo and Arak. If using them in recipes, blanch the kernels in salted water and then rub them in a towel to remove their skins. Their natural green color makes these an attractive ingredient and garnish for many dishes in many parts of the world. Whole, they are used in stuffings, pilafs, stews, and pâtés, and they have a special affinity for pork. Skinned and chopped, they are used to garnish desserts such as Baklava, custards, and all manner of Middle Eastern rice dishes and pastries. Ground pistachios are used in an Afghan dessert, Abrayshum Kabaub (rolled omelet) and Sambsay Sheereen (fried pastry).

PITA BREAD

OTHER: pocket bread, *khubz, eish shami,* Arab or Syrian bread

Breads accompany every meal in the Middle East, and there are a number of varieties, with and without pockets, but flat, round pita is the most commonly known. As it bakes, it puffs quickly to form a natural pocket, which is perfect for stuffing with all kinds of salads and sandwich fillings. It is now available almost everywhere, in supermarkets, Middle Eastern bakeries and markets, and natural-food stores. You will find it made with white or whole wheat flour, sometimes sprinkled with sesame seed.

STORAGE: It can be stored at room temperature or in the refrigerator for up to 5 days, or frozen for longer storage.

PREPARATION AND USE: You may wish to freshen pita breads before serving by either steaming them or baking for a few minutes in a 350° oven. In the Middle East, these are often used, torn into pieces, to mop up delicious sauces at meals. Cut crosswise in half (which will give you 2 "pockets"), they can be filled with any description of salads and sandwich fillings. Try filling them with BASTOURMA and LABNI (see under CHEESES), for a sandwich called "Armenian Delight." They are sometimes toasted to serve as a dipper for Taramosalata (see recipe under TARAMA). We like to split pita into two circles to be buttered and sprinkled on the unbrowned side with various spices or herbs and then baked until crisp to serve as an unusual bread with salads and soups.

POMEGRANATE

OTHER: Chinese apple

FRENCH: *grenade* GERMAN: *Granatapfel* ITALIAN: *melagrana*
SPANISH: *granada*

The pomegranate is a red, smooth-skinned fruit the size of an orange that has crimson, jewel-like seeds enclosed in bitter white membrane. These are the seeds Persephone, daughter of Ceres, the Roman goddess of agriculture, ate while married, against her will, to the lord of the underworld and, according to the myth, because she ate them, she had to return to him for four months every year—and that's why we have four months of winter. The pomegranate is an ancient fruit that grows all over the Middle East and also in California so it is likely you will find it in the fall in specialty grocery stores and some supermarkets. Buy large fruits that are firm and not at all shrunken. GRENADINE (see THE FOODS OF EUROPE section) is made from these.

STORAGE: Store whole pomegranates in the refrigerator for up to 2 weeks. Cut ones should be wrapped airtight in plastic wrap for use as soon as possible. The seeds can be frozen for up to 2 weeks, after which time they become watery.

PREPARATION AND USE: These are often split to eat with your fingers, picking out each seed, as a snack, for which purpose 1 pomegranate will easily serve 2. The seeds are a popular garnish and ingredient for dishes both sweet and savory, such as Samakah Harrah, a stuffed baked fish, and atop sweet custards. In Mexico, they garnish Chiles en Nogada, peeled chiles stuffed with a sweet meat stuffing topped with a ground walnut or pecan and cream cheese sauce. The seeds of tart pomegranates are oftentimes dried in the Middle East to sprinkle over meat dishes (see ANARDANA in THE FOODS OF ASIA section). POMEGRANATE JUICE is used along with the seeds to flavor and color sauces, as in the popular stew made with chicken or duck, known as Fesanjan.

POMEGRANATE JUICE AND SYRUP

This is used in Middle Eastern sauces as a seasoning and flavoring. To obtain juice from fresh pomegranates, cut in half and juice in a juicer that has a handle to lower the top and press out the juice, or juice on a reamer as you would an orange, but take care to cover your clothes because the juice can stain. Another method is to remove the seeds from the pomegranate and squeeze them in a cheesecloth bag. Fortunately, the tart-flavored juice is widely available in Middle Eastern markets and in health food stores, so we don't have to wait for pomegranate season and juice them ourselves. In a pinch, substitute GRENADINE (see THE FOODS OF EUROPE section), using 2 tablespoons grenadine, 1 tablespoon lemon juice, and 1 tablespoon water for each 4 tablespoons pomegranate juice called for.

STORAGE: Unsweetened juice should be refrigerated; it will keep for up to 5 days. It will keep frozen for months. The more common sweetened syrup will keep indefinitely in the refrigerator.

USE: Freshly squeezed juice is often served as a breakfast drink. When sweetened with sugar, it makes a refreshing drink called Sharbat Rumman. The syrup is popularly used to add acidity to Middle Eastern dishes such as the Persian Fesanjan, which is also garnished with the seeds. It can add a sweet-and-sour taste to many dishes and, in Lebanon, it adds a tart flavor to sautéed okra.

PRESERVES

Preserves in the Middle East tend to be sweeter than American jams and jellies. You will find a wide range of them in Middle Eastern markets, including Greek rose petal (*glyko triantofallo*), Arabian citron (Roubb-al-Kabbâb), and Israeli Jaffa orange.

STORAGE: As any preserve—store in a dark place and refrigerate after opening.

USE: An assortment of preserves is offered on a tray to a guest in many Middle Eastern countries. The guest takes a spoonful of his chosen one, follows it up with a glass of water, and then wishes the hosts good health. It is customary to serve coffee or liqueurs after this small ritual. Preserves are also stirred into water to make a sweet drink, or are served as they are for dessert.

PURSLANE

OTHER: pussley or portulaca

ARABIC: *baqli* FRENCH: *pourpier* GERMAN: *Portulak* INDIAN: *kulfa* ITALIAN: *portulaca* or *procellana* LEBANESE: *farfhin* or *baqleh* SPANISH: *verdolaga*

You will not find purslane in stores, as it is considered a weed, but you may very well have one of the many varieties growing in your yard, especially around roses or tomatoes. It is a highly nourishing green with a mildly sour taste that is popular in the Middle East, Europe, and Latin America. Pick the tender leaves and flowers early in the morning or late in the afternoon when they are crisp. The tender shoots are the most delicious of all.

STORAGE: Rinse very well, wrap in paper towels, and store inside a plastic bag in the refrigerator for use within a week.

PREPARATION AND USE: Allow 1 cup per serving. Pick out and discard the seeds from the center of any clusters. In the Middle East, this is most commonly used as a salad ingredient as in the Lebanese Slatat al-Farfhin, along with tomatoes and cucumbers with a dressing of lemon juice, olive oil, and garlic. Like okra, it has a thickening effect on soups and sauces. To serve as a vegetable, simmer in salted water for 8 to 10 minutes until tender; season with butter or a mild cream sauce, or toss with bacon drippings. Drizzle with vinegar to serve as a relish.

QAMARADIN

OTHER: *amardeen*

This is an Arabic sweetmeat sold in thin sheets in Middle Eastern markets. It is made from a puree of apricots that has been spread out in a thin layer and sun- or oven-dried. You can make this at home from fresh pitted apricots that have been pureed in a blender with sugar to taste. Spread the resulting liquid ¼" to ½" deep in a shallow baking pan and dry in a low oven.

STORAGE: It will keep in the refrigerator indefinitely.

USE: These are often cut in strips to serve as a snack food or are soaked in water overnight and then eaten with sugar for breakfast. It can also serve as an easy-to-make cake or pastry filling.

QUINCE

ARABIC: *sfarjal* FRENCH: *coing* GERMAN: *Quitte* GREEK: *kythonia* ITALIAN: *cotogna* SPANISH: *membrillo*

Quinces are one of the most ancient of all fruits and are widely used throughout the Middle East and Europe. Fresh ones, which weigh about 8 ounces apiece and look like golden, pear-shaped apples, can be found occasionally in specialty produce shops during the fall, and perhaps our renewed national interest in exotic foods will result in a more abundant supply from growers. Ripe ones are yellow and always have a delicious perfume-like aroma. Take care in handling them as they bruise easily.

STORAGE: After ripening, they can be stored for up to a month in the refrigerator.

USE: Quinces must be cooked in order to be eaten, and they have a high pectin content, so they make exquisite jams and compotes (one quince is often added to a batch of other fruit preserves for that reason). They are often cooked with lamb or chicken dishes in the Middle East, added to Tagines in Morocco, and stuffed in Persian recipes. Middle Eastern quince preserves usually have rose water added as a flavoring. In Iraq, a drink is made by adding ½ teaspoon crushed dried pits to 1¼ cups of water and simmering for 5 minutes and then sweetening to taste. The pits are also chewed as a kind of "cough drop." We like quince baked in the same manner as apples and in fruit tarts.

Another popular use for quince in Europe and in Latin America is in the making of a thick, concentrated quince paste cooked with sugar, which is formed into bars and sliced to serve as a dessert, or as a topping for mild cheese. It is called *membrillate* (see ATE in THE FOODS OF LATIN AMERICA section.)

RAKI

See ANISE-FLAVORED LIQUEURS

RAS EL HANOUT

Ras el Hanout, which means, literally, "head of the shop," is an exotic aromatic spice combination, sold in Moroccan spice shops (épiceries) that varies from shop to shop, ranging in complexity from a few aromatics to up to 50 flavorings and spices. When purchased in Morocco, it probably will contain various ingredients that are purported to be powerful aphrodisiacs. It can, in Middle Eastern recipes, be used in place of the aromatic spices (cinnamon, mace, nutmeg, and allspice) called for in recipes. It is not unlike CURRY POWDER or GARAM MASALA, except for the addition of dried flowers, and either could substitute in a pinch, especially with the addition of a tiny bit of crushed lavender and rose. A simple version, containing readily available ingredients, is made as follows.

RAS EL HANOUT

1	whole nutmeg	For ¼ cup
2	6-inch sticks cinnamon, broken up	
3	dried rosebuds *or* ½ teaspoon rose water	
1	teaspoon white peppercorns *or* ground white pepper	
½	teaspoon ground mace	
½	teaspoon ground turmeric	
½	teaspoon ground ginger	
½	teaspoon paprika	
½	teaspoon cayenne (ground red pepper)	
¼	teaspoon anise seed	
6	allspice berries	
4	cardamom pods (white or green), seeds only	
2	whole cloves	
	Pinch of dried lavender	

Combine ingredients in container of electric blender and process until all ingredients are finely ground.

STORAGE: Pack into an airtight container and store in a cool, dark place or in the refrigerator for up to 6 months.

USE: Use in cooking Moroccan recipes that call for it.

RAWBI

"Rawbi" is the Arabic word for the culture or "starter" used in making yogurt, or laban as it is called in the Middle East. A fine rawbi is highly prized, going on for years and years by saving enough from each fresh batch of yogurt to make a new batch, though homemade yogurt, after 20 or 30 batches, begins to have a fermented taste. It is as commonly borrowed by neighbors, like our proverbial cup of sugar. When you find particularly fine yogurt, reserve ¼ cup of it to use as a rawbi for making a quart of yogurt.

RICE

ARABIC: *roz* GREEK: *rizi* PERSIAN: *chilau* TURKISH: *pirinc*

Long-grain rice is a staple dish served with almost every meal in the Middle East except in Morocco where bread is the favored starch (Cous Cous is usually a Friday lunch dish). Some rather rare Persian rices can be purchased in bulk in Middle Eastern markets, including *domsiah*, which is very expensive, *darbori*, and several others. BASMATI rice (see under RICE in THE FOODS OF ASIA section) is popular there as well.

STORAGE: Store all types of rice in an airtight container in a cool, dark place. Dry rice will easily keep for a year. Leftover cooked rice can be cooled, fluffed with a fork, and refrigerated or frozen. Thaw if frozen, and sprinkle with 1 tablespoon water per cup of rice to reheat slowly in a heavy saucepan or in the oven. [Or fluff and put in sieve or colander over 1″ boiling water in pot (do not let rice touch water) and steam for 5–7 minutes.]

PREPARATION AND USE: (Directions for cooking plain long-grain and *basmati* rice appear in THE FOODS OF ASIA section.) Middle Eastern cooks usually add some butter, SÂMNA, or oil to rice when cooking and seldom use water as the cooking liquid. Most often a pilaf is made with the addition of raisins, nuts, spices, and various broths, and it is often colored yellow with saffron or turmeric. In Iran, rice is made into either a dish called Chelo (plain rice topped with various other foods and often formed into a ring) or Pollo, in which rice is mixed with other ingredients, pilaf-style, and baked in a buttered dish to form a crisp bottom crust. Rice is served in some form with almost every Arabic meal, some diners choosing to eat it at the beginning and others waiting until the end of the meal. Armenian Kufta are stuffed lamb meatballs, which are served with rice. Rice is used in the making of rice puddings such as Afhan Daygtcha, flavored with cardamom, and Muhallabia.

ROSE PETALS

IN MOROCCO: *rous el word* IN TUNISIA: *chachiouard*

Dried rose petals (usually from pink damask roses) are an essential ingredient in Tunisian cooking. They can be purchased in some Middle Eastern markets, and can be ordered by mail (see SHOPPING SOURCES). Greek markets sell a Greek rose petal jam, *glyko triantofallo,* which is very sweet.

STORAGE: Airtight, in a cool, dark place, it will keep for up to 6 months.

USE: Powdered rose petals are added to spice mixtures such as RAS EL HANOUT used in Tunisian lamb and fish Tagines, and in Cous Cous recipes. In Iranian cooking, they are mixed with mint and cucumbers and served in cold soup with yogurt.
 The jam makes an exotic spread on freshly baked breads.

ROSE WATER OR ESSENCE
See THE FOODS OF ASIA section

SAHLAB
OTHER: *salep* or *salop*

IRAQI: *baraghoush*

 This powdered starch, extracted from tubers of any of various male orchids, is available in bulk in Middle Eastern markets. Substitute 2½ teaspoons ARROWROOT POWDER (see THE FOODS OF ASIA section) or 1 tablespoon cornstarch for 1 teaspoon of sahlab in recipes for cooked food.

STORAGE: It will keep indefinitely in an airtight container in a cool place.

USE: In Greece, this is mixed with hot water to make a popular bland-tasting drink. In Lebanon, it thickens a pudding of the same name, flavored with either orange-flower water or rose-water and decorated with pistachios. Like KISHK, it is used as a thickener for stews, but doesn't have the tart flavor of kishk.

SÂMNA

 This is the Egyptian version of Indian GHEE (see THE FOODS OF ASIA section) made by slowly boiling butter (often made from buffalo milk) until the water has evaporated and the milk solids have cooked away. The result is a cooking oil with a butter flavor. You will find a cow's milk version in many Middle Eastern markets. In Palestine, there is a variant called *samneh,* which has a reddish color. In Morocco, SMEN is used.

STORAGE: Because the milk solids have been cooked away this can be stored indefinitely in a cool place without refrigeration.

PREPARATION AND USE: To make sâmna, boil butter slowly until the milk solids have browned and are sticking to the sides of the pan. Strain twice through a damp towel or cheesecloth to remove every last bit of milk solid. This is used as an all-purpose oil for sautéeing, in stews, etc., but only in dishes that are to be served warm. Butter and margarine are used as well, but they burn rapidly in cooking because they contain milk solids.

SEEDS

A variety of seeds, such as melon, pumpkin, watermelon, and squash, are sold in Middle Eastern markets by bulk.

STORAGE: In an airtight container they will keep indefinitely.

PREPARATION AND USE: Seeds are roasted and salted to serve as snacks. In Greece, they are called *pasatempo* (to pass the time) and are sold by street vendors of the same name. To roast the seeds at home, wash and dry them well. Sprinkle with salt and bake in a shallow pan at 375°, stirring often, until golden.

SEMOLINA

See THE FOODS OF EUROPE section

SESAME SEEDS

OTHER: *benne*

GREEK: *sousame* IN MOROCCO: *jinjelan*

General information appears in the HERBS, SPICES, AND SEASONING BLENDS section. In the Middle East, these are toasted to sprinkle as a garnish over cooked dishes, but are perhaps most widely used to make TAHINI and as a source of oil for cooking.

SMEN

To make smen, cow's or sheep's butter is boiled until all water has evaporated and the milk solids have cooked away (see SÂMNA). The remaining liquid is salted, and stored in earthenware jugs. Alternatively, it may be strongly flavored with ZA'ATAR (see HERBS, SPICES, AND SEASONING BLENDS section), which also keeps it from spoiling. Paula Wolfert, in her book *Couscous and Other Good Food From Morocco,* gives directions for making several variations. It looks like Gorgonzola cheese, and tastes a bit like it, too. In Morocco, you can buy smen that is 1½ years old—in fact, it is chic there to claim your smen is *years* old.

STORAGE: In Morocco, this is stored in earthenware jugs in a cool place for years. It will keep in your refrigerator indefinitely.

USE: Smen is used as an all-purpose cooking oil for Moroccan Tagines. It is used in Tangier in the making of Cous Cous with lamb, saffron, cinnamon, raisins, pumpkin, and almonds.

SMID
OTHER: *smead*

Smid is finely ground SEMOLINA (see THE FOODS OF EUROPE section for general information), which can be purchased in bulk in Middle Eastern markets.

STORAGE: Like any grain, it will keep indefinitely in an airtight container in a cool place.

USE: Most commonly used in cakes and in doughs for filled cookies, and toasted in butter to make confections.

SUMAC
ARMENIAN: *soumakh* GERMAN: *Sumach* ITALIAN: *sommacco*
LEBANESE: *summaq* SPANISH: *zumaque*

A tart ground spice made from sumac berries that looks like chili powder. It is an important souring agent, especially in Lebanon, and will be found in all Middle Eastern markets. When mixed with thyme it is called ZATAR (see SEASONING BLENDS). Should you have access to a "red," "elm leaf," or Sicilian sumac tree that has ripe, hairy red berries, you have your own source of supply. Avoid other sumacs, because they won't have the proper flavor, and especially those with white berries, because they are the poisonous variety of sumac.

STORAGE: As any ground spice.

USE: This is often used to lend a sour taste to grilled meats and kababs in place of lemon juice. It is commonly sprinkled over tomato and cucumber salads or dips such as Baba Ghanoush (made with charred eggplant) or Hummus (pureed chick-peas), with an added drizzling of olive oil. Sprinkle it over any Middle Eastern dish where an astringent taste is desirable.

TABIL

Tabil is a Tunisian combination consisting of equal portions of red pepper flakes, toasted caraway seeds, toasted coriander seeds, and minced garlic.

STORAGE: Unless you wish to make it fresh for each use, stir some oil into it to dampen the spices and prevent the garlic from drying out, and then store in the refrigerator indefinitely.

USE: Tabil is commonly used in flavoring meat dishes. It is sautéed in fat or added to the liquid in which meat is cooked at the beginning of the cooking time.

TAHINI
OTHER: *tahina, taheeni*

IRAQI: *rashi*

An oily paste of ground raw white (hulled) sesame seeds, which is popular throughout the Middle East. It is found in many supermarkets today, in natural-food stores, and in all Middle Eastern markets. It can be made with some success at home by grinding the seeds with a small amount of water in a blender or food processor but it will not ever be as smooth as the commercial product. Chinese SESAME SEED PASTE (see THE FOODS OF ASIA section) found in Asian markets, is much stronger in flavor because the seeds are roasted.

STORAGE: This becomes rancid very rapidly, so refrigerate or freeze it after opening and plan to use it up within a month or so.

PREPARATION AND USE: This can be served as is for a dipping sauce, but is usually used as an ingredient in the making of all kinds of dips and sauces, particularly the ubiquitous Hummus Bi Tahina (see HUMMUS) which is a blend of pureed chick-peas, garlic, and lemon served as a sauce or a dip for bread with many Middle Eastern meals. Always stir tahini well to reblend it with its oil, which has a tendency to float on top. When making any kind of tahini sauce, always blend water with the tahini first, and then add the required amount of lemon juice, which whitens the sauce. If it lumps with the addition of liquid, just add more liquid gradually until it smooths out.

TARAMA
OTHER: *atarama*, salted carp roe, "caviar"

These tiny orange eggs (roe) of the grey mullet, tuna, or carp are sold in bottles in all Greek and most Middle Eastern markets. In some Greek markets, tarama is sold directly from the barrel. This is the same thing as BOTARGO, but is packaged differently and is usually much moister, which makes it a great deal easier to use in sauces. Even though it is a type of caviar, it is not expensive.

STORAGE: Because this is highly salted it will keep for months in the refrigerator, even after opening.

PREPARATION AND USE: Soak the tarama in cold water to cover for 5 to 10 minutes before using to rid it of some of its salt. Use just a bit as a seasoning for mayonnaise to be used as a sauce with poached fish or as a dip for raw vegetables. In Greece, this is most commonly made into an hors d'oeuvre spread by beating it with olive oil, lemon, garlic, and fresh bread that has been soaked in water and then squeezed out and torn into pieces until it has a consistency almost like mayonnaise. The same mixture can be formed into small fritters, Taramo Keftides, and fried to serve warm as an appetizer with lemon wedges. The basic dip is made as follows:

TARAMOSALATA

For 2 cups, or approximately 8 servings

Serve this creamy, pale pink puree as a dip with raw cucumbers or pieces of PITA BREAD. Or use it as a salad dressing or as a spread for buttered bread for canapés.

    4 ounces tarama
       Cold water for soaking
    4 slices firm white bread, crusts removed (Pepperidge Farm
          is a superior brand)
   ⅓ cup cold water
    1 small white onion *or* the white part of 4 scallions, finely
          chopped
   ⅓ cup fresh lemon juice
    1 cup olive oil
    1 teaspoon chopped fresh dill (optional)
       Salt and white pepper, to taste
       Minced parsley, to garnish

Place tarama in a small bowl, cover with cold water, and let soak for 10 minutes to remove excess salt; drain. Meanwhile, tear the bread in pieces, sprinkle with ⅓ cup cold water, and let soak. Then squeeze out as much of the moisture as possible.

Place the tarama, bread, onion, and lemon juice in the container of an electric food processor or blender. Puree for a few seconds; then add the oil through the feed tube or lid. Stop the motor often to scrape the sides of the bowl, pushing the mixture into the blades. Add the dill and continue processing until the mixture is very pale pink and creamy, and has the consistency of mayonnaise. Taste for seasoning and add salt and white pepper as needed. Chill thoroughly, during which time it will thicken considerably.

Serve very cold, sprinkled with fresh parsley.

TO PREPARE IN ADVANCE: This can be stored in the refrigerator for up to 5 days.

TSIRI

OTHER: *tsere*

Tsiri are slender dried fish, approximately 5″ long, sold in Greek markets. They have a flavor and consistency comparable to BOMBAY DUCK (see THE FOODS OF ASIA section).

STORAGE: They will keep indefinitely stored airtight in a cool, dry place.

PREPARATION AND USE: These are generally grilled (preferably outdoors, as they have a very unpleasant odor), and then marinated in olive oil and lemon juice to serve as an appetizer with crackers.

WARKA

IN ALGERIA: *dioul*   IN TUNISIA: *malsouqua*

Warka is a Moroccan pastry used in that country to make Bstilla, in Tunisia to make Brik, and in Algeria to make a variety of fried pastries called Diouls. It is not sold commercially, but Paula Wolfert, authority on Moroccan food, discovered that it is actually the same thing as Chinese Spring Roll Skins, but made with wheat starch instead of semolina flour or all-purpose flour. Many assume it is the same thing as FILO PASTRY, which can be used as an adequate substitute. Chinese Spring Roll Skins are not recommended as a substitute in making Bstilla, as they toughen in cooking, but can be used for Briks. We suggest Paula's book, *Couscous and Other Good Foods From Morocco*, for an enlightening discussion of the intricacies of making and using this dough.

YOGURT

ARAB: *laban zabadi* ARMENIAN: *madzoon* GREEK: *yiaourti*
IRANIAN: *mast* LEBANESE AND SYRIAN: *laban* TURKISH: *yoğurt*

Yogurt, which is the easiest of all dairy products to digest, seems to have originated in the Middle East, where it is an essential part of the diet. It is interesting to note that the Biblical reference to the Land of Promise, which flowed with milk and honey, is more accurately translated as flowing with yogurt and honey. People make it in their homes almost as a family ritual, from the milk of cows, sheep, goats, and even camels. It is believed to have great curative qualities and to promote good health and longevity. In the United States, we are fortunate to be able to buy excellent yogurt in supermarkets and natural-food stores, as well as yogurt starters to make our own. If you decide to dabble in yogurt making, try to find some Bulgarian yogurt or starter, which will give your yogurt an exceptionally fine flavor.

STORAGE: Freshly made yogurt can be stored for up to 3 weeks in the refrigerator.

USE: Yogurt has infinite uses in Middle Eastern (and Indian) cooking. It is served plain as a sauce with meat, vegetables, or pilaf; thinned with water to serve as a drink; made into a delicious Lebanese cheese called LABNI (see under CHEESES); made into soup and into sweetened desserts and dessert sauces; and, when stabilized with cornstarch, used to thicken stews and other cooked dishes. The Lebanese mix it with BULGHUR WHEAT and ferment the mixture to make KISHK.

Yogurt can be stabilized (prevented from curdling) for sauces by whisking it with cornstarch, and then bringing to a simmer and cooking for a minute or two over low heat just until thickened. Use 2 teaspoons cornstarch for each 1 cup yogurt. In making stews, the meat is removed, and the meat juices, sautéed onions, garlic, and seasonings are then folded into the thickened sauce and simmered briefly to blend the flavors.

ZA'ATAR

LATIN: *Origanum cyriacum*

There is always confusion over this and ZATAR, especially in Moroccan recipes. This is a Moroccan herb, and is a cross between thyme, oregano (wild marjoram) and marjoram. It is sold dried in markets in Morocco, but will not be found in this country. Substitute a mixture of the three herbs in equal amounts.

USE: Za'atar grows wild everywhere in Morocco. It is known to have antiseptic powers and has a calming effect on the digestion. It is used as a flavoring for Tagines (stews) and for butter to be used in cooking.

ZATAR

OTHER NAMES: *zahtar, zatore, zaatar*

This seasoning blend of sumac, thyme, marjoram, and salt is available in Middle Eastern markets.

STORAGE: As any spice.

USE: Sprinkle as a sort of seasoning salt over kebabs, breads, dips, and LABNI (see CHEESES in this section). It adds a yellow color, besides a tart flavoring.

THE FOODS
OF
REGIONAL
AMERICA

A NATION OF NATIONS

Walt Whitman, the great American poet who spent his lifetime celebrating the dignity of the individual and the brotherhood of humankind, understood well the structure of America when he wrote, "Here is not merely a nation, but a teeming nation of nations." We are all the descendants of immigrants—even our "native" Americans, the Indians, came from someplace else.

For the most part, the motives for immigration, though sometimes political and religious, were chiefly economic. Millions of Europeans settled into ethnic pockets in our huge northeastern industrial cities. Each group had its own particular foods and they clung tightly to the security and comfort of their Old World cooking traditions.

A number of dishes, and sometimes whole cuisines, would become associated with certain cities and regions of America: Cioppino, the Italian Fisherman's Wharf Stew in San Francisco, the Polish sausages of Chicago, the cuisine of the French Huguenots in Charleston, the cooking of the Acadians who settled in the marshland parishes of Louisiana, after being exiled by the British from Nova Scotia. But we have gone too far south too quickly. Let's go back to the beginning, to the English in their "New England."

The Pilgrims, who landed in the dead of winter in 1620, were by no means hardy explorers or even hunters. They were London tradespeople who knew nothing of hunting or fishing, or even berry picking. The credit for their survival must be given to three basic food items completely native to the North American continent: corn, beans, and squash.

The European wheat and pea crops that the Pilgrims planted failed miserably; however, the three Indian items, planted as the Indians suggested, prospered. These three fundamental items are still cornerstones of the American diet. For example, simple Indian corn was nourishingly good just boiled. The English quickly learned, though, that when it was dried and ground into powder, and then mixed with hot water and honey, it would produce a "hasty pudding." This hasty pudding, if left to cool overnight, hardened into a semi-rigid mass that could then be cut, sliced, and fried, drizzled with maple syrup or honey, and served for breakfast as a hot panbread. The northeasterners also made a type of stew of corn and lima beans, which still retains its original Indian name—succotash. Over the next hundreds of years, New Englanders skillfully innovated with over twenty popular varieties of fresh and saltwater fish, from herring, mackerel, and blue fish to haddock and cod. Codfish from Newfoundland that has been salted and dried in the same manner for the past 300 years is the main ingredient of the stern Cape Cod Boiled Dinner. Also easily found on most New England menus today is thickly sliced brown bread served with pots of oven-baked Boston beans, broiled lobsters, steamed clams, and a "white" French stew called a *chaudre,* which the New Englanders renamed chowder. In their seasons, you can find Cranberry Muffins and Blueberry Pancakes and, if you're very lucky, somebody's Beach Plum Jam. The English adapted very well to their "New England." Their dishes adapted well, too. For example, their sweet custard and spongecake dessert called Trifle, when of necessity converted to the contents of the American larder, resulted in a custard-based Maple Bread Pudding.

It wasn't long after the English settled New England that they were joined by the Dutch, who settled New Amsterdam (New York). Trailblazers crossed the Appalachian Mountains west, and the Germans from the south of Germany with their livestock, seed, and farm equipment set up the model for the American farm near Lancaster, Pennsylvania. Their descendants are known today as the Pennsylvania Dutch (originally "Deutsch"). By about 1880, the dispersion of the American immigrant was pretty much complete and the location of the center of the country's population lay about 100 miles east of Chicago.

Today many Americans are still clustered in the central eastern sections of industrial America. And, as each of these cities is in itself a miniature United Nations, it is not surprising to find that there is less "foreign" food prejudice here than there is abroad. In our celebrations of births, weddings, Bar Mitzvahs, and wakes, we have become better acquainted with each other's foods. The Italians serve with pride their Sicilian pizza with crisp green peppers and mushrooms. The Hungarians offer their goulash with dumplings, and also their stuffed whole cabbage with sauerkraut. And the Czech-Americans, aside from their noodles and breads, give us a robust duck with sauerkraut dressing. Along with their standard white and wheat loaves, American markets have found they can also sell Lithuanian potato bread, Czech caraway rye bread, and Armenian pocket bread with sesame seeds. The northeastern seaboard of America, as well as the mid-western heartland, is well supplied with Old World dishes. In the nonindustrial South, however, the table is different.

The immediate potential of America's Southland was agricultural; consequently it attracted few immigrating European workers. Instead, it attracted French, English, and Spanish planters from the Caribbean. And these planters brought in slaves from West Africa to provide the labor for the huge plantations. The foods of the South were based upon this ethnic mix overlaying a simple Indian corn, bean, and squash cuisine. Corn was the basic staple and it is difficult even today to imagine a southern meal without either corn bread, corn dodgers, hush puppies, corn pones, Pan Flats, spoon bread, johnnycakes, hoecakes, or grits. Other memorable southern specialties include Fried Chicken, She-crab Soup, Deviled Crabs, Fried Catfish, black-eyed peas, turnip greens, ham, bacon, Candied Sweet Potatoes, Pecan Pies, and pecans cooked in a brown sugar syrup to make confections called Pralines. New Orleans and the Louisiana bayous have a special magic all of their own with a French influence that has created the fish dish, Pompano en Papillote. And the exiled Acadians from Nova Scotia introduced a distinctive Cajun cuisine that was seasoned with ground sassafras leaves (filé) and contributed dishes such as Jambalaya (rice simmered with assorted meats and spices) and Gumbo (a mixed ingredient stew).

In 1848, gold was discovered in California and, thirteen years after that, came the Civil War. At this point the South started its slow transformation into an industrial society, adding a minor German and Italian influence to its already well-established cuisine.

The best and fastest way to get to the California gold fields was by water, but it cost less to travel by oxcart. This mass migration of easterners to the West caused another giant stirring of the American melting pot. Hundreds of thousands of these adventurers of all national backgrounds stayed in the West and added their particular ethnic food specialties to the existing Indian-Mexican-Spanish-Chinese-Russian-Scandinavian cuisines. And those who returned to the East brought back with them a newly expanded dimension of taste, and recipes for Burritos (rolled wheat tortillas with beans and meat filling), Chile con Queso (a peppery cheese and green chili dip), abalone steaks, guacamole (avocado dip), buffalo roasts, Sour Cherry Pie, Chop Suey, Alaska King crab, smoked sockeye salmon, Swedish Pancakes, Norwegian Flatbread, and Kissel, a glorious Russian fruit dessert.

There was a time when America enjoyed a culinarily distinctive geography, when it was possible to tell where people were from by what they ate. Today, the purity of our ethnic tables has begun to blur or, rather, to blend into a homogeneous medley of "Americanized" foods, creatively using the ingredients to be found in the following pages.

ASHES, CULINARY

We refer here to the charred remains of certain plants used by native American Indians to color, flavor, and add mineral content to foods. The ashes, mixed with water, make a highly alkaline liquid which is added to recipes in which BLUE CORN is an ingredient, and stabilizes the blue color of these foods. The Creek and Seminole indians use hickory, the Navajos use juniper, and the Hopis use *chamisa* (four-winged saltbush). The ashes are not sold commercially, and are mentioned here for their intrinsic interest.

STORAGE: Stored in an airtight container, it will keep indefinitely.

PREPARATION AND USE: To make culinary ashes, bushes are cut down, cleaned of extraneous debris, and stacked on top of each other in a cleared outdoor spot to a height of five feet. The bushes are then burnt until only ashes remain. The ashes are sifted before storage.

The ashes are always used in making Piki, a tissue-thin blue corn bread cooked on a hot stone that is unique to Hopi culture.

BACON AND BACON DRIPPINGS

Bacon is a cured and usually smoked meat product made from the belly of pigs. Bacon and bacon drippings are often called for as ingredients in regional recipes. There are many more types of bacon available to the consumer than the pre-sliced packaged type found in every supermarket, and the flavor varies depending on how it was smoked. Bacon that has been cured and not smoked has white fat and paler meat than smoked bacon, which has yellow fat and rose-colored meat.

There is a good deal of controversy over the potential health dangers to the consumer from the addition of nitrates and nitrites used during the curing process to enhance both color and flavor of pork products. There is some medical evidence that these substances are carcinogenic, so their use is restricted by law to limited amounts. Many of the health-conscious avoid them altogether, and bacon cured without their use is available in some health food stores and specialty meat markets. Our advice is to read labels, as these items must be listed on packaged products. When purchasing slab bacon from smokehouses, ask whether or not these chemicals were used (probably they were).

Your choice of which bacon to use in a dish will, of course, make a difference in the authentic taste of a regional recipe, and often these recipes specify certain types. Slab bacon is smokier in flavor than packaged super-market types, and is worth the trouble it takes to seek it out for special dishes. Listings of the different types follow this entry.

STORAGE: If smoked in one piece, bacon can be stored for months, though it may form surface mold. Sliced packaged bacon, stored in the refrigerator, will keep for up to a week or, if frozen, for up to a month. Cooked bacon can be refrigerated for 5 days or frozen for 2 months. Canadian bacon, especially if pre-sliced in packages, is more perishable, and should be refrigerated for use within 3 or 4 days, or frozen for use within a month.

PREPARATION AND USE: When bacon is called for as an ingredient in a recipe, it is usually diced or cut in pieces and partially cooked. Other ingredients are then added to it and the bacon drippings. If the drippings are not to be used, save them for other cooking uses. Remove the sediment by pouring the warm drippings through several layers of cheesecloth or a clean kitchen towel. Store in the refrigerator to use in the cooking of beans, in making corn bread, and in many dishes in which a smoky bacon flavor is desirable.

Bacon is America's most popular breakfast meat. It is usually sliced to be pan-fried until crisp, drained on paper towels, and served as an accompaniment to eggs, waffles, Cornmeal Mush, French Toast. In the United States, it is often sautéed with calf's liver and onions, and used in the cooking of lima beans. Cured (but not smoked) bacon is often used to line terrines and casseroles for meat loaves and pâtés.

Crisp chopped bacon and the pan drippings are used by the Pennsylvania Dutch in a hot, sweet salad dressing thickened with cornstarch, and also in Hot Potato Pancakes. They also add bits of crisp bacon to a basic batter to make Bacon Muffins. Manhattan Clam Chowder contains potatoes, celery, tomatoes, bacon, and thyme. Thick sliced bacon is used in the cooking of cabbage in the South: the bacon is chopped into small pieces, rendered until crisp, and then removed from the pan; onion slices are then sautéed in the drippings, and chopped cabbage added to cook for 10 minutes. The reserved crisp bacon pieces serve as a garnish for the finished dish.

Bacon or salt pork is often used in recipes for Baked Beans. A Hawaiian appetizer, Rumaki, wraps strips of bacon around chicken livers and water chestnuts to be broiled and served on toothpicks. The Hopi Indians have long cooked cubed bacon with pinto beans to serve with Blue Corn Tortillas and a green vegetable as a main meal. Bacon drippings are also used in cooking dried sweet corn on the reservations. Pueblo Indians cook bacon and greens with pinto beans and place the pot on an asbestos mat for especially slow cooking. Crumbled cooked bacon can be rubbed into any type of beef to be roasted to add flavor, or combined with barbecue sauce to use in basting spareribs.

CANADIAN BACON

This is not the fat-streaked smoky "bacon" we think of as bacon, but a lean, cured and smoked pork loin roll, from the eye of the pork loin, available in most supermarkets. It has almost no fat and is more like ham than bacon. It is most often used, thinly sliced and baked or sautéed, for dishes like Eggs Benedict (poached eggs on a slice of Canadian bacon on a buttered English muffin, covered with hollandaise sauce). It lacks the fat of most bacons so, to prevent toughening when pan-frying, add a bit of oil to the pan, and slash the rind to prevent curling. A whole piece can be cooked and glazed like ham and served in the same manner, allowing approximately 5 ounces per serving.

COUNTRY-CURED BACON

This type of bacon is sold in some gourmet specialty shops and in the same places as country-cured hams, such as SMITHFIELD and KENTUCKY hams (see under HAMS, COUNTRY STYLE). It is salty, quite strong-flavored, and more expensive than regular bacon. Because of its high salt content, it keeps longer, but the salt called for in recipes in which it is used should be adjusted accordingly.

SLAB BACON

This term simply means that the cured and smoked bacon has not been sliced. Many people prefer to buy bacon this way, cutting away the rind and slicing it to the desired thickness as needed, believing that it tastes better. It does keep longer than sliced bacon, for months actually, because less of the surface is exposed to air. In visiting specialty meat markets around the country, we have found some delicious examples of slab bacon. One that stands out especially in our memory is a black-pepper-coated bacon in Oregon. The rind from slab bacon is cooked with various greens in Southern "soul" (soul-food) cooking.

SLICED BACON

Packaged sliced bacon is sold in three thicknesses in every supermarket: "Regular" has 16 to 20 slices per pound, "thin" has about 36, and "thick" has about 12. It is the type of bacon usually used in recipes unless others are specified.

BEACH PLUM

A small wild plum that grows on bushes in sandy soil close to the shoreline on the Atlantic coast, from New England to Virginia. The trees bloom in the springtime on Cape Cod, and the plums ripen in September and October, at which time their skin color turns from pink to dark purple. The flesh is juicy when ripe, but the thick, deep purple skin is too sour to be eaten raw. They were appreciated by the Indians of the Atlantic Coast because they were not eaten by birds. Beach plums and jelly made from them are sold in New England and along the coast of the northern Atlantic states in local markets and at roadside stands.

STORAGE: Store ripe plums in the refrigerator for use within a few days. Underripe plums can be ripened at room temperature and then refrigerated.

PREPARATION AND USE: The fruit, minus its sour skin and hard seed, can be eaten raw, but is not particularly flavorful. The primary use for these plums is in making jams and jellies used as a spread for bread. Six cups of beach plums to 6 cups of sugar is the usual proportion specified. The pit is usually removed with the rounded end of a hairpin through the stem end. Ripe plums don't have enough natural pectin to set the preserves, so some underripe ones are usually added to the kettle for their additional pectin. The preserves are often served as a condiment, like cranberry sauce, with roast duck or pork.

BEANS

Beans and corn were the Colonists' first vegetables. Dried beans, called "pease" by the Colonists, were traded by the local Indians. In the early days, because there was no refrigeration, beans were often simmered slowly for several days until they could be eaten. Beans were often "parched" by soaking in salt water and heating on hot sand, to serve as a snack and hunting ration.

General purchasing information, storage, and basic cooking directions for dried beans are described under BEANS, DRIED, in THE FOODS OF LATIN AMERICA section. Following are the beans, dried and fresh, most commonly called for in American regional recipes.

BLACK BEANS

See under BEANS, DRIED, in THE FOODS OF LATIN AMERICA section

BLACK-EYED PEA

OTHER: yellow-eyed pea, cow pea

Because these tiny oval beans with a black (or sometimes yellow) spot on their inner curve came originally from Africa, general information on purchasing, storage, and preparation will be found in THE FOODS OF AFRICA section under BLACK-EYED PEA. They have an earthy flavor and are an important part of soul food cooking in America's southern states, where they are often called "cow peas" because of their original use as animal fodder. They are sold in most every supermarket both dried and canned, and are occasionally available fresh in the summertime, either shelled or still in their tough pods.

USE: Almost invariably, these are cooked in the United States with some sort of flavorful pork, be it ham hocks, bacon, or salt pork. In the South, they are served in a rather soupy state with their liquid, which is called "pot likker," and hot corn bread is the traditional accompaniment. It is a southern tradition to cook black-eyed peas with hog jowls to serve before noon on New Year's Day—it is supposed to bring good luck. A famous southern dish called Hopping John combines them with rice, hot peppers, and salt pork. They often appear in soups, casseroles, and bean salads. Yellow-eyed peas are used in Southern Baked Beans, with salt pork, brown sugar, molasses, mustard, vinegar, onions, and garlic.

CHICK-PEAS

See under BEANS in THE FOODS OF THE MIDDLE EAST section

CRANBERRY BEANS

OTHER: shellouts, shell beans (in Ohio and Indiana)

Fresh pods containing cream-colored beans with red streaks are available in the Midwest and New England during a very brief season in the summer. They have a nutlike flavor and turn a creamy white and lose their streaks as they are cooked. You may be able to find them in a fancy-produce market, but a Latin American or Hungarian grocery store is a more likely source because they are especially popular in those cuisines. Dried cranberry beans, already removed from their pods, are more readily available. Much of America's supply of dried beans is exported to Italy, where they are used in Minestrone. PINTO BEANS, and even PINK BEANS (see under BEANS, DRIED, in THE FOODS OF LATIN AMERICA section), can be substituted for dried cranberry beans in most recipes with little difference in taste or texture. They are plumper than pinto beans and have very tough outer skins.

STORAGE: Fresh beans can be stored in a paper bag in the crisper of the refrigerator for up to 4 days. They should be shelled from their pods and cooked as soon as possible for best flavor.

PREPARATION AND USE: Buy 3 pounds of fresh cranberry beans in their pods for 4 servings. The outer pods are tough, so you will find it easiest to get inside if you peel a strip with a vegetable peeler from the outer curved edge of the pod. Shell them, and use a small knife to make a cut at the inner

632

curve of the bean so it will cook more quickly. Place in a pot with a generous amount of water and cook just until tender, 10 to 20 minutes. Drain and add seasonings, preferably only butter, salt, and pepper.

One pound of dried beans will serve 4 to 6. The dried beans are cooked like any bean. In New England, they are made into a dish called Cranberry Bean Succotash with onions, corn, and cream.

GREAT NORTHERN BEANS

These rather large, plump white beans, grown mostly in the Midwest, are widely available. They have a mild flavor and mealy texture. They can be used interchangeably with other white beans including CANNELLINI (see under BEANS, DRIED, in THE FOODS OF EUROPE section).

USE: This is an excellent bean to use in all kinds of dishes that call for white beans, from the French bean and sausage casserole, Cassoulet, to hearty vegetable soups and baked bean dishes. They are often used in Baked Beans, though not as often as NAVY BEANS. In Kentucky, they are cooked with Bourbon and coffee. When pureed as in the following recipe, they are a sophisticated accompaniment to roast meats or chicken.

WHITE BEAN PUREE

1	pound (about 2½ cups) great northern beans (or substitute NAVY BEANS)	For 8 servings
7	cups water	
2	medium carrots, scraped	
1	large onion, stuck with 1 whole clove	
2	cloves garlic, peeled	
1½	teaspoons chopped fresh thyme leaves *or* ½ teaspoon dried, crumbled	
4	tablespoons butter	
1	cup heavy (whipping) cream	
2	teaspoons salt	
	White pepper to taste	
	Freshly grated nutmeg, to garnish	

Rinse and pick over the beans. Place in a saucepan of at least 4-quart capacity with 7 cups of cold water. Bring to a boil and cook for 2 minutes. Remove from the heat, cover, and let stand for 1 hour.

Add the carrots, onion, garlic, and thyme to the pot, and simmer slowly, covered, for 2 hours or until the beans are tender. Drain and reserve the cooking liquid. Remove the clove and place beans, carrots, onion, and garlic in a food mill or electric food processor, 2 cupfuls at a time, and puree.

Return the mixture to the saucepan and beat in the butter, cream, and seasonings, beating until the mixture has the consistency of mashed potatoes. Reheat, stirring constantly, just until hot.

Serve hot, sprinkled lightly with freshly grated nutmeg.

TO PREPARE IN ADVANCE: This will keep in the refrigerator for up to 3 days. Reheat gently in a double boiler, thinning the mixture if necessary with the reserved liquid from cooking the beans.

KIDNEY BEANS

White kidney beans are the famous Italian CANNELLINI (see under BEANS, DRIED, in THE FOODS OF EUROPE section), but are seldom seen in this country. Red kidney beans, with their meaty flavor, are one of our country's most popular beans, and are also a favorite bean in many European countries. They are considered the world's second most important bean, second only to SOYBEANS (see under BEANS, DRIED, in THE FOODS OF ASIA section). The darkest colored ones are usually canned, the paler ones dried. They are grown in California, Michigan, and New York, and are sold in all supermarkets, either dried or canned.

USE: At one time, Hopi Indians used a paste of the cooked beans instead of pine pitch for gluing turquoise into jewelry. Red kidney beans are commonly used in delicatessen salads and are often used in preference to red beans or pinto beans for Chile con Carne (often made with venison in Texas), preferably as a side dish so diners can add to their own taste, and in Southwestern Chili Beans, combined with Jack cheese, chili powder, and fresh CILANTRO (see CORIANDER in the HERBS, SPICES, AND SEASONING BLENDS section). Their meaty flavor makes them particularly suitable for cooking with sausages or serving with barbecued meats. We enjoy them in the following salad.

FOUR BEAN SALAD

For 10 to 12 servings

Our version of what has become a classic Western dish.

1   cup dried CHICK-PEAS, rinsed and soaked
1   cup dried NAVY BEANS, rinsed and soaked
5   teaspoons vegetable oil
1   cup dried red kidney beans, rinsed and soaked
1   (10-ounce) package frozen "baby" lima beans
¾   cup olive oil
3   tablespoons wine vinegar or lemon juice

634

1 teaspoon sugar
8 scallions, finely sliced, including the green shoots
2 cloves garlic, minced
½ cup minced parsley

Drain the chick-peas and place in a pan with 6 cups water and 1 tablespoon oil. Simmer, covered, 45 minutes; then add the drained navy beans, and continue simmering just until both are tender but not bursting, about 1 more hour. Add boiling water if they seem dry. Meanwhile, drain the kidney beans and simmer them separately in 3 cups water with 2 teaspoons oil for about 1½ hours until they are tender. Cook the baby limas according to package directions just until crisp-tender. Drain all the beans and place in a large mixing bowl. In a small bowl, whisk together the remaining ingredients and pour over the hot beans. Toss them gently in the dressing; cool, and then chill.

For best flavor, serve at room temperature.

TO PREPARE IN ADVANCE: This can be refrigerated for up to 4 days. After 24 hours, the salad can be freshened with a sprinkling of chopped parsley before serving.

LIMA BEANS

OTHER: butter beans (in the South), Madagascar beans

These are large or small, flat, kidney-shaped beans that range in color from pale green to tan. There are also yellow, red, and black varieties, which are not sold commercially but which are cultivated on Indian reservations. Fresh limas, either "baby" or the larger "Fordhook," are sold in some supermarkets most of the year, and especially during their peak season in the summer. Look for fresh looking, crisp pods. Shelled fresh limas are sold as well—their skins should be tender, not tough. More widely available are frozen or canned limas—the frozen are far better than the canned.

STORAGE: Fresh limas should be stored in their pods in the refrigerator for use within 3 days, and should be shelled just before use. Cooked or canned limas, after opening, can be stored for up to 4 days in the refrigerator.

PREPARATION AND USE: Buy 3 pounds unshelled limas for 4 servings. Cook fresh shelled limas in salted water just to cover for 10 minutes or so, just until tender. Frozen limas should be cooked according to package directions, keeping in mind that undercooking is better than overcooking. Canned limas require only rinsing and warming in a small amount of water. Dried limas do not double or triple in size as do other beans when cooked, but plump up only slightly.

The word "succotash," which comes from the Indian word *m'sickquatash* meaning boiled corn, is applied to a dish of lima beans and corn that has an unlimited number of regional variations. For instance, in New England, it is cooked with cream, and the Pennsylvania Dutch add tomatoes, milk, and brown sugar. The Pennsylvania Dutch also bake limas in a casserole with bacon, onion, green pepper, tomatoes, mustard, and brown sugar and, in Lancaster County, they are cooked with potatoes, milk, and butter. In the Southwest, they are cooked with both salt pork and bacon drippings, onion, garlic, vinegar, and tomato soup in a dish called Barbecued Limas. Lady Bird Johnson, during her stay in the White House, served limas cooked with mushrooms, chili powder, and grated Cheddar.

NAVY BEANS

OTHER: pea beans

This is another popular American white bean, smaller than Great Northern, grown primarily in Michigan, and sold dried in most markets. They are nearly indistinguishable from pea beans, so we list them here as one. These are the beans we most often substitute for CANNELLINI (see under BEANS, DRIED, in THE FOODS OF EUROPE section) in Italian recipes, because they hold their shape so well when cooked.

USE: These are the preferred beans for Boston Baked Beans, prepared with salt pork, brown sugar, and molasses, and traditionally served with Boston Brown Bread and Coleslaw. Vermont Baked Beans are flavored with maple syrup. In the Ozarks, a bit of ground ginger is added to the cooking water for baked beans in the belief that it prevents stomach distress. The early Colonists used navy beans in White Pease Soup, made with beef, turnips, and bacon.

Navy beans are excellent to use in any ethnic recipe calling for white beans, be it a casserole or a soup. They are good in salads, in which case they should be marinated while still hot (but after being rinsed of their cooking liquid), in a good garlicky vinaigrette. In Oklahoma, Navy Bean Salad is flavored with chopped sweet pickles and lemon juice. Pennsylvania Dutch Bean Salad is flavored with diced dill pickles and hard-cooked eggs. They are particularly famous in Senate Navy Bean Soup, originated in the dining room in the Senate Building in Washington, D.C.

PINTO BEANS

See under BEANS in THE FOODS OF LATIN AMERICA section

RED BEANS, SMALL

OTHER: Mexican chili bean

This slightly sweet, dark red bean, sold dried in many markets, especially in the Southwest and in Louisiana, is darker in color than the pink bean, or *rosada*, used in Latin American cooking.

USE: This bean is best known for its use in the Creole dish of Red Beans and Rice, in which it is usually cooked with onion, garlic, thyme, and a ham bone that has been sawed or cracked open so the marrow leaks out during the cooking. (These regional recipes have many variations, each cook claiming his or her recipe as the "original.") The dish is traditionally served in New Orleans with a light salad dressed with tarragon vinegar and oil.

RED BEANS AND RICE

For 6 servings

This dish should have the consistency of stew—not too thick, and not too soupy.

1 meaty ham bone or smoked ham hock
1 pound dried small red beans, (about 2½ cups), washed
     and picked over
4 ounces salt pork, diced, blanched, and drained
1 large onion, minced
¾ cup minced celery
2 cloves garlic, minced
¼ cup chopped parsley
1 dried red chili, crumbled
1 bay leaf
½ teaspoon *each* chopped basil and thyme, *or* a pinch *each* of
     dried
   Salt and freshly ground pepper, to taste

TO SERVE:
6 cups cooked Carolina rice
2 sliced scallions, including part of the green tops
   Tabasco sauce

To obtain the most flavor from a ham bone, cut it into 3″ sections with a hack saw, or ask the butcher to do this for you.

Soak the beans overnight in 6 cups cold water, or quick-soak by bringing them to a boil for 2 minutes, covering, and setting aside for an hour.

In a stew pot or Dutch oven, sauté the ham bone or ham hocks, salt pork, onion, and celery until the meat is lightly browned and the onion is transparent. Add the garlic and sauté briefly. Add the beans and the remaining ingredients, bring to a simmer, and cook slowly, covered, for 1½ hours.

637

Remove cover and cook 30 to 45 minutes longer, until the beans are tender. Meanwhile, remove the ham bone or hock, trim off and dice the meat and return it to the pot, discarding any bones and gristle. Taste, and adjust seasoning as is necessary. Serve over steamed rice, sprinkling each serving with sliced scallions. Serve Tabasco sauce as a table condiment.

TO PREPARE IN ADVANCE: Refrigerate up to 3 days or freeze up to 3 months. Reheat gently in a heavy saucepan.

SOYBEANS

See under BEANS in THE FOODS OF ASIA section

SPLIT PEAS

Green and yellow dried split peas, made from the field pea and garden pea, respectively, are sold in most supermarkets. Don't confuse them with the split golden gram (*mung dal*) sold in Asian markets, which are the split form of green mung beans. Some are labeled "quick-cooking." They are particularly popular in Southern and Pennsylvania Dutch cooking.

PREPARATION AND USE: These cook more quickly than dried beans and don't require presoaking. Cover with 4 parts water and simmer for 30 to 45 minutes, depending on whether you wish them to keep their shape or be soft enough to puree. (Read package directions for "quick-cooking" types.)

Split peas are often cooked with ham bones to make thick, hearty Pennsylvania Dutch soups, and substitute for BLACK-EYED PEA(S) in the Southern specialty, Hopping John. Mormon Split Pea Soup contains pork, onion, and diced potatoes. The yellow type were served in Mongole Soup made with tomato juice and onions at all of the official inauguration banquets for Franklin Delano Roosevelt. Today, they are often cooked with onion and then pureed with herbs and cream to accompany roast fowl or meats.

TEPARI BEANS

This small bean, which grows wild in the Southwest, is higher in protein than most beans, and has a flavor that is highly prized. There are white, black, and mottled light brown varieties, all of which have wrinkled skins and veins. The white are cultivated by the Hopis, who traditionally plant "three for the table and two for the rabbits" in order to harvest a good crop. They can be purchased in some markets in Arizona and the Southwest. Navy beans can be substituted, but with some difference in flavor.

USE: These are cooked with bacon or salt pork, or cooked like PINTO BEANS (see under BEANS, DRIED, in THE FOODS OF LATIN AMERICA section) in any Southwestern recipe.

BLACKSTRAP MOLASSES

See MOLASSES

BUTTERNUT

OTHER: white walnut

This native American nut grows in New England, especially in Vermont. It is not widely cultivated because it is extremely difficult to shell and because its relatively large percentage of oil makes it go rancid very quickly.

STORAGE: Store in the freezer for use within a month.

USE: Crack the shell with a hammer and remove. Use as walnuts in cookies, candies and cakes. It is classically used in Vermont in Maple Nut Frosting for cakes.

CALCIUM HYDROXIDE

See SLAKED LIME

CANE SYRUP, PURE

OTHER: ribbon cane syrup, cane juice

FRENCH: *jus de canne*

This is a dark brown syrup made from sugar cane. It is extremely sweet and has the consistency and clarity of heavy MAPLE SYRUP. It is available wherever Creole or Caribbean ingredients are sold. If not available, SORGHUM SYRUP, or 2 parts dark corn syrup and 1 part dark molasses, can be substituted.

STORAGE: After opening, store in the refrigerator for use within 3 months.

USE: This syrup is used in making some corn bread recipes, and is poured like maple syrup over New Orleans breakfast cakes such as Calas (deep-fried fritters made from rice flour), Pig's Ears (large pieces of crisp fried dough), and Pain Perdu (a version of French Toast flavored with lemon rind). It is also used to make Gâteau de Sirop (syrup cake), and a soul-food dessert called Sweet Potato Pudding, made with grated sweet potatoes, milk, eggs, raisins, and spices. In New Orleans, it is often cooked to the consistency of taffy and is called "la cuite," derived from the French word *cuire*, to cook. "La cuite" is so thick that it can be wrapped around a stick and dipped in nuts to make a lollipop for children. The syrup is used as a flavoring for tropical rum drinks in the Caribbean, and was used in Artillery Punch, invented by veterans of the Revolutionary War in Chatham, Georgia.

CATSUP
OTHER: ketchup

This word is derived from the Indonesian *ketjap,* a term used for a sauce added to food for extra flavor. In the United States, it is a tomato-based sauce made with sugar, vinegar, onion, garlic, and spices, and sold in every supermarket. Supermarket types, such as Heinz, Del Monte, etc., do not contain chemicals. It is possible to buy catsup made without white sugar in health food stores.

STORAGE: It will keep indefinitely, even after opening, on the pantry shelf.

USE: Used primarily as a condiment for hamburgers, hot dogs, and the like, catsup is also used a great deal in regional recipes, such as Shaker Flank Steak (the Shakers made their own catsup from fresh tomatoes), Pennsylvania Dutch Meat Loaf, Baked Beans, South Carolina's Pinebark Stew (made with fresh fish, bacon, potatoes, curry powder, and Tabasco), Rhode Island Clam Chowder, and Southwestern Barbecued Spareribs. It is used a great deal by Chinese-Americans in the preparation of Chinese dishes.

CHEESES

Canadian and American cheeses are more often specified in regional American recipes than imported cheeses. We have dealt with the subject of cheese in depth in THE FOODS OF EUROPE section, and we refer you there for general information, storage, and definition of types. An alphabetical listing of the primary domestic types is as follows:

American: A generic term for all of the Cheddar-type cheeses made in America. It includes the pasteurized process cheese, sold in individually wrapped slices for sandwiches. Processed cheese is often specified in recipes because it melts well into sauces and doesn't separate like natural cheese. We always prefer natural cheeses for their superior flavor.

"Blue": As a general rule, the flavors of American "blue" cheeses don't compare well to the finest European examples when served as table cheeses, but they have the same texture and tang, so are fine for use in most recipes. However, there are at least three outstanding examples of domestically made "blues" that make fine eating cheeses: Oregon Blue from Central Point, Oregon; Minnesota Blue from Fanibault, Minnesota, packaged by Treasure Cave; and Maytag Blue from Iowa. "Blue" cheeses are used in salad dressings, spreads, quiches, as a topping for grilled steaks, and other uses described under CHEESE, "BLUE," in THE FOODS OF EUROPE section.

BLUE CHEESE SPREAD FOR APPLES

For 12 or more servings

Joan Baeder, who gave us this simple yet satisfying recipe, sets the spread next to a bowl of red apples, and provides a small board and an apple slicer/corer so the apples can be freshly cut as needed.

    8 ounces cream cheese, at room temperature
    6 ounces "blue" cheese of your choice
    3–4 walnut halves, to garnish

TO SERVE:
    4 red Delicious apples, cored and cut in wedges

Note: Apple wedges that are cut in advance should be dipped in a mixture of 1 cup water and 1 tablespoon lemon juice or 1 teaspoon granulated vitamin C (ascorbic acid) to prevent discoloration on standing.

Whip cream cheese in electric mixer or in food processor fitted with the steel blade until it is very creamy. Add the blue cheese and mix until well combined, scraping the sides of the bowl often with a rubber spatula.

Mound the mixture in the center of a large serving plate, and stud the nuts into the surface for decoration. Surround with apple wedges and provide a spreading knife.

TO PREPARE IN ADVANCE: Store, covered, in the refrigerator. Bring to room temperature before serving.

Brick: One of the few cheeses that originated in America, this is a semi-soft Wisconsin cheese that is usually sold in bricks. It is golden colored and has a medium-strong flavor when young, but becomes very strong with age. It is seldom specified and is a cheese to be used with discretion in cooking.

Cheddar: Most of America's cheese products are in this category. They are labeled "mild," "mellow," and "sharp," depending on how long they have been aged, and range in color from white to dark orange, which has nothing to do with their flavor.

Cheddar is very widely used in the United States in such regional dishes as Grits Casserole, New England Corn and Cheese Soufflé, Canadian Cheese Soup, Southwestern Tortilla Soup, Western Omelets, California Hot Chicken Salad (with mayonnaise and celery, and topped with grated Cheddar). The Pueblo Indians use it in Nambe Governor's Pudding, made with bread, raisins, sugar, cinnamon, and vanilla. In Maine, it is used with eggs as a pie filling for Cheddar Pie, which is eaten for breakfast. Cheddar Biscuits, served cold, were a favorite of Martin Van Buren, and often served in the White House when he was in residence. In the Southwest, Cheddar is used in place of Mexican cheeses in Cheese Enchiladas and in Chile con Queso, a hot chili and cheese dip. There are some outstanding regional types:

Canadian Cheddars: These are among the finest domestic eating Cheddars. There are several labels that are widely distributed. "Black Diamond" is golden and very well aged.

Colby Cheddar: A soft, mellow, orange Cheddar named for the town in Wisconsin where it originated.

Coon Cheddar: A well-aged, dark orange cheddar with sharp flavor.

Longhorn Cheddar: A mellow, golden-orange Wisconsin cheddar named after the Longhorn breed of cattle, and sold in wax-coated cylinders.

New York Cheddars: There are several makers, whose names will appear printed on packages or stamped on the rinds. "Cooper Cheddar" is golden and mellow; "Herkimer" is pale and quite sharp in flavor.

Smoked Cheddar: Cheddar with a smoky flavor, used primarily as a snack and rarely used in cooking. Several of the top Cheddar makers also produce this type.

Tillamook Chedder: A well-aged, orange cheddar from Oregon, which ranges from mild to quite sharp, and is sold in paraffin bricks in many West Coast supermarkets. A salt-free type is more pungent than the others.

Vermont Cheddar: Excellent aged cheddar which is often white, sometimes golden, and has a sharp, distinctive flavor. One version, called Vermont Sage, is flavored with that herb.

Cottage: A very mild, fresh cow's milk cheese with large or small curds sold in 8-, 16- and 32-ounce containers in the dairy section of every supermarket. It is available creamed (with 4 to 8 percent cream added), low-fat, dry, or whipped. It is usually eaten as is as a diet foot, but is a common ingredient in recipes for pasta casseroles, baked goods, and desserts. The carton is usually stamped with an expiration date. The Pennsylvania Dutch, who call cottage cheese *schmierkäse*, use it to make a Cheese Custard Pie flavored with nutmeg. It is sometimes substituted for RICOTTA (see CHEESE, SOFT, UNRIPENED, in THE FOODS OF EUROPE section) in such dishes as Lasagne. Jewish-Americans use dry cottage cheese in Blintzes (thin pancakes with a cheese filling served with jam).

Cream cheese: Soft, white Philadelphia-style cream cheese is a mild, fresh cheese available in every supermarket. Cheese shops carry a superior type that does not have gummy emulsifiers, which is preferred for most uses. The "Neufchatel" type of cream cheese is lower in butterfat (and calories), but contains more moisture. Cream cheese is used in many appetizer dips and cheese spreads. In New England, it is mixed with honey to use as a cake filling or dessert sauce. Combined with grated Cheddar and gelatin, it is made into a cheese ring served at buffets in the Midwest. It is the traditional icing ingredient for Carrot or Zucchini Cake, and we like it especially for Paul's mother's Pumpkin Cake, the recipe for which will be found with the PUMPKIN entry.

Creole cream cheese: Sold only in Louisiana or through mail-order, this is a unique cream cheese that tastes more like thick sweet cream than the Philadelphia type. It is sold in 12-ounce containers, the bottom of which contains the drained curds topped with thin fresh cream. In southern Louisiana, this is eaten for breakfast with sugar and fruit, or with salt and pepper.

Jack cheese: Also called Monterey Jack and Sonoma Jack, this is a mild-flavored, ivory-colored cheese created in California. It is actually of the Cheddar family, but is usually marketed very young. Though now manufactured in many parts of the country, the best examples are still from California.

Jack cheese has a wonderful, melting creaminess in cooking, especially in Southwestern dishes with chiles, and in California Crabmeat Mornay. It is widely used in the Southwest as a substitute for Mexican cheeses in Enchiladas, Quesadillas (tortillas filled with melted cheese), and as a topping for Refried Beans. It is also used in place of MOZZARELLA (see CHEESE, SEMISOFT, in THE FOODS OF EUROPE section) on top of Pizza. An aged type, called "dry Jack," is very like fine aged Cheddar. Some varieties are flavored with hot peppers (*jalapeños*), and are used as snacking cheeses. Domestic MUNSTER is often recommended as a substitute.

Munster: The domestic version of this German cheese is mild and buttery, not unlike Jack. One version is flavored with caraway seeds. It is used in the same manner as Monterey Jack as a substitute for Mexican cheeses. It is used specifically in Pennsylvania Dutch Noodle Cheese Ring, flavored with paprika.

CHICKEN FAT

OTHER: *schmaltz*

Delis, ethnic markets, and supermarkets in cities with large Jewish populations sell rendered chicken fat. When labeled "schmaltz," it has been cooked with onion (sometimes with garlic) to give it extra flavor. The cracklings, or crisp pieces of skin, are called *grebenes,* and are sold in some Jewish markets.

STORAGE: Store in the refrigerator for use within a week, or freeze for longer storage.

PREPARATION AND USE: To make "schmaltz," cut up the skin and pieces of fat from a whole chicken. Place them in water to cover and boil until most of the water has evaporated. Add chopped onion and cook slowly until the onion and pieces of skin are brown. Strain to use as cooking fat, seasoning, or as a rich spread for bread or MATZO(S) (see THE FOODS OF THE MIDDLE EAST section).

Chicken fat is an essential ingredient in Chopped Chicken Liver. *Grebenes* are used to garnish that dish or Kasha Varnishkes (buckwheat groats and noodles) or are served plain atop toast as a snack. They are commonly used in Passover dishes.

CHICORY

This is the white tap-root of a special variety of chicory (not the same as the salad greens), which is dried, roasted, and ground to use as a coffee substitute or flavoring for coffee. It is imported from Europe and sold in packages or in bulk in markets in southern Louisiana. "French Market" coffee, made of very dark, roasted coffee beans and flavored with chicory, is widely distributed throughout the country.

STORAGE: Chicory absorbs moisture, so must be stored airtight. It will keep in a cool place for up to 6 months, but it loses flavor on standing.

USE: Ground chicory gives New Orleans coffee its distinctive aroma and flavor. One teaspoon of ground chicory to every 4 teaspoons ground coffee is the usual amount.

CHITTERLINGS
OTHER: chitlins

Chitterlings are the small intestines of a pig, and an important ingredient in Louisiana and southern soul-food cookery. They are sold by pork butchers in the southern states, often cleaned and boiled and cut in 2″ pieces. Only those from freshly slaughtered pigs should be used.

STORAGE: Cleaned and boiled chitterlings can be stored in the refrigerator for use within 2 days. Fresh ones should be cleaned and boiled before storage.

PREPARATION AND USE: One pound of chitterlings is the usual amount for 1 serving. They must be thoroughly cleaned very soon after the pig is butchered, and this is often done by the butcher. If this has not been done, empty and turn inside out, and soak in salted water for 24 hours washing repeatedly. Cut away and discard most of the fat that adheres to them.

Chitterlings are used in sausages called ANDOUILLE (see under SAUSAGE, COOKED, in THE FOODS OF EUROPE section), made by the French, and by the Acadians in Louisiana at Boucheries (hog butchering parties). They are popularly prepared in the South either by simmering in a spicy tomato sauce until tender, or by dipping cooked pieces in beaten egg and cracker crumbs and deep-frying to serve with collard or turnip greens, black-eyed peas, and corn bread, with a cruet of vinegar in which hot chiles have steeped for a week or longer, for seasoning.

CITRIC SALT
OTHER: sour salt

These are small crystals of an extract from lemons and limes sold in bottles in supermarkets catering to a Jewish population.

STORAGE: In an airtight container in a cool place, they will keep indefinitely.

PREPARATION AND USE: The crystals are used to impart an acidulous taste to soups, such as Borscht (beet soup) and Holishkes (sweet-and-sour stuffed cabbage rolls). A mixture of lemon juice and salt can be used as a substitute. For ½ teaspoon citric salt called for in a recipe, add 3 tablespoons lemon juice and ¼ teaspoon salt; taste, and adjust seasoning as necessary.

COLLARDS
OTHER: "greens"

Collards are a variety of cabbage, closely related to kale, that do not form heads. They are one of many greens termed EFO in Africa (see THE FOODS OF AFRICA section). Collards are almost synonymous with the term "soul food." The greens are sold fresh in produce markets in some parts of the country, especially in the southern states, all year. Look for unblemished, dark green leaves. Frozen collards are also sold in many supermarkets. Substitute turnip greens, mustard greens, or kale.

STORAGE: Wrap in damp paper towels and store in a plastic bag in the crisper of the refrigerator for use within a few days.

PREPARATION AND USE: One pound of collards will serve 2. Wash the greens very well and remove any tough stems or discolored leaves. Chop in bite-sized pieces and place in a pan with ½ cup water and salt to taste. Simmer 15 to 20 minutes until tender; then drain and season to taste. If very young and tender, collards can be used as a salad ingredient. Mature greens generally require more cooking than other greens.

Melted butter, bacon drippings, or a splash of vinegar in which hot chiles have steeped for a week or longer, are traditional seasonings. In the South, collards are often simmered for hours on the back of the stove with bacon, salt pork, or hog jowl, but such long cooking tends to make the greens bitter and is not necessary to make the greens tender. The resulting savory juice is called "pot likker," and is traditionally served with hot corn bread. Collards are often served with pan-fried fish, fried chicken, or pork chops, and are used as a flavoring in southern-style Split Pea Soup.

CONCH

(pronounced CONK)

Conchs are large, spiral-shelled mollusks with a delicious sweet-flavored meat, found in Florida, along the Gulf Coast, and in the West Indies. It is best to buy them right off the fishing boats in Florida, but they are sold frozen (cooked or uncooked) or canned in many markets in the Gulf States and along the Eastern Seaboard.

STORAGE: Fresh conch should be stored in the refrigerator for use as soon as possible. After opening, canned conch can be stored in the refrigerator for up to 3 days. Frozen conch should be kept frozen, and then thawed in the refrigerator overnight before using.

PREPARATION AND USE: Uncooked conch is very tough and rubbery and requires special treatment. Remove it from the shell and blanch for 3 minutes in water to which salt and lemon juice have been added. Drain. It can now be used in soups and stews, which should be slow-simmered. If it is to be pan-fried or used in fritters, slice it or leave whole and place in fresh water to cover with salt and simmer for 2 to 4 hours until it is fork tender. It may then be sliced to pan-fry, or diced to make fritters. In Florida, it is often marinated in lime juice after it is cooked, to make a salad with onions, tomatoes, and chopped parsley. The well-known Bahamian Chowder features conch, and Italian-Americans, who call it *scungilli,* serve it hot with Marinara Sauce. It is often used as a filling for omelets or served with scrambled eggs.

CORN

OTHER: maize

Corn is the only cereal grain native to the New World and was introduced by the Iroquois Indians to the Colonists. It had long been of great nutritional and religious significance not only to the Indians of North America, but to the Incas, Aztecs, and Mayans of Mexico, and Central and South America. It has become one of the most important crops in the United States, the entire plant being used for human consumption and for animal fodder.

There are many varieties and colors of corn, from "flint" corn, which was the original corn introduced to the settlers but is of little importance today, to "popcorn" to "field" corn, which is dried to use in making HOMINY, and MASA for tortillas (see THE FOODS OF LATIN AMERICA section) to the "sweet" corn with which we are most familiar, sold fresh, canned, or frozen in every supermarket. White sweet corn is much lower in nutrients (including vitamin A) than yellow sweet corn. Blue corn (see CORN, BLUE) is grown only in Arizona and New Mexico, where it is sold in markets that specialize in Indian groceries.

Fresh corn is in season from May through December, and is best purchased from roadside stands where it has just been picked. When buying fresh corn, look for unblemished, snug husks and evenly spaced, firm kernels. Brown "silk" at the husk end indicates juicy kernels. Avoid any that show signs of decay or worms, or that have soft kernels.

STORAGE: Fresh corn loses flavor quickly, so wrap in damp paper towels to store in the refrigerator for use within 24 hours. Cooked corn or canned corn, once opened, can be stored in a nonmetal container in the refrigerator for up to 3 days. Store frozen corn in freezer until use.

PREPARATION AND USE: For corn on the cob, allow 1 to 2 ears per serving. One ear of corn will yield approximately ⅔ cup of kernels.

To prepare and cook corn on the cob, remove husks and silk, and cut off both ends. Place in a generous amount of water to which one teaspoon of sugar per ear of corn, but no salt, has been added. Cover and cook for 5 minutes, and then test for doneness. Serve hot with butter, salt, and pepper. Alternatively, corn on the cob can be cooked in the husk, after the silk has been removed, if it is soaked in cold water for 30 minutes. Roast it in a 400° oven for 30 to 40 minutes, or in hot coals for 10 minutes. Kernels removed from the cob can be simmered in water to cover for 4 to 5 minutes, and then drained and seasoned as desired.

Corn is the most popular vegetable in the United States, and appears in many regional recipes. Fresh corn dumplings are simmered over Chile Stew by the Pueblo Indians of the Southwest. Corn was often dried for storage by the Indians and the early settlers during winter months, to be made into soup, CORNMEAL, masa for tortillas, or hominy. It is still popular in the Southwest, especially in Green Corn Pudding and Green Corn Tamales. Corn Chowder is a popular New England and Pennsylvania Dutch soup.

Corn is an essential ingredient in succotash, prepared with various BEANS, depending on the region. It also appears in griddle cakes called Corn Cakes, which vary from region to region, in Pennsylvania Dutch Corn Relish, and Corn Fritters. It is very often combined with green chiles in the cooking of the Southwest.

CORN, BLUE

This strain of corn, cultivated around the pueblos near Taos, New Mexico, has a more delicate and slightly more bitter taste than white or yellow corn, and a distinctive blue color, which is of great religious importance to many American Indian tribes. It is sold in whole dried kernels or as cornmeal *(harina azul* or *harinella)* in markets in New Mexico and can be ordered by mail.

STORAGE: In an airtight container in a cool place it will keep indefinitely.

PREPARATION AND USE: Blue corn is ground into meal for a variety of dishes in the Southwest. It is difficult to grind at home without a hand grinding mill, it can be done with a mortar and pestle and a good deal of effort. See CORNMEAL, BLUE for more information.

CORN, DRIED

OTHER: parched corn, Shaker dried corn

BY THE HOPIS: *kutuki*

In the days before refrigeration, sweet corn was often dried by the Indians, the Shakers, and by the Pennsylvania Dutch. Dried sweet corn is still available today in stores that sell Pennsylvania Dutch specialties. It is made from the finest fresh sweet corn and has an excellent flavor. Field corn, when specially treated and dried becomes HOMINY, and is used to make *nixtamal* for MASA (see THE FOODS OF LATIN AMERICA section). Parched corn is dried sweet or field corn that has been soaked in salt water and then toasted to give it a deep corn flavor. It is sold as a snack item in many health food stores and in some supermarkets.

STORAGE: In an airtight container in a cool place for up to a year.

PREPARATION AND USE: Dried sweet corn must be reconstituted, just like dried beans, for use in soups and dishes such as succotash. Parched corn was used as a provision by Indian hunters who ate it without cooking it, or boiled it into a simple soup.

In Pennsylvania Dutch recipes, we have found dried sweet corn is used whole or ground in soups, as an accompaniment to roast chicken or meat, or made into Dried Corn Salad with cabbage, green pepper, and cider vinegar. To prepare Creamed Corn to serve as a vegetable, use 1 cup of dried corn for 4 servings. Soak overnight in a saucepan in 2 cups of milk. The next day add 1 cup heavy cream, 2 tablespoons butter, 1 teaspoon sugar, and salt and pepper. Bring to a simmer, lower the heat, and cook, stirring often, for 30 minutes. Serve as an accompaniment to roast chicken, ham, or pork.

CORN FLOUR

A finely milled flour, finer than cornmeal, but with the taste of cornmeal. It has not been chemically treated as has MASA HARINA ("instant corn flour"— see THE FOODS OF LATIN AMERICA section), so the flavors are not similar and they should not be substituted for each other. It is sold in Louisiana in supermarkets, and in health food stores nationwide.

STORAGE: Like any flour, it will keep indefinitely in an airtight container in a cool place.

USE: In southern Louisiana, this type of flour is preferred for dredging seafood and vegetables to be deep-fried.

CORNMEAL, BLUE

SPANISH: *harina azul* or *harinella*

Cornmeal ground from blue corn (see CORN, BLUE) is widely used by the Pueblo Indians. It is sold in New Mexico and can be ordered by mail (see SHOPPING SOURCES).

STORAGE: It will keep in the refrigerator for up to 3 months.

PREPARATION AND USE: The commercially sold cornmeal needs to be ground finer in a blender or food mill before use in recipes.

Blue cornmeal is used to make cornbread and tortillas in the Southwest, and some recipes combine it with wheat flour for those items. The Hopi Indians make their staple bread, Piki, by roasting and grinding dried blue corn into a meal and making it into a batter which is then darkened with CULINARY ASH. The batter is spread very thin on a long hot stone to cook on one side. The paper-thin pancake is then tightly rolled to make a "loaf." The same bread is sometimes made with white or yellow cornmeal and is dyed red or yellow with vegetable dyes to serve on special occasions. Other dishes include Hopi Hush Puppies, served with beans or stews instead of bread, Blue Corn Dumplings made with bacon drippings, milk, and baking powder, and steamed on top of stews, Blue Frying-Pan Bread, and a drink with powdered milk called Piñole. The Hopis also make a mush called Finger Bread, eaten with the fingers with stews called Huzuskuki. The leftover is sliced and fried for breakfast the following day, like Cornmeal Mush.

The following recipe for Blue Corn Tortillas has been adapted from *Hopi Cookery* by Juanita Tiger Kavena, an excellent source of information on Hopi culture.

BLUE CORN TORTILLAS

For 12 tortillas

These are traditionally served with beans.

    2 cups very finely ground blue cornmeal (or 1⅔ cups
          blue cornmeal and ⅓ cup sifted all-purpose white
          flour)
1–1½ cups water

Combine cornmeal and water in a bowl, mixing until the dough is moist and pliable. Do not add so much water that the dough is sticky. Shape the dough into 12 balls. One at a time, flatten a ball and place between two plastic bags or pieces of oiled waxed paper. Pat with hands, roll with a rolling pin, or flatten in a tortilla press (see TORTILLAS, CORN). Lightly grease a griddle or skillet and cook each tortilla over medium heat, turning once, to brown lightly on both sides.

CORNMEAL, YELLOW OR WHITE

Cornmeal is an American ingredient sold in supermarkets everywhere. It is available in yellow or white, either roller ground ("enriched"), or stone- or water-ground on millstones, a process that preserves more of the nutrients. There is also a quick-cooking type. The best kind to buy is that which retains the whole grain. It is labeled "unbolted," and contains the hull and germ of the corn. It is sold in health food stores and can be used interchangeably with other types in recipes. Yellow cornmeal has more nutrients than white cornmeal, specifically vitamin A. BLUE CORNMEAL is sold in New Mexico and can be ordered by mail (see SHOPPING SOURCES). A type of cornmeal called POLENTA (see THE FOODS OF EUROPE section) is sold in Italian markets.

STORAGE: The supermarket type will keep indefinitely in an airtight container in a cool place. The "whole grain" type should be refrigerated for use within 3 months.

PREPARATION AND USE: To make 4 servings of Cornmeal Mush, sprinkle ½ cup of cornmeal into 2½ cups of boiling water to which ½ teaspoon of salt has been added. Stir often over low heat for 25 to 30 minutes until it is thick. Spoon into bowls, top with pats of butter, and serve as a breakfast porridge. Alternatively, spoon it into a loaf pan or a buttered empty soup can and chill. Unmold, slice in ¾" slices, dip in flour, and fry in bacon drippings or butter to serve with maple syrup or cane syrup.

Recipes using cornmeal abound in the southern United States, where it is used to make corn bread or muffins, Tamale Pie, hush puppies, in fact, dozens of variations of bread, biscuits, muffins, and pancakes. Corn dodgers, hoecakes, corn pone are terms used interchangeably for a mixture of cornmeal, salt, and water formed by hand and baked, fried, or cooked on a griddle or on the blade of a hoe! Hush puppies, so called because they were supposed to quiet the hounds, made of cornmeal, onion, buttermilk, and baking powder, are served as a starchy accompaniment to many southern meals, and in the Ozarks are made into turnovers, with fillings of meat, shrimp, or vegetables. Other southern cornmeal preparations include Crackling Bread, Skillet Corn Bread, and Fried Catfish breaded with cornmeal. White stone- or waterground cornmeal is often preferred in southern recipes, specifically in Kentucky Spoon Bread.

In New England, Johnnycakes (Jonny Cakes in Rhode Island) get their name from a corruption of Journey Cakes, corn cakes that could be put in the pocket and eaten as a ration on long journeys. They are usually made with molasses and served with maple syrup. Corn bread is the traditional stuffing for turkey in New England.

The Pennsylvania Dutch save scraps of pork to cook with cornmeal, and add onions, herbs and spices, and a healthy dose of ground black pepper. This mixture is then chilled until firm in loaf pans. The resulting dish, Philadelphia Scrapple (called "panhaus" by the Pennsylvania Dutch), is cut into ½" slices and fried until brown to serve for breakfast, or as a base for small roast game birds. (There is a commercially sold canned version of this dish, but it is traditionally homemade in Pennsylvania.) Pennsylvanians also make Cornmeal Griddle Cakes with buttermilk. In Texas, cornmeal patties are made by ranchers to fry and serve with beans and stews. In the Southwest, cornmeal is often combined with chiles in such dishes as Tamale Pie. In the Old West, it was used in stuffing for fresh trout. American-Italians love Polenta, a cornmeal mush topped with a zesty sauce, and even make Gnocchi (dumplings) out of cornmeal. The Romanian equivalent of Polenta is Mamaliga, one version of which is baked with layers of goat cheese and topped with sour cream. And cornmeal even shows up as a cookie ingredient in the following "tried-and-true" recipe given to us by Marion Cunningham, editor of the latest edition of *The Fannie Farmer Cookbook,* and a consultant in the writing of this book.

CORNMEAL PIÑON COOKIES

1   cup sweet (unsalted) butter, softened   For 4 dozen 2″ cookies
½   cup dark brown sugar, firmly packed
1   cup powdered sugar
2   teaspoons pure vanilla extract
1   cup yellow cornmeal
1⅓ cups all-purpose flour
½   teaspoon salt
½   cup piñon nuts (pine nuts), lightly toasted

Preheat the oven to 350°.

Combine the butter, brown sugar, and powdered sugar in a large mixing bowl. Beat until smooth. Stir in the vanilla, ⅔ cup of the cornmeal, flour, and salt. Beat until well blended. Work the piñon nuts evenly into the dough.

Break off about 1 tablespoon of dough and form into a ball. Repeat until all dough is used. Roll each ball in the remaining cornmeal to coat; place about 2″ apart on a cookie sheet. Flatten each ball until ¼″ thick.

Bake in the center of the oven for 10 to 15 minutes, or until slightly colored around the edges. Remove and cool on racks.

TO PREPARE IN ADVANCE: These will keep in an airtight container at room temperature for up to a week or, frozen, for up to 6 months.

CORNED BEEF

BRITISH: salt beef (or "bully" beef, if canned)

The term "to corn" comes from an Old English word for coarse salt (the size of corn kernels) used to make the brines for preserving meat. Though meats have been treated thus for hundreds of years, the term has become almost synonymous with "corned beef" as it is served in a New England Boiled Dinner. The usual cuts are brisket, plate, and bottom round, with the brisket considered the choicest because it is slightly sweeter in flavor. Fresh meat is placed in a heavily salted brine, usually with the addition of SALTPETER (see THE FOODS OF EUROPE section) to preserve a pink color, and pickling spices for flavor. The meat is then cured for 6 to 8 weeks. Corned beef can be purchased in pieces of varying sizes, from specialty butchers, corned on the premises, or in supermarkets sealed in plastic bags. Corning mixtures vary, with some being extra-spicy and some containing more garlic than others, so you will be wise to find a brand or source you like and stick with it. Canned corned beef and packaged sandwich slices, both precooked, are also sold in most supermarkets, but are inferior in texture and flavor.

STORAGE: Corned beef in its brine will keep a long time in the refrigerator, but becomes increasingly salty as it waits. Leftover cooked meat can be stored a week or longer in the refrigerator if tightly wrapped.

PREPARATION AND USE: Allow ½ pound corned beef per person. Remove any wrapping and place the meat in a large pot with all of the spices from the package. Cover with a generous amount of water and simmer for approximately 3 hours until very tender when pierced with a long-pronged fork.

Some cooks save the broth (which can be quite salty) to use in making soups and cooking beans. Corned Beef is most traditionally served as part of a New England Boiled Dinner, with wedges of cabbage and whole vegetables such as carrots, potatoes, and turnips poached in the cooking broth at the end of the cooking time, and is usually accompanied with spicy mustard or horseradish sauce. Leftovers are made into sandwiches, Corned Beef Hash (a great favorite of President McKinley), Plymouth Succotash (corn, navy beans, and corned beef), Potato Salad and soups.

COUNTRY-STYLE HAM

See HAMS, COUNTRY-STYLE

CRAB

The coasts of North America are known for their many varieties of crab. Because crab is hardly known in other countries, it must indeed be considered an ethnic ingredient. We will discuss the various types of fresh and frozen crab indigenous to various parts of North America, and then describe the types of canned crabmeat you are likely to find.

When buying live crab, buy it on the day you are going to cook it from a reliable fish market and take care that it is alive and kicking. If it has been kept on crushed ice, its reactions will be slow. Any cooked crabmeat purchased in a fish market should smell sweet and fresh. If it smells strong, don't buy it.

STORAGE: Live crab should be purchased on the day of use and refrigerated until just before cooking. Raw crabmeat should be cooked within 24 hours of the crab's demise. Cooked crabmeat can be refrigerated for use within three days. Freezing crabmeat damages its flavor and texture, but should be done if it is not to be used quickly. Use frozen crabmeat within 3 months.

PREPARATION AND USE: When buying crabmeat, figure on 1 pound for 3 servings if it is to be the main course. Crabs in their shells are harder to estimate because they vary so in size, but an average Dungeness crab will serve 1 or 2, depending on appetites. Live crabs should be cooked in plenty of boiling water. Often salt or spices called CRAB BOIL (see under SEASONING BLENDS in the HERBS, SPICES, AND SEASONING BLENDS section) are added to the water. Depending on the size of the crab, it will cook in 5 to 15 minutes, the shell turning bright red when cooked. Care should be taken not to overcook or the meat will be stringy.

Frozen crabmeat should first be thawed for 6 to 8 hours in the refrigerator. Frozen crab used as an ingredient in other dishes should be firmly blotted with paper towels to prevent it from watering down a dish during cooking.

Crabmeat has a sweet, delicate flavor, so it should not be served with the ubiquitous red "cocktail" sauce which James Beard calls "the red menace"; and which is much too strongly flavored. Simple cooking and simple sauces, such as butter and seasoned mayonnaise, are best. A recipe for Crab Omelet borrowed by Martha Washington from Dolly Madison contained chopped eggplant, tomatoes, and thyme. Crab Soup has long been a popular southern dish, and has been served in the White House since it was first built. Along the South Atlantic Seaboard, especially in Delaware, Crab Cakes, made with onion, mayonnaise, and cracker crumbs, have long been popular. On the West Coast, recipes abound for Crab Dip, Crab Canapés, and Crab Mornay.

CANNED CRAB

Canned crab is sold in 6- to 8-ounce cans in every supermarket. The most common variety is "snow crab," a market name for various types of "spider crab," much of which is imported from Japan. Occasionally one can find Alaska king crab back meat. Canned crabmeat varies greatly in price depending on the type. It tends to be stronger in flavor than fresh or frozen.

STORAGE: After opening, store in a nonmetal container as you would fresh cooked crabmeat, in the refrigerator for use within 2 days.

PREPARATION AND USE: Canned crabmeat is precooked. Pick over it carefully to remove any small bits of cartilage. Its liquid is usually used in recipes but, if it is to be sautéed, rinse it lightly and blot dry.

FRESH AND FROZEN CRAB

Alaskan king crab: A huge variety of crab, weighing 8 to 10 pounds, with large claws and legs. It has snow-white meat, brilliantly edged in red. A smaller variety, called "red crab," is very similar in flavor and texture. It is almost always shipped frozen, and is precooked before packaging right on the fishing boat. One can buy the choice meat or the split crab legs in the shell in fish markets everywhere. Because of the size it is one of the easiest types of crab to eat as is, or to use as an ingredient, but take care to remove any small pieces of cartilage. Allowing 8 to 10 ounces per serving, it is often served simply cracked, but the legs can be split, brushed with butter, and broiled.

Blue crab: A bluish-colored crab weighing between 6 and 16 ounces, found along the Atlantic and Gulf coasts, and sold in markets primarily in those areas. It is the crab most familiar to Americans and is the same variety as soft-shelled crab, but hasn't yet shed its hard shell. It is boiled and cleaned to serve, and is often dipped in batter and fried. One Southern preparation places boiled crabs on steamed rice to serve with Rusty Gravy, made by cooking oil and flour to a dark roux, adding onions, celery, green pepper, garlic, tomato juice, and TABASCO.

Buster crab: A term that describes a blue crab in the process of shedding its shell to become a soft-shelled crab. It is especially prized and is shipped on ice to many specialty fish markets. It must be cleaned like a SOFT-SHELLED CRAB.

Dungeness: A green West Coast crab, named for a fishing village on the Strait of Juan de Fuca in Washington, available fresh from Washington to Baja California. When cooked, it has fine shreds of pink meat in the claws and LUMP CRABMEAT in the body. Whole ones, weighing between 2½ and 3 pounds are sold raw or precooked in West Coast markets beginning in January, and the meat is shipped frozen or canned to other parts of the country. Fresh, it is usually served cracked (one per person) with a mayonnaise dip, but also finds its way into casseroles and Deviled Crab preparations.

Lump crabmeat: Solid lumps of white meat taken from the body of the crab. The finest Florida and Maryland crabmeat is this especially meaty type, sold cleaned, in refrigerated cans in those areas, where it is quite expensive. "Backfin" is from the back of the crab, and is in smaller pieces, but is considered just as fine.

She crab: A female blue crab with bright orange roe, which is considered a great delicacy in the Southern Atlantic states, where both meat and roe are incorporated into recipes for soup.

Softshelled crab: This blue crab that has shed its shell is a specialty of the Southern Atlantic states, where it is in season from June through August. It must be cleaned to remove the spongy material from underneath and from its front apron: the fish market where you buy it will do this for you. The smaller they are the better. Two or three of these make one serving, and they are usually coated with beaten egg, and then rolled in cracker crumbs or seasoned flour to be sautéed or deep-fried and served with drawn butter. They are eaten shell and all.

Stone crab: Only the large claws of this crab, found along the coast of Florida and Cuba, are eaten. They are removed from the live crab, which is then returned to the ocean to grow a new one. The claws are cooked by the fishermen on the boat and then sold to restaurants or frozen. They are a local specialty, but can be found frozen in some specialty fish markets. The delicate clawmeat is best enjoyed warm with melted butter or mayonnaise for dipping, but can substitute for other types of crab in recipes.

CRACKLINGS

This term applies both to the crisp pieces of brown skin from roasted pork or to what is left from the rendering of pork or poultry fat, and to thin slices of FAT BACK or SALT PORK that have been cooked until crisp and curled. These are sold in some specialty meat markets in the southern states and in places that have large open-air "farmer's markets." They are generally lighter in flavor than CHICHARRÓN (see THE FOODS OF LATIN AMERICA section). Chicken cracklings are virtually the same thing as *grebenes* (see CHICKEN FAT), sold in Jewish markets.

STORAGE: These are best the day they are cooked, but can be refrigerated or frozen and reheated to serve.

PREPARATION AND USE: Cracklings are often made at home in the South from thin square slices of fat back or salt pork, which are rendered until crisp and curled. These are served warm or cold as a snack with a light sprinkling of salt. In the South, cracklings are often served atop cooked greens as a garnish or utilized in the making of corn bread, as in the following recipe for Crackling Bread.

CRACKLING BREAD

For 6 to 8 servings

This is traditionally served from the iron skillet in which it is made.

4 ounces FATBACK, diced (or 4 ounces salt pork, diced),
    blanched in boiling water for 2 minutes, and drained
    Butter, drippings, or oil, as necessary to make ⅓ cup
    drippings
1 cup white or yellow cornmeal
1 cup all-purpose flour
¾ teaspoon salt
1 cup buttermilk *or* sour milk
2 large eggs, beaten

Fry the diced, blanched pork in 10″ iron skillet until crisp. Drain, reserving the drippings. Measure ⅓ cup drippings, adding butter or oil if necessary to make the required amount, and return to the skillet. In a bowl, combine the remaining ingredients in their order listed and beat until smooth. Pour into the skillet and sprinkle the cracklings over the top.

Bake at 425° for 15 to 20 minutes, until firm. Cool for 10 minutes; then cut into wedges to serve warm as an accompaniment to COLLARD GREENS, Country Ham, and other southern dishes.

CRAYFISH

OTHER: crawfish or crawdad

FINNISH: *keitetyt* FRENCH: *écrevisse* GERMAN: *Flusskrebs* ITALIAN: *gamberi di fume* NORWEGIAN: *kraftor* SPANISH: *cangrejo de rio*

These freshwater crustaceans look like tiny lobsters and have sweet white meat in their tails. They are found in Lake Michigan, in the Pacific Northwest, and in Louisiana and California, and are usually about 6″ long, twice the size of the European type, which are popular especially in France and in Finland. But nowhere are they more celebrated than in Creole cooking. In Louisiana, they can be purchased live during their season from February to June. Frozen whole crayfish, or their tail meat, can be purchased in some fish markets and by mail. If you are in New Orleans, you had better call these "*craw*fish," or they won't know what you want.

STORAGE: Fresh crayfish should be refrigerated and cooked as soon as possible after purchase. Frozen ones will keep for up to 3 months.

PREPARATION AND USE: If they are to be the main course, allow at least 1 dozen per person, and many more if they are tiny, as they tend to be in New Orleans. Live crayfish tend to be gritty, so soak them in cold water for 10 minutes or so. Frozen ones are usually precooked or can be thawed to cook as fresh. Usually only the easily removed tail meat is specified in recipes but, if the crayfish are served as the main course, the claws are served, too, and are sucked to obtain their juices and meat. Melted butter is served for dipping the succulent tail meat. There is a shell-like fin on the top of the tail which should be pulled off, and the threadlike intestinal vein usually comes with it. If it doesn't, it should be cut away before the crayfish is eaten because it has a bitter flavor. They should be simmered like live CRAB, but will take only 5 to 8 minutes, depending on their size. Their shells turn red when cooked. The fat that adheres to the shelled tail meat is often specified for use in New Orleans recipes. A stock made of all the shells and other discarded portions is often specified as well.

Whole cooked crayfish often garnish fancy food platters because they look like perfect miniature red lobsters. Creole cookery includes many ways to prepare the tail meat. It is sautéed or used in bisques or stews. The popular Crawfish Étouffée literally means smothered crawfish, which it is, with an herb-flavored tomato sauce in the following stew recipe.

CRAWFISH ÉTOUFFÉE

1½ cups minced onion   For 4 servings
  2 tablespoons olive oil or vegetable oil
  1 small clove garlic, minced or pressed
  2 ripe tomatoes, peeled, seeded, and chopped
  2 tablespoons butter
  3 scallions, minced, including some of the green part
  ¼ cup crayfish stock, chicken broth, or white wine
  2 pounds shelled crawfish tails
  ¼ cup crawfish fat
  ¾ teaspoon *each* fresh basil, marjoram, thyme, and rosemary,
       minced, *or* ¼ teaspoon *each* of the dried herbs,
       crumbled

TO SERVE:
     Steamed Carolina rice

Sauté the onion in the olive oil in a small heavy skillet (not iron), just until transparent. Add the garlic, stir briefly, and add the tomatoes. Cook slowly, stirring often, for 20 minutes or so until quite thick.

Melt the butter in a heavy saucepan and cook the scallions briefly. Add the tomato mixture, the stock or wine, crawfish tails, fat, and herbs. Simmer, stirring often, for 15 to 20 minutes. Serve hot with rice.

TO PREPARE IN ADVANCE: Cook only 10 minutes after adding the crawfish tails; cool and refrigerate. Reheat gently for serving the next day.

CREOLE MUSTARD

This local Louisiana specialty is a mustard made from brown mustard seeds, as is Dijon (see under MUSTARD, FRENCH, in THE FOODS OF EUROPE section), but given extra spiciness with horseradish. It is sold in gourmet specialty shops and in stores that specialize in Creole ingredients.

STORAGE: After opening, store in the refrigerator indefinitely.

USE: This is very often specified in Creole recipes. Substitute any strong mustard.

DANDELION GREENS

FRENCH: *pissenlit* GERMAN: *Löwenzahn* ITALIAN: *dente de leone* SPANISH: *amargon*

The wild or cultivated dandelion plant is related to the dahlia. The small, tender pointed leaves are slightly bitter and have the best flavor if they are picked before the flower appears. The greens can be purchased in markets during the spring, but are easiest to find on lawns. The cultivated ones tend to be milder in flavor than the garden weed variety.

STORAGE: Wrap in damp paper towels and store in a plastic bag in the refrigerator for use within 3 days. To freeze, clean as described below, and then scald the leaves in boiling water for just 2 minutes. Chill in ice water; then drain well and pack into a freezer container, leaving ½" space at the top for expansion. They can be kept in the freezer without losing much quality for up to 6 months.

PREPARATION AND USE: If you have gathered these yourself, be sure to wash them thoroughly to remove any traces of weed-killer or other sprays. A popular way to cook them is to render some chopped bacon in a pan and toss in the greens with seasonings such as garlic and a bit of vinegar, cover, and cook just until wilted and tender. Frozen dandelion greens, when thawed, should be cooked like fresh.

The very tender fresh leaves add spiciness to salads. The Pennsylvania Dutch cook the greens as a vegetable and dress them with a sweet-and-sour sugar-vinegar sauce made with bacon drippings. They are often part of what is referred to as a "mess of greens" used in soul-food cooking, and in the version of Gumbo traditionally made with seven types of greens, Gumbo Z'Herbes.

FAT BACK

OTHER: pork fat

This is the firm, clear fat covering the loin of pork, often used as an ingredient in Southern recipes. It is fresh, neither smoked nor cured. SALT PORK that has been blanched, can be substituted. When rendered, fat back becomes LARD (see THE FOODS OF ASIA section).

STORAGE: Tightly wrapped in the refrigerator, it will keep for up to 4 days or, frozen, for up to 6 months.

PREPARATION AND USE: In the South, fat back is cut in thin square slices to render into curled CRACKLINGS. The rendered fat is used as a cooking fat in many Southern and New England recipes for greens or beans. It is also used to line baking pans for pâtés and Terrines in French cooking.

FIDDLEHEAD FERN

This is the tightly curled head of the common ostrich fern, which grows wild in Canada's maritime region and in the New England states. **When open and mature, they are poisonous and only the part that is tightly curled is edible.** But, during the spring, from early May to the middle of July, the tightly curled shoots are gathered. They are sold fresh only in local markets, especially in Quebec. Their flavor has been described as somewhere between artichokes, asparagus, and mushrooms. Frozen and canned ones are occasionally sold in shops carrying gourmet delicacies, and are expensive. The canned type don't taste much like fresh, and are a waste of money.

STORAGE: Wrap fresh fiddleheads in damp paper towels and store in a plastic bag in the refrigerator for use within 3 days.

PREPARATION AND USE: If fresh ones have been gathered, pull off the brown sheaths. Fiddleheads can be served raw in salads, or cooked in lightly salted water to cover for 3 to 4 minutes, until just tender to be served with melted butter or hollandaise sauce. Frozen should not be thawed before cooking, and require only enough simmering to thaw them.

They can be cooked with salt pork and garlic, or creamed to serve on toast. They are sometimes deep-fried to serve as an appetizer, or marinated in a light vinaigrette to serve as a salad. We have enjoyed pasta tossed with fresh fiddleheads in a delicate cream sauce, which emphasized their woodsy flavor.

FILÉ

(FEE-lay)
OTHER NAMES: gumbo filé, sassafras powder

Young leaves from sassafras trees, which grow wild along the Gulf of Mexico, were dried and ground and sold originally by the Choctaws in New Orleans markets to use as a flavoring and thickening for Creole soups and stews. It had a flavor that slightly resembled THYME and SAVORY (see HERBS,

SPICES, AND SEASONING BLENDS section) and was called filé. Today, filé powder is sold on the spice shelves of most supermarkets and gourmet specialty shops (it may also contain thyme or other herbs), or it can be ordered by mail from shops that carry Creole ingredients.

STORAGE: As any powdered spice.

PREPARATION AND USE: This powder acts quickly as a liaison, or thickening agent. If boiled, it becomes stringy, so it is stirred in only after the soup or stew has been removed from the heat and, once added to a soup, it does not reheat well or freeze well, so should be added only a few minutes before the soup is to be served. One to 2 teaspoons of filé thicken 3 quarts of soup, which should be allowed to stand for 5 minutes or so for the flavor to mellow before serving.

Filé is one of the most important seasonings of Creole Gumbo, a dark rich soup, which is made with seafood or chicken, or simply with an assortment of green vegetables, in which case it is called Gumbo Z'Herbes, a descendent of the Caribbean Callaloo (see under CALLALOO GREENS in THE FOODS OF LATIN AMERICA section). Unlike some soups, Gumbo tastes better if it is cooled and refrigerated overnight and then reheated to serve, and it is only then that the filé, and possibly any tender shellfish, which would suffer from overheating, should be added. An alternate thickening for Gumbo is fresh okra, which is added at an earlier point in the cooking. Purists never use *both* okra and filé in the same dish.

HAMS, COUNTRY STYLE

Ham—the smoked or cured hind leg of pork—is one of America's favorite meats. Up until the 20th century, fresh ham and bacon were rubbed with salt or submerged in brine for a month or so and then smoked in rural smokehouses over fires made of maple or hickory wood. They were then rubbed with pepper and sewn into muslin bags to hang in a barn until needed. These hams are still available in markets and smokehouses in Virginia, Kentucky, Maryland, Tennessee, and Pennsylvania, and are widely available through mail order (see SHOPPING SOURCES). They can, in some instances, be purchased fully cooked, but most require cooking. Whole hams, half hams, and ham pieces are available. Whole hams are usually "long-cut," which means they were cut at the point where the pelvic bone meets the backbone, and at the fetlock point, so they look different from the short, squat whole hams most of us are used to. They are salty and very flavorful. A similarly treated SLAB BACON (see under BACON) is usually sold by the same processors.

STORAGE: To store country-style hams, remove any plastic wrapper (don't worry about the oftentimes moldy surface, which can be scrubbed away), place in a muslin bag, and hang in a cool, dry place for up to 2 years. It needs air circulating around it to prevent excessive mold from forming. Don't refrigerate any uncooked aged ham because the texture changes; it should be refrigerated only after cooking or cutting. Cooked ham can be refrigerated or frozen indefinitely.

PREPARATION AND USE: Always read and follow the directions that come with the ham, because nobody knows better than the packer how these hams should be stored, soaked, and cooked. Scrub away the mold in hot water with a stiff brush or nylon scrubber. As a general rule, a country-style ham must be soaked for 12 hours (sometimes for as long as 36 hours) in several changes of cold water, the length of time depending upon its age and how much salt you wish to rid it of.

Unless the ham is precooked, it must be simmered slowly. You will need a very large pot or roasting pan to hold it. Place it in water to cover and bring to a simmer. After 10 minutes or so, skim away any scum that has risen to the surface, and continue cooking, at the merest simmer, for 2½ hours; then let it cool completely in its liquid. Use a sharp knife to cut away the skin, but leave the fat, which will prevent the ham from drying out during baking. Glaze or decorate the ham as desired and then bake at 400° for 25 to 30 minutes until glazed. These hams can also be braised.

Country-style ham is usually served in paper-thin slices. In Maryland and Virginia, it is often served to make small sandwiches with Beaten Biscuits, made of flour with a minimum amount of fat, and hand-beaten or pounded with a mallet for 2 to 3 hours. In one favorite Southern preparation, the ham is cut in 1″ slices with a good border of fat, and fried, turning several times, until brown. The slices are kept warm in the oven while a gravy is made. Ham Gravy is made from rendered ham fat, flour, and warm milk, cooked until thick; Red Eye Gravy is made by deglazing the pan with strong coffee. The flavorful bone and any scraps are saved for cooking beans, spoon bread, and dishes such as Red Beans and Rice. The scraps are used on the Gulf Coast in Picadillo à la Creollo, a hash-like mixture served inside hollowed-rolls called Moyettes, which are deep-fried until crusty.

Following are examples of some country-style hams.

Country Style: A generic term for cured hams, which may or may not be smoked.

Kentucky: Kentucky hams are particularly prized for southern soul-food cooking because they are the leanest and because the heavy smoke flavor penetrates clear to the bone.

Pennsylvania Dutch: Ham cured in spiced vinegar and sugar and then smoked over apple or hickory wood. Unlike most country-style hams, they are "short-cut" and are fully cooked and ready to eat.

Smithfield: A trade name for a specific dry-cured, aged ham available un-cooked or fully cooked only from Smithfield, Virginia. This is the most famous of all of America's hams and has been enjoyed for over a hundred years. Gwaltney is the oldest company producing these hams, which can be ordered by mail (see SHOPPING SOURCES) or through specialty butcher shops. The meat is dark red and highly flavorful. During the long curing and aging process, the meat loses approximately 30 percent of its moisture. Whole hams come in a fabric bag in which they are intended to be hung until they are cooked. Smithfield Hams were served by Martha Washington, topped with a brown sugar and sherry glaze.

Sugar-Cured: Ham cured in brine to which brown sugar or molasses has been added. This is not to be confused with the trade name of "Honey Baked Hams," which are not country-style.

Virginia: A generic term for a country-cured, hickory-smoked ham made from a hog that has been fed a diet of peaches, peanuts, or acorns, which gives the dark reddish brown meat a very distinct, rich flavor. They may be cured for a shorter period of time than a SMITHFIELD, and are smoked over different woods. One Virginia method of preparation is to skin it after cooking and then bake with a glaze of currant jelly, horseradish, and a bit of dry mustard.

Williamsburg: This ham, from the same producers as SMITHFIELD hams, has a milder cure than a Smithfield.

HOG JOWL

OTHER: bacon square

Hog jowl is the fatty cheek of a pig, cured and smoked in the same manner as BACON. Unless "country-cured" in smokehouses like country-style ham (see HAM, COUNTRY STYLE), it is quite inexpensive, and can be used as an economical bacon substitute. It is sold in many supermarkets in the South.

STORAGE: If tightly wrapped in foil, it will keep for up to a week in the refrigerator, or up to a month in the freezer.

PREPARATION AND USE: The usual amount of hog jowl specified in recipes is ½ pound for 4 to 6 servings. It can be sliced and cooked like bacon, but is traditionally used in Southern cooking to flavor Black-Eyed Peas, which is served before noon on New Year's Day for good luck. It is often cooked in one piece with turnip or collard greens and dried red chiles, and then sliced to serve topped with sliced scallions, "pot likker," and corn bread.

HOG MAW

Hog maw is the stomach of a pig. It is popularly used in Pennsylvania Dutch and Southern soul-food cooking, and is sometimes sold in supermarkets in those areas. It can usually be obtained by special order through butchers.

STORAGE: Fresh hog maw should be cleaned and used within 24 hours. Cooked (prepared by the butcher), it can be stored in the refrigerator up to 3 days, or frozen for up to a month.

PREPARATION AND USE: Wash thoroughly and remove all membranes. Recipes often recommend soaking it in 1 quart water, 1 cup vinegar, and ¼ cup salt for 30 minutes, and then rinsing and removing all fat. It is sometimes cooked with CHITTERLINGS until tender and then fried until crisp. More often, it is stuffed with a sausage mixture. One average hog maw will hold 4 pounds of raw stuffing, and, when cooked, will serve 6 to 8.

The classic way of preparing this is to stuff it with a combination of 2 pounds seasoned pork sausage mixed with 2 pounds of onions and potatoes. The Pennsylvania Dutch add apples. The maw is then sewn closed and simmered like a giant sausage for 3 hours; then drained, placed in a roasting pan, and baked, basting with butter, until it is browned. It is served hot or cold.

HOMINY

SPANISH: *pozole*

Hominy is a native American food, introduced by the American Indians to the early Colonists, consisting of whole kernels of dried corn that have been treated and soaked to remove the germs and hulls. This is done either mechanically ("pearl" hominy) or chemically with baking soda, SLAKED LIME, or lye ("lye" hominy). It is virtually the same thing as *nixtamal* (see under CORN, DRIED) used to make MASA for Tamales and tortillas (see THE FOODS OF LATIN AMERICA section). Broken kernels are called "samp." White or golden hominy is sold in 29-ounce cans in most supermarkets, and is available dried in some health food stores and Latin American markets.

STORAGE: Dry hominy can be stored in an airtight container in a cool place for up to a year. Cooked or canned hominy, once opened, can be stored in the refrigerator for use within a few days, or frozen.

PREPARATION AND USE: To make hominy from dried corn kernels dissolve ¼ cup baking soda or slaked lime in 4 quarts of cold water. Add 4 cups of dried corn kernels and leave to soak overnight. The next day, simmer the mixture for 3 hours until the hulls are loose and the kernels have puffed, adding more water as necessary to keep the hominy covered. Drain, rinse well, and rub to remove the hulls. At this point the hominy can be dried, pressure canned, or frozen for future use. To serve, simmer 4 hours until tender.

Allow ⅓ cup of dried hominy or ⅔ to 1 cup cooked or canned hominy for each serving in most recipes. A 29-ounce can, drained, contains 3½ cups, enough for 4 to 6 servings, depending on the recipe. Dried hominy must be treated like a bean and soaked; then cooked for 3 to 4 hours in water (or milk) until it is tender. When tender, it is often beaten with butter to whiten and season it. Canned hominy is precooked and needs only warming.

Hominy is sometimes served as a potato substitute or used as a soup ingredient, specifically in Pozole, a term used both for the type of hominy used, and an American Indian soup popular in the Southwest and in Mexico. The Pueblo Indians add hominy to Jackrabbit Stew. In the South, it is often seasoned and layered with Cheddar cheese or sour cream and onions in a casserole and baked, or flavored with onions, green peppers, and bacon fat. Cooked hominy can be used in place of corn in any succotash recipe.

HOMINY GRITS

When whole hominy is ground, the particles are called hominy "grits." White is preferred over yellow. Grits are sold in coarse, medium, or fine grains, which are interchangeable in recipes. One type of grits is "quick-cooking."

STORAGE: In an airtight container in a cool place it will keep indefinitely.

PREPARATION AND USE: One cup of grits, when cooked, will serve four. Grits are cooked in exactly the same manner as CORNMEAL. They are often served for breakfast in the South, as a cereal, or as baked or fried mush, which is made by pressing cooked grits into a buttered pan and chilling it; then slicing to dip in seasoned flour and fry in bacon drippings. Grits are the traditional accompaniment to a slice of country-style ham and Red Eye Gravy (see under HAMS, COUNTRY-STYLE) made from the pan drippings and black coffee. Grits are used in all sorts of casseroles, such as Garlic Grits (made with garlic-flavored process cheese). They are often served with bacon and pan gravy, and in the Southwest are made into a spoon bread with sour cream and chiles. The varieties of preparation seem endless. A famous New Orleans breakfast dish is Grillades and Grits, as prepared in the following recipe.

GRILLADES AND GRITS

1½ pounds veal or beef round, cut into 4 slices,   For 4 servings
       approximately ½" thick
½   cup flour
1   teaspoon salt
¼   teaspoon black pepper
3   tablespoons lard, bacon drippings, or vegetable oil
2   medium onions
1   large green bell pepper, (seeds and membranes removed)
       chopped
¼   cup minced celery, including leaves
2   cloves garlic, minced
2   tablespoons butter
2   cups peeled chopped tomatoes, fresh or canned (drained)
½   teaspoon chopped fresh thyme, *or* a healthy pinch of dried
       thyme, crumbled
1   bay leaf
     Tabasco sauce to taste

GRITS:
5   cups water
1   teaspoon salt
1   cup hominy grits (not quick-cooking)

If using veal steaks, pat them dry. If using beef rounds, pound them with a mallet to half their original thickness; pat dry. Combine the flour, salt, and pepper in a grocery bag, add the meat, and shake until the meat is coated; remove meat, shaking off excess flour.

Heat the lard in a large skillet. Brown the meat on both sides in the lard and remove from the pan. Pour out the lard, leaving any flavorful brown crusty bits in the bottom of the skillet. Use the same skillet to sauté the onions, green pepper, celery, and garlic in the butter until the onion is transparent. Add the tomatoes, thyme, and bay leaf. Bring to a boil; then lower the heat and simmer for 5 minutes.

Meanwhile, start cooking the grits by bringing the 5 cups water to a boil with 1 teaspoon salt in a small saucepan. Lower the heat and pour the grits into the simmering water slowly, stirring constantly, until all are added and the mixture is smooth. Cover and cook on the lowest possible heat for 25 to 30 minutes.

Return the meat to the pan and cook slowly until the meat is tender when pierced with a knife (about 20 minutes), covering the skillet if the sauce becomes too thick. Add a few shakes of Tabasco sauce and taste; add more Tabasco and salt if needed.

To serve, mound the hot grits on warm serving plates. Top each with a steak and a portion of sauce.

INDIAN NUT

See PIÑON NUT

JERKY

Jerky, a powerhouse of energy and the same thing as African BILTONG (see THE FOODS OF AFRICA section), was originally wind-dried pulled meat or game used as a hunting provision and winter sustenance by American Indians. At one time it was made primarily from buffalo and other wild game such as venison and rabbit. It was either sun-dried or smoked next to the fires inside tepees, and Indian women took pride in the thinness of the strips of meat. Hunters still make it from all types of game, sometimes soaking it in brine or adding seasonings before drying. Commercial versions, sold in supermarkets and sporting good stores are usually made of beef with many different seasonings—some are as highly seasoned as PASTRAMI. Jerky that has been pounded to the fineness of sawdust and then mixed with fat and dried fruit is called pemmican.

STORAGE: Both jerky and pemmican can be stored for up to 3 months at room temperature without loss of quality, and can be refrigerated or frozen for years. To retain flavor, store in an airtight container.

PREPARATION AND USE: To make jerky, lean beef or game is cut into 4″ squares. Using a very sharp knife, it is sliced into a long, ¼″ thick strip by cutting the first slice to within ¼″ of the bottom, turning the meat and slicing downward to ¼″ of the bottom, turning, cutting, until it is in one long thin strip.

It is then stretched, or "jerked," strung along one side with thread, and hung in the sun to dry. If protected from moisture at night, it will dry in 3 to 4 days. It can also be dried on racks on a screened porch, but takes up to a week to dry. Today, jerky is more often oven-dried on a rack at 150° for 12 hours.

Seldom used today as a survival food, jerky is often eaten by Americans as a snack. It can be cut into squares and cooked in soups or stews, or soaked until soft and then fried with onions and chiles. The Hopi Indians cook it with eggs, make it into hash, use it in Tamale filling, or broil it until crisp to serve as a lean bacon. Hawaiian jerky, *pipikaula,* is served at luaus. Fine jerky makes an interesting appetizer on picnics, served with various dips, such as mustard or barbecue sauce.

JERUSALEM ARTICHOKE

OTHER: sun choke

FRENCH: *topinambour* GERMAN: *Erdartischocke* ITALIAN: *topinambur* SPANISH: *cotufa* or *pataca*

This tuber was cultivated by the American Indians long before the arrival of Columbus. It looks like ginger-root and, in spite of its name, it is not related to the globe artichoke. The name is believed to be a corruption of the Italian word *girasole,* meaning sunflower, because these tubers are from a certain type of sunflower. The name "artichoke" was given to them by Samuel de Champlain, who found them growing in a garden in 1605 and thought their flavor resembled that of artichokes. Actually, they are more potato-like in flavor, though they contain no starch at all. They are sold fresh in supermarkets during the winter months, especially in the West. Look for heavy ones that are blemish-free and, if they are to be peeled, buy those with the smoothest skins to facilitate peeling.

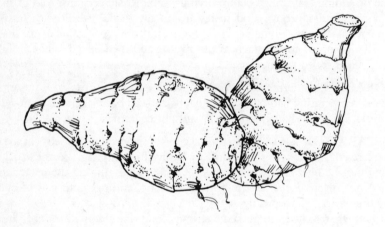

STORAGE: In a cool, airy spot or in the refrigerator, they will keep for up to a week. Once cooked, they can be refrigerated for up to 2 days.

PREPARATION AND USE: Allow 3 to 4 of these small tubers per person, or approximately 1 pound for 2 generous servings. Scrub, cover with water and salt, and simmer 8 to 10 minutes until tender; then peel, if desired. Alternately, they can be rubbed with oil to bake like potatoes. After cooking, they can be mashed to serve as is, dipped in batter to cook as fritters, or sliced and marinated to use in salads. To fry them, boil for 2 to 3 minutes, rub off the skin, cut into slices, and deep-fry or pan-fry them.

They are used as a relish ingredient, and are served, especially in France, where they are very popular, with cream and a flavoring of fresh chives. American-Italians are especially fond of them sautéed in olive oil with tomatoes and fresh basil. American Indians like to cut them into ⅛″ slices and fry them in bacon drippings, like home-fried potatoes.

These are often eaten in the fingers like a radish or used as a salad ingredient, in which case they can be peeled, but it is not necessary and it is a bit difficult to do so, even with a vegetable peeler. When peeled, they darken very quickly when exposed to air, so drop them into a bowl of cold water to which you have added a bit of lemon juice or granulated vitamin C (ascorbic acid) to keep them white until they are to be used. They are sometimes used in Chinese dishes as a substitute for water chestnuts though they lose their crisp quality if overcooked.

MAPLE SUGAR

This is a very sweet sugar made by evaporating the sap of the maple tree until it becomes solid. It is twice as sweet as granulated sugar.

STORAGE: It will keep, refrigerated and tightly wrapped, for up to 6 months.

PREPARATION AND USE: If used as a sugar substitute, be sure to mix it with at least an equal measure of granulated sugar to compensate for its super-sweetness. Maple sugar is used primarily to mold into candies in Vermont, and as a filling in hand-dipped chocolates sold in candy shops. In New England, it is often used in the preparation of Pickled Pears.

MAPLE SYRUP

This sweet, rich syrup is made by condensing the sap gathered by tapping various types of maple trees growing in the eastern regions of Canada and in New England. The process was taught to the early settlers by the American Indians. Pure maple syrup is sold in most supermarkets or can be ordered by mail in several grades: "A" is the best for use as a table syrup, "B" is darker, stronger, and used mostly for cooking. Maple-flavored syrup, which is lighter in taste and less expensive, but which does contain real maple flavor as well as "imitation" maple syrup (flavored with FENUGREEK—see HERBS, SPICES, AND SEASONING BLENDS section—among other things), is also sold. When pure maple syrup is simmered to a spreadable consistency it is called "maple butter." Both syrup and butter are sold in most supermarkets. There is a new "powdered" form available by mail (see SHOPPING SOURCES), which is crystalized maple syrup and can be made into either syrup or butter.

STORAGE: Though high in sugar content, real or imitation maple syrup spoils quickly at room temperature. Once opened, store in the refrigerator. Powdered maple keeps indefinitely in an airtight container in a cool place.

USE: Maple syrup is usually served warm over waffles and pancakes. It makes an excellent sauce for ice cream, and is often used in icings for cakes, bread pudding, and candies, such as Maple Fudge. A New England specialty is Maple Sugar Pie, either with a plain custard or a chiffon filling. It is often used in flavoring vegetables, such as carrots and sweet potatoes and is used as the sweetener in Vermont Baked Beans. Once used as a liquid for boiling hams and sausages, when it was plentiful and cheap, it is now used primarily as a topping for breakfast specialties, including Cornmeal Mush or grits.

Maple butter is used as is, or sometimes mixed with BUTTERNUTS, for cake icings. Powdered maple is mixed with water to the desired consistency and used as a convenience item by people who need to store it for long periods of time.

MOLASSES

Molasses is a by-product of the refining of cane sugar and is available in three grades, from the smooth, sweet, dark amber syrup from the first boiling to the dark molasses from the second boiling to the rough brown "blackstrap" molasses from the third boiling. Light and dark molasses are sold in bottles in most supermarkets. Blackstrap molasses is sold in some supermarkets and in health food stores. Molasses of all grades is sold either "sulphured" or "unsulphured," depending on whether sulphur was used in the refining process. The unsulphured, a favorite of health food enthusiasts, is generally lighter in color and has a richer flavor. Sorghum "molasses" is a syrup made from sorghum (see SORGHUM SYRUP).

STORAGE: Refrigerate after opening for storage of up to 2 months.

USE: Light molasses is mild in flavor and often used as a table syrup over breakfast specialties such as pancakes, waffles, Cornmeal Mush, and grits. The dark is used primarily as a rich flavoring in regional specialties, and blackstrap is favored by many in the same dishes for its distinct flavor and purportedly high mineral content.

Molasses was used as the primary sweetener in the United States until the mid-1800s, and many of the dishes in which it was used have become American classics. Examples are Boston Baked Beans, Pennsylvania Dutch Shoofly Pie, Anadama Bread (made with cornmeal and lard), Scripture Cake, and Gingerbread. Spice Cookies, 6" in diameter, are called Joe Froggers in Marblehead, Massachusetts, where they were created by an old Black man named Joe who lived next to a frog pond. The cookies were a favorite with fishermen, who traded rum for them, because they kept well on trips. In the

Ozarks, it is used with scraps of country-style ham and corn mixed with egg and milk to make fritters, or is cooked with vinegar to make taffy, which is pulled and stretched with buttered hands. The Pennsylvania Dutch use it to make Molasses Cake with sour milk, raisins, and spices; doughnuts called Fastnacht Kuckas; and in their famous Moravian Christmas Cookies. In Missouri, it is the flavoring for Molasses Pie and Squash Custard Pie. It is often used in the South in Sweet Potato Pone, as a topping for Fried Salt Pork, in Barbecue Sauce, and in old recipes for Pecan Pie. Molasses was mixed with butter to use as a spread by the Pioneers. And Indian Pudding, made with cornmeal and topped with vanilla ice cream, is an old New England specialty.

INDIAN PUDDING

For 6 servings

Many old recipes specify that part of the milk be reserved to pour over the pudding during the final 30 minutes of baking. We prefer it made this way.

4   cups milk
½   cup stone-ground yellow cornmeal
⅓   cup unsulphured molasses
½   cup light brown sugar
2   tablespoons butter
1   large egg, beaten
1   teaspoon freshly grated orange rind
1   teaspoon ground cinnamon
1   teaspoon ground ginger
¼   teaspoon freshly grated nutmeg

FOR SERVING:
1   quart vanilla ice cream *or* sweetened whipped cream

Butter a 5- to 6-cup soufflé or baking dish, or six 8-ounce ramekins for individual servings. Preheat oven to 275°.

Bring the milk to a simmer in a 3- or 4-quart saucepan. Sprinkle the cornmeal into the pan gradually, and cook, stirring constantly, over low heat for about 10 minutes, until the mixture has the consistency of porridge. Remove from the heat and whisk in the remaining ingredients.

Pour the mixture into the baking dish(s), smoothing the top(s). Bake the large pudding for approximately 2 hours; the small ones for approximately 45 minutes, until firm in the center. Serve slightly warm, topped with ice cream or whipped cream.

TO PREPARE IN ADVANCE: Cool, and refrigerate overnight. Bring to room temperature; then warm slightly in a low oven before serving.

MUSTARD GREENS

OTHER: Chinese or Oriental mustard

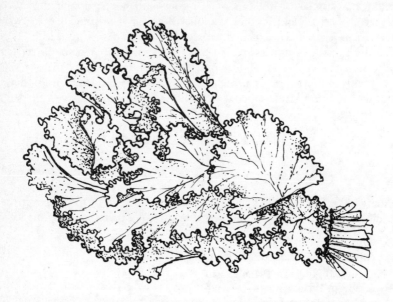

General information on purchasing, storage, and use of mustard greens will be found in THE FOODS OF ASIA section. Sharp-flavored mustard greens, not to be confused with a Chinese variety of cabbage sometimes called Mustard Cabbage, are almost as important to southern soul-food cookery as their cousin, COLLARDS. The type cultivated in the South is usually a curly-leafed variety. Mustard greens are sold nationwide in many supermarkets, fresh or frozen.

USE: Mustard greens are used in the South in the same manner as collards, but they require less cooking time to become tender.

NASTURTIUM

OTHER: Indian cress, *capuchina, nasturcia*

FRENCH: *capucine* GERMAN: Kapuzinerkresse ITALIAN: *naturzio*

Nasturtiums are commonly grown throughout Mexico and the United States for their bright yellow, orange, and red flowers and peppery-tasting leaves. Seeds are available at nurseries.

STORAGE: Store in refrigerator for use as soon as possible.

PREPARATION AND USE: Leaves and flowers add a peppery taste to salads and to vinegars. The stems can be minced to flavor cheese spreads or to add to salads. The ripe berries, which resemble capers, can be pickled in salted vinegar and used like capers in salads, sauces, and marinades. The flowers are especially good to use as a pretty, edible garnish on salads and vegetable dishes.

OKRA

General information on purchasing, storage, and preparation of fresh okra will be found under OKRA in THE FOODS OF AFRICA section; dried okra under OKRA in THE FOODS OF THE MIDDLE EAST section. The early slaves in the South brought okra seeds with them from Africa, introducing okra to the United States. That found in American supermarkets may be either long and tapered, or short and chubby.

USE: Fresh okra is widely used in regional dishes in the United States. Okra Pilau, made with rice, was a favorite preparation of the early slaves. In Louisiana, okra is used for its mucilaginous quality for thickening many versions of Gumbo. In New Orleans, it is often cooked as a vegetable dish with bacon fat, tomatoes, curry powder, and brown sugar. A Southern specialty is pickled okra, made with vinegar, dried red chiles and, occasionally, with dill. Another Southern and Texan method of preparation is to coat okra, sliced or whole, with cornmeal to be deep-fried—when served with Tartare Sauce, this dish is called Okra Oysters. Kentucky Burgoo, a stew made of veal, bacon fat, chicken, and assorted vegetables, usually contains okra.

PASTRAMI

Pastrami is a spicy, pepper-coated smoked beef, closely related to CORNED BEEF, except cut from the boneless plate or flank, which are located by the rib section, next to the brisket. It is a descendant of the Romanian Pastrama (*pastra* is the Romanian word for preserve), originally made with pork and lamb. It is very popular in New York City, and is sold nationwide in Jewish delicatessens and in some supermarkets in whole pieces, or sliced in packets. It can vary greatly in quality, so your best bet is to search out a good source and stick with it. There is a turkey pastrami as well. SALTPETER (see THE FOODS OF EUROPE section) is almost always used in making it which gives it its rosy color, and it may contain other chemicals as well.

STORAGE: Whole or sliced pastrami in its original package can be stored for several weeks (or longer, according to package directions) in the refrigerator. Sliced pastrami from a deli, if tightly wrapped in plastic wrap, will keep for 4 to 5 days in the refrigerator.

PREPARATION AND USE: It can be served hot or cold and is ready to eat. It can become tough if over-heated, so your best bet is to slowly simmer a whole piece, or steam just a few slices until warm. If too peppery for your taste, simmering it will briefly tone it down.

It can be used in place of corned beef in many recipes. The classic way to serve it is thinly sliced and piled an inch high on rye bread with a "shmear" of sharp mustard, which has usually been mixed with a bit of kosher dill pickle juice.

PAWPAW

OTHER: papaw

This fruit is often confused with the PAPAYA (see THE FOODS OF LATIN AMERICA section) because the two fruits have similar names and are of similar color. The pawpaw, however, is native to North America. It is about 6″ long, has many seeds, and a rather strong aroma. The rich flavor is similar to that of bananas. They grow wild, especially in the Ozarks, but are not much cultivated, and are seldom found in markets.

STORAGE: Unripe pawpaws should be wrapped in paper towels and stored in a cool place until they ripen. Ripe ones will keep for 2 to 3 days in the refrigerator.

PREPARATION AND USE: Pawpaws are served in the same manner as melon or small papaya. Allow 1 for 2 servings, and remove the many large seeds. These seeds are often strung in the Ozarks for use as beads.

Pawpaw Butter is highly prized in the Ozarks. To make it, remove the skin and seeds from 6 large pawpaws to yield 6 cups of pulp. Place in a heavy pot with water and simmer for 8 minutes. Add 1 tablespoon powdered pectin, 3 cups of sugar, and a pinch of salt. Boil hard for 5 minutes while stirring;

then lower the heat and cook for 5 minutes longer. Spoon into containers for refrigerator storage or seal in canning jars according to manufacturer's directions. Serve as a spread for bread or muffins.

PEANUTS

OTHER: groundnut, monkeynut, goober
(See under GROUNDNUT in THE FOODS OF AFRICA section for foreign-language names)

Peanuts are native to Brazil, but have a long agricultural history in the United States. George Washington Carver, the highly acclaimed black scientist, was known for developing hundreds of products from peanuts, including not only peanut butter, but flour, ink, and a type of board used in insulation. There are two primary types of peanuts available, the Virginia and the Spanish. The Virginia type, which is longer, has a stronger flavor than the Spanish. Both are sold raw or roasted, salted or unsalted, in or out of their shells. They are also sold vacuum-packed in jars or in cans, usually heavily salted. Also sold in every supermarket is peanut butter, either smooth or chunky. These often contain preservatives. Natural peanut and other nut butters can be purchased in health food stores.

STORAGE: Peanuts can go rancid quickly so it is best to store them in the refrigerator. In their shells, they can be stored for up to 6 months; shelled, for only 3. Peanut butter, once opened, should be stored in the refrigerator.

PREPARATION AND USE: To roast peanuts, shell them but leave their skins on. Spread on a shallow baking pan and bake at 325° for 20-30 minutes, stirring often. Remove the skin from one or two to see how brown they've gotten.

Peanut butter is easily made at home in a blender or electric food processor, and is tastier than store-bought. Let the roasted peanuts cool before processing 1 cupful at a time in the blender, 2 cupfuls in the food processor, until the desired texture is obtained. It may be necessary to add a tablespoon or more of peanut oil if the mixture is too dry. Season, if desired, with salt.

One southern soul-food method of preparation is to boil raw peanuts in their shells in heavily salted water until tender, then serve with plenty of napkins as an appetizer or snack, to be shelled as they are eaten. Peanut soup is popular in Williamsburg, Virginia, and in Georgia. Peanuts are used in many African-American dishes such as Groundnut Stew (see under GROUNDNUT in THE FOODS OF AFRICA section), and in Chinese, Southeast Asian, and Indian dishes. Peanut butter is used in sandwiches, cookies and fudge, nationwide. Peanuts are a flavorful addition to salads as in the following recipe for Pea Slaw.

Pea, Cabbage, and Nut Slaw

For 8 servings
To double recipe for 16 servings, see Note

This takes only minutes to make and is ideal for picnics and many other summer meals.

SLAW MIXTURE:
1 (10-ounce) package frozen tiny peas, thawed
½ head cabbage, cored, and cut crosswise in fine shreds
1 cup roasted peanuts
¼ cup sliced scallions

DRESSING:
⅔ cup mayonnaise
¼ cup Shallot Vinaigrette (see under VINEGAR), *or* French
    or Italian salad dressing of your choice
½ teaspoon celery seeds
    salt and pepper to taste

Note: When doubling recipes for slaws, potato salads, macaroni salads, etc., you will probably find you need less than double the amount of dressing. As a general rule, make 1½ times the dressing (i.e., 1 cup mayonnaise, ⅜ cup salad dressing, etc.). Your salad won't be soupy and you can always add a little more mayonnaise or vinegar if it seems dry.

Combine the slaw ingredients in a large mixing bowl. Stir together the dressing ingredients and pour over the slaw. Mix well; chill.

TO PREPARE IN ADVANCE: This salad keeps well in the refrigerator for up to 5 days, though the nuts gradually lose their crunch.

PEMMICAN
See under JERKY

PINE NUT
See PIÑON NUT

PIÑON NUT
OTHER: Indian nut, pine nut

HOPI: *tuva*

For general information, see PINE NUT, in THE FOODS OF EUROPE section. The variety of piñon nut from native American trees in the Rocky mountains is quite small and rather hard to come by. They are not nearly as common as the longer and thinner Portuguese type and chubbier Chinese type sold in most Italian, Middle Eastern, and Latin American markets. American Indian families gather them in the fall by shaking the trees until the ripe nuts fall out of the cones to the ground. You are most likely to find these labeled as "Indian nuts" in nut shops and health food stores, either in their shells or shelled.

STORAGE: Shelled nuts can be stored in the refrigerator for up to 3 months, and can also be frozen, but lose some of their texture if kept frozen for more than 2 months. Nuts in their shells can be stored for up to a year in the freezer.

PREPARATION AND USE: To shell piñons, wash them well and spread on a shallow baking pan. Roast at 350° for about 20 minutes, stirring several times. While still hot, place between damp cloths and roll vigorously to remove the shells. Use in the same manner as imported pine nuts.

American Indians have long ground these nuts and boiled them in water. The fat that floats to the top of the water is skimmed off to use as a cooking oil, and the liquid is used as a gravy. They also grind them and mix with cornmeal for breads and mush. The roasted nuts are often soaked in salted water for flavoring and returned to the oven to dry and serve as snacks.

PRICKLY PEAR CACTUS

For general information on purchasing, storage, and use of prickly pear cactus, see NOPALES in THE FOODS OF LATIN AMERICA section.

The Hopi Indians have long gathered fresh cactus pads in the spring to simmer whole with sweet corn in water to cover. The cactus is then chopped and cooked to a thick, mucilaginous juice which is used as a dip for Hopi Finger Bread, a Cornmeal Mush made with blue cornmeal (see CORNMEAL, BLUE), which is eaten with the fingers.

PUMPKIN

Pumpkin, a winter squash, was being cultivated by the Indians when the first Colonists arrived. Besides being boiled or roasted, it was dried and ground by the Indians to use like cornmeal. Whole pumpkins, weighing an average of 18 pounds, as well as cut pieces, can be purchased in the fall and winter in supermarkets nationwide. The flowers are edible as well (see SQUASH BLOSSOM in THE FOODS OF LATIN AMERICA section). Look for clean pumpkins with smooth skins. The smaller ones are said to be the most tender. Pumpkin is also sold in 16-ounce cans as a puree, which is a good and very convenient substitute for fresh pumpkin in many recipes. The seeds, PEPITAS (see THE FOODS OF LATIN AMERICA section), can be purchased in many supermarkets, and in health food stores.

STORAGE: A whole pumpkin will keep in a cool place for at least a month, or in the refrigerator for 4 months. Canned pumpkin, once opened, should be transferred to a nonmetal container for use within 4 days, or frozen for up to 4 months.

PREPARATION AND USE: Two pounds of fresh pumpkin will yield 2 cups of cooked, pureed pumpkin, enough for 4 servings in most recipes. To boil, it is seeded, cut up, and peeled and simmered in salted water for 20 to 30 minutes until tender. Alternatively, the pieces can be brushed with butter or oil and baked at 350° for 40 to 45 minutes, brushing with fat from time to time, to be served as a vegetable.

Whole pumpkins are traditionally made into Jack-o'-Lanterns for Halloween, and into Pumpkin Pie for Thanksgiving. The early Colonists often baked pumpkins whole, filling them with spices, MAPLE SUGAR, and milk, creating a very early version of Pumpkin Pie. Steamed Pumpkin Pudding and Pumpkin Butter were also popular. Later, pumpkin was sweetened with MOLASSES to use as a pie filling, which has become a national classic. The Pennsylvania Dutch make a traditional Pumpkin Layer Cake frosted and filled with sweetened and spiced whipped cream. Pumpkin Bread with piñons (see PIÑON NUT) was made by the Pueblo Indians. Pumpkin has long been used as a soup ingredient not only in the United States but in France. It is one of the most popular vegetables in Yugoslavia, where it is called *bundeva,* and in Poland, where it is called *dynia,* and it is cooked in both countries with cream and herbs to serve as a vegetable, or used as a pie filling in strudel pastry (see STRUDEL LEAVES in THE FOODS OF EUROPE section).

Today, in the United States, pumpkin is used in muffins, mousses, soufflés, ice cream—the list is endless. Paul's mother makes a superior Pumpkin Cake, as in the following recipe.

PUMPKIN CAKE WITH CREAM CHEESE ICING AND PECANS

For 16 servings

This is the holiday counterpart of carrot cake—dark orange and spicy! This is a new version of a cake from our first cookbook, *The Pleasure of Your Company.*

CAKE:
- 2 cups sugar
- 4 eggs
- 1 cup vegetable oil
- 2 cups (a 1-pound can) pumpkin
- 2 cups all-purpose flour
- 2 teaspoons baking soda
- ½ teaspoon salt
- 2 teaspoons ground cloves
- 2 teaspoons ground cinnamon
- 1 teaspoon finely grated orange rind (zest)

ICING:
- 6 ounces cream cheese
- 1 (1-pound) box of powdered sugar
- 4 ounces (¼ pound) butter
- 1 teaspoon vanilla extract
- 2–3 teaspoons Grand Marnier

DECORATION:
- 1 cup chopped pecans

Place the sugar and the eggs in the bowl of an electric mixer and beat until smooth and creamy. Add the oil and pumpkin and continue beating until well blended.

Sift together the flour, baking soda, salt, cloves, and cinnamon. Add these to the pumpkin mixture and mix until thoroughly combined.

Pour the batter into an ungreased 10-inch tube pan (angel food pan) and bake at 350° for 55 to 60 minutes. Let the cake cool in the pan for 1 hour before turning it out.

To make the icing, place all the icing ingredients in a bowl and beat them until smooth. Spread the icing over sides and top of cake (don't forget center hole) and decorate the top with the chopped pecans.

TO PREPARE IN ADVANCE: This cake really should be made 2 or 3 days before serving, as the flavor improves on standing. The cake freezes perfectly, iced or not. (When freezing an iced cake, place it in the freezer unwrapped; then when it is solid, wrap it in foil and seal tightly. To serve, unwrap and then defrost at room temperature for about 8 hours.)

QUINCE

See THE FOODS OF THE MIDDLE EAST section

RICE, CAROLINA

The long-grain Carolina type of rice, which is the one most popularly cooked throughout the United States, was originally developed in the Carolinas but is now produced in a number of other states. There are two types: "polished," which cooks easily into fluffy separate kernels, but has most of its nutrients removed in the processing, and "converted," which is somewhat less fluffy, but more nutritious. Most of our brown rice is long-grain unpolished rice, which retains all of its nutrients and has a more assertive, nutty flavor than white rice. Short-grain rice is sometimes called "pudding rice" in the States because it is stickier, and in Louisiana it is called "broken" rice and may even be pounded to break the grains to make them even stickier for certain dishes. "Instant" rice is precooked and dehydrated, during which processes it loses most of its personality. We don't use it. WILD RICE is not a rice at all, but a grass.

STORAGE: White rice keeps better than brown rice. In an airtight glass jar in a cool place, white rice will keep for up to 6 months. If too warm, it becomes bug-infested. Brown rice does not keep well, so store it in the refrigerator.

PREPARATION AND USE: Rice is generally boiled or steamed and, as a general rule, triples in size during the process. Plan on approximately ⅓ cup of raw rice (1 cup after cooking) per serving. In boiling, one uses an unlimited amount of water (as in cooking pasta), so the results are easy to control. White boiled rice is cooked in about 15 minutes, brown in 35. In steaming, a specific amount of water is used for each type: "polished" uses twice its bulk, "converted," 2½ times, and "brown," 3 times. The rice is poured into simmering water, stirred, covered, and cooked over the lowest possible heat until the water has been absorbed; approximately 22 minutes for white rice, 42 minutes for brown. It used to be necessary to wash rice because millers used to coat it with glucose to make it look better, and many nutrients were rinsed away with the coating, but that step can be omitted if the rice you buy is the American supermarket type and it looks clean. Add about a teaspoon of salt per cup of rice when using either method.

Rice is becoming more and more popular in this country as part of the increasing interest in all types of Asian cooking, but has a long history in American cooking, especially in the South where it was originally cultivated. "Dirty" Rice is a Cajun dish of long-grained rice cooked with chicken gizzards and livers. It has a delightful flavor, but a rather unappetizing color, which gives the dish its name. A New Orleans specialty is Calas (rice fritters). In Charleston, rice is baked with bacon fat, onions, tomatoes, ground mace, and red pepper; when the grains are almost cooked, shrimp are stirred in and the cooking finished to make the famous Shrimp Pilau or Perloo, long a southern favorite. Rice Pudding with Almonds, as served at the New York restaurant Delmonico's, was a favorite of Ulysses S. Grant. Andrew Johnson liked Red Rice, cooked with bacon, tomatoes, onions, and garlic; and rice was added to waffle batter by the Van Burens. Spanish rice, made with tomatoes, onion, and garlic, was popular in the West, and was turned into Mexican Rice with the addition of chiles and bacon. Rice was half the basis for New Orleans Red Beans and Rice, the recipe for which appears in this book (see RED BEANS, SMALL under BEANS), but also for Jambalaya, as in the following recipe.

JAMBALAYA

SHRIMP AND STOCK: For 8 to 10 servings
- 2 pounds large raw shrimp
- 2 cups dry white wine
- 2 cups water
- 1 lemon, sliced
- 1 cup celery leaves and diced celery
- 2 teaspoons Shellfish Boil (see CRAB BOIL)
- 2 cloves garlic, sliced

BASIC TOMATO-HAM-SAUSAGE SAUCE:
- 2 tablespoons bacon drippings
  Salt pork or ham fat
- 4 medium onions, minced
- 2 cloves garlic, minced
- 1 pound lean ham, cubed
- 4 pounds ripe tomatoes, peeled, seeded, and diced *or* 2 (28-ounce) cans crushed tomatoes in tomato puree
- 1 pound highly spiced sausages (chorizo, longaniza, kielbasa, or other)
- 3 green bell peppers (seeds and membranes removed), diced
- ½ cup minced celery, including leaves
- ½ cup minced fresh parsley
- 1 tablespoon chopped fresh thyme *or* 1 teaspoon dried thyme leaves, crumbled
- 2 bay leaves

FINAL PREPARATION:
- 2¼ cups long-grain Carolina rice, preferably "converted"
- 1 pound fresh scallops, rinsed and cut in bite-sized pieces
- 4 scallions, thinly sliced, including part of the green

Start one day ahead by cooking and marinating the shrimp. Shell and devein the shrimp, but reserve shells. Place the shrimp with their shells in a 2½- to 3-quart saucepan. Add the wine, water, sliced lemon, celery, Shellfish Boil, and sliced garlic. If necessary, add more water to cover all ingredients. Bring to a boil, lower the heat, and simmer very slowly for 1 minute. Remove from the heat and cool. Refrigerate in the cooking liquid overnight.

The sauce should also be made one day before serving. In a large skillet, melt the bacon drippings, or sauté the salt pork or ham fat until it has rendered some of its fat. Add the onions, and sauté until transparent. Stir in the garlic and cubes of ham, cook briefly, then add the tomatoes. Cook 10 minutes uncovered; with mixture simmering, add the sausage, cut in bite-sized pieces, green peppers, celery, parsley, thyme, and bay leaves. Simmer covered for 30 minutes; remove the lid and simmer uncovered for another 30 minutes or so until the sauce is quite thick. Refrigerate overnight.

About 35 minutes before serving, strain the shrimp and vegetables from the marinade, reserving the marinade. Heat the prepared sauce in a 6-quart or larger Paella pan or in a large stove-top-to-table serving casserole that has a lid. Add the marinade and bring to a rapid boil. Sprinkle in the rice and press it down into the liquid with the back of a spoon. Cover the pan, lower the heat, and simmer slowly for 15 minutes. Remove the lid and lightly mix in the raw scallops, the cooked shrimp, and the scallions, distributing them evenly. Cover, and cook very slowly 4 to 5 minutes longer.

The Jambalaya is now ready to serve from its cooking dish. If there is excess liquid remaining in the bottom of the pan, boil over high heat for a minute or two until evaporated.

TO PREPARE IN ADVANCE: The shrimp and the basic sauce should be cooked the day before. Finish cooking just before serving. Any leftovers can be stored in the refrigerator for up to 3 days. Reheat gently, adding water if the mixture is too thick.

RICE FLOUR

Finely ground rice, which is white if made from white rice, or cream-colored if made from brown rice, is sold in health food stores. It is used in some New Orleans recipes for breakfast fritters, called Calas, and by many Americans who are allergic to wheat products. White rice flour is sold in Asian markets—see RICE FLOUR in THE FOODS OF ASIA section for general information.

SALT PORK
OTHER: white bacon

Cut from the side of the hog, this white fat has been cured in salt, but not smoked like bacon. It is sold in most supermarkets, usually in square chunks weighing 6 to 8 ounces, and varies in salt content. The best has a streak of lean meat through it.

STORAGE: Wrapped tightly and stored in the refrigerator, it will keep for a month or longer. It can be frozen, but loses something in the process.

PREPARATION AND USE: Salt pork is used primarily as a seasoning. If it is too salty (you might fry a piece to test it), cut it up as called for in the recipe, simmer for 5 to 10 minutes in water to cover, drain, and rinse; then proceed with the recipe.

Salt pork is an important New England ingredient, traditional in Boston Baked Beans, Clam Chowder, Pork Apple Pie, and in the original New England Boiled Dinner. In Martha's Vineyard, a dish of salt pork, potatoes, and onions cooked by fishermen along the waterfront is called Scooting Along the Shore. A simple Succotash Soup made of limas, corn, and salt pork was a favorite of John Quincy Adams. In the South, it is used in the cooking of COLLARDS and MUSTARD GREENS, which are traditionally served with vinegar in which hot peppers have steeped. It is used in New Orleans in the making of Gumbo, and in that special version using a variety of greens, Gumbo Z'Herbes. Another Louisiana salt pork dish is Congri, salt pork simmered with cowpeas (see BLACK-EYED PEA), onions, and rice. The Pennsylvania Dutch use it in making G'shtuptafel Lewir (stuffed liver). In Wyoming, it is essential for Son-of-a-Gun Stew, made with veal heart, sweetbreads, and brains. The Hopis dice it to make a dish of Baked Sweet Corn and Pinto Beans.

SAUSAGES

Most American sausages originated in Europe, so information on their classifications and specific descriptions appear in THE FOODS OF EUROPE section under SAUSAGE. There are some that are distinctly American and are found locally, in farmer's markets or sausage shops. They are listed below.

CREOLE SAUSAGES

Acadians traditionally gather in Louisiana for all-day hog butchering parties called Boucheries, where all types of sausages are made, cooked, and consumed. Creole sausages, called "boudin," or "little pudding" (the same as the French term for blood sausage, but it applies to all sausages here) can be purchased locally or ordered by mail. There are no perfectly adequate substitutes for them, but we make suggestions for some that are approximations. *Boudin blanc* is made from fresh pork shoulder, rice, and seasonings and, when cooked, the interior becomes very soft, like a stew. There is no substitute. *Boudin rouge* is a fully cooked and smoked blood sausage. *Saucisse boucaner* is a smoked pork sausage, for which KIELBASA (see SAUSAGE, DRY AND SEMI-DRY, in THE FOODS OF EUROPE section) makes an adequate substitute. *Andouille* is a lean pork sausage made of CHITTERLINGS seasoned with vinegar and red pepper, which is usually cut in ½″ slices and fried to serve, or is used as an ingredient in Gumbo. It is different from the French version because it contains rice. *Chaurice* is a highly spiced fresh sausage of ground veal, beef, and pork, flavored with thyme, clove, bay leaf, nutmeg, and a good deal of red and white pepper, which is still popular for barbecues. Spanish CHORIZO or LONGANIZA (see THE FOODS OF LATIN AMERICA section), seasoned with extra red and white pepper, make the best substitutes. *Fromage de tête* is HEAD CHEESE (see under SAUSAGE, COOKED, in THE FOODS OF EUROPE section), sometimes made from bits of meat other than from the head. These sausages are not often used as ingredients, though *andouille, chaurice*, or *saucisse boucaner*, might be used as a Gumbo ingredient, or be added to Jambalaya, a dish that consists of rice and whatever fish, poultry, or meat is available to the cook.

PENNSYLVANIA DUTCH

Farmer's markets in areas where there is a large Amish population have many varieties of all kinds of sausages from LIVERWÜRST to HEAD CHEESE (see under SAUSAGE, COOKED, in THE FOODS OF EUROPE section). "Souse" is a sausage made of bits of pork cooked with onion and is denser than the usual head cheese. "Lebanon bologna" is a local specialty of Lebanon, Pennsylvania, which is a coarse, rather sour-tasting bologna that has been flavored with a lactobacillus culture and then briefly air-dried. Please note that *schmierkäse*, which is a soft, spreadable sausage in Germany, is the word for cottage cheese in Pennsylvania Dutch.

OTHER REGIONAL SAUSAGES

Throughout the Midwest and on the East Coast where there are large settlements of immigrants, sausage making still flourishes. In ethnic neighborhoods, one can find Czech sausages, Serbian sausages, and Polish sausages of all description, which are available only locally. Milwaukee, with its large German population, is the home of Fred Usinger sausages, some of which are distributed throughout the country and are of generally excellent quality.

SCHNITZ

These dried, whole or quartered sweet apples are used in Pennsylvania Dutch cookery. They can be purchased locally in areas with a large Amish population or bought in 8-ounce packages by mail. Apples dried in this manner were preserved for year-'round use. Dried apple rings, sold in natural-food stores, can be substituted, though they are less dense.

STORAGE: Schnitz will keep in an airtight container in a cool, dark place for up to a year.

PREPARATION AND USE: Soak schnitz in water to cover for 2 hours; sliced dried apples only 30 minutes.

The classic dish for these apples is Schnitz and Knepp (apples and dumplings), a very old Pennsylvania Dutch recipe in which a 3-pound piece of ham is simmered for 2 hours in water to cover; then the soaked apples are cooked with the ham for 1 more hour; and then the whole is topped with baking powder dumplings, which are steamed for 15 minutes. These apples are often mixed with other dried fruits and simmered to make compotes to accompany meals or to serve as dessert.

The Pennsylvania Dutch use dried apples to make the filling for Dried-Apple Pie, for which they are soaked overnight and then simmered for an hour with orange juice and rind, and pureed. The mixture is then sweetened with sugar and flavored with cinnamon, placed in a pie shell, and covered with a lattice pastry top to be baked at 375° for 40 minutes. Dried-Apple Cake, made with molasses and spices, is usually topped with vanilla ice cream.

SLAKED LIME

OTHER: calcium hydroxide

Slaked lime, a white powder used in the making of HOMINY and *nixtamal* (see under CORN, DRIED, in THE FOODS OF LATIN AMERICA section), can be purchased in well-stocked pharmacies or hardware stores that carry canning equipment. It has a long history of use in pickling in the rural sections of the United States.

STORAGE: It will keep indefinitely in an airtight container in a cool, dry place.

PREPARATION AND USE: Directions for using slaked lime to make HOMINY will be found with that listing. It is also used in the manufacture of MASA HARINA, "prepared corn flour." (See THE FOODS OF LATIN AMERICA section.)

Soaking cucumbers in water to which some form of lime has been added gives them incomparable crispness. [Our recipe for Super Crisp Pickle Chips appears in our book, *With Love from Your Kitchen* (Tarcher).] The chemical does not actually dissolve in water, so any residue should be thoroughly washed away in the numerous rinsings specified in the recipes that call for it. Do not worry about getting the mixture on your hands—it is not caustic. In fact, "lime water" was, and still is, given to children for stomach upset.

SORGHUM SYRUP

OTHER: sorghum "molasses"

This is a sweet, molasses-like syrup made from sweet sorghum, a plant resembling sugar cane, grown in Kentucky, Indiana, and Tennessee. It was a staple ingredient in the South during the Civil War. It was traditional where it was grown to have "sorghum boils," similar to "maple sugar boils" in Vermont. It is sold in health food stores and is valued for its high mineral content.

STORAGE: Like molasses, this spoils quickly, so store in the refrigerator after opening. It will keep for up to 2 months.

USE: This has long been used as a sweetener, like molasses, in recipes in the South. It was often used as a substitute for CANE SYRUP, in everything from cakes to cookies to whiskey. It is also used as a syrup over breakfast specialties, such as pancakes, waffles, and Corn Cakes. In Kentucky, it is used in Sorghum Cake, made with sour milk and spices and baked in a loaf pan, and is often served as a spread for biscuits in Tennessee.

SOURDOUGH

This fermented dough used as leavening in making bread has been used around the world for thousands of years. It has become most famous in North America, however, where prospectors and pioneers came to be called "sourdoughs" because of their reliance on it. Sourdough French bread has risen to its culinary heights in San Francisco. Sourdough "starter" may be borrowed, purchased from bakeries, or it can be made easily at home. Some cooks have kept their starter going for 20 years! Crystals to make starter are sold in health food stores and gourmet specialty shops.

STORAGE: Sourdough starter should always be kept in a nonmetal container because it will corrode metal during long storage. A crock with a rather loose-fitting lid is ideal. Active starter can be refrigerated or frozen, but will be killed if its temperature exceeds 95°. If stored at room temperature, it will need to be "fed" once a week by adding flour and water to it.

PREPARATION AND USE: There are three ways to get a starter going.

1. Purchased or borrowed starter (all you need is 2 to 4 tablespoons) should be put in a nonmetal, 8-cup container. Add 2 cups of white flour (bleached or unbleached) and 2 cups of warm water (not over 115° or the yeast will be killed). Cover with a towel (not the lid) and let stand for 3 to 4 hours at room temperature until it is bubbly. Stir, cover loosely, and refrigerate.

2. A basic starter can also be made with yeast. Dissolve 1 package active dry yeast in 1½ cups warm water or milk with 1 tablespoon sugar or honey. Add 2 cups of white flour, cover loosely, and let stand for 24 hours until it smells slightly sour. Stir to collapse the bubbles and store in the refrigerator, loosely covered, for 3 days before using it.

3. A "wild yeast" starter, which gathers wild yeast spores from the air, is very tricky to make, and not at all necessary when the other, easier methods are equivalent.

If you use your "starter" at least once a week, it needs no special attention except to replace what you have used with equal amounts of flour and liquid, either water or milk, stir, and return it to the refrigerator. If you don't use it that often, remove about one-fourth of the starter about every 10 days and replace it with an equal amount of flour and liquid. (The part you remove can be frozen for future use and needs only to be thawed and brought to room temperature.) This process "feeds" the starter and keeps it active.

The starter is always brought to room temperature before use.

We don't consider ourselves experts in sourdough baking, and there are excellent books that deal with the subject. Sourdough is used for many recipes besides French bread. It makes excellent biscuits and rye bread and is used in Alaska to make sourdough pancakes with wild blueberries. In Texas, it is made into biscuits with lard. Our favorite sandwich is made with fresh sourdough rolls filled with a chicken salad freshly made with mayonnaise, sour cream, and walnuts, and just a bit of vinaigrette dressing for tang.

SPLIT PEAS

See under BEANS

SQUASH BLOSSOM

General information on purchasing, storage, and use of squash blossoms will be found in THE FOODS OF LATIN AMERICA section. American Indians have long gathered squash blossoms in the morning before they open. They were added to stews or stuffed with a dough made of blue cornmeal and bacon drippings to be baked, or were dipped in batter to be fried and served as fritters or as a garnish for soup.

TABASCO SAUCE

This is the trade name of the world's best known hot sauce and has become almost a generic term for all liquid red-pepper seasoning sauces. Tabasco is made in New Iberia, Louisiana, of tabasco peppers, vinegar, and salt. Other brands are Louisiana, and Red Rooster, to name a few.

STORAGE: It will keep for up to 6 months on the pantry shelf. It oxidizes and loses flavor if stored longer.

USE: These hot sauces are used, drop by drop, to spice up all kinds of soups, stews, dips, and sauces. It is a common table condiment, especially in the South.

TOMATOES, GREEN

For general information on purchasing, storage, and use of red, or ripe, TOMATOES, see THE FOODS OF EUROPE section.

Green tomatoes are simply unripened tomatoes. They were picked by the early settlers when the first frost threatened, and there were also those last tomatoes on the vine that never ripened, so many ways of using them up were devised. Green tomatoes can be purchased in many supermarkets all year, though they are most easily found in the early fall. Do not confuse them with Mexican "green tomatoes" (see TOMATILLO in THE FOODS OF LATIN AMERICA section).

STORAGE: Store in the refrigerator or they will ripen unevenly and turn blotchy.

PREPARATION AND USE: For most uses, allow one tomato per serving. Small tomatoes are usually used in relishes; larger ones are used for frying.

Piccalilli is a New England relish made from red and green tomatoes, red and green bell peppers, cucumber, vinegar, celery, and brown sugar. The Pennsylvania Dutch make a green tomato relish called Chow Chow, served as one of the many "sweets and sours" served with every meal. They are used in Wyoming to make Green Tomato Pie, in which sliced tomatoes are mixed with sugar, cloves, cinnamon, flour, and vinegar. The Pueblo Indians make Green Tomato Stew with squash blossoms, corn, and zucchini. In the South, they are cut into ¼″ slices, dipped in flour, and fried in bacon drippings to be topped with crisp bacon for serving. In Pennsylvania, brown sugar is almost always sprinkled over green tomatoes that are fried, and often cream is added to the pan during the cooking to make a gravy to spoon over them.

VINEGAR, APPLE CIDER

Cider vinegar was invented by the Colonists, and was originally made from either sweet or hard cider. It quickly became a staple and was sold in general stores from huge barrels with spigots. The process was speeded up by adding a brown slimy membrane composed of yeast and bacteria, called a "mother," from an old batch. It is the most popular vinegar in the United States, and is sold in bottles in every supermarket. It is not as tart as white vinegar. All brands are similar.

STORAGE: Indefinitely on the pantry shelf.

USE: Cider vinegar has long been used in pickling, specifically for Piccalilli, Chow Chow, and Spiced Peaches, served as a side dish with many meals. Old-timers in New England still consider it a tonic, and often down a jigger of vinegar before meals to aid the digestion.

WILD RICE

OTHER: Indian rice, tuscarora rice

Wild rice is not actually rice, but the seed of a water grass. For many years it was harvested by Chippewa Indians from wild grass growing at the edges of the lakes in the northern United States, but now it is being commercially cultivated as well, and is more uniform in size and of generally better flavor and quality. It is sold in supermarkets and gourmet specialty shops in 4-ounce boxes and is very expensive. It has a strong, nut-like flavor and chewy texture. The specific type being cultivated in California is larger grained, costs approximately 25 percent less, and is of excellent quality, though it is still a luxury item.

STORAGE: Store in an airtight container in a cool dry spot, like any grain. Leftover rice can be stored in the refrigerator for up to 5 days.

PREPARATION AND USE: Though expensive, wild rice goes a lot farther than other rices, with 1 cup making 3½ cups of cooked rice, or 4 to 6 servings. It can be extended by mixing it after cooking with cooked brown rice or BULGHUR WHEAT, or can be cooked with another grain in the proportion of 2 parts grain to 1 part wild rice. It tends to be dirty and must be thoroughly rinsed. It can be boiled in unlimited salted water, or steamed like rice (see under RICE, CAROLINA) using 4 cups of water (or broth or part white wine) to 1 cup of wild rice and cooking for 35 minutes or so. To keep the special crisp texture, don't overcook it.

Cooked wild rice can be seasoned with butter to serve and is complemented by sautéed mushrooms (for which it has a special affinity), onions, and chopped nuts. Leftover rice should be steamed over simmering water just until heated. It is an excellent accompaniment to all kinds of fowl and is often combined with chopped giblets and sherry to be used as a stuffing for them and for baked whole fish. The Chippewa Indians cooked it to serve with wild game or made it into a breakfast porridge. Today, it is being used in many imaginative ways—in soups, stuffings, and even in cold salads, as in the following recipe.

WILD RICE PECAN SALAD

1 cup (4 ounces) wild rice, cooked and drained   For 6 servings
¼ cup Shallot Vinaigrette (see under VINEGAR), *or* any
     seasoned vinegar and oil dressing of your choice
4 scallions, cut in ¼″ slices
¾ cup pecan halves, toasted at 350° for 10 minutes
     Zest of 1 orange, coarsely chopped, *or* 2 teaspoons freshly
     grated orange rind
     Salt and freshly ground black pepper to taste

Variation: The recipe may be made with ½ cup brown rice in place of ½ cup of the wild rice to cut costs. With some menus, we like to add a sprinkling of homemade curry powder to the recipe.

Toss the rice while still slightly warm with the Shallot Vinaigrette in a serving bowl. Chill. Add remaining ingredients. Serve chilled or at room temperature.

TO PREPARE IN ADVANCE: Store, covered, in the refrigerator. Serve within 3 days.

YUCCA FRUIT

The large, sweet fruit from wild yuccas are easily knocked off the tall plants with sticks when they are ripe during July and August in the Southwest. This is an old custom with American Indians and those interested in wild foods, as yucca fruits are not sold commercially. The young leaves and tender shoots of the plant are used by the Hopis and other Indians of the Southwest to make baskets.

STORAGE: Ripened fruit will keep in a cool place for up to 5 days, or in the refrigerator for up to 2 weeks.

PREPARATION AND USE: The fruit is diced and boiled until thick and then mashed to serve as a spread. It can also be baked, whole, at 300° for 2 hours and then cut open to remove the ball of seeds and fiber in the center.

The pulp is used by the Hopis in pies or turnovers, or shaped into bars and dried in the sun or in a low oven to make an Indian candy.

RECOMMENDED ETHNIC COOKBOOKS

The following is not intended to be a comprehensive listing of every ethnic cookbook, but those we have found to be most authentic, authoritative, and inspiring.

HERBS, SPICES, AND SEASONING BLENDS

David, Elizabeth. *Spices, Salt and Aromatics in the English Kitchen*. London: Penguin Books, 1970.

Hériteau, Jacqueline. *Herbs*. New York: Grosset & Dunlap, Inc., 1975.

Hooker, Alan. *Herb Cookery*. San Francisco: 101 Productions, 1970.

Humphrey, Sylvia Windle. *A Matter of Taste: The Definitive, Seasoning Cookbook*. New York: The Macmillan Co., 1965.

McNair, James K. *The World of Herbs & Spices*. California: Ortho Books, 1978.

Sunset Books. *How to Grow Herbs*. California: Lane Publishing Co., 1972.

Witty, Helen, and Colchie, Elizabeth Schneider. *Better Than Storebought*. New York: Harper & Row, 1979.

AFRICAN

Hachten, Harva. *Kitchen Safari*. New York: Atheneum Publishers, 1970.

Karsenty, Irène and Lucienne. *La Cuisine Pied-Noir (Cuisines de Terroir)*. Paris: Éditions Denoél, 1974.

Odarty, Bill. *A Safari of African Cooking*. Detroit: Broadside Press, 1971.

van der Post, Laurens, and the Editors of Time-Life Books. *African Cooking*. New York: Time-Life Books, 1970.

Wilson, Ellen Gibson. *A West African Cookbook*. New York: M. Evans & Co., Inc., 1971.

ASIAN

Brennan, Jennifer. *The Original Thai Cookbook*. New York: Richard Marek Publishers, 1981.

Chang, Wonona W. and Irving B., and Kutscher, Helene W. and Austin H. *An Encyclopedia of Chinese Food and Cooking*. New York: Crown Publishers, 1970.

Chen, Esther. *Introductory Traditional Chinese Regional Cuisine*. Seattle: Esther Chen (5610 12th N.E., Seattle, WA 98015), 1976.

Claiborne, Craig, and Lee, Virginia. *The Chinese Cookbook*. Philadelphia and New York: J.B. Lippincott Co., 1972.

Green, Karen. *Japanese Cooking for the American Table*. Los Angeles: Tarcher, 1982.

Hom, Ken, and Steiman, Harvey. *Chinese Technique*. New York: Simon & Schuster, 1981.

Jaffrey, Madhur. *An Invitation to Indian Cooking*. New York: Alfred A. Knopf, 1973.

Jaffrey, Madhur. *Madhur Jaffrey's World-of-the-East Vegetarian Cooking*. New York: Alfred A. Knopf, 1981.

Kuo, Irene. *The Key to Chinese Cooking*. New York: Alfred A. Knopf, 1980.

Mei, Fu Pei. *Pei Mei's Chinese Cookbook*, Vols. 1 and 2. Taipei: T&S Industrial, 1969 and 1974.

Miller, Gloria Bley. *The Thousand Recipe Chinese Cookbook*. New York: Grosset & Dunlap, 1970.

Ngô, Bach, and Zimmerman, Gloria. *The Classic Cuisine of Vietnam*. New York: Barron's, 1979.

Shurtleff, William, and Aoyagi, Akiko. *The Book of Tofu*. Brookline, Mass.: Autumn Press, Inc., 1975.

Rau, Santa Rama, and the Editors of Time-Life Books. *The Cooking of India*. New York: Time-Life Books, 1969.

Sahni, Julie. *Classic Indian Cooking*. New York: William Morrow & Co., 1980.

Solomon, Charmaine. *The Complete Asian Cookbook*. New York: McGraw-Hill Book Co., 1976.

Steinberg, Raphael, and the Editors of Time-Life Books. *The Cooking of Japan*. New York: Time-Life Books, 1969.

Steinberg, Raphael, and the Editors of Time-Life Books. *Pacific and Southeast Asian Cooking*. New York: Time-Life Books, 1970.

Tsuji, Shizuo. *Japanese Cooking, a Simple Art*. Tokyo and New York: Kodansha International, Ltd., 1980.

Wong, S. T. Ting, and Schulman, Sylvia. *Madame Wong's Long-Life Chinese Cookbook*. Chicago: Henry Regnery Co., 1977.

Yueh, Jean. *The Great Tastes of Chinese Cooking*. New York: Times Books, 1979.

Yeuh, Jean. *Dim Sum and Chinese One-Dish Meals*. New York: Irena Chalmers Cookbooks, Inc., 1981.

EUROPEAN

Bailey, Adrian, and the Editors of Time-Life Books. *The Cooking of the British Isles*. New York: Time-Life Books, 1969.

Beck, Simone; Bertholle, Louisette; Child, Julia. *Mastering the Art of French Cooking*. New York: Alfred A. Knopf, 1961.

Beck, Simone. *New Menus From Simca's Cuisine*. New York: Harcourt Brace Jovanovich, 1979.

Brown, Dale, and the Editors of Time-Life Books. *The Cooking of Scandinavia*. New York: Time-Life Books, 1968.

Bugialli, Giuliano. *The Fine Art of Italian Cooking*. New York: Times Books/Quadrangle—The New York Times Book Co., Inc., 1977.

Caggiano, Biba. *Northern Italian Cooking*. Arizona: H.P. Books, 1981.

Child, Julia, and Beck, Simone. *Mastering the Art of French Cooking, Volume Two*. New York: Alfred A. Knopf, 1970.

Claiborne, Craig; Franey, Pierre; and the Editors of Time-Life Books. *Classic French Cooking*. New York: Time-Life Books, 1970.

David, Elizabeth. *A Book of Mediterranean Food*. London: Penguin Books, 1958.

David, Elizabeth. *French Country Cooking*. London: Penguin Books, 1951.

David, Elizabeth. *Italian Food*. London: Penguin Books, 1954.

David, Elizabeth. *Summer Cooking*. London: Penguin Books, 1955.

DiVecchio, Jerry Anne, Ed. *Sunset Italian Cook Book*. Menlo Park, CA: Lane Publishing Co., 1981.

Feibleman, Peter S., and the Editors of Time-Life Books. *The Cooking of Spain and Portugal*. New York: Time-Life Books, 1969.

Field, Michael and Frances, and the Editors of Time-Life Books. *A Quintet of Cuisines*. New York: Time-Life Books, 1970.

Fisher, M.F.K., and the Editors of Time-Life Books. *The Cooking of Provincial France*. New York: Time-Life Books, 1968.

Grigson, Jane. *The Art of Making Sausages, Pâtés and Other Charcuterie*. New York: Alfred A. Knopf, 1968.

Grigson, Jane. *English Food*. London: Macmillan London Ltd., 1974.

Grigson, Jane. *Good Things*. New York: Alfred A Knopf, 1971.

Giusti-Lanham, Hendy, and Dodi, Andrea. *The Cuisine of Venice and Surrounding Northern Regions*. New York: Barron's Educational Series, 1978.

Hazan, Marcella. *The Classic Italian Cookbook*. New York: Harper's Magazine Press, 1973.

Hazan, Marcella. *More Classic Italian Cooking*. New York: Alfred A. Knopf, 1979.

Johnston, Mireille. *The Cuisine of the Sun, Classic Recipes From Nice and Provence*. New York: Vintage Books, a Division of Random House, 1979.

Hazelton, Nika Standen, and the Editors of Time-Life Books. *The Cooking of Germany*. New York: Time-Life Books, 1969.

Lang, George. *Cuisine of Hungary*. New York: Atheneum Publishers, 1971.

Levy, Faye. *La Varenne Tour Book*. Seattle: Peanut Butter Press, 1979.

McNair, James. *Adventures in Italian Cooking*. San Francisco: Ortho Books, 1980.

Olney, Richard. *Simple French Food*. New York: Atheneum Publishers, 1972.

Papashvily, Helen and George, and the Editors of Time-Life Books. *Russian Cooking*. New York: Time-Life Books, 1969.

Pépin, Jacques. *A French Chef Cooks at Home*. New York: Simon & Schuster, 1975.

694

Pépin, Jacques. *La Technique*. New York: Quadrangle/The New York Times Book Co., 1976.

Pépin, Jacques. *La Methode*. New York: Times Books, 1979.

Root, Waverly, and the Editors of Time-Life Books. *The Cooking of Italy*. New York: Time-Life Books, 1968.

Root, Waverly, *The Food of France*. New York: Random House, 1958.

Scott, Jack Denton. *The Complete Book of Pasta*. New York: William Morrow & Co., 1968.

Sheraton, Mimi. *The German Cookbook*. New York: Random House, 1966.

Troisgros, Jean and Pierre. *The Nouvelle Cuisine of Jean and Pierre Troisgros*. Translated by Roberta Wolfe Smoler. New York: William Morrow & Co., 1978.

Vergé, Roger. *Roger Vergé's Cuisine of the South of France*. New York: William Morrow & Co., 1980.

Wechsberg, Joseph, and the Editors of Time-Life Books. *The Cooking of Vienna's Empire*. New York: Time-Life Books, 1961.

Willan, Anne. *Basic French Cookery*. Tucson: H.P. Books, 1980.

Willan, Anne, & l'Ecole de Cuisine la Varenne. *French Regional Cooking*. New York: William Morrow & Co., 1981.

Wolfert, Paula. *Mediterranean Cooking*. New York: Quadrangle/The New York Times Book Co., Inc., 1977.

LATIN AMERICAN

de Leon, Josefina Valazquez. *Mexican Cook Book for American Homes*. Mexico City: Acadamia de Cocina Velazquez de Leon, 1956.

Hansen, Barbara. *Mexican Cookery*. Tucson: H.P. Books, 1980.

Kennedy, Diana. *Cuisines of Mexico*. New York: Harper & Row, 1972.

Kennedy, Diana. *Recipes From the Regional Cooks of Mexico*. New York: Harper & Row, 1978.

Kennedy, Diana. *Tortilla Book*. New York: Harper & Row, 1975.

Leonard, Jonathan Norton, and the Editors of Time-Life Books. *Latin American Cooking*. New York: Time-Life Books, 1968.

Ortiz, Elizabeth Lambert. *The Complete Book of Caribbean Cooking.* New York: M. Evans & Co., 1973.

Ortiz, Elizabeth Lambert. *The Complete Book of Mexican Cooking.* New York: M. Evans & Co., 1967.

Wolfe, Linda, and the Editors of Time-Life Books. *The Cooking of the Caribbean Islands.* New York: Time-Life Books, 1970.

Villa, Angelo, and Barrios, Vicki. *Adventures in Mexican Cooking.* Edited by Marjorie and Clyde Childress. San Francisco: Ortho Books, 1978.

Middle Eastern

Chantiles, Vilma Liacouras. *The Food of Greece.* New York: Atheneum Publishers, 1975.

Corey, Helen. *The Art of Syrian Cookery.* New York: Doubleday & Co., 1962.

Daisy, Ina. *The Best of Bagdad Cooking, With Treats From Tehran.* New York: Saturday Review Press/E.P. Dutton & Co., 1976.

Farah, Madelain. *Lebanese Cuisine.* Portland, Oregon: Madelain Farah, 1972.

Khayat, Marie Karam, and Keatinge, Margaret Clark. *Food From the Arab World.* Beirut: Khayats, 1959.

Nickles, Harry G., and the Editors of Time-Life Books. *Middle Eastern Cooking.* New York: Time-Life Books, 1969.

Roden, Claudia. *A Book of Middle Eastern Food.* New York: Alfred A. Knopf, 1974.

Shepard, Sigrid M. *Natural Food Feasts From the Eastern World.* New York: Arco Publishing, Inc., 1979.

Theoharous, Anne. *Cooking and Baking the Greek Way.* New York: Holt, Rinehart and Winston, 1977.

Wolfert, Paula. *Couscous and Other Good Food From Morocco.* New York: Harper & Row, 1973.

Zane, Eva. *Middle Eastern Cookery.* San Francisco: 101 Productions, 1974.

Regional American

Balsley, Betsy, Ed., and the Food Staff of the Los Angeles Times. *The Los Angeles Times California Cookbook.* New York: Harry N. Abrams, Inc., 1981.

Beard, James. *James Beard's American Cookery.* Boston: Little, Brown and Co., 1972.

Beard, James. *The New James Beard.* New York: Alfred A. Knopf, 1981.

Bentley, Virginia Williams. *Bentley Farm Cookbook.* Boston: Houghton Mifflin Co., 1975.

Brown, Dale, and the Editors of Time-Life Books. *American Cooking.* New York: Time-Life Books, 1968.

Brown, Dale, and the Editors of Time-Life Books. *American Cooking: The Northwest.* New York: Time-Life Books, 1970.

Brown, Helen Evans. *Helen Brown's West Coast Cook Book.* Boston, Little, Brown and Co., 1952.

Cannon, Poppy, and Brooks, Patricia. *The President's Cookbook.* New York: Funk & Wagnall's, 1968.

Cunningham, Marion, and Laber, Jeri, Editors. *The Fannie Farmer Cook Book, 12th Edition.* New York: Alfred A. Knopf, 1980.

De Masters, Carol. *Dining in Milwaukee.* Seattle: Peanut Butter Press, 1981.

Early, Eleanor. *New England Cookbook.* New York: Random House, 1954.

Feibleman, Peter S., and the Editors of Time-Life Books. *American Cooking: Creole and Acadian.* New York: Time-Life Books, 1971.

Foley, Joan and Joe. *The Chesapeake Bay Fish and Fowl Cookbook.* New York: Macmillan Publishing Co., 1981.

Geise, Judie. *The Northwest Kitchen.* Los Angeles: J.P. Tarcher, 1982.

Greene, Bert. *Honest American Fare.* Chicago: Contemporary Books, 1981.

Groff, Betty, and Wilson, José. *Good Earth and Country Cooking.* Harrisburg, PA: Stackpole Books, 1974.

Hughes, Phyllis, Ed., *Pueblo Indian Cookbook.* Santa Fe: Museum of New Mexico Press, 1972.

Junior League of New Orleans. *The Plantation Cookbook.* New York: Doubleday & Co., 1972.

Kafka, Barbara. *American Food & California Wine.* New York: Irena Chalmers Cookbooks, Inc., 1981.

Kavena, Juanita Tiger. *Hopi Cookery.* Phoenix: University of Arizona Press, 1978.

Lee, Jimmy. *Soul Food Cook Book*. New York: Award Books, 1970.

Leonard, Jonthan Norton, and the Editors of Time-Life Books. *American Cooking: The Great West*. New York: Time-Life Books, 1971.

Leonard, Jonathan Norton, and the Editors of Time-Life Books. *American Cooking: New England*. New York: Time-Life Books, 1970.

Marks, Rowena McLean, and McDermott, Betty. *California Cooks*. Los Angeles: The Ward Ritchie Press, 1970.

Masterton, Elsie. *The Blueberry Hill Menu Cookbook*. New York: Thomas Y. Crowell Co., 1965.

The Original Picayune Creole Cook Book. New Orleans: The Times-Picayune Publishing Co., 1901, 1906, 1916, 1922, 1928, 1936.

Platt, June. *June Platt's New England Cook Book*. New York: Atheneum Publishers, 1971.

Shenton, James P; Pellegrini, Angelo M.; Brown, Dale; Shenker, Israel; Wood, Peter; and the Editors of Time-Life Books. *American Cooking: The Melting Pot*. New York: Time-Life Books, 1971.

Walter, Eugene, and the Editors of Time-Life Books. *American Cooking: Southern Style*. New York: Time-Life Books, 1971.

Wilson, José, and the Editors of Time-Life Books. *American Cooking: The Eastern Heartland*. New York: Time-Life Books, 1971.

Witty, Helen, and Colchie, Elizabeth Schneider. *Better Than Storebought*. New York: Harper & Row, 1979.

INTERNATIONAL

de Groot, Roy Andries. *Feasts for All Seasons*. New York: McGraw-Hill Book Co., 1966.

Field, Michael. *Michael Field's Culinary Classics and Improvisations*. New York: Alfred A. Knopf, 1967.

Green, Karen. *The Great International Noodle Experience*. New York: Atheneum Publishers, 1977.

International Association of Cooking Schools. *International Association of Cooking Schools Cookbook*. New York: Irena Chalmers Cookbooks, Inc., 1981.

Katzen, Mollie. *The Moosewood Cookbook*. Berkeley: Ten Speed Press, 1977.

Meyers, Perla. *The Peasant Kitchen*. New York: Random House, 1975.

Price, Mary and Vincent. *A Treasury of Great Recipes*. New York: Ampersand Press, 1965.

Wilde, Mary Poulos. *The Best of Ethnic Home Cooking*. Los Angeles: J.P. Tarcher, 1981.

SHOPPING SOURCES

The following listing are sources we have found ourselves or have found specially recommended in ethnic cookbooks. Those which have an asterisk (*) following their names deal in mail-order. Write for price lists and enclose a self-addressed, stamped envelope. Some of these sources charge for their catalogues and deduct the cost of it from the first purchase. Some also have minimum orders.

If you know of good sources that we have missed, we should very much appreciate your sending information to us at:

Diana and Paul von Welanetz
P.O. Box 692
Pacific Palisades, CA. 90272

HERBS AND SPICES

Magic Garden Herb Co.
P.O. Box 332
Fairfax, CA 94930

Estus
1499 67th Street
Emeryville, CA 94608

Nature's Herb Co.
281 Ellis St.
San Francisco, CA 94102

Kitazawa Seed Co. (plants, seeds)
1748 Laine Ave.
Santa Clara, CA 95051

Taylor's Herb Gardens, Inc.
(plants, seeds)*
1535 Lone Oak Rd.
Vista, CA 92084

Carpilands Herb Farm
(plants, seeds)*
Silver Street
Coventry, CT 06238

The United Society of Shakers
Sabbathday Lake
Poland Spring, ME 04274

Deer Valley Farm
R.D. 1
Guilford, NY 13780

Paprikás Weiss
1546 Second Ave.
New York, NY 10028

The Spice Corner
904 S. 9th St.
Philadelphia, PA 19147

Greene Herb Gardens
Greene, RI 02827

Meadowbrook Herb Garden
Route 138
Wyoming, RI 02898

Hilltop Country Inn & Shop
P.O. Box 1734
Cleveland, TX 77327

Horticultural Enterprizes
P.O. Box 810082
Dallas, TX 75381

Market Spice, Inc.
P.O. Box 2935
Redmond, WA 98073

AFRICAN INGREDIENTS

We have had no luck in locating good mail-order sources for African ingredients. Items such as palm oil, cassava, and gari, can often be found in well-stocked Latin American markets.

ASIAN INGREDIENTS

CHINESE

Kwong On Lung Co.
680 N. Spring St.
Los Angeles, CA 90015

Wing Chong Lung Co. Grocery
922 S. San Pedro St.
Los Angeles, CA 90015

Southeastern Food Supplies*
400 NE 67th St.
Miami, FL 33138

Lee's Oriental Gifts and Foods*
3325 Bailey Ave.
Buffalo, NY 14215

Kam Man Food Products*
200 Canal St.
New York, NY 10013

Wing Woh Lung Co.*
50 Mott St.
New York, NY 10013

Wing Fat Co., Inc.
33-35 Mott St.
New York, NY 10013

Oriental Import-Export Co.
2009 Polk St.
Houston, TX 77003

Super Asian Market
2719 Wilson Blvd.
Arlington, VA 22201

Wang's Co.
800 Seventh St., NW
Washington, DC 20001

Chinamart Trading Co.
210 Spadina Ave.
Toronto, Ontario
Canada

INDIAN

Bazaar of India*
1131 University Ave.
Berkeley, CA 94702

Bezjian Grocery*
4725 Santa Monica Blvd.
Los Angeles, CA 90029

Mr. K's Gourmet Foods & Coffee
Stall 430, Farmer's Market
6333 W. 3rd St.
Los Angeles, CA 90036

House of Spices*
76-17 Broadway
Jackson Heights, NY 11373

Passage to India Gifts
127 E. 28th St.
New York, NY 10016

Antone's Import Co.*
4234 Harry Hines Blvd.
Dallas, TX 75219

House of Rice*
4122 University Way NE
Seattle, WA 98105

Top Banana Ltd.
1526 Merivale Road
Ottawa, Ontario
K2G 3J7 Canada

JAPANESE

Safe and Save
2030 Sawtelle Blvd.
Los Angeles, CA 90025

K. Sakai Co.
1656 Post St.
San Francisco, CA 94115

Pacific Mercantile Grocery*
1925 Lawrence St.
Denver, CO 80202

Far East Trading Co.*
2835 N. Western Ave.
Chicago, IL 60618

Star Market*
3349 N. Clark St.
Chicago, IL 60657

Jung's Oriental Food Store*
1140 E. 9th St.
Des Moines, IA 50316

Yoshinoya*
36 Prospect St.
Cambridge, MA 02139

Sun Sun Co.
34 Oxford St.
Boston, MA 02111

Asian Food Market*
217 Summit Ave.
Jersey City, NJ 07306

Katagiri Co.*
224 E. 59th St.
New York, NY 11022

Japan Imported Foods
808 N.W. 6th St.
Oklahoma City, OK 73106

Mikado
4709 Wisconsin Ave., N.W.
Washington, DC 20016

KOREAN

East-West Food Center
3300 W. 8th St.
Los Angeles, CA 90005

SOUTHEAST ASIAN
(Thai, Indonesian,
 Vietnamese, etc.)

Jaynell Dutch Import
3113 W. 6th St.
Los Angeles, CA 90020

Ann's Dutch Import Co.*
4537 Tujunga Ave.
North Hollywood, CA 91604

Bangkok Market*
4757 Melrose Ave.
Los Angeles, CA 90029

Hillcrest Oriental Food Center
540 University Ave.
San Diego, CA 92103

Merapi Inc.
139 White St.
Danbury, CT 06810

Vietnam House*
242 Farmington Ave.
Hartford, CT 06105

Thai Grocery, Inc.*
5014 N. Broadway
Chicago, IL 60640

De Wildt Imports, Inc.*
R.D. #3
Bangor, PA 18013
(Mail-order only)

EUROPEAN INGREDIENTS

Conte di Savoia
555 W. Roosevelt Rd.
Chicago, IL 60607

Maison Glass (European &
domestic gourmet specialties)*
52 E. 58th St. Dept. W
New York, NY 10022

Manganaro Foods (Italian)*
488 9th Ave.
New York, NY 10018

Paprikás Weiss*
1546 2nd Ave.
New York, NY 10028

LATIN AMERICAN INGREDIENTS

Santa Cruz Chili & Spice Co.
P.O. Box 177
Tumacacori, AZ 85640

Catalina's Italian Market
1070 N. Western Ave.
Los Angeles, CA 90029

Del Rey Spanish Foods
Central Market, Stall A-7
317 S. Broadway
Los Angeles, CA 90013

Jones Grain Mill (dried herbs)
Grand Central Market
317 S. Broadway
Los Angeles, CA 90013

Casa Lucas
2934 24th St.
San Francisco, CA 94110

La Palma
2884 24th St.
San Francisco, CA 94110

Chapala Market
605 N. Milpas St.
Santa Barbara,CA 93103

El Molino Foods
1078 Santa Fe Dr.
Denver,CO 80204

La Preferida Inc.
3400 W. 35th St.
Chicago, IL 60632

Central Grocery Co.*
923 Decatur St.
New Orleans, LA 70116

Bueno Mexican Foods*
P.O. Box 293
Albuquerque, NM 87103

Josie's Best Mexican Foods*
1731 2nd St. 1130 Agua Fria St.
P.O. Box 5525
Santa Fe, NM 87501

Casa Moneo*
210 W. 14th St.
New York, NY 10011

Pecos River Spice Co.
500 East 77th
New York, NY 10162

Beaverton Foods*
P.O. Box 687
Beaverton, OR 97075

La Mexicana
10020 14th, SW
Seattle, WA 98146

International Safeway
1330 Chain Bridge Rd.
McLean, VA 22101

MIDDLE EASTERN INGREDIENTS

Manukian's Basturma and
   Soujouk Co.
International Foods
1720 S. Orange Ave.
Fresno, CA 93702

G.B. Ratto and Co.
821 Washington St.
Oakland, CA 94607

Acropolis Food Market*
1206 Underwood, NW
Washington, DC 20012

Skenderis Greek Import*
1612 20th St., NW
Washington, DC 20009

Athens Imported Food*
City Market 84-84
Indianapolis, IN 46204

Progress Grocery
915 Decatur
New Orleans, LA 70116

Cardullo's Gourmet Shop*
6 Brattle St.
Cambridge, MA 02138

Model Food Importers*
113-115 Middle St.
Portland, ME 04111

Gabriel Importing Co.
2461 Russell
Detroit, MI 48207

Mourad Grocery
13847 Hamilton St.
Highland Park, MI 48203

Morgan's Mexican and
Lebanese Foods
736 S. Robert St.
St. Paul, MN 55107

K. Kalustyan
123 Lexington Ave.
New York, NY 10016

Sahadi Importing Company
187 Atlantic Ave.
Brooklyn, NY 11201

Ellis Bakery
577 Grant St.
Akron, OH 44311

Athens Pastry Import*
2545 Lorain Ave.
Cleveland, OH 44113

Near East Market
602 Reservoir Ave.
Cranston, RI 02910

Sayfy's Groceteria
265 Jean Talon, E.
Montreal, Quebec
H2R 1S9 Canada

T. Eaton Co.
190 Yonge St.
Dept. 205
Toronto, Canada M5B 1C8

REGIONAL AMERICAN INGREDIENTS

All of the following deal in mail-order, and prices or catalogues are given upon request.

Broadbents Food Products (Kentucky
hams, sausages, pickles)*
6321 Hopkinsville Rd.
Cadiz, KY 42211

Colonel Bill Newsom's Hams
(Kentucky country hams)*
127 N. Highland Ave.
Princeton, KY 42445

C.S. Steen Syrup Mill, Inc.
(pure cane syrup and *la cuite*)*
P.O. Box 339
Abbeville, LA 70510

Bourgeois Meat Market
(Creole sausages)*
519 Schriever Highway
Thibodaux, LA 70301

Jugtown Mountain Smokehouse
(slab, sliced, and Canadian bacon,
and smoked poultry, nitrate free)
P.O. Box 366
Flemington, NJ 08822

Gwaltney of Smithfield (Smithfield
and Williamsburg hams)*
P.O. Box 489
Smithfield, VA 23430

Joyner Smithfield Hams
  (Smithfield hams)*
Box 387
Smithfield, VA 23430

Green Mountain Sugar House
  (maple syrup, sugar, Vermont
  Cheddar cheese)*
Box 341
Ludlow, TX 05149

Harrington's in Vermont (corncob-
  smoked hams, bacon, poultry)*
Main St.
Richmond, VA 05477

MISCELLANEOUS

CHEESES

Cheese-of-all-Nations*
153 Chambers St.
New York, NY 10007

SAUSAGE CASINGS

Tatarowicz's*
390 Broadway
Bayonne, NJ 07002

Sedro Industries
P.O. Box 8009
Rochester, NY 14606

RECIPE INDEX

APPETIZERS

Blue Cheese Spread for Apples, 641
Escargots in Pasta Shells, 375–376
Felafel, 569–570
Fonduta, 345–356
French Bread Croutons, 371
Hummus Bi Tahina, 597–598
Mozzarella Marinara, 341–342
Nacho Appetizer Platter, 528–529
Quesadillas with Epazote, 526
Saganaki, 578
Sesame Brie Wafers, 339
Spinach Pâté, 337

BEEF

Grillades and Grits, 666–667
Ropa Vieja, 530–531
Steak with Four Peppercorns, 57–58
Vivi's Tamale Pie, 82–83

BREADS (See also FLATBREADS)

Crackling Bread, 656–657
Lahvosh Sandwich Roll, 599–560

CHICKEN

Chicken Lenore, 441–442
Chicken Mogli, 66–67
Chicken Suprêmes in Mustard Cream,
    404–405
Chicken Suprêmes in Paprika-Champagne
    Sauce, 53–54
Fancy Taste Chicken, 62–63
Kung Pao Chicken (Chicken with Charred
    Chiles and Peanuts), 160–161

DESSERTS

Amaretto Cream with Raspberries, 316–317
Apple Tart with Almond Filling, 315
Chocolate Chip Hazelnut Cookies, 388–389
Chocolate Soufflé, 363–364
Cornmeal Piñon Cookies, 652
Fiesta Flan, 79
Figgy Pudding, 589–590
Flaming Mango Topping for Ice Cream, 539
Fudge Walnut Torte, 364–365
Indian Pudding, 671
Pralin Cream, 426–427

Pumpkin Cake with Cream Cheese Icing and
    Pecans, 678–679
Ravani, 587-588
Sesame Seed Brittle, 72

DRESSINGS

Japanese Country Dressing, 297
Miso Salad Dressing, 223
Raspberry Vinegar, 468
Shallot Vinaigrette, 467
Taramosalata, 621–622
Tomatoes with Fresh Basil Dressing, 461

DUCK

Confit d'Oie, 368–369
Crisp Duckling with Green Peppercorns and
    Kumquats, 58–60

DUMPLINGS

Pot Stickers with Sauce, 305–306
Rye Bread Dumplings, 431

EGGS

Barley Soufflé, 415
Fresh Vegetable Frittata, 347–348
Quiche Printanière, 352–353

FILLINGS

Chinese Chicken Filling, 593–594
Feta Filling, 593
Hugh's Filling for Peking Pancakes,
    157–158
Spinach Filling for Filo, 592–593

FISH

Crawfish Étouffée, 658
Fillets de Sole Troisgros, 455–456
Gravlax and Gravlax Sås, 432–433
Hot and Spicy Szechuan Shrimp, 145–146
Shellfish Boil, 83
Tempura, 291–292

FLATBREADS

Blue Corn Tortillas, 650
Chilaquiles, 559
Flour Tortillas, 560–561
Hugh's Peking Pancakes, 249

Flatbreads, *cont.*

Injera, 117
Rotis, 265

GARNISHES. *See* **SEASONINGS**

NOODLES. *See* **PASTA**

PASTA

Cavatelli Caruso, 413–414
Fettuccine with Shiitake Cream Sauce, 228
Linguine with Broccoli, 418
Pasta alla Puttanesca, 22
Pasta Tricolore, 18–19

PASTES AND POWDERS. *See* **SEASONINGS**

PORK

Barbecued Roast Pork, 187
Salcisse e Fagioli (Italian Sausage and Bean Casserole), 322–323

PORRIDGE

Eba (Cassava Porridge), 101
Mealie Meal Porridge, 107–108

RICE

Easy Sushi Rice, 262–263
Jambalaya, 681–682
Red Beans and Rice, 637–638
Risoto con Funghi Secchi, 400–401
Sizzling Rice Soup, 263–264
Wild Rice Pecan Salad, 690

SALADS

Belgian Endive Walnut Salad, 326
Ensalada de Nopalitos, 544
Four Bean Salad, 634–635
Jícama Salad with Cilantro, 535
Parsley Salad, 55–56
Pea, Cabbage, and Nut Slaw, 676
Serbian Salad, 357
Szechuan Noodle Salad, 253
Tabooli, 574–575
Thai Cucumber Salad, 300
Tomatoes with Fresh Basil Dressing, 461
Wild Rice Pecan Salad, 690

SAUCES

Black Bean Sauce, 136–137
Creamy Clam Sauce for Pasta, 416–417
Indonesian Peanut Sauce, 199
Mint Chutney, 48–49
Pesto, 423
Quick Basic Brown Sauce, 435–436
Red Chile Sauce, 514–515

Salsa Cruda, 511
Sancerre Sauce, 51
Shabu-Shabu, 176–178
Sorrel Sauce, 458
South African Fruit Curry, 108–109
Tempura Dipping Sauce, 293
Tomato Chutney, 165
Welsh Rarebit, 469

SEASONINGS

Almond Paste, 314–315
Berberé, 96–97
Caramelized Lemon Zest, 470
Chili Powder, 81–82
Garam Masala, 88
Gremolata. (*See under* Veal Stew alla Milanese, 39)
Harissa, 596
Hot Curry Powder, 85
Madras Curry Paste, 85–86
Niter Kibbeh, 110–111
Pralin, 426
Ras el Hanout, 615
Serundeng, 168
Tomato-Herb Mustard, 389–390

SOUPS

Aromatic Beef Noodles, 142–143
Basic Bouillon, 327
Basic Cream of Vegetable Soup, 394
Callaloo Soup, 492
Chicken Groundnut Stew, 105–106
Chile Verde, 557–558
Creamy Lamb Stew with Herbs, 70
Doro Wat, 97–98
Oxtail Chinoises, 73–74
Papou's Greek Stew, 608–609
Preserved Vegetable Soup, 255
Sancocho, 537
Sizzling Rice Soup, 263–264
Sopa de Chiles Poblanos, 570
Sopa de Frijol Negro, 487–488
Székely Gulyás, 437
Veal Stew alla Milanese, 39–40

STEWS. *See* **SOUPS**

VEAL

Grillades and Grits, 666–667
Truffle-Stuffed Veal Chops, 385–386
Veal Stew alla Milanese, 39–40

VEGETABLES

Alu Gobi (Curried Cauliflower and Potatoes), 131–132
Baked Peas with Pancetta, 410

Broccoli with Oyster Sauce, 245
Chiles en Nogada, 501–502
Chorizo Chile Beans, 522–523
Croûte Aux Champignons, 399
Cucumber Sushi Rolls (*Kappa-Maki*), 261–262
Flageolets, 324
Fresh Vegetable Frittata, 347–348
Imam Bayildi, 586–587

Linguine with Broccoli, 418
Raita, 88–89
Ratatouille Niçoise, 373–374
Red Beans and Rice, 637–638
Stir-Fried Long Beans, 137
Tempura, 291–292. (*See also* Tempura Dipping Sauce, 293)
Tomatoes with Fresh Basil Dressing, 461
White Bean Puree, 633–634

GENERAL INDEX

Note: The page numbers in italic denote the main entry of the listed ingredient.

abalone, 125
ablemanu, 107
Accent. *See* monosodium glutamate
achee (ackee). *See* akee
achiote
  adobo de, and condimentado. *See* recado
    colorado seeds, 478–479
acitrón (candied cactus), 479
Adam's fig. *See* plantain
aduki (adzuki). *See* azuki
agar, *126–127*, 308
Aji-No-Moto. *See* monosodium glutamate
ajwain, 127
akee, 480
albi. *See* taro root
alimentary paste, *See* konnyaku
  Chinese style. *See* Won Ton wrappers
alligator pear. *See* avocado
allspice, 16–17
almond
  bitter, 312–313
  earth. *See* chufa
  oil, 313
  paste, 314–315
  powder, 127–128
amaranth, *128*, 491
amardeen. *See* qamardin
amaretti, 313, *316–317*
amazu shoga. *See under* ginger pickled, 190
amchoor (dried mango), 128
Anaheim chile. *See* chile verde
Anardana, 48, *128–129*
anchovy, 317
  paste (essence), 318
ancient eggs. *See* eggs, 1000 year old
andouille sausage, 443
angelica, *318*, 330
angostura (bitters), 480
anise, *17*, 72, 73
  flavored liqueurs, 566
  pepper. *See* Szechuan peppercorns
aniseed. *See* anise
annato seeds. *See* achiote seeds
ao nori (seaweed), 271
Appenzell cheese, 343
apple brandy. *See* calvados
Arak. *See* anise-flavored liqueurs
arborio. *See* rice, Italian

arhal dal. *See under* dal, 174. *See also* pigeon
  pea
arrowhead . *See* arrowroot
arrowroot, (Asia): 129–130; (Latin
    America): 481
  powder, 130, 617
  starch, 130, 481
artichoke, Jerusalem, 668–669
arugula, 319
asafetida, 50, *130–132*
ashes, culinary, 628
asparagus, 133
ata (African condiment). *See* shatta; (Asian
    flour). *See* atta
ate (fruit paste), 481–482
atta, 132
avocado, 482–483
  leaves, 483
azafrán (Mexican saffron), 65, *483–484*
azuki (beans), 135
  paste, 308

bacalao (salted fish), 484
bacon and drippings, 628–630
  Canadian, 630
  Chinese, 132
bagoong (bagoongalamang). *See* shrimp
    paste, Southeast Asian
bajra (bullrush millet), 109
balsam pear. *See* melon, bitter
bamboo
  leaves, 133
  shoots, 133–134
bamiya (bamya, bamies). *See* okra
banana leaves, 484–485
Banon cheese, 356
baobab, *95*, 101, 106
bara elaichi. *See under* cardamom, 24
barbecued roast duck. *See* duck, roast
barbecue sauce, Chinese, 134. *See also* hoisin
    and chee how
bar-le-duc, confiture de, 319–320
barley and pearl barley, 320–321
  pressed, 134–135
basil, 17–18
basteda, 566
bastourma (dried beef), 567–568
battuto alla Genovese. *See* pesto

Bauernwürst, 439
bay laurel. *See* bay leaf
bay leaf, 19–20
   Indonesian. *See* daun salaam
Bayonne ham, 386
bay rum berries, 20
beach plum, 630–631
bean curd (custard), 139–140
   dried sticks, 140–141
   fermented, 141
beans
   (Asia): 135–139; azuki, 135; black, salted
     and fermented, 135–136; long
     (asparagus, Chinese green, chopstick,
     ribbon bean), 137; mung (green gram),
     138; soybeans, dried (yellow, soya,
     great bean), 138–139
   (Middle East): 568–572; chick-peas,
     568–570; fava (*bob*, broad, horse,
     Windsor, shell bean), 570–571; lentils,
     571–572; lupini, 572
   (Regional America): 631–639; black-eyed
     pea (yellow-eyed, cow pea), 631–632;
     cranberry (shell-outs, shell bean),
     632–633; great northern, 633; kidney,
     634; lima (butter, Madagascar),
     635–636; navy (pea beans), 636; red
     beans, small (Mexican chili) 636–637;
     split-peas, 638; tepari, 638–639
beans, dried
   (Europe): 321–325; borlotti, 322;
     cannellini (Tuscan, white kidney), 322;
     flageolets, 323–324; lentil (champagne,
     blond), 324–325
   (Latin America): 485–488; black (turtle),
     486–488; pink (rosada, Mexican red),
     488; pinto, 488
   refried. *See* frijoles refritos
   threads. *See* cellophane noodles
bêche-de-mer, 147
beef
   corned, 652–653
   dried. *See* jerky, biltong, carne seca
beefsteak leaves. *See* shiso
Belgian endive, 325–326
bellelay (cheese), 343
bel paesa, 340
Bengal gram. *See* channa dal *under* dal, 173
beni shoga. *See under* ginger, pickled, 190
benne. *See* sesame seeds
berberé, 53, 93, *96–97*, 110
besan, 148
bharat, 572
Bierwürst, 449
bigarde. *See* orange, Seville
biltong, 95, 96, *98–99*, 329
bird peppers. *See* dried chiles *under* chiles,
   Asian

bird's eye chiles. *See* dried chiles *under* chiles,
   Asian
birds' nests, 148–149
bissybissy. *See* cola nut
bittern. *See* nigari
biznaga. *See* acitrón
blachan. *See* shrimp paste, Southeast Asian
black-eyed pea, 631–632
black gram. *See under* dal, 174–175
black mushrooms. *See* mushrooms, dried
black pudding sausage, 444
blood sausage, 444
Blutwürst, 444
Bockwürst, 439
bok cho. *See* vinegar rice, Chinese
bok choy, 151–152
bologna, 444
Bombay duck, 149–150
Bonbel cheese, 340
boquerónes, 317
borage, 20–21
botargo, *572–573*, 621
bottle gourd. *See* squash, bottle
boudin blanc, boudin noir (sausage), 445
bouillon, *326–327*, 369
   cubes and granules, 327–328
Boule de Périgord, 356
bouquet garni, 15, 40, 74, 76, 80
Boursin cheese, 337
bovril, 328
Bratwürst, 445
Braunschweiger, 445
Brazil nut, 489
breadfruit, 489–490. *See also* jackfruit
Brie, 338
brinjal, hairy. *See* melon, hairy
brionne. *See* chayotte
broccoli, Chinese, 150
   rabe. *See* rape
brown gravy sauce. *See* molasses, Chinese
   bead
Bryndza cheese, 356
bucatini pasta, 413
Bucheron cheese, 356
buckwheat (groats), 328–329
bulghur wheat, 48, 55, 328, *573–575*
bünderfleisch, 329–330
burdock root. *See* gobo
butter
   palm, 112
   ghee, 189–190
butter beans. *See* lima beans
butterbur. *See* coltsfoot
butternut, 639

cabbage, Oriental, 151–153: bok choy, choy
   sum (chard, Chinese chard, white
   mustard), 151–152; celery cabbage

(napa, nappa, Chinese lettuce), 152–153; snow. *See* Red-in Snow
caciocavallo cheese, 340
cactus. *See* nopales, prickly pear, tuna
caerphilly cheese, 343
cajeta, 490
calabaza (calabazilla), 490–491
calcium hydroxide. *See* slaked lime
callaloo greens (callilu, callau), 290, *491–492. See also* malanga, amaranth
Calpis, 153
caltrop. *See* water chestnut
calvados (apple brandy), 330
camarón seco, 492–493
Camembert, 339
Canadian bacon, 630
candied fruit, 330
candlenut, 153–154
cane syrup, pure, 639–640
cannelloni, 413
Cantonese sausage. *See* sausage, Chinese pork
capers, 21–22
Capelli d'Angelo, 413
Cappelletti pasta, 413
capuchina. *See* nasturtium
carambola, 154
caraway seed, *22–23*, 32, 33
cardamom, 23–25
cardoon, 331
carne seca, 493. *See also* jerky, biltong
carob, 575–576
carom seeds. *See* ajwain
cashew nut, 155
cassareep, 494
cassava
    (Africa): 99–101, 102, 103, 290
    Latin America): 494–495. *See also* gari
    flour. *See* tapioca meal, 495–496
cassia. *See* cinnamon blossoms, 155
catsup, 640
cavetelli pasta, 413–414
caul, *332*, 440
cayenne, 25
ceci. *See* chick-peas
celery
    cabbage, 152
    root (celeriac, knob, turnip-rooted), 331, *333–334*
    seed, 25–26
cellophane noodles, 235–236
century eggs. *See* eggs, 1000 year old
cèpe mushrooms, 400
cervelas sausage, 449
channa dal. *See under* dal, 175
    flour. *See* besan
chanterelle mushrooms, 401–402
chapatis, 121

chard, Chinese. *See* cabbage, Oriental
chappati flour. *See* atta
charoli nuts, 156
chasoba, 236
chayote, 496–497
cheddar cheese, 344
chee how sauce, 156–158
cheese
    (Europe): 334–357
    (Latin America—"quesos"): 497–504
    (Middle East): 576–581
    (Regional America): 640–643
    See also individual listings
cherimoya fruit, 504
cherries, sour, 581–582
chervil, 26
Cheshire cheese, 344
chestnuts (Marrons), 357–360
    fresh, 357; canned, 359; dried, 359– 360; flour, 360; preserved. *See* Kuri-no-Kanro-ni
Chèvre Valençay cheese, 356
chicharrón, 504–505
chicken . *See* recipe index
    fat, 643–644
chick-peas, 321
chicory, 325, *644*
chikuwa. *See* kamaboko
chiles
    (Asia): 159–161; dried, 159; fresh, 161
    (Latin America): 505–521; canned, 512–513; dried, 513–521; fresh, 506–512; powdered, 520
    paste, 96, 159, *192. See also* piripiri
chili
    oil, 161–162
    sauce, 162
Chinese apple. *See* pomegranate
Chinese egg noodles, 237
Chipolata sausage, 439–440
chitterlings (chitlins), 644–645
chives, 27
    Chinese, 27
chocolate, 361–364
    bittersweet, 361; coating, (couverture), 361; cocoa, 362; dietetic, 362; Mexican, 521; milk, 362; semisweet and sweet, 362–363; unsweetened, (baking), 364; white, 385
chop suey greens. *See* crysanthemum greens
chorizo (chourico), 45, 440, *521–523*
choy sum. *See under* cabbage, Oriental
chrysanthemum greens, 163–164
chuchu. *See* chayote
chufa, 365–366
chutney, 164–165
cilantro. *See* coriander
cinnamon, 27–28

citric salt, 645
citron, 582
citronella root. *See* lemon grass
citrus leaves, 165–166
ciubritsa, 366
clams, dried, 166
cloud ears. *See* mushrooms, dried
cloves, 28
coconut, 166–167
    milk (cream), 168–169
    oil, 112, *169*
    syrup, 170
cocoyam. *See* taro root
cod, salted and dried, 366–367
cola nut, 101–102
collards, 102, *645–646. See also* haak
coltsfoot, 170
comino. *See* cumin
conch, 646
conchiglie pasta, 414
confit d'oie, 367–369
Congo pea. *See* pigeon pea
consommé, 369
Copocollo ham, 386
coriander, 29–32
    fresh, 30; seed, 31
corn, 647–648
    baby sweet, 170–171; blue, 648; dried,
        524, 648–649; flour, 649; husks, 524
corned beef, 652–653
cornichons, 369–370
cornmeal, 649–650
cornstarch, *171*, 302
cotechino sausage, 440
cous cous, 28, 65, 77, 116, 454, *583*
cow pea. *See* black-eyed pea
crab, 653–656
    boil, 83
cracklings, 656–657
cranberry beans, 325, 632
crayfish (crawfish), 657–658
cream, clotted. *See* eishta
cream of tartar, 95
crema Danica, 339
crème fraîche, 51, *370*, 380
Creole mustard, 658
Creole sausages, 683–684
crépinette, 440–441
croutons, *370–371*, 408
crowberry. *See* lingonberry
cubebe pepper, 60
cucumber, sweet. *See* melon, tea
culatello ham, 387
cumin, 23, *32–33*
currants, 371–372
curry
    leaves, 171–172
    powder, 35, *84*, 108
cuttlefish, dried, 172

daikon, *172–173*, 232
dal, 31, 113, 129, *173–174*, 247
Danablu, 350
dandelion greens, 319, 659
dasheen. *See* taro root
dashi, *176*, 202, 223, 241, 273
date, 583–584
    Chinese, 178; red, 178; Indian. *See*
        tamarind
daun pandan, 178–179
daun salaam, 172, *179*
Derby(shire) cheese, 344
Devonshire cream, 370, *372*
dibs (syrup), 584–585
Dijon mustard,s36403
dill, 33–34
    fresh, 33
    seed, 34
dioul. *See* warka
Ditali pasta, 414
djon djon (mushrooms), 525
dock. *See* sorrel
Dolcelatte cheese. *See* Gorgonzola
Domiati cheese, 576
Doro Wat, 93, 97
double Gloucester cheese, 344
dragon eyes. *See* longan
duck
    feet, *179*, 180
    liver, cured, 180
    preserved and salted, 180
    roast, 180–181
    sauce. *See* plum sauce
Dungeness crab, 655
Dunlop cheese, 344
dura. *See* sorghum
durian fruit, 181

eau de vie, 330, 356, 380, 392
eba, 100, 101, 104
Edam cheese, 344
efo, *102*, 113, 645
egg barley pasta, 414–415
eggplant, 372–373
    (Africa–"brinjal"). *See* garden eggs;
        Japanese, 181–182; (Middle East):
        585–587
eggs
    quail, 182–183
    salted and preserved, 183
    shrimp, 279–280
    1000 year old, 183–184
egg roll wrappers, 182
egusi seeds, 102
eishta, 372, *587*
elbow pasta, 415
elephant ears. *See* gobo
elubo. *See* yam
Emmenthaler cheese, 345

endive, Belgian or French, 325–326
epazote, 525–526
Épices Fines, 86
escargot, 374–375
Esrom cheese, 340

fagara. *See* peppercorns, Szechuan
farfel. *See* egg barley pasta
farfalle pasta, 416
farina (flour), 587–588
farina dolce. *See* chestnut flour
fat back, 656, *659–660*
fava beans, 570–571
fecula. *See* potato starch
feijao. *See* beans, azuki
felafel mix, 588
fennel, 34–35
    Florentine (sweet, Roman, Florence),
        376–377
fenugreek, 35–36
Feta cheese, 356, 576–577
fettuccine, 416
fiddlehead fern, 660
fide noodles, 605, 416
fideos, (noodles), 416, *527*
fig
    Indian or Barbary. *See* tuna
    Smyrna, 589–590
filé, 106, 112, *660–661*
filo pastry, 356, 458, *590–594*
Fines Herbes, 26, 55, 75, *87*
Finnan haddie, 377–378
fireek. *See* bulghur wheat
fish
    dried, Chinese, 184–185
    Southeast Asian, 185
    maw. *See* swim bladder
    sauce, 185–186
Five Spice Powder, 73, *186–187*, 232, 246.
    See also panch phora
flor de calabaza. *See* squash blossom
flours
    atta, 132; besan (chick-pea), 148; cassava.
        See tapioca; elubo (yam). *See under* yam;
        gari (cassava), 103–104; gluten, 192;
        kinako, 204; masa harina, 540–541;
        rice, 115; semolina, 453–454; teff
        (millet), 116–117
flowers and flowerbuds
    borage, 20–21; capers, 21–22; cassia,
        155; crystallized, 378–379; cloves, 29;
        golden lilies, 194; Jamaica, 534;
        lavender, 45–46; manzanilla, 539; rose
        petals, 616–617; saffron, 65–67; squash
        blossom, 554–555. *See also* kewra, and
        rosewater
foie gras, 379–380
Fontina cheese, 345
fraises des bois, 380

Frankfurters, 445
frijoles refritos, 527–529
fresadilla. *See* tomatillo
frizzes (frizzie), 449
fruit, candied, 330
fruta bomba. *See* papaya
fu, 187–188. *See also* gluten flour
fufu, 92, 93, 100, 104, 107, 115, 118
fuki. *See* coltfoot
fusille pasta, 416

gado gado, 188
gai lat (mustard), 49
galanga root, 36–37
galuska, 417
gammon. *See* ham, Chinese
Garam masala, 24, 29, 32, 46, 77, 87, 148,
    246
garbanzos. *See* chick-peas
garden eggs, 103
gari, 100, 101, *103–104*
garlic, 37–39
Gaslevertov. *See* liver sausage
gelatin
    agar, 126–127
    konnyaku, 207
    leaf, 380–381
gemelli, pasta, 417
genmai cha (tea), 189
génoise, 381
gervais, 335
ghee, 108, 110, *189–190*
ginger, 41–43
    pickled, 190
    red candied (preserved), 42, 184, *191*
    subgum, 191
ginkgo nuts, 191–192
girolle. *See* chanterelle
Gjetost cheese, 346
glace de viande, 381–382
gluten flour, 192
gnocchi, 382–383
gobo, 193
golden lilies, *194*, 249
goober. *See* groundnut and peanut
gooseberry, Chinese. *See* kiwi
goosefoot. *See* epazote
Gorgonzola cheese, 350
gourd. *See* kampyo
    bitter. *See* melon, bitter
Gouda, 346
gouta cheese (goat), 597
grains of paradise. *See* malagueta pepper
    under peppercorns
gram. *See* dal
granadilla, 529–530
grape leaves, 356, *594–595*
grapeseed oil, 383
grass jelly, 194

Gravlax, 33
grebenes, 544, 656
green almond. *See* pistachio nut
green chile salsa, 530–531
green gram. *See* mung dal *under* dal, 175
greens
    crysanthemum, 163
    chop suey, 163
green tomatoes, Mexican. *See* tomatillos
Gremolata, 39, 40
grenadine, 384
grits, hominy, 665–667
gros sel (sea salt), 69
groundnut, 93, *104–106*. *See also* peanut
groviera cheese, 346
Gruyère, 346–347
guanábana fruit, 531–532
guanciale, 384, 410
guava, 532–533
Guinea corn. *See* sorghum
Guinea pepper. *See* malagueta pepper *under*
    peppercorns
guru nut. *See* cola nut

haak, 195
haddock, smoked. *See* Finnan haddie
haisein sauce. *See* hoisin
haloumi cheese, 48, 577
hams
    Chinese, 196
    (Europe): 384–388
    (Regional America): country-style,
        661–663
ham choy. *See* mustard greens, Oriental
harissa, 268, *595–596*
hasu. *See* lotus root
hazelnut oil, 388–389
head cheese, 446
hearts of palm, 215, 325, *583*
herbes de Provence, 383, *389–390*
herbs, 13–15. *See also* individual listings
herrings, 390–392
    kippered, 390–391
    salt, 391
hichimi togarashi. *See* seven spice seasoning
hijiki (seaweed), 272
hog jowl, 663
    maw, 664
hoisin sauce, 156, 157, *196–197*
holuski, 417
holy basil. *See* basil
hominy, 664–665
    grits, 665–667
honewort. *See* mitsuka
honey, 596
    black. *See* pekmez
horseradish, 43–44

hummus, 597–598
hundred-year-old eggs. *See* eggs, 1000 year
    old

Indian cress. *See* nasturtium
    rice. *See* wild rice
    nut. *See* piñon nut
Injera, 93, 116, *117*
ito-kezuri-katsuo, 197

jackfruit, 198
jaggery, 66, 165, *198–199*
jalapeños. *See* chiles, Latin America
Jamaica flower, 534
Jarlsberg cheese, 347
jee choy, 272
jellyfish, dried, 199–200
jerky, 98, 329, *667*. *See also* biltong
Jerusalem artichoke, 668–669
jícama, 534–535
juda's ear. *See* cloud ears *under* mushrooms,
    dried
jujubes. *See* dates, Chinese
juniper berries, 44–45
junsai, 200

kadaifi pastry, 598
kaffir corn, 109
kalamata (olives), 608
kalongi, 45
kamaboko, 200–201
kampyo (kanpyo), 201
kanten. *See* agar
karashi, 201–202
kari leaves. *See* curry leaves
kasha, 329
kashkaval cheese, 348
kasseri, 340, 342, *577–578*
katakuriko, 202
katschkawalj cheese, 578–579
katsuo-bushi, 140, 176, *202*, 216
kefalotri cheese, 579
keffir lime leaves, dried. *See* citrus leaves
kemiri nut. *See* candlenut
kentjur. *See* galanga
ketchup. *See* catsup
ketjap manis, 198, 199, *203*
kewra, 203
khubz. *See* pita bread
kidney beans, 634
Kielbasa, 450
kimchi, 152, *204*
kinome, 204–205
kirsch, 313, 330, *392*
kishk, 598–599
kiwi, 205
Knackwürst (Knoblauch), 446

kobe beef, 205
kochu chang, 205–206
kohlrabi, 206
kola nut. *See* cola nut
kombu (kelp), 176, *274*, 308
konnyaku, *207*, 240
kopanisti cheese, 579
krupek, 207
kubu. *See* kombu
kuka powder, 95, *106*
Kuminost cheese, 348
kumquat, 59, *208*
Kuri-No-Kanro-Ni, 208–209
kuzu, 209

labni cheese, 579, 611
ladyfingers. *See* okra
lahvosh, 599–600
la Kama, 600
lakertha, 600–601
lalu powder, 95, *106*
laos. *See* galanga
lard
  (Asia): 209
  (Latin America): 535
lasagne, 417
lavender, 45–46
leaf fat. *See* lard
leaf mustard. *See* mustard
Leberkäse, 446
leche quemada. *See* cajeta
leek, 392–393
  Japanese. *See* onion, long
Leicester cheese, 348
lemon
  curd, 394–395
  grass, 210–211
  pickled, 601
  preserved, 601–602
lentils, 571–572
lentisk. *See* mastic
lettuce, Chinese. *See* celery cabbage, 152
Leyden cheese, 341
lima beans, 635–636
limes, dried, 602–603
lingonberry, 395
linguiça sausage, 450
linguine, 417–418
litchi (litchee), 211
Liptauer cheese, 23
liver sausage, 446
locust bean. *See* carob
lombia. *See under* dal, 175
longan, 211–212
longaniza sausage, 536
loquat, 212

lotus
  buds. *See* golden lilies
  leaves, 133, *212–213*
  paste, 213
  root, 213–214
  root flour, 214
  seeds, 214–215
lox. *See* salmon, smoked
lumache pasta, 418
lumpia wrappers, 157, *215*, 266
lupini beans, 572
Lyonnaisse sausage. *See* salame

macadamia nut, 216
maccheroni (macaroni), 418
mace, 46
Madiera wine, 395–396
Madras-style curry powder, 32, 108
mafalda pasta, 418
mahleb (Persian spice), 603
maize. *See* corn
Malagueta peppercorns, 20, *60*
malanga, 536–538. *See also* callaloo
maldive fish, *216*, 279
maltose, genuine. *See* sugar, malt
manchego cheese, 348–349
mandarin orange. *See* mikan
mandarin pancakes. *See* Peking pancakes
manestra, 419
mangetout. *See* snow peas
mango, *217*, 538–539
  squash. *See* chayote
mangosteen, 217
manicotti, 419
manzanilla (flower), 539
maple sugar, 669
  syrup, 669–670
marjoram, *47*, 52
  wild. *See* oregano
Marmite, 381, *396*
marrons. *See* chestnuts
Marsala wine, 396–397
maruzze. *See* conchiglie
marzipan, *397*, 314
masa, 664
  fresh, 540
masa harina, 540–541
  trigo, 541
masala, 218
mascarpone, 335
mastic, 603–604
matsutake, 230
matzo, 604
  meal, 604–605
mazur dal, 175
mealie and mealie meal, 107–108
meat substitutes, 298

medlar, Japanese. *See* loquat
melon
  bitter, 218–219
  hairy, 219
  silk. *See* okra
  tea, 220
  tree. *See* papaya
  winter, 220–221
membrillate. *See* quince, 614
metélt pasta, 419
Mettwürst, 447
Mexican tea. *See* epazote
mikan, 221
millet, 93, 107, *109–110*, 155
milo, 109, 115
Ming Dynasty eggs. *See* eggs, 1000 year old
mint, 47–48
mirin, *222*, 224, 241
mirleton. *See* chayote
miso, 164, *222–223*, 232, 234
mitsuba, 223–224
mizithra cheese, 580
mochi, *224*, 274
mochiko. *See* flour, rice
mo-er. *See* cloud ears *under* mushrooms, dried
molasses, 670–671
  Chinese bead, 224–225
mole (chile sauce), 542
monkeynut. *See* groundnut
monosodium glutamate (MSG), 225
Montrachet cheese, 357
moo shoo pork skins. *See* Peking pancakes
morcilla sausage, 447
morel mushrooms, 402
morella cherries. *See* cherries, sour
mortadella sausage, 457
mostaccioli, pasta, 419
mostarda, 397–398
mozzarella, 341
MSG. *See* monosodium glutamate
muloukia, 32, 102, *605*
mung bean flour, 225–226
Muenster (Munster), 349
mushrooms, 398–402
  (Asia), dried, 226–229
  fresh, 229–232
mushroom soy. *See* soy sauce
mustard, 49–50
  (Europe): 402–405
  greens, 672
  oil, 165
  Oriental, 232–233
  powder, Japanese, 201

nam prik, 233
napa. *See* celery cabbage, *under* cabbage, Oriental

naranja agria. *See* orange, Seville
nasturtium, 672–673
natto, 233–234
net fat, 332
Neufchâtel cheese, 335
niboshi, 234
nigari, 140, *234–235*
nigella, 45
niger oil, 110
niter kibbeh, 96, 97, *110–111*
nixtamal. *See under* corn, dried
noodles
  (Asia): 235–241; (Middle East): 605–606. *See also* pasta
nopales, 543–544. *See also* tuna
nori, 122, 140, *273*
nouilees, 419
Nudeln, 419
nuka, 241–242
nuoc nam, 186
nutmeg, 50–51
nuts
  butternut, 639
  Brazil, 489
  cashew, 155
  charoli, 156
  cola nut, 101–102
  groundnut, 104–106
  ginkgo, 191–192
  kuri-no-kanro-ni, 208–209
  pine, 423–424, 610. *See also* piñon
  pistachio, 610

Occhi di Lupo, 419
oils
  chili, 161
  coconut, 169–170
  hazelnut, 388–389
  Middle Eastern, 606
  niger, 110
  niter kibbeh, 110–111
  olive, 407–408
  palm, 112
  smen, 618–619
  walnut, 468
okome. *See* short grain *under* rice, Oriental
okra, 111–112, 673
  dried, 606
olives
  Chinese cured, 243
  (Europe): 405–407
  (Middle East): 607–609
  oil, 407–408
ombene. *See* cola nut
onion, long, 243–244
orange, Seville, 408–409
  mandarin. *See* mikan

717

flower-water, 609
oregano, 47, *51–52*
one hundred unities, 243
orgeat, 312
orgeat syrup, 409
orzo pasta, 419

palm, hearts of, 533
  palm butter, 112
  palm nuts. *See* palm butter
  palm oil, 112–113
pancakes, Peking, 248–250
pancetta, 384, *409–410*
panch phora (panchphoran), 246
pandanus. *See* daun pandan
panir cheese, 124, *246–247*
panko (Japanese bread crumbs), 247
panocha. *See* piloncillo
papar. *See* pappadum
papaya, 544–545
pappadum (Indian flat breads), 247
paprika, 52–54
Parmesan. *See* Parmigiano
Parmigiano cheese, 352
parsley 54–55
  Chinese or Japanese. *See* coriander
passion fruit. *See* granadilla
pasta, 410–421. *See also* noodles
pastini, 419
pastrami (Regional America), 673
pastry, puff, 421
pâté à choux (cream puff pastry), 382
patis. *See* fish sauce
pawpaw, 674–675
pazote, Jerusalem oak. *See* epazote
peanuts (Regional America), 675. *See also*
    groundnut
  oil, 248
  sauce (Indonesian), 199
pea pods. *See* snow peas
pecorino cheese, 354
Peking pancakes, *248–250*
pekmez (molasses), 609–610
pemmican. *See under* jerky
penne pasta. *See* mostaccioli
pepitas (pumpkin seeds), 550
pepper, seven-spice. *See* seven spice
    seasoning
pepper. *See also* peppercorns, 56–61
  cubebe, 60
  malagueta, 20, 60
  anise. *See* Szechuan, 61
  piripiri (African), 92
  sweet, 546–547
peppercorns, black, white, 56–61
  cubebe, 60
  green, 57, 58

pink, 60
  Szechuan (Chinese or Japanese
    peppercorns), 61
  malagueta, 60
perilla. *See* shiso
Pernod, 422
pesto, 18, 19, *422–423*
Petit-suisse, 335
peynir, 580
Pickapeppa sauce, 547
pickles, Chinese, 250–251
  ginger. *See* ginger, subgum
pigeon pea, 113–114
pignola. *See* piñon nut
pigweed. *See* eqazote, amaranth
pilafs, 16
piloncillo sugar, 548
pimientón (Spanish paprika). *See* paprika
pine nut, 423–424, 610. *See also* piñon nut
pinocchios. *See* pine nut
piñon nut, 676–677
pinto beans, 488
pipián, 549. *See also* mole
piripiri, 92, *114*
pistachio nut, 610
pita bread, 610–611
plantain, 549–550
Player's #3 cigarette tin, 114
plum duck. *See* duck, roast
plum sauce, 251–252
polenta, 424
pomegranate, 611–612
  juice and syrup, 384, *612*
  seeds, dried. *See* anardana
poppy seeds, 63
  filling, 425
pork, barbecued roast, 252–253
pork, roast, 253–254
portulaca. *See* purslane
Port-Salut (Port-du-Salut), 342
potato starch, 425
pozole. *See* hominy
Prague powder. *See* saltpeter
pralin (praline paste), 425–427
prawns (dried, powder). *See* shrimp, dried
preserves, 427, *612–613*
presunto ham, 387
prickly pear cactus, 677. *See also* tuna
prosciutto, 387
provolone, 342
puff pastry. *See* pastry, puff
pumpernickel, *427–428*, 430. *See also*
    Schwartzbröt
pumpkin (Regional America): 677–679
  seeds. *See* pepita
pumpkin, green (West Indian). *See* Calabaza
purple laver. *See* jee choy
purslane, 613

pussley. *See* purslane
Pyramide cheese. *See* Chèvre Valençay

qamaradin, 613–614
Queensland nut. *See* macadamia nut
queso (cheese, Latin America): 498–504
quince, 614

raclette, 349
radish, Japanese (white). *See* daikon
raita, 132
raji, 109
rajma dal, 175
rambutan, 256
ramen. *See* noodles (Asia)
rape, 428
Ras el Hanout, 16, 37, 45, 46, *615*
ravioli, 419
rawbi, 615
recado colorado, 478, *550–551*
red beans, small, 636–637
red chili sauce, Mexican, 551
red gram. *See* pigeon pea
Red-in-Snow, 256–257
red roast pork. *See* pork, barbecued roast
reukon. *See* lotus root
rice
  bran. *See* nuka
  Carolina, 680–682
  crusts, dried, 263–264
  flour, 115, *264–265*, 682
  honey. *See* sugar, malt
  Italian, 529
  Middle Eastern, 616
  Oriental, 257–263
  paper, 265–266
  sticks. *See* noodles
  wild, 689–690
ricotta, 336
rigatoni, 419–420
Romano cheese, 354–355
Roquefort, 351
rose hips, 429–430
rose petals, 616–617
rose water, 266–267
rose wine spirits, 267
rosemary, 63
rotelle pasta, 420
roti flour, 267
rum, Jamaican, 552
Route di Carro, 420
rye, 430, 431

saffron, 65
  Mexican. *See* azafrán
sage, 67–68
  Derby, 349
sahlab, 617

Saint Maure cheese, 357
sake, 224, 231, *268*
salame, 451
saligua. *See* borlotti
salmon, cured, 431–433
  smoked, 433–434
salsa, green chile, 530–531
salsa jalapeña, 552
salsiccia, 442
salt, 68–69
  citric, 645
saltpeter, 98, *434*
salt pork, 682–683
sambals, *268*, 595
sâmna, 617–618
Samsoe cheese, 349
sansho, 276
sapodilla, 553
sapsage, 335
Sandellenwürst, 447
sassafras powder. *See* filé
satsuma imo, 269
sauces
  chee how, 156
  chili (Asia), 162
  fish (Asia), 185
  French, 434–436
  hoisin, 196–197
  Ketjap manis, 203
  See also recipe index
saucisse, 447
  d' Espagne. *See* chorizo
saucisson, 452
sauerkraut, 436–437
  Chinese. *See* preserved vegetables, Chinese
sausage
  casings, 452–453
  Chinese liver, 269
  Chinese pork, 270
  cooked, 442–448
  Creole, 683–684
  fresh, 439–442
  Italian link, 441–442
  liver, 446
  Mexican. *See* chorizo
  Pennsylvania Dutch, 684
  semi-dry and dry, 448, 452
  Spanish. *See* longaniza
savory, 69–70
Sbrinz, 355
scallions, pickled, 270
scallops, dried, 270
Schinkenwürst. *See* bologna
Schmaltz. *See* chicken fat
Schnitz, 684–685
Schwartzbröt, 453
screwpine. *See* daun pandan
sea cucumber. *See* beche-de-mer

sea tangle. *See* kombu
sea urchin. *See* uni
seaweed, dried, 271–274
seeds and seedpods
  achiote, 478–479
  ajwain, 127
  anise, 17
  black gram, 174–175
  caraway, 22–23
  cardamom, 23–25
  cayenne, 24
  celery, 25–26
  coriander, 31
  cumin, 32–33
  dill, 34
  egusi, 102
  fennel, 34–35
  fenugreek, 35–36
  kalongi, 45
  Middle Eastern, 618
  monkey bread (baobab), 95
  mustard, 49–50
  nutmeg, 50–51
  okra, 111–112
  pepitas, 546
  poppy, 63
  sesame, 71–72
  star anise, 72–73
  vanilla bean, 78–79
sel gris, 68
sembei, 275
semolina flour, 328, 453
Serrano ham, 387
sesame seeds, 71–72
  (Middle East): 618
  paste, 276
  oil, 197, *275*
seven spice seasoning, 276–277
shaddock (fruit), 553–554
shallot, 454–456
shark's fin, 277
shatta, 114, *115*, 119
shao hsing, 305
shellouts. *See* cranberry beans
sheriya noodles, 606
shichimi. *See* seven spice seasoning
shiitake, 231
shiso, 278–279
shoga. *See* ginger, pickled
shoyu, 140
shrimp
  chips, 233
  dried, 279. *See also* camoron seca
  eggs, 279–280
  paste, Chinese, 280
  Southeast Asian, 280–281
shirata kombu, 274
slaked lime, 685

smallage, 26
smen, 618–619
smid, 619. *See also* semolina
snail. *See* escargot
snobber (snobore). *See* pine nut
snow cabbage. *See* Red-in-Snow
snow peas, 282
soffrito, 40, 41
sorghum, 109, *115–116*
  syrup, 639, 686
sorrel, 102, *456–458*
sourdough, 686–687
sourgrass. *See* sorrel
soursop. *See* guanabana
soybean cake. *See* bean curd
soy flour. *See* kinako
soy sauce
  Chinese, 282
  Indonesian, 283–284
  Japanese, 284
  mushroom, 282
  Tamari, 284
spaghetti, 420
Saplen cheese. *See* Sbrinz
Spanish sorrel. *See* muloukia
spearmint, 47
spice Parisienne. *See* Épices Fines
spinach, Chinese. *See* amaranth
sprats, dried. *See* fish, dried, Southeast Asian
squash, bottle, 285
  blossom, 554–555, 687
squid, dried, 285
star anise, 72–74
Star beer, 116
starches
  gari, 103–104
  kuzu, 209
  arrowroot powder, 130, 481
  cornstarch, 171
  polenta, 424
  potato starch, 425
  tapioca, 555–556
star fruit. *See* carambola
Stilton cheese, 351
string cheese, 580–581
strudel leaves, 458–459
sugar
  Barbados, 555
  European term, 459–460
  malt, 285–286
  rock, 286
  slab, 286
Sülze sausage, 448
sumac, 619
sun yee, 134
sushinori. *See* seaweed
swallows' nests. *See* birds' nests
sweet cumin. *See* fennel

sweet potato, Japanese. *See* satsuma imo
swim bladder, 287
Swiss cheese, 349
syrup, golden, 383

Tabasco sauce, 687–688
tabil, 620
Tabooli, 48, 55
tagliatelle pasta, 420
tahini (tahina, taheeni), 71–72, 276, *620*
Takuan (Japanese pickle), 288
taleggio cheese, 342
tamara (roe), 620–622
Tamari. *See* soy sauce, Tamari
tamarind, 24, 154, 268, *288–289*
tampala. *See* amaranth
tangerine peel, dried, 289
tangerine, winter. *See* mikan
tapioca, 99, 100, *555–556*
tarhonya noodles, 420
taro root, 289–290
tarragon, 74–76
teff, 93, 104, 109, *116–117*
Telemes cheese. *See* feta
tempeh (bean cakes), 290–291
tempura-ko (flour), 291–292
tempura oil, 292
tentsuyu, 292–293
teriyaki sosu, 293
Tête de Moines (monk's head) cheese, 343
Tientsin. *See* preserved vegetables, Cantonese
ti leaves, 294
temperance nut. *See* cola nut
Thuringer sausage, 448
thyme, 76–77
tiger needles. *See* golden lilies
Tilsit cheese, *340*, 349
tofu. *See* bean curd
tomate (de cáscara, verde). *See* tomatillo
tomatillo, 556–558
tomatoes, 460–462
  canned, 462
  paste, 462
tomatoes, green (Regional America), 688
tonkatsu sosu, 294
tororo imo. *See* yama-no-imo
tortellini, 19, 420
tortillas, corn, 558–560
  flour (de harina), 560–561
Toulouse sausage, 442
trahana (Greek noodles), 606–607
trefoil. *See* mitsuba
trepang. *See* bêche-de-mer
truffles, 463–464
Trufflewürst, 447
tsiri (dried fish), 622
tsukemono, Japanese pickled vegetables, 295
tubettini, 420

tulum cheese, 581
tuma cheese, 581
tuna (fruit), 561
Turkish bacon. *See* bastourika
turmeric, 49, *77–78*, 110
turnip, salted (preserved), 295–296
Tuscarora rice. *See* wild rice
tybo, 349

ugli fruit, 562
umeboshi (pickled plums), 296
umeshu (plum liquor), 296–297
uni (sea urchin), 297
urad dal, 176

Vainilla de Papantla (Mexican vanilla), 78, 79
Valodi Tojasos Teszta (Hungarian pasta), 54
Van de Hum liqueur, 117–118
vanilla bean, 78–79
varak, 240, *298*
vark, 32
veal, 39
vegetable brains. *See* akee
vegetarian meat substitutes, 298
vegetables, preserved
  (Cantonese), 254
  Chinese, 254–255
  Szechuan, 255
vermicelli, 420
vermicelli. *See* noodles, cellophane
  soybean. *See* harusame *under* noodles, cellophane
Vermouth, 464–465
Vesiga (sturgeon marrow), 465
vinegar, apple cider, 688–689
vinegar, 466–468
vinegar, dill, 34
vinegar, rice, Chinese, 299
  Japanese, 299–300

walnut oil, 468
warka (Moroccan pastry), 591, *622*
wasabi (Japanese horseradish), 213, 241, *300–301*
wat, 39, 53, 96. *See also* Doro Wat
water chestnut, 301
  powder, 302
water lily root. *See* lotus root
Weisswürst, 442
Wensleydale cheese, 350
Westphalian rye. *See* pumpernickel
wheat starch, 302
white bacon. *See* salt pork
white fruit. *See* ginko nut
  fungus. *See* cloud ears *under* mushrooms, dried
  radish. *See* daikon

721

wild marjoram. *See* oregano
wild rice, 689–690
wine, fermented rice (wine ball), 303–304
wine, rice, Chinese, 304
   Japanese. *See* sake
wine, rice (cooking). *See* mirin
winter mushrooms. *See* black or "winter"
   mushrooms *under* mushrooms, dried
witloof chicory. *See* Belgian endive
Won Ton wrappers (skins), *304–306*, 411
Worcestershire sauce, 288, *469*
wormseed. *See* epazote

Yakidoufu (firm bean curd), 139
yam, giant or white, 92, 93, *118–119*

Yama-No-Imo, 307
yams, 118–119. *See also* Yama-No-Imo
yam cakes. *See* konnyaku
yerba buena. *See* mint, 47
yogurt, 66, 132, 599, 615–616, *622–623*
yokan, 308
yucca fruit, 690

zampone sausage, 324, *442*
za'atar (herb), 623
zatar, 619
zatar (seasoning blend), 624
zest, 470
ziti pasta, 421
zwieback, 471